# Handbook for Practice Learning in Social Work and Social Care

*of related interest*

**The Post-Qualifying Handbook for Social Workers**
**Edited by Wade Tovey**
ISBN 978 1 84310 428 5

**Competence in Social Work Practice**
**A Practical Guide for Students and Professionals**
2nd edition
*Edited by Kieran O'Hagan*
ISBN 978 1 84310 485 8

**The Child's World**
**Assessing Children in Need**
*Edited by Jan Horwath*
ISBN 978 1 85302 957 8

**The Developing World of the Child**
**Edited by Jane Aldgate, David Jones, Wendy Rose and Carole Jeffery**
*Foreword by Maria Eagle MP*
ISBN 978 1 84310 244 1

**Social Work and Disadvantage**
**Addressing the Roots of Stigma through Association**
*Edited by Peter Burke and Jonathan Parker*
ISBN 978 1 84310 3646

**Making an Impact**
**Children and Domestic Violence – A Reader**
2nd edition
*Marianne Hester, Chris Pearson and Nicola Harwin*
*With Hilary Abrahams*
ISBN 978 1 84310 157 4

**See You in Court**
**A Social Worker's Guide to Presenting Evidence in Care Proceedings**
*Lynn Davis*
ISBN 978 1 84310 547 3

**Enhancing Social Work Management**
**Theory and Best Practice from the UK and USA**
*Edited by Jane Aldgate, Lynne Healy, Barris Malcolm, Barbara Pine, Wendy Rose and Janet Seden*
ISBN 978 1 84310 515 2

**Developments in Social Work with Offenders**
*Edited by Gill McIvor and Peter Raynor*
ISBN 978 1 84310 538 1

# Handbook For Practice Learning in Social Work and Social Care

Knowledge and Theory

Second Edition

*Edited by Joyce Lishman*

Jessica Kingsley Publishers
London and Philadelphia

Originally published in 1991
as *Handbook of Theory for Practice Teachers in Social Work.*

This edition first published in 2007
by Jessica Kingsley Publishers
116 Pentonville Road
London N1 9JB, UK
and
400 Market Street, Suite 400
Philadelphia, PA 19106, USA

*www.jkp.com*

**Library of Congress Cataloging in Publication Data**
Handbook for practice learning in social work and social care : knowledge and theory / edited by Joyce
Lishman. -- 1st American paperback ed.
        p. cm.
        Rev., expanded and updated ed. of: Handbook of theory for practice teachers in social work. London : J.
Kingsley, 1991.
        Includes bibliographical references.
        ISBN 978-1-84310-186-4 (pbk. : alk. paper) 1. Social service. 2. Human behavior. 3. Social work educa-
tion. I. Lishman, Joyce. II. Handbook of theory for practice teachers in social work.
        HV40.H2825 2007
        361.0071'1--dc22

                                                        2007026949


**British Library Cataloguing in Publication Data**
A CIP catalogue record for this book is available from the British Library

ISBN 978 1 84310 186 4

Printed and bound in Great Britain by
Athenaeum Press, Gateshead, Tyne and Wear

**Acknowledgement**
With special appreciation to Claire Booth who has coped with a rather IT-illiterate editor.

# Contents

# Section 4: The Context of Assessment and Intervention

# Section 5: Reflective and Evidence-Based Practice

# INTRODUCTION

## Joyce Lishman

While the context of practice teaching and practice learning has changed significantly since the first publication of the *Handbook of Theory for Practice Teachers* in 1991, the need for a reference volume of theory, knowledge, research and evidence dedicated to practice learning and its teaching and assessment remains. This new edition of the Handbook has been substantially changed and updated to reflect and represent the changed world of social work and social work education.

Section 1 is about our understanding of the structural, social and individual influences which may lead us to become users of social work services. Chapter 1 addresses the importance of understanding the relevance of social policy in a devolved United Kingdom to the work we do. Chapter 2 further addresses structural influences on both society and individuals. Chapter 3 is retained from the original volume and in my editor's note preceding it I explain why. This chapter admirably integrates and applies to our practice the range of knowledge, theory, research and evidence we should be using and the complexity of doing so.

Chapters 4, 5 and 6 recognize the importance and relevance of a structural understanding of our life circumstances but also examine the need to understand individual emotional development, including the role of unconscious thoughts and feelings.

Section 2 deals with assessment. Chapter 7 examines assessment in a holistic way and how it contributes to effective practice in social work, social care and integrated services. Chapters 8, 9 and 10 examine assessment in specific contexts, i.e. child care, community care and criminal justice. Chapter 11 examines more general issues in relation to risk assessment and management.

Section 3 is about intervention. The Handbook presents a range of methods of intervention including cognitive behavioural social work, task-centred practice, crisis intervention, family therapy and group care. It does not have a specific chapter on psychosocial intervention but the theme of psychosocial assessment and intervention, I hope, underpins this volume. Each of these is a useful tool but needs to draw carefully on the conclusions of assessment. The use of 'an assessment' and thereafter an 'appropriate intervention' is not a one-off event but the interaction continues. Assessment may lead to changes in social work intervention over time. We also need to be careful not to assume that an initial assessment automatically leads to a specific method of intervention. For example, an assessment which is predominantly psychosocial may quite rightly be followed by a cognitive behavioural intervention. An initial method of intervention may change: we need to be flexible. Following a revised assessment and using an evidence base, we may need to change, in partnership with our service user, for example, from a task-centred intervention to a psychosocial one. We need to be vigilant in continuing to address structural issues in intervention.

Rochford's Chapter 16 on loss with the editor's addendum is included from the previous volume. Loss, we should remember, and also problems about attachment underpin a considerable part of social workers' intervention. Chapter 17 examines group care, a sometimes neglected but crucial area of social work intervention, and usefully examines it in the context of an evidence-based practice (see Chapter 24). Chapter 18 focuses specifically on how social work and social care can empower service users and advocate for them. More broadly in Chapter 19 we reflect on the role of social work in community development.

Section 4 addresses the context of assessment and intervention. Chapter 20 examines law, social policy, assessment, intervention and the evidence base in child care and child protection, i.e. it is a case study of how as social workers we must analyse and integrate these very different strands, policy, law and knowledge and research into our practice.

Chapter 21 examines the interdisciplinary context of social work and partnership working. Chapter 22 addresses the practice of social work in its organizational context with the requirements of organizational change which are a given.

Section 5 follows from this chapter. As professional social workers we need to be fully engaged in reflective practice, evaluation and evidence-based practice.

The task for social work students, practice teachers and more generally social workers is highly complex: to understand and apply in assessment and intervention law, social policy and research in relation to complex individuals who do not neatly fit into the broad parameters of policy or of research findings.

I hope this book helps students and practitioners to practise in a more knowledge-based way to meet the needs of individual service users and carers and ensure that we maintain a focus on how we can improve on the outcomes of our practice.

# Section 1: Understanding

## CHAPTER I

# THE SOCIAL POLICY CONTEXT OF PRACTICE LEARNING

*Steven M. Shardlow*

## Introduction: what is the relevance of social policy for practice learning?

Social workers are expected to have a broadly-based professional understanding that integrates knowledge derived from a range of academic and professional disciplines into a coherent and usable form, which can be directly applied in practice. Such an expectation may sometimes create an impression, especially for the neophyte social worker, that almost all forms of knowledge have relevance for social work. It is reasonable to expect that a strong, substantial and persuasive argument should be made to justify why social workers should acquire knowledge derived from any given cognate academic or professional discipline, and vice versa, to limit the expectations about the knowledge that social workers should acquire. Hence, three questions arise. First, what is the justification for the assertion that social workers need to acquire knowledge about a particular domain, in this case social policy? Second, what in particular about this discipline should they understand? Third, in what ways can practice teachers assist students during periods of practice learning with the acquisition of a relevant understanding of social policy? This chapter presents a discussion of and suggested answers for these questions. As a starting point a preliminary question can be posed: 'if social workers knew nothing of social policy would they necessarily be worse as practitioners?' To answer this question, a kind of 'acid test' of the utility of social policy knowledge, it is necessary to explore the nature of social policy as a discipline.

## What is social policy?

Mapping the content and boundaries of social policy is not a simple matter; the very breadth and scope of the discipline seem almost boundless – busy practice teachers can be heard to groan in unison, 'Not another boundless set of knowledge to acquire and to assist students to grasp'. It is perhaps not then surprising to note that Alcock, Payne and Sullivan (2000) compare the discipline to a elephant: something which can be recognized on sight but which is 'notoriously difficult to describe' (see, for example, p.1 which develops Esping-Andersen's framework (1990)[1] by allowing the inclusion of a southern European model of welfare). More concretely, Blakemore suggests reasons for what he terms the 'lack of identity of social policy': it is 'a relatively new' subject (the origins lie in the early part of the twentieth century) and it is 'a "magpie" subject [...] that has taken sparkling treasures from other disciplines such as economics, philosophy, politics and sociology' (Blakemore 2003, p.3). This suggests a natural affinity with the discipline of social work, which is often taken to possess similar characteristics. To help resolve some of these problematics both succinctly and helpfully, Alcock (2003) proposes a definition of social policy which suggests that it comprises both academic discipline and also a form of social action. If we develop this notion a little further, social policy might be seen as having as four-cornered character, being a field for study that contains a discrete group of subject areas (the *content* of the discipline), which may be approached through a set of common *principles* or concepts. These common principles constitute a *political arena for social action*, at both national and municipal levels, and that have the potential for realization through the enactment and delivery of a particular set of policies, which are specifically *social* in character. These italicized notions benefit from further exploration.

CONTENT

According to Spicker (1995) 'social policy' is usually taken to include the study of education, health, housing, social security and social work.[2] This view is echoed by Erskine who contends that the 'most common and traditional approach, within the United Kingdom, used to conceptualise to social policy is through these "big five social services"' (Erskine 1998, p.17).[3] However, Erskine also comments that the point of departure for thinking about social policy may not be these big 'five social services' but through consideration of:

- social issues (for example, the changing demographic structure of many industrially developed countries to an increasing proportion of the population over the age of 75, who are presumed to require additional financial and social support, relative to the employed population)

- social problems (for example, the extent of poverty, the impact of unemployment or the increasing incidence of HIV/AIDS)

- the experiences of social groups (for example, black people, children, older people, those with a disability and so on).

PRINCIPLES

Principles provide another vantage point from which we can unlock the core of social policy. Value positions or philosophical principles, which may be either aspirational (i.e. are required to realize a better society according to a given some value position) or normative (i.e. describe required behaviour in the social field and may contain mechanisms for enforcement), underpin social polices. Blakemore proposes a way of understanding these principles by suggesting that they may, at various times, have the force of being 'moral standards' which provide justification for beliefs; 'rules' which specify behaviour; and 'ideas' which underpin social policy (Blakemore 2003, pp.17–18). The values or principles that are most often referred to are:

- altruism and reciprocity

- citizenship

- equality (egalitarianism; equality of opportunity)

- freedom and rights

- equity and social justice

- social needs (satisfaction and wants).

These principles are often interpreted through their application to one of several different perspectives or political orientations. Some of the most commonly articulated are:

- communitarianism (socialism)

- conservativism

- feminism

- neo-liberalism

- social democratism

- postmodernism.

This configuration of principles, perspectives and political orientations connect strongly with social work (for example, the satisfaction of social need and want and the realization of social justice). They find expression through professional ethics and values, although often expressed in different terminology, that are very much the concern of social work).

## THE POLITICAL ARENA

When approached from the perspective of the political arena, social policy provides an understanding of the forces that shape policy, the way in which these policies are implemented and an evaluation of their impact. For example, in the United Kingdom, social policy in the political arena can be explored through an examination of the New Labour government's (1997–) agenda for policy change, which is badged as the 'Third Way' – this is an ideology neither entirely of the 'left' nor 'right' which purports to change the nature of politics through 'modernization'. However, some commentators, Powell (1999) for example, have suggested that there has never been a set of 'New Labour' social policies which cohere around a 'big idea' that can compare with the 'big idea' of the 1945 Labour government of Clement Atlee (an ex-social worker) which is credited with the creation of the Welfare State. The contested nature of the relationship of social policy to political forces provides an excellent mechanism for teachers to promote understanding of the discipline, as discord provides a sharp tonal distinction to better appreciate the nature of this relationship.

## THE SOCIAL CONTENT OF POLICY

Not all government policy is 'social' policy, although many policies have a social dimension, as so far as they affect people. Miller (1999) grappled with defining and containing the nature of social policy and resolved the problem by referring back Donnison's long-standing definition of social policy:[4]

> What distinguishes a policy as 'social' is [...]the fact that it deals with the distribution of resources, opportunities and life chances between different groups and categories of people.[...] It follows that every Government department, programme and policy may have social aspects. Meanwhile social policies always have other aspects which for many people will be more important. Health and education services, for example, are primarily designed to raise general standards of health and learning without much regard to their distribution or distributional consequences. Policies for these services become social in the sense defined here, when they deal with the allocation of resources and opportunities between potentially competing groups, and – as a consequence which may be more distant but equally important – with relations between groups in society, their status and self-respect, their power and their access to broader social opportunities. (Donnison 1975, p.26)

This comment encapsulates to the 'essence' of social policy, helpfully for those, such as social work students who seek to comprehend its complexity in a single graspable statement.

## SOCIAL POLICY AND SOCIAL WORK

In day-to-day practice social work students will encounter people whose experiences represent the realization of particular social policies.

On a visit to an older disabled person, the student may learn that the service user's weekly allowance of home care has been significantly reduced. The student can be encouraged to explore the reasons for this reduction and may discover that it is not related to the individual's level of need but to the operation of a policy shift at local or national level whereby less funding is available to support this type of home care due possibly to the budget being exhausted.

A direct appreciation of the policy context allows the student to recognize how policy frameworks contain professional practice, and how these enhance or constrain opportunities for the delivery of high quality social work. This then provides the answer to the first question posed at the start of this chapter; the acid test – the utility of knowledge about social policy for social work students and practitioners. Without an understanding of the social policy context in the above example, the social work student would not be able to make an informed assessment of need and how that need might be met.[5] Having dealt with the first question, we have established the importance of social policy for social work and can shift our attention to the second question addressed by this chapter – which aspects and areas of social policy students should understand.

## Current and recent policy domains in the UK

If students of social work need some knowledge of social policy, then we require a principle to delineate necessary from supplementary knowledge. Clearly they cannot be expected to have a detailed knowledge of the entire scope of the discipline. Help is at hand, in that the conventional division of social policy into the 'big five' policy areas (education, health, housing, personal social services) serves social work students well.[6] An overall knowledge of these areas is necessary if their practice is to be grounded on an understanding of the social world. Students should be familiar with the current policy emphasis in these 'big five' areas of social policy – in other words, with the policy aims and aspirations that government is seeking to achieve – and the underlying principles for any given policy approach. To this effect, only most schematic capture of recent policy trends is possible here. It is helpful to compare some of the key social policy initiatives as developed by the Conservative government (1979–97) with those of the current New Labour government (1997– ).

## EDUCATION

- 1979–1997: Policies designed to promote the notion of consumer choice in education: the removal of responsibilities and powers from local education authorities (LEAs) and the granting of increased powers to schools through local management (LMS); the introduction of 'league tables', which purport to demonstrate the academic performance of individual schools and facilitate cross-school comparisons; and, perhaps most significantly, the introduction of a national school curriculum with tests (SATS) to measure the performance of individual children.

- 1997–: Policies designed to give increased power to parents, increase the numbers of children who achieve academic success and enable those at school to become good citizens. Initiatives taken include the following: an increase in the number of teachers; the introduction of Sure Start to provide a secure entry point for those under five to the education system; the introduction of the Education Maintenance Allowance (EMA) to increase the number of those from economically deprived backgrounds who remain in education; an increase in the number of those attending university, such that by 2010 50 per cent of 18-year-olds will benefit form higher education. In 2006 government sought to introduce measures to promote greater independence for schools and to turn the LEAs into the commissioners of education rather than the providers.[7]

## HEALTH

- 1979–1997: Policies designed to introduce market principles into the allocation of the scare resource of health care. The most significant development was the NHS and Community Care Act (1990), which introduced an internal market in the NHS with the intention that money should follow the patient. GPs became fundholders who were able to purchase health care, active encouragement was given to the private sector, a significant number of new private hospitals being built.

- 1997–: Policies intended to increase the efficiency and effectiveness of the Health Service, notably the creation of treatment centres for routine operations as one key measure to reduce waiting times for treatment; a major increase in investment year on year leading to increased numbers of medical staff being trained; and an increase in the number of employed doctors and nurses.

## HOUSING

- **1979–1997**: Policies introduced that were designed to increase the number of people who owned their own property, with the intention of creating a society where as many as possible had a stake in the economic stability of the country. The most notable policy was the establishment of the 'right to buy', under which many local authority tenants purchased their homes, combined with very significant reductions in the number of social housing units constructed.

- **1997–**: Policies flagged as 'delivering decent homes for all'; this is being achieved, according to government, by increasing the numbers of social housing units constructed and by increasing the capital investment in existing local authority housing stock.

## SOCIAL CARE

- **1979–1997**: Prime policy objective was the introduction of the 'mixed economy of welfare' to reduce the proportion of social care provided directly by local government and to increase the opportunity for not-for-profit and private organizations to provide various forms of social care: the introduction of the 'purchaser/provider' split in the NHS and Community Care Act (1990), which mirrored developments in the health sector.

- **1997–**: Major policy objective to modernize the provision of social care and to increase efficiency while valuing people who receive social care. Performance-led management through comparative indicators of standards and levels of service delivery (for example, the star ranking of local authority social services departments) was introduced, substantial change in organization arrangements was made through the creation of new national regulatory and inspectorial bodies and services for young people increasingly diverged from those for adults.

## SOCIAL SECURITY

- **1979–1997**: Policies designed to reduce economic dependency on the state and to promote self-reliance. For example, unemployment benefit was replaced with the jobseeker's allowance, which emphasized limited social security provided for being unemployed per se; stringent eligibility tests were introduced for various social benefits.

- **1997–**: Policies designed to protect those in work and to provide encouragement to work, while protecting those unable to work; to provide a more equal distribution of income, in particular by reducing family poverty. Tax credits to lessen the tax burden on these on low incomes, a minimum wage and the New Deal initiative to help lone parents into employment were all introduced. The Disability Rights Commission (DRC) was established to seek to counter discrimination against disabled people.

This juxtaposition of the current government approach to the 'big five' areas of social policy with the approach of the previous government, albeit in a brief and highly schematic format, allows students to grasp the character of social policy, in particular the unity or absence of underlying principles evident in the policies pursued by different governments. Knowledge of current policies provides a context for students who are undertaking an agency-based period of practice learning – a context to better understand the lived reality of the service user.

## Key policy themes

Students need a broad-brush understanding of social policy in the 'big five' areas, yet the exploration of current policy themes may be a particularly pertinent way for social work students to develop their understanding of social policy, however, although selecting which issues to concentrate upon is inherently problematic. Ellison and Pierson (1998) have identified several 'social movements' as the key contemporary issues: gender, race, ecology, the changing dimensions of poverty, consumerism, and policy in a European context. Examination of these aspects of social policy may help to guide a student's developing knowledge.

### SOCIAL MOVEMENTS

Developing a theoretical and practice-based understanding of the impact upon people's lives of such key contemporary issues as age, disability, gender, race, sexuality (or other attributes that may impact on people's lives, e.g. through social exclusion or discrimination) is a core and fundamental aspect of social work practice and professional learning (QAA 2000). These themes are discussed from a social work perspective in relevant social work literature and are likely to be familiar to both practice teachers and students – an extended discussion from a policy perspective is not therefore needed here. Nonetheless, social work students may be asked to consider the extent to which discussion is differently framed about age (or any of the other key contemporary issues listed above) when approached from a policy perspective rather than a professional social work practice perspective. Comparing the way that different bodies of literature treat a particular theme is something that practice teachers may encourage generally – not just in relation to social policy and social work.

While many of these key contemporary issues are found in parallel discussions in social policy and social work literature, some are not. For example, 'ecology' as an issue does not figure strongly within social work. Possibly increased emphasis should be given to looking for sustainable social work futures (for example, the construction of new residential units that are energy efficient) that reflect concern for both people and the environment.

### POVERTY

'Poverty' is a key policy theme for social workers, encountered daily in professional practice. In their review of social policy for social workers, Walker and Walker (2002) devote most of the discussion to poverty with the incisive comment:

> The majority of social work service users are poor, yet poverty as an issue is too often marginalised in social work training, even though it is a greater cause of social exclusion than are 'race' and gender with which it also overlaps. (Walker and Walker 2002, p.52)

Poverty is generally understood in three ways. First: 'absolute poverty', which was defined by the United Nations as: 'A condition characterised by severe deprivation of basic human needs, including food, safe drinking water, sanitation facilities, health, shelter, education and information. It depends not only upon income but also on access to services' (United Nations 1995, p.57). Second: 'overall poverty',[8] defined by the United Nations as:

> Lack of income and productive resources to ensure sustainable livelihoods; hunger and malnutrition; ill health; limited or lack of access to education and other basic services; increased morbidity and mortality from illness; homelessness and inadequate housing; unsafe environments and social discrimination and exclusion. It is also characterised by lack of participation in decision-making and in civil, social and cultural life. It occurs in all countries: as mass poverty in many developing countries, pockets of poverty amid wealth in developed countries, loss of livelihoods as a result of economic recession, sudden poverty as a result of disaster or conflict, the poverty of low-wage workers, and the utter destitution of people who fall outside family support systems, social institutions and safety nets. (United Nations 1995, p.57)

Third: social exclusion. The prime minister, Tony Blair, has described social exclusion as: 'a shorthand label for what can happen when individuals or areas suffer from a combination of linked problems such as unemployment, poor skills, low incomes, poor housing, high crime environments, bad health and family breakdown' (The Scottish Office 1999).

Since the so-called 'rediscovery of poverty' in the 1960s,[9] academic and political interest in the subject waned somewhat until 1997 when Tony Blair gave his famous policy commitment, at Toynbee Hall, to end child poverty within 20 years and to lift 700,000 children out of poverty by 2001. The measurement of poverty is problematic. There is no officially used measure of poverty in the UK. A standard measure of poverty commonly used across much of Europe is the proportion of the population living on less than half of the average income (DWP 2006),[10] and a report by UNICEF using such statistics placed the UK as the nineteenth worst (of the 23 OECD countries) in terms of the number of children living in poverty, with almost 20 per cent of children living below the poverty line (UNICEF Innocenti Research Centre 2000, p.4).[11] If this is correct, there appears to be little chance of meeting the objective of eradicating poverty in the UK during the next ten years. Moreover, using the same statistical measure, in the final quarter of the twentieth century, poverty has increased in both the numbers living in poverty and the depth of poverty: for example, the poorest 10 per cent of the population were 12 per cent worse off in 1996 than in 1979 (Gordon 2001, p.62). However, these figures should be treated with some caution. Certainly, they demonstrate that change is occurring, but Johnson, Tanner and Thomas (2000) have demonstrated that this mode of calculating poverty is very sensitive to changes in the income of the richest. For example, in the 1980s higher incomes increased dramatically – hence increasing the 'average' income – hence increasing the numbers living in poverty as measured by HBAI statistics.

The impact of poverty on the individual will vary greatly by place and time. Blakemore (2003) invited readers to identify which of the following were necessities and to compare the results against the findings of a study by Gordon *et al.* (2000) in order to better understand the notion of poverty. You may like to complete their exercise.

Which of the following items do you think are necessities?

- A damp-free home.
- Beds and bedding for everyone.
- A mobile phone.
- The opportunity to attend weddings and funerals.
- A refrigerator.
- A warm, waterproof coat.
- A home computer.
- A television set.
- Toys (for example, dolls or teddies).
- Celebrations on special occasions.
- A meal in a restaurant or pub every month.
- Three meals a day for children; two meals a day for adults.
- A deep freezer.
- Fresh fruit and vegetables daily.
- A hobby or leisure activity.
- A telephone.
- A washing machine.
- A car.

The results of Gordon's survey for comparison are to be found at the end of this chapter in Table 1.1 taken from Blakemore (2003, p.81).

Poverty is not the only way to understand the experience of some marginalized groups. The 1990s saw the rise to prominence of another term, 'social exclusion', which has many similarities with the notion of 'poverty'. 'Social exclusion' often refers to exclusion from the labour market or educational opportunity. Social workers spend a considerable proportion of the time engaged in work with people who live in poverty and they need to understand the nature, extent and impact of poverty and social exclusion. The only certain route out of poverty is through employment – although even that may not be sufficient as many jobs are low paid and do not lift people out of poverty. Furthermore the effects of living in poverty for a period of time are pernicious and do not just disappear with increased income.

## COMPARATIVE AND INTERNATIONAL SOCIAL WELFARE
A key element of social policy discourse is concerned with the comparison of welfare systems in different countries and how these impact on the lives of the citizens. Arguably,

through such comparisons, judgements can be made about how to secure given levels of welfare at the most effective cost, the impact of certain policy initiatives and the effects of ideological shifts on the delivery of welfare. If government were a rational process, and it clearly is not, such comparison might inform more policy development in a systematic and thorough manner. There are different comparative schema. Titmus (1974), the originator of comparative classifications of different policy regimes, developed a three-point classification, comprising the residual, the achievement and the redistributive models. Currently, however, the conventional starting point to explore comparative social welfare is through the work of Esping-Andersen (1990, 1996). He described a three-point classificatory system of the 'regimes of welfare capitalism'. The three different types of regimes identified are named according to the dominant political characteristics of the countries where they are typically found: neo-liberal (American), social democratic (Scandinavian) and corporatist (Franco-German). These different types of welfare regime are 'ideal types' (i.e. the pure form, as described by Esping-Andersen, may not be found in any actual nation, but countries will have some if not all of the features of the particular type of regime that they most closely resemble). Esping-Andersen suggested that these welfare regimes differed along two fundamental dimensions:

1.  'Decommodification' – a measure of the extent to which welfare goods and services are provided through bureaucratic distribution processes according to the needs of recipients rather than through the operation of market mechanisms.

2.  'Stratification' – a measure of the extent to which access to welfare goods and services is determined by factors such as inequalities of income or social class.

These and similar frameworks (for example, Abrahamson 1992, which includes a southern European model of welfare) provide a mechanism by which social work students can reflect upon the nature of the welfare regime in which their social work practice is located.

There is an interface between international social policy and social work at many different levels: much discussion about social work in various countries is less concerned with the micro-level of day-to-day practice than with the social policy, legal frameworks and organizational structures in respect of social work. In seeking to define different types of international social work, Midgely comments that some argue that social workers need: 'a global awareness that enhances the ability of social workers to transcend their preoccupation with the local and contextualize their role within a broad global setting' (Midgley 2001, p.25). Put crudely, social workers need to understand how the forces of globalization lead to social change, perhaps through the relocation of jobs to another country, and how the welfare regime can or cannot respond to such challenges – and most particularly what is social workers' part in the process. Exploring social policy in an international context can thus provide insights for the social work practitioner which help to generate understanding the local and regional level.

## DEVOLUTION, DIFFERENCE AND IDENTITY

Within the UK, one state within the British Isles,[12] a seismic shift has taken place in the political structures and consequent policy frameworks during the past 30 years. In 1998, the passing of the Scotland Act (and comparable legislation for Wales and Northern

Ireland), firmly announced that devolution had become a major element of the political landscape in the UK. The UK had been one of the most centralized states within the European Union prior to devolution. Devolution is a growing force which will continue to exercise an influence in the different countries within the UK as the countries develop different social policies. Practitioners need to be aware of these differences if they move to a different country within the UK. Moreover the differences can be explored in relation to national identity and provide an opportunity for student practitioners to recognize that different forms of policy are possible and realizable (Payne and Shardlow 2002).

In the various countries that comprise the UK, the implications of being a member of the EU are ever more strongly felt in many aspects of life. Geyer comments that EU social policy has not, as yet, 'radically restructured the UK social policy regime', as 'EU social policy is so variable and interwoven in the UK social policy regime it is extremely difficult to disentangle causal relationships and gauge its true impact' (Gyer 2003, p.293). At present, member states have primary responsibility for the delivery of social policy. Whether this will ultimately continue remains to be seen.

## Practice learning and social policy

Social policy and social work as disciplines share, as if siblings, a common heritage rooted in the early years of the twentieth century. Conventionally, the origin of modern social work in the UK is famously located in the slums of late nineteenth-century London[13] (Younghusband 1981, p.11). If social work first emerged as praxis (the practical performance of a skill), then the idea of social policy first emerged through the development of social administration (the forerunner of social policy) as a field of study. Conventionally, the origin of social policy is taken to date from the establishment of the Department of Social Science and Administration at the London School of Economics (LSE) in 1912. This shared heritage suggest that those engaged in the practice of social work and the implementation of social policy should have something in common and perhaps something to learn from each other. Both social work and social policy as disciplines have a long-standing engagement with practical learning: the differences and similarities in the approaches adopted have been explored by Scott and Shardlow (2005).

Practice teachers should actively encourage students to identify examples where the impact of social policy directly affects the lives of service users – this is most strongly evident where a change in policy has occurred. Through such examples students are to better understand the opportunities for practice that are complementary with or compensatory for current policy social policy.

## Conclusion

This chapter began by posing three questions: whether social policy is a necessary discipline for social workers to have knowledge of, if so, what they should learn about the discipline, and how practice teachers might help students to acquire the necessary knowledge of this knowledge domain. An argument has been advanced that knowledge of social policy is required, while an exploration of the discipline has suggested some important knowledge areas that students would benefit from acquiring. Throughout the chapter, ways in which practice teachers can assist students have been suggested. Underlying these examples and suggestions has been a common principle: that the practice teacher can best assist the student by encouraging and suggesting ways in which social work can be explored within a social policy context. In this way the academic materials presented in a class setting can be enriched and enlivened.

**Table 1.1 Items deemed to be necessities in a sample survey of public opinion that compares the results for two years**

|  | % of population | |
| --- | --- | --- |
| Item | 1999 | 1983 |
| A damp-free home | 94 | 96 |
| Beds and bedding for everyone | 95 | 97 |
| A mobile phone | 8 | – |
| The opportunity to attend weddings and funerals | 81 | – |
| A refrigerator | 89 | 77 |
| A warm, waterproof coat | 87 | 87 |
| A home computer | 11 | – |
| A television set | 58 | 51 |
| Toys (for example, dolls or teddies) | 84 | 71 |
| Celebrations on special occasions | 83 | 69 |
| A meal in a restaurant or pub every month | 27 | – |
| Three meals a day for children; two meals a day for adults | 91 | 82 |
| A deep freezer | 55 | – |
| Fresh fruit and vegetables daily | 87 | – |
| A hobby or leisure activity | 79 | 64 |
| A telephone | 72 | 43 |
| A washing machine | 77 | 67 |
| A car | 36 | 22 |

Taken from Blakemore (2003, p. 89). Source: Gordon *et al.* (2000, p.44).

## Notes

1  A detailed account of Esping-Andersen's model is not provided in the text as Blakemore's model is in essence similar, with the addition of another category of welfare system.
2  The book refers to policies that concern the distribution and allocation of social work rather than professional practice skills.

3 He uses the same terms except for 'social work', which becomes more helpfully the broader notion of 'personal social services'.

4 Originally this definition was developed for the Irish government.

5 As required by the National Occupational Standards, (for example, Key Role One 'Prepare for, and work with individuals, families, carers, groups and communities to assess their needs and circumstances' (Skills for Care 2002).

6 In large measure these are a policy response to the 'five giant evils' which were identified by Beveridge (1942) in his eponymous Report as disease, idleness, ignorance, squalor and want.

7 This parallels developments in health care and social care.

8 'Overall poverty' similar to a concept previously used, 'relative poverty'.

9 This is usually credited to two academics, Townsend and Abel-Smith, who wrote about rediscovering poverty after Rowntree's *Third York Survey* in the 1950s had indicated a marked decline: most notable was Townsend's book *Poverty in the United Kingdom* published in 1979.

10 Usually termed HBAI – Households Below Average Income statistics.

11 Poland and Turkey by this definition had less child poverty than the UK.

12 The archipelago to the north-west of Europe, known by its correct geographical name as the British Isles, comprises a complex set of countries and dependencies which share an interwoven history of conquest, oppression and empire, yet have distinct cultural identities and are likely to diverge in their approach to the realization of social policy and social welfare.

13 Similar work developed about the same time in other countries, notably the US. Interestingly, the UK example is often referred to not just in a UK context but internationally as a precursor of modern social work.

## References

Abrahamson, P. (1992) 'Welfare pluralism: towards a new consensus for a European social policy.' In L. Hantrais, M. O'Brien and S. Mangen (eds) *Cross National Research Papers 6: The Mixed Economy of Welfare.* Leicester: European Research Centre, Loughborough University.

Alcock, C., Payne, S. and Sullivan, M. (2000) *Introducing Social Policy.* Harlow: Pearson.

Alcock, P. (2003) 'The discipline of social policy.' In P. Alcock, A. Erskine and M. May (eds) *The Student's Companion to Social Policy.* 2nd edn. London: Blackwell.

Alcock, P. and Craig, G. (eds) (2001) *International Social Policy: Welfare Regimes in the Developed World.* Houndmills, Basingstoke: Palgrave.

Alcock, P. and Erskine, A. (2002) *Blackwell Dictionary of Social Policy.* Oxford: Blackwell.

Beveridge, W. (1942) *Social Insurance and Allied Services* (The Beveridge Report). Cmnd 6404. London: HMSO.

Blakemore, K. (2003) *Social Policy: An Introduction.* 2nd edn. Maidenhead: Open University Press.

Donnison, D.V. (1975) *An Approach to Social Policy.* Dublin: National Economic and Social Council and Republic of Ireland Stationery Office.

DWP (2006) *National Statistics First Release. Households Below Average Income (HBAI).* London: Department for Work and Pensions. Retrieved 10 February 2007 from www.dwp.gov.uk/asd/ hbai2005/first_release_0405.pdf.

Ellison, N. and Pierson, C. (eds) (1998) *Developments in British Social Policy.* Houndmills, Basingstoke: Macmillan.

Erskine, A. (1998) 'The approaches and methods of social policy.' In P. Alcock, A. Erskine and M. May (eds) *The Student's Companion to Social Policy.* Oxford: Blackwell.

Esping-Andersen, G. (1990) *The Three Worlds of Welfare Capitalism.* Cambridge: Polity Press.

Esping-Andersen, G. (1996) *Welfare States in Transition.* London: Polity.

Gordon, D. (2001) 'The British poverty and social exclusion survey.' In G. Kelly and M. Tomlinson (eds) *Joblessness and Poverty. Proceedings of a Joint Seminar Vol. 1.* Belfast: DSD and QMB.

Gordon, D., Alderman, L., Ashworth, K., Bradshaw, J. *et al.* (2000) *Poverty and Social Exclusion in Britain.* York: Joseph Rowntree Foundation.

Gyer, R. (2003) 'The European Union and British social policy.' In N. Ellison and C. Pearson (eds) *Developments in British Social Policy*. Basingstoke: Palgrave Macmillan.

Hick, S. (2003) *Introduction to Social Work and Social Welfare*. Ottawa: Carleton University. Retrieved 2 April 2005 from http://socialpolicy.ca/52100/.

Higher Education Academy (2005) *Social Work and Social Policy*. York: Higher Education Academy. Retrieved 2 April 2005 from http://www.swap.ac.uk/.

Johnson, J., Tanner, S. and Thomas, R. (2000) 'Money matters: Measuring poverty, wealth and unemployment.' In S. Kerrison and A. Macfarlane (eds) *Official Health Statistics: An Unofficial Guide*. London: Arnold.

Midgley, J. (2001) 'Issues in international social work.' *Journal of Social Work 1*, 1, 21–35.

Miller, S. (1999) 'Social policy and social welfare systems.' In J. Baldock, N. Manning, S. Miller and S. Vickerstaff (eds) *Social Policy*. Oxford: Oxford University Press.

Payne, M. and Shardlow, S.M. (eds) (2002) *Social Work in the British Isles*. London: Jessica Kingsley Publishers.

Powell, M. (ed.) (1999) *New Labour, New Welfare State?* Bristol: Policy Press. QAA (2000) Social Policy and Administration and Social Work. Gloucester: Quality Assurance Agency. Retrieved 23 March 2003 from http://www.qaa.ac.uk/crntwork/benchmark/benchmarking.htm.

QAA (2000) *Social Policy and Administration and Social Work*. Gloucester: QAA. Retrieved 23 March 2003 from http://www.qaa.ac.uk/academicinfrastructure/benchmark/honours/socialwork.pdf

Scott, D. and Shardlow, S.M. (2005) 'Developing learning beyond the campus: increasing vocationalism and declining pedagogy?' In H. Burgess and I. Taylor (eds) *Effective Learning and Teaching in Social Policy and Social Work*. London: RoutledgeFalmer.

Skills for Care (previously TOPPS England) (2002) National Occupational Standards for Social Work. London: Skills for Care. Retrieved 10 February 2007 from www.skillsforcare.org.uk/ view.asp?id=140.

Spicker, P. (1995) *Social Policy: Themes and Approaches*. Hemel Hempstead: Harvester Wheatsheaf.

The Scottish Office (1999) *Opening the Door to a Better Scotland*. Edinburgh: The Scottish Office. Retrieved from http://www.scotland.gov.uk/library/documents-w7/sima-03.htm

Titmus, R. (1974) *Social Policy An Introduction*. London: Allen & Unwin.

UNICEF Innocenti Research Centre (2000) *Innocenti Report Card No. 1 June 2000*. A league table of child poverty in rich nations. Florence: UNICEF. Retrieved 3 January 2006, from www.unicef.org.ne/advocacy/publications/Report_Card_-_Poverty_1.pdf

United Nations (1995) *Report of the World Summit for Social Development*. Copenhagen 6–12 March. New York: United Nations.

Walker, C. and Walker, A. (2002) 'Social policy and social work.' In R. Adams, L. Dominelli and M. Payne (eds) *Social Work: Themes, Issues and Critical Debates*. 2nd edn. London: Palgrave.

Younghusband, E. (1981) *The Newest Profession: A Short History of Social Work*. Sutton, Surrey: Community Care/IPC Business Press.

## Further reading

To obtain a richer understanding of the nature of social policy, social work students may be encouraged to explore some of the following core text books:

- the *Blackwell Dictionary of Social Policy* (Alcock and Erskine 2002)

- *International Social Policy: Welfare Regimes in the Developed World* (Alcock and Craig 2001) distance learning materials (Hick, 2003)

- major journals, such as *Journal of Social Policy* and *Journal of European Social Policy, Social Policy and Administration*

- the Social Policy and Social Work (SWAP) Subject Centre (Higher Education Academy, 2005).

## CHAPTER 2

# STRUCTURAL APPROACHES TO SOCIAL WORK

*Ann Davis*

## Introduction

The International Association of Schools of Social Work and the International Federation of Social Workers (2001) have usefully defined 'social work' as a profession that:

> promotes social change, problem solving in human relationships and the empowerment and liberation of people to enhance well-being. Utilising theories of human behaviour and social systems, social work intervenes at the points where people interact with their environments. Principles of human rights and social justice are fundamental to social work.

The IASSW notes that 'the holistic focus of social work is universal, but the priorities of social work practice will vary from country to country and from time to time depending on cultural, historical, and socio-economic conditions'.

Working with this definition of social work challenges those delivering qualifying and post-qualifying UK social work education (in the field and the universities) to give explicit recognition to the ways in which contemporary UK society is structured. The IASSW definition also suggests that at the heart of social work are concerns with individuals and their lives which reflect issues of rights, inequalities, social justice and the exercise of political and professional power. As social work in the four countries of the UK responds to a situation of organizational and educational change, this approach to understanding the remit of social work provides an important focus for the critical consideration of its evolving development. It is a helpful reminder of the distinct contribution of social work both across and within national boundaries.

Social work, positioned as it is between the mainstream and the margins (Davis and Garrett 2004; Jones 1998), is mandated to respond to complex situations which reflect public issues as well as private pain (Becker and MacPherson 1988). In working with these situations, social workers need to develop abilities to recognize the ways in which social, cultural, historic and economic forces are reconfiguring the public and the private arenas in which social work is practised. Social workers need to employ a critical appreciation of how and why social structures, processes and institutions shape and are shaped by the lives, experiences, choices, opportunities and agency of people who become users of social work services. This appreciation needs to be actively used to inform social work assessments of the situations of service users as well as the decisions practitioners make about their interventions in these situations.

The importance of knowledge-based structural awareness is recognized in the Quality Assurance Agency's benchmarks for social work education: 'Social work, both as an occupational practice and as an academic subject, evolves, adapts and changes in response to the social, political and economic challenges and demands of contemporary social welfare policy, practice and legislation (QAA 2000, s.2.2.3). Social work students need to be equipped with the knowledge to understand and critically analyse the range of academic perspectives which seek to explain 'the social processes (associated with, for example, poverty, unemployment, poor health, disablement, lack of education and other sources of disadvantage) that lead to marginalisation, isolation and exclusion and their impact on the demand for social work services' (QAA 2000, s.3.1.1).

Such knowledge has traditionally been delivered as part of the social science inputs to social work education programmes, and as such has often been left at the margins of social work theory and practice. Because of this positioning students have found themselves struggling to use this knowledge in relation to their practice. One consequence of this, as a number of commentators have noted, is the ambivalence and confusion amongst social workers as to how they might address the poverty, inequalities and social exclusion experienced by service users (Barry and Hallett 1998; Davis and Wainwright 2005; Dowling 1999; Jones 1998; Manthorpe and Bradley 2002).

This chapter argues that structural approaches to social work need to promote structural awareness in ways that actively embed it in both the theory and the practice of social work. This means that social work education (in UK universities and in the growing range of practice agencies and settings offering practice learning to social work students) needs to disseminate evidence of structural inequalities and its consequences for citizens. It needs to support practitioners in making meaningful connections between structural analysis and the everyday practice of social work. It is work of this kind that is key to developing creative and energizing forms of practice which recognize and challenge oppression, stigma and other manifestations of inequality and disadvantage in the lives of service users, their households, groups and communities.

This chapter in considering structural approaches to social work starts by referencing the knowledge base which can be used to develop structural awareness of contemporary Britain. It then considers two approaches to theorizing this awareness. The first is a maintenance approach; the second is a critical structural approach. The implications of each are discussed in relation to social work theory and practice. Finally, the chapter describes one way of working with these issues that has been developed by the author and colleagues at the University of Birmingham as a first-year module on the undergraduate and masters social work programmes.

## Developing structural awareness in the UK context

In 1989 Pond observed that, in the UK:

> The distribution of economic awards between different groups in the population and different parts of the country, is an important determinant of the nation's economic and social structure. Economic and social inequality are inextricably

intertwined, and the distribution of income and wealth, the extent of poverty and privileges, have their effects on living standards, life chances and opportunities. Individuals' health and well-being are influenced by their position in the labour market, income and access to economic resources. Thus, class differences in health have persisted despite an overall improvement in national standards.

Moreover, inequalities in wealth have political implications, providing the wealthiest individuals with access to economic, social and sometimes political power. For this reason, inequalities can become self-perpetuating, having an influence on the institutions that reinforce the class structure. (Pond 1989, p.44)

Almost two decades later this observation about the significance of inequality as a major element of the structural context of UK social work still stands (Pantazis and Gordon 2000). Income inequality has grown faster in the UK since the 1980s than in any other industrialized country except for New Zealand (Hills 1995). In 1979 the post-tax income of the top tenth of the income earning population was around five times that of the bottom tenth; by the mid-1990s that ratio had doubled (Hills 2004). One in four children in the UK lived in poverty in 2005 compared with one in eight in 1979 (Piachaud 2005). In 2003 relative poverty amongst working age adults without children had increased to record levels whilst poverty amongst unemployed people in the UK remained the worst of 11 EU countries with comparable data (Hills and Stewart 2005).

The UK continues to be characterized by high levels of relative poverty. This derives from marked geographical as well as social class, gender and ethnic inequalities in income, health chances, education achievements and physical environments (Lister 2004). Evidence in relation to social exclusion demonstrates that the groups deemed to be on the margins of society are now more deeply disadvantaged than those in the same position a decade ago. (Hills and Stewart 2005; Preston 2005). When the Labour government came into office in 1997 it faced levels of inequality and poverty that were unprecedented in the UK in the post-war period. In recognizing this situation and its impact on society it introduced policies explicitly designed to address and reduce poverty and social exclusion (Jordan 2000).

Recent analysis of the impact of these policies suggests that there is little evidence that they have resulted in a major reversal of existing trends (DSS 1999; DWP 2004). Intergenerational mobility, for example, a measure of the extent of equality of economic opportunity or life chances, has declined markedly in Britain since the 1950s as income inequality has risen. This trend appears to be associated with the relationship between family income and educational attainment. It results in Britain, when compared to other countries in Europe and North America, being on the lower rungs of comparative tables (Blanden, Gregg and Machin 2005).

The forces which have created this situation of widening inequality in the UK include transforming changes in demography and the impact of globalization on the economy and the labour market as well as the responses of successive UK governments in managing these factors through economic and social policies. The consequences have been that a growing section of UK citizens have had to bear a disproportionate reduction in their material, social and physical well-being. These citizens include those living in areas of relatively high unemployment, those lacking educational qualifications, younger and older workers, ethnic minority communities, asylum seekers and disabled people (Hills and Stewart 2005; Pratt 2002). There is a significant research literature that contains the testimonies of such citizens, a literature that eloquently conveys the impact of inequality and exclusion on daily lives and aspirations (Barham and Hayward 1991; Begum, Hill and Stevens 1994; Beresford and Turner 1997; Beresford *et al.* 1999; Daly and Leonard 2002; Kempson 1996).

Social workers in the UK have contact on a daily basis with the casualties of an unequal social order. The research which has tracked the impact of structural inequalities on the lives, opportunities and aspirations of UK citizens suggests that the majority of those who have contact with social workers come from the ranks of those who have least. This is a reflection of the structural inequalities which shape society and the consequent insecurity and lack of resources.

As Schorr observed in the early 1990s, 'the most striking characteristics that clients of social services have in common are poverty and deprivation' (Schorr 1992, p.8). More than a decade later this situation remains unchanged. The responses of social work practitioners to this situation are all too often ones that actively contribute to a process which Lister describes 'Othering the poor', a stance which reduces people in poverty 'to passive objects – in either the benign form of helpless victim or the malign spectre of the lazy, work-shy, welfare dependant. This passive characterization contributes to the social distancing of "them" from "us"' (Lister 2004, p.125). Alternative stances which recognize and work with the considerable strengths that are evidenced in poor and socially excluded communities in the UK are all too rare amongst social workers (Beresford and Croft 1993; Green 2000; Holman 1998).

Knowledge of the patterns, processes and experiences of inequality and social exclusion in contemporary Britain is therefore a critical starting point for developing structural awareness in social work. Such knowledge needs to embrace an understanding that:

> 'Inequality' constitutes a key overarching structural dynamic which can operate at interpersonal, local, national and international levels in a wide variety of social, economic, political and cultural spheres; 'social exclusion' is a consequent process, though not a necessary one, linked to inequality; 'poverty' is a state or condition, but not a necessary one, linked to both inequality and social exclusion. (Williams 1998, p.13)

Social workers utilizing this perspective will develop that understanding of the nature of diversity and difference in contemporary Britain and the ways in which the distribution of resources impacts on individuals, households, groups and communities. This will enhance their knowledge of the nature, distribution and use of power including a recognition of the ways in which power is embedded in political processes as well as in personal encounters (Harris 1997).

## Theorizing structural awareness

Hardiker and Barker suggest that when a social worker views a situation in which he or she is involved solely in structural terms, he or she can be totally incapacitated when working out where and how to intervene in that situation. To counteract this effect they suggest that it is necessary to 'disaggregate different levels of analyses to avoid reductionist explanations and misdirected interventions' (Hardiker and Barker 1988, p.106). The different levels of analysis they outline provide a useful orientation to thinking about how structural awareness can be used to inform social work practice. The levels are:

1.  *Structural*, i.e. an understanding of inequalities and how they are reinforced through social class, gender, age, disability, ethnicity and regional difference.

2.  *Organizational*, in terms of needs and resources and their distribution in relation to personal difficulties and way in which social work intervention gives people access to available resources.

3.  *Interactional or psychosocial* in terms of the way in which private difficulties can be understood as influenced by structural as a well as personal forces.

Whilst this orientation to developing a structural awareness offers a start to thinking about the relationship of structural awareness to practice interventions, it leaves open the question of theorizing structural awareness. At each level questions need to be asked about the range of theoretical perspectives which can be used to develop analyses which are robust enough to generate alternative practice options. In other words, structural awareness needs to be theorized if it is to fully inform creative social work practice.

In seeking to develop structural approaches to social work practice, social workers will find two contrasting approaches to theorizing their knowledge of structural inequalities in the current social work literature. The roots of these approaches are in the political and professional debates which have characterized social work, since its inception, as a profession working with the political, moral and social dilemmas of an unequal society. They both seek to address, rather than ignore, structural issues and provide a starting point from which to develop theorized structural approaches to contemporary social work. The first approach promotes the view that social workers should understand the structural dimensions of the societies in which they work and practise in ways that uphold and maintain the given order. The second promotes the view that social workers in understanding the structural givens with their associated processes and institutions, should, in working with service users, challenge the world in which they live in order to change it for the better.

## A maintenance approach

An example that is worth exploring in relation to the first approach is the maintenance approach; a term coined by Martin Davies in his book *The Essential Social Worker: A Guide to Positive Practice*. Davies views social work as an activity 'concerned with maintaining each individual and society as a whole, and with negotiating the interdependent relationship between each individual and society: it is a policy of reconciliation'. He describes the role of the social worker in relation to this definition as being one that seeks 'to reconcile marginal individuals to their social position, while helping them improve it; and she has to reconcile society to the existence of marginal groups, while simultaneously working to secure improved conditions for them' (Davies 1994, p.59). In operating as it does at the interface of the individual and society, Davies asserts that 'the essence of social work is maintenance: maintaining a stable, though not a static, society, and maintaining the rights of and providing opportunities for those who in an un-planned, uncontrolled community would go to the wall' (Davies 1994, p.202). Social workers for Davies are 'maintenance mechanics oiling the interpersonal wheels of the community' (Davies 1994, p.57).

In this formulation social workers focus on ensuring that people who are referred to them are assisted to cope with the difficult issues in their lives. To do this they provide in-formation about resources and opportunities which might make a difference. They may also need to exercise their authority in situations where risk or vulnerability require a statutory response. In doing this work they draw on their knowledge of what works for individuals and their families – their practice wisdom. At an organizational level they recognize need and grant access to resources in the ways that are framed by their em-ploying agencies. In doing so they seek to help rather than harm the individuals with whom they are working.

This approach, whilst recognizing the impact on individuals of an unequal social or-der, promotes the view that the role of social work should be to work, as effectively as they can, within that order, so as to assist people to make adjustments to and cope with their situations. As such it sets clear limits on the remit of social work practice. Davies has argued that the existence and survival of social work is dependent on two conditions. First, that social workers retain a 'broad respect for the political and economic viability of their society and its underlying political philosophy. Second, that 'the state itself… must retain a broad commitment to a fair, just and humanitarian society in which the rights of each individual, and especially of each most vulnerable citizen, are given due consideration' (Davies 1984, p.32).

Given these two conditions, the maintenance approach is not concerned with chal-lenging the structural status quo. This does not mean that social workers should not raise questions about the direction and distribution of resources and the discrimination and stigma which service users may experience. Advocacy and empowerment are part of the repertoire that social workers need to undertake the role they have been given. However, such activities have clear limits and should not to be confused with the kind of political activity which any citizen might decide to take in a democratic society to bring about political and social change. The scope of professional interventions are bounded by or-ganizational structures and procedures designed to deliver on the state's mandate for social work.

While Davies' formulation gives explicit recognition to the structural framework in which the maintenance work of social workers take place, it offers little analysis of its dy-namics. While referring at times to 'disadvantage' and 'deprivation' alongside 'deviance' and 'vulnerability' as characterizing the lives and identities of those using social work services, he gives little consideration to the social, political and economic forces shaping the social construction and understandings of these conditions. Davies argues that the existence and survival of social work depends on practitioners who in 'implicitly or ex-plicitly accepting a consensus view of the state, must retain broad respect for the political and economic viability of their society and for its underlying political philosophy' (Davies 1994, pp.59–60). As Dominelli observes, this suggests that 'engaging in politi-cal issues, particularly those which challenge the existing social order, falls outside the

remit of the "maintenance" practitioner, who views society as being basically benign'
(Dominelli 1998, p.4).

## A critical structural approach

A contrasting approach to theorizing structural awareness is to be found in the rich
stream of social work literature emerging from the late 1960s which is characterized
by the centrality it has given to the importance of structurally contextualizing individual
situations and difficulties. This critical structural approach embraces radical social work
(Bailey and Brake 1975; Corrigan and Leonard 1978; Langan and Lee 1989), feminist
social work (Dominelli and McCleod 1989; Orme 1998), critical social work (Adams,
Dominelli and Payne 2002; Fook 1993), anti-oppressive social work (Dominelli
1998, 2002), structural social work (Mullaly 2003) and transformational social work
(Adams, Dominelli and Payne 2005). These texts cover a wide range of political, professional, philosophical and personal positions, and as a consequence cannot be viewed as
constituting a unitary approach (Payne 2005). But the term 'approach' is used here to
highlight the shared core ideas that offer an alternative to the maintenance approach
outlined by Davies.

A critical structural approach is one which questions the existing social order. It
views this order as unequal, socially divisive and unjust. It rejects the account of the
nature of the state taken by the maintenance approach. It argues that the state in maintaining dominant interests sustains inequality and associated forms of oppression.
Because of this social workers need to question accounts which suggest that the state
plays a neutral, humanitarian role with respect to its citizens. In doing so they need to
recognize that any maintenance role they assume with respect to state welfare policies
and institutions serves to perpetuate inequality and its associated oppressions,
disadvantages and stigma.

Critical structural social work texts argue that social workers need to engage with
the myriad ways in which the nature of social structures and state power constructs social
work as an element of state control and oppression. In doing this social workers need to
understand how the lives and opportunities of service users shape and are shaped by
structural factors. Practice which is underpinned by this understanding is concerned
with both challenging and seeking to change oppressive and dominant structures and
processes. Critical structural social work practice is also concerned with transforming
the relationships between social work and service users in directions that empower,
emancipate and give voice to those who have least.

The radical social work perspective, which was an early influence on the development of critical structural approaches, focused on social class as the major and
determining site of inequality and oppression. Subsequent contributions from feminist,
anti-oppressive and critical social work perspectives have opened up consideration of
the diverse and overlapping dimensions of power, inequality and oppression in contemporary society. For critical structuralists, society is characterized by structured conflicts
of interest which are played out in a number of different spheres and are experienced simultaneously and serially by individuals. In understanding and working with this
knowledge links need to be made between structural awareness and the accounts that

service users give of their predicaments. Social work practice that is developed in the light of this analysis must be informed by knowledge about how social, economic and political structures shape lives and must be responsive to the diversity of voices and perspectives of those who live those lives.

A critical structural approach offers much to developing analyses of the structural level of Hardiker and Barker's (1988) framework. However, a long-standing criticism of this approach is that in emphasizing the impact of social, economic and political structures and processes on the theory and practice of social work it fails to engage convincingly with the organizational and interactional levels of analysis. This failure has resulted in relatively little being offered to social workers concerned with developing structurally informed practice in ways that engage effectively with both social work agencies and service users' lives (Fook 2002; Payne 2005).

More recent social work and social welfare texts have begun to redress this situation. Adams, Dominelli and Payne (1998); Batsleer and Humphries (2000); Lister (2004); Williams (1998) and Williams, Popay and Oakley (1999), amongst others, offer fruitful ways of furthering understanding of the organizational and interactional levels. These make use of the idea of agency in order 'to characterize individuals as autonomous, purposive and creative actors, capable of a degree of choice' (Lister 2004, p.124) despite the cultural and structural constraints they experience. Lister argues persuasively that current theorizing of agency provides a way to transcend the dichotomy between structuralist and individualist approaches to understanding welfare practice. For Williams et al. this means recognizing 'the capacity of people to be creative, reflexive human beings, that is to be active agents in shaping their lives, experiencing, acting upon and reconstituting the outcomes of welfare policies in various ways' (Williams et al. 1999, p.47). An approach which offers a great deal to understandings of the situations of both service users and social workers

In developing ideas of agency in relation to social work theory and practice Batsleer and Humphries highlight the importance of listening to the testimony of oppressed and marginalized individuals and groups who are voicing their concerns about their situations. They suggest that 'The idea of agency is more than individual' and usefully explore the way in which 'political agency' contributes to 'making common cause out of…shared ends, entering into dialogue about shared and different common interests and needs' (Batsleer and Humphries 2000, p.16). In furthering this work Lister provides a taxonomy which, in representing the dimensions of agency on continua which span the personal, the political, the everyday and the strategic, is particularly helpful in framing thinking about the directions that structurally informed social work theory and practice could take (Lister 2004, p.130).

## Developing structural social work approaches

These two broad approaches to theorizing the structural offer contrasting analyses of, and ways of working with, knowledge of structural issues. They provide different starting points for social workers in training and practice. The first, in arguing for maintenance within given conditions, promotes a consensual view of practice in which recognition of the discrimination suffered by vulnerable groups is dealt with through advocacy within organizational and political givens. The second, in arguing for change of existing structures which perpetuate inequality, promotes an adversarial view of practice which simultaneously seeks to alleviate and transform the conditions in which oppressed clients find themselves.

Developing structural social work approaches amongst social workers in qualifying and post-qualifying education involves work in both university and practice settings. In delivering on this in the context of the qualifying courses at the University of Birmingham, we offer a first-term module called 'Identity, Social Processes and Social Inclusion'. It has been designed to deliver on the QAA benchmark requirements as well as providing a foundation on which students can build a structurally informed approach to social work theory and practice. The aim of the module is to introduce students at the beginning of their qualifying programme to a socially informed consideration of theory and practice in working with individuals and groups who are excluded, disadvantaged and oppressed by the systematic inequalities of poverty, gender sexuality, ethnicity, class, disability and age.

The module is offered over eight weeks in one-day sessions. In each of the morning sessions the focus is on issues of social process and identity in contemporary Britain. The morning sessions combine lectures drawing on sociology and social policy knowledge delivered by social work academics and service users with seminars in which students discuss selected texts. The programme is launched with a morning session on identity and personal experience. In this session students are invited to explore and share their experiences of identity formation. It is a session which builds a body of student-generated knowledge about diversity and difference, oppression and esteem in contemporary society. It also serves to introduce students to the wealth of experiential knowledge that they hold as a group. In the afternoon session students consider the characteristics of inequality and social exclusion in Britain and the ways these are experienced by individuals and groups who use social work services.

In the following six morning sessions six sites of identity are considered – gender, sexuality, ethnicity, class, disability and age. In the afternoon sessions these identities are revisited through a series of presentations from social work academics as well as service users and practitioners who are involved in projects which seek to positively address issues of social exclusion. In these sessions knowledge about the experiences of those who find themselves with least in our society is shared, as well as a range of practice responses to these experiences. The final session of the module is used to assist students to make the links between learning on this module and their professional practice skills and values.

This module is taken before students engage with social work theory and practice modules and they are invited to take forward their learning in order to critically contextualize what they are offered on these later modules. In university-based assignment work as well as practice-based portfolio work students are asked to provide evidence of how they have, practically and theoretically, applied their knowledge about the impact of structural issues, on the lives of service users.

## Conclusion

The success of modules, like the one developed in Birmingham, which aim to develop a structural awareness amongst qualifying social workers as well as a critical appreciation of how that awareness can be theorized, depends on social work educators in universities and the field creating supported spaces for students to explore and reflect on structural approaches to social work theory and practice (see, for example, Davis and Wainwright 1996). This means that educators need to actively develop practice learning opportunities within and outside placement agencies that actively seek to develop the learning undertaken by students in the university.

This will involve educators on both sites supporting students to find out about the local, national and international evidence of the inequalities and oppression experienced by those individuals, families and communities who use social work services (for an example, see Singh Cooner 2005). It will involve educators in encouraging students to critically reflect on what they learn about the policies and procedures of health and social work agencies and their impact on marginalized and excluded citizens. It will involve practice teachers in encouraging students to develop their practice creativity in assessing, intervening and reviewing their work with individuals, families and groups in a structurally informed way. Finally, it requires that social work students on placement and at the university are given time to share their evolving thoughts and feelings about what working with structural approaches offers to them as critically reflective practitioners.

## References

Adams, R., Dominelli, L. and Payne, M. (eds) (1998) *Social Work: Themes, Issues and Critical Debates.* Basingstoke: Macmillan.

Adams, R., Dominelli, L. and Payne, M. (eds) (2002) *Critical Practice in Social Work.* Basingstoke: Palgrave Macmillan.

Adams, R., Dominelli, L. and Payne, M. (eds) (2005) *Social Work Futures: Crossing Boundaries, Transforming Practice.* Basingstoke: Palgrave Macmillan.

Bailey, R. and Brake, M. (eds) (1975) *Radical Social Work.* London: Edward Arnold.

Barham, P. and Hayward, R. (1991) *From the Mental Patient to the Person.* London: Routledge.

Barry, M. and Hallett, C. (eds) (1998) *Social Exclusion and Social Work.* Lyme Regis: Russell House Publishing.

Batsleer, J. and Humphries, B. (eds) (2000) *Welfare, Exclusion and Political Agency.* London: Routledge.

Becker, S. and MacPherson, S. (eds) (1988) *Public Issues, Private Pain: Poverty, Social Work and Social Policy.* London: Social Services Insight Publications.

Begum, N., Hill, M. and Stevens, S. (1994) *Reflections: Views of Black Disabled People on their Lives and Community Care.* Paper 32.3. London: CCETSW.

Beresford, P. and Croft, S. (1993) *Citizen Involvement: A Practical Guide for Change.* London: BASW/Macmillan.

Beresford, P. and Turner, M. (1997) *It's Our Welfare: Report of the Citizens Commission on the Future of the Welfare State.* London: National Institute of Social Work

Beresford, P., Green, D., Lister, R. and Woodward, K. (1999) *Poverty First Hand: Poor People Speak for Themselves.* London: Child Poverty Action Group

Blanden, J., Gregg, P. and Machin, S. (2005) *Intergenerational Mobility in Europe and North America.* London: Centre for Economic Performance.

Corrigan, P. and Leonard, P. (1978) *Social Work Under Capitalism.* London: Macmillan.

Daly, M. and Leonard, M. (2002) *Against All Odds: Family Life on a Low Income in Ireland*. Dublin: Institute of Public Administration/Combat Poverty Agency.

Davies, M. (1984) *The Essential Social Worker*. 2nd edn. Aldershot: Gower.

Davies, M. (1994) *The Essential Social Worker*. 3rd edn. Aldershot: Arena.

Davis, A. and Garrett, P.M. (2004) 'Progressive practice in tough times: Social work, poverty and division in the 21st century.' In M. Lymbery and S. Butler (eds) *Social Work Ideals and Practice Realities*. Basingstoke: Palgrave.

Davis, A. and Wainwright, S. (1996) 'Poverty work and the mental health services.' *Breakthrough 1*, 1, 47–56.

Davis, A. and Wainwright, S. (2005) 'Combating poverty and social exclusion: Implications for social work education.' *Social Work Education 24*, 3 (April), 259–73.

DSS (1999) *Opportunity for All: Tackling Poverty and Social Exclusion*. London: DSS.

DWP (2004) 'Households below average income: An analysis of the income distribution 1994/5–2002/03.' Leeds: Corporate Document Services.

Dominelli, L. (1998) 'Anti-oppressive practice in context.' In R. Adams, L. Dominelli and M. Payne (eds) *Social Work: Themes, Issues and Critical Debates*. Basingstoke: Macmillan.

Dominelli, L. (2002) *Anti-oppressive Social Work Theory and Practice*. Basingstoke: Palgrave Macmillan.

Dominelli, L. and McCleod, E. (1989) *Feminist Social Work*. Basingstoke: Macmillan.

Dowling, M. (1999) *Social Work and Poverty*. Aldershot: Ashgate.

Fook, J. (1993) *Radical Casework*. London, Sage.

Green, R. (2000) 'Applying a community needs profiling approach to tackling service user poverty.' *British Journal of Social Work 30*, 287–303.

Hardiker, P. and Barker, M. (1988) 'A window on child care, poverty and social work.' In S. Becker. and S. MacPherson (eds) *Public Issues, Private Pain: Poverty, Social Work and Social Policy*. Insight/Carematters books.

Harris, J. (1997) 'Power' in M. Davies (ed.) *The Blackwell Companion to Social Work*. Oxford: Blackwell.

Hills, J. (2004) *Inequality and the State*. Oxford: Oxford University Press.

Hills, J., Le Grand, J. and Piachaud, D. (eds) (2002) *Understanding Social Exclusion*. Oxford: Oxford University Press.

Hills, J. and Stewart, K (eds) (2005) *A More Equal Society? New Labour, Poverty, Inequality and Exclusion*. Bristol: Policy Press.

Holman, B. (1998) *Faith in the Poor*. Oxford: Lion Publishing.

International Association of Schools of Social Work/International Federation of Social Workers (2001) *International Definition of Social Work*. Addis Ababa: IASSW. Retrieved from www.iassw-aiets.org.

Jones, C. (1998) 'Social work and society.' In R. Adams, L. Dominelli and M. Payne (eds) *Social work: Themes, Issues and Critical Debates*. Basingstoke: Macmillan.

Jordan, B. (2000) 'Tough love: Social work practice in UK society.' in P. Stepney and D. Ford (eds) *Social Work Models, Methods and Theories: A Framework for Practice*. Lyme Regis: Russell House Publishing.

Kempson, E. (1996) *Life on a Low Income*. York: Joseph Rowntree Foundation.

Langan, M. and Lee, P. (eds) (1989) *Radical Social Work Today*. London: Unwin Hyman.

Lister, R. (2004) *Poverty*. Cambridge: Polity Press.

Manthorpe, J. and Bradley, G. (2002) 'Managing finances.' In R. Adams, L. Dominelli and M. Payne (eds) *Critical Practice in Social Work*. Basingstoke: Palgrave Macmillan.

Mullaly, B. (2003) *Structural Social Work: Ideology, Theory and Practice*. 2nd edn. Ontario: Oxford University Press.

Orme, J. (1998) 'Feminist social work.' In R. Adams, L. Dominelli and M. Payne (eds) *Social Work: Themes, Issues and Critical Debates*. Basingstoke: Palgrave Macmillan.

Pantazis, C. and Gordon, D. (eds) (2000) *Tackling Inequalities*. Bristol: Policy Press.

Payne, M. (2005) *Modern Social Work Theory*. 3rd edn. Basingstoke: Palgrave Macmillan.

Piachaud, D. (2005) 'Child poverty: an overview.' In G. Preston (ed.) *At Greatest Risk: The Children Most Likely to be Poor.* London: CPAG.

Pond, C. (1989) 'The changing distribution of income, wealth and poverty.' In C. Hamnett *et al.* (eds) *The Changing Social Structure.* London: Sage.

Pratt, L. (2002) *Parallel Lives? Poverty among ethnic groups in Britain.* London: Child Poverty Action Group.

Preston, G. (ed.) (2005) *At Greatest Risk: The Children Most Likely to be Poor.* London, CPAG.

QAA (2000) *Subject Benchmark Statements: Social Policy and Administration and Social Work.* Gloucester: Quality Assurance Agency. Retrieved from http://www.qaa.ac.uk/academzinfrastructure/ benchmark/honours/socialpolicy.asp.

Schorr, A. (1992) *The Personal Social Services: An Outsider's View.* York: Joseph Rowntree Foundation.

Singh Cooner, T. (2005) 'Dialectical constructivism: Reflections on creating a web-mediated enquiry-based learning environment.' *Social Work Education 24,* 4 375–9.

Williams, F. (1998) 'Agency and structure revisited.' In M. Barry and C. Hallett (eds) *Social Exclusion and Social Work.* Lyme Regis: Russell House Publishing.

Williams, F., Popay, J. and Oakley, A. (eds) (1999) *Welfare Research a Critical Review.* London: UCL Press.

## CHAPTER 3

# TOWARDS SOCIAL THEORY FOR SOCIAL WORK

*Pauline Hardiker and Mary Barker*

## Editor's note

Sadly Pauline Hardiker died in August 2004. She had, as I asked, provided a brief update to her original chapter. Because it was very specifically linked to the Diploma in Social Work (CCETSW) requirements and competences I have not included it in this new edition since future readers will be involved with new honours degrees in social work.

I have, however, included the original chapter in her memory and because, in 1991, it was a seminal paper (and remains so in 2007) to enable practice teachers and students to consider how they might critically examine and apply a range of theoretical approaches to understand and conceptualize their practice, not as a 'pick and mix' but from an integrated conceptual base (see also Chapter 2 in the present volume). We need this for understanding in a holistic way service users who require social work and social services, for assessment, for intervention and for a continuing evaluation of how effective our interventions are in responding to and meeting the needs of service users.

Hardiker and Barker use child care and child protection as a case example for their argument (in Chapter 20 Buckley deals with current child care and child protection research, knowledge, policy and practice). Hardiker and Barker's chapter remains relevant to current social work practice:

> An identifying characteristic of social work is the great range of human situations it addresses: this encompasses not only people's predicaments but also their social situations. The work requires a breadth of discipline knowledge, derived not only from social sciences but also from other bodies of knowledge (e.g. law, psychiatry and philosophy). Furthermore social workers need to be sufficiently familiar with them to make informed choices. (p.41)

As Hardiker and Barker go on to comment wryly: 'a tall order'!

Hardiker and Barker's chapter possibly pioneered and certainly promoted problem-based learning in the development of social work practice and education. Problem-based learning (Burgess and Taylor 2005) in Hardiker and Barker's chapter involves using a specific exercise, based on a problematic situation presented to a social worker, which requires students, practice teachers and academics to examine and review a full range of possible theoretical or empirical explanations or approaches to understanding, assessment or intervention which they might employ and provide an evidence-based rationale for their choice.

In reviewing the exercise it is clearly based on theory and empirical knowledge. While the references to research findings appear historical, i.e. before 1990, they are not irrelevant in 2007, and remain part of the evidence base for social work. Students could usefully be asked to update the research base of the exercise as part of a problem-based learning task.

As Hardiker and Barker argue, the exercise – where students are required to examine assumptions critically, explicit or implicit, in the statements given, and identify the theoretical frameworks from which they are drawn – is 'mind-blowing'. It also represents a commitment to evidence-based practice in terms of the sources, derivations and validity of social work theory and knowledge (for example, is it empirically tested or does it represent a useful 'theory of meaning'? see Chapter 24 in the present volume). It enables students to begin to identify rather more specifically, on the basis of the nature of the evidence provided, what themes, concepts and frameworks relevantly apply and should be used for a specific piece of practice.

Hardiker and Barker introduce the concept of ideology, i.e. 'a set of ideas and beliefs which is systematic enough to convey an underlying attitude to society, shared by members of a social group' (p.45). Such ideologies may be implicit and taken for granted: professions may each have a set of ideological assumptions which are not shared. Entrants to social work need to think very clearly and critically about the ideologies and assumptions they 'take for granted'. These assumptions may conflict with those of users of services and other professionals.

Hardiker and Barker helpfully identify an ideological base to political trends and policies and practices. As they suggest, an attempt to understand the ideological base of trends in policies and practices is another way of breaking through the assumptions and stereotypes which may determine action. It may also increase the range of alternative approaches considered.

Hardiker and Barker remind us of ongoing and historical tensions in social work where we need to engage with powerful human predicaments. They also challenge us to reflect on whether a specific approach taken – for example, individual/psychosocial, structural or advocacy – could potentially have damaging or exploitative implications for users of services.

The final section of Hardiker and Barker's chapter argues the relevance of knowledge in social work but suggests that a key function of social work education is *enlightenment* in the liberal education tradition. This involves a 'humbling' function, where we recognize the centrality of uncertainty in social work and social services and adopt an approach which abandons 'isms' and tries to examine critically a potential dogma or ideology by reference to empirical knowledge and to make a balanced judgement in terms of use and application. This is particularly relevant to risk assessment and management which present current complex issues where we need to review carefully relevant evidence (see the chapters in Section 2 on assessment in the present volume).

Hardiker and Barker *also* counsel us to recognize the 'non-Utopian' element of social work where we grapple with the tensions between working with private pain and meeting the requirements of social control when the two may be interlinked. As Hardiker and Barker argue:

> Any social worker who claims to have 'cracked' child abuse after completing…a lifetime's career in practice will have failed to grasp some of these messages. Any social theorist or politician who fails to appreciate that *some* human predicaments brook of *no* solutions is also being Utopian or entirely unrealistic. (p.50, emphasis mine)

In conclusion, this chapter continues to address fundamental issues and themes for social work practice in relation to the range of personal and social issues it needs to address (for example, from empowerment to social control), and the tensions that this involves. It addresses critically the dangers of using ideology and 'isms', or fads and fashions, to underpin our practice and stresses the need for us to use critically and evaluatively knowledge and evidence. Finally, it asks us to consider carefully whether unwittingly our interventions may be less than helpful: this underpins the need for a sophisticated use of evaluation and evidence-based practice (see Chapter 24 in the present volume).

> to practice without theory is to sail an uncharted sea; theory without practice is not to set sail at all. (Susser 1968, p.v)

> Without a social theory the social worker is at the mercy of a thousand discouragements. (Marshall 1946, p.1)

## Introduction

In this chapter, we discuss the general theme of discipline knowledge for social work. Other chapters in this volume present specific theories from the social sciences (e.g. loss and bereavement; attachment theory) and models of social work intervention (e.g. behavioural; crisis intervention).

An identifying characteristic of social work is the great range of human situations addressed; this encompasses not only people's predicaments but also their social situations. The work requires a breadth of discipline knowledge, derived not only from the social sciences, but also from other bodies of knowledge (e.g. law, psychiatry and philosophy). Furthermore, social workers need to be sufficiently familiar with them to make informed choices, to keep up to date with advances and to discard redundant theories. This is a tall order indeed. Practitioners, therefore, often adopt a pragmatic stance, claiming to use whatever approach appears to work in a particular case. However, social workers are rarely as arbitrary as this implies; their practices are influenced and constrained by their agencies, by the nature of the cases, and by changing ideas of the role of the state in welfare (Briar and Miller 1971; Hardiker and Barker1981; Loewenberg1984).

For example, social workers practise from an agency-specific location, so child abuse referrals are processed through a variety of legal and administrative systems and are assessed in different ways, e.g. neglect, incest, family dysfunction (Hardiker and Barker 1985). Hardiker, Exton and Barker (1991, p.112) suggest in relation to preventive child care:

> Problem definition and assessment is not a simple, objective measure but a complex process which involves values, principles, agency policies and procedures, the current legal position and the perspectives of social workers and their managers. Similar situations may or may not lead a client to seek help, a social worker to open a case file, a court to make an order.

Furthermore, child abuse assumes different forms in relation to the nature of injuries and patterns of parenting. These perceived variations also shape the types of interventions chosen. Very serious physical injuries may involve police, courts and probation officers, whereas less serious ones may be processed through community facilities and self-help groups. Finally, child abusers differ in respect of their age, gender, socio-economic status, race, ethnicity and neighbourhood, i.e. typically, social inequalities (Frost and Stein1989).

The poverty lobby suggests that the parenting of many young, working-class mothers living in deprived communities may be too readily labelled as child abuse instead of being recognized as adequate coping in stressful circumstances.

It has been suggested in this introduction that, in spite of the wide range of discipline knowledge available to social workers, they are rarely in a position to choose whatever theory or approach they please. Frameworks for practice are shaped by the nature of problems referred, circumstances of families, and agency functions and resources.

## Social theory for social work

Where can one look for principles and frameworks of knowledge which will help social workers to find a way through this range of discipline knowledge? One way in which this is attempted on the Leicester MA in social work course is through a sequence we have called 'Social Theory for Social Work'. It is studied in the final academic block of this two-year post-graduate course, when students have already received teaching in many of the contributory disciplines, and in social work theory and methods. They have also completed two practice placements and their practice study. They are, therefore, relatively well versed in both theory and practice.

It is probably best to convey the nature of this sequence through the use of an exercise, taken from the social theory course. This example concerns approaches to child abuse (though any field of practice could have been selected, and the analysis offered is intended to be transferable).

### EXERCISE
The students are asked to think of a general statement about child abuse and to write it down (working individually).

Students are then handed the following list of statements about child abuse (taken from the literature or illustrating a commonly held view) and asked to compare them with their own individual statements. It is anticipated that most of the students' statements will have parallels in the list, and that there may even be clusters of typical responses (e.g. bonding and family systems):

1. Fatal battering has been shown to occur where young, unstable, deserted and un-happy women associate with young, psychopathic and criminal men (Smith 1975; Smith, Henson and Noble 1974, p.575).

2. Neither parent has had any experience of a normal loving home and I think they need a sustaining and nurturing experience themselves to enable them to cope with the demands and stresses of their own small children (Court 1985, p.x; this statement illustrates some of Kempe's theories).

3. By definition, however, the child who has been abused has demonstrably not bonded with its abusing parents (London Borough of Brent 1985, p.97).[1]

4. Mr X is repeating patterns of abusive parenting which he experienced in his own family.[2]

5. This episode of abuse reflects some of the ways in which this child is scapegoated within her family (Vogel and Bell 1968).

6. This child's 'failure to thrive' has partly arisen because his aversive temperamental attitudes have shaped his interaction with Mr and Mrs X who found him difficult to parent (Iwaniec, Herbert and McNeish 1985a, 1985b).

7. The relationship between the parents is problematical. Mr and Mrs X wish to avoid conflict because they fear their marriage will break down. Mrs X opts out of the family and Mr X becomes over-involved with his daughter. This abuse maintains the pattern (Bentovim et al. 1988).[3]

8. Boundary roles within this family have weakened external and internal inhibitory mechanisms which might have protected the child against abuse (Finkelhor 1984).

9. This family is socially isolated in the neighbourhood.[4]

10. J's delinquency is a symptom of the abuse she has experienced in her family.[5]

11. The infant mortality rate in this deprived district is two and a half times higher than that in 'leafy suburbia' (Black Report 1980; Westergaard and Resler 1975; Whitehead 1987).

12. Mr X's assault on his daughter is the cause not the symptom of this family's difficulties (Feminist Review Collective 1988).

13. Welfare agencies have underreacted or overreacted to the signs of physical injury notified to them (Dingwall, Eekelaar and Murray 1983; for types of agency response see Aldrich 1979; Benson 1982; Cook 1977).

14. The problem of child abuse should be addressed at a much earlier stage in the community, e.g. education programmes, self-help and parent-craft groups (Browne, Davies and Stratton 1988; see also Chandler, Stone and Young 1989).

15. The identification of risk groups by the Area Review Committee is sexist, racist and discriminates against vulnerable working-class families (Ahmed, Cheetham and Small 1986; Equality for Children 1983; Frost and Stein 1989; Hardiker and Curnock 1984; Holman 1988; Parton and Parton 1988).

16. The Child Protection Register polices problem populations and dangerous families (Parton 1985; Parton and Small 1989; Rojeck, Peacock and Collins 1989; Spitzer 1975).

*Note:* It is important to remember that this exercise is presented as a teaching device, not a comprehensive theory of or approach to child abuse; otherwise, the presentation over-simplifies and caricatures perspectives which are normally appropriately more complex. The exercise has also been used with groups of practice teachers.

### REVIEW

In discussion, the students are asked to identify some of the assumptions underlying the statements (which may be implicit or explicit), and the different theoretical frameworks they represent (Stainton Rogers, Harvey and Ash 1989).

This exercise is quite 'mind-bending' for anyone who attempts it, as we rarely, if ever, attempt to write down the full range of possible explanations or approaches to any particular social work situation (Curnock and Hardiker 1979). The students are then asked to contribute to the discussion the statements about child abuse that they themselves wrote down, and to try to identify the assumptions underlying those. Often, their own statements add even more to the range of views, e.g. child abuse as a rediscovered problem-definition; the relationship between sexual abuse and adult psychiatric difficulties.

The discussion leads into an analysis of the exercise, in which an attempt is made to look for themes/frameworks/concepts which underlie this diversity, and help social workers to make more sense of the whole. This approach is demonstrated in the next section, and again is related to the exercise on child abuse, for the purpose of illustration. The following themes are discussed:

1. Identifying concepts and theoretical traditions.

2. Value positions and ideologies.

3. Explanations and interventions.

## Themes and frameworks of social theory

### IDENTIFYING CONCEPTS AND THEORETICAL TRADITIONS

The statements listed above are derived from the authors' reading and understanding of the literature on child abuse (which is less than exhaustive). A first stage in learning about social theories for social work is the ability to recognize particular concepts and theories. This may not be easy for social work practitioners, who have sometimes internalized them so that they are 'taken for granted' and not questioned. For instance, many of the statements use the concept of parenting as crucial to the understanding of the problems (e.g. numbers one to six). Bonding is identified in the third statement, and boundary roles in the seventh and eighth. Risk groups are suggested in statements 15 and 16. Such concepts are significant tools in increasing understanding and achieving a common discourse, and readers are invited to identify others.

Sometimes the theoretical approach underlying such concepts is relatively clear. For example, a psychodynamic approach is evident in the second statement, and a behavioural one in the sixth. A sociological view is implied in the eleventh, and organizational theory in the thirteenth. Again, readers should be able to identify others.

It will be obvious that the same concept may be used in different theoretical approaches. For example, parenting may be understood in psychodynamic ways (Statements 2 and 3), or in behavioural terms (the sixth statement). Intergenerational patterns of parenting may be analysed in terms of cycles of deprivation (the fourth statement) or the persistence of the patriarchal family (the twelfth).

In the same way, units of analysis (e.g. the family) may be considered from different perspectives, such as cultural (number nine) or systems (number eight).

Identification of such theoretical underpinning can give pointers to social workers in the way of further study. For instance, behavioural methods are often used in 'common sense' ways, but a better grasp of principles and techniques can achieve much more. The concept of 'bonding' has gained wide acceptance and usage, but is often misused, and the term has widely differing meanings and implications.

## VALUE POSITIONS AND IDEOLOGIES

Another framework for understanding social work and social policy is in terms of the value positions which underlie actions and choices (Fox 1982; Freeman 1983).[6] Fox compares two schools of thought represented in child care legislation, policies and practices: 'kinship defenders' and 'society-as-parent protagonists'. The 'kinship defenders' see the natural or biological family as being the best environment for almost all children. They emphasize class and economic variables, rather than parental inadequacy and culpability, as factors associated with poor standards of care. For example, Holman (1976, 1988) stressed the link between child separation and poverty, advocating more supportive services to enable good parenting to take place. The 'society-as-parent protagonists', on the other hand, place great importance on the need to defend children against neglectful and abusive parents, by the beneficient interventions of state welfare. Rowe and Lambert (1973) for instance, emphasized the psychological need of children for early placement in secure, permanent substitute families, in preference to long-delayed reclamation by their parents. In our exercise, Statements 2, 11 and 15 can be seen as examples of the 'kinship defender' position, whereas Statements 1, 3 and 12 might represent the views of the 'society-as-parent' view. Readers may be able to see similar links in other statements. Of course, any of these statements may be appropriate to individual cases, and there is overlap between the two perspectives, but realization of the social values underlying policy trends and actions may remind us of other important objectives. It also helps us to unpack over-generalized phrases such as 'best interests', 'the welfare of the child' and 'parents' rights', which may camouflage great differences in interpretation and preferred action.

The concept 'ideology' suggests yet another way in which some of these theory-practice links can be explored (see Hardiker 1981; Hardiker and Barker 1981, Chapter 7; Smith 1977; for an exploration of these ideologies). By 'ideology', we mean a set of ideas and beliefs, which is systematic enough to convey an underlying attitude to society, shared by members of a social group. Ideologies may be difficult to identify because they are often implicit and taken for granted by those who hold them. However, they may have a profound effect on choices and decisions, sometimes representing the interests of one social group (e.g. parents) as against others (e.g. lawyers), and carrying considerable emotional weighting.

The statements about child abuse may be analysed in terms of the ideologies which seem to underpin them. For instance, the first example may represent a judicial ideology, which emphasizes legal rights and duties, and due punishment for offenders. It draws attention to the deviance which may underlie serious child abuse, which might lead to a punitive disposal. A welfare ideology, on the other hand, would focus on the needs of the families concerned, and the ways in which they could be helped (possibly through therapeutic and resource-based interventions). Statements 2 to 10 exemplify this attitude. Number 14, however, calls attention to possibilities of addressing child abuse through community participation and empowerment, in accordance with a developmental ideology. Proponents of this viewpoint would be concerned with poverty and disadvantage, and would consider the possibilities of changing systems rather than people. Statement 13 carries this approach further towards a radical view, in suggesting that the actions of state institutions may themselves be part of the problem.

Ideologies are complex and multidimensional, and it is not suggested that they can be adequately studied in such simple ways. However, an attempt to understand the ideological basis of trends in policies and practices is another way of breaking through the assumptions and stereotypes which may determine action. It may also increase the range of alternative approaches considered.

Some strongly held ideologies are sustained at the cost of vulnerable social groups. For example, powerful ideologies about family privacy, parental rights and patriarchy have probably maintained some forms of child abuse, and limited access to sources of help. Sexual abuse is a prime instance. From some feminist perspectives and also research evidence (Dobash and Dobash 1980; Feminist Review Collective 1988; Pahl 1985), families are not safe places for many women and children, and alternative living and relational forms are circumscribed through social and economic policies, limited day care resources, housing legislation and familial ideologies.

Good questions to ask ourselves, in seeking to understand any pervasive social problem, are 'Whose interests are being served?' and 'Are the interests of one social group being met at the expense of others?'. Some social problems persist because all of us have social and psychological investments in maintaining them.

## EXPLANATIONS AND INTERVENTIONS

The literature on child abuse is currently entering a relatively 'scientific' phase, in which strong links are made between explanation and intervention, and some very exciting helping approaches have been initiated (Browne et al. 1988; Glaser and Frosh 1988; Walker, Bonner and Kangman 1988). For example, behaviour modification programmes are devised to change the behaviour of parents who abuse their children through over-chastisement or lack of cuddling; boundary roles in families may be redefined and clarified in order to alter power balances between father/daughter and husband/wife, respectively, thereby reducing the risk of incestuous liaisons.

However, we should be aware that different social science disciplines tend to use different levels of analysis to explain social problems. Characteristically, psychology is concerned with the study of individuals and small groups; sociology with social institutions and social processes; and social policy with political economy and welfare organizations. These levels of analysis suggest different units of intervention: parents or parent–child dyads; families and social networks; social legislation and welfare agencies.

As referrals normally come to social service departments in terms of individuals and families, it is, perhaps, understandable that theories which are directly concerned with these units of intervention often seem more relevant and applicable, e.g. play therapy and family casework. However, other social sciences direct us towards other units of intervention, such as schools, communities or agency procedures.

Sometimes, a further connection is made, in that work with individuals is considered as 'social control' and work with communities as 'social change'. However, it is important to recognize that the unit of intervention should not necessarily determine the objectives of the work (Cockburn 1977; Cowley *et al.* 1977; Leonard 1984; Rein 1970). Work with individuals can include social change objectives, e.g. helping them to have a better appreciation of their social situation and how they can work towards influencing it (conscientisation). Conversely, work directed towards communities may be more concerned with dampening social protest than with empowerment of residents. Examples may be drawn from the field of child abuse. For instance, work with parents and children may appropriately take the form of family work, or of a unitary systems approach (Herbert 1988) which would identify a wider range of targets. Work with adolescent girls may be directed towards re-socializing them into traditional gender roles or towards empowering them to choose another lifestyle outside the nuclear family (Hudson 1985,1989). Possibilities of addressing child abuse at a community level (e.g. through education programmes, self-help groups or social policies in relation to poverty and housing) should also be kept in mind (Smale *et al.* 1988).

## REVIEW

In this section, we have explored some ways in which relatively tight links are made between causal explanations and types of social work interventions. These links may derive from specific theoretical approaches, e.g. behavioural and family systems, or from particular units of analysis, e.g. child, parent, neighbourhood. It was also argued, however, that the unit of analysis should not necessarily determine the objectives of the intervention.

Our earlier discussion on values and ideologies may also help us to clarify some of these issues because it reminds us that social work relies on other sources of understanding besides social science disciplines. Understanding is based on an amalgam of ideas, beliefs, interests and hunches which may indicate a particular attitude or approach on the part of the social worker. For example, a behavioural or family systems intervention suggests a welfare ideology, whereas a community support project points to a developmental ideology.

As any social worker knows, practice is never as abstract as these arguments imply, because our profession is an art as well as a science. England (1986) refers to the importance of skills such as the use of self, intuition, meaning and subjectivity in the art of social work. All these dimensions – values and ideologies, skills in the use of self and intuition – may help us to understand ways in which social science knowledge should inform social work practice rather than take it over (Timms and Timms 1977). The next section explores some of the ways in which a psychosocial approach brings these several sources of knowledge and understanding together.

## Theorizing the psychosocial

Social work is more than applied sociology, applied psychology or social policy and administration – though, as we have seen, it relies on and borrows heavily from these disciplines. First, social workers necessarily use psychosocial terms such as 'coping', 'functioning', 'self-determination', 'loss and change', 'good-enough' parenting, rather than relying on terms central to other disciplines such as 'personality', 'role', 'social institution', and 'poverty'. Second, social work is a purposeful and value-based rather than solely conceptual exploration. Therefore, if they were not already to hand, social workers would need to create such terms as 'person–environment fit', 'person-in-situation', 'psychosocial functioning'. These equations may be informed by psychodynamic, behavioural, social-ecological or critical theories, but they still amount to 'more than' their theoretical underpinnings.

Such psychosocial perspectives are sometimes adopted in the child abuse literature. For example, O'Hagan (1989) argues that 'social work categorizations' are needed to address the varieties of child sexual abuse and differential indications for intervention; these categorizations relate to child protection, family and social context, and resources. Joan Court's report on the Beckford family was informed partly by psychodynamic ideas but was also based on a broad psychosocial perspective which considered communication, stresses, environmental resources, accounts and values (Court 1985).

It has been suggested, though, that social workers also need to move beyond theoretical conceptualizations (even those of a psychosocial variety). This is one reason why the term 'practice theories' is so useful. Hardiker and Barker (1986, 1988) illustrate these in relation to child protection work. For example, social workers rely on many faculties in assessing family situations: thinking, feeling, empathizing, observing and doing. This enables them to locate their purposes in relation to clients and to agency functions. For example, they may try to understand these in the following ways:

- *Clients' situations*: relationships, feelings, needs which cannot be met, disabled and disabling families.

- *Workers' roles and agency functions*: the pain of working with families who have experienced abuse, problems of involvement and detachment, anxieties around statutory intervention.

- *The inalienable elements in social work*: working with shades of grey rather than 'cut and dried' situations or responses; trying to decide whether to enable a family to split up or stay together; determining who is the client; being brokers in lesser evils (e.g. preventing the need for more intrusive interventions).

These examples illustrate ways in which social workers rely on many sources in their attempts to understand and work with painful human predicaments. However, a psychosocial approach (like any other) can be exploitative, even damaging. Practitioners must secure a clear value base, knowledge frameworks and practice skills if they are to be 'altruists under social auspices' (Timms and Timms 1977). The chapters in this book on models of understanding human development and social work intervention provide further directions for the pursuit of professional competence, ethically based.

The next section raises more general issues of the functions of theory in social work. Again, many of the examples will be drawn from the field of child abuse.

## Some functions of knowledge in social work

It is not only the substantive nature of knowledge which differentiates one form of explanation or understanding from another in social work; the functions of knowledge vary also. Social theory identifies at least three functions of knowledge in social work:

1.  enlightenment in the liberal education tradition.

2.  boundary-defining.

3.  metaphorical and semantic.

### ENLIGHTENMENT

The liberal education tradition serves an enlightening function when it enables us to understand and explore some ways in which 'things are not what they seem'. This is sometimes referred to as a 'romance' phase in learning and most of us will be able to recall such experiences in our lives (Harris 1985; Towle 1954). But enlightenment must function rather more profoundly than this in professional education, and some clues are now suggested.

*Humbling*
In the grand literature and discourses of the humanities and the sciences, knowledge should help us to locate ourselves in the universe. Pearson, Treseder and Yelloly (1988) illustrate this succinctly:

> The theory of the unconscious as Freud…described it, is one which insists that 'the ego is not master in its own house'. This, he suggested, was the 'third blow' to human narcissism that had been delivered by science: the first having been Copernicus's revelation that the earth was not the centre of the solar system, and the second Darwin's assertion that human beings were of animal descent.
>
> In this sense, Freud's work was a continuation of the humbling experience of modernity and rational enquiry – whereby the process of scientific enlightenment stripped humankind of its naive illusion that it stood at the centre of the universe. (p.21)

Sadly, social science literature does not always appear to facilitate this humbling function, perhaps because, 'all seekers after truth believe that the truth will set them free'. Ashdown and Clement Brown (1953) understood these issues profoundly:

It seems obvious that such a service calls for wide and liberal training so that the psychiatric social worker may see what she is doing in perspective, against a background of historical change and social movement, and *may escape the insidious error that 'wisdom shall die', or was born, with her own or any other generation.* (p.228, our italics)

This is a reminder that our own struggles in learning and even inspirations may only bring us to the early stages of the understanding of those who have gone before.

### Non-dogmatic

The history of social work illustrates some ways in which it has been besieged by different 'isms': biologism, Freudianism, behaviourism, genericism, Marxism, anti-sexism, anti-racism. Though social work, like any other practice, changes in different generations, any profession monopolized by one ideology is a type of dogma. Social theory should enable teachers, practitioners and students to think through complex issues rather than starting arguments with 'isms', which may too readily function as thoughtstoppers. Professional education should enable social workers to locate and identify the frames of reference and value bases through which we all think and write; this should dissolve dogmatism, especially if efforts are made to read literature with which one is not sympathetic (for example, Rojeck *et al.* 1989).

### No Utopia

There are no safe hiding places in social work, whether these are sought in methods, client groups, settings, theories or value positions. This is a very conservative statement and, if misinterpreted, encourages paralysis and negative attitudes. This is hardly the intention! An illuminating exposition of this stance can be found in a paper written by an Australian welfare administrator (Green 1976):

> social control is about private pain as well as public issues. Social workers are more than control agents in the name of the socio-economic status quo, they are part of those social processes that protect themselves, their clients and the community from excessive anxiety and distress and intolerable discomfort.
>
> Unfortunately, not all personal pain is political… And sometimes we are subject to what is a confidence trick of significant appeal, that of politicising all personal pain for our own protection. (p.67)

Whether one's orientation is personal or political, casework or social policy, another non-Utopian function of social theory is to grasp ways in which social work – even at its best – can only achieve modest goals. Freud (Breuer and Freud 1955) understood this in relation to psychoanalysis: 'much will be gained if we succeed in transforming your hysterical misery into common unhappiness' (p.393).

Any social worker who claims to have 'cracked' child abuse after completing a short training course or even a lifetime's career in practice has failed to grasp some of these messages. Any social theorist or politician who fails to appreciate that some human predicaments brook of no solutions is also being Utopian.

## BOUNDARY-DEFINING

Though the parameters of social work are permeable and loosely defined, social theory functions to locate the boundaries of permitted and required practice in every age (see Bailey 1980; see also Heywood 1978; Packman 1981). For example, Gordon (1988) traces the history of welfare services in relation to child abuse and family violence in America in different eras: child saving, reform and economic amelioration, psychiatry and familialism and (latterly) anti-family ideologies. This meant that child abuse itself was defined in different ways, from cruelty, neglect and poverty through to family dysfunction and patriarchal violence. Parton (1985)[7] also traces some ways child abuse was rediscovered as a social problem in this country in the 1970s. This is a reminder that problems in child care are ever with us, but that these have historically been defined in different ways. Social workers are part of these changing problem-definitions, but their practices can be better understood if they are located in relation to social and historical changes.

Thus, social theory informs rather than determines practice by outlining some of the boundaries of the activity; this lays bare some of the choices available to practitioners (such as family support or freeing for adoption). Moreover, if interventions in child abuse are increasingly based on statutory orders (Parton and Parton 1988), social workers may not be wholly free to reverse the trend, though an understanding of the issues raises some lessons for practice; work to empower parents has to be embraced much more seriously in these circumstances.

Hardiker *et al.* (1991) explored some of these boundary-defining functions in relation to preventive child care: 'social work practice has to be understood in the context of client careers, agency objectives and social policies, i.e. that the methods and resources used have little meaning unless they are contextualised in this way' (p.225).

Another way of describing this function is to point out that there will always be a hiatus between theory and practice, i.e. that an understanding of the social, historical and personal reasons for the construction of social problems and welfare responses does not necessarily provide the practitioner with pointers to direct interventions:

> The fact of...the social origin does not preclude treatment on an individual basis. The reverse is true; treatment on an individual basis [must] proceed at the same time that the theory suggests that the 'ailment' and ultimately the 'cure' is extra-individual. (Jacoby 1975, p.141)

Jacoby is explaining here how an understanding of some of the structural sources of, say, child abuse and risk registers need not prevent practitioners helping individual families caught up in these processes. Different understandings and interventions can coexist because they are different forms of activity. We may add that, not only should understandings not preclude interventions, these activities should interact in social work practice informed by social theories.

## METAPHORICAL AND SEMANTIC

Social scientists sometimes read social work language too literally, which is surprising, given their 'critical' functions. The main section of this chapter, which outlined a range of different explanations for child abuse, was an exercise in the literal use of language, i.e.

that child abuse may relate to bonding, family systems, social isolation, etc. It is important not to leave the literal argument here, though, because concepts should not be reified (i.e. assumed to have a concrete form). The first stage in understanding the metaphorical functions of social theories is to prefix knowledge-statements with the words, 'as if'. Supervisors of social workers frequently invite them to hypothesize about a referral, using a range of 'as if' statements. No explanation should ever monopolize a practitioner's repertoire.

A further stage in metaphorical work involves an understanding of the broader purposes which language serves in practice (Novak and Axelrod 1979; Philp 1979). This was alluded to briefly in the discussion of psychosocial perspectives above, because the person–society connection can be explored through a variety of theories: psychodynamic, behavioural, feminist and sociological (Leonard 1975; Webb 1981). The suggestion here is not that any type of theory serves equally well a particular social problem, such as child abuse, but that social theory for practitioners needs to go further than explanation and understanding. For example, it was seen earlier that a range of social science disciplines may analyse child abuse and ways in which it is controlled. But what purposes are social workers fulfilling that they need to find explanations of such circumstances? The purposes derive from the remit of social workers in contemporary Britain, which is to assess needs and to help reintegrate people engaged in abusing interactions into civil society. Needs may be explained psychologically or socially, but they have to be represented psychosocially. Families caught up in these situations have problems in coping with child abuse, whether the main reasons lie with them in their situations or with the intrusions of social controllers, or both.

Social theory should provide a language which speaks for 'child abusers' as persons, rather than as deviants, to the powerful social control agents who make decisions (Novak and Axelrod 1979; Philp 1979). This is one dimension of preventive child care, when social workers are engaged in delabelling vulnerable families or negotiating the removal of names from a child protection register. Scientific language alone is not adequate in these circumstances; we have to speak metaphorically about 'good-enough parenting', coping under stress, providing 'adequate protection' for pre-school children, listening to stories about how other parents handle similar difficulties. If social workers fail to hold on to these psychosocial equations when they speak for families in courts and case conferences, they are no longer fulfilling social work purposes.

## Conclusion

This chapter explored selected social theories and some functions of knowledge in social work. An exercise illustrating different ways in which psychosocial equations can be worked out was outlined. The brief for this chapter was manifestly ambitious and calls for several books rather than a brief paper! Nevertheless, we hope we have conveyed some of the ways in which we continue to struggle with these eternal issues and try to make social theory illuminating rather than paralyzing for ourselves, our students and practice teachers. This book for practice teachers is transparently welfare oriented, i.e. the papers illustrate different helping and needs-based approaches. This is, of course, the structural space which social work still inhabits in contemporary Britain. It is important to remember that this 'space' straddles much larger social institutions, such as the judicial system, a welfare state which is being fundamentally restructured and also those oases of social transformation in which social changes are taking place. Social work has to address structural realities, such as punishment in the community; the new Children Act; the move to private and voluntary-based welfare; growing inequalities in health care; disease, ageing and disabilities; homelessness and poverty. Though needs-based helping approaches are relevant as never before, the challenge lies in making psychosocial equations which firmly address the structural realities of our changing society.

## Notes

1   The following books illustrate different explanations of bonding, from psychoanalytical to social learning theories: Bowlby (1988), Kempe and Kempe (1978), Sluckin, Herbert and Sluckin (1983).
2   This statement is often associated with a crude cultural transmission theory (Keith Joseph), but intergenerational patterns can be explained in various ways: ethological, psychodynamic, behavioural, cognitive, structural and patriarchal: see Quinton and Rutter (1988), Rutter and Madge (1976).
3   A rather different family systems approach is illustrated in Dale *et al.* (1986).
4   There is a variety of theoretical explanations for the socially patterned nature of child abuse. The social isolation view derives from Garbarino and Gilliam (1980); Gelles and Cornell (1985) explain abuse in relation to culturally sanctioned patterns of physical chastisement; Gil (1979) analyses ways in which societies and families are structurally violent; the NSPCC presents evidence of a social-epidemiological and social-pathology kind. These theories explain the links between social class and abuse in different ways.
5   A good example of this type of link being made can be found in an excellent paper by a paediatrician: Lynch (1988). 'Treatment model' explanations of female delinquency are critically debated in recent feminist criminology: Carlen and Worrall (1987), Morris (1987), Worrall (1989).
6   Further value positions, laissez-faire and children's rights are also developed in Harding (1990).
7   See also Dingwall (1986), Parton and Small (1989) Rojeck, Peacock and Collins (1989) Spitzer (1975).

## References

Ahmed, S., Cheetham, J. and Small, J. (1986) *Social Work with Black Children and their Families.* London: Batsford/BAAF.

Aldrich, H.E. (1979) *Organisations and Environments.* London: Prentice Hall.

Ashdown, M. and Clement Brown, S. (1953) *Social Service and Mental Health: An Essay on Psychiatric Social Workers.* London: Routledge.

Bailey, J. (1980) *Ideas and Intervention: Social Theory for Practice.* London: Routledge and Kegan Paul.

Bentovim, A., Elton, A., Hildbrand, J., Tranter, M. and Vizard, E. (1988) *Child Sexual Abuse within the Family: Assessment and Treatment.* London: Butterworth and Co.

Benson, J.K. (1982) 'A framework for policy analysis.' In D. Rogers and D. Whetten (eds) *Inter-Organisational Coordination.* Ames, IA: Iowa State University Press

Black Report (1980) *Inequalities in Health.* Report of a research group chaired by Sir Douglas Black. London: DHSS.

Bowlby, J. (1988) *A Secure Base: Clinical Applications of Attachment Theory.* London: Routledge.

Breuer, J. and Freud, S. (1955) 'Studies in hysteria.' In James Strachey (ed.) *The Standard Edition of the Complete Psychological Works of Sigmund Freud,* Volume 2. London: Hogarth Press.

Briar, S. and Miller, H. (1971) *Problems and Issues in Social Casework.* New York: Columbia University Press.

Browne, K., Davies, C. and Stratton, P. (eds) (1988) *Early Prediction and Prevention of Child Abuse.* Chichester: Wiley.

Burgess, H. and Taylor, I. (eds) (2005) *Learning and Teaching in Social Policy and Social Work.* London: Routledge Falmer.

Carlen, P. and Worrall, A. (eds) (1987) *Gender, Crime and Justice.* Milton Keynes: Open University Press.

Chandler, S., Stone, R. and Young, E. (1989) *Kidscape: Keeping Yourself Safe, A Programme for Nursery Aged Children.* Corby: Pen Green Family Centre.

Cook, K.S. (1977) 'Exchange and power in networks of interorganisational relations.' *Sociological Quarterly 18*, 62–82.

Cockburn, C. (1977) *The Local State: Management of Cities and People.* London: Pluto Press.

Court, J. (1985) 'Independent social worker's report, 8th September 1981.' In London Borough of Brent, *A Child in Trust: The Report of the Panel of Inquiry into the Circumstances Surrounding the Death of Jasmine Beckford.* London: Borough of Brent.

Cowley, J., Kaye, A., Mayo, M. and Thompson, M. (1977) *Community or Class Struggle?* London: Stage 1.

Curnock, K. and Hardiker, P. (1979) *Towards Practice Theory: Skills and Methods in Social Assessment.* London: Routledge.

Dale, P., Davies, M., Morrison, T. and Waters, J. (1986) *Dangerous Families: Assessment and Treatment of Child Abuse.* London: Tavistock.

Dingwall, R. (1986) 'The Jasmine Beckford affair.' *Modern Law Review 49*, 3, 489-507.

Dingwall, R., Eekelaar, J. and Murray, T. (1983) *The Protection of Children: State Intervention and Family Life.* Oxford: Blackwell.

Dobash, R.E. and Dobash, R. (1980) *Violence Against Wives: A Case Against the Patriarchy.* London: Open Books.

England, H. (1986) *Social Work as Art: Making Sense of Good Practice.* London: Allen and Unwin.

Equality for Children (1983) *Keeping Kids out of Care, Crisis and Consensus in Child Care Policy.* London: NCOPF.

Feminist Review Collective (1988) *Family Secrets: Child Sexual Abuse.* Feminist Review 28. London: Routledge.

Finkelhor, D. (1984) *Child Sexual Abuse.* New York: Free Press.

Fox, L. (1982) 'Two value positions in child care.' *British Journal of Society Work 12*, 3, 265–90.

Freeman, M.D.A. (1983) *The Rights and Wrongs of Children.* London: Frances Pinter.

Frost, N. and Stein, M. (1989) *The Politics of Child Welfare: Inequality, Power and Change.* London: Harvester Wheatsheaf.

Garbarino, J. and Gilliam, G. (1980) *Understanding Abusing Families.* Cambridge, MA: Lexington Books.

Gelles, R. and Cornell, C. (1985) *Intimate Violence in Families.* Beverly Hills, CA: Sage.

Gil, D. (1979) *Child Abuse and Violence.* New York: AMS Press.

Glaser, D. and Frosh, S. (1988) *Child Sexual Abuse.* Basingstoke: Macmillan/BASW.

Gordon, L. (1988) *Heroes of their own Lives: The Politics and History of Family Violence.* London: Virago Press.

Green, D. (1976) 'Social control and public welfare practice.' In P.J. Boas and J. Crawley (eds) *Social Work in Australia: Responses to a Changing Context.* Melbourne: International Press.

Hardiker, P. (1981) 'Heart or head: The function and role of knowledge in social work.' *Issues in Social Work Education 1*, 2, 88–111.

Hardiker, P. and Barker, M. (eds) (1981) *Theories of Practice in Social Work.* London: Academic Press.

Hardiker, P. and Barker, M. (1985) 'Client careers and the structure of a probation and after-care agency.' *British Journal of Social Work 15*, 6, 599–618.

Hardiker, P. and Barker, M. (1986) *A Window on Child Care Practices in the 1980s.* Research report. Leicester: Leicester University School of Social Work.

Hardiker, P. and Barker, M. (1988) 'A window on child care, poverty and social work.' In S. Becker and S. Macpherson (eds) *Public Issues, Private Pain: Poverty, Social Work and Social Policy.* London: Social Services Insight Books.

Hardiker, P. and Curnock, K. (1984) 'Social work assessment processes in work with ethnic minorities – the Doshi family.' *British Journal of Social Work 14*, 1, 23–47.

Hardiker, P., Exton, K. and Barker, M. (1991) *Policies and Practices in Preventive Child Care*. Research Report to the Department of Health. Aldershot: Avebury.

Harding, L. (1990) *Perspectives on Child Care Policy*. London: Longman.

Harris, R.J. (ed.) (1985) *Educating Social Workers*. Leicester: Association of Teachers in Social Work Education.

Herbert, M. (1988) *Working with Children and their Families*. London: Routledge/Leicester BPS.

Heywood, J.S. (1978) *Children in Care: The Development of the Service for the Deprived Child*. 3rd edn. London: Routledge.

Holman, R. (1976) *Inequality in Child Care*. London: Child Poverty Action Group.

Holman, B. (1988) *Putting Families First*. Basingstoke: Macmillan Educational.

Hudson, A. (1985) 'Feminism and social work: Resistance or dialogue?' *British Journal of Social Work 15*, 6, 635–55.

Hudson, A. (1989) 'Troublesome girls: Towards alternative definitions and policies.' In M. Cain (ed.) *Growing Up Good: Policing the Behaviour of Girls in Europe*. London: Sage.

Iwaniec, D., Herbert, M. and McNeish, A.S. (1985a) 'Social work with failure-to-thrive children and their families. Part I: Psychosocial factors.' *British Journal of Social Work 15*, 3, 243–59.

Iwaniec, D., Herbert, M. and McNeish, A.S. (1985b) 'Social work with failure-to-thrive children and their families. Part II: Behavioural social work intervention.' *British Journal of Social Work 15*, 4, 375–89.

Jacoby, R. (1975) *Social Amnesia: A Critique of Conformist Psychology from Adler to Laing*. Boston: Beacon Press.

Kempe, R.S. and Kempe, C.H. (1978) *Child Abuse*. London: Fontana.

Leonard, P. (1975) 'Explanation and education in social work.' *British Journal of Social Work 5*, 3, 325–33

Leonard, P. (1984) *Personality and Ideology: Towards a Materialist Understanding of the Individual*. London: Macmillan.

Loewenberg, F.M. (1984) 'Professional ideology, middle range theories and knowledge building for social work practice.' *British Journal of Social Work 14*, 4, 309–322.

London Borough of Brent (1985) *A Child in Trust: The Report of the Panel of Inquiry into the Circumstances Surrounding the Death of Jasmine Beckford*. London: London Borough of Brent.

Lynch, M. (1988) 'The consequences of child abuse.' In K. Browne, C. Davies and P. Stratton (eds) *Early Prediction and Prevention of Child Abuse*. Chichester: Wiley.

Marshall, T.H. (1946) 'Basic training for all types of work.' In Nuffield College, *Training for Social Work*. London: Oxford University Press.

Morris, A. (1987) *Women, Crime and Criminal Justice*. Oxford: Blackwell.

Novak, M.W. and Axelrod, C.D. (1979) 'Primitive myth and modern medicine.' Special book review of E. Kübler-Ross, *On Death and Dying. Psychoanalytic Review 66*, 3, 443–9.

O'Hagan, K. (1989) *Working with Child Sexual Abuse*. Milton Keynes: Open University Press.

Packman, J. (1981) *The Child's Generation*. Oxford: Basil Blackwell and Martin Robertson.

Pahl, J. (1985) *Private Violence and Public Policy*. London: Routledge and Kegan Paul.

Parton, C. and Parton, N. (1988) 'Women, the family and child protection.' *Critical Social Policy 24*, winter, 38–49.

Parton, N. (1985) *The Politics of Child Abuse*. Basingstoke: Macmillan.

Parton, N. and Small, N. (1989) 'Violence, social work and the emergence of dangerousness.' In M. Langan and P. Lee (eds) *Radical Social Work Today*. London: Unwin-Hyman.

Pearson, G., Treseder, J. and Yelloly, M. (1988) *Social Work and the Legacy of Freud: Psychoanalysis and its Uses*. Basingstoke: Macmillan.

Philp, M. (1979) 'Notes on the form of knowledge in social work.' *Sociological Review 27*, 1, 83–111.

Quinton, D. and Rutter, M. (1988) *Parenting Breakdown: The Making and Breaking of Intergenerational Links*. Aldershot: Avebury.

Rein, M. (1970) 'Social work in search of a radical profession.' *Social Work 15* (US), 2, 13–28.

Rojeck, C., Peacock, G. and Collins, S. (1989) *The Haunt of Misery: Critical Essays in Social Work and Helping.* London: Routledge.

Rowe, J. and Lambert, L. (1973) *Children Who Wait.* London: Association of British Adoption Agencies.

Rutter, M. and Madge, N. (1976) *Cycles of Disadvantage.* London: Heinemann.

Sluckin, W., Herbert, M. and Sluckin, A. (1983) *Maternal Bonding.* Oxford: Blackwell.

Smale, G., Tuson, G., Cooper, M., Wardle, M. and Crosbie, D. (1988) *Community Social Work: A Paradigm for Change.* London: National Institute for Social Work.

Smith, G. (1977) 'The place of "professional ideology" in the analysis of "social policy".' *Sociological Review 25*, 4, 843–65.

Smith, S.M. (1975) *The Battered Child Syndrome.* London: Butterworth.

Smith, S.M., Henson, R. and Noble, S. (1974) 'Social aspects of the battered baby syndrome.' *British Journal of Psychiatry 125*, 568–82.

Spitzer, S. (1975) 'Towards a Marxian theory of deviance.' *Social Problems 22*, 5, 638–51.

Stainton Rogers, W., Harvey, D. and Ash, E. (1989) *Child Abuse and Neglect: Facing the Challenge.* London: Batsford/Open University.

Susser, M. (1968) *Community Psychiatry: Epidemiologic and Social Themes.* New York: Random House.

Timms, N. and Timms, R. (1977) *Perspectives in Social Work.* London: Routledge and Kegan Paul.

Towle, C. (1954) *The Learner in Education for the Professions.* Chicago, IL: University of Chicago Press.

Vogel, E.G. and Bell, N.W. (1968) 'The emotionally disturbed child as the family scapegoat.' In G. Handel (ed.) *The Psychosocial Interior of the Family: A Source-book for the Study of Whole Families.* London: George Allen and Unwin.

Walker, C.E., Bonner, B.L. and Kangman, K.L. (1988) *The Physically and Sexually Abused Child: Evaluation and Treatment.* Oxford: Pergamon Press.

Webb, D. (1981) 'Themes and continuities in radical and traditional social work.' *British Journal of Social Work 11*, 2, 143–58.

Westergaard, J. and Resler, H. (1975) *Class in a Capitalist Society: A Study of Contemporary Britain.* London: Heinemann.

Whitehead, M. (1987) *The Health Divide: Inequalities in Health in the 1980s.* London: Health Education Council.

Worrall, A. (1989) 'Working with female offenders.' *British Journal of Social Work 19*, 2, 77–94.

## CHAPTER 4

# THE PLACE OF ATTACHMENT THEORY IN SOCIAL WORK WITH CHILDREN AND FAMILIES

*Jane Aldgate*

## Introduction

Attachment has long been seen as significant in children's development. Trying to make sense of the theory is not easy, partly because of its complexity and partly because it has seen many interpretations. The centrality of the construct of 'attachment' in child welfare work has been exemplified by writers such as Fahlberg (1981, 1994), Howe (1995) and Aldgate and Jones (2006).

The chapter begins by suggesting that attachment has been used to justify a range of policies at central government level. It goes on to outline the origins and definitions of attachment and contemporary thinking, which sees children's attachment and the adult caregiving relationship as two parallel, connected systems. The chapter then discusses how patterns of attachment develop, and asks if attachment is a universal construct. It draws attention to recent research which addresses issues for children with multiple attachments and the impact of loss on attachment, with special reference to children looked after by the state. There is then discussion of whether attachments are set for life in childhood or can be changed. The last part of the chapter addresses the application of attachment in social work practice. It makes a case for a positive, strengths approach to using attachment in practice and outlines the place of attachment in assessment, planning and review, and direct work with children. The chapter ends by emphasizing how important it is that workers themselves are supported to undertake demanding, direct work with children and families.

## Attachment in contemporary policy

Attachment theory has been much used and abused in child care policy and practice. The application of attachment has often gone far beyond its actual meaning and application. The importance of children being 'attached' to families has been used to justify a range of policies from family support to permanency planning for adoption. Sure Start programmes, for example, are designed to help improve parenting relationships with children. The primary legislation for children across the different countries of the UK introduced in the 1980s and 1990s emphasizes the importance of children growing up in families (see, for example, Department of Health 1990). Recognition of the importance of parents to children has also informed policies about shared parental responsibility for parents living apart from their children (Department of Health 1990) and contact for looked-after children, on the grounds that maintaining contact with families will enhance children's well-being in most cases and aid reunification (Cleaver 2000).

Children's need for secure stable and lasting relationships with caring adults has been used to justify policies to find permanent alternative homes for looked-after children. One of the main indicators of the Department of Health's Quality Protects initiative is 'to ensure that children are securely attached to carers capable of providing safe and effective care for the duration of childhood' (Berridge 2000, p.4) and the importance of secure attachments underpins recent policies on adoption (see Adoption Policy Review Group, Scottish Executive 2005; Thoburn 2002). Cynically, one might argue that setting local authorities targets for the adoption of looked-after children may be also driven by cost but, nevertheless, the argument for providing safe, loving, permanent homes for children is a powerful one.

Knowledge about attachment has progressed much since the 1980s. Definitions and applications of attachment have been revisited and refined. This chapter attempts to return to the origins of attachment theory in order to unravel and re-knit our understanding of the place of attachment in children's development. It also outlines the most common usage of attachment theory in contemporary texts (see, for example, Howe 2001; Aldgate and Jones 2006). The chapter looks at new research evidence on the application of attachment within today's diverse patterns of family life.

## The origins of attachment theory

No discussion of attachment can begin without reference to John Bowlby, whose writings introduced attachment to the British public in the 1950s (Bowlby 1951, 1953, 1958). Bowlby has been much misread. Since the mid-1990s, there has been a re-evaluation of Bowlby's work, based on careful rereading of his ideas from the 1950s to the 1980s (see Aldgate and Jones 2006; Howe 1995, 2001). There is now substantial research evidence to show that attachment between children and carers exists in every known culture, though there are variations in expected attachment behaviours and caregiving responses (Quinton 1994; van IJzendoorn and Sagi 1999).

Bowlby believed that attachment behaviour is a specific biological response which arises from a desire of an individual, either adult or child, to seek security and protection from harm through proximity to an attachment figure who is seen as stronger and wiser, with the ultimate aim of survival from predators and, thereby, preservation of the species (Bowlby 1958). This biological approach to attachment is, in Bowlby's view, an evolutionary adaptation to self-preservation. As Cassidy (1999) suggests, 'within this framework, attachment is considered a normal and healthy characteristic of humans throughout the life span, rather than a sign of immaturity that needs to be outgrown' (p.5). Attachments, therefore, can last over time and can be formed at any stage of the life cycle (Howe 1995). The key characteristics are that an attachment relationship is part of a wider affectional relationship: that one person sees the other as stronger and wiser and as someone to turn to when he or she is afraid.

## What is attachment?

Sometimes, attachment is mistakenly talked about by practitioners as if it embraces the whole emotional relationship between a parent and child. A child is described as 'well attached' to new foster carers, for example, when he or she seems to be settling in a placement and babies only several weeks old and their parents are sometimes said to be 'attached or bonded to each other'. This is a misunderstanding of the theory. Attachment was never designed to describe the full range of developing behaviours and emotions between children and their carers.

Attachment is only one part, albeit an important one, of a whole range of affectional behaviours which develop between infants and parents. All children will show affectional behaviour towards their carers from their first weeks of life, as Murray and Andrews' work on the social baby illustrates (Murray and Andrews 2000). Indeed, the sensitive caring for infants and the positive affection shown towards them is a rehearsal for caregiving behaviour that supports the development of healthy attachments. Contemporary thinking suggests that attachment behaviours develop in children around six to seven months old (Aldgate and Jones 2006; Daniel 2006; Mussen et al. 1990).

Attachment is concerned with the behaviour and emotions that occur in particular situations where a child is stressed or fearful of perceived danger. In these circumstances, children show attachment behaviour by seeking the proximity of another (usually an adult but might be another child) who is perceived as stronger and wiser and who will make them feel safe.

It is related to two behavioural systems:

* the exploratory behavioural system

* the fear behavioural system.

When a young child feels safe, the attachment behavioural system is inactive. Children who feel calm and safe are more likely to be sociable and want to explore the world around them. By contrast, children's curiosity or exploratory behaviour system will be suppressed when they are afraid and attachment behaviour will be activated. It is only in situations when children are afraid or stressed that they will exhibit attachment behaviour. The aim of their behaviour is not to seek the affection from the person they see as an attachment figure who can protect them, but to regain a state of equilibrium. Children may employ many behaviours, such as signalling, moving towards an adult or crying out to get physically close to the adult, in order to regain that state of equilibrium. What children actually do to seek proximity will be influenced by cultural expectations.

Attachment figures are individuals whom children see as stronger and wiser than themselves and who will protect them when they seek safety. Such figures will often also provide affectional relationships for children in a wider sense but children turn to them as attachment figures only when they seek to lessen their fears. Usually the attachment figures will be parents, but this is not always so. Children's patterns of attachment will be influenced by what their attachment figures do, not who those caregivers are – a factor to which Bowlby was alert early on (Bowlby 1958). Therefore, a range of significant adults in children's lives can become attachment figures.

Until fairly recently, a common assumption among writers (see, for example, Bowlby 1958; Fahlberg 1981), has been that there would be a hierarchy of attachment figures, with one primary attachment figure, who would generally be the mother, although Bowlby and others have been careful to talk about 'mothering' figures. This view has now been challenged, partly influenced by the growing body of research on the diversity of child-rearing patterns worldwide (Quinton 1994) and partly influenced by the changing nature of the family in contemporary UK society. As we will see later, it is now thought that children can have good attachments to multiple caregivers under certain conditions (Howes 1999). Nevertheless, all children learn to adapt their attachment behaviour to the responses of their attachment figures, known as caregivers. This is why the role of the caregiver, either single or multiple, is so important in attachment theory.

Although the idea of a 'bond' as a reciprocal emotional connection between two individuals 'attached' to each other has been revised, the idea of an attachment bond is still valid. The attachment bond develops over time. An attachment bond cannot exist by itself unless it is part of a wider affectional bond between that child and another person. Affectional bonds can exist between children and a whole range of individuals who are significant in their lives. There are many circumstances when such affectional bonds exist between individuals throughout life. For instance, affectional bonds exist between friends, partners and relatives in many different circumstances but an attachment bond is only part of such a relationship when one individual sees the other as an attachment figure who is stronger and wiser (Aldgate and Jones 2006; Cassidy 1999). As will be shown later in the chapter, attachment bonds are relevant to long-term relationships between children who are separated from their parents.

## Seeing attachment and caregiving as two linked systems

Contemporary writers tend to use the term 'attachment relationship' and, in the longer term, 'attachment bond', only to describe the child's attachment relationships with the adults. The response from the adult to children's attachment needs is now seen as a separate system, known as the caregiving system (see Cassidy 1999).

The 'caregiving relationship' refers to those aspects of the caregiver's behaviour that promote the development and maintenance of attachment behaviour within the child. This includes the provision of nurturance and emotional availability, sensitivity, affection and other behaviours, which promote the child's security (Ainsworth et al. 1978). Such responses may have a cultural element, depending on expected child-rearing practices (Quinto 1994), but every sensitive caregiver will have the universal aim of responding appropriately to the child's stress and fear.

Attachment theory stresses the importance of caregivers' sensitive response to children's attachment behaviour. The importance of this sensitivity cannot be emphasized too much. Specifically, the degree of sensitivity or lack of it in caregivers over the first years of children's development will influence the development of children's internal organization of their attachment behaviour and their internal working model of how they see the world around them.

Factors within children, such as temperament, are likely to influence the amount of effort needed to promote a sensitive response. As Howe suggests, a difficult baby is likely to provoke a different reaction in a parent than a contented baby (Howe 1995). In turn, this may affect the caregiving response to attachment needs. How caregivers respond is the critical factor that will influence children's representations of how they see their relationships with others in their world. Solomon and George (1999), for example, have distinguished between three groups of caregivers, which can be broadly classified as:

- those who provide a secure base

- those who reject and thereby deactivate the infants' attachment behaviours

- uncertain and helpless parents who provide disorganized caregiving.

These parenting styles seems to be universal across cultures and are present in societies where children have multiple carers as much as in those where they spend their days with only one or two individuals. Sensitive caregivers who have several children will also be able to respond differently and appropriately to each individual child (Green 2003; Howe 1995). It is worth echoing Howe's point here, that no parent is expected to be perfect within these dimensions but only to be, as D.W. Winnicott suggested in 1965, 'good enough'. For further details of caregiving styles, see Howe (1995, 2001).

Separating out the child's behaviour and emotions from those of the adults is a helpful way of understanding attachment in the context of other aspects of a parent-child relationship. Parents and other attachment figures are not 'attached' to their children – they have sensitive, caregiver relationships responding to children's attachment behaviours. Adults also provide many other facets of parenting. Parents can be teachers, playmates or those who set guidance and boundaries. It is important, for example, when assessing caregiving in relation to attachment, to analyse the context in which the assessment is being made. A child trying to gain a parent's attention to engage in play is not engaging in attachment behaviour (Aldgate and Jones 2006).

Emerging research in Japan, the USA and England has suggested that there may be many influences on adults' caregiving ability, including the ecology of their circumstances and their relationships with other adults (Solomon and George 1999). How far childhood experiences of attachment carry over into adult caregiving behaviour is a debatable matter and it seems important not to make assumptions about caregiving behaviour based on parents' histories. Researchers now tend to believe that patterns of behaviour are not set for life and can be disconfirmed (Howe 1995; Schaffer 1998). Both children and adults can change their behaviour given the right circumstances, as will be discussed later.

## Attachment patterns and the development of internal working models

Although attachment is a specific part of children's development, it has consequences for other parts of children's development, because children learn to set their expectations about those around them from caregivers' responses to their attachment behaviour. They internalize the responses of caregivers to them into an internal working model. This initially sets a pattern of expectation for subsequent experiences. As Aldgate and Jones (2006) suggest:

> Through the development of the internal working model, children learn that they can or cannot trust others to protect them and have to develop appropriate defensive strategies for dealing with caregivers' behaviour. In so doing, they begin to construct a view of the world around them that reflects how they have experienced adults' responses to their need to find proximity and security when attachment behaviour has been aroused. The consequence of this learning process triggered by attachment behaviour is that children learn to incorporate within themselves, through the internal working model, expectations and beliefs about their own and other people's behaviour. The internal working model creates for the child a sense of self, other people, and the relationship between self and others. (Aldgate and Jones 2006, pp.78–9)

It is now recognized that children's early attachment patterns are likely to influence their responses to adults outwith the family and to their siblings and peers. Some children who are at risk of harm because of child protection concerns, may well have experienced inconsistent or rejecting caregiving behaviour. For example, those who have experienced parents' inconsistent response through substance misuse, have learnt to rely on themselves. Those whose attachments have been ambivalent or disorganized may display behaviours such as helplessness, aggression, or attention-seeking (Howe 2001). It is because patterns of attachment can have such a serious effect on children's behaviour and on children's perception of those in their world that attachment becomes so important to children's well-being and development. Attachment disorders influence children's behaviour beyond the context of the immediate situation of the fear which triggers initial attachment behaviour. Many children who experience serious problems of regulating their emotions and behaviour will have experienced poor attachments.

## Classifications of attachment patterns

Classification of attachment patterns in children were initially developed by Ainsworth and colleagues, from studying children in Uganda in the 1970s (Ainsworth *et al.* 1978). Currently, it is usually agreed that there are four patterns of attachment: avoidant, secure, ambivalent, and disorganized (see Howe 1995, 2001). This classification is now generally accepted by professionals as a guide to assessing children's patterns of attachment. Howe (2001) summarizes the patterns as follows:

1.  Secure attachment patterns: children experience their care-giver as available, and themselves positively.

2.  Ambivalent patterns: children experience their caregiver as inconsistently responsive, and themselves as dependent and poorly valued.

3.  Avoidant patterns: children experience their caregivers as consistently rejecting, and themselves as insecure but compulsively self-reliant.

4.    Disorganized patterns: often associated with children who have suffered severe maltreatment: children experience their caregivers as either frightening or frightened, and themselves as helpless, angry, and unworthy.

(Howe 2001, pp.201–202).

## Is attachment universal?

Patterns of attachment seem to be present in all countries and can be measured across cultures. Van IJzendoorn and Sagi (1999), who have studied patterns of attachment across different countries extensively, conclude:

> Not only the attachment phenomenon itself but also the different types of attachment appear to be present in various western and non-western cultures. Avoidant, secure and resistant attachments have been observed in the African, Chinese and Japanese studies; even in the extremely diverging child-rearing context of the Israeli kibbutzim, the differentiation between secure and insecure attachments could be made. (van IJzendoorn and Sagi 1999, p.728)

In spite of this common ground, which confirms the universality of attachment, there can be striking differences across cultures in the proportions of children who are in the different categories identified by Ainsworth and colleagues (1978). It is within these different proportions of categories that cultural differences can be identified. This does not undermine the case for the universal application for attachment but rather strengthens it in recognizing that attachment behaviours will be influenced by expectations of what is 'the ideal child' in different cultures and by expectations of adult behaviour within a given society (Aldgate and Jones 2006).

This is a complex field and this chapter can only introduce the key ideas. Practitioners will need to study the detail of these patterns because there is a growing body of research that suggests children's attachment patterns are associated with patterns of social and emotional behaviour that can be recognized. Key texts in this are, for example, Aldgate and Jones (2006), Crittenden (1995), Howe 1995, 2001), Howe, Brandon and Schofield (1999).

## Children and multiple attachments

One of the criticisms laid at the door of early attachment theorists was that they focused too heavily on one primary attachment figure, usually the mother, at the expense of other significant adults in children's lives who might also be attachment figures, although it must be emphasized that Bowlby was quite clear that children could have more than one attachment figure (Bowlby 1958).

In today's diverse family lifestyles, that view about hierarchy of attachments has been revised, influenced by a greater understanding about attachment in different cultures across the world. In contemporary times in many countries, children often spend their days looked after by several different adults both within and outwith their own families. This has led developmentalists in the USA, like Howes (1999), to suggest that it is helpful to look at a child's network of attachment relationships rather than concentrating on a primary attachment figure.

It is suggested by Howes (1999) that children who have multiple carers from the outset or who acquire them by spending time with other adults, such as extended family or in day care, may have patterns of attachment that are spread more evenly among them. Children's internal working models will relate to the quality of all the attachment relationships in their network. This new line of thinking suggests that children who experience multiple carers from early on will give equal weight to each experience. Furthermore, the quality of attachment will influence outcome, and two secure attachments, for example, will be more powerful than one that is insecure.

Developments about thinking in terms of a network of attachments suggest a more creative approach to viewing attachments within a context of supporting families in the community. Further developments in this area deserve a watching brief. As the research develops, we shall begin to be more certain about the impact of different experiences on children. Whatever the final outcomes are, one thing is certain: ongoing multiple attachments are very much part of the lives of many children and should be taken into account in assessing a child's attachment behaviour.

## Loss and attachment

While having several attachment figures may influence the way we now think about attachment, children will still be affected when they experience separation from a main attachment figure. This is especially so if this happens involuntarily, for example, when a child is removed from parents or experiences a breakdown in a care placement. It also applies where children have lost carers through parental separation or death. Irrespective of previous experiences of attachment, where children have been involuntarily separated from their attachment figures, they will find this a frightening experience, because they do not know to whom to turn to help them return to a state of equilibrium. This is why children who have been abused still want to be with their parents, even if their attachments to them are insecure.

Bowlby suggested that children separated from adult attachment figures will go through a process of protest, despair and detachment (Bowlby 1958). Howe has refined Bowlby's process into five stages, including numbness and shock, yearning, anger and resentment, disorganization and adjustment (Howe 1995).

How children recover from such loss will depend on the security of their attachments before separation and what happens next. A short parental absence may cause distress but trust and positive attachments can be restored if the child is returned quickly to sensitive caregivers. The most enduring images of such experiences come from the films of brief separations of children from their parents in the 1950s (Robertson 1952), which showed poignantly children's strong emotions on separation and return. Similarly, the replacement of the lost attachment figure with another is important to children's well-being. This is why Fahlberg (1994) suggests that: 'minimizing the trauma of separations and losses and working to facilitate the development of new attachments are complementary rather than competitive tasks...' (Fahlberg 1994, p.168).

It has been known for many years that children who lose an attachment figure through death need to grieve that loss in an age appropriate way. Children's expression of grief may well be influenced by what is expected of them culturally but this does not invalidate their need to grieve and come to terms with their loss (see Jewett 1984). Age will also affect children's reactions to loss. Age can be a protective factor in very young children who have not yet developed selective attachments, while school-aged children may have the cognitive ability 'to understand situations and develop strategies for dealing with them' (Rutter 1985, p.606). Children thought most vulnerable are those aged between six months and four years (Daniel 2006). Daniel believes that children in this age group:

> may react to separation by regression to less autonomous behaviour. During these early years children lack the cognitive skills to comprehend the events leading to separation and this coupled with the propensity for magical thinking, means young children are highly likely to blame themselves for the loss. (Daniel 2006, p.193)

Aldgate and Jones (2006) summarize for workers three fundamental principles in all cases where children are separated from attachment figures:

1.    Children will react to their loss in the light of their previous experiences of attachment.

2.    Children should to be allowed to express their feelings about loss.

3.    Children need sensitive caregiving to help them through experiences of loss.

(Aldgate and Jones 2006, p.83)

## Loss and the care system

Children who have lost attachment figures by coming into the care system are very much at risk of further harm through insensitive caregiving responses to their attachment needs. Children who come to their placements with insecure attachment behaviour are likely to test the parenting capacity of the majority of carers. If this leads to further separations, the children's sense of being unloved and unlovable will only increase. Placement breakdown has been shown to be an ongoing problem in two decades of research across the UK (see, for example, Berridge and Cleaver 1987; Department of Health 1991; Department of Health and Social Security 1985; Kelly 1995; Ward, Macdonald and Skuse, forthcoming). Concerns about the impact of loss on children's well-being have led policy-makers to set targets for stability (see Berridge 2000) and to stress the importance of children maintaining connections with their kin (e.g. Department of Health 1990; Scottish Office 1997).

## Attachments and socio-genealogical connectedness

A different way of looking at attachment for children separated from their families comes from the theory of socio-genealogical connectedness, a construct which endorses the importance of attachment but puts less emphasis on actual contact and more on the information about attachment figures that children possess (Owusu-Bempah 2006; Owusu-Bempah and Howitt 1997): 'A basic tenet of the theory is that the degree to which children identify with their parents' backgrounds is dependent on the amount and quality of information they possess about their parents (Owusu-Bempah and Howitt 1997, p.201).

Socio-genealogical connectedness is a useful map through the minefields of attachment and contact for all children who live in separation from one or both parents. It also offers a way of dealing with situations where coming face-to-face with parents is likely to cause children further significant emotional harm. Socio-genealogical connectedness does not see contact as a sine qua non in promoting the retention of attachments; rather, it complements attachment theory in suggesting that children's knowledge of significant, absent attachment figures will influence their internal working models of themselves and those around them. It supports the idea of an attachment bond persisting over time and space.

The theory has relevance to any child who is living apart from a long-term attachment figure. Owusu-Bempah suggests that maintaining connectedness through relationships with family members and other significant adults can give children continuity to enhance their emotional well-being (Owusu-Bempah 2006). Research would support these arguments. Marsh and Peel (1999), for example, noted the significance of attachment bonds in their study of young people leaving care, even if there had been no contact with family members for several years.

## Continuities and discontinuities of working models in children and adults

One of the key questions relating to attachment theory is the extent to which early patterns can be modified or discontinued. The answer seems increasingly to be in the affirmative, providing that new attachment figures are found who can respond to children's attachment needs sensitively and can be committed enough to handle any intervening behaviour which may test carers' staying power.

Information about how discontinuities occur is emerging. Recent research in the USA on attachment between small children and alternative carers (such as extended family and foster carers) suggests that the process of making new attachments is similar, whenever it occurs. In other words, children construct their attachment relationships on the basis of repeated and frequent interactions with new caregivers. Children are able to reorganize their attachment behaviour on the basis of being with sensitive caregivers who respond consistently to their needs (Aldgate and Jones 2006; Howes 1999).

It is, however, not so easy for some children to make new attachments. Those who have had repeated experience of feeling emotionally unsafe will find it very hard to show trust in new relationships with adults. This is one of the key factors that makes recovery from serious maltreatment so difficult (Jones and Ramchandani 1999). The caregiver (such as a foster-carer) who looks after a toddler with previous experiences of inconsistent caregiving may find that the child will not trust him or her for a very long time. Some children may need to learn, almost from scratch, that a caregiver can be a consistent and safe attachment figure. A useful detailed description of children's patterns of behaviour and the inputs needs to bring about change may be found in Howe (1995).

Although there is still a widely held view that the cumulative effect of childhood patterns will be carried into adult life and will influence caregiver behaviour towards the next generation (see, for example, Howe *et al.* 1999), it is now known that the pattern of those relationships is not fixed. They can be 'discontinued' and, like children, adults can 'disconfirm' or change the way they have learnt to see others. Intergenerational research on parenting has shown that many intervening experiences (including relationships with new carers, professionals and adult partners) can influence individuals' working models and their states of mind, both through childhood and into adulthood (Bowlby 1953; Berlin and Cassidy 1999; Howe 2001; Rutter, 1985; Rutter and Quinton, 1984).

## The social work role in attachment – knowing about attachment and child development

Any social worker embarking on working with attachment issues needs to be well informed about child development and particularly about the impact of different attachment patterns on children's behaviour at different ages and stages. They also need to understand the impact of parenting styles and inputs on the development of attachment patterns. Helpful texts in this area are *Child Development for Child Care and Child Protection Workers* (Daniel, Wassell and Gilligan 1999), *The Child's World* (Horwath 2001) and *The Developing World of the Child* (Aldgate *et al.* 2006). Howe has also produced helpful texts specifically on attachment (Howe 1995; Howe *et al.* 1999).

## Embracing a positive approach of contemporary psychology

Taking seriously the work needed to help children become securely attached demands a sea of change in attitudes of social workers and others working with children. Psychology has an increasing interest in strengths, wellness, well-being and potential for change (Lorion 2000; Schaffer 1996, 1998). There is an urgent need in social work to depart from the idea that vulnerable children will be held back by their pasts and to understand how change can be effected. Furman, for example, has written extensively about how children survive abuse and adversity. His work emphasizes how attitudes can influence the reappraisal of past adversities and can contribute to quality of life (Furman 1998): 'It's natural to think that our past has an effect on how our future will turn out, but we rarely look at it the other way round. The future – that is what we think it will bring – determines what the past looks like' (Furman 1998, p.81).

## An attachment perspective for social workers

Taking up the positive psychology approach, Howe outlines the essential features of what he calls an 'attachment perspective' for social workers. This 'recognises that relationships are where things can go wrong in the first place, but equally relationships are generally the place where things are eventually put right' (Howe 2001, p.204). Howe also advocates the professional relationship as the means by which change can be

achieved: 'Support and understanding provided within the context of a confiding relationship have been found to promote psychological well-being, esteem, confidence and
resilience' (Howe 2001, p.204).

Social workers have three key roles to play within an attachment perspective:

1. assessment

2. planning

3. direct work with children, parents and carers.

## Assessment

Contemporary child welfare policy across the UK identifies sound assessment as the
foundation for helping safeguard and promote the welfare of children. In England and
Wales, the *Framework for the Assessment of Children in Need and their Families* (Department of
Health, Department for Education and Home Office 2000) incorporates aspects of attachment within the triangular model design to assess children's needs, parenting and
other wider factors in children's ecology. The practice guidance accompanying this system stresses the importance of attachment in children's development (Rose and Aldgate
2000), while the domain of children's developmental needs also pays attention to emotional and behavioural development and family and social relationships, all necessary to
the assessment of attachment.

There are also classic tests for assessing attachment such as the stranger test developed by Ainsworth in the 1970s (see Howe et al. 1999). These can be used in context of
a wider assessment to help identify patterns of attachment in young children, remembering it is important not to attribute every aspect of children's behaviour to the quality of
his or her attachments.

The Assessment Framework (Department of Health *et al.* 2000) also incorporates
caregiving behaviour in relation to attachment within the domains of parenting capacity,
especially that of emotional warmth. Accompanying tools developed by Cox and
Bentovim (Department of Health, Cox and Bentovim 2000) also have relevance for the
assessment of appropriate caregiving. The Department of Health's Framework can be
supplemented by applying tools to assess the impact of childhood attachment on adults.
Contemporary approaches aimed at helping practitioners are moving towards the line
taken by Main in the USA. Main's tool for assessing attachment in adults (Main and
Goldwyn 1994; see also Hesse 1999; Howe *et al.* 1999) stresses that it is what individuals have made of experiences of attachment rather than the experiences themselves that
are important (see Aldgate and Jones 2006).

The ecological approach of the assessment system with its emphasis in the third side
of the triangle on wider relationships, school and community also provides a context for
assessing the potential for positive multiple attachments which may supplement parental
caregiving. There is increasing interest in the role of kinship care to provide continuity
and stability for children (see, for example, Broad 2001; Hunt 2001). The book by Jack
and Gill (2003) on 'the missing side' of the triangle has a helpful guide for assessing factors in the child's wider world, including the potential of adults in the community such
as teachers and youth leaders to become mentors and attachment figures.

Scotland is now developing its own system for the assessment of children called *Getting it Right for Every Child* (Scottish Executive 2005). This system of assessment, planning, recording and review is based around a triangle of children's ecology seen from the perspective of the child, and provides useful questions for practitioners from a child's perspective about attachments and other aspects of parenting.

## Planning and review

Legislation across the four countries of the UK requires that children are consulted about any decisions that will affect their lives. Though such consultation may be variable (see, for example, Department of Health 2001), there is evidence that children are able to articulate their views about their relationships with others and where they wish to live (Grimshaw and Sinclair 1997).

Planning and reviewing of children should have meaning and purpose and should consider any impact of proposed change on children's development. Planning for new attachments can be positive and may mark a turning point for some children. Planning for looked-after children is necessary to try to find the best possible parenting figures with whom children can form new attachments. An essential ingredient for success is that children are ready to accept new attachments and that work has been done with them to ensure this is so. Careful planning also helps to avoid placement changes with further loss of attachment figures, which are likely to be interpreted by children as even more evidence of their unworthiness.

## Direct social work

Useful though assessment and planning systems are, they do not substitute for good communication skills and direct work with children and families. A review of social work in Scotland (Social Work Review Team, Scottish Executive 2005) commented on the damage the change of role from direct worker to care-manager had done to practice.

Direct work can be effective in helping children to move from one place to another and to manage loss and change. Until recently, direct work as described in the early 1990s (see, for example, Aldgate and Simmonds 1991) seemed to have become lost to mainstream social work practice. Recent developments have indicated a renaissance of manuals of guidance for this kind of work (see Aldgate *et al.* 2006). It is imperative that direct work is reclaimed in order that children are helped to come to terms with their past and move on. Direct work can:

- help children feel they are valued and have champions

- prepare children for change

- show children their perspectives on attachments figures are acknowledged

- give children permission to express their feelings about loss and change

- use techniques such as life story work and eco-maps to help children retain socio-genealogical connections.

Working and supporting parents to improve their caregiving behaviour is also a direct part of the social work role, supplemented by linking parents to groups who may enhance their self-esteem. Social workers need to give parents time and expertise to prepare for change if children are looked after. There is also a role to help parents maintain and manage contact if appropriate. If a plan involves children being adopted, social workers must not abandon parents but help them to come to terms with the loss of their child. Some of the most helpful practice advice in this area comes from the earlier texts (see, for example, Aldgate 1991; Maluccio and Sinaloglu 1981).

Complementary to working with parents is the preparation and support of new attachment figures. There are excellent texts on supporting foster carers (see, for example, Triseliotis, Sellick and Short 1995; Thomas 2005), as well as many publications from the British Association of Adoption and Fostering Agencies.

## Nurturing the workers

Finally, in today's world of targets and outcomes, important as they are, it must be recognized that those working with children should be supported, since the work is demanding and calls for self-awareness and considerable skill. Children have told researchers they appreciate workers who can be their champions (Department of Health 1996). They also appreciate those who explain clearly and honestly what is going to happen to them and listen to their side of the story. Time and reliability are also required: commodities in short supply in social work practice. Above all, children want workers who see them as the whole child, not as a child with problems (Rose 2006).

Such work demands of workers self-awareness of their own childhood, a capacity to separate children's emotions from their own feelings of anger or sadness about what has happened to children, and a resolve not to let this influence their motivation for action. In short, workers undertaking the role of direct worker with children need to ensure they themselves have access to trusted adults to support and supervise their work. In the managed environment of social work, it is time to move to an ecology in the workplace of learning and nurture so that workers are empowered to engage in effective direct work with children. In the 1950s, Bowlby suggested that, if society valued its children, it must cherish their parents. Social workers in the twenty-first century cannot promote secure attachments in children or help improve sensitive caregiving in their parents unless they themselves are cherished and supported effectively.

## References

Ainsworth, M.D.S., Blehar, M., Waters, E. and Wall, S. (1978) *Patterns of Attachment.* Hillsdale, NJ: Erlbaum.

Adoption Policy Review Group, Scottish Executive (2005) *Report of Phase Two Secure and Safe Homes for Our Most Vulnerable Children Scottish Executive Proposals for Action: A Consultation Paper.* June. Edinburgh: Scottish Executive.

Aldgate, J. (1991) 'Attachment theory and its application to child care social work: An introduction.' In J. Lishman (1991) (ed.) *Handbook of Theory for Practice Teachers in Social Work.* London: Jessica Kingsley Publishers.

Aldgate, J., Jones, D., Rose, W., and Jeffery, C. (eds) (2006) *The Developing World of the Child.* London: Jessica Kingsley Publishers.

Aldgate, J. and Jones, D. (2006) 'The place of attachment in children's development.' In J. Aldgate, D. Jones, W. Rose and C. Jeffery (eds) *The Developing World of the Child*. London: Jessica Kingsley Publishers.

Aldgate, J. and Simmonds, J. (eds) (1991) *Direct Work with Children*. London: Batsford.

Berlin, L. and Cassidy, J. (1999) 'Relations among relationships contributions from attachment theory and research.' In J. Cassidy and P.R. Shaver (eds) *Handbook of Attachment: Theory, Research and Clinical Applications*. New York and London: The Guilford Press.

Berridge, D. (2000) *Placement Stability* Quality Protects research briefing. London: Department of Health, Research in Practice, Making Research Count.

Berridge, D. and Cleaver, H. (1987) *Foster Home Breakdown*. Oxford: Blackwell.

Bowlby, J. (1951) *Maternal Care and Mental Health*. WHO Monograph Series No. 2. Geneva: World Health Organisation.

Bowlby, J. (1953) *Child Care and the Growth of Love*. Harmondsworth: Penguin Books.

Bowlby, J. (1958) 'The nature of the child's tie to its mother.' *International Journal of Psycho-Analysis 39*, 350–3.

Broad, B. (2001) *Kinship Care: The Placement Choice for Children and Young People*. Lyme Regis: Russell House Publishing.

Cassidy, J. (1999) 'The nature of the child's ties.' In J. Cassidy and P. Shaver (eds) *Theory, Research and Clinical Applications*. New York and London: The Guilford Press.

Cleaver, H. (2000) *Fostering Family Contact: A Study of Children, Parents and Foster Carers*. London: The Stationery Office.

Crittenden, P.M. (1995) 'Attachment and psychopathology.' In S. Goldberg, R. Muir and J. Kerr (eds) *Attachment Theory: Social, Developmental and Clinical Perspectives*. Hillsdale, NJ: Analytic Press.

Daniel, B. (2006) 'Early childhood: Zero to four years.' In J. Aldgate, D. Jones, W. Rose and C. Jeffery (eds) *The Developing World of the Child*. London: Jessica Kingsley Publishers.

Daniel, B., Wassell, S. and Gilligan, R. (1999) *Child Development for Child Care and Protection Workers*. London: Jessica Kingsley Publishers.

Department of Health (1990) *Principles and Practice in Guidance and Regulations*. London: Her Majesty's Stationery Office.

Department of Health (1991) *Patterns and Outcomes in Child Placement*. London: Her Majesty's Stationery Office.

Department of Health (1996) *Focus on Teenagers: Research into Practice*. London: Her Majesty's Stationery Office.

Department of Health (2001) *The Children Act Now – Messages from Research*. London: The Stationery Office.

Department of Health, Cox, A. and Bentovim, A. (2000) 'The family pack of questionnaires and scales.' In Department of Health, *Framework for the Assessment of Children in Need and their Families*. London: The Stationery Office.

Department of Health and Social Security (1985) *Social Work Decisions in Child Care*. London: Her Majesty's Stationery Office.

Department of Health, Department for Education and Home Office (2000) *Framework for the Assessment of Children in Need and Their Families*. London: The Stationery Office.

Fahlberg, V. (1981) *Attachment and Separation*. London: British Agencies for Adoption and Fostering.

Fahlberg, V. (1994) *A Child's Journey Through Placement*. London: British Agencies for Adoption and Fostering.

Furman, B. (1997) *It's Never too Late to Have a Happy Childhood: From Adversity to Resilience*. London: BT Press.

Green, J. (2003) 'Concepts of child attachment.' Paper given at the President's Interdisciplinary Conference, Dartington Hall, 12–14 September.

Grimshaw, R. and Sinclair, R. (1997) *Planning to Care: Regulations, Procedure and Practice Under the Children Act 1989*. London: National Children's Bureau.

Hesse, E. (1999) 'The adult attachment interview: Historical and current perspectives.' In J. Cassidy and P. Shaver (eds) *Handbook of Attachment: Theory, Research and Clinical Applications*. New York and London: The Guilford Press.

Horwath, J. (ed.) (2001) *The Child's World: Assessing Children in Need*. London: Jessica Kingsley Publishers.

Howe, D. (1995) *Attachment Theory for Social Work Practice*. Basingstoke: Macmillan.

Howe, D. (2001) 'Attachment.' In J. Horwath (ed.) *The Child's World: Assessing Children in Need*. London: Jessica Kingsley Publishers.

Howe, D., Brandon, M. and Schofield, G. (1999) *Attachment Theory, Child Maltreatment and Family Support*. London: Macmillan.

Howes, C. (1999) 'Attachment relationships in the context of multiple carers.' In J. Cassidy and P.R. Shaver (eds) *Handbook of Attachment – Theory, Research and Clinical Applications*. New York and London: The Guilford Press.

Hunt, J. (2001) *Friends and Family Care – A Scoping Paper for the Department of Health*. London: The Stationery Office.

Jack, G. and Gill, O. (2003) *The Missing Side of the Triangle*. Barkinside: Barnardo's.

Jewett, C. (1984) *Helping Children Cope with Separation and Loss*. London: Batsford.

Jones, D.P.H. and Ramchandani, P. (1999) *Child Sexual Abuse – Informing Practice from Research*. Oxford: Radcliffe Medical Press.

Kelly, G. (1995) 'Foster parents and long-term placements: Key findings from a Northern Ireland study.' *Children and Society 9*, 2, 19–29.

Lorion, R.P. (2000) 'Theoretical and evaluation issues in the promotion of wellness and protection of "well enough".' In D. Cicchetti, J. Rappaport, I. Sandler and P. Weissberg (eds) *The Promotion of Wellness in Children*. Washington, DC: Child Welfare League of America.

Maluccio, A.N. and Sinanoglu, P.A. (1981) *The Challenge of Partnership: Working with Parents of Children in Foster Care*. New York: Columbia University Press.

Main, M. and Goldwyn, R. (1994) 'Predicting rejection of her infant from a mother's representation of her own experience. Implications for the abused – abusing intergenerational cycle.' *Child Abuse and Neglect 8*, 203–217.

Marsh, P. and Peel, M. (1999) *Leaving Care in Partnership: Family Involvement with Care Leavers*. London: The Stationery Office.

Murray, L. and Andrews, L. (2000) *The Social Baby*. Richmond, Surrey: C.P. Publishing.

Mussen, P.H., Conger, J.J., Kagan, J. and Huston, A.C. (1990) *Child Development and Personality*. 7th edn. New York: HarperCollins.

Owusu-Bempah, K. (2006) 'Socio-genealogical connectedness: Knowledge and identity.' In J. Aldgate, D. Jones, W. Rose and C. Jeffery (eds) *The Developing World of the Child*. London: Jessica Kingsley Publishers.

Owusu-Bempah, K. and Howitt, D. (1997) 'Socio-genealogical connectedness, attachment theory, and childcare practice.' *Child and Family Social Work 2*, 199–207.

Quinton, D. (1994) 'Cultural and community influences.' In M. Rutter and D.F. Hay (eds) *Development Through Life: A Handbook for Clinicians*. Oxford: Blackwell Science.

Robertson, J. (1952) *A Two-year-old Goes to Hospital*. (Film: 16mm, 45 min.; sound. Distributors: Tavistock Child Development Research Unit. London; New York University Film Library; United Nations, Geneva.)

Rose, W. (2006) 'The developing world of the child: Children's perspectives.' In J. Aldgate, D. Jones, W. Rose and C. Jeffery (eds) *The Developing World of the Child*. London: Jessica Kingsley Publishers.

Rose, W. and Aldgate, J. (2000) 'Knowledge underpinning the Assessment Framework.' In Department of Health, *Assessing Children in Need and their Families: Practice Guidance*. London: The Stationery Office.

Rutter, M. (1985) 'Resilience in the face of adversity: Protective factors and resistance to psychiatric disorder.' *British Journal of Psychiatry 147*, 598–611.

Rutter, M. and Quinton, D. (1984) 'Long-term follow-up of women institutionalised in childhood: Factors promoting good functioning in social life.' *British Journal of Developmental Psychology 2*, 191–204.

Schaffer, H.R. (1996) *Social Development.* Oxford: Blackwell.

Schaffer, H.R. (1998) *Making Decisions about Children.* Oxford: Blackwell.

Scottish Executive (2005) *Getting it Right for Every Child: Proposals for Action.* Parts 1–4. Edinburgh: Scottish Executive.

Scottish Office (1997) *The Children (Scotland) Act 1995, Regulations and Guidance, Volume 2, Children Looked After by Local Authorities.* Edinburgh: The Stationery Office.

Social Work Review Team, Scottish Executive (2005) *21st Century Review of Social Work – Interim Report.* Edinburgh: Scottish Executive.

Solomon, J. and George, C. (1999) 'The measurement of attachment security in infancy and childhood.' In J. Cassidy and P. Shaver (eds) *Handbook of Attachment: Theory, Research and Clinical Applications.* New York and London: The Guilford Press.

Thoburn, J. (2002) *Adoption and Permanence for Children who Cannot Live Safely with Birth Parents or Relatives.* Quality Protects Research Briefing. London: Department of Health, Research in Practice, Making Research Count.

Thomas, N. (2005) *Social Work with Young People in Care.* Basingstoke: Palgrave Macmillan.

Triseliotis, J., Sellick, C. and Short, R. (1995) *Foster Care: Theory and Practice.* London: Batsford.

van IJzendoorn, M.H. and Sagi, A. (1999) 'Cross-cultural patterns of attachment, universal and contextual dimensions.' In J. Cassidy and P.R. Shaver (eds) *Handbook of Attachment: Theory, Research and Clinical Applications.* New York and London: The Guilford Press.

Ward, H., Macdonald, I. and Skuse, T. (forthcoming) *Looking After Children: Longitudinal Cohort Study – Final Report to the Department of Health.* Loughborough: University of Loughborough.

## CHAPTER 5

# ERIKSON'S LIFE CYCLE APPROACH TO DEVELOPMENT

*Alastair Gibson*

At certain ages or points in our lives, according to Erikson's (1965) life cycle approach to development, we encounter expectable life crises which create a conflict within ourselves as individuals and between ourselves and significant other people in our lives. How we cope with these conflicts affects the development of our personality and patterns of behaviour. In the development of this theoretical approach, Erikson has provided a framework for those working in the helping or caring professions whose role is to assess and understand the individual personality.

This is very much a psychosocial theory; although it may owe its roots to certain aspects of Freudian theory, it is firmly committed to the importance of relationships as a central factor in the development of personality. There are important features from psychodynamic theory which are inherent in an understanding of the life cycle approach and it would be useful to mention these briefly before considering the life crises.

First, the concept of the ego assumes importance. The ego is the central functioning part of the personality which is conscious, aware and determines our day-to-day activities and relationships in a rational, reality-based way. The ego, however, is only a part of the personality and attention is given to the unconscious part, or, as identified by Melanie Klein (1960) and Ronald Fairbairn (1952), the split part which forms the inner world of the individual.

In studying the life cycle with its psychodynamic core, we understand that there are situations experienced and feelings engendered which are so painful or stressful to the developing ego that they become subject to the intervention of ego defence mechanisms (Rycroft 1968). Briefly, there are two principal methods of defence in the very early formative years which are relevant to the helping professions. The first is introjection, whereby feelings and experiences are taken inside, both physically through the mouth and emotionally through responses to external stimuli. To the baby this is an unconscious process, but the feelings remain in our inner world as a significant determinant of our personality. This process of introjection begins with the baby's identification of familiar people, familiar patterns of behaviour and feelings associated with these. By introjecting these perceptions and feelings, the infant absorbs them into the developing personality.

For example, if the baby introjects the caring, nurturing parts of the carer, this may be reflected at a later stage in life in a giving, open personality. Similarly, if the baby introjects the depriving or rejecting parts of the carer, this may result in a non-giving, withholding personality. As a positive defence mechanism, the process of introjection may help a child cope with separation, or separation anxiety, by providing something of the presence of an absent carer within the child, which may help the child tolerate the crisis.

The other main method of defence is projection, whereby we put or project onto other people whatever is felt to be personally intolerable; whatever we fear or are anxious about is inside us and is very painful. We may cope by denying and repressing, or we may actually get rid of it by placing it onto someone else. Thus, for example, angry feelings that we find intolerable in ourselves are projected onto another, whom we now allow ourselves to identify as angry, while we, despite the fact that these feelings are really our own, regard ourselves as calm. A young child may have very powerful feelings of rage if his or her needs are frustrated – for example, as a baby, if food is not provided when hungry, or, as a toddler, if movement and the chance to explore is restricted or if the carer is not available when needed. The power of such feelings of anger may be quite terrifying to the infant. Anger may, therefore, be a very unsafe emotion to own and express, and crises later in life may be distorted either by an avoidance of anger at all costs or by an undercurrent of anger impeding relationships which might involve constant projections of angry feelings on to others.

If the use of such defences is a predominant feature of early years, they may form a large unconscious part of ourselves. This unconscious part, our inner world, may affect our ability to deal with the demands of the real world, and as a result, the ego may be poorly equipped to cope with later crises. In any assessment of need which we undertake, we may not in everyday language use the term 'ego', but we are assessing another person's 'ego strength'. By this, I mean that we assess the conscious ability to tolerate a reasonable level of frustration or difficulty and to be able to problem-solve with a reasonable level of assistance. If the unconscious or split part of our personality is considerable, the conscious self, the ego, is less likely to be able to respond constructively to task-centred or cognitive behavioural approaches and may require a more sustaining approach which acknowledges the potentially strong emotional deficits which may influence behaviour.

In life cycle theory, the first five or six years of life are deemed most significant because of the development of inner and outer worlds, because of the strength of unconscious processes and of the potential use of infantile defence mechanisms. How many of us can remember anything from our first two years of life? In fact, what is your earliest memory? Yet, Erikson, in common with other psychodynamic theorists, points to the earliest years as being the most significant in our development of personality, and we have little, if any, conscious memory of these major experiences. However, it is essential that anyone who applies this theoretical framework to practice does so with sensitivity and an awareness that this is a dynamic theory. A difficult early life does not automatically result in a difficult later life. Studies into resilience (Clausen 1995) have introduced the concept of 'turning points', where a young person's negative experiences, often associated with anti-social behaviour and deviant labelling, may be influenced by significant life events, such as the influence of an understanding teacher or a parent who comes off drugs. Such positive experiences have been shown to change the course of a person's life.

Erikson saw each life crisis as a conflict, characterized by a pull in different directions. The word 'versus' appears in each stage. For example, the first stage is seen as basic trust versus basic mistrust. From the outset it should be made clear that Erikson does not assume that the successful resolution of each stage requires absolute goodness, be it complete basic trust, complete autonomy or whatever. Psychological health is not seen as that. Erikson's own words are 'favourable ratio' (Erikson 1965, p.262), which conveys the element of balance in considering the outcome of these crises. For example, the assimilation of some mistrust into one's personality would be vital, otherwise one might have a totally naïve, potentially dangerous faith that everything is good and safe. The importance of avoiding a mechanistic interpretation of the life cycle framework is reinforced by Winnicott's early studies. In considering conditions which children required for their needs to be met, he wrote:

> These conditions need only be good enough, since a child's intelligence becomes increasingly able to allow for failures and to deal with frustrations by advance preparation. As is well known, the conditions that are necessary for the child's individual growth are…in a state of qualitative and quantitative change relative to the infant's or the child's age and changing needs. (Winnicott 1957, p.3)

The various crises which form the life cycle are a process. Thus, if one achieves a favourable ratio of basic trust, one is as well prepared as possible for the next stage. Equally, failure to achieve a favourable ratio is likely to make the resolution of succeeding life crises more problematic. In the first 18 months of life, the baby is confronted with the crisis of basic trust versus basic mistrust, which corresponds to Freud's oral sensory stage (Brown 1961) where the mouth is the focus of sensory stimulation. The word 'basic' is not used lightly. It refers to a fundamental sense of trust, of inner confidence in the outer world, that forms the core of one's adult personality. Absence of such basic trust can be a feature of those whose adult personalities are withdrawn in schizoid or depressive states, and this stage of the life cycle assumes considerable importance if we consider our work with people of any age who have particular difficulty forming attachments, making satisfactory relationships or trusting. Can we work effectively with them without specifically trying to help them rebuild a sense of basic trust?

The baby at this stage has to develop a sense of what is good and what is bad by a process of introjection and projection. The desired outcome is a favourable ratio of basic trust with a healthy sense of mistrust to allow future experiences to be evaluated realistically. From a social work perspective, this theory implies that a baby has particular needs which have to be met by parents or substitute carers. We must try to understand what a baby, without the power of word formation, without formed cognitive thought processes, feels when, for example, the pangs of hunger become distressing or a colic pain upsets or when physical pain is administered by someone. The depth of feeling is not tempered by rationalization. It is probably a bitter rage and identifies the person associated with the feeling as wholly bad. 'In introjection we feel and act as if an outer goodness had become an inner certainty. In projection, we experience an inner harm as an outer one: we endow significant people with the evil which is actually within us' (Erikson 1965, p.240). The bad feelings translate to the world as a bad place, i.e. not to be trusted. The act of feeding, by breast or bottle, may restore feelings of goodness which are taken in through the mouth and psychologically introjected. Cuddles, hold-ing and physical demonstrations of affection are also very important in conveying to the baby that feeling of goodness which results in the acquisition of basic trust.

Erikson is quite specific that this is not purely a mechanical approach and that the amount of trust acquired in no way depends on how much food is given or how much the baby is held. Trust is created because the parent or carer is sensitive to the child's needs, meets those needs within a consistent framework which begins to have some meaning for the baby and establishes his or her own trustworthiness. The building of trust depends very much on the quality of the relationship between baby and primary carers. What, therefore, if the carer came through his or her childhood with an unfa-vourable ratio of basic trust? Here the work of Bowlby (1969) and Rutter (1981) on the formation of attachment is significant. The reciprocal basis of a bond, where, for exam-ple, baby offers rewards to father/mother/carer just as much as father/mother/carer of-fers them to baby, seems to relate closely to Erikson's views on the establishment of basic trust. As a baby develops a sense of attachment to primary carers based on their relative reliability, and as the carers enjoy caring for their baby, an affectional bond develops, which, if the carers remain sensitive to the child's changing needs, will allow the child to move into the wider world without the continuing physical presence of the primary attachment figure.

Continuity and consistency in terms of helping the baby attach meaning to the outer world also relate to Rutter's research into the number of different carers in a young baby's life. Although the evidence is somewhat limited, Rutter (1981) suggests that up to five carers could be involved in the care of a baby without there being harmful psycho-logical effects, provided these carers were responsive and stimulating. This research was an important factor in changing child care practices, and nurseries could not meet regis-tration requirements if they did not provide such consistency of care. The formation of a bond and attachments may well be impeded if the early care of a baby is chaotic and lacking the stability of contact with recognizable people over a prolonged period. Here again we must try to speculate how it must feel to a baby to be left to cry with hunger for a long period with no certainty that food will be provided. In the same way, how does a baby react when there is no recognizably consistent figure to whom to relate or attach? Given the potentially intense feelings, if the world is felt to be an unsafe or untrustwor-thy place at this stage, there is a strong possibility that it will remain an unsafe place, with consequent inhibiting effects on the individual's ability to tackle subsequent life crises.

The second stage, autonomy versus shame and doubt, coincides with the physical development of muscular control, including the anal sphincter, and Freud's anal stage (Brown 1961). Erikson places the onset of this life crisis in the second year of life, but clearly a baby in the first year displays some kind of autonomy when squirming away from someone or resisting a feed. Thus there is a relationship between all the life crises and it may be true to say that features of each crisis exist before the chronological time for the crisis arrives. The particular nature of each crisis is, however, seen as age related. For example, 'under normal conditions, it is not until the second year that he [the infant] begins to experience the whole critical opposition of being an autonomous creature and being a dependent one' (Erikson 1965, p.263).

At this stage the crisis is about who controls, and, in the context of toilet training, 'holding on' and 'letting go'. Physically, the infant is becoming more mobile, crawling and walking, and beginning to experience the pleasures of being able to do things and wanting to do things. Anything of value within the house which is within reach becomes vulnerable to the exploring infant. Getting the infant out of nappies and toilet trained assumes significance for parents. Compromise and balance are critical in order to avoid, at one end of the spectrum, the all-powerful child who becomes terrified by the lack of meaningful boundaries, and, at the other end, the heavily restricted, overly controlled or punished child, who experiences meaningless shame and doubt. There is no neat interpretation or application of this stage, however, and it is essential to have as much assessment information as possible. The adolescent who sets fire to the school may be a product of an indulged childhood, so unsure of his boundaries that he resorts to extreme measures in order to elicit some control from others, or, on the other hand, he may be the product of very restrictive parenting against which he is now rebelling. Equally, the parent who tries to keep the house spotless and prevents a child's development of autonomy may also be reacting to too much freedom as a child by imposing her own rigid boundaries or she may be identifying with the restrictions placed on her by her own parent.

In practical terms, the relationship between child and carer determines so much of the outcome of this stage. The carer who is not stressed about toilet training, who is prepared to wait till the infant seems ready and who is prepared to tolerate the interest in faeces will not unduly inhibit the acquisition of autonomy. The carer who can let the infant explore his or her surroundings, protecting against danger, will also enhance the sense of autonomy. If, however, the infant experiences the pain of punishment, the anger of a carer who clears up the mess or the restriction of having to do things, including the toilet, when other people want, the balance of shame and doubt may be excessive. Shame is the kind of feeling of fear one gets of being completely exposed and of being looked at, the kind of feeling that makes one wish the ground would swallow one or that one could be invisible. The risk, according to Erikson, of too much shaming is that the individual may try to get away with things or indeed reacts by defiant shamelessness. Erikson links the origins of doubt to Freud's anal stage of development. The pleasure in the passing of faeces makes the infant aware of the back of the body. If the infant feels shame when those faeces which felt so good to pass are treated with revulsion by the carer, Erikson argues that doubt may be established when that part of the body which cannot be seen by the owner, as it were, attracts such an interest in its control from others. Holding on at this stage can turn into an obsessional holding on in adult life. This could be a compulsive need to be in control of self or others at all costs. Letting go could be more positive if it is a relaxed feeling of toleration, but could be translated into more destructive activity if it becomes a release of harmful, pent-up emotions. At this stage the infant learns by repeating actions and activities, with boundaries being imposed by carers and by learning from the knocks and bumps of mistakes. The child who is prevented from standing on his or her own feet at this stage, may repress feelings of anger and may become the obsessive adult, the compulsive neurotic, the personality lacking self-esteem. If one were to summarize the aims of the first two life crises, they might be: 'the world is an OK place, and I'm an OK person'.

The third stage, described as initiative versus guilt, may broadly be expected to become critical between the ages of four and six years, although one cannot be too rigid, and links with Freud's oedipal complex (Brown 1961). There is often a degree of confusion about the differences between initiative and autonomy and between guilt and shame or doubt. Initiative implies more than autonomy, because it suggests an ability to set something in motion, to make the first move, to plan and to act independently. Because of this element of personal volition and ability, the negative aspect is one of guilt about one's intentions and the actions that one has implemented.

Physically and mentally the child has an energy which enables it to form relationships with others in a more complex way than before. Multiple relationships develop in terms of adults, siblings and playmates. Cognitively, the child is able to begin to reason and deduce, but still carries that part of thinking which could be described as 'magical' in the sense that fantasy and wish fulfilment can make it seem possible to achieve anything. While this may produce good feelings if the results are pleasurable, the feelings may be bad where the results are painful. For example, the death of a parent or carer at this stage, if the child magically assumes some causative part in it, may leave deep anxiety, fear and guilt. Within this particular framework of understanding personality development, this stage is potentially traumatic, as fantasy has to become transformed into reality and the child begins to understand concepts of right and wrong, fair play and deferred gratification and the requirements of social conformity.

Jealousy and rivalry seem to be major features of the conflict at this stage and this is particularly so in those families where a new baby has to be integrated by a brother or sister at this age. Families who foster children may also find that this age presents difficulties for the child of the family or the fostered child. The main arena for the rivalry is seen as the battle for the affections of the parent of the opposite sex, where the fantasy that the son can possess his mother or the daughter her father is, under normal circumstances, doomed to failure. Freud paid particular attention to the concept of sexuality and at this stage the awareness of genitals in boys and the absence of them in girls. If, however, we take a broader, more relationship-oriented view, and also acknowledge the cognitive developments in the child's personality, we may begin to understand something of the potential turmoil taking place within the child. This is a transitional time when the child is moving from a very self-centred basis of relating to a much wider basis. The child has to come to terms with different ways of interpreting the world and the possibly intense relationship within the family has to be modified. Again, the relationship with parents or carers will affect the child's progression through this stage. Psychological health may be maintained if the child is not made to feel that his or her behaviour is wrong or unduly threatening. Ideally, the child continues to feel the affection of both parents and gradually gives up the desire to possess the parent of the opposite sex and begins to identify with the parent of the same sex. The child is then prepared in this transitional stage to develop wider relationships. Within our society, this is almost a blueprint for ideal personality development. What happens, however, to the child in care who is deprived of the presence of two parents? What happens to the child in a single parent family? In reality, there does not have to be any difference. There are likely to be other adults or children in everyone's life, and the process can be experienced whatever the family composition.

From practice experience it would appear that the life crisis as indicated by Erikson is a critical part of development and that individuals are critically affected by experiences at this stage. There is a relationship-seeking energy at this age which needs to find some kind of outlet in people of the same and opposite sex. In whatever setting the child lives, there are implications for the behaviour of significant adults in helping the child achieve a favourable ratio of initiative, a sense of purpose and awareness of self. Guilt does appear to be unavoidable as there are so many activities that cannot be completed at this age, including being the partner of one's parent, that some guilt must be engendered. This can be exacerbated, for example, if a parent of the same sex dies leaving the child with the parent of the opposite sex. Fantasy and reality overlap, creating a potential for either massive guilt or an excess of initiative in the form of extreme risk taking.

These three stages of life crises mark the most critical of the formative stages because of the intensity of experiences and the repression which is needed to help the child cope with everyday events. If a child has a favourable ratio of basic trust, autonomy and initiative, there is a healthy psychological foundation. It is impossible to imagine a child who has not repressed feelings and experiences, and therefore within this model everyone has a potentially neurotic part of their personality. The less favourable the ratio, the more potential repression, and, it is fair to assume, the less equipped one is to tackle subsequent life crises realistically. Nevertheless, in assessing a child's development, it is important to recognize the totality of experience. In their research on children who had come through a childhood marked by adversity, Masten and Coatsworth noted, 'successful children remind us that children grow up in multiple contexts – in families, schools, peer groups...teams, religious organisations, and many other groups – and each context is a potential source of protective as well as risk factors' (Masten and Coatsworth 1998, p. 216). This becomes even more relevant as the life cycle progresses.

The fourth stage is rooted more in conscious memory and covers the primary school years, industry versus inferiority. Freud called this the 'latency stage' (Brown 1961), because the violent drives and turmoil which characterized the earlier years become dormant at this point pending the onset of puberty. Within our psychosocial framework we tend to find that memory of this period is clearer, and whereas the anxiety-provoking experiences of earlier stages are more prone to repression or selective recall, the anxiety of this period is within the conscious part of the ego. The conflict now is about the acquisition of knowledge and skills as a preparation for life in adult society against a feeling of inadequacy or failure. School obviously becomes the focus for much of this conflict, but home life continues to play an important part.

It is usually not difficult to remember teachers and how they made one feel. Nor is it usually too difficult to remember one's own reactions and behaviour. It is all too easy to place a child in an inferior role at this stage, and all children find some way of coping, finding the inner strength or playing the fool or fighting the system, for example. Here one may see that the ability to cope with outside pressures depends on ego strength which derives from a favourable ratio from previous stages.

Particularly relevant, but not exclusively, is the result of the autonomy versus shame and doubt conflict. The child who harbours inner doubt or shame has a propensity for feelings of inadequacy and low self-esteem and is, therefore, less well prepared for the pressures than the child who has a more favourable experience. Relationships are also widening and peer group identification is becoming a more significant part of personality. There are conflicts inherent in trying to meet the requirements of adults and trying to meet the need to identify with friends and peers. Again, the child who has a sense of purpose and initiative, who is not restrained by the oedipal pressure to cement relationships with a particular member of the family, will be better equipped to find a satisfactory balance.

The onset of puberty, the move into secondary education and adolescence mark the fifth stage of the life cycle, identity versus role confusion. If one considers the fundamental importance of a sense of identity to the individual personality, of being a specific person within an understood environment, one gets an impression of the potential depth of conflict inherent in this life crisis. Such is the fundamental importance that one can begin to appreciate why, at this stage, there is the potential for behaviour to mirror the pattern of earlier conflicts which have not been satisfactorily concluded. For example, a lack of basic trust may inhibit the formation of an identity outwith very narrow, 'safe' surroundings. A sense of shame and doubt may result in behaviour that might be delinquent or repetitive as the adolescent struggles inwardly to establish some satisfactory meaning. Oedipal attachments from Erikson's stage of initiative versus guilt may affect the adolescent's attempt to wrestle with relationships and to establish a sexual identity.

For every adolescent, this is a time for testing: testing themselves and testing other people in relation to themselves. If one reviews the previous life crises, one can see that a favourable ratio will have established a sense of security, purpose and meaning which form a basis for this part of the life cycle, but this does not imply that such an adolescent will avoid the fights with significant adults which form part of the testing behaviour. The concern is how the adolescent appears in the eyes of others and how to connect what knowledge and skills have been acquired with future work or study. Ethnic origin may be a factor, and Erikson has been criticized for his predominantly white, Eurocentric approach in his reference to ethnic self-doubt and a denial of one's roots being part of Negro identity (Robinson 1995). However, a more realistic interpretation of Erikson's framework for the twenty-first century needs to look at the individual within the wider community. Ethnic identity may be a matter of pride in the culture or the community which exists around the individual, and issues of identity may be less a matter of racial or ethnic confusion. However, it can be argued that in area more hostile to one's ethnicity, issues of identity could be much more problematic. Sexual identity could be seen in the same way: sensitive and understanding family and friends may promote a sense of identity, whereas homophobic attitudes may promote a more negative outcome of role confusion. This stage also includes, very powerfully, an occupational identity. The absence of employment opportunities may have a significant effect on the developing personality at this stage of life.

Within families there is the potential for conflict. Parents need to understand that the rivalry for the mother's affection between father and son, for example, is part of a separation process, a reworking of an earlier unresolved stage. The teenager is in the process of loosening attachments, but if families overreact to behaviour there is a danger that the teenager is expelled or leaves before the natural adjustment has taken place. Psychological health at this stage results in the acquisition of a personal identity with which one is reasonably comfortable, for in some ways the conflicts of this stage are never satisfactorily resolved or completed. Adults are quite capable of behaviour which could be described as adolescent or childish because of its delinquent or selfish aspect, for example. If, however, one has acquired a comfortable sense of identity, one is prepared for the next psychosocial crisis which is the fusion of that identity with another's.

The sixth stage is described as one of intimacy versus isolation and covers the period of young adulthood which may begin in the teens and last through the twenties. One of the more contentious aspects of this theory centres on genitality and, sexual relations, and questions tend to be raised about the importance for psychological health of sexual intimacy. Erikson (1965) attempts to provide a context by describing the ideal of genitality as:

1.     mutuality of orgasm

2.     with a loved partner

3.     of the other sex

4.     with whom one is able and willing to share a mutual trust

5.     and with whom one is able and willing to regulate the cycles of

(a)  work

(b)  procreation

(c)  recreation

(d)  so as to secure to the offspring, too, all the stages of a satisfactory development.

(p.257)

Such a definition raises all kinds of issues, not least about the relative importance of orgasm, heterosexual love and procreation. Since Erikson wrote, attitudes and social policy have changed significantly, and the identification of a loved partner as being only of the opposite sex would be regarded as discriminatory. The factors influencing sexual orientation remain subject to some speculation. Rathus (2006) refers to a number of studies which suggest that there may be an interaction between hormonal and genetic factors and childhood experiences, but there is no conclusive evidence about the primary significance of any one of these factors.

If one subscribes to Erikson's view that satisfactory sexual relations serve to make sex less obsessive and make any form of overcompensation or displacement less necessary, it is also important to consider what kind of sublimation, displacement or overcompensation people employ and which may be unhealthy psychologically. Does, for example, a satisfactory level of intimacy require an outlet in physical sex? In this area of human development, there is a risk that we apply our own standards, based on our own experiences, to other people and make judgements accordingly. If we exist in a sexually active heterosexual relationship, do we accept that someone in a celibate relationship is as 'normal' as we see ourselves? The person in the celibate relationship may have lots of close friends, feel comfortable with the close friendships and may feel contentment which could be described as a positive balance of intimacy.

Another way of looking at what might be a satisfactory ratio of intimacy is to consider the object relations definition of mature dependency (Fairbairn 1952) (see also

Chapter 6 in the present volume). Very briefly, this suggests that a healthy relationship is based on a capacity to put something of oneself into a relationship and to accept something back from the other person, based on an acceptance in reality of each other as individuals. This requires a degree of trust in others, a sense of autonomy in the self and a mature attitude to unresolved parent–child issues. The legacy of previous life crises is therefore as much in evidence at this stage, and studies in marital fit (Pincus and Dare 1978; Skynner and Cleese 1983) show a tendency for unconscious influences to be at work in determining one's choice of partner. There is, for social work, relevance in the potential correlation between lack of satisfactory experiences in early childhood and the inability in adulthood to form satisfactorily intimate relations with other adults.

It is also possible for heterosexual couples who have apparently achieved a satisfactory relationship to be living in 'quasi' intimacy, which in effect isolates them as a couple rather than as individuals. Shared emotional needs might draw them unconsciously together, and inhibit their ability or desire to share themselves with any other. Such a reaction has particular relevance to the next stage in the life cycle, which Erikson describes as generativity versus stagnation. There is a strong emphasis placed on the adult's need to help provide the next generation and to guide and develop that generation.

Although this life crisis includes such a direct reference to the next generation, there is more to generativity than simply having children or wanting to have children. Generativity also includes creativity, which could be artistic or employment based, and concepts of productivity. Implicitly it refers to that concept of adult mature dependency and suggests that there are psychological rewards for adults who can meet other people's needs, who have others dependent upon them. This element of give and take in a relationship is linked to psychological health in adulthood. The adult who is still emotionally dependent, who is 'needy' in relationship terms, may have those needs met by encouraging the dependency of others. Such a relationship is clearly not mature dependency.

As an illustration of the life cycle concept, babies are now being born to adults and these babies are experiencing parenting or care from adults whose personalities have evolved through the kind of experiences we have considered. The important question at this stage is how much of the adult personality is based on reality and an honest acknowledgement of past experiences and how much is based on a fantasy. If feelings have had to be repressed in order to cope with the pressures of day-to-day life, the external part of one's personality which is presented to others may be a gross distortion, superficially fine, but in reality trying to keep in check a lot of troubling feelings. The other consideration is the relative importance of bearing and raising children. Here too the issue of the woman's role in society as opposed to the man's needs to be considered, and personality theory cannot be separated from sociology. The traditional caretaking role of women and providing role of men needs to be challenged and evaluated within the concept of this life crisis. Generativity is about using mental and physical energy to meet needs of mind and body, is about having the opportunity to expand one's self, one's ego, and to channel one's libidinal energy. Failure to do so results according to Erikson in a 'pervading sense of stagnation and personal impoverishment' (1965, p.258). Attitudes to employment, gender and family roles are crucial factors at this stage of adult life. The final life crisis is seen as ego integrity versus despair and refers to the conflict in old age when the end of one's life becomes imminent, but could reflect a crisis facing younger people who have a terminal illness. If we look first at old age, Erikson says:

> only in him who in some way has taken care of things and people and has adapted himself to the triumphs and disappointments adherent to being, the originator of others or the generator of products and ideas – only in him may gradually ripen the fruit of these seven stages. (Erikson 1965, p.259)

Old age is placed firmly at the top, the culmination of crises of childhood and adulthood, the stage to which adults progress. Ego integrity is about a realistic acceptance of one's past life, an acceptance of one's life as it actually was and an understanding that all events, pleasant or painful, combined to form one's individual self. Ego integrity is about valuing one's individual self.

The favourable part of this life crisis suggests maturity and wise adulthood – progression – and there are important implications for social workers working with older people. Not only does it seem vital to avoid the kind of care which encourages childlike dependency and regression, but it also seems vital to work therapeutically towards a fostering of ego integrity. Erikson states quite clearly his belief that if one can achieve a feeling of ego integrity, death becomes less frightening. In the same way, perhaps the younger person imminently approaching death may need help to integrate past life experiences even though the life cycle is incomplete. In working with older people there may be a tendency to leave potentially painful experiences alone and not cause upset. This kind of attitude may enhance regression as it has the same kind of basis as the relationship between the over protective parent and the dependent child. It may say more about the worker's needs or fears than it does about the old person's potential. Despair implies that time is now too short. Practically, despair may result in regressed behaviour, such as bitter feelings that other people are getting better treatment, or pathetically clinging dependent behaviour. Each example in its way suggests that the old person has given up hope of trying other ways to achieve integrity. Despair, according to Erikson, is signified by the fear of death: it could also be signified by a desire for one's life to end. A life that is seen as having had no sense of worth, of purpose or of meaning leaves the individual bitter – 'if only' becomes the predominant thought. Again, societal attitudes towards old age need to be considered. Do we value old people for their experience? A combination of valuing old age and valuing individuals may help promote a sense of purpose in workers that ego integrity is as crucial a part of personality development as any earlier stage of the life cycle.

## Strengths and weaknesses

Ryckman (2004) points to the absence of empirical research to underpin Erikson's theory on the first four stages he identifies and the need for additional research to examine, among other things, identity development among a wider range of racial and ethnic groups. Lefrancois (1999) also identifies the lack of experimental validation, but confirms that the theory is most helpful as a framework for describing and interpreting changes which are experienced during one's life. Lefrancois (1999) refers to studies which have used the Erikson Psychosocial Stage Inventory and cites the research of

Brookins (1996), which confirmed that those who had a formed a sense of identity by late adolescence had significantly more positive self-concepts than those who were still struggling with identity.

Much corroborative research has been undertaken in studies on attachment and resilience. Rutter (1999) indicated that the number of negative factors, rather than any one in particular, may be far more significant in determining whether a child becomes a resilient adolescent or adult. These factors could be emotional, interpersonal, educational and structural (for example, poverty), and serve to support Erikson's psychosocial theory. There are many findings from attachment studies which confirm the positive effects of a sense of belonging and feeling of comfort in preparing children for the realities of adult life. Gilligan (1999) has postulated that children cope better with adversity in adult life if they have had the experience of reliable adults in their social network.

## References

Bowlby, J. (1969) *Attachment and Loss: 1. Attachment.* Harmondsworth: Pelican.

Brookins, C.C. (1996) 'Exploring psychosocial task resolution and self-concept among African-American adolescents.' *Perceptual and Motor Skills 82,* 803–810.

Brown, J.A.C. (1961) *Freud and the Post-Freudians.* Harmondsworth: Pelican.

Clausen, J. (1995) 'Gender, contexts and turning points in adult lives.' In P. Moen, G. Elder and K. Luscher (eds) *Examining Lives in Context – Perspectives on the Ecology of Human Development.* Washington, DC: American Psychological Association

Erikson, E. (1965) *Childhood and Society* Harmondsworth: Penguin.

Fairbairn, W.R.D. (1952) *Psychoanalytic Studies of the Personality.* London: RKP.

Gilligan, R. (1999) 'Children's own social networks and network members: Key resources in helping children at risk.' In M. Hill (ed) *Effective Ways of Helping Children.* London: Jessica Kingsley Publishers.

Klein, M. (1960) *Our Adult World and Its Roots in Infancy.* Pamphlet. London: Tavistock.

Lefrancois, G. (1999) *The Lifespan.* London: Wadsworth.

Masten, A. S. and Coatsworth, J. D. (1998) 'The Development of competence in favourable and unfavourable environments – Lessons from research on successful children.' *American Psychologist 53,* 2, 205–220.

Pincus, L. and Dare, C. (1978) *Secrets in the Family.* London: Faber.

Rathus, S. (2006) *Childhood and Adolescence.* London: Thomson.

Robinson, L. (1995) *Psychology for Social Workers: Black Perspectives.* London: Routledge.

Rutter, M. (1981) *Maternal Deprivation Reassessed.* Harmondsworth: Penguin.

Rutter, M. (1999) 'Resilience Concepts and Findings: Implications for Family Therapy.' *Journal of Family Therapy 21,* 119–44.

Ryckman, R.M. (2004) *Theories of Personality.* London: Thomson.

Rycroft, I.C. (1968) *A Critical Dictionary of Psychoanalysis.* Harmondsworth: Penguin.

Skynner, R. and Cleese, J. (1983) *Families and How to Survive Them.* London: Methuen.

Winnicott, D.W. (1957) *The Child and the Outside World.* London: Tavistock.

## CHAPTER 6

# A PSYCHODYNAMIC APPROACH TO SOCIAL WORK

## Judith Brearley

## Introduction

Perhaps more than ever before, social workers need in-depth understanding to make sense of the issues clients bring and to guide them in their responses. 'Anxiety from puzzlement and from feeling overwhelmed by human problems is best alleviated when we understand what is going on' as Sutherland (Scharff 1994, p.277) has indicated. The degree of complexity and risk in social work seems to have multiplied. Their entire environment has become ever more turbulent, with heightened stress in the community, new social problems, severe tensions between needs and resources, frequent structural reorganizations and a pervasive climate of uncertainty, anxiety and even fear. Social workers' practice is more often subject to public scrutiny and critical appraisal, often with unfair allocation of blame.

At first sight it may seem far-fetched to suggest that an approach deriving from psychoanalysis might have something valuable to offer in this state of affairs. How can thinking that emphasizes personal feelings and relationships possibly have anything to do with societal injustice and legal constraints? Yet it is clear that 'use of self' is one of the main resources the social worker possesses, allowing helpful mediation between the wider society and some of its most vulnerable members. Social workers agonize over questions like 'How unsafe is it to keep that child at home? 'Why does this person always become his own worst enemy?' 'Why does that client hate me so much when I'm only trying to help?' 'How did we come to such a bad decision in that meeting?' 'Supposing he's violent to me when I visit? It felt really scary last time!'

Psychoanalysis itself would not claim to answer such questions directly, but they are amenable to scrutiny by the approach we call 'psychodynamic'. The aims of this chapter are to provide definitions of 'a psychodynamic approach' and of its main concepts, to summarize briefly the work of those psychodynamic theorists whose ideas have most relevance for social work and to show with illustrations from the literature how this approach can be useful in the actual practice of social workers grappling with specific complex problems brought by their clients. But first, some definitions.

> Psychodynamic thinking is predominantly concerned with certain key relationships, namely, those between the self and significant other people, past and present experience, and inner and outer reality, with simultaneous focus on both the

actual relationships and those built up internally from experience and with special emphasis on the processes of these relationships and interactions (Brearley 1995).

The term psychodynamic refers to those theories which stress the importance of unconscious mental processes and which involve the acceptance of such central psychoanalytic concepts as transference and resistance. (Yelloly 1980)

By psychodynamic we refer to the entire theory and practice which derives from Freud and which has been expanded and modified subsequently by the work of Melanie Klein and object-relations theorists, as well as by such other influences as Bowlby's attachment theory. (Preston-Shoot and Agass 1990, p.11)

By psychodynamic thinking we mean an approach informed by attachment theory, psychoanalysis and systems theory, which together offer ways of understanding the complexity and variability of the ways in which individuals develop and relate to one another within particular social contexts, via a focus on their past and present relationships. (McCluskey and Hooper 2000, p.9)

The boundaries of psychodynamic thought have widened out considerably over the years as a result of the cross-fertilization of ideas, new research findings and the testing-out of ways to apply this growing understanding to practice across the range of caring professions. It is now seen to have as much relevance for groups and organizations as for individuals and families (Obholzer and Roberts 1994). A most significant feature has been the growing rapprochement between disciplines. Earlier distrust or hostility between, say developmental psychology and psychoanalysis, has been replaced by areas of common ground, constructive acceptance of difference and valuable complementarities. Of particular interest is the way that neurobiological findings are now amply confirming the emphasis placed by modern psychoanalysis on the vital need for responsive care giving during the earliest years of life (Gerhardt 2004).

## Psychoanalytic concepts of relevance for social workers

For Freud (see Brown 1961; Jones 1974) and all later psychoanalytic theorists, the unconscious is a central concept on which most other ideas about mental functioning are based. The idea was already familiar in the nineteenth century, but Freud was the first to chart its territory, discover how it worked and investigate it systematically. He regarded mental life as operating on several levels:

- *the conscious*, as the sum total of everything of which we are aware

- *the preconscious*, as the reservoir of everything we can remember: 'knowledge and thoughts…outside consciousness but not held back by the counterforce of repression' (Sandler, Dare and Holder 1973, p.16)

- *the unconscious*, as that vast area of internal life where all our more primitive impulses and repressed images and their associated emotions are stored and whence they continue to influence our behaviour. Freud inferred the existence of the unconscious from interpretations of dreams and also on the logical grounds that some of our activity is not consciously initiated, but flows out of us as if it comes from 'another'. As we sometimes say, 'I must have been beside myself to do that!' Such behaviour, which is often self-destructive, must have a source. Freud pointed out the logicality and irrationality of the unconscious, its allusive, distorted quality, the fact that it is not located in time or space and is communicated symbolically rather that in words, all characteristics familiar to us through our own dreams.

Freud saw the development of character in an individual as the outcome of a three-cornered struggle between unconscious aggressive and sexual impulses and instincts, which he called the id; the superego (that is the internalized images of critical parents and other authority figures), which acts as a conscience and gradually develops moral values; and the more conscious mediating ego trying to manage and relate to the demands of external reality. These competing forces within an individual's mental life may be resolved with varying degrees of success by a variety of techniques, such as sublimation, reaction-formation and symptom-formation, known collectively as defences.

The key to understanding defences is the concept of anxiety. Anxiety is ubiquitous in human nature. It is at times intolerably painful and it can seriously affect a person's ability to function normally. The greater the degree of anxiety in relation to a person's tolerance and ability to manage it, the more will there be a need to construct defences against it. Very young children whose security is threatened by separation from parents show by desperate crying how vulnerable to panic and terror they are (see Chapter 4 in the present volume). Individuals as they grow through life develop a repertoire of defensive strategies to protect themselves from the impact of their most painful experiences and the nightmarish anxieties to which these give rise. At the time, a particular way of coping seemed to be the only option and felt absolutely vital for their very survival. This is why defences are long-lasting and extremely hard to relinquish even when they have served their initial purpose. They then tend to become problematic in their own right. It is important to bear in mind that anxiety and its associated defences operate not only at an individual level but also between couples, in families, in groups and in organizations.

It might be helpful for us to think about some of the defences we commonly encounter. For example, why is it that some memories can be easily recalled, even though 'quite forgotten', whereas the memory of other experiences seems buried, split off and completely inaccessible? Repression, a central concept of Freud, explains the latter type of forgotten memory. The term describes the unconscious process whereby certain feelings, ideas and experiences are pushed into hiding and disowned because they are too painful, shameful of threatening to be acknowledged consciously at the time. Such objectionable feelings, e.g. irrational distrust or overdependence, do not simply disappear, but remain in the psyche, almost as a foreign body. They are liable to resurface later in coded form in emotions, behaviour and relationships, especially between spouses, parents and children.

*Denial* is a defence which is relatively easy to perceive in operation. All of us want to keep unpleasant reality at bay and there are times when a temporary buffer is needed against the pain of a well-nigh intolerable realization. The loss by death of a spouse, child or parent is a clear example of this, as is the diagnosis of a feared illness. Practically everyone in such a situation react at first by saying, 'No, it's not true. I don't believe it!

This can't be happening to me.' There is then often a delay before other feelings of distress emerge. The denial proves useful as a cushioning device, at least for a short time.

Aspects of Freud's theory were built on in different ways by Freud's daughter, Anna (Freud 1968), and Klein (1988). Kleinian ideas have proved the more accessible, have led to much further debate and seem to have more relevance for social work practice and therefore will be emphasized here. Klein (1988; see also Segal 1985; Mitchell 1986) described two psychological 'positions' each with their own characteristic anxieties and defensive ways of responding. The first, the 'persecutory or paranoid-schizoid position', begins to develop in the earliest months of life. It involves very primitive and intense anxieties about being left alone with terror, about not surviving or falling apart. These are known as persecutory anxieties and the defences against them are said to be splitting and projection.

Splitting arises from the existence of utterly contradictory feelings which seem impossible to countenance simultaneously and which are therefore kept in separate compartments. The very young baby cannot yet understand that the mother who feeds and cares is also the one who sometimes goes away and fails to meet needs. The image of the parent is therefore divided into a good and a bad figure; one idealized, the other hated. This process can be seen when a baby suddenly shifts from a quite blissful state to one of rage and despair, in children's stories of wicked witches/fairy godmothers and in adults who rigidly polarize their experiences and perceptions of others in extreme fashion, being either extremely disparaging or overly positive. Social workers often find themselves on the receiving end of splitting when clients compare them with other workers, for example, talking of the health visitor in glowing terms while scathingly criticizing the social worker. (The roles could just as easily be reversed.) It is as if the client is unwittingly attempting to drive a wedge between the various agencies involved; unless the workers are tolerant and self-aware the manoeuvre often succeeds, to the detriment of the work. Mattinson and Sinclair (1981) describe such processes in vivid detail.

Projection nearly always accompanies splitting. It occurs when a feeling or characteristic which in reality belongs to the self is first externalized and then ascribed to another person. The unconscious aim is to get rid of an unwanted part of the self by dumping it into someone close at hand, such as a marital partner. Not only negative qualities are projected, as we see when people cannot recognize or accept their own positives and instead strongly idealize someone else.

Klein (1960) called her second position the 'depressive position', and suggests that this develops at a later stage of infancy when the child discovers that the good and bad figures are different aspects of the selfsame person. The child may then believe, with a sense of guilt and sadness, that his or her hateful feelings could magically destroy the loved parent. Winnicott (1984) helpfully described it as 'the development of the capacity for concern' (p.100) and saw it as a stage towards maturity and reciprocity. The inevitable conflict between love and hate for the same person is not bypassed by the 'either/or' strategies of splitting and projection, but rather by tolerating the ambivalence involved, and working through the realistic regrets towards a sense of reparation. There is recognition and acceptance that significant other people may sometimes let us down, but that this is not an ultimate disaster. The nature of the anxiety associated with this phase is concerned less with personal survival and more with fears of being destructive rather than creative in close relationships. The depressive position, like the paranoid-schizoid one, is never totally worked through. Remnants of it will always persist in the form of anxieties, especially ambivalence and guilt, which may come to the fore at different developmental stages such as adolescence and mid-life. These are times when inability to tolerate the extremely painful feelings involved may be enacted in drug-taking, promiscuity, unresolved grief and even suicide.

Whenever people meet, their feelings for each other are always affected not only by the immediate occasion but also by association with past experiences, both good and bad. To the extent that this happens, most often unconsciously, the past is being revived and relived in the present. Freud called this phenomenon 'transference', and the concept remains a central one in psychodynamic thought, invaluable in all forms of relationship work. It originates in childhood and is usually the outcome of much-repeated or pervasive series of interactions with caregivers, as for example when a child's efforts and achievements are constantly disparaged. The impact of such responses from those on whom the child is most dependent is to create residues, fantasies, expectations and assumptions which in turn profoundly affect later relationships. The person so treated in the past may well have very shaky confidence and self-esteem and is therefore likely to perceive any critical comment with particular sensitivity and to interpret reactions of others as put-downs. Furthermore these interpretations will influence others in subtle ways through behaviour which elicits from them the very response most feared.

Social workers are often puzzled and discomfited by unwarranted reactions from clients; all the worker's best efforts may be met with misunderstanding, resentment, blame, aggression or exploitation. A person damaged by early ill-treatment is tragically identified with his or her parents' negative views and yet at the same time protests against these. Attempts to communicate to others what has been suffered often takes the form of re-enacting the behaviour previously experienced. This is the 'negative transference' to which social workers are particularly subject, given the vulnerability and parlous circumstances of their clients, coupled with the fact that their work may involve compulsion and allocation of very limited resources, often at times of crisis.

Kleinians have very usefully extended these ideas into two further concepts. 'Projective identification' is one of the most powerful and primitive means of communication we have, akin to that between very young infants and their parents. It is the unconscious disowning of feelings felt to be unmanageable by dumping them onto someone else. This process is so powerful that the other person actually begins to experience those emotions of attributions as his or her own. The unconscious aim is not only to get rid of the feelings but also to convey their significance to another person who may be better able to survive them and make sense of them. This concept helps to make sense of some of the very irrational transactions that go on in families and between couples. It is also an important factor in the helping relationship itself and if we can gain insight into what is happening between worker and client we can begin to understand at a much deeper level what the problem is really about. This is achieved by making use of the 'counter-transference', those intense feelings and extremely disturbing reactions stirred up in the worker by the client's story, behaviour and especially by his or her transference and projected emotions. Monitored carefully to screen out what is personal to the worker, which of course requires good self-awareness, these reactions provide valuable indications of what the client most wants to communicate. It then offers the chance to experience and think jointly about the feelings; essential processes which have until then been bypassed.

Finally, mirroring or the reflection process (Hughes and Pengelly 1997; Mattinson 1975) is worth discussion as it relates closely to the above concepts and is often encountered in social work supervision. An important clue to its presence is when a supervisee behaves out of character, as if he or she has been seduced or manipulated into the client's way of thinking or feeling. This viewpoint is then expressed forcefully or defensively to the supervisor as if were the supervisee's own. Alternatively, a worker may have become so confused about what is going on that aspects of the client's behaviour are unconsciously re-enacted in supervision in an attempt to convey what is hard to put into words. A further example is provided by the social worker who leaves an interview feeling unusually burdened with anxiety or distress, feelings which have probably been dumped onto him or her by the client and who then in turn attempts to leave those unwanted emotions with the supervisor. Such transactions are very complex and disturbing, involving as they do many of the unconscious processes outlined so far. The value of understanding them, through careful use of the supervisor's counter-transference, is that it prevents the worker from being blamed for over-identification and helps both parties to see with greater clarity the strength and nature of the client's problem.

## Specific contributions of selected psychodynamic theorists

The classical Freudian view proves least helpful when we come to explore ideas of human development and motivation, but more recent psychodynamic thinking has much to offer in these areas. Mention has already been made of Klein's concepts. The work of Winnicott (Jacobs 1995; Kahr 2002) is highly valued by social workers, especially those working with children and families and in residential and day care. His descriptions of transitional objects, playing, the 'false self', the anti-social tendency, primary maternal preoccupation and the 'good-enough' mother are all extremely fruitful concepts for social work practice.

The work of both Erikson (1965) and Bowlby (1969) is fully discussed in its own right elsewhere in this handbook (see Chapters 4 and 5 in the present volume). Each of them thinks psychodynamically and their theories share some common ground. Erikson's (1965) conceptualization of development stages encompasses the whole life cycle and firmly places the individual within family, social and cultural contexts, emphasizing the relationship between these. As Fonagy (2001) demonstrates, Erikson's concern to identify the determinants and long-term effects of 'basic trust versus mistrust' closely parallels the analysis of secure and insecure attachment and the role of caregivers which is central in the work of Bowlby (1969) and Ainsworth and colleagues (1978). Their formulation of attachment theory (Holmes 1993, 2001) has proved to be both scientifically rigorous and clinically useful for all working with human relationships. It is unfortunate that for a long time conflict and hostility existed between psychoanalysts and attachment theorists. This grew out of Bowlby's criticisms of the Kleinians' overemphasis on the world of fantasy and the psychoanalysts' suspicions of Bowlby's collaboration with ethnologists and his much greater use of observational studies and empirical research. Fortunately these tensions are now being replaced by mutual respect and collaboration.

Scotland's two great psychoanalysts, Fairbairn (1952) and Sutherland (1989), are now acknowledged internationally (Scharff and Scharff 2005) as among the pioneers of the British 'object relations' approach – a leading-edge aspect of psychodynamic thinking which originated in reaction to Freud's overemphasis on drives, instincts and intrapsychic phenomena. Its other proponents include Klein (1988), Guntrip (1968), Balint (1968), Winnicott (1958) and Bowlby (1969). The term 'object relations' probably requires explanation at this point. Such terminology is unfortunate as it implies something impersonal, whereas the opposite is in fact the case, as the central focus is on what it means to be human. The term actually means 'relationships with significant other people and their internal representations'. Gomez (1997) offers a helpful overview. Fairbairn's (1952) thinking about human motivation is fundamentally different from that of Freud. Fairbairn believed that what persons require and seek most assiduously is emotional contact with others. The infant is oriented to other people (its 'objects') from the very start and the pressing urge to seek and maintain relationships continues throughout life. These significant relationships are gradually internalized and by this means early experiences set a pattern which shapes future expectations of involvement. Bowlby's notion of 'internal working models' echoes this. Satisfying relationships form the developing person's sense of a real and effective self. If the essential unconditional loving care has not been available, then survival, development and maturity are all threatened. The centrality of the human encounter, both in the growth of the person and in therapeutic relationships, is fundamental in Fairbairn's thinking. Sutherland was Fairbairn's colleague and biographer (Sutherland 1989) and made a massive contribution in his own right to the application of these ideas in the caring professions through a large body of publications (Scharff 1994) and his key roles in establishing both the Tavistock Clinic and the Scottish Institute of Human Relations.

## Applications of psychodynamic understanding in social work practice
### CHILD PROTECTION AND INTER-AGENCY COMMUNICATION
See also Chapters 20 and 21 in the present volume.

Since 1973 there have been over 30 detailed inquiries concerning deaths of children abused and neglected by their caregivers, the most recent in Scotland being that of Caleb Ness (Edinburgh and the Lothians Child Protection Committee 2002). In each case the responsible services collectively failed to protect the child. These inquiries provide a wealth of evidence of primitive emotions and irrational transactions in operation, and salutary descriptions of how such feelings and processes surface in destructive behaviour and relationships, not only in the family but also in and between the workers and their agencies. In one recent most serious case, that of Victoria Climbié who died in 2000, Lord Laming's report identified, among very many instances of extremely bad practice, several missed opportunities to save her life which involved poor communication between agencies (Lord Laming 2003). One structural explanation given for this problem is that lines of accountability within an agency tend to be 'vertical' and that this acts as a barrier to 'horizontal' communication between staff in different agencies. Psychodynamic thinking offers further reasons. Woodhouse and Pengelly (1991) carried out thorough research using interdisciplinary case discussion groups involving social workers, health visitors, general practitioners and couple counsellors. Their find-ings highlight the central part played by collectively held unconscious anxiety and asso-ciated defences, which, they point out, 'distort perceptions of oneself, of others and of events, leading to inappropriate and ineffective responses to reality' (p.11). They identify key anxieties and characteristic ways of defending against them for each profession and convincingly show how these produce strong impediments to constructive collabora-tion. Their view was that social workers coped with their conflict of feelings towards bad parents by tending to blame other professionals, who in turn were seeking to offload their own intolerable anxiety about child protection into the 'dustbin' of social services departments.

The 'distorted perceptions' mentioned above can be seen in the tendency for diffi-culties originating at the societal or organizational level to become personalized. They then find expression in conflict between individuals or in scapegoating processes. Mar-tin Ruddock was the social work team manager at the centre of another child protection tragedy, that of Kimberley Carlile in 1986. In his submission to the Inquiry he wrote:

> I was faced with an overwhelming body of work, which meant I could deal with none of it to anything approaching the degree of competence which I would normally demand of myself and was forced to adopt a method of working whereby some tasks were not dealt with at all. (Ruddock 1998, p.93)

Despite being commended for his insight integrity, the response to his experience was generalized and dismissive. Reflecting on this ten years later (Ruddock 1998), Ruddock regretted having focused mainly on his own response to the stress, because this allowed external factors to be overlooked and effective job performance defined as the result of individual competence rather than job demands and the organizational environment. He would now, with hindsight, have placed emphasis on the cause of stress rather than the reaction to it, that is to say, on the work environment or system rather than on individual pathology.

ORGANIZATIONAL UNDERSTANDING AND ORGANIZATIONAL CONSULTANCY

Menzies Lyth, a Kleinian psychoanalyst and organizational consultant, was one of the first to show, through her classic study of hospital nursing in the 1950s ('The Function-ing of Social Systems as a Defence against Anxiety', 1959) how work-related anxieties, such as being close to suffering and death, resonate with people's primitive fantasies and personal insecurities to bring about socially structured defences – for example, denial of feelings, depersonalizing the nurse–patient relationship and distrust between staff members (reprinted in Menzies Lyth 1988). These then become a pervasive part of the functioning of an entire institution, to the detriment of quality of care. Similarly, for social workers without adequate support, the distress, disturbance and tragedy of clients may well amplify their anxieties to an intolerable degree, making collective defensive functioning inevitable.

There is every indication that newly emerging features of organizational life are combining to increase such difficulties significantly. In a paper, 'The Vanishing Or-ganisation', Cooper and Dartington (2004) eloquently identify the sociological and psychological elements of this new 'order'. These include the centrality of networks and networking; emphasis on outcomes, evidence-based practice and best value; external target-setting and monitoring of performance; and moves away from relationship-based to procedure-based and legalistic responses in, for example, child protection work. Risk awareness and risk management (see Chapter 11 in the present volume) figure large in people's awareness, reflecting deep survival anxieties, compounded by a crisis of trust, preoccupation with system failures, tension between complexity and control and continual institutional instability. In this climate the work setting is not experienced as a source of security; mutual commitments are weaker and a sense of alienation may be much greater. The authors suggest that some form of containment allowing workers' experiences to be processed through the medium of relationships will remain vital if too much vulnerability and destructiveness is to be avoided and competence and a sense of purpose is to be safeguarded.

An old French saying, 'The fish does not know that it lives in water until it is already on the bank!', is a reminder of how important it is to understand the complex medium which constitutes the workplace. How might practitioners develop such understanding? It is not easy for social workers under pressure to find the space for acquiring a more reflective and objective stance. One way forward, in addition to good staff supervision, is to refine one's observation skills. Systematic observation of babies and young children has always been a central element of training for child psychotherapists. Trowell and Miles (1991) believe this powerful learning tool has much to offer social workers and multidisciplinary groups. It enhances awareness of the environment, of people's interactions and non-verbal behaviour and of issues of race and gender, all invaluable in making accurate assessments of and responding effectively in complex, emotionally charged situations. Supportive seminars enable extremely painful observations to be tolerated, so that workers can reflect on their meaning rather than taking flight in premature action or avoidance. A valuable account of how observations in health care settings can promote better understanding of organizational transactions and processes is given by Hinshelwood and Skögstad (2000).

Skilled external organizational consultancy is an economical and underused resource for enabling social workers to make sense of and manage institutional dilemmas. At times of change, in conflict situations and when developing new ways of collaborative working, an outsider with no vested interests may be able to provide containment, defuse tensions and promote new insights. This may be done by means of regular meetings with a staff group, work with an individual in a key role (often a manager) or an occasional away-day. The consultant aims to provide a safe space in which all participants can be heard and their views respected. Possible causes and effects of the difficulty are explored, taking into account those often overlooked, such as historical and environmental factors, hidden agendas and misunderstandings, inadequate or inappropriate communication and the sheer pace of change. This almost always results in a calmer and more cooperative atmosphere, with less blame and scapegoating and a greater degree of shared creative thinking. The process is more like attending a car-maintenance class than taking one's car to the garage. That is to say, the problem is not handed over to be sorted out by someone else, but instead the consultees learn the skills to resolve issues themselves. Such an approach using psychodynamic understanding to the full is well-documented with many detailed case examples (Brearley 2002, 2005; Huffington *et al.* 2004; Menzies Lyth 1988, Obholzer and Roberts 1994).

COUNSELLING SKILLS IN SOCIAL WORK PRACTICE

It is important to dispel some persistent myths about psychodynamically-informed social work intervention; for example, that it has necessarily to be long term, based on exploring the client's early life and aimed at promoting insight. These features are integral to some psychotherapies, but it is misleading to think of social work in this way. The confusion arises from not distinguishing psychotherapy and counselling as professions in their own right from the selective use of some of their understanding and skills to inform social work practice. Sudbery (2002, p.157), writing about therapeutic social work, states: 'an understanding of social work is incomplete if attention is placed solely on task-completion, or solely on societal issues, or solely on material problems…good practice in social work necessarily requires attending to relationships'. He identifies several ways in which this can be achieved: ensuring that the working relationship is empathic and even-handed, appreciating the symbolic restorative significance of meeting basic needs, conveying acceptance of angry and aggressive responses and attending to the quality of the client's relationship to him or herself in areas such as self-criticism, self-destructiveness and guilt. Seden (1999) offers a comprehensive exposition of the precise skills involved and concludes:

> The range and scope of social work tasks mean that if the more advanced counselling and communication skills are used, within current legislative mandates, to facilitate classic social work processes of assessment, intervention and evaluation, practice competence in social care is considerably enhanced. (Seden 1999, p.151)

## Conclusion

This chapter has clarified psychodynamic concepts and explored their potential relevance for social work practice. The essence of a psychodynamic approach is that it recognizes the importance of feelings and that it emphasizes relationships – between self and significant other people, between past and present experience and between inner and outer reality.

Tension between people's internal and external worlds is particularly crucial for social workers, who so often find themselves struggling to act as mediators in areas where those worlds seem irreconcilable. This role is all the more difficult because of the chronic absence of consensus in our society about the nature of the social work task, the extent of scapegoating when things go wrong, the resultant impact on morale and the frequent, often defensive, organizational restructurings of both social work education and practice. A split may be discerned among social workers' views about assessment and intervention: one emphasizes environmental factors to the exclusion of emotions; the other – just as extreme – stresses the leading role of feelings and relationships but underestimates the significance of the environment (see Chapter 3 in the present volume). Complex reality cannot be simplified in these ways. Very many clients' problems are indeed rooted in poverty and disadvantage. Gross inequalities of access to health care, housing, education and unemployment undoubtedly exist, but structural explanations throw little light on why some people abuse their children while others in similar social circumstances do not. It is important to seek remedies through political action and better social policies, but these do not address all the needs of couples in conflict, of children facing successive foster home breakdowns or of people with chronic mental health problems

Practical help cannot be effectively delivered unless its emotional significance to clients is well understood. It follows that social workers must address themselves both to their clients' inner problems and to their social context. Also, crucially, they must work at the interface and address the interaction and tensions between these.

Fulfilling the potential of a psychodynamic approach has implications for qualifying and post-qualifying training. Its principles should be as applicable to teaching methods as to content, with academic understanding integrated with professional and personal experience. An experiential component is vital to making sense of the ideas at a deep level. Growing self-awareness enables the social worker to distinguish his or her own personal material from what the client brings to the encounter and to pick up accurately the underlying communications. This is fostered through high quality supervision, a crucial requirement which provides containment, a different perspective, shared accountability and essential reflective space. There are also important implications for how social workers are deployed, resourced and managed. If the larger systems are malfunctioning, for example, though inadequate staffing, poor relationships with other agencies or remote management, then front-line workers cannot possibly provide a 'good-enough' service and disastrous consequences become more likely. If these psychodynamic ideas could foster better awareness at all levels then damage might be limited and the quality of services enhanced.

*Editor's note*: This chapter can usefully be read in conjunction with Chapter 5: both chapters clearly elucidate the range of psychodynamic theory on which we can draw.

## References

Ainsworth, M.D., Blehar, M.C., Water, E. and Wall, S. (1978) *Patterns of Attachment*. Hillsdale, N J: Erlbaum.

Balint, M. (1968) *The Basic Fault*. London: Tavistock.

Bowlby, J. (1969) *Attachment and Loss*. London: Hogarth and the Institute of Psychoanalysis.

Brearley, J. (1995) *Counselling and Social Work*. Buckingham: Open University Press.

Brearley, J. (2000) 'Working as an organisational consultant with abuse encountered in the workplace.' In U. McCluskey and C-A. Hooper (eds) *Psychodynamic Perspectives on Abuse: The Cost of Fear*. London: Jessica Kingsley Publishers.

Brearley, J. (2005) 'Application: Organisational Consultancy.' In J. Scharff and D. Scharff (eds) *The Legacy of Fairbairn and Sutherland*. London: Brunner-Routledge.

Brown, J.A.C. (1961) *Freud and the Post-Freudians*. London: Pelican.

Cooper, A. and Dartington, T. (2004) 'The vanishing organization. Organizational containment in a networked world.' In C. Huffington, D. Armstrong, W. Halton, L. Hoyle and J. Pooley (eds) *Working Below the Surface: The Emotional Life of Contemporary Organisations*. London: Karnac.

Erikson, E. (1965) *Childhood and Society*. Harmondsworth: Penguin.

Fairbairn, W.R.D. (1952) *Psychoanalytic Studies of the Personality*. London: Routledge and Kegan Paul.

Fonagy, P. (2001) *Attachment Theory and Psychoanalysis*. New York: Other Press.

Freud, A. (1968) *The Ego and the Mechanisms of Defence.* London: Hogarth Press and Institute of Psycho-analysis.

Gerhardt, S. (2004) *Why Love Matters: How Affection Shapes a Baby's Brain.* London: Brunner-Routledge.

Gomez, L. (1997) *An Introduction to Object Relations.* London: Free Association Books.

Guntrip, H. (1968) *Schizoid Phenomena, Object Relations and the Self.* London: Hogarth and Institute of Psycho-analysis.

Hinshelwood, R.D. and Skögstad, W. (2000) *Observing Organisations: Anxiety, Defence and Culture in Health Care.* London: Routledge.

Holmes, J. (1993) *John Bowlby and Attachment Theory.* London: Routledge.

Holmes, J. (2001) *The Search for the Secure Base: Attachment Theory and Psychotherapy.* London: Brunner-Routledge.

Huffington, C., Armstrong, D., Halton, W., Hoyle, L. and Pooley, J. (eds) (2004) *Working Below the Surface: The Emotional Life of Contemporary Organisations.* London: Karnac.

Hughes, L. and Pengelly, P. (1997) *Staff Supervision in a Turbulent Environment: Managing Task and Process in Front-line Services.* London: Jessica Kingsley Publishers.

Jacobs, M. (1995) *D W Winnicott.* London: Sage Publications.

Jones, E. (1953) *The Life and Work of Sigmund Freud.* London: Hogarth Press. Abridged by L. Trilling and S. Marcus (1964). Harmondsworth: Penguin.

Kahr, B. (ed.) (2002) *The Legacy of Winnicott.* London: Karnac.

Klein, M. (1988) *Envy and Gratitude and Other Works 1946–1963.* [First published by Hogarth Press, 1975.] London: Virago Press.

Lord Laming (2003) The Victoria Climbié Inquiry Report. Cmd 5730. London: HMSO.

Mattinson, J. (1975) *The Reflection Process in Casework Supervision.* London: Institute of Marital Studies.

Mattinson, J. (1988) *Work, Love and Marriage: The Impact of Unemployment.* London: Duckworth.

Mattinson, J. and Sinclair, I. (1981) *Mate and Stalemate.* Oxford: Blackwell.

McCluskey, U. and Hooper, C-A. (eds) (2000) *Psychodynamic Perspectives on Abuse: The Cost of Fear.* London: Jessica Kingsley Publishers.

Menzies Lyth, I. (1988) *Containing Anxiety in Institutions.* London: Free Association Books.

Mitchell, J. (1986) *The Selected Melanie Klein.* Harmondsworth: Penguin.

Obholzer, A. and Roberts, V. (eds) (1994) *The Unconscious at Work: Individual Organisational Stress in the Human Services.* London: Routledge.

Preston-Shoot, M. and Agass, D. (1990) *Making Sense of Social Work: Psychodynamics, Systems and Practice.* Basingstoke: Macmillan.

Edinburgh and the Lothians Child Protection Committee (2002) *Report of the Caleb Ness Enquiry.* Edinburgh: City of Edinburgh Council. Available at www.edinburgh.gov.uk/socialwork/calebness/calebness.html

Ruddock, M. (1998) 'Yes and but and then again, maybe.' In R. Davis (ed.) *Stress in Social Work.* London: Jessica Kingsley Publishers.

Sandler, J., Dare, C. and Holder, A. (1973) *The Patient and the Analyst: The Basis of the Psychoanalytic Process.* London: George Allen & Unwin.

Scharff, J. (ed.) (1994) *The Autonomous Self: The Work of John D Sutherland.* New Jersey: Jason Aronson Inc.

Scharff, J. and Scharff, D. (eds) (2005) *The Legacy of Fairbairn and Sutherland.* London: Brunner-Routledge.

Seden, J. (1999) *Counselling Skills in Social Work.* Milton Keynes: Open University Press.

Segal, J. (1985) *Phantasy in Everyday Life.* Harmondsworth: Penguin.

Segal, J. (1992) *Melanie Klien.* London: Sage Publications.

Sudbery, J. (2002) 'Key features of therapeutic social work: The use of relationship.' *Journal of Social Work Practice 16,* 2, 149–62.

Sutherland, J. D. (1989) *Fairbairn's Journey into the Interior.* London: Free Association Books.

Trowell, J. and Miles, G. (1991) 'The contribution of observation training to professional development in social work.' *Journal of Social Work Practice 5,* 1, 51–60.

Winnicott, D.W. (1958) *Collected Papers: Through Paediatrics to Psycho-analysis.* London: Tavistock Publications.

Winnicott, D.W. (1984) *Deprivation and Delinquency.* Edited by C. Winnicott, R. Shepherd and M. Davis. London: Routledge and Kegan Paul.

Woodhouse, D. and Pengelly, P. (1991) *Anxiety and the Dynamics of Collaboration.* Aberdeen: University Press.

Yelloly, M. (1980) *Social Work Theory and Psychoanalysis.* Wokingham: Van Nostrand Reinhold.

# Section 2: Assessment

**CHAPTER 7**

# MODELS OF ASSESSMENT

*Daphne Statham and Patricia Kearney*

## Introduction

This chapter reviews the specific contribution social work makes to assessments, the context in which those assessments are made and the different models used. It argues that person-centred or personalized assessments require the social worker to be a problem solver and an outcomes approach. This is consistent with social work principles and government policies, and is effective.

## Social work and assessment

There are numerous definitions of 'assessment' in the literature. Crisp *et al.* (2005) in their review of textbooks and frameworks chose Coulshed and Orme's defintion of it as:

> an ongoing process, in which the client participates, the purpose of which is to understand people in relation to their environment; it is the basis for planning what needs to be done to bring about change in the person, the environment or both. (1998, p.16)

Over the past 20 years, the state has taken an increasing interest in assessment and how it is carried out. The result is a collection of assessment frameworks that are used across social work, social care, health and education (Department for Education and Skills 2004, Department of Health 2006, Department of Health, Department for Education and Employment and The Home Office 2001). All focus on the key areas on which evidence should be sought within this multi-organizational and multidisciplinary context.

Social work's contribution to this process is shaped by its values and theories. For example, Scotland's Framework for Social Work Education states that:

> Social work is a moral activity in the sense that social workers make and follow up difficult decisions about human situations that directly benefit or harm an individual or group. They should be able to understand moral reasoning and to make decisions in difficult ethical situations, especially where there are conflicting moral obligations. (Scottish Executive 2003, p.19)

The international definition of social work also identifies this moral and ethical component of social work as a result of its commitment to human rights and social justice:

The social work profession promotes social change, problem solving in human relationships and the empowerment and liberation of people to enhance well-being. Utilising theories of human behaviour and social systems, social work intervenes at points where people interact with their environments. Principles of human rights and social justice are fundamental to social work. (International Federation of Social Workers and International Association of Schools of Social Work 2004)

Uncertainty and complexity are at the centre of social work because it specializes in situations where there are no known solutions: 'where you are damned if you do and damned if you don't' (Brand, Reith and Statham, 2005a). It is important to understand that this is the nature of the social work task not an unfortunate consequence of it.

For this reason, social work can never be a technical activity based simply on assessment formats, models or methods. Conflicts and uncertainty are endemic in social work and hence in assessment, whatever framework or method is used. Conflict is a necessary condition for the start of any assessment between people, between people and organizations or between organizations. This may originate in differences in views about what has happened, what should happen, the risks and how they should be managed who is, or thinks they should be, the beneficiary of any intervention.

No assessment framework or model is value free or neutral and all are value based. It is a tool that implements a particular conception about the function of social welfare, assumptions about the capacities of people using services and their place in society, whether they are children, young people or adults. These conceptions are based on policy definitions that formulate the role of social welfare, the contribution of social work and social care at a particular time and in a specific society (Hardiker, Exton and Barker 1991).

However, there are often contradictions in policies. For example, even though, throughout the UK, the current trend is to emphasize people's rights and responsibilities as citizens and the UN Convention on the Rights of the Child, there are exceptions. For example, young offenders and people with severe mental health problems are often seen less as citizens and more as potential risks to public safety. The management of these contradictions falls heavily at the point where the person using services and the front-line worker meet and have to be managed in assessment.

Therefore, there are a number of influences on how an assessment framework is implemented, not all of them explicit. These include current policy trends, professional codes of practice, the attitudes of the workers, their managers, the organizations involved and the available knowledge.

## THE KNOWLEDGE RESOURCE FOR ASSESSMENT

Social work shares with other professions, using knowledge to underpin its practice. The social care research base is less well developed than in health or education, but it is growing. Its knowledge comes from a range of sources as identified in *Types and Quality of Social Care* (Pawson *et al.* 2003):

- organizational knowledge
- practitioner knowledge

- user knowledge

- research knowledge

- policy community knowledge.

This collective resource guides assessment. It indicates where the evidence for effective practice is strong, where it is weak and where there are gaps.

The social work knowledge resource includes human development and social systems theories, but unlike other professions does not claim exclusive rights to a territory of knowledge or skill. Brand *et al.* (2005a) argue that this is not a deficit but rather that it is counterproductive to do so. While all professions need knowledge of the organizations and professions with which they work closely, for social workers this knowledge is central. The social worker's role is to bring together a range of information and resources so that the support is personalized. In addition to working with individuals and their social networks, this requires the capacity to move between systems and to cross into the borders of other professions and organizations in ways that command confidence and trust from them.

## The characteristics of social work assessment
### HOLISTIC OR PERSONALIZED ASSESSMENT
The holistic approach to assessment originates in the black, women's and disability liberation movements. All strove to address the failure of social work and social care to deliver competent practice and services to these groups (Ahmad 1990; Butt and Box 1996; Dominelli and McLeod 1989; Hamner and Statham 1989; Morris 1993; Oliver, 1983). The holistic approach builds on the social model of disability that sees blocks to independence arising from social attitudes, disabling systems and environments. The approach also stresses the need for attention to people's ethnicity, culture and history because together they form their identity and influence life options. In Northern Ireland the McLernon report (Social Services Inspectorate 1998) identified the risks of failing to focus on the individual in their wider personal and social context as opposed to a limited concern with eligibility for a service. The principles of holistic assessment and the social model of disability are embedded in the new policy of personalization (Department of Health 2006; Leadbeater 2005).

So, while social work used to claim the holistic approach as its own, the policy of personalization is now the imperative in health, education, housing and environmental services. In each the purpose of holistic assessment is to improve an aspect of the person's well-being: their health, educational attainment or living environment. Social work's distinctive feature continues to be maintaining a 360-degree focus on the personal, social and economic situation of individuals, families, groups and communities (Brand *et al.* 2005a). The approach is based on the social model that was developed by the disability movement. It sees blocks to independence arising from social attitudes, systems and a disabling environment rather than the impairment itself (Campbell and Oliver 1996; Oliver 1993). The ethnicity, culture and history of an individual are crucial in social work assessment because together they form people's identity, influence the life options open to them and the attitudes of some people towards them and their abilities.

## WORKING WITH COMPLEXITY AND UNCERTAINTY

Social workers are no longer central in the majority of assessments. They are mainly involved when there is complexity, risks are uncertain or high, there is conflict, or decisions involve the limitation of the rights of the individual either as parent or as citizens.

Clarity about roles and responsibilities is very important. An assessment may be led by:

- the social worker

- another professional or a multidisciplinary team

- social care, health care or education support workers with support from the social worker or another professional

- the person using services as part of self-assessment.

Whichever model is used there will be tensions that have to be managed (Brand *et al.* 2005a). These arise because social workers have multiple accountabilities for:

- promoting the outcomes people using services want

- rationing or gatekeeping resources

- fulfilling legal and statutory responsibilities

- meeting the requirements and procedures of their organization

- working with the different priorities of other professions and organizations involved

- fulfilling the Codes of Conduct of the Regulatory Councils.

For example, direct payments assessment focuses on eligibility for service and not what, who, how or when support is provided. The intention is that the person using the service determines what support will enable him or her to have as much control over his or her life as possible and how best to achieve this. However, some organizations are restricting what the finance can be used for in spite of this intention (Commission for Social Care Inspection 2005).

Holding the focus on the strengths and expertise of people using services is very difficult for another reason. The responsibility of social work to create and maintain working arrangements with other organizations and professions creates centrifugal forces that can draw the focus away from people using services (Brand, Reith and Statham 2005b). This focus can be lost when workers concentrate only on administrative arrangements within and between organizations.

Government assessment frameworks for children and young people (DfEs and DH 2001) and for adults (DH 2001) are multidisciplinary. Different organizational perspectives and priorities have to be heard and negotiated. Justifications for assessments have to convince in a multi-organizational and multidisciplinary context. It is very easy for the service user and the outcomes he or she wants to achieve to become marginalized during these processes.

### INTEGRATING WHAT TO DO WITH HOW TO DO IT AND EXPLAINING WHY

Effective social work assessment integrates *what* to do with *how* and *why* to do it and achieves congruence between them. Knowledge of different assessment models is not enough to ensure effective practice. Direct practice is modified when these models are set within the intellectual, moral, organizational and policy frameworks in which social work is practised.

There are parallels between the assessments carried out with people using services and the formative and summative assessments of students. The practice teacher with responsibility for assessing the student's capacity to practice, has an excellent opportunity to model congruence, participation and openness, even when the news is bad. Modelling good practice provides a sound basis for students subsequently to achieve greater congruence themselves between what they know and what they actually do. Some of the parallels include demonstrating:

- that assessment models and tools are subsets of the main task of user-focused and student-focused assessment

- how a positive role model of not only *what* but *how* to do it gives the experience quality. Good practice is learnt from observation and support within a learning environment, not from learning from negatives or poor practice

- a position of 'determined ignorance' at first contact and not making assumptions about people. Students can bear in mind what it feels like if assumptions are made about them

- questions that elicit the perspective of the person and that will require useful answers

- how to use this knowledge to appreciate the expertise and skills of the person whether service user or student.

Good assessment skills go beyond working with people in need. They ensure that individual practitioners and their organizations take an intellectually and morally robust approach to systems and procedures, so that they are properly used as helpful tools rather than becoming barriers to working alongside people using services.

## The policy context for assessment

The policy context within which assessment in all the countries of the UK takes place specifies:

- social care values and how they must be expressed in practice

- what constitutes competent practice

- that children, young people and adults, including parents and carers, have a voice, are shown respect and listened to

- multidisciplinary/multiprofessional/multi-organizational practice and services

- person-centred or personalized assessments in both the care and the control aspects of the work

- a priority on safeguarding the public, and being tough on crime and anti-social behaviour.

## Assessment in practice

The evidence is that achieving holistic/personalized practice is very difficult. People using services consistently report that their experience and expertise has not been respected or that the assessment was culturally inappropriate (Turner and Evans 2004, Butt and Box 1996) even if this is the intention of the worker.

The skills essential to the assessment process are:

- recognizing the legal component in practice situation

- managing multiple accountability – to the law, to oneself, to employers and to professional norms – through clarity about which values guide practice in what circumstances, the knowledge relevant to decision-making, and awareness of role boundaries

- collecting information and analysing it against the legal component and an understanding of the role

- managing practice dilemmas, again by reference to values, knowledge, decisions-making frameworks, and boundaries

- assessing risk

- using evidence to advocate for a particular outcome

- challenging discrimination

- working in partnership with services users

- networking and teamworking, including differentiating and negotiating professional roles, and establishing a common value system.

(Summary of Preston-Shoot (1998) in Crisp *et al*. 2003, p.10)

To this list can be added knowledge of the organization's procedures for complaints, policies on equality, health and safety, and working with aggression and violence. Multi-organizational or multiprofessional working involves both the worker and people using services handling different pressures and priorities. It is a misconception to see assessment as a process that primarily involves only two people – the person using services and the worker. Identifying who is and needs to be involved is ironically a key task in keeping assessment person focused.

It is small wonder that given this range of knowledge workers find it difficult to be person centred. The danger is that rather than being part of a supportive framework for competent practice, all this knowledge brings so much noise into process that attention is diverted away from listening to and respecting the individual, family, group or community. Added to this is a predominant 'blame culture' in many social care organizations that militates against learning from mistakes (Bostock *et al.* 2005). This context helps to explain why there is often a disjunction between what the social worker knows and what he or she actually does.

A minority of the skills listed by Preston-Shoot relate to working directly with people using services. They, like social workers, bring their concerns into the assessment: expectations about how they will be seen, a dislike of feeling dependent, and fears about whether they are eligible for a much-needed service, whether their liberty will be curtailed or lost whether children will remain at home or be removed. These concerns can impact on the behaviour of the person using services, and in the case of control functions because of fear or anger lead to aggressive or violent behaviour (Department of Health 2001a). The first contact between the worker and the person using the services is crucial and it is hard to recover from a bad start (Thoburn, Lewis and Shemmings 1995). Workers in referral and intake teams can have a significant impact on subsequent interactions (Learner and Rosen 2004).

## Assessment models

At least three different models of intervention in assessment coexist at present. Often colleagues and people using services will be very aware of 'the way it is done here' (Marsh and Fisher 1992) even though this is not formally acknowledged. There will also be differences in approach between workers and managers. People using services often talk of being 'lucky' in having a worker who listens to and shows respect for them (Turner and Evans 2004).

### ADMINISTRATORS AND GATEKEEPERS TO SERVICES

Under this approach a worker adopts, or an organization expects the worker to adopt, an administrative approach to assessment because the primary objective is rationing scarce resources. This transforms the approach of *any* assessment framework essentially into ticking boxes regardless of its intentions. The event will be highly focused and economic in the use of time. Workers avoid eliciting information that moves them too far away from what the organization needs to reach a decision about eligibility and which scarce resource is allocated. This model avoids time-consuming efforts to be creative and preventative. The assessment may follow faithfully the areas covered in an holistic framework, but the spirit, the process and a personalized outcome are all lost. Targets for the numbers of assessments completed and timescales will be easily met. The cost of this approach is the loss of the uniqueness of each person's life. Resources may be allocated inappropriately and wasted. At its worst the service user's strengths and those in his or her network will be undermined. Some people refuse support on these terms and are sifted out of the system; some will return when in crisis, because timely help had not been given.

### EXPERTS IN OTHER PEOPLE'S PROBLEMS

Workers who see themselves in this role assume that they understand the problems of people using services. Whether the client is an individual, a family, group or a community, the worker is the main actor in problem-solving. The expert approach differs from the administrative approach because the worker is more likely to see a situation as unique; but it is based on the worker's assessment rather than that of the individual, the family or others in the individual's support network. Communication focuses on areas that workers consider important. Once they have reached that judgement, further questioning concentrates on collecting additional evidence that supports or refines their analysis. This is the opposite of 'determined ignorance', where the concerns and responses of people using services are central.

Although these two broad groups would see no similarities between their approaches, for people using services the outcome is very similar. The assessment is not person centred and does not establish a process of participation in social problem solving. The worker's assumption is that there has been a partnership, but the service user will be clear that it was the worker's views that predominated and that their own concerns were of a secondary order (Marsh and Fisher 1992; Balloch and Taylor 2001). Workers are central in managing the traffic of communication and so minimize communication between people using services and those in their support network. There is a strong tendency to underestimate the strengths in the service user's situation and this often leads to a deficit model of assessment. Both approaches can severely limit the range of perspectives which are brought together, the resources which are accessed, the conflicts which identified and negotiated, and who needs to be involved. The areas most likely to be neglected are finance, housing, transport and the environment. These are often the most important for people using services (Turner and Evans 2004), but the least relevant to the organization and the use of its resources.

## THE WORKER AS EXPERT IN PROBLEM-SOLVING

Workers who are experts in problem-solving have a very different approach to the previous two described, which is characterized by assumptions that:

- problem definition is a collaborative exercise in which everyone involved, including the worker's organization, have a perspective

- the individual, family, group or community is a major source of information about the problem and ways of addressing it in both care and control issues

- views about the source of the problem, preferred outcomes and the risks involved may conflict

- the worker contributes information about resources and facilitates access to them

- negotiation and conflict resolution are key areas for the worker, with people using services, within his or her own organization and with other organizations

- the worker is 'determinedly ignorant' of the outcome of assessment or responses to it at the beginning of the process.

Smale, Tuson and Statham (2000) introduced the idea of 'marginality' to describe:

> The worker's ability to operate effectively as a participant and as an observer in any circumstance, to become neither part of the problem-perpetuating behaviours, nor to slip unintentionally into being a permanent part of the solution, nor remaining impotently on the outside of the networks of people with whom he or she is involved. (p.178)

This is an uncomfortable position to hold, whether working with people using services or with colleagues within or outside the worker's organization. The position, however, enables the social worker to act as a broker or 'go-between' in assessments where there are tensions, conflicting perspectives and different priorities (Kearney, Levin and Rosen 2000). These are the essential material from which a way forward will emerge.

The worker has to understand the detailed nature of a specific problem, the range of ways of trying to resolve it, who needs to be involved and the consequences of the alternatives. A key requirement is the capacity to listen and to establish sufficient trust for communication in often the most inauspicious circumstances. These skills are described in the National Occupational Standards for Social Workers (Skills for Care 2002) and for Social Care and Health Care staff (Skills for Care 2005). They are not only significant in working with individuals and families but also with multi-organizational and multidisciplinary contexts. Kearney *et al.* (2000) describe the role of the social worker in negotiating between different organizations to ensure people using services whose needs cross organizational boundaries get a tailored and reliable service.

The essential skills required is an ability to get alongside people to develop a problem-solving partnership. This means demonstrating empathy and authenticity. Empathy is the ability of the worker to stand alongside other people so that they can communicate what they are thinking and feeling, how they perceive the situation and what they want. It is hard work and requires listening, hearing, comprehending and communicating in ways that are consistent with the culture, communication requirements and needs of the people involved. It is important to apply this approach to working with colleagues and other professionals, and to expect this approach from a supervisor about one's own work, as well as to people using services. It does not to turn professionals into 'clients', but takes a professional, not a personal, stance towards all working relationships and decision-making. As with people using services, initial contacts between workers will have a long-term impact on the capacity to work together effectively. Empathy is the foundation on which collaborative interpersonal problem solving and conflict negotiation is based. All of us have the capacity to demonstrate empathy with certain groups of people or in certain situations. Often this is based on our personal experience, history and culture. Registered social workers have to develop the capacity to stand alongside when people's life experience is very different from their own because of gender, ethnic descent, disability, age, religion, social class or sexuality, or because people are viewed, and often view themselves, as troublesome.

Authenticity, or demonstrating genuineness, is essential to building trust, particularly in situations where the liberty of the individual is at stake or where parenting or caring capacities are being challenged. It is a characteristic people using services value. Often described as being open, honest and up-front even when the news is bad, authenticity is seen by Smale *et al.* (2000) as a cluster of behaviours, attitudes and knowledge that are synthesized in the person of the worker:

> the congruence between what the person says, what he fells and what he does: the worker's ability to relate to others with personal integrity, 'person to person', while at the same time being aware of and using his own feelings and values, a well as the resources of his organisational role and the other roles he occupies. (p. 204)

To reach this position when there is so much noise coming from the context surrounding an assessment requires commitment to a value base and a practice approach that highlights skills in negotiating between differing and often conflicting perspectives of what is 'reality', the 'truth', or what is 'realistic'. A framework that identifies the outcomes people want to achieve enables the worker to maintain the focus on the people using services in a problem-solving approach to assessment.

### IMPLEMENTING A PROBLEM-SOLVING APPROACH: THE OUTCOMES MODEL

Nichols, Quereshi and Bamford (2003) argue that an outcomes model helps the worker to keep the work person centered and operate a problem-solving approach. Outcome is defined as the impact, effect or consequence of help received. The starting point for the assessment is the service users' 'preferred outcome'. This preference is taken as the reference point in negotiating the agreed outcomes that all will work towards. Holding the focus on outcomes prevents people becoming lost in the process of identifying resources available or slipping rapidly into routine services. Conflicts of perspective, judgement and interest are carefully recorded and have to be negotiated during the assessment and managed in the implementation of a plan. The process of working to this point is crucial because 'there are no good outcomes without good processes' (Turner and Evans 2004, p.56). The emphasis on outcomes is now part of government policy in all the countries of the UK.

Nichols *et al.* (2003) argue that if social care and social work organizations are to deliver current social policy, knowing how to implement an outcomes approach is integral to their core business. The strengths of an outcomes approach to assessment are that it:

- changes the status of the person using services from being assessed to becoming an active participant in the process

- requires an holistic approach that uses a social model

- manages the external noise that the numerous demands from the organization, government and resource scarcity and gives the process a clear focus on listening and understanding the distinct perspectives of service users and others who are significant in their lives

- moves from a primary concentration on problems to one on strengths, aspirations and the service user's or carer's priorities.

- clarifies differences in perspective between all those involved, including the worker's organization and others involved

- forces the worker and his or her organization to think creatively, and beyond routine solutions, consider what can be done to achieve the best possible outcome

- promotes inter-organizational working because people using services do not think in compartments but about what would make a difference in their lives.

Nichols *et al.* (2003) distinguish three broad functions for social care interventions in promoting well-being:

1. Maintenance outcomes.

2. Change outcomes.

3. Service process outcomes.

*Maintenance outcomes*
Maintenance outcomes are those where continuing support is necessary to maintain a person's quality of life to keep them safe, to have social contact, recreation or leisure and to have control over their lives. Maintenance includes trying to support an individual whose health is deteriorating so that he or she remains as independent as possible for as long as possible. Increasing emphasis is placed on this function because an ageing population means that a growing number of people need support to manage long-term conditions. While this is seen very much as a health function, the role of social work in working with personal, relationship and social issues is key to achieving good outcomes for people that improve the quality of their lives.

*Change outcomes*
Change outcomes involve time-limited work that aims to improve people's confidence, enable them to regain skills or develop new ones, to reduce risks – including offending behaviour – or to improve communication between the individual and others. It is similar to the task of supporting people to use the platforms provided by the state so that they can manage their problems (Leadbeater 2004). The role of the social worker in managing change will vary from short-term support to enable people to return to using mainstream services to long-term support that supports children, young people and adults with transitions.

Whether the outcome is maintenance or change, attention to service processes are crucial. Using an outcomes approach means charting the impact of services and the way they are delivered: it is not only what is provided, but how that gives a service its quality (Turner and Evans, 2004). The outcome of a service process could be that people feel respected, that their experience and ethnic descent and culture are recognized, that they have as much control over their lives as possible and that their choices have been respected as far as possible.

*Service process outcomes*
Service process outcomes relate to the impact made by how the service is delivered. The importance of this outcome has consistently been demonstrated by research carried out by service users. It is not only what support is provided but the way that it is deliver that makes a quality service. Nichols *et al.* (2003) identify two components to service process

outcomes: the staff – their competence, personality and their attitude to people using services – and the organization's capacity to provide the flexibility that enables the service to be personalized.

## Conclusion: establishing and maintaining the integration of what to do with how to do it and explaining why

It is vital that students understand just how difficult it is to achieve this congruence between what to do, how to do it and explaining why, and do not simply think in technical terms about assessment frameworks. Frameworks should be an aid to a complex activity and not a mechanistic process to conform to. The integration of what to do with how to do it and explaining why is even more difficult for the registered social worker to maintain if he or she is not working in a practice environment that supports this process. The social work degree gives an opportunity to establish the foundations for such integration of worker with workplace. This then becomes something that needs to be addressed and reviewed on a regular basis throughout a career in social work. This learning applies to organizations as well as to individual students and workers. Because good assessment practice requires effective working relationships with colleagues and organizations and because supervision should mirror good assessment practice, supervisors and managers shaping practice settings need to consider the following questions about the service they are accountable for:

- Is there a dissonance between what social workers know and what they do?

- Do people using this service report that their expertise and experience is not recognized in assessments?

- Are we making use of the models of good assessment practice available?

- How do our service users rate our assessments?

- Are we operating a deficit model when working with people using services when the policy framework is about maximizing their capacity and developing personalized services?

## Note: standards in social work education in Scotland

Students on these programmes must understand that social work is a moral activity in the sense that social workers make and follow up difficult decisions about human situations that directly benefit or harm an individual or group. They should be able to understand moral reasoning and to make decisions in difficult ethical situations, especially where there are conflicting moral obligations.

Practice is seen as an essential element of the new qualification. Development of the students' skills and abilities in practice is based on the fact that practice is *a setting* for learning, *a way* of learning and *an essential part* of the learning that students must complete.

# References

Ahmad, B. (1990) *Black Perspectives in Social Work.* Birmingham: Venture Press.

Balloch, S. and Taylor, M. (2001) *Partnership Working: Policy and Practice.* Bristol: Policy Press.

Brand, D. Reith, T. and Statham, D. (2005a) 'The need for Social Work Intervention: A Discussion Paper for the 21st Century.' Social Work Review, Scottish Executive, 19 December.

Brand, D., Reith, T. and Statham, D. (2005b) *Roles and Tasks of Social Workers.* Unpublished Paper: GSCC.

Bostock, L., Bairstow, S., Fish, S. and Macleod, F. (2005) *Managing Risk and Minimising Mistakes in Services to Children and Families.* London: Social Care Institute for Excellence.

Butt, J. and Box, L. (1996) *Social Care and Black Communities.* London: HMSO.

Campbell, J. and Oliver, M. (1996) *Disability Politics: Understanding our Past, Changing our Future.* London: Routledge.

Commission for Social Care Inspection (2005) *Direct Payments, What are the Barriers.* London: Commission for Social Care Inspection.

Coulshed, V. and Orme, J. (1998) *Social Work Practice: An Introduction.* Basingstoke: Macmillan.

Crisp, B., Anderson, M., Orme, J. and Green Lister, P. (2003) *SCIE Knowledge Review 1: Learning and Teaching in Social Work Education.* London: Social Care Institute for Excellence. Retrieved from www.scie.org.uk/publications/knowledgereviews/kr01.asp.

Crisp, R., Anderson, M.R., Orme, J. and Green Lister, P. (2005) *Learning and Teaching in Social Work Education: Textbooks and Frameworks on Assessment.* London: Social Care Institute for Excellence.

Department for Education and Skills (2004) *Every Child Matters: Change for Children.* London: Department for Education and Skills.

Department of Health (2001a) *National Task Force on Violence to Social Care Staff: A Safer Place.* London: Department of Health. Retrieved from http://www.gov.uk/violencetaskforce.

Department of Health (2001b) *National Service Framework for Older People.* London: Department of Health.

Department of Health (2006) *Our Health, Our Care, Our Say.* White Paper. London: Department of Health.

Department of Health, Department for Education and Employment and The Home Office (2001) *Framework for the Assessment of Children in Need and their Families.* London: HMSO.

Dominelli, L. and McLeod, E. (1989) *Feminist Social Work.* London: Macmillan.

Hamner, J., and Statham, D. (1989) *Women and Social Work: Towards Women Centred Practice.* Houndsmill: Macmillan.

International Federation of Social Workers/International Association of Schools of Social Work (2004) *Ethics in Social Work, Statement of Principles.* Bern: IASSW. Available at http://www.ifsw.org/en/p38000324.html.

Hardiker, P., Exton, K. and Barker, M. (1991) 'The policy context of prevention in child care.' *British Journal of Social Work 21,* 4, August, 341–359.

Kearney, P., Levin, E. and Rosen, G. (2000) *Alcohol, Drugs and Mental Health Problems: Working with Families.* London: National Institute for Social Work.

Leadbeater, C. (2004) *Personalisation through Participation: A New Script for Public Services.* London: DEMOS.

Learner, E. and Rosen, G. (2002) *Duty First: Developing Practice with Children and Families Duty Teams.* London: National Institute for Social Work/Social Care Institute for Excellence.

Marsh, P. and Fisher, M. (1992) *Good Intentions: Developing Partnership in Social Services.* York: Joseph Rowntree Foundation.

Morris, J. (1993) *Disabled Lives: Many Voices, One Message.* York: Joseph Rowntree Foundation.

Nichols, E., Quereshi, H. and Bamford, C. (2003) *Outcomes into Practice: Focusing Practice and Information on the Outcomes People Value.* York: Social Policy Research Unit, York University.

Oliver, M. (1983) *Social Work with Disabled People.* London: Macmillan.

Oliver, M. (1993) *Disability, Citizenship and Empowerment.* Workbook K665, Disabling Society. Milton Keynes: Open University Press.

Pawson, R., Boaz, A., Grayson, L., Long, A. and Barns, C. (2003) *Knowledge Review 3: Types and Quality of Knowledge in Social Care.* London: Social Care Institute For Excellence. Retrieved 25 February 2007 from www.scie.org.uk/publications/knowledgereviews/kr03.asp.

Preston-Shoot, M., Roberts, G. and Vernon, S. (1998) 'Developing a conceptual framework for teaching and assessing law within training for professional practice: Lessons from social work.' *Journal of Practice Teaching 1,* 41–51.

Scottish Executive (2003) *The Framework for Social Work Education in Scotland.* Edinburgh: Scottish Executive. Retrieved from www.scotland.gov.uk.Resource/Doc/47021/0025613.pdf.

Skills for Care (2002) *The National Occupational Standards for Social Work.* Leeds: Skills for Care. Retrieved from www.skillsforcare.org.uk/view.asp?id=582.

Skills for Care (2005) *The National Occupational Standards for Social Work.* Leeds: Skills for Care. Retrieved from www.skillsforcare.org.uk/files/cd/England/Main.htm.

Smale, G., Tuson, G. and Statham, D. (2000) *Social Work and Social Problems: Working Towards Social Inclusion and Social Change.* Basingstoke: Palgrave.

Social Care Institute for Excellence (2003) *Learning and Teaching in Social Work Education: Assessment.* London: Social Care Institute for Excellence.

Social Services Inspectorate (1998) *Community Care from Policy to Practice: The Case of Mr Frederick Joseph McLernon (deceased).* Belfast: Department of Health and Social Services.

Thoburn, J., Lewis, A. and Shemmings, D. (1995) *Paternalism or Partnership: Family Involvement in the Child Protection Process.* London: HMSO.

Turner, M. and Evans, C. (2004) 'Users influencing the management of practice.' In D. Statham (ed.) *Managing Front Line Practice.* London: Jessica Kingsley Publishers.

# CHAPTER 8

# ASSESSMENT AND CHILDREN

*Brigid Daniel*

## Introduction

Assessment must be the cornerstone of all social work with children and all assessment must be underpinned by a sound understanding of children's developmental needs. Everybody has some knowledge about children. And of course, everyone has their own childhood experience as a reference point. It is helpful for students to recognize that such knowledge can serve as a useful starting point for practice, but that it is limited precisely because it is so idiosyncratic. This is why theories, and the results of research carried out to test theories, are so important, as they enable us to locate our individual experience and views within a conceptual framework.

The main argument in this chapter is that, in order to carry out effective assessments, social workers need to draw upon the existing body of knowledge about child development to guide them in the gathering of information about the individual child (see Chapters 4 and 5 in the present volume). They then need to re-examine that information within a theoretical context and analyse what it means for this particular child. Then they must plan intervention that offers protection from harm and, above all, aims to make the child's life better and happier.

## Framework for assessments

### DEPARTMENT OF HEALTH FRAMEWORK

In England and Wales assessment is principally carried out within the structure of the Department of Health's *Framework for the Assessment of Children in Need and Their Families* (Department of Health 2000). An equivalent framework is being developed in Scotland (Scottish Executive 2005). The Department of Health framework was developed as a result of studies that showed that the child protection system was preoccupied with risk at the expense of a broader consideration of need. Too many families who were vulnerable and had unmet needs, it was suggested, were being filtered out of the system by the rigorous process of assessment of risk. These families were subsequently not receiving support that might have prevented future referrals and might have improved the well-being of children. The call was for a refocusing of the system with a greater attention to children's needs (Department of Health 2000). In order to assist practitioners to sharpen their attention on children's needs, an assessment framework was developed that was rooted in evidence about child development.

Considerable detail about the framework is provided in *The Child's World*, which provides a very valuable source of information for students and qualified practitioners (Horwath 2001). The framework is presented as a triangle with 'safeguarding and promoting the child' at the centre which is to be assessed by considering:

- the child's developmental needs

- the parenting capacity

- family and environmental factors.

An important theoretical underpinning of the framework is the ecological approach that locates the individual within layers of systems from immediate family up to wider society (Bronfenbrenner 1989).

### LIMITATIONS AND ENHANCEMENTS

In a comprehensive evaluation of the impact of the framework, Cleaver *et al.* (2004) found that, despite logistical difficulties in carrying out full assessments, practitioners welcomed the conceptual framework that was provided. The study found that more active attempts were made to involve parents, and that in comparison with the findings of previous studies parents were more likely to feel consulted, involved and included at all stages. However, it was very evident that to carry out a comprehensive assessment took time. As has been found in other studies, this study found that it is often tempting to leapfrog over assessment into the provision of services, but in the long term it is a false economy if the services are not suitable for the child and his or her family (Daniel 2002).

Before this study Horwath had already cautioned against the danger of the 'lop-sided' triangle where assessment does not cover all three strands equally (Horwath 2002). This caution was evidenced in the evaluation which indicated that among the referrals least likely to progress to initial assessment were those related to financial or housing problems, meaning that at the very early stages there is inadequate appreciation of, and therefore assessment of, these environmental factors upon children. Practitioners are not recognizing that: 'there is compelling evidence to support the contention that poverty and low income increase the pressures on parents, make the job of parenting more difficult, and increase risks of neglect and other harmful behaviours' (Spencer and Baldwin 2005, p.36).

The most pervasive critique of the framework has been that it does not pay sufficient attention to risk (see Chapter 11 in the present volume). Cooper (2003) draws on theories of risk and probability to show just how difficult it would be to explicitly build formal risk assessment into the framework, but he argues that the framework does encourage social workers to look explicitly at the impact of parenting behaviour upon the child. He also points out that wherever there is a need there is risk.

The concept of need can offer a guiding principle for the social worker if he or she assesses the extent and immediacy of need. For example, one child may be in immediate need of state protection from a violent parent; another may need supplementary support to make up for some lack of stimulation.

The framework for assessment can further be enhanced by incorporating knowledge of the factors that are associated with resilience. 'Resilience' describes a process of adaptation to difficult life experiences. When children experience difficult and poten-tially damaging life experiences they may develop some predictable emotional prob-lems. However, some children, who can be described as resilient, come through relatively intact and show emotional well-being. Resilience is known to be associated with having at least one secure attachment relationship, an appreciation of the worth of others and of yourself, a sense of the ways in which you can have some control over your own life, good friendships and school experiences and a sense of belonging to a commu-nity (Werner 2000). Social workers can draw on this knowledge when assessing ways in which children's resilience can potentially be nurtured (Daniel and Wassell 2002).

## Developmental pathways

Assessments can provide snapshots of where a child is, but they must also include infor-mation about how they have got where they are now, and where they are likely to go from here. The concept of developmental pathways is, therefore, a helpful one for social workers carrying out comprehensive assessments (Bowlby 1988). There are a range of healthy pathways that children can follow, and supportive parenting will help them to find these pathways. However, all of us can be deflected towards less emotionally healthy pathways by a single traumatic event or more chronic unsupportive conditions (see Figure 8.1).

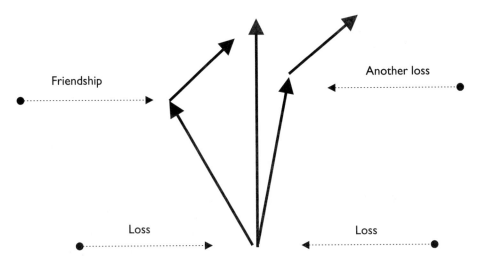

*Figure 8.1 How events can deflect people onto different developmental pathways*

One of the best ways to map the child's pathway to date is to construct a detailed chro-nology of events and of professional intervention. A good chronology is invaluable and no assessment is complete without one.

There is now an emerging body of evidence about the kind of chronic circumstances that can impact upon children's developmental pathways; for example, Cleaver, Unell and Aldgate (1999) have pulled together the evidence about the impact of domestic abuse, parental mental health problems and substance misuse.

## Assessing children's developmental needs

It is clearly not possible to offer extensive details of child development here; instead, one main theme will be highlighted for each stage and linked with helpful theoretical concepts to demonstrate the way in which theory must underpin assessment. It must also be stressed that assessment is not the sole province of social workers. Social workers cannot and should not carry out a detailed assessment of all dimensions of a child's development, but they will often be in the key position of bringing all the information together and making sense of what it all means.

### EARLY YEARS

Babies are utterly dependent and highly vulnerable; they have an inherent need to attach and to assert that need (Bowlby 1998). Unlike some species, whose young are quickly able to fend for themselves, humans bear offspring which are very immature at birth and for whom a considerable amount of development is still to occur, especially of the brain (Glaser 2000).

Because babies are highly dependent upon a mature carer during their early years they are also highly vulnerable to failures in such care, whether the failures are of omission or commission. It may be difficult for students to grasp the reality of what can happen to tiny babies; for example, it can be shocking to hear that in a three-year period approximately three children under the age of ten were killed or seriously injured each week and that 83 per cent of the victims were under the age of two (*Guardian* 2003, cited in Dent and Cocker 2005). Similarly, it can be difficult to believe that toddlers can be subjected to sexual abuse. Without this knowledge, though, social workers may either miss signs of harm or potential harm to young children, or be so outraged that someone can harm a young baby that they are of no assistance to the situation. Reder and Duncan (1995) have developed a theoretical explanation which helps to explain why people can end up harming very young children and which, therefore, may assist the student to assess the circumstances of a young child. Their explanation is rooted in that very vulnerability and dependence of young children and links with the fact that attachment needs are expressed very overtly and powerfully.

Reder and Duncan draw upon psychoanalytical and family systems traditions to propose that all children hold a meaning to their parents and some meanings can contribute to them being harmed. For, example, some children are expected to fulfil some of the parent's unmet dependency needs; others carry the legacy of stressful events at the time of their conception. Reder and Duncan suggest that when assessing parenting meaning can be explored at different levels.

- *Cultural beliefs*: does the parent carry cultural expectations about children that might lead to unreasonable demands or harm?

- *Family history*: did any significant events coincide with the time of conception or birth of the child – for example, the death of a partner?

- *Parent's unresolved conflicts*: is the child being expected to resolve the parent's own caring and dependency needs?

- *Current interaction*: is the child being used to impact upon the parental relationship, for example, as a distance regulator?

- *The child's history*: are there factors in the child's history that may be render him or her vulnerable, such as being conceived by rape, a traumatic birth, a premature birth and so on?

- *The child's characteristics*: are there ways in which the child behaves, or factors such as whom the child resembles, that may increase the risk of harm?

The attachment needs of children can be overwhelming and can be misinterpreted by parents. Risks to children can flow from inappropriate attribution of intent, for example, a parental response to a crying baby as 'He's deliberately winding me up!' Similarly, parents may overestimate their children's stage of development, as can be evidenced by comments such as 'She needs to learn to use the potty,' made of a year-old child.

## SCHOOL YEARS

Children's emotional and cognitive processes need to be maturing during early and middle school years to enable them to thrive in a range of out-of-home settings.

Social workers do not need to be experts in psychological assessment, but they do need to have a sufficient understanding of theories of cognitive and emotional development in order to work effectively in partnership with other professionals such as educational psychologists and teachers. For example, knowledge of child development tells us that by the middle school years children should have reasonably well developed levels of self-control, competence and autonomy (Masten and Coatsworth 1998). They should have moved from the younger child's need for adult control and external monitoring towards being more able to inhibit inappropriate and impulsive responses. For many children it is not until they are required to fit within the structured school environment that behavioural control problems become apparent. There is existing empirical and theoretical information to guide social workers with the assessment of emotional maturity. For example, studies of parenting have indicated that children's emotional competence is promoted by a combination of warmth and clear boundaries, or what is known as 'authoritative parenting' (Baumrind 1971; Maccoby and Martin 1983).

Children's cognitive processes gradually become more complex as they mature and language becomes increasingly sophisticated and incorporates more abstract concepts. The best-known theorist on cognitive development is Piaget (1952). He postulated that cognitive development occurs through a process of assimilation, where new learning is incorporated into existing learning, and accommodation, where existing thought processes are adapted to take account of the new information. Social workers must take cognitive development very seriously and must ensure that they have good, comprehensive information about the child's level of cognitive ability.

## ADOLESCENCE

Young people are likely to have a smoother transition through adolescence if they have a healthy sense of identity, self-esteem and self-efficacy.

Adolescence is a time of internal change and external transition. All we already know about attachment theory would indicate that people find it easier to cope with changes and transitions if they feel loved, secure and supported. Many young people who come to the attention of social workers in their teenage years are facing up to an accumulation of stressors that have been affecting their developmental pathway from early years. As they move into adolescence the potential for the pathway to take a sharp turn for the worse becomes greater. For example, as young people move into adolescence the negative impact of mixing with anti-social peers can become greater (Bender and Lösel 1997).

Issues of attachment remain as important, if not more important, for troubled young people. Many referrals relate to young people who are in conflict with their parents and it is helpful to bear in mind, during the assessment process, that the imminence of more independence can highlight existing anxious attachments. A young person's sense of identity will be closely bound up with their sense of self-esteem, which also flows from earlier attachment experiences and opportunities for achievement. Self-efficacy is under-pinned by attribution theory and relates to the explanations we give to ourselves for why things happen. People with a low sense of self-efficacy tend to blame themselves for bad things that happen to them, to see problems as enduring and to expect to experience fail-ure and difficulties in all arenas (Petersen and Seligman 1985). In a nutshell, people with low self-efficacy do not have a sense of hope about the future: a sad situation for someone on the brink of adulthood to find themselves in.

## Keeping children at the heart of the process

It is remarkable how much assessment activity occurs without any direct work with the child. In their study of assessment practice Cleaver et al. (2004) found that there 'was lit-tle evidence of informing or consulting children during the assessment and planning processes' (p.248). This is despite the fact that the importance of direct communication with, and involvement of, the child is stressed throughout the guidance material. Horwarth found three main reasons for practitioner failure to engage directly with children during the assessment process:

1.    perception of lack of time to develop meaningful relationships with children

2.    lack of confidence in having appropriate communication skills, especially when more enhanced communication skills were required

3.    failure to collaborate with other professionals to ensure that communication is established with children.

(Horwath 2002)

What is startling about these findings is that the ability to communicate with children should be a core skill of all social workers involved in child care and protection work. The starkest reminder of the dangers of not speaking directly to the child came in the Laming report into the death of Victoria Climbié (Lord Laming 2003). All the profes-sionals involved from all the disciplines failed to make it a priority to spend meaningful time with Victoria and failed to find a way to engage in effective communication with her. Therefore, it is essential that from a very early stage social work training must em-phasize the importance of professional confidence and instil a firm focus on the child.

There is no doubt that there are time constraints in statutory social work, especially during child protection investigations. Social workers who are confident of their role and have a sound focus on the need to involve the child will make it a priority to ensure that they spend time with the child. Even when time is pressured it is possible for a skilled worker to convey the message to the child that they take his or her views seriously. Different social workers can use a short time with a child very differently: one may bombard the child with information or questions and exude anxiety; the other may sit quietly with the child, offer a few opening comments, listen to what the child has to say and offer reassurance.

Bannister (2001) describes three stages in the process of engaging with children and ascertaining their views. She suggests that first it is important to gain the child's trust by building rapport; then to provide a space within which the child feels safe to express his or her needs. Finally, the child requires reassurance that he or she has been listened to and that his or her views will be considered.

Bannister explicitly draws upon existing knowledge and theories of child development in her practice guidance. For example, she highlights the key role of play in child development and suggests that play provides a good vehicle for rapport building. For guidance on the creation of a safe space she draws on the language of client-centred approaches in suggesting that the practitioner show the child 'unconditional regard' (Rogers 1951). She also draws on attachment theory to emphasize the fact that the assessment process entails the forming of a relationship between the child and assessor and that this relationship must be respected. The detachment stage must therefore be carefully planned and the child must be given honest information about what will happen next and who will be involved. Here we can see how valuable it is to draw on a range of theoretical approaches when working with children.

## MESSAGES FROM STUDIES THAT ASK CHILDREN

As with all the issues discussed in this chapter, there is a body of existing information that provides a backdrop for gathering the views of a specific child. A range of studies have been carried out that have actively sought the views of children about different aspects of the child care and child protection processes and services.

Children report that involvement in investigations, medical examinations, case conferences, children's hearings and court systems is stressful and that they feel anxiety about loss of control and being inextricably entangled in a system with uncertain outcomes (Hallett et al. 1998; NCH Action for Children 1994; Taylor and Roberts 1993; Westcott and Davies 1996). Children who were consulted for the Scottish Audit and Review of Child Protection described similar concerns. Those who had received therapeutic help, though, were positive about it (Scottish Executive 2002b).

Wilson et al. (2004) carried out a systematic review of studies of foster care and found that children:

- are generally positive about their care

- want to be treated as a member of the family

- want to be loved and encouraged

- need to have respect for their individuality and differences but do not want to be made to feel different

- feel their birth families are important to them

- need better explanations of why they entered care
- do not want to be moved unnecessarily
- want their views to be heard.

However, they also found that children wanted workers to:

- take time to explain to them what is happening and why
- listen to and respect their views and experiences
- believe what they said
- talk to the people they thought were important
- provide them with something to remind them of what was decided.

Studies such as these are illustrative for a number of reasons. First, of course, they provide invaluable information about what children find supportive and helpful. Second, they demonstrate that children can provide coherent and insightful in their own views if asked. If children can be successfully involved in research studies then they can also be involved in their own assessment process. Stalker has also demonstrated that children with profound impairments of communication can offer vivid and coherent views about their lives in response to sensitive, carefully paced enquiry, using communication aids where necessary (Connors and Stalker, 2003).

In Scotland, a Children's Charter for child care and protection has been developed following consultation with children and young people (Scottish Executive 2004). The aim of the charter is to place expectations on the professionals from the perspective of the child. The charter sets out what all children should expect of all professionals from any agency:

- Get to know us.
- Speak with us.
- Listen to us.
- Take us seriously.
- Involve us.
- Respect our privacy.
- Be responsible to us.
- Think about our lives as a whole.
- Think carefully about how you use information about us.
- Put us in touch with the right people.
- Use your power to help.
- Make things happen when they should.
- Help us be safe.

(Scottish Executive 2004, p.2)

These statements fit squarely with existing theory about children's needs during professional intervention and provide a very useful checklist for social workers embarking upon assessment of a child's circumstances.

## OBSERVATION

Just as it is important to involve the child in the process of assessment, it is equally important for the assessor to integrate information based on direct observation of the child in different settings (Bridge and Miles 1996; Fawcett 1996). As Fitzpatrick, Reder and Lucey (1995) assert, 'assessment begins with observation, and even the first meeting in the waiting room is an opportunity for the professional to observe aspects of the child's development and functioning' (p.63). Such observations provide invaluable insights into the child's functioning and interaction with the physical and social world. Again, it is essential to consider children's behaviour in the context of knowledge of healthy developmental trajectories, set within theoretical frameworks. For example, observation of a happy pre-school age child in a secure setting where toys are available will provide a scene of happy exploration and play interspersed with excited and questioning interaction with a caregiver. Attachment theory provides an explanation of this behaviour: during these early years children use the secure base of the attachment figure as a springboard from which to explore the world of objects and the world of other people (Bowlby 1998). This early play and exploration lays the foundation for further social, emotional and cognitive development. This can be contrasted with the sad picture of the behaviour of neglected children, as described in a comparative study of the impact of various forms of abuse and neglect (Egeland, Sroufe and Erickson, 1983). At 24 months of age the children in this study lacked enthusiasm in problem-solving tasks, showed less flexibility and alternated passive with aggressive behaviour. They were more likely to show behaviour consistent with insecure attachment and to demonstrate less affection and initiate less play with mothers. Here the foundations are being laid for incremental delay in social, emotional and cognitive development. Therefore, when faced with assessing a potentially neglectful situation, it is very sensible to find naturalistic ways to observe the child's demeanour and behaviour (Tanner and Turney, 2000). If we bring all these strands together we have a model for this essential element of assessment:

- there is available research information about the kind of behaviour that tends to be associated with various forms of abuse and neglect

- there is a theoretical framework that offers an explanation for that behaviour

- there is a method that allows the practitioner to gauge whether this child shows this kind of response.

This model can be drawn on for children at all stages of development and can be underpinned by different theoretical approaches. For example, children are often referred with a constellation of behavioural problems. While attachment theory can be very helpful for understanding the emotional reasons for the development of behavioural problems, it may not always provide the most useful framework for the analysis of the specific way in which the distress is manifested. Behavioural theories can provide a helpful lens through which behaviour can be observed because they offer explanations for how behaviour is triggered and reinforced (Herbert 1987). Chapter 12 in the present volume provides more information about behavioural and cognitive-behavioural approaches.

During the initial phases of assessment it would not be unusual to be provided with a catalogue of concerns about the child and a list of worrying behaviours such as aggressive outbursts, violence to other children, violence to animals, verbal or physical threats to teachers and parents, soiling, stealing, lying and disregard for personal safety. If social workers rely solely on this type of evidence they are in danger of having skewed impressions of the children involved. It is, therefore, very important for the social worker to find opportunities to observe a referred child in as many situations as possible. The child should be observed with parents, and this should not be confined to observations of maternal interaction. If there is a father or father figure who is important to the child then he must be included in the assessment process (Daniel and Taylor 2001). The child should also be seen in the company of other children and other adults, and a nursery or school is likely to offer the best opportunity for this. Observation can provide all sorts of useful information and questions can be asked of the observations.

### WHAT IS THE RATIO OF DIFFICULT BEHAVIOUR TO NON-PROBLEMATIC BEHAVIOUR?
It is very important not to dismiss the concerns of others about a child's difficult behaviour: there is nothing more likely to impair good interdisciplinary working relationships than a teacher's real concern about the child's presentation in a classroom not being heard. At the same time the key role of the social worker who is carrying out a comprehensive assessment is to maintain objectivity. To do this the child should not be assessed only via the information provided by others. Direct observation, coupled with careful recording can provide accurate information about exactly how much of the time the child is showing difficult behaviour.

### WHAT ARE THE ANTECEDENTS AND CONSEQUENCES OF BEHAVIOUR?
There are all sorts of consequences to difficult behaviour that may be rewarding and reinforcing for some children. Rewards may include increased adult attention, exclusion from a stressful classroom or learning task, a parent being called to the school and admiring responses from other children. The dispassionate social worker can bring new eyes to the situation and is in an ideal position to consider the scenario from the child's perspective. When there is an outburst the observer can note the triggers or antecedents to that behaviour and can then note the immediate consequences. They are also in an ideal position to observe the conditions that promote and reinforce more appropriate behaviour.

### TO WHAT EXTENT CAN THE CHILD CONTROL HIS OR HER OWN BEHAVIOUR?
Uninhibited behaviour will be obvious during observation, especially when a child responds to mild or no provocation with impulsive aggression. Other children with challenging behaviour may be observed to use aggression in a more controlled way towards a particular end. This should, again, be obvious to the observer.

### HOW DOES THE CHILD RELATE TO YOU?
During the process of assessment a social worker is in an ideal position to learn about the child's inner working model of relationships from observing the way the child relates to him or her. Attachment theory proposes that we all develop templates for relationships in

response to early attachment experiences. These inner working models are then played out in the context of new relationships. So, for example, a child with an anxious avoidant attachment pattern may respond to the social worker with coldness and distance, even after a prolonged assessment period (see also Howe *et al.* 1999) for a detailed account of the way that inner working models are transported to different relationships).

## Children's worlds

There is an important strand of sociological theory that provides a helpful counterbalance to a potential within social work to focus upon children as vulnerable and either the victims of adult violence or the recipients of adult help. Sociologists have pointed out that 'childhood' is a social construct and that understandings of what is a 'child' shift and change over time and across cultures (James and Prout, 1997).

This theoretical lens offers social workers a useful reminder that children are active participants in the world. They have individual views, feelings and important peer networks. Children exist in a world of other children and this world poses threats and also offers support. For example, the largest proportion of calls to ChildLine are from children who describe being bullied by other children. At the same time, a study of calls to ChildLine (Scotland) about abuse and neglect showed that when children talked of seeking help they often mentioned turning to friends (Scottish Executive 2002a). Emond carried out a study of young people who were looked after and accommodated in residential settings. She found that they developed webs of support that built on their different strengths and abilities. The young people offered each other advice and emotional support and looked out for each other's welfare (Emond 2003).

The message for assessment practice is that it is all too easy to underestimate both the extent to which children may be frightened of other children and also how important their peer networks can be to them. Having good friendship skills and having intimate friends is associated with long-term well-being and helps to nurture resilience in the face of adversity. Social support is, therefore, as important for children as it is for adults (Thompson 1995). Theories of friendship indicate that children tend to move from friendship based on proximity and convenience towards friendship based on mutual interests and support. When assessing children's lives it is therefore important to take account of their peer network and what it means to them.

## Conclusion

In order to carry out effective assessments of children social workers need to draw on a range of theoretical perspectives. First it is essential to base all assessment on an understanding of child development and knowledge of the key developmental tasks at different stages. This will enable the assessment of the extent to which the child's developmental needs are not being met, and the extent of risk that healthy development will be compromised. To facilitate assessment it is necessary to be prepared to enter the child's world and to try, as far as possible, to see the world from his or her perspective. The best way to do this is to find an effective way to communicate meaningfully with the child.

Finally, in the welter of procedure, policy and multi-agency demands, it is all too easy to lose sight of the purpose of assessment. Assessment can become an end in itself, and an 'assessment paralysis' can set in (Reder and Duncan, 1999). The ultimate aim of assessment must be to improve children's lives and social workers must keep this as their central focus. Using their understanding of children's developmental needs, therefore, social workers must develop plans that aim to provide supports to meet their needs, including any need for protection from harm.

## References

Bannister, A. (2001) 'Entering the child's world: Communicating with children to assess their need.' In J. Horwath (ed.) *The Child's World: Assessing Children in Need.* London: Jessica Kingsley Publishers.

Baumrind, D. (1971) 'Current patterns of parental authority.' *Developmental Psychology Monographs 4,* 1, 99–102.

Bender, D. and Lösel, F. (1997) 'Protective and risk effects of peer relations and social support on antisocial behaviour in adolescents from multi-problem families.' *Journal of Adolescence 20,* 661–78.

Bowlby, J. (1988) 'Developmental psychiatry comes of age.' *The American Journal of Psychiatry 145,* 1, 1–10.

Bowlby, J. (1998) *Attachment and Loss.* Vol. 2. London: Pimlico.

Bridge, G. and Miles, G. (1996) *On the Outside Looking In: Collected Essays on Young Child Observation in Social Work Training.* London: CCETSW.

Bronfenbrenner, U. (1989) 'Ecological systems theory.' *Annals of Child Development 6,* 187–249.

Cleaver, H., Unell, I. and Aldgate, J. (1999) *Children's Needs – Parenting Capacity: The Impact of Parental Mental Illness, Problem Alcohol and Drugs Use, and Domestic Violence on the Development of Children.* London: The Stationery Office.

Cleaver, H., Walker, S. and Meadows, P. (2004) *Assessing Children's Needs and Circumstances: The Impact of the Assessment Framework.* London: Jessica Kingsley Publishers.

Connors, C. and Stalker, K. (2003) *The Views and Experiences of Disabled Children and their Siblings: A Positive Outlook.* London: Jessica Kingsley Publishers.

Cooper, A. (2003) 'Risk and the framework for assessment.' In C. Calder and S. Hackett (eds) *Assessment in Child Care.* Lyme Regis: Russell House Publishing Ltd.

Daniel, B. (2002) 'Assessment practice in cases of child neglect: A developmental project.' *Practice 13,* 4, 21–38.

Daniel, B. and Taylor, J. (2001) *Engaging with Fathers: Practice Issues for Health and Social Care.* London: Jessica Kingsley Publishers.

Daniel, B. and Wassell, S. (2002) *The Early Years: Assessing and Promoting Resilience in Vulnerable Children I.* London, Jessica Kingsley Publishers.

Dent, R.J. and Cocker, C. (2005) 'Serious case reviews: Lessons for practice in cases of child neglect.' In J. Taylor and B. Daniel (eds) *Child Neglect: Practice Issues for Health and Social Care.* London: Jessica Kingsley Publishers.

Department of Health (2000) *Framework for the Assessment of Children in Need and their Families.* London: The Stationery Office.

Egeland, B., Sroufe, L.A. and Erickson, M. (1983) 'The developmental consequences of different patterns of maltreatment.' *Child Abuse and Neglect 7,* 459–69.

Emond, R. (2003) 'Understanding the residential group.' *Scottish Journal of Residential Child Care 1,* 1, 30–40.

Fawcett, M. (1996) *Learning Through Child Observation.* London: Jessica Kingsley Publishers.

Fitzpatrick, G., Reder, P. and Lucey, C. (1995) 'The child's perspective.' In P. Reder and C. Lucey (eds) *Assessment of Parenting: Psychiatric and Psychological Contributions.* New York and London: Routledge.

Glaser, D. (2000). 'Child abuse and neglect and the brain – a review.' *Journal of Child Psychology and Psychiatry 41,* 1, 97–116.

Hallett, C., Murray, C., Jamieson, J. and Veitch, B. (1998) *The Evaluation of the Children's Hearings in Scotland, Vol. 1 Deciding in Children's Interests.* Edinburgh: The Scottish Central Research Unit.

Herbert, M. (1987) *Conduct Disorders of Childhood and Adolescence.* New York: Wiley.

Horwath, J. (ed.) (2001) *The Child's World: Assessing Children in Need.* London: Jessica Kingsley Publishers.

Horwath, J. (2002) 'Maintaining a focus on the child? First impressions of the Framework for the Assessment of Children in Need and Their Families in cases of child neglect.' *Child Abuse Review 11,* 4, 195–213.

Howe, D., Brandon, M., Hinings, D. and Schofield, G. (1999) *Attachment Theory, Child Maltreatment and Family Support.* London: Macmillan Press.

James, A. and Prout, A. (1997) *Constructing and Reconstructing Childhood: Contemporary Issues in the Sociology of Childhood.* 2nd revised edn. London and Philadelphia: Falmer Press.

Lord Laming (2003) *The Victoria Climbié Inquiry.* London: HMSO.

Maccoby, E.E. and Martin, J. (1983) 'Socialization in the context of the family: Parent–child interaction.' In E.M. Hetherington (ed.) *Handbook of Child Psychology: Socialization, Personality and Social Development.* Vol. 4. New York: Wiley.

Masten, A.S. and Coatsworth, J.D. (1998) 'The development of competence in favorable and unfavorable environments.' *American Psychologist 53,* 2, 205–220.

NCH Action for Children (1994) *Messages from Children: Children's Evaluations of the Professional Response to Child Sexual Abuse.* London: NCH Action for Children.

Petersen, C. and Seligman, M.E.P. (1985) 'The learned helplessness model of depression: Current status of theory and research.' In E. Beckham (ed.) *Handbook of Depression: Treatment, Assessment and Research.* Homewood, Il: Dorsey Press.

Piaget, J. (1952) *The Origins of Intelligence in Children.* New York: International Universities Press.

Reder, P. and Duncan, S. (1995) 'The meaning of the child.' In P. Reder and C. Lucey (eds) *Assessment of Parenting: Psychiatric and Psychological Contributions.* London and New York: Routledge.

Reder, P. and Duncan, S. (1999) *Lost Innocents: a Follow-Up Study of Fatal Child Abuse.* London and New York: Routledge.

Rogers, C. (1951) *Client-Centred Therapy.* Boston, MA: Houghton Mifflin.

Scottish Executive (2002a) *An Analysis of Calls to Childline on the Subject of Child Abuse and Neglect.* Edinburgh: Scottish Executive. Available at: www.scotland.gov.uk/Topics/People/Young-People/ children-families/17834/10637.

Scottish Executive (2002b) *Messages from Young People who have Experienced Child Protection Proceedings.* Edinburgh: Scottish Executive. Available at: www.scotland.gov.uk/Topics/People/Young-People/ children-families/17834/10636. Accessed 24 January 2004.

Scottish Executive (2004) *Protecting Children and Young People: The Charter.* Edinburgh: Scottish Executive.

Scottish Executive (2005) *Getting It Right for Every Child.* Edinburgh: Scottish Executive.

Spencer, N. and Baldwin, N. (2005) 'Economic, cultural and social contexts of neglect.' In J. Taylor and B. Daniel (eds) *Child Neglect: Practice Issues for Health and Social Care.* London: Jessica Kingsley Publishers.

Tanner, K. and Turney, D. (2000) 'The role of observation in the assessment of child neglect.' *Child Abuse Review 9,* 5, 337–48.

Taylor, C.J. and Roberts, J. (1993) 'Child sexual abuse: The child's perspective.' In H. Ferguson and R. Gilligan and R. Torode (eds) *Surviving Childhood Adversity: Issues for Policy and Practice.* Dublin: Social Studies Press.

Thompson, R.A. (1995) *Preventing Child Maltreatment Through Social Support.* Thousand Oaks, London, New Delhi: Sage.

Werner, E. (2000) 'Protective factors and individual resilience.' In J. Schonkoff and S. Meisels (eds) *The Handbook of Childhood Intervention.* Cambridge, MA: Cambridge University Press.

Westcott, H. and Davies, G.M. (1996) 'Sexually abused children's and young people's perspectives on investigative interviews.' *British Journal of Social Work 26,* 451–74.

Wilson, K., Sinclair, I., Taylor, C., Pithouse, A. and Sellick, C. (2004) *Knowledge Review 5: Fostering Success: An Exploration of the Research Literature in Foster Care.* London: Social Care Institute for Excellence.

## CHAPTER 9

# ASSESSMENT: FROM REFLEXIVITY TO PROCESS KNOWLEDGE

*Michael Sheppard*

Assessment is most characteristically associated with the early stages of social work intervention. It is, so the argument goes, required, before any action can be taken. The quality of that action depends, in turn, on the quality of the assessment that takes place. Assessment is, of course, essential to these early stages. It would, however, be a mistake to limit assessment in this way. Assessment occurs, or should occur, at all times. It is quite obvious, with a little thought, that constant evaluation and re-evaluation of circumstances is required if the practitioner is to keep track of changes and developments in clients' circumstances. Indeed, even where circumstances do not change, additional information can lead to practitioners reflecting on their initial judgements, and revising their judgements. Assessment, therefore, is central to the conduct of social work practice.

Gambrill (1997) neatly summarizes some of the major functions of assessment. They are, she suggests:

1.  identifying problems

2.  clarifying problems

3.  detecting the characteristics of clients and their environments that influence problems

4.  interpreting and integrating the data collected

5.  selecting outcomes to focus on.

This process helps highlight the relationship between assessment and actions. It also emphasizes the substantive dimensions of assessment. Focusing on problems (or needs) means paying attention to the detailed circumstances underlying mental health, child abuse, learning disability, and so on, which provide the 'stuff' of social work practice.

In recent years, however, attention has increasingly moved from just focusing on the substantive areas of assessment, to the processes by which social workers make judgements and decisions which then lead to their assessments. This leads us away from looking at areas on which social workers focus, to the ways in which they actually think when making assessments. It is the quality of that thinking which, it is now apparent, is crucial to the quality of the assessment made. How, in other words, do social workers come to the conclusions they do when they make assessments? What constitutes good quality practice in this respect? How rigorous are social workers when they make assessments? Such questions are not purely academic, for it is the quality of thinking upon which the assessment, and consequently the intervention is to a considerable degree, dependent. Understanding better these thinking processes has been termed by Sheppard (1998) as 'process knowledge', and it has become clear that developing this process knowledge is of considerable importance in social work. This chapter will focus on some of the main dimensions of this process knowledge that have emerged through theoretical developments and empirical research.

## Reflexivity

### WHAT GOES ON IN A SOCIAL WORKER'S MIND WHEN HE OR SHE CONDUCTS AN ASSESSMENT?

At the heart of assessment is reflexivity. To conduct good assessment, the practitioner must be reflexive. Reflexivity has been defined in two ways. The social worker is:

- an active thinker, able to assess, respond and initiate action

- a social actor, one who actually participates in the situation with which he or she is concerned in the conduct of his or her practice.

(Sheppard 1998)

Reflexivity involves, then, both detachment and involvement, with a recognition that in seeking to make sense of a situation, the social worker needs to account for their own actions and motivations. It also involves a recognition of the assumptions underlying their own assessments. These relate to the knowledge forms they are using, and their own position as a practitioner, particularly the assumptions which underlie the nature and conduct of the role of the social worker (Sheppard 1995a, 1995b).

Thus the reflexive practitioner shows a high degree of self-awareness, role awareness and awareness of assumptions underlying their conduct of practice. What, however, happens when the social worker actually confronts a new situation? What are the mental processes which may occur? Above all, the social worker is trying to create some meaning out of a range of information – stimuli if you like – with which he or she is confronted. This can be in the form of written information, verbal information, observation and so on. Information does not of itself tell social workers the story. They need to make sense of it, but they also need to examine it: how convincing is the information they have?

### WHAT DO REFLEXIVE SOCIAL WORKERS DO WHEN CONFRONTED BY A REFERRAL?

To achieve these kinds of evaluations and to go through processes which will enable them to create meaning, social workers utilize various mental processes. We can start at the point of referral, with information which may have been recorded. At this point the reflexive social worker undergoes a process of *Critical Appraisal*. This refers to analysis undertaken by social workers through which they seek to make initial judgements about the nature and quality of the information they have received. Referrals are not straightforward pieces of information, but require such appraisal.

One element of this is *Focused Attention*. Social workers get a range of information, and they need to decide which bits are important and which are less important. Social workers tend to focus on particular pieces of information to a greater degree than other pieces. For example, a child care social worker may pay particular attention to a slap on the face which a young person has received from his or her parent. The reason why is obvious; it may be part of possible child abuse. The practitioner would want to explore this further: what were the circumstances under which it happened? What were the intentions of the parent who did it? Has it happened more than once? What degree of damage occurred as a result? And so on. Here we have the social worker concentrating on a particular facet of information which is important because it relates to a central part of his or her role. Nevertheless, the point is that the worker does not assume too much. The slap may be less serious than it appears, or an accident, and so on.

Focused Attention is an important element of the social worker's cognitive processes when making assessments. This is the first stage of a process by which the social worker 'sifts' information, emphasizing particular aspects, and through which they construct meanings, i.e. make sense of a situation.

Another element of Critical Appraisal is *Querying Information*. At the heart of this is a refusal to take information that has been provided at face value. We might find, for example, that in a referral for possible child abuse, the parents had been described as awkward and defensive when doctors sought to investigate the situation. This is a serious label, when the character of the parent can play an important part in the assessment being made. If it were repeated, unchecked, then it could disadvantage the parents when they tried to present their own story. Questions need to be asked: were, in fact, the parents being defensive when the doctor saw them? If they were, how far was it down to the doctor's manner – was the doctor him- or herself difficult, for example? In any case, confronting powerful high status professionals like doctors over an issue such as possible child abuse can itself feel threatening. How far were the parents acting in an understandable way in the circumstances? Such questions allow us (potentially) to shift our attention from some enduring and negative characteristic, to the circumstances in which the behaviour took place. Such querying does not require us to discard the possibility that the parents are, in fact, defensive, but it requires that such a claim should be demonstrated.

Social workers also *Evaluate Information*. This occurs where they seek to assess the quality and comprehensiveness of the information they have received. Social workers may look at various aspects of the information received, and, so to speak, present it with penetrating questions. Again, taking a referral for child abuse, the social worker may simply have one bit of information – that the stepfather of a young child was 18 years old, and the referrer may be questioning his capacity to parent, and raise the issue of whether a bruise on the child's head was caused by this man. However, such information is limited, and the social worker could legitimately ask what he or she really knows about him. There might be nothing about his experience with children; he might be black, living in a predominantly white area. How far might that impact on the kinds of perceptions which underlay the referral? Such issues involve the asking of questions which do not immediately flow from the information to the referral itself, but which rather, to some degree, form the information that is lacking. The capacity to ask such questions reflects experience and knowledge, and an awareness that a deeper understanding of the situation is required to avoid jumping to conclusions.

A final element of the initial process of critical appraisal involves making *Causal Inferences*. Causal Inferences are inferences made by social workers from information they initially receive, which can then be built into hypotheses about underlying features of the problem or situation. It is about 'going behind' statements made in the initial information received, in an attempt to make more sense of the situation. Take, for example, the last situation mentioned. Here we have a young stepfather, who is black, in a predominantly white area, about whom allegations of abuse have been made. It may be that some abuse has occurred. Alternatively the social worker may consider the possibility of racism: is this a situation where allegations are being made for a racist motivation, or even because cultural norms and expectations are different? The possible focus switches from the presenting problem of possible abuse to the possibility of a racist-motivated referral – a very different matter. The focus switches from the actions of the stepfather to the motivation of the referrer. Of course, the social worker may be maintaining an open mind, but it involves two potentially radically different ways of understanding the situation.

## Hypothesis generation

Hypothesis generation is a key element of the reflexive process of assessment. Hypotheses are propositions about the situation which make sense of it. Whole case hypotheses are propositions made which sum up the case as a whole. They are, from the point of view of the social worker, their 'definition of the situation'. For the reflexive social worker this will always be a 'working definition', capable of change as new information emerges. Such hypotheses are both provisional and probabilistic. That is, they are the best the social worker can come up with at the time, given the information at her or his disposal, and they represent a likely (the most likely) correct way (as far as the social worker is concerned) of defining the situation. In fact the second part of that comment should be revised. Properly understood, such propositions should be the ones which are least likely to be wrong. Placing an emphasis in this way enables us to be looking for information which would contradict the hypothesis, and leave us open to the possibility of revising the hypothesis.

*Whole case hypotheses*: ideally, the social worker would be aware of more than one possible hypothesis, because it is in this awareness that he or she is better able to compare and hence revise hypotheses. We may, for example, have a child 'acting out', presenting challenging behaviour. We may, for example, define a case as fundamentally one of abuse. The 'acting out' is a response to the experience of abuse. Alternatively we may define it as being about a 'clash of wills' between parents and child, and the challenging behaviour represents part of that clash of wills. It could instead be a matter of loss or bereavement: the child's behaviour arising within the context of his or her emotional response to the loss. The point is that, depending on the definition of the situation, radically different approaches may be made to intervention. Varying, possibly, from registration on the child protection register, to therapeutic direct work with the child.

Another feature of social work assessments is the use of *partial case hypotheses*. These are hypotheses which, rather than seeking to make a general definition of the situation, focus on particular facets. In any one case and at any point in time there can be a wide number of these partial case hypotheses. There are two types. The first is understanding hypotheses. These are propositions which help make sense of particular aspects of a case. If, for example we have a case involving possible abuse of a male child, where there are two parents and the boy in the family, and they know that there is a threat of redundancy for the father who is the only breadwinner, the social worker may generate hypotheses about each individual. The boy may, for example, be seen as awkward and challenging, the father as rigid and the mother as indecisive, unable to challenge the two males. Hypotheses may be made about particular crisis situations. Where there has been a serious argument or altercation, the social worker may make propositions about why it occurred (for example, the child may have 'wound' the father up), the father may have been short-tempered because of anxiety arising from the threat of redundancy, and so on. The point is, with limited information, hypotheses like these enable social workers to provide themselves with a direction through which they can explore matters in more detail. Thus, having hypothesized about the importance of the threat of redundancy, they may explore this avenue further, seeking to discover its likelihood, the effect it had had on the father, and whether it might have had any impact on him in the crisis situation.

*Others' hypotheses* are propositions social workers make about other people's hypotheses. This apparently complex idea is not that far-fetched: it is an attempt to make sense of what another person meant or intended when they gave information. 'Exactly what did they mean when they said that?' is the question being answered. For example, a paediatrician may refer a family without directly alluding to possible abuse, while nevertheless noting the explanation given by parents for, say, some bruising to the head of their child. The referral itself might be interpreted by the social worker to indicate that the paediatrician was suspicious, and that it was the social worker's task to explore matters further. If that point was not noted in the referral, then this idea that the paediatrician was 'suspicious' would be a hypothesis, one about what the consultant was actually thinking.

## Speculative hypotheses

The third group of hypotheses is speculative or forward looking. Here social workers do not simply rely on information before them, or inferences from that information, but imagine the possibilities and consequences of those possibilities. They consider possible actions they might undertake in response to the situation, which are characterized by what we might call 'if…then' statements (*if* I did this, *then* that would be the consequence).

One form of speculative hypothesis is the *Intervention Hypothesis*, which refers to the actions a social worker might undertake in relation to a problem, and what the outcome would be. There can be considerable variation in the complexity of these intervention hypotheses. We might come across a case where a teenager is apparently manifesting challenging behaviour to his father. If, for example, his mother died when he was young and he had received no counselling, we may hypothesize an unresolved grief reaction which would require therapy. The 'if…then' here is if he receives appropriate grief counselling, then his challenging behaviour will diminish.

*Procedural hypotheses* are another form of speculative hypotheses. These focus on procedures which may need to be invoked. These can involve, for example, strategy meetings, child assessment orders, child protection case conferences and so on. These are again 'if…then' statements (if we fail to get a satisfactory explanation for the bruising then we will need to call a case conference). These, in some respects, are straightforward, in that they are invoking established procedures. However, behind them appropriate judgement is required, so that what exactly constitutes an unsatisfactory explanation is clear, as are the circumstances under which a conference would be called.

*Client behaviour hypotheses* constitute a third group of speculative hypotheses. Here the social worker speculates about a client's behaviour, including how he or she will behave in particular situations. These are perhaps the most complex hypotheses, because they involve not considering your own actions as social worker (as with, for example, intervention hypotheses) but the likely actions of someone else. These hypotheses often involve active empathy on the part of the social worker in the attempt to answer the question: what is the client likely to do in a particular circumstance? This is not simply intuitive; it requires a clear appreciation of the client's circumstances. This kind of thing goes on all the time. How will the parents react if we move to a child protection conference? How will they react if I challenge them over some behaviour? Should I attempt to be sympathetic towards a situation I know not to be good in the long run, in order to enable the client to feel understood, and so I may influence him or her better in the future? If we placed a child in foster placement A, would he or she be likely to respond positively? And so on.

## Rules

It is all very well our discussing abstract notions such as critical appraisal and hypothesis generation. These clearly result from cognitive (thinking) processes undertaken by social workers, and are central to the practical enquiring mind which is required to carry out social work assessments. They reflect, at least in part, the reflexive orientation of social work practitioners. However, how do these thinking processes connect with the actual substance of practice? With the observations on cases made by social workers, the application (when it occurs) of knowledge? How do the hypotheses, in other words, connect with the content of the hypotheses – what they are about?

It is now apparent that social workers employ background rules which are, so to speak, available for them to refer to in any situation. What seems to occur is that social workers have a vast range of rules which help them to explain social life. They do not necessarily consciously think of them as rules, but they bring them to bear when confronting the range of situations characteristic of social work. The rules, which are descriptive, represent background 'knowledge' about the ways in which social situations work.

What does this mean in real terms? Well, the kind of rule we are talking about might be: 'Behavioural problems in children are (or can be) the result of inadequate bonding with an (adult) attachment figure.' Now this is not the only kind of rule which can operate. Another might be: 'Teenagers tend to be more difficult and behavioural problems can be the result of their life stage.' Both these rules relate to behavioural problems, but they are not necessarily consistent with each other. Indeed, they can be different or contradictory. This does not matter, because the social worker is calling upon a range of alternative background rules which may be applied to a situation where there are child behaviour problems. The key is the 'adequacy of fit' between the rule being used and the situation confronted. Taking the two rules we have mentioned, it would be a matter of sorting out which of the two was most consistent with the client's circumstances.

These background rules become activated by facets of the case identified by the social worker, which we have earlier referred to as the result of 'focused attention'. A case, therefore, which involved child behaviour problems might then invoke, for example, the 'grief reaction' hypothesis (identified above in the case of the teenager), as well as, indeed, other possible hypotheses. As applied to the particular case, the rules provide the substantive content out of which hypotheses about the case emerge.

## Substantive rules

Social workers actually employ a number of different types of rules. Substantive rules are rules that are used by social workers to enable them to make sense of cases or understand particular facets of them – where, for example, they identify, say in supervision, what they consider to be salient aspects of a case. Some of these reflect views which are widely held, and not confined to social work as a profession. This is the case where, for example, a 'generation gap' might be invoked as an explanation for troubles between a young person and their parent. That kind of rule might be more precisely expressed as: 'A wide age gap can cause difficulties in parent–child relationships.' The same kind of rule can emerge where a parent is young and considered likely, because of their age, to make mistakes: 'Young people, because of their youth and inexperience, can be poor parents.' Where such features as young parenthood or age gap are observed, these rules enable the social worker to interpret the situation, and indeed, characteristically develop hypotheses about the case.

The 'can' in the statements is significant. It is important to appreciate that rules are not hard and fast, but represent possibilities in relevant situations. What social workers are looking for is a 'fit' between the rule and the situation they are confronting. However, there is generally more than one possible rule which can be relevant to a particular situation. The statements can be no more than probabilistic, and this underlies the tentativeness with which such statements must often be made. There may be some 'firming up' when information is gathered which confirms or disconfirms the hypothesis, but the hypothesis must always be provisional, because it is always possible that it could turn out to be wrong.

## Application rules

Application rules are rules about the way in which knowledge or experience should be applied. They are, in effect, rules about the way substantive rules should be applied. Social workers may be more or less tentative in the way they apply substantive rules, dependent, to a considerable degree, on the comprehensiveness of the information they have before them (as well as their opportunity to consider and synthesize that information). However, tentativeness also reflects the social world. Where humans are able to make their own decisions and take their own actions – and this of course extends to clients – such tentativeness is well founded, because an individual's actions can always confound any predictions or observations made by social workers. Any substantive rule applied, no matter how confident the social worker is in applying it, can only ever be probabilistic.

One general way in which application rules are utilized by social workers is in relation to how they should look at and in particular weigh up the evidence. When they do this, social workers are looking at different facets of a case, but also operating with a rule: 'Do not use the information uncritically.' This can be the case, for example, when using checklists or indicators of child abuse. It is, social workers understand, no use simply applying such checklists to particular situations. They need to be aware of the limits to the checklists and the particular and unique nature of the situations with which they are dealing.

Another application rule relates to self-awareness, an important part of the reflexivity adopted by social workers. Here the social worker seeks to be aware of his or her self and motivations. An example of this might relate to the issue of race. Here, if a white social worker were working with a black family the social worker might – as some certainly do – need to consider where he or she was coming from and any racism he or she manifested. Clearly, if the social worker were influenced by racist views, this could affect the assessment of the case. Here, the rule would be: 'Be aware of your own potential for racism when making assessments of black families.'

Other application rules can be more specific. Just as social workers would seek to be aware of their own motivation when making assessments, so they may need to be aware of the motivations of referrers. Again using the example of a black family in a predominantly white area, it is important to be aware that a referral might be more than it at first appears. The referral might reflect the racist perspectives of the referrer, or even just an insular ethnocentrism which leads to the referrers misunderstanding the behaviours of a black family. Many social workers, furthermore, are aware that, in general, child protection referrals can be made, from time to time, for malicious reasons, rather than because of a real concern for the welfare of children. Such referrals are at times made when divorce proceedings, including those relating to the child's residence, are being considered. A rule in this case might be: 'Referrers can have a malicious intent when making child protection referrals during divorce proceedings.'

## Rules and formal knowledge

Rules, as we have seen can involve elements which are not necessarily confined to social workers, i.e. they do not simply reflect professional knowledge. The notion that problems can emerge in a family where the generation gap is wide, for example, is not one confined to social workers alone. The origin of these rules may be in life experience or the perceptions that are held by people in particular groups or cultures. Where the rules are more specific to social work they might emerge from practice experience. However, they are also important in relation to formal knowledge, the kind of knowledge which has been researched, written down and applied to practice. Rules, or the use of rules, are a central feature in the way social workers are able to translate generalised knowledge and ideas to the specifics of the individual case. If we were to ask: what is the process by which social workers are able to relate formal knowledge to practice? – or more precisely, to integrate them – then it is the use of rules which helps us to understand this process. Essentially, where remembered, knowledge is formulated in the form of rules, which are then available and can emerge when relevant, and identified as such by the social worker, to a practice situation.

Social workers tend not to overtly identify knowledge in relation to their practice, although at times it is implicit in their assessments and actions. Where it does emerge, it does so in the context of rules. For example, a social worker may be aware that some sex offenders are interested in both sexes rather than confining themselves to one. When used to understand a situation where sex abuse may have occurred, they would have a rule such as: 'Sex offenders do not have an exclusive preference on the basis of sex in their choice of victims.' Another issue may be about the cycle of abuse. Here social workers may consider abuse to be more likely where the perpetrator was themselves abused as a child. The rule here would be: 'If someone is abused in their childhood, they may go on as adult to abuse children themselves.'

Another area in which formal knowledge may play a part is in the use of 'technical language'. In social work the main sources of technical language are concepts from the social sciences. These concepts are important because they 'give form' to what would otherwise be vaguely understood ideas about the way the social world operates. A term like 'expressed emotion', when used in relation to schizophrenia, provides a way of looking at this mental health problem which would not be possible without awareness of this issue. In the case of expressed emotion, research on intervention provides us with guidance as to effective practice. Concepts provide a basis on which to give meaning to – to make sense of – particular situations.

It is worth remembering, of course, that concepts from social science often find their way into general (lay) use of language. Notions, for example, 'networking', are used frequently to describe the social or professional behaviour of individuals, and such language use does not require a social science degree. Nevertheless, technical language is widely used by social workers and is incorporated into their accounts of practice. Such language, therefore, helps form the substantive content of the hypotheses that they generate. When discussing cases, they use a wide range of technical language. Examples include labelling, support (systems and structures), rejection, (low) self-esteem, depression, genogramme, scapegoating, reconstituted family, stereotyping, statementing, gender (as opposed to sex), internalizing (external rejection), extended family, paranoia, learned response, (psychological) defensive/defences, challenging behaviour, rigid behaviour/parenting and so on. Of course, one issue will always be the extent to which such terms are used correctly, and in general it would appear social workers were fairly accurate in the use of such language. Indeed, it may not so much be in the employment of one or two terms through which social work expert use of language is identifiable, but in the range of terms being used.

## Final comments

After Schon (1991a, 1991b), we used to talk of 'reflective practice'. In social work, from 1995 onwards, this was increasingly replaced by the idea of 'reflexive practice' as outlined above. More recently, through a series of empirical research studies, we have begun to identify the mental processes undertaken in order to be reflexive. These mental processes, so far as we understand them, have been outlined in this paper.

As we understand more – and this can only occur through a retroductive combination of theory and empirical research – we are able to delineate more clearly these mental processes. Once overtly identified, they can become a form of knowledge – *process knowledge*. We are able to pass on this knowledge and help students and practitioners become better in its use. Thus, by developing notions of focused attention, querying information, information evaluation, whole case, partial case and speculative hypotheses, as well as various forms of rules, we can actually teach students how to think rigorously about their practice.

Process knowledge is the new paradigm of knowledge in social work, and is absolutely crucial in identifying components of rigorous practice. It is central to assessment, and enables us to consider how formal (product) knowledge may be used for practice, as well as the ways in which life experience, practice experience and wisdom may be synthesized by the social worker.

## References

Gambrill, E. (1997) *Social Work Practice: A Critical Thinker's Guide.* Oxford: Oxford University Press.

Schon, D. (1991a) *The Reflective Practitioner.* 2nd edn. Aldershot: Arena.

Schon, D. (1991b) *Educating the Reflective Practitioner.* Oxford: Jossey Bass.

Sheppard, M. (1995a) *Care Management and the New Social Work.* London: Whiting and Birch.

Sheppard, M. (1995b) 'Social work, social science and practice wisdom.' *British Journal of Social Work 25,* 265–93.

Sheppard, M. (1998) 'Practice validity, reflexivity and knowledge for social work.' *British Journal of Social Work 28,* 763–81.

## Further reading

Cooper, B. (2001) 'Constructivism in social work: Towards a participative practice viability.' *British Journal of Social Work 31,* 5, 721–38.

Houston, S. (2001) 'Beyond social constructioniam: Critical realism and social work.' *British Journal of Social Work 31,* 845–62.

Sheppard, M., Newstead, S., DiCaccavo, A. and Ryan, K. (2000) 'Reflexivity, process knowledge and the intellectual imagination: A classification and empirical study.' *British Journal of Social Work 30,* 465–88.

Sheppard, M., Newstead, S., DiCaccavo, A. and Ryan, K. (2001) 'Comparative hypothesis assessment and quasi triangulation as process knowledge assessment strategies in social work practice.' *British Journal of Social Work 31,* 6, 863–87.

Sheppard, M. and Ryan, K (2003) 'Practitioners as rule using analysts: A further development of process knowledge in social work.' *British Journal of Social Work 33,* 2, 157–77.

White, S. (1997) 'Beyond retroduction? Hermaneutics, reflexivity and social work practice.' *British Journal of Social Work 27,* 5, 739–53.

Taylor, C. and White, S. (2001) 'Knowledge, truth and reflexivity: The problem of judgement in social work.' *Journal of Social Work 1,* 1, 37–61.

## CHAPTER 10

# ASSESSMENT IN CRIMINAL JUSTICE

*Gill McIvor*

## Introduction

The focus of this chapter is assessment in criminal justice and, more specifically, the content and purpose of assessments undertaken by probation officers (in England and Wales) and criminal justice social workers (in Scotland). In England and Wales major changes to the professional training of probation officers were introduced in the latter part of the 1990s with the ending of social work training as a qualifying route for probation officers and its replacement by an academic degree and linked vocational qualification. Under the new arrangements, practice development assessors have a key role in assessing and supporting probation trainees (Knight and Ward 2001). In Scotland social work with offenders has developed as a specialist area of practice since the introduction of central government funding and associated National Objectives and Standards in 1991 (Social Work Services Group 1991). However, it remains firmly embedded within generic pre-qualifying training.

As this chapter will demonstrate, despite important changes in the organization of probation services,[1] in the context in which services are provided and in the nature of the work undertaken, assessment remains a core task for probation officers.[2] As Boswell concluded from her study of the knowledge, skills and qualities required of probation officers: 'The process of assessment, whether for report-writing or record-keeping purposes, measuring progress or needs, or considering action and outcomes, constitutes one of the major tasks of the probation service' (Boswell 1996, p.39).

Similarly, the probation inspectorate for England and Wales (Her Majesty's Inspectorate of Probation (HMIP)) observed in their introduction to a thematic inspection of offender assessment and supervision in 1999 that 'good offender assessment and clear supervision plans are the building blocks for effective practice' (HMIP 1999, p.3) while Aubrey and Hough (1997, p.1) have argued that 'identifying the nature of offenders' problems or needs and assessing whether these are related to the offending are pivotal tasks in probation supervision'.

Although it is not possible to avoid reference to risk assessment in this chapter, given its increasing prominence in criminal justice assessment, the chapter focuses upon assessment within probation practice in a broad sense. A more detailed consideration of risk assessment and associated issues is provided in Chapter 11 in the present volume.

## Assessment in criminal justice: a brief historical overview

Historically, assessment in probation has been most closely associated with the preparation of reports to the courts, the purpose of which has changed over the last century. Smith (1996) provides a useful analysis of the development and changing focus of court reports. He describes how, in the early part of the twentieth century, probation officers' reports to the courts took the form of pleas in mitigation. However, with the increasing emphasis in social work on social diagnosis, supported by the ascendancy of scientific theories and research, the focus of reports shifted towards diagnosis to assist the court in determining the most appropriate disposal for the offender. The role of assessments in providing social diagnosis and prognosis was formalized by the Streatfeild and Morrison reports in 1961 and 1962 respectively. The function of Social Inquiry Reports[3] (court reports), according to Streatfeild, was to provide three types of information which it was assumed were readily available:

(a) information about the social and domestic background of the offender which is relevant to the court's assessment of his culpability

(b) information about the offender and his surroundings which is relevant to the court's consideration of how his criminal career might be checked

(c) an opinion as to the likely effect on the offender's criminal career of probation or some other specified form of sentence.

(Home Office 1961: para 335, quoted in Smith 1996, p.136)

Arguably the Streatfeild Report in particular defined the purpose of Social Inquiry Reports for the next two decades. However, during this time the quality of reports came under growing criticism with probation officers 'increasingly criticised for making personal moral judgements in the guise of professional assessments and of contributing to erratic and discriminatory sentencing' (Worrall 1997, pp.80–81). Although the impact of reports on sentencing outcomes has been a topic of considerable debate (and arguably remains unresolved),[4] subsequent evidence has emerged to suggest that the *quality* of reports may have a bearing upon whether a custodial or non-custodial sentence is imposed (Gelsthorpe and Raynor 1995).

During the 1980s and 1990s successive legislative and policy developments in England and Wales encouraged an increasing focus on the *offence* rather than the *offender*. In the first instance, this reflected a growing disenchantment with the treatment-focused, rehabilitative orientation of probation practice and a concomitant shift in emphasis towards gatekeeping and system change, the latter being supported by the Home Office's first *Statement of National Objectives and Priorities for the Probation Service* (Home Office 1984). Subsequent policy documents highlighted a key role for the probation service in helping to reduce the use of custodial sentences, while the Criminal Justice Act 1991 proscribed the circumstances in which the courts were required to consider Social Inquiry Reports (which the legislation also renamed Pre Sentence Reports) before passing sentence. This Act also heralded a shift in sentencing practice towards 'just deserts' in which the seriousness of the offence and the harm perpetrated by it were to be given greater consideration than the offender's previous criminal behaviour. However, Worrall (1997) has argued that the origins of courts reports 'are clearly rooted in the

rehabilitative individualized approach to sentencing which emphasises personal histories and circumstances and it has not been easy to adapt them to a "just deserts" approach
which focused more on the offence than the offender' (p.79).

Although, as Worrall (1997) has indicated, the concept of risk in the context of reports to the courts was first alluded to by Curnock and Hardiker (1979) in arguing that
reports should balance the risk posed with the offender's need and available resources, it
became an increasingly prominent focus of probation reports and probation practice
during the 1990s. This coincided with a re-emerging interest in the capacity for probation intervention to impact positively on offenders' behaviour (subsequently redefined
as 'what works' or 'effective practice') alongside research findings that suggested that the
intensity of services provided to probationers should be related to the risk that they
would re-offend (otherwise referred to as the 'risk principle' (see, for example, Chapman
and Hough 1998)).

As Aubrey and Hough (1997) observed, existing National Standards for Pre Sentence Reports in England and Wales at that time (Home Office 1995) stipulated that
probation officers should undertake a thorough *needs* assessment when preparing Pre
Sentence Reports and developing supervision plans for probationers.[5] By 2002, the
National Standards required that Pre Sentence Reports explicitly identified the risk of
re-offending, risk of serious harm to the public and risk of self-harm and included attention to factors relevant to achieving an understanding of the offence (Home Office
2002). The significance of risk in respect of report-writing practice is further underlined
in the most recent version of the National Standards in which whether or not a full
assessment is required is determined by a calculation of the risk of reconviction and an
initial screening of the risk of harm (Home Office 2005).

Therefore whilst ostensibly having the potential to serve as a mechanism for limiting
intervention by the state, adoption of the risk principle in probation policy and practice
(accompanied by parallel concerns about the effective management of serious and
violent offenders) instead brought about a subtle shift from *needs* to *risks* as the basis for
assessment and intervention, resulting in what Smith (2004) has argued has been the
most important change in the work of the probation service over the last decade.

In Scotland, the focus and purpose of probation has also changed over the last 100
years from punishment to supervision to treatment to welfare and, more recently, to
public protection (McNeill 2005). As in England and Wales, this has had an important
influence on the content and purpose of Social Enquiry Reports (SERs). For example, although the most recent National Standards for Social Enquiry Reports describe the purpose of reports as being to 'provide the court with information and advice they need in
deciding on the most appropriate way to deal with offenders' (Scottish Executive 2003,
para 1.5) this includes 'assessing the risk of re-offending, and in more serious cases the
risk of possible harm to others...[and] requires an investigation of offending behaviour
and of the offender's circumstances, attitudes and motivation to change' (Scottish
Executive 2003, para 1.6). Here, then, as in the rest of the UK, assessment practice is
increasingly driven by concerns about risk and, as in England and Wales, this has had
important implications for the focus of assessments and manner in which they are
undertaken.

## The development and use of structured approaches to assessment

As the previous discussion indicates, the focus of offender assessment in probation and criminal justice social work has changed over time. This has been accompanied by a change in the methods used in probation assessments that can be broadly defined as a shift from unstructured practice underpinned by professional judgement to increased structure and consistency through the use of standardized tools (Robinson and Dignan 2004). The increasing use of structured approaches to assessment – and, in particular, the use of actuarial methods for the assessment of risk – reflects the growing influence of managerialism and 'actuarial justice' (Feeley and Simon 1994) upon probation practice.

The initial focus of actuarial tools – reflecting the objectives of probation practice at the time – was on predicting the likelihood of a custodial sentence being imposed by the courts as a means of assisting practitioners to identify those offenders for whom alternatives to imprisonment should be considered. In Scotland, for example, the *National Objectives and Standards for Social Work Services to the Criminal Justice System* (Social Work Services Group 1991) provided detailed guidance on the appropriate content of reports and encouraged social workers to target community-based social work disposals upon offenders who would otherwise be at risk of receiving a sentence of imprisonment. A standardized instrument for measuring risk of custody – the Dunscore – was developed in the early 1990s for use in the Scottish context (Creamer *et al.* 1993). Similarly, in England and Wales, the development of a risk of custody assessment tool (Bale 1987) was consistent with Home Office policy to reduce the unnecessary use of imprisonment by diverting from custody those offenders for whom a community-based disposal might suffice (Home Office 1990).

During the 1990s, however, with an increasing emphasis upon effective practice and increasing policy preoccupation with public protection, the emphasis shifted from assessing risk of custody to assessing the risk of reconviction and the risk of harm. Some assessment tools – such as the Offender Group Reconviction Score (OGRS) (Copas 1995) that predicted the percentage likelihood of being reconvicted – were based purely upon static historical data (such as sex, age, number of previous convictions, etc.). Stephens and Brown (2001) have criticized OGRS2 (the revised version of the original tool) on a number of grounds, not least because it is based entirely on 'static' variables despite growing evidence that social factors (or 'dynamic' variables) can have an impact on the risk of re-offending. They also argued that by predicting reconviction, OGRS2 underestimates the risk of re-offending, especially in relation to crimes that tend to be under-reported to the police. Moreover, and this is a criticism that can be applied to actuarial predictors more generally, OGRS2 predicts the likely reconviction rate among a group of 'similar' offenders, but it cannot specify *which* individuals will re-offend. Despite the apparent 'objectivity' of OGRS2, Stephens and Brown found wide variations in probation officers' calculation of OGRS2 using Police National Conviction data. The most common 'mistakes' included the miscalculation of the offenders' ages and the exaggeration of previous criminal history by basing the calculation on offences rather than convictions (which may include several offences).

Subsequent assessment tools have become more sophisticated and include a structured assessment of the offender's circumstances and needs. The first tool of this kind to be widely used in England and Wales and in Scotland was the Level of Service Inventory – Revised (LSI-R) that had been developed in Canada and adapted for use in the UK context (Andrews and Bonta 1995). The development of needs/risk assessment tools such as the LSI-R drew upon accumulating evidence about which factors are most strongly related to an increased likelihood of recidivism (also referred to as 'criminogenic needs'). Aubrey and Hough (1997), in a review of existing probation practice, concluded that needs assessment tools could improve and maintain the quality and consistency of assessment, assist in the allocation of resources, document the needs of offenders subject to supervision and assess the effectiveness of supervision in addressing/reducing offenders' needs. In short, needs assessment was linked to problem identification, intervention planning, service development and outcome measurement.

LSI-R could be regarded as an improvement upon tools that were based solely upon static factors because in theory it could assist in identifying areas upon which subsequent intervention might focus and it was valued by practitioners because of its relative ease of administration. As its use by probation officers and social workers grew and as structured assessments became recognized as an important component of probation practice (for various reasons including their ability to underpin defensible decisions – see Chapter 11 in the present volume) so were other assessment tools developed in the UK. In Scotland, for example, the Social Work Services Inspectorate developed the Risk Assessment Guidance and Framework (RAGF), which is a structured tool combining actuarial indicators with clinical or professional judgements. It incorporated assessments of risk of re-offending, criminogenic need and risk of harm. The RAGF used the same predictive factors as OGRS2 but there was no algorithm to determine precise levels of risk and judgements were made using 'high', 'medium' or 'low' descriptions (Social Work Services Inspectorate 2000). Practitioners who had used the RAGF regarded its ability to identify risk of harm, its ease of use, its compatibility with other risk assessment procedures and its ability to predict violent offending as strengths. It was also viewed by social workers as assisting professional judgements of risk and encouraging a more structured approach to assessment and case planning. On the other hand, its predictive ability was not known and it was regarded by some practitioners as too time consuming to complete and insufficiently objective (McIvor and Kemshall 2002).

ACE (Assessment, Case Recording and Evaluation System) was developed by researchers at the University of Oxford in conjunction with Warwickshire Probation Service (Roberts et al. 1996). Its aim was to improve the quality of reports to the courts and to enhance the consistency and quality of assessment practice. It focused on both static factors and on other social and personal variables known to be associated with offending and included a section on offender self assessment, thereby enabling offenders to contribute directly to the assessment process. ACE was intended to enable probation officers to identify and prioritize 'criminogenic' needs (that is, needs that are directly related to the individual's offending) and to link offenders to appropriate interventions. It was also developed to serve as a case recording instrument and to facilitate – through repeated administration – the monitoring of offenders' progress over the course of supervision. Gibbs (1999), in a survey of staff trained in the use of ACE, found that it had generally achieved its aims and was easy to incorporate into practice. However, she also found that some staff were resistant to its use on the grounds that it allowed them less autonomy and could be 'de-skilling'. Robinson (2003) found that probation officers also regarded the LSI-R as de-skilling, eroding professional discretion and contributing to de-professionalization through reducing the amount of 'indeterminancy' in probation practice. To compensate for this, some probation officers portrayed the LSI-R as a reflection of their own assessment rather than an alternative to it or emphasized the importance of professional judgement in completing the LSI-R.

A comparison of the predictive capacity of LSI-R and ACE (Raynor *et al.* 2000) concluded that both were reasonably effective in assessing needs and evaluating the effectiveness of probation practice, though ACE was slightly more effective at measuring change over time because it contained a larger number of dynamic items. Aye Maung and Hammond (2000) found that ACE was more likely than LSI-R to be viewed by probation officers as assisting in the preparation of Pre Sentence Reports and contributing to the development of supervision plans, though ACE was more often regarded as burdensome and repetitive to administer and neither tool was considered to be very good at predicting the risk of harm. A fuller discussion of the relative merits of these tools and OASys (see below) is provided by Merrington (2004).

Similar developments with respect to the development and use of risk assessment tools have been taking place in the youth justice setting. The Youth Justice Board (2004) has emphasized the multifaceted nature of assessment as a mechanism for identifying needs, understanding the young person's offending and planning interventions to meet those needs, and has also stressed the importance of involving the young person and, where appropriate, his or her parents or carers in the assessment process. A version of the LSI-R – the Youth Level of Service/Case Management Instrument (YLS/CMI) – has been developed for use with young offenders under 18 years of age. However, another tool – Asset – was developed for the Youth Justice Board by the Probation Studies Unit at the University of Oxford, drawing upon their prior experience of developing ACE, and it is now more widely used than the YLS/CMI. Asset consists of a core profile that focuses upon static and dynamic factors linked to offending, an offender self-assessment form and a risk of serious harm assessment (to be completed in relevant cases). It is intended for use with young offenders aged between 10 and 17 years and, according to the Youth Justice Board National Standards (Youth Justice Board 2000), should be completed both at the beginning and end of intervention, to enable an assessment to be made of change over time (Baker 2004). Asset is now used by all Youth Offending Teams in England and Wales and by an increasing number of practitioners in Scotland (Baker 2004), though further information about its predictive accuracy is required.

## OASYS

The most significant advance in offender assessment in England and Wales in recent years has been the development by the Home Office of a common assessment tool for use by the probation and prison services. The development of the Offender Assessment System (OASys) began in 1998, it was first used in 2001 and by 2003 it was universally implemented in probation areas (Merrington (2004). However, its introduction across the prison estate has taken longer to achieve. OASys, as the probation inspectorate

(HMIP 2005, p.8) have indicated, 'was designed to support, and to be a crucial component of, the overarching "what works" strategy that placed prime importance on the assessment of offenders and the consequent targeting of interventions'.

OASys is intended for use with offenders aged 18 years and older (with Asset being appropriate for younger offenders). Sharing many features in common with earlier tools (such as ACE) it includes an assessment of risk of reconviction, risk of serious harm and needs linked to offending. The incorporation of a supervision or sentence plan enables change to be measured over time while an offender self-assessment can assist staff in assessing the offender's motivation and likely response to interventions, refine the risk analysis and track changes over time. Risk of reconviction and needs assessments are based on a combination of static and dynamic (social and personal) factors. Completion of an OASys assessment triggers further specialist assessments as required (for example, basic skills, violence or substance misuse) and can point to the relevance of specific interventions. By highlighting unmet needs and identifying gaps in the range of available interventions it may also assist in resource planning and allocation.

Initially OASys was paper-based but an electronic version was subsequently developed. Its functions and the contexts in which it should be used have been proscribed in a series of Home Office circulars. Home Office Guidance indicates that an OASys assessment should be undertaken for all 'standard delivery' Pre Sentence Reports, all community penalties imposed, residents of approved probation premises, adults serving six months or more in custody, young offenders serving one month or more in custody and those released from prison on licence (National Probation Service 2005). Courts in England and Wales now have an option of requesting either a 'fast delivery' or 'standard delivery' PSR based on the seriousness of the offence. The former should be completed within five working days using OGRS and the OASys risk of harm screening tool while the latter will involve a longer adjournment for a full OASys assessment.

A probation inspection published in 2005 reported that probation areas had made significant progress in implementing OASys though a number of shortcomings were also identified. For example, it was postulated that the setting of targets for completion of OASys assessments may have been at the expense of their quality, both at the assessment stage and throughout the supervision process. Although assessments took, on average, two hours to complete, this was not regarded by the inspectors as overly resource intensive 'given the importance of accurate and thorough assessment and planning, especially at the start of supervision' (HMIP 2005, p.11).

Since the Criminal Justice Act 1991, probation officers in England and Wales have been required to pay increasing attention to the risk of harm presented by the offender when undertaking assessments. Powis (2002, p.1) defines 'risk of serious harm' as 'offenders' risk of causing serious harm either to themselves or others'. OASys and ACE (and, in Scotland, the Risk Assessment Guidance and Framework developed by the Scottish Executive) incorporate an assessment of risk of harm. However a thematic inspection of practice in England and Wales (HMIP 2005) concluded that staff tended to regard risk of harm in OASys as an add-on to the assessment rather than being a central component and expressed concern about the quality of risk of harm screenings undertaken at court for 'fast delivery' reports because they lacked consideration of the wider range of issues that would have been identified though a full OASys assessment.

## The limitations of structured assessments

The development of actuarial assessment tools can be regarded as a manifestation of managerialism in probation which is also linked to increasingly close cooperation between different criminal justice agencies (Robinson and Dignan 2004). This is particularly evident in relation to sexual offending where formal arrangements have been instituted in England and Wales for multiprofessional assessment and management of offenders. However, Horsefield (2003) has argued that tools incorporating dynamic factors may serve more to support organizational claims that public protection is being addressed than to provide a substantively better predictor of risk.

Writing from a North American perspective, Silver and Miller (2002) have argued that actuarial assessment tools tend to facilitate resource management rather than a response to need. In other words, assessments become resource led rather than needs led. Like other commentators (e.g. Creamer and Williams 1996), Silver and Miller suggest that group-based methods of assessment and predication can further discriminate against already marginalized and stigmatized groups:

> As a social science practice, actuarial risk assessment assists in legitimating the involuntary detention of groups of individuals not for something they have done wrong but for something it is estimated they might do based on the previous behaviour of the group with which they are statistically associated. (Silver and Miller 2002, pp.155–6)

Bhui (1999) has argued that risk assessments, because they are based on data (such as police data) that reflect discriminatory processes in wider society, can disadvantage black offenders and cautions that while actuarial methods may play a useful role as a precursor to informed clinical assessment, 'practitioners must guard against…the illusion of clarity which such tools can give' (p.177).

More generally, concerns have been expressed about the applicability of standardized risk assessment tools for certain groups of offenders. For example Gibbs (1999) found that some probation officers believed that ACE was limited in its usefulness with some offenders, for whom more specialist assessment tools were required, while Aye Maung and Hammond (2002) observed that both ACE and LSI-R were not regarded as suitable for all groups of offenders. Similarly, a survey of social workers in Scotland found that generic tools such as the LSI-R were regarded as less suitable for young offenders, women, those with mental health problems or perpetrators of domestic abuse (McIvor and Kemshall 2004). Holsinger, Lowenkamp and Latessa (2003) found that Native Americans had higher LSI-R scores than white Americans both overall and in relation to many of the individual domains, while women had lower scores than men in most domains (apart from health/emotional issues and financial issues). Although women's offending tends to be underexplored and less well understood than offending by men, it is now recognized that they are likely to have different 'criminogenic needs' (Hedderman 2004). Risk and needs assessments are likely to be highly gendered because the factors that they incorporate are drawn predominantly from studies of men (Shaw and Hannah-Moffat, 2000, 2004).

At a practical level, Robinson (2003) has argued that studies of structured instruments have highlighted the resource demands associated with gathering the relevant information and completing the associated paperwork, and has suggested that staff need to receive positive reinforcement if their commitment to a particular tool is not to decrease over time (for example, through being able to see how the data thus generated are used to determine service priorities and for the purposes of evaluation and quality assurance). This is likely to be increasingly important as successive generations of risk-needs assessment tools become increasingly sophisticated and, at the same time, more resource-intensive to complete. Merrington (2004, p.67) stresses that 'a balance has to be struck between technical performance and fitness for purpose' while, according to Robinson (2003):

> For designers of risk/needs assessment instruments, achieving a balance between comprehensiveness and user-friendliness has been a significant problem. As prediction and assessment methods have become more sophisticated, so the instruments themselves have tended to become more lengthy and to place ever greater demands on practitioners' time. (p.36)

This may explain why the probation inspectorate (HMIP 1999) found that many officers regarded assessment processes as bureaucratic and mechanical and not well suited to meeting operational needs.

## The advantages of structured approaches to assessments

The introduction of more structured assessment procedures in probation was initially regarded as desirable to increase the consistency and quality of assessments and to promote equity of treatment of offenders. Subsequently, however, the 'what works' initiative encouraged offender assessments to be articulated in terms of risk and criminogenic needs as the basis for resource allocation (Robinson 2003). Despite their limitations, it is now acknowledged that structured approaches to offender assessment can offer certain benefits, though it has been argued that that assessment tools in probation practice should be regarded as assisting a structured assessment rather than as providing a diagnostic function (Aubrey and Hough 1997). Robinson (2003) has also observed that, despite some of the limitations previously discussed, probation officers broadly welcomed the introduction of more structured assessments because they provided them with additional assurances over and above professional judgement and made them feel more secure in the conclusions that they reached.

Robinson (2003) has summarized the benefits of structured assessment tools as follows:

1.  Promote consistency between assessments.

2.  Contribute to improvements in the quality of Pre Sentence Report writing and supervision planning.

3.  By being grounded in relevant 'evidence', enhance the defensibility of assessments and decisions flowing from them.

4.  Predict the risk of reconviction.

5.  Inform decisions about the nature and level of supervision that is appropriate in individual cases.

6.  Provide a basis for measuring the effectiveness of intervention.

7.  Provide managers with information about the nature and extent of offenders' needs at the service level and in so doing inform service development.

Just as the purpose of assessments is wide-ranging, so too does assessment require that probation officers and social workers possess a range of qualities, knowledge and skills. As Boswell (1996, p.40) found, when undertaking assessments practitioners need to 'blend interviewing and diagnostic skills with particular bodies of knowledge' and she emphasizes the importance of verifying and contesting information rather than simply collecting it. It is also important to recognize that while structured approaches may offer certain advantages over unstructured professional judgement (for example, they tend to be more accurate in predicting risk), they cannot replace it.

In addition to identifying the types of intervention that would be appropriate for individual offenders, Furniss, Flaxington and MacDonald (2001) have argued that assessment by the authors of court reports and supervising officers/case managers has a important role to play in motivating offenders and preparing them to participate in programmes. As Robinson (2005) and others (e.g. Burnett and McNeill 2005) have argued, there is a growing body of research evidence that points to the importance of the relationship between the offender and the supervising officer as a vehicle for encouraging and supporting change. Trotter (1999) emphasizes the importance of pro-social modelling as a means of eliciting cooperation by 'involuntary clients' while a meta-analysis by Dowden and Andrews (2004) showed that the quality of interpersonal relationships between offenders and their supervisors was an important element of effective practice. In this regard, Smith (1996) concludes that 'PSRs have been most effective, and have developed in the most positive directions, when their writers have been not only technically competent but also morally engaged' (p.153) while Robinson and Dignan (2004, p.17) have argued that 'offenders cannot be treated solely as actuarial subjects…effective practice requires a "human link"', and Robinson (2005 p.314) has observed 'that neither offenders, nor those who supervise them, are best served by arrangements which limit opportunities for forming working relationships'. In her discussion of the skills required for assessment in probation, Boswell (1996, p.41) concludes that:

> In the assessment process generally…officers…referred to or reiterated… honesty, warmth, intuition (based on life and work experience), risk-taking and acceptance… As they described the place of particular skills, knowledge and qualities in assessment, many officers also explained that the process sometimes required, for its success, the injection of social work methods of intervention.

Despite a redefinition of professional territory having occurred since the late 1990s (Robinson 2005; Robinson and Dignan 2004) in which low-risk offenders are assigned to non professionally qualified staff and increasing use is made of specialist resources to address particular needs, assessment is still regarded as a core probation officer task. That said, there is evidence that in England and Wales supervision became increasingly fragmented in response to organizational changes – essentially a shift from 'generic' to 'specialist' arrangements – occasioned by allocation practices predicated upon risk. The consequence, as Robinson (2005, p.309) has argued, was that 'staff *either* conducted assessments and wrote reports *or* delivered programmes, *or* managed "public protection" (that is, high risk of harm) cases' (original emphasis). Although assessment and report-writing were still regarded as core probation tasks, Robinson found that they were viewed as mundane and de-skilling by probation officers and as contributing to lower levels of job satisfaction compared with other aspects of practice (such as supervising high risk offenders or programme delivery) that were associated with greater prestige. Perhaps this is why recent Home Office sponsored research found that staff were resistant to the re-introduction of generic working and a reduction in the specialist functions of teams in the context of the new arrangements for offender management under the National Offender Management Service (PA Consultancy Group and MORI (2005).

## Assessment, intervention and case management

Assessment in the probation setting is not simply a matter of providing information to the courts to assist sentencing decisions. Good quality assessment is also critical as a means of ensuring that the interventions provided are appropriate to the offender's needs and identifying how motivated offenders are to respond to the services provided (HMIP 1999). As the probation inspectorate (HMIP 1999, p.4) have argued:

> it is reasonable to expect that good assessments form the basis for sensible plans for the supervision of offenders in the community which describe what will happen, how progress will be achieved, and what the outcomes are intended to be.

However, Burnett (1996) found little evidence that the content of supervision and services provided were related to assessed risk and criminogenic needs and the subsequent inspectorate report on assessment found that, while many probation services were using a variety of assessment tools, supervision plans were often of poor quality and did not draw explicitly upon assessments. Assessments were being undertaken, it seemed, as an end in themselves rather than as a basis for making informed judgements for future practice. The report recommended that there should be better integration of information derived from assessments in supervision plans (HMIP 1999).

Of particular concern to the probation inspectorate in a more recent thematic inspection (HMIP 2005) was the finding that 'many still regard OASys completion as an extra bureaucratic task to be completed rather than as a tool to assist in the management of an offender' (p.16). Offenders, it appeared, rarely participated jointly in the production of the supervision plan (despite Trotter's (1999) emphasis on the importance of active client involvement in goal setting to encourage and sustain motivation) and the inspectors concluded that there was increasing scope for OASys data to inform planning and service provision and to measure organisational performance.

Studies elsewhere have also highlighted the limited use made by probation officers of risk-needs assessments to formulate supervision plans and inform the management of offenders. For example, Bonta *et al.* (2004) found that in Manitoba, Canada, actions incorporated in probation action plans were more likely to have been included as a requirement by the court than to have been identified through the assessment of risk and needs. A corollary was that identified criminogenic needs were usually not a focus for intervention and minimal use was made of external recourses to assist in addressing them.

Arguably, a consequence of the fragmentation and loss of continuity that flowed from the increasing specialization of probation functions in England and Wales in the late 1990s was poorly developed case management practice which, in turn, resulted in high levels of attrition from probation groupwork programmes (Robinson and Dignan, 2004). In this respect it is interesting, therefore, to note that the integration of assessment and case management functions under the new arrangements for offender management under the National Offender Management Service appeared to have had the effect of reducing attrition rates before and after sentence (PA Consultancy Group and MORI 2005).

## Conclusion

This chapter has outlined key developments in the assessment of offenders by probation officers and social workers. These developments have been located within wider policy developments that have in part been predicated upon the changing nature of available 'expert knowledge'. While the focus of assessments in criminal justice, their purported purposes and the manner in which they are undertaken has shifted over the last century or so, assessment has remained a core probation task. The increasingly 'scientific' approach to assessment that has emerged in more recent decades offers the potential for assessments to contribute to allocation decisions, intervention planning and practice evaluation to be realized, and for the information derived from assessments to play an increasingly important role in profiling need and service planning. That said, the limitations of actuarial methods need to be recognized (including their potential to inculcate a false sense of 'security' on the part of practitioners and managers) and the role of professional judgement that draws upon relevant knowledge and skills – including skills in engaging and motivating offenders – duly acknowledged.

*Editor's Note*: A more general examination of risk assessment and management follows in the next chapter.

## Notes

1   This includes the creation of the National Probation Service in April 2001 and the more recent establishment in June 2004 of the National Offender Management Service (NOMS) aimed at improved coordination of the prison and probation services. It was established following the recommendations of the Carter report (2003) and subsequent Home Office response (2004).

2   The term 'probation officer' will be used to refer also to criminal justice social workers unless the context indicates otherwise.

3   Called Social Inquiry reports in Scotland.

4   This issue is complicated not least because high levels of convergence between the recommended disposal in reports and the actual sentences imposed may reflect 'second guessing' of the sentencer's intentions by the report author rather than the persuasive capacity of the latter's arguments.

5   National Standards were introduced in England and Wales and in Scotland in the late 1980s/early 1990s. They identify the minimum expected standards of practice in relation, for example, to the frequency of contact with offenders on supervision. In the current context, National Standards identify the areas that practitioners should focus upon when preparing reports for the courts.

# References

Andrews, D.A. and Bonta, J. (1995) *The Level of Service Inventory – Revised Manual.* Toronto: Multi-Health Systems Inc.

Aubrey, R. and Hough, M. (1997) *Assessing Offenders' Needs: Assessment Scales for the Probation Service.* Home Office Research Study 166. London: Home Office.

Aye Maung, N. and Hammond, N. (2000) *Risk of Re-offending and Needs Assessments: The User's Perceptive.* Home Office Research Study 216. London: Home Office.

Baker, K. (2004) 'Is asset really an asset?' In R. Burnett and C. Roberts (eds) *What Works in Probation and Youth Justice: Developing Evidence-based Practice.* Cullompton: Willan.

Bale, D. (1987) 'Uses of the risk of custody scale.' *Probation Journal 34,* 4, 127–31.

Bhui, H. (1999) 'Race, racism and risk assessment: Linking theory to practice with black mentally disordered offenders.' *Probation Journal 46,* 3. 171–81.

Bonta, J., Rugge, T., Sedo, B. and Coles, R. (2004) *Case Management in Manitoba Probation.* Ottawa: Public Safety and Emergency Preparedness Canada.

Boswell, G. (1996) 'The essential skills of probation work.' In T. May and A.A. Vass (eds) *Working with Offenders: Issues, Contexts and Outcomes.* London: Sage.

Burnett, R. (1996) *Fitting Supervision to Offenders: Assessment and Allocation Decisions in the Probation Service.* Home Office Research Study 153, London: Home Office.

Burnett, R. and McNeill, F. (2005) 'The place of the officer–offender relationships in assisting offenders to desist from crime.' *Probation Journal 52,* 3, 221–42.

Carter, P. (2003) *Managing Offenders, Reducing Crime.* London: Prime Minister's Strategy Unit.

Chapman, T. and Hough, M. (1998) *Evidence Based Practice: A Guide to Effective Practice.* London: The Home Office.

Copas, J. (1995) 'On using crime statistics for prediction.' In M. Walker (ed.) *Interpreting Crime Statistics.* Oxford: Clarendon Press.

Creamer, A., Ennis, E. and Williams, B. (1993) *The Dunscore: A Method for Predicting Risk of Custody within the Scottish Context and its Use in Social Enquiry Practice.* Dundee: University of Dundee Department of Social Work.

Creamer, A. and Williams, B. (1996) 'Risk prediction and criminal justice.' In G. McIvor (ed.) *Working with Offenders.* Research Highlights in Social Work 26. London: Jessica Kingsley Publishers.

Curnock, K. and Hardiker, P. (1979) *Towards Practice Theory.* London: Routledge Kegan Paul.

Dowden, C. and Andrews, D. (2004) 'The importance of staff practice on delivering effective correctional treatment: A meta-analysis. *International Journal of Offender Therapy and Comparative Criminology 48,* 203–14.

Feeley, M. and Simon, J. (1994) 'Actuarial justice: The emerging new criminal law.' In D. Nelken (ed.) *The Futures of Criminology.* London: Sage.

Furniss, J., Flaxington, F. and MacDonald, A. (2001) 'The role of audit in the holistic assessment of programme effectiveness.' *Probation Journal 48,* 3, 171–8.

Gelsthorpe, L. and Raynor, P. (1995) 'Quality and effectiveness in probation officers' reports to sentencers.' *British Journal of Criminology 35,* 2, 188–200.

Gibbs, A. (1999) 'The assessment, case management and evaluation system.' *Probation Journal 46,* 3, 182–6.

Hedderman, C. (2004) 'The "criminogenic" needs of women offenders.' in G. McIvor (ed.) *Women who Offend.* Research Highlights in Social Work 44. London: Jessica Kingsley Publishers.

Her Majesty's Inspectorate of Probation (1999) *Offender Assessment and Supervision Planning: Helping to Achieve Effective Intervention with Offenders.* London: HMIP.

Her Majesty's Inspectorate of Probation (2005) *Realising the Potential: A Short Focused Inspection on the Offender Assessment System (OASys).* London: HMIP.

Holsinger, A.M., Lowenkamp, C.T. and Latessa, E.J. (2003) 'Ethnicity, gender and the Level of Service Inventory – Revised.' *Journal of Criminal Justice 31,* 4, 309–20.

Home Office (1984) *Statement of National Objectives and Priorities for the Probation Service.* London: Home Office.

Home Office (1990) *Supervision in the Community: A Framework for Action.* Cmd. 966. London: Home Office.

Home Office (1995) *National Standards for the Supervision of Offenders in the Community.* London: Home Office.

Home Office (2002) *National Standards for the Supervision of Offenders in the Community (Revised).* London: Home Office.

Home Office (2004) *Reducing Crime – Changing Lives: The Government's Plans for Transforming the Management of Offenders.* London: Home Office.

Home Office (2005) *National Standards 2005.* London: Home Office.

Horsefield, A. (2003) 'Risk assessment: Who needs it?' *Probation Journal 50,* 4, 374–9.

Knight, C. and Ward, D. (2001) 'Qualifying probation training: Implications for social work education.' *Social Work Education 20,* 2, 175–86.

McIvor, G. and Kemshall, H. (2002) *Serious Violent and Sexual Offenders: The Use of Risk Assessment Tools in Scotland.* Edinburgh: Scottish Executive Social Research.

McNeill, F. (2005) 'Remembering probation in Scotland.' *Probation Journal 52,* 1, 23–38.

Merrington, S. (2004) 'Assessment tools in probation.' In R. Burnett and C. Roberts (eds) *What Works in Probation and Youth Justice: Developing Evidence-based Practice.* Cullompton: Willan.

Morrison Report (1962) *Report of the Departmental Committee on the Probation Service.* Cmnd. 1650. London: HMSO.

National Probation Service (2005) *National Probation Service Briefing No 26: OASys Information.* London: National Probation Service.

PA Consultancy Group and MORI (2005) *Action Research Study of the Implementation of the National Offender Management Model in the North West Pathfinder.* Home Office Online Report 32/05, London: Home Office.

Powis, B. (2002) *Offenders' Risk of Serious Harm: A Literature Review.* RDS Occasional Paper No 81. London: Home Office.

Raynor, P., Kynch, J., Roberts, C. and Merrington, S. (2000) *Risk and Needs Assessment in Probation Services: An Evaluation.* Home Office Research Study 211, London: Home Office.

Roberts, C., Burnett, R., Kirby, A. and Hamill, H. (1996) *A System for Evaluating Probation Practice.* Probation Studies Unit Report 1. Oxford: University of Oxford Centre for Criminological Research.

Robinson, G. (2003) 'Implementing OASys: Lessons from research into LSI-R and ACE.' *Probation Journal 50,* 1, 30–40.

Robinson, G. (2005) 'What works in offender management?' *The Howard Journal 44,* 3, 307–318.

Robinson, G. and Dignan, J. (2004) 'Sentence management.' In A. Bottoms, S. Rex and G. Robinson (eds) *Alternatives to Prison: Options for an Insecure Society.* Cullompton: Willan.

Scottish Executive (2003) *National Objectives for Social Work Services in the Criminal Justice System: Standards Social Enquiry Reports and Associated Court Services.* Edinburgh: Scottish Executive.

Shaw, M. and Hannah-Moffat, K. (2000) 'Gender, diversity and risk assessment in Canadian Corrections.' *Probation Journal 47,* 3, 163–72.

Shaw, M. and Hannah-Moffat, K. (2004) 'How cogitive skills forgot about gender and diversity.' In G. Mair (ed.) *What Matters in Probation.* Cullompton: Willan.

Silver, E. and Miller, L.L. (2002) 'A cautionary note on the use of actuarial risk assessment tools for social control.' *Crime and Delinquency 48,* 1, 136–61.

Smith, D. (1996) 'Pre-sentence reports.' In T. May and A.A. Vass (eds) *Working with Offenders: Issues, Contexts and Outcomes.* London: Sage.

Smith, D. (2004) 'Probation and social work.' *British Journal of Social Work 35,* 621–37.

Social Work Services Group (1991) *National Objectives and Standards for Social Work Services in the Criminal Justice System.* Edinburgh: The Scottish Office.

Social Work Services Inspectorate (2000) *Risk Assessment Guidance and Framework.* Edinburgh: Scottish Executive.

Stephens, K. and Brown, I. (2001) 'OGRS2 in practice: An elastic ruler.' *Probation Journal 48*, 3, 179–87.

Streatfeild Report (1961) *Report of the Interdepartmental Committee on the Business of the Higher Criminal Court.* Cmnd. 1289. London: HMSO.

Trotter, C. (1999) *Working with Involuntary Clients: A Guide to Practice.* London: Sage.

Youth Justice Board (2000) *National Standards for Youth Justice.* London: Youth Justice Board.

Youth Justice Board (2004) *Assessment, Planning Interventions and Supervision, Key Elements of Effective Practice Edition 1.* London: Youth Justice Board for England and Wales.

Worrall, A. (1997) *Punishment in the Community: The Future of Community Justice.* London: Longman.

# RISK ASSESSMENT AND MANAGEMENT: AN OVERVIEW

## Hazel Kemshall

## Introduction

Risk has become a core feature of late modern life (Beck 1992) and the 'risk industry' is 'big business' (Adams 1995). In this climate, risk, and particularly its accurate and reliable assessment, has gained increased significance in the policy and practice of social care, social work and criminal justice (Kemshall 2002a, 2003; Kemshall *et al.* 1997). The reasons for this are complex,[1] but in short can be attributed to the demise of the welfare state, the 'New Right' reduction of the state from the 1970s onwards, and a shift from what has been termed the 'welfare society' to the 'risk society' (Giddens 1998; Kemshall 2002a). Aharoni (1981) has described the welfare state as a 'no risk' society in which citizens were promised protection from various risks (such as ill-health through national insurance), and the welfare state is epitomized by a collective, social insurance approach to risks in which the citizen can expect the state to provide a safety net. Within this social insurance approach, social work flourished as a key mechanism for tackling personal, family and social ills. Such ills were largely characterized as no fault (Doyal and Gough 1991) and expressed through the language of need, although receipt of such services could be both exclusionary and stigmatizing (Leonard 1997).

Within the risk society protection is only afforded to the citizen in exceptional cases, and welfare is residual rather than universal. Citizens are encouraged to be responsible and self-manage life's risks (Rose 1996), and universal needs are replaced with residual or targeted needs. Jordan (1998) has called this 'the new politics of welfare' in which only genuine needs will be met, and social justice is achieved through the labour market and not through welfarism. Table 11.1 contrasts the key features of the welfare and risk societies.

**Table 11.1 From welfare society to risk society**

| Welfare society | Risk society |
|---|---|
| Universal welfare | Residual welfare |
| Risk protection | Risk promotion |
| Social insurance | Social justice |
| 'No fault' exposure to risk | The 'prudential' citizen |

From Kemshall 2002a, p.40. Reproduced with the kind permission of the Open University Press.

In this climate, preoccupations with need have been increasingly replaced by preoccupations with risk as evidenced by the use of risk in policy documents, practice guidance, rationing strategies and targeting policies (Kemshall *et al.* 1997). While it may be an overstatement to suggest that the language of need has been replaced by the language of risk (Kemshall 2002a), there is extensive evidence that the universalism of need has been replaced by targeted strategies of risk avoidance, prevention and management (Langan 1998; Parton 1994; Parton, Thorpe and Wattam 1997). Risk assessment and risk management are key tasks for practitioners in social care, social work and criminal justice (Kemshall and Pritchard 1996; Parsloe 1999).

Broadly speaking the implications for workers have been:

- The rationing of services on the basis of risk.

- Emphasis upon regulating risky behaviours rather than upon ameliorating need.

- An increasingly compulsory element to service use.

- Risks outweigh rights.

(See Kemshall 2002a)

## What is risk?

Traditionally risk has been defined as the 'chance' or likelihood that a particular behaviour or event will occur. In its original sense in around the sixteenth century, the word 'risk' was value-neutral – it could be something good or bad – but by the latter half of the twentieth century risk had become increasingly associated with events or behaviours carrying negative consequences or impacts. Not withstanding praise and reward for risk-taking behaviours such as entrepreneurship or high risk sports, risk, particularly within health, social work and probation, is usually associated with the assessment of 'bad risks' (e.g. re-offending, harm to self or others, harm to children) and the raison d'être for interventions is risk avoidance, prevention or reduction. Service entitlement is often expressed in terms of risk, and resource allocation is risk-driven (Kemshall 2002a). Conversely, protective factors (often expressed as the inverse of risk factors) can result in de-prioritization, particularly for 'at risk' children. 'Chance' and 'likelihood' have been superseded by formal, often statistically-based calculations of probability (Brearley 1982), or structured assessment tools to guide the assessment activities of practitioners.

Risks across the spectrum of social care and criminal justice can be placed into two general categories:

- those risks which people *pose to others*

- those risks to which people are exposed – better understood as *vulnerability to risk(s).*

### POSING RISKS TO OTHERS
This framing of risk is most common within criminal justice, and to a lesser extent in forensic mental health. In common parlance it is often associated with the assessment of

'dangerousness', and more recently with public protection and the appropriate management of high-risk and high-profile offenders in the community such as sex offenders (Kemshall 2003). The core features of this approach are:

- The person assessed is seen as a poser of risk to others (sometimes vulnerable others such as children).

- Risk is defined as harmful behaviour to others.

- The purpose of risk assessment is to accurately identify risky persons and risky behaviours.

- The purpose of risk management is the reduction or avoidance of risks to others.

- The rights, and to some extent the liberty, of posers of risk can be limited in the interest of protecting others and preventing future risks.

(From Kemshall 2002b, p.124)

## VULNERABILITY TO RISK(S)

Assessing exposure to risk is more common within health, social care and social work, and includes assessing the risk of self-harm. Some of those vulnerable to risk are exposed to the risk presented by others, children, for example, to the abuse of adults, elders to the abuse of carers and so on. The reduction of risks to the one may result in the restriction of rights, liberty and activities of the other, or require the complex balancing of rights and risks. In some cases, vulnerability may result in a person posing risks to others and assessment is not necessarily clear-cut. Mentally ill persons, for example, can be characterized as both 'at risk' and as 'posing a risk' (Kemshall 2002b), with those mentally ill persons who fail to comply with medication regimes more likely to commit homicide and suicide than those who do comply (Boyd Report 1994), and social care deficits to vulnerable mental health users have been implicated in subsequent risk management failures (Blom-Cooper, Hally and Murphy 1995; Sheppard 1995). In such cases there is often significant tension between risks and rights, although policy development in the mental health arena from the late 1990s onwards has tended to favour risk management, public protection and compulsory treatment (Home Office and Department of Health 1999). However, distinguishing between the assessment of risk to others, and the assessment of vulnerability may assist practitioners in carrying out and justifying this delicate balancing act, and in matching interventions to the complex array of vulnerability and risk factors that may be present in any individual case.

The core features of vulnerability assessments are:

- Accurate identification of the risks to which the person is exposed and why.

- The likely impact or consequence(s) of the risks to the person.

- Whether the risks are externally posed, or are endemic to the person and their circumstances.

- Whether the risks are acceptable – those externally posed by others (such as adult offenders to children) are usually less acceptable.

- For risks arising from the person and their situation a key question is whether the risk should be run. What are the costs and benefits of the risk?

- Balancing the desirability of reducing risk against the likely reduction of choice, independence and autonomy of the individual. For example, the reduction of risk for older persons through the use of residential care.

- Risk management strategies are usually characterised by a desire to achieve this balance and to resolve where possible tensions between autonomy, quality of life, rights and risks.

(From Kemshall 2002b)

Vulnerability assessments are also likely to assist those practitioners working with older persons or vulnerable adults, where rights and risks must be balanced, and where intrusions to manage risk effectively often erode or limit both independence and quality of life.

As stated, there are some individuals who fall into both the 'posing a risk' and 'vulnerability' categories. For example, some young offenders will fall into both categories and in Scotland a number of children coming before Children's Panels will require assessments of both vulnerability and risk. The use of the above frameworks can enable practitioners to 'cover all the bases' and ensure that a balanced approach to risk and vulnerability is made in both the interests of the service user and potential victims.

## Risk assessment – key principles and difficulties

The last decade has seen an explosion of formal risk assessment tools and techniques in social care, social work and criminal justice. The purpose of risk assessment in individual cases is to:

- identify the risk of what, to whom, when and why

- specify clearly the behaviour or event of concern

- calculate the likelihood or probability that the risk will occur

- identifying the conditions, circumstances and situations in which the risk might occur

- estimate the likely impact of the risk

- calculate the consequences of the risk and who might be exposed to and harmed by the risk.

(Adapted from Kemshall 2002b)

Practitioners and managers are making risk assessments in a climate of high accountability and blame (Parton 1991), and Carson (1996) has noted that risk assessment is a highly fallible task. It is essential therefore that risk assessment can meet the standards of *defensibility*, or, as Carson puts it, whether a 'responsible body of co-professionals would have made the same decision' (1996, p.4). This is particularly pertinent for those agencies carrying out risk assessments in the public eye and where risk failures present threats to organizational credibility. In these circumstances it is essential that practitioners make *defensible decisions*, that is, decisions that can stand the test of hindsight bias scrutiny when risk failures have occurred. The core components of a defensible decision are that:

* reasonable steps have been taken

* reliable assessment methods have been used

* information is collected and thoroughly evaluated

* decisions are recorded

* staff work within agency policies and procedures

* staff communicate with others and seek information they do not have.

(Kemshall 1998, 2001)

Defensible decisions are also enhanced by the proper use of risk assessment tools with a proven track record of reliability. Inquiries in both mental health and child protection highlight the lack of defensibility at both practitioner and management level, and staff and managers should consider the key components of defensibility as the minimum standards for case work and as an important quality assurance mechanism for ensuring appropriate service delivery on risk.

## RISK ASSESSMENT METHODS

The centrality of risk to much work in health, social work and criminal justice has fuelled extensive research into risk assessment tools and methods. Bonta (1996), for example, has written on the long developmental history of risk assessment tools for offenders, and the constant refinement of such tools in the pursuit of accuracy and reliability. In brief, the clinical and largely subjectively based individualized assessment of professionals has been discredited due to high degrees of human error and fallibility due to bias, faulty decision-making processes and flaws in subjective inference (see Kemshall 2001 for a full review). Actuarial risk assessment, based largely on static risk factors such as age, gender and previous history/behaviour, has a higher success rate and is based upon statistical calculations of probability (for example, as used in the insurance industry, Green 1997). However, by the late 1990s pure actuarialism was itself subject to criticism on the following grounds: statistical fallacy, limitations of the meta-analytic studies it was based upon and low base rates for the most problematic behaviours/risks.

## STATISTICAL FALLACY

In essence, this is the problem of transferring the aggregated risk factors based upon group, statistical information to an individual case. Aggregated reconviction data based upon white, male offenders does not transfer to women or ethnic minority offenders, and risk profiles and circumstances can change over time – hence insurance companies revise their premiums over time. Such probability scores are also limited in actual case application. For example, a 60 per cent score of reconviction after sentence for an offender only means that that particular offender has a six in ten chance of reconvicting, not whether that individual actually will. It still remains a matter of case-by-case judgement to determine whether the offender is likely to be in the 60 per cent reconviction group, or the 40 per cent non-offending group. Most predictive scores cluster at around the 40–60 mark and where chances are almost even. This does not greatly assist practitioners tasked with making difficult decisions about liberty, quality of life, risk of harm or child protection. Where behaviours are less frequent in the population as a whole, such as acts of extreme violence, *the base rate* (that is, the known frequency of the behaviour in the population as a whole) is low, and this again makes prediction very difficult. Transfer to child protection and other social work risks has been problematic because the base rates for the behaviours of concern are low (Corby 1993).

Meta-analysis has been the preferred research methodology for the generation of actuarial risk factors. This is a statistically-based technique that analyses the outcomes of a large body of primary research studies. These outcomes are then aggregated to produce the core factors that have statistical significance for risk prediction (McGuire 1997). However, this approach has been critiqued for its inability to appropriately distinguish between factors and impacts, and a failure to appropriately examine and account for multivariant effects (Copas 1995; Mair 1997).

Despite considerable criticism, actuarial assessment can be used to:

- Establish those risk predictors that have a proven track record (e.g. previous convictions for reoffending).

- Establish the relevant base rate for the behaviour/risk of concern.

- It can increase the accuracy of risk assessment.

- It can increase levels of consistency and reliability across practitioners.

(Adapted from Kemshall 2001, p.16)

Since the late 1990s dynamic risk factors have been seen as crucial to more effective risk assessment (Gendreau, Little and Goggin 1996). As the name implies, dynamic risk factors are those that change over time, are situationally specific and may be amenable to change through treatment or interventions (e.g. drug use). Research does not support their use without static factors, nor should their assessment supplant actuarial assessment. However, dynamic factors are important in establishing treatment/intervention plans, and in focusing scarce resources on what can be changed (Raynor 1999).

More recently greater emphasis has been placed upon the development and use of holistic risk assessment methods, combining static and dynamic factors into structured assessment tools that utilise both actuarial methods and structured interviewing techniques by practitioners. These tools have gained acceptance in work with offenders (see Kemshall 2001 for a review), and to a lesser extent in work in child protection (Adcock 1995; Munro 2002). The actuarial component assists in establishing basic probability information on likely risks, and the structured interviewing aids practitioners in focusing on the right dynamic factors to both refine prediction but also to assist with the formulation of risk management plans, treatment and intervention choices (Raynor 1999). Increasingly these tools adopt a multifactorial approach and practitioners are encouraged to consider a range of risks the potential impacts and consequences of such risks, and the likely outcome of any risk management plans. The approach draws extensively on decision theory and attempts to encourage practitioners to consider a range of possible options in a systematic and evidenced way. This technique has potentially much to offer in the complex world of child protection, and particularly where practitioners must balance vulnerability and harm, risks and rights (see Munro 2002, Chapter 7, for a full discussion). Decision trees allow workers to speculate more rigorously about the outcomes of their decisions on users and others, and to weigh more transparently and empirically the decision choices available to them.

CHOOSING RISK ASSESSMENT TOOLS

Risk assessment tools must aid practitioners to make defensible decisions (Kemshall 1998), and should be chosen for their 'fitness for purpose'. In considering tools, practitioners, managers and policy-makers should have regard for the following key features of tools – these are presented as those which should be considered as *essential* and those considered as *desirable*.

Research indicates that the following are essential features of risk assessment tools:

- The tool must be validated for use against a relevant population.

- The risk factors used in the tool must have a proven track record of reliability and predictability.

- The tool must be able to differentiate between low, medium and high risk.

- The tool must have inter-rater reliability (consistency across users).

- The tool must assist workers to make relevant risk management plans.

The following can be understood as desirable features of risk assessment tools:

- user friendly

- resource lean

- 'easy' for training staff to use appropriately

- transparent and accountable in process of use (particularly important in those cases where assessment decisions are subsequently challenged).

(Adapted from McIvor and Kemshall 2002, p.51)

If workers understand these criteria and how they have been used to select risk assessment tools they are more likely to accept and use them with integrity. They should form the essential rubric by which managers and policy makers choose risk assessment tools.

## Dealing with error

Risk assessment is a highly fallible enterprise, and errors are costly, not only in terms of organisational and practitioner credibility, but also to the victims of such mistakes (Monahan 1993). It is essential that practitioners avoid both overprediction and underprediction. In an arena where the professional and personal stakes are so high it is important that we understand and can avoid error. Moore (1996) helpfully defines error types and their implications (see Table 11.2).

## Table 11.2: Prediction outcomes

| | | Prediction | |
|---|---|---|---|
| O | Yes | A<br>True positive<br>prediction | B<br>False negative<br>prediction |
| U | | | |
| T | | | |
| C | No | C<br>False positive prediction | D<br>True negative prediction |
| O | | | |
| M | | | |
| E | | | |

Reproduced from *Risk Assessment: A Practioner's Guide to Predicting Harmful Behaviour* (Moore, 1996).

Box A and D are correct predictions, that a risk will occur (true positive) or that it will not (true negative). Box B identifies those cases in which a risk is not predicted but does occur, and Box C identifies those cases in which a risk is predicted but does not occur. In Box B the consequences can be severe with victims and members of the public being harmed. Box C cases result in over-intervention, misplaced resources and infringements on individuals' rights and liberties. Perversely, Box B and C errors can be reduced but usually only by transferring errors between them, and not by increasing true positive or true negative predictions. The rate of Box B and C errors is often a matter of what society finds tolerable and acceptable – for example, Box C errors are readily accepted where paedophiles are concerned and the attitude to over-prediction is 'better safe than sorry'. This 'precautionary principle' (Hood and Jones 1996) can be very powerful and leads to net-widening, over-intrusion and defensive (rather than defensible) practice (Kemshall 1998).

Errors can be very costly for practice and for practitioners. Blame is easily allocated, particularly at an individual level, and the spectre of blame can result in risk inflation and overly defensive practice. The latter has serious repercussions for service users as it leads to unnecessary intrusions/interventions/treatments and an erosion of rights, liberties, quality of life and choice.

### SOURCES OF ERROR
There are many sources of error, but they can be broadly categorized under the following headings: human (e.g. bias), organizational (a preference for the precautionary principle in all cases) or methodological (e.g. the statistical fallacy above). The main methodological error sources have been discussed above, and this section will focus on human and organizational sources.

### Human error
Human errors occur for a number of reasons, not least because subjective inference is unreliable and decision-making is based on partial information, such as the self-report of the person whose risk is being assessed (Milner and Campbell 1995). Inappropriate value judgements have also been implicated in false risk assessments, including child protection where 'unreal optimism' about the cooperation of parents and the progress of

children has been misplaced (Beckford Inquiry, London Borough of Brent 1985). Practitioners also prefer to utilize case-based information at the expense of actuarial data or tools (Glaser 1973), resulting in Box B and C errors. Case-based reasoning can also be 'intuitive', but such reasoning is open to the 'confirmatory bias' (only factors that confirm initial beliefs are seen) and can lend itself to a 'creeping determinism'; that is, causal connections between actions and events are imputed where none actually exist (Fischoff 1975). Munro has explored how these factors play a negative role in child protection risk assessments with practitioners failing to revise initial assessments in the light of new information, and where workers are slow to refine their initial views of parents despite signs to the contrary (1999, 2002). Intuitive reasoning is also flawed by discriminatory beliefs and values, and by the personal experiences of the worker (Munro 2002). While intuitive reasoning may positively assist 'practice wisdom' (Schon 1983), it is important that this does not result in short-cut, 'lazy' thinking (Kemshall 1998), but is made explicit and is well grounded in the evidence (Munro 2002). In the event of a risk management failure, how well a practitioner can account for such reasoning will be central to the defensibility of the decision.

*Organizational failings*
Organizational failings are also responsible for risk failures. Reder, Duncan and Gray (1993) in an examination of numerous child protection failures have noted a range of organizational flaws that contribute to poor risk assessment and management. Most notable are workers operating alone without appropriate levels of supervision and support, ill-trained and faced with competing demands in environments of low resource. Such features are characteristic of most public sector organizations charged with risk assessment and its management. It is therefore important that senior agency managers recognize the potential for systemic flaws and attempt to combat them by:

- clear agency policies, procedures and priorities

- appropriate training and supervision of staff

- encouraging peer review and support

- allocating high-risk cases only to those workers equipped to manage them

- ensuring that staff have the skills and competence to deal with risk, and that such skills and competencies are regularly updated.

In addition, risk failure(s) tend to result in organizations pursuing the precautionary principle on risk, that is a 'better safe than sorry' defensive position in response to a previous disaster (Hood and Jones 1996). This inevitably leads to overassessment of risk, risk-inflation and net-widening, with the consequent result that agencies over-intrude, focus resources too widely, and cannot adequately target genuinely high-risk cases (Kemshall 1998).

*Methodological error*
Methodological errors stem from misuse of probability data and lack of attention to relevant base rates (Monahan 1981). In recent years statistical methodologies have developed to incorporate something called the 'ROC' adjusted score – in effect an

actuarial prediction free from base rate limitations (Mossman 1994). This has improved the predictive scores of recent assessment tools for violence and sexual offenders (see Kemshall 2001 for a full review), and enables better comparison between the various risk assessment tools.

There are numerous sources of error but they can be reduced by improved methods, increased rigour and professionalism by workers, and good management practice by the agencies involved (see Kemshall 1998; Munro 1996, 2002).

## Risk management

The effective management of high-risk persons, situations and behaviours is a crucial feature of most social care, health and criminal justice agencies. It is an arena in which the credibility and professionalism of agencies is severely tested, especially in the light of serious incidents or risk management failures. It is therefore essential that risk management is informed by clear principles and the most effective strategies of intervention.

### PRINCIPLES OF RISK MANAGEMENT

Based upon a general public health approach (for example, in drug abuse), harm reduction has been seen as a central principle of effective risk management (Laws 1996). Risks cannot necessarily be removed, and no society is risk free, but risks can be credibly identified and reduced by sound and well-matched interventions (Kemshall 2001). This approach acknowledges that reduction in the frequency of risky behaviours is a gain and reduces the volume of victims, and that any reduction in harmful behaviours and their effects is worth having. Other key principles are:

- Interventions should be proportionate to the risks – both over and under intrusion should be avoided.

- Risk management should be just and fair, and not discriminate disproportionately against certain sections of the population.

- Risks and rights should be balanced (although there is at present a tendency to emphasize risks, notably where victims are especially vulnerable, e.g. children, older persons).

- Risk management should be defensible but not precautionary.

Principles are not always adhered to, either in individual work or in the corporate approach to risk taken by agencies. The precautionary principle tends to breed over-intrusion, and this can be exacerbated where potential or actual victims are vulnerable.

There is also growing evidence that some risk management policies and approaches can inadvertently result in discriminatory interventions, for example, the overuse of compulsory mental health treatment for ethnic minorities on the grounds of risk (Kemshall 2002a; Ryan 1999).

### INTERVENTION STRATEGIES

Combined strategies focusing on specific risky behaviours, conditions and circumstances have been evidenced as the most effective for risk management (Kemshall 2001). Programmes to change behaviours are now well established, particularly those rooted in cognitive-behavioural work (see Scottish Office Social Work Inspectorate 1997 for an example of those designed for sex offenders), and attention to the following four areas has proved the most rewarding for risk reduction:

- changing patterns of deviant behaviour

- correcting distorted thinking and educating to pro-social thinking

- educating on impact of behaviours and 'victim empathy'

- increasing social competence, problem-solving skills and personal efficacy.

(From Beckett *et al.* 1994; Bush 1995; Kemshall 2001, p.40)

These areas have a wider application beyond work with sex offenders to high-risk behaviours generally (Kemshall 2001) although they have been more extensively evaluated with offenders.

Such programmes need to be supported by the following factors:

- Integrity of programme delivery.

- Amenability and motivation to the treatment/intervention from the risky person.

- The change process is well-timed and harnesses motivation.

(See Kemshall 2001, p.41).

Programmes are often an important feature of broader risk management strategies comprising monitoring and surveillance; enforcement, control and sanctions; incentives to self-risk management; rewards for non-risky behaviour and clear sanctions for risky behaviour (see, for example, work with drug abusers). In terms of individual case management, this requires practitioners to:

- reduce risky behaviours or events by improving the person's coping and/or choice mechanisms, and by strengthening their protective factors

- provide and enhance support networks to prevent situations and behaviours from deteriorating

- implement strategies to protect potential victims and vulnerable persons 'at risk', including appropriate enforcement of rules, requirements, agreements

- regularly monitor to note and act on any changes in individual or situational factors that may result in risk

- assist the person with self-risk management strategies

- provide a clear contingency plan in the event of risk management breakdown and/or absence of key worker

- provide speedy access to support services

- provide continuity of case management.

Balance in the overall risk management strategy is important, and strategies that combine the promotion of internal controls with the imposition of clear external ones are increasingly stressed as the route to effective risk management.

## Conclusion

Risk is a central feature of modern life and we are living in what Frank Furedi has called a 'climate of fear' (1997). This has pervaded all aspects of our lives, not least those public sector arenas charged with assessing and managing the risks posed by their users. They are also highly accountable arenas infused with scrutiny and blame. In this climate it is essential that workers and managers make well-informed decisions based on the evidence and rooted in assessment tools and management techniques well supported by the available research evidence. Working with risk will remain a risky business, but with the assistance of sound methods and defensible decision-making it can be well managed.

## Note

1   See Kemshall 2002a for a full review.

## References

Adams, J. (1995) *Risk*. London: UCL.

Adcock, M. (1995) *Framework for Risk Assessment*. London: Wilson and James.

Aharoni, Y. (1981) *The No-Risk Society*. Chatham, NJ: Chatham House.

Beck, U. (1992) *The Risk Society: Towards a New Modernity*. London: Sage.

Beckett, R., Beech, A., Fisher, D. and Fordham, A.S. (1994) *Community-Based Treatment for Sex Offenders: An Evaluation of Seven Treatment Programmes*. A report for the Home Office by the STEP team. London: Home Office.

Beckford Inquiry, London Borough of Brent (1985) *A Child in Trust: the Report of the Panel of Inquiry into the Circumstances Surrounding the Death of Jasmine Beckford*. Presented to the London Borough Council and to Brent Health Authority by members of the Panel of Inquiry, London Borough of Brent.

Blom-Cooper, L., Hally, H. and Murphy, E. (1995) *The Falling Shadow: One Patient's Mental Health Care 1978–1993*. London: Gerald Duckworth and Co.

Bonta, J. (1996) 'Risk-needs led assessment and treatment.' In A.T.Harland (ed.) *Choosing Correctional Options That Work*. Thousand Oaks, CA: Sage.

Boyd Report (1996) *Report of the Confidential Inquiry into Homicides and Suicides by Mentally Ill People*. Steering Committee of the Confidential Inquiry. London: Royal College of Psychiatrists.

Brearley, C.P. (1982) *Risk and Social Work: Hazards and Helping*. London: Routledge and Kegan Paul.

Bush, J. (1995) 'Teaching self-risk management to violent offenders.' In J. McGuire (ed.) *What Works: Reducing Reoffending: Guidelines from Research and Practice*. Chichester: John Wiley.

Carson. D. (1996) 'Risking legal repercussions.' In H. Kemshall and J. Pritchard (eds.) *Good Practice in Risk Assessment and Risk Management, Vol. 1*. London: Jessica Kingsley Publishers.

Copas, J. (1995) *Some Comments on Meta-analysis*. Warwick: Department of Statistics, Warwick University.

Corby, B. (1993) *Child Abuse: Towards a Knowledge Base*. Buckingham: Open University Press.

Doyal, L. and Gough, I. (1991) *A Theory of Human Need*. Basingstoke: Macmillan Press.

Fischoff, B. (1975) 'Hindsight = foresight: The effect of outcome knowledge on judgement under conditions of uncertainty.' *Journal of Experimental Psychology, Human Perception and Performance 1*, 288–99.

Furedi, F. (1997) *Culture of Fear: Risk-Taking and the Morality of Low Expectation*. London: Cassell.

Gendreau, P., Little, T. and Goggin, C. (1996) 'A meta-analysis of the predictors of adult offender recidivism.' *Criminology 34*, 575–607.

Giddens, A. (1998) *The Third Way: The Renewal of Social Democracy.* Oxford: Polity Press.

Glaser, D. (1973) *Routinizing Evaluation.* Rockville Maryland: National Institute of Mental Health.

Green, J. (1997) *Risk and Misfortune.* London: UCL.

Home Office and Department of Health (1999) *Managing Dangerous People with Severe Personality Disorder: Proposals for Policy Development.* London: Home Office and Department of Health.

Hood, C. and Jones, D.K.C. (1996) *Accident and Design: Contemporary Debates in Risk Management.* London: UCL Press.

Jordan, B. (1998) *The New Politics of Welfare.* London: Sage.

Kemshall, H. (1998) *Risk in Probation Practice.* Aldershot: Ashgate.

Kemshall, H. (2001) *Risk Assessment and Management of Known Sexual and Violent Offenders: A Review of Current Issues.* Police Research Series 140. London: Home Office.

Kemshall, H. (2002a) *Risk, Social Policy and Welfare.* Buckingham: Open University Press.

Kemshall, H. (2002b) 'Risk assessment and management.' In M. Davies (ed.) *The Blackwell Companion to Social Work.* Oxford: Blackwell Publishing.

Kemshall, H. (2003) *Understanding Risk in Criminal Justice.* Buckingham: Open University Press.

Kemshall, H., Parton, N., Walsh, M. and Waterson, J. (1997) 'Concepts of risk in relation to organisational structure and functioning within the personal social services and probation.' *Social Policy and Administration 31*, 3, 213–32.

Kemshall, H. and Pritchard, J. (eds) (1996) *Good Practice in Risk Assessment and Risk Management, Vol. 1.* London: Jessica Kingsley Publishers.

Langan, M. (1998) *Welfare: Needs, Rights and Risks.* London: Open University and Routledge.

Laws, D.R. (1996) 'Relapse prevention or harm reduction.' *Journal of Research and Treatment 8*, 3, 243–7.

Leonard, P. (1997) *Postmodern Welfare.* London: Sage.

Mair, G. (ed.) (1997) *Evaluating the Effectiveness of Community Penalties.* Aldershot: Avebury.

McGuire, J. (1997) 'A short introduction to meta-analysis.' *VISTA 3*, 3, 163–76.

McIvor, G. and Kemshall, H. (2002) *Serious Violent and Sexual Offenders: The Use of Risk Assessment Tools in Scotland.* Edinburgh: Scottish Executive, Social Research Crime and Criminal Justice.

Milner, J.S. and Campbell, J.C. (1995) 'Prediction issues for practitioners.' In J. Campbell (ed.) *Assessing Dangerousness: Violence by Sexual Offenders, Batterers, and Child Abusers.* London: Sage.

Moore, B. (1996) *Risk Assessment: A Practitioner's Guide to Predicting Harmful Behaviour.* London: Whiting & Birch.

Monahan, J. (1981) *The Clinical Prediction of Violence.* Beverley Hills, CA: Sage.

Monahan, J. (1993) 'Limiting therapist exposure to Tarasoff liability: Guidelines for risk containment.' *American Psychologist 48*, 242–50.

Mossman, D. (1994) 'Assessing predictions of violence: Being accurate about accuracy.' *Journal of Consulting and Clinical Psychology 62*, 4, 783–92.

Munro, E. (1996) 'Avoidable and unavoidable mistakes in child protection work.' *British Journal of Social Work 26*, 795–810.

Munro, E. (1999) 'Common errors of reasoning in child protection work.' *Child Abuse and Neglect 23*, 8, 745–58.

Munro, E. (2002) *Effective Child Protection.* London: Sage.

Parsloe, P. (1999) *Risk Assessment in Social Care and Social Work.* London: Jessica Kingsley Publishers.

Parton, N. (1991) *Governing the Family: Child Care, Child Protection and the State.* London: Macmillan.

Parton, N. (1994) 'Problematics of government, (post) modernity and social work.' *British Journal of Social Work 24*, 1, 9–32.

Parton, N., Thorpe, D. and Wattam, C. (1997) *Child Protection: Risk and the Moral Order.* Basingstoke: Macmillan Press.

Raynor, P. (1999) 'Risk, needs and effective practice: The impact and potential of new assessment methods in probation.' Paper presented to the British Criminology Conference, July.

Reder, P., Duncan, S. and Gray, M. (1993) *Beyond Blame: Child Abuse Tragedies Revisited.* London: Routledge.

Rose, N. (1996) 'Governing "advanced" liberal democracies.' In A. Barry, T. Osborne and N. Rose (eds) *Foucault and Political Reason: Liberalism, Neo-Liberalism and Rationalities of Government.* London: UCL Press.

Ryan, P. (1999) *Assertive Outreach in Mental Health.* Nursing Times Clinical Monographs 35. London: Nursing Times.

Schon, D.A. (1983) *The Reflective Practitioner.* New York: Basic Books.

Scottish Office Social Work Inspectorate (1997) *A Commitment to Protect: Supervising Sex Offenders: Proposals for More Effective Practice.* Edinburgh: Scottish Office.

Sheppard, D. (1995) *Learning the Lessons: Mental Health Inquiry Reports Published in England and Wales between 1969 and 1994 and their Recommendations for Improving Practice.* London: Zito Trust.

## Further reading

Nash, M. (1999) *Police, Probation and Protecting the Public.* London: Blackwell Press.

# Section 3: Intervention

## CHAPTER 12

# COGNITIVE BEHAVIOURAL SOCIAL WORK

*Geraldine Macdonald*

## A theoretical leveller

Learning theory is an approach that sits well with the value base of social work. The likelihood of success depends upon establishing an effective working relationship between the social worker and the person using services, such that the latter can contribute their particular knowledge of their circumstances. In other words, it is an inherently collaborative approach. Its rationale and principles are shared with people and the evidence suggests this improves outcomes. Once people have acquired an ability to think cognitive-behaviourally, they become more adept at analysing and intervening in problematic situations, without recourse to professional intervention.

## Learning theories

Learning theories describe the variety of means whereby we acquire certain ways of behaving, thinking and feeling, whether these are desirable or undesirable, social or anti-social. While each method of learning operates simultaneously and interactively, it is helpful for understanding, assessment and planning, to consider them separately in the first instance.

### RESPONDENT LEARNING

Respondent learning, also known as classical or Pavlovian conditioning (Pavlov 1927), is concerned with those behaviours over which we experience little conscious control. They are often concerned with emotional arousal. Human beings are 'programmed' automatically to respond in particular ways to certain stimuli. Threats (unconditioned stimuli) trigger a range of physiological changes such as sweating, raised heartbeat (unconditioned responses). Such reactions serve a useful purpose, preparing us physiologically to either escape or deal with the situation head on i.e. the 'fight/flight' mechanism. However, sometimes we find ourselves responding with immense anxiety to stimuli that pose no threat, for example, confined spaces, crowds, certain animals or insects. We find ourselves reacting inappropriately angrily to stimuli (people or situations) that present little or no provocation.

Sometimes, this is because an unconditioned stimulus (e.g. a threat) has been either dramatically or repeatedly paired with a neutral one, and the latter has acquired the anxiety-eliciting properties of the unconditioned stimulus. The best-known example of repeated pairing is an experiment in which this pairing was deliberately engineered, known as 'Little Albert' (Watson and Raynor 1920).

> Little Albert was startled (unconditioned response) when a loud noise sounded behind him (unconditioned stimulus).

> He played with a pet rat (conditioned [neutral] stimulus) just before the loud noise (unconditioned stimulus).

> He began to get startled (conditioned response) when he saw the rat (conditioned stimulus).

> Rat = conditioned stimulus. Startle at rat = conditioned response.

Albert also experienced stimulus generalization. His conditioned anxiety response generalized to other furry animals. One very bad experience with a policeman (a 'dramatic pairing') can generalize to other police officers. Children for whom cuddles have become the precursor to sexual abuse (repeated pairing) may well react anxiously to anyone attempting to show affection or reassurance in this way.

Clearly, not all fears and phobias develop in this way. Some are learned by a process of modelling (see pages 173 and 181). Others just seem to 'happen'. Whatever the aetiology, the respondent theory of learning holds an important key to addressing problems of anxiety, aggression and misplaced sexual arousal. For example, if the psychologists concerned in the above experiment had gradually introduced Albert to the pet rat without the loud noise occurring, the evidence suggests that Albert's startle reaction would disappear. This is known as respondent extinction. One of the key reasons that phobias persist, even when a person recognizes that it is irrational, is that they either organize their lives so that they avoid the feared object, or else they withdraw from the situation as soon as possible. In other words, they escape. This means that they never have the opportunity to learn that nothing dreadful will happen and that they can cope. Further, the relief they experience when escaping from threatening situations negatively reinforces their escape response (see page 171).

## OPERANT LEARNING

Operant learning is also known as instrumental or Skinnerian conditioning, after the psychologist whose work established this theory of learning (Skinner 1953, 1971). We talk about operant behaviour because, from an early age, human beings show strong signs of wanting to influence (operate upon) their environment (both physical and social), which responds to our attempts in a variety of ways, sometimes positively, sometimes aversively. Some of these consequences just happen, as when we reach out and touch something with sharp edges. Sometimes we organize the world so that certain behaviours attract certain kinds of consequences, designed either to encourage or discourage their occurrence. Sensible parents will go out of their way to show their pleasure when children play collaboratively, or try to do things for themselves. They will withdraw their approval when children misbehave, or will impose sanctions.

Learning can happen unawares, and without anyone intending it. Some children learn that the only way to get their parents' attention is by misbehaving. Others learn that it pays to be aggressive, or that it is best not to be noticed. In none of these situations do the children or the adults necessarily intend that this is what they should learn. Understanding operant learning is therefore essential knowledge in undertaking good quality assessments, in all fields.

Operant theory focuses on the relationship between behaviour (behaviour – 'B'), the circumstances in which the behaviour occurs (the antecedents – 'A'), and the events that follow it (the consequences – 'C'). Hence the approach to assessment in cognitive behavioural work is often referred to as the 'ABC' approach.

Consequences following behaviour can be reinforcing or punishing, or neutral. The key processes underpinning operant learning are therefore reinforcement, punishment and extinction. In learning theory, the terms reinforcement and punishment have very precise meanings. Both are defined solely in terms of the effect they have on the behaviour they follow. Something may look quite 'unrewarding' – the intention may be quite different – but if something strengthens behaviour then, in cognitive behavioural terms, it is a reinforcer. If shouting at a child for arguing results in more arguing, then for this child shouting is a reinforcer, whatever the carer intended or however aversive we think shouting is.

A reinforcer then is anything that increases the probability of the behaviour that precedes it. In other words, a reinforcer is anything that strengthens behaviour. We can reinforce behaviour in one of two ways.

*Positive reinforcement*
In behavioural terms we only use the term positive reinforcement when:

- the consequence is presented contingent upon the behaviour

- that behaviour becomes more likely to occur because, and only because, the consequence is presented when the behaviour occurs.

If, every time James plays with his food rather than eating it, his carer spends time cajoling and encouraging him, and he continues to play with his food at mealtimes, we can hypothesize that cajoling and encouragement are positively reinforcing his behaviour.

*Negative reinforcement*
Negative reinforcement also increases the probability of the behaviour that precedes it, but this time it does so by ending something that increases the preceding behaviour. Typically something unpleasant is escaped, or avoided, or terminated after the behaviour has occurred. Mother dislikes seeing the children fighting (aversive stimulus – antecedent), Mother yells at them (operant response/behaviour) – children stop fighting (termination of aversive stimulus) – Mother yells next time the children fight (we deduce that Mother's behaviour has been negatively reinforced by its effect on the children's fighting). Other everyday examples: if we are prone to headaches and find a certain medication alleviates the pain quickly we are more likely to use it again in the future. The termination of the headache is what reinforces the use of the medication. When addiction is established, one of the drivers for misuse is the alleviation of aversive symptoms. Negative reinforcement is not to be confused with punishment. Negative reinforcement is, by definition, something that strengthens behaviour.

### Punishment

A punisher is anything that decreases the probability of the behaviour that precedes it. It might be a critical comment, a fine or a slap. From the wrong person, it might be a compliment. Not all students welcome approbation from their teachers, and public praise in a class of 14-year-olds might – unintentionally – weaken ('punish') the very behaviour it was intended to strengthen.

### Extinction

If a particular reinforcer has maintained a behaviour and that reinforcer ceases to arrive, then the behaviour will decrease.

### Antecedents

One of the things we gradually learn in the course of our interaction with the environment is that certain behaviours are only reinforced (or punished) in certain circumstances. The socially competent among us quickly learn what behaviours are likely to be reinforced in what settings, and behave appropriately. Such learning is known as stimulus discrimination and is a part of the process we normally refer to as socialization. People act as discriminative stimuli. Some children will be more forthcoming with one teacher than another because experience teaches them that the one will probably provide encouragement and reinforcement, while another will most likely be dismissive or critical.

## SOCIAL LEARNING THEORY

Social learning theory provides a more complex account of human behaviour, drawing on respondent and operant learning, and adding cognitive factors. Modelling (also called imitative, observational or vicarious learning) is the process at the heart of social learning theory. Modelling accounts for the acquisition of a vast range of behaviours, both simple and complex, and some responses that we do not designate as skills, such as reacting with anxiety to thunderstorms or being brave in the face of danger. While complex skills will also require physical practice for good performance, simple skills can often be acquired on the basis of one example (one-trial learning), making it an economical and efficient mode of learning. Again, it does not have to happen consciously or intentionally.

In an early experiments, Bandura illustrated the process of modelling, and how it relates to reinforcement (Bandura 1965). He randomly allocated a number of nursery children to three groups. Each group was shown a film of a child (the 'model') beating up a life-size Bobo doll (plastic doll), often accompanied by a distinctive phrase, such as 'Pow, boom, boom'. The incident was identical in each, but in the first film the model was rewarded for his behaviour with sweets, soft drinks and praise ('reinforcement condition'); in the second film his behaviour was punished by spanking and a telling off ('punishment condition'); and in the third film nothing happened to the model following his behaviour ('no consequence' condition). After viewing the film each child was placed in a room with lots of toys, including a replica of the Bobo doll. Children who had watched the 'reinforcement' film or the 'no consequence' film imitated the aggressive behaviour of the model much more than children who had seen the model being punished. Interestingly, when all children were offered incentives for imitating the aggressive behaviour, all children behaved equally aggressively.

Clearly, perception and information processing play key parts in the process of observational learning:

> Humans do not respond simply to stimuli; they interpret them. Stimuli influence the likelihood of particular behaviours through their predictive function, not because they are automatically linked to responses occurring together. In the social learning view, contingent experiences create expectations rather than stimulus–response connections. (Bandura 1977, p.59)

Modelling involves a process that cannot be directly observed; the theory suggests that the learner observes, stores information, anticipates outcomes. As well as the concept of 'single trial learning', it includes the use of symbols (learning from what is heard or read), attention, memory and expectations of reward or punishment, success or failure.

Another reason why Bandura pressed for the inclusion of cognition in the understanding of behaviour is the demonstrable ability of people to regulate their own behaviour 'from within'. That is to say we determine some of the consequences of our own behaviour. For instance, we can deny ourselves the pleasure of a coffee break until we have finished the task we are engaged on or we can reward ourselves for a job well done either with something tangible (the purchase of a record) or with a mental 'pat on the back'. Similarly we can perform certain behaviours, sometimes for long periods, that are not intrinsically rewarding (or extrinsically reinforced) by dint of long-term goals towards which we strive. All these things, and others, point to the need to acknowledge that cognitions play an important part in the process of learning.

## COGNITIVE THEORY

The importance of cognition, particularly in relation to depression and other mental health problems, has been reinforced, and its role explored in the work of clinicians such as Aaron Beck (1978), Albert Ellis (Ellis and Greiger 1977) and Meichenbaum (1985), and theorists such as Teasdale (1993) and Brewin (1996). The evidence suggests that in order to help those with depression, and a number of other mental health conditions, it is helpful directly to attend to faulty cognitions and ways of thinking, including faulty reasoning. The best known cognitive theory, which exemplifies the theoretical principles underpinning cognitive approaches, is that of Beck.

Beck uses three key concepts in accounting for depression:

1. 'Cognitive triad' denotes the very negative way in which depressed persons typically regard themselves, their current situations and their prospects. In later writings Beck uses the term 'negative cognitive shift' (1995) indicating a systematic filtering out of pertinent positive information, and acceptance of negative self-relevant information. Thus, rather than being pleased about the series of compliments paid to her about her appearance, Melissa leaves the party worrying that, because no one mentioned her hair, it must be because it looks dreadful. When James received feedback on his progress in the group, he finds it hard to believe any of the positive things said to him by other groups members, but amplifies the things they say he still needs to work on.

2.   'Schemata' denotes the particular ways in which depressed persons have of looking at the world based on models derived from previous experience. This is perhaps best thought of as the opposite of 'rose-tinted spectacles'. Children who had adverse experiences of parenting may acquire negative ways of thinking about themselves (I'm unlovable; I make things go wrong; I drive people away) and of others (people will eventually let you down).

3.   Faulty information processing or cognitive distortions are cognitive errors that arise from biased schema. Thus the depressed woman whose partner terminates their relationship will probably conclude that no one wants her (negative over-generalization). Other 'errors' are dichotomous thinking, in which only one or both of two extremes are considered; and selective abstraction, the tendency of depressed people typically 'home in' on the negative aspects of situations, to the exclusion of other, positive and equally valid ones.

Beck does not view such patterns of thinking as causal, but rather as having a major (or primary) role to play in the development of the condition, once triggered: 'I view deviant cognitive processes as intrinsic to the depressive disorder, not a cause or consequence' (Beck 1987, p.10). In other words, people have basic schemas or beliefs about themselves and the world which are latent (dormant) until activated by a stressor. Once activated, the negative automatic thoughts that follow contribute to maintaining the depressed mood. Teasdale's work supports this hypothesis (1983, 1993).

## Salient features of the cognitive behavioural approach

1.   The approach is essentially evidence based. Respondent, operating and social learning theories, and the interventions which derive from them, enjoy strong empirical support. Cognitive interventions have generally grown out of clinical practice, and the theory-building and testing have followed. Cognitive behavioural interventions enjoy strong empirical support, particularly in the area of mental health and self-control (including pain control).

2.   The approach is inherently empirical, with each intervention regarded as a mini-experiment. Is there actually a change in the problem? Have unwanted behaviours decreased and wanted behaviours increased? Has a new skill been learned, and is it being used? Cognitive behavioural workers would argue that this is an ethical requirement for all practice. Only by careful monitoring and with a degree of humility can we ensure that people using services get a good deal. Ensuring early feedback that something isn't working can save time and resources, and alert us to the possibility that we have missed something in our assessment, underestimated something in our intervention plan or failed to provide sufficient support for what can be demanding programmes. Changing behaviour, whether our own or that of others, is not easy.

3.   In order to evaluate the work, it is necessary to set clear and specific goals at the outset, and to measure the state of affairs before intervention (the 'baseline'), during intervention, and after intervention. This is the simplest kind of mini-experiment (there are more sophisticated kinds – see Bloom and Fischer 1982).

Now some key questions that are often asked about cognitive behavioural approaches.

1. What do cognitive behavioural workers think about causation? Cognitive behavioural workers recognize three sets of interacting causes. First, genetic or biological causes, such as inborn personality differences, disability, illness, injuries and the effects of drugs and alcohol. Second, historical causes (distal antecedents) – factors arising from someone's learning history which impact on their thinking and behaviour in the present. For example, parenting style is often shaped by our experience of parenting, including the expectations people have of children. Third, contemporary causes of behaviour: the factors in a person's current environment that regularly precede behaviour (proximal antecedents) or follow it (consequences). Contemporary causes of behaviour usually attract most attention because these are the causes that are most susceptible to change.

2. What about insight? Insight is important. Human beings want to understand why they – and others – behave the way they do. We can only speculate about this. The most useful insights are those that focus on the what? when? where? and how? – which often yield plausible hypotheses regarding 'why?'. It is therefore preferable to use the term 'psychological awareness'. We are interested in teaching people to think cognitive behaviourally. This includes helping them to put together a picture of how they, or others, have come to think, feel and behave the way they do, including distal antecedents, i.e. things that happened in the past. Sometimes this understanding is brought about using a formal teaching approach, sometimes it is embedded in the process of helping, i.e. routinely explaining what we are doing and why, and getting them to reflect on their own experiences of change.

3. Does the relationship with people using services matter? Yes, as much as in any other approach, but with some possible differences of emphasis. First, the relationship is seen as a necessary but not sufficient condition of change. It sets the scene for effective helping. Second, cognitive behavioural workers concentrate on those aspects of relationships that research suggests are particularly important to people, namely empathy, warmth and genuineness. Similarly, in group work, the focus in on the encouragement of client behaviours that are summed up as 'group cohesion'. At a more individualized and specific level, we use friendly comments and such, to try to help people feel less anxious or less guilty; to make them feel valued or that they have done well. Third, we try to work in a collaborative way, combining the unique knowledge that the person with whom we are working has about their situation with our knowledge of cognitive behavioural approaches. The evidence suggests that this is important in sustaining relationships, and maximizing the likelihood of good outcomes, e.g. Webster-Stratton (1998).

4. So what's different? What is different is the structured, open and – relative to some approaches – transparent way in which we go about our work, and a willingness to be more directive and make concrete suggestions for actions. There is also a stronger focus on evidence gathering, which results in a greater use of charts, graphs and other forms of data collection, and on working collaboratively to develop hypotheses about what is happening and what might help, and whether it works.

## Assessment

Assessment is a distinct phase which holds the key to successful intervention. A cognitive behavioural assessment will start broadly, exploring the development of problems over time, including discussions of those experiences in the past that may well be impacting on the present, particularly in terms of attitudes, beliefs and expectations, not all of which will be immediately available to the user. Thereafter, it will focus on the target problems and those more immediate causes (proximal antecedents and consequences) in which it is possible to intervene. Problems need to be defined very precisely. 'She is aggressive' needs to be turned into what she does, in what circumstances (time, place, people present) and with what level of intensity and frequency. Goals need to be equally specific and generally more modest than is usual, e.g. 'reduce the number of tantrums and increase time spent in cooperative play' rather than 'improve her behaviour'. Where there are a number of problems to deal with, these need to be prioritized. Problems need to be sufficiently important to the user that he or she is likely to persist with it, and at the same time feasible to be dealt with. On the grounds that nothing reinforces like success, it is a good idea to start small if at all possible.

### BASELINE

How often does the behaviour occur now? Sometimes it is easy to get a baseline, the baseline may be zero: not up before midday for the last year, never washes without a fight. Or it can be more awkward to get a baseline: talked about delusions on average four times a day over a three-week baseline period; screamed an average of 30 minutes a night over two weeks. People with whom the student is working will need help to keep records. Sometimes the student will need to do some direct observations. With behaviours that can't be observed or measured in a concrete way, one can use a simple rating scale, for example, 0–10 as a rating of anxiety in a specific situation, or a standardized questionnaire, e.g. the Beck Depression Inventory. Throughout the intervention the student should repeat the measures at regular intervals.

### ABC ANALYSIS

Once the behaviour has been defined clearly, the ABC analysis is undertaken. For example, the behaviour of interest is the child refusing to do what the parent says (the goal being to increase the number of times the child does what the parent says without making a fuss); the antecedents are a request or direction from parent; the consequences are the parent gives up and lets the child do what he or she wants or bargains with the child. The analysis might lead the worker to decide, as a first shot, to try to arrange a change in the antecedents and consequences. The worker rehearses the parent in making requests clearly and firmly, and helps him or her to work out new, effective consequences for compliance and non-compliance.

Another example, with respondent behaviour in mind: the problem behaviours are feeling anxious when alone out of doors and avoiding going out; the antecedent is going out or approaching the street or supermarket; the consequences are avoiding anticipated anxiety (negative reinforcement) and receiving a lot of fuss from the partner (positive reinforcement). In this case, the worker might decide to institute a programme of rapid exposure to the feared situations and also attempt to bring in the partner as a co-therapist to help with the exposure programme and provide more appropriate consequences, that is, praise for effort. Note these are just examples – no assumptions about particular problems can be made without an individualized and detailed analysis.

In each of these cases the worker would explore the role of cognition, with a view to targeting these if necessary. Does the parent have age-inappropriate expectations? What motivation does she attribute to the child? Does the agoraphobic believe that she is going to collapse or have a heart attack, or become a laughing stock? These may need to become the specific focus of intervention.

## Intervention techniques
### BASED ON OPERANT LEARNING
*Positive reinforcement*
This is about devising a programme which ensures that the wished-for behaviour is positively reinforced as quickly as possible. Positive reinforcement should initially be delivered every time the behaviour occurs (continuous schedule of reinforcement). So, whenever four-year-old Graham puts his toys away when asked, his parent gives him a marble for his jar or a piece of Duplo towards a his model.

While continuous schedules of reinforcement produce rapid increases in the rate of performance, these increases are not very durable. Later on, reinforcement should be thinned out so that the behaviour is reinforced less and less frequently and less predictably (intermittent schedules of reinforcement). This is the best way to ensure that a newly learned behaviour becomes resistant to extinction. When Graham is routinely and reliably responding to his parents' requests, his parents will give him a marble or a Duplo piece every other time he responds, or every few times. If his behaviour deteriorates, they will be advised to return to a continuous schedule of reinforcement, and gradually try to 'stretch' the time between reinforcement.

It is worth taking the trouble to familiarize oneself with the detail of reinforcement schedules, since not only does this make the construction of programmes of help easier and more likely to succeed, but it is also important for assessment purposes.

Where it is necessary to use 'tangible' reinforcers, such as food, these should be paired with 'social reinforcers', such as praise, and the tangible reinforcers gradually withdrawn. When Graham's parents reinforce his behaviour with stars or activities, they also praise him and give him cuddles, or tousle his hair. Finding out what someone values (or dislikes), whether one is considering tangible or social reinforcers is crucial. One can usually do this by asking what people opt to do when left to their own devices.

Chaining entails reinforcing someone for completing one part of a chain of behaviour, then two parts, then three parts, until they can complete the entire chain (before reinforcement). Chaining is a very common component of work with people with learning difficulties, who need to learn ordinary skills of daily living, such as dressing, cooking, using public transport (Carr and Collins 1992). In backwards chaining, the worker does all parts of the chain except the last, which the user is helped to do, and is then reinforced. When competent with this, the worker does all parts except the last two, which the user does and then is reinforced, and so on.

Shaping (also called successive approximation) means reinforcing a behaviour somewhat like the desired behaviour and then raising the standard for reinforcement step by step, until the behaviour is occurring. This is another effective way of teaching skills, such as social skills. For example, in training a social work student in 'active listening' the teacher might begin by reinforcing simply looking at the speaker, then require other non-verbal signs of attentiveness and concern, and then perhaps some verbal encouragement.

Points systems, which may be used with older children and teenagers, include the familiar star chart and the token economy. They are a means of providing immediate reinforcers (the star or token) which are later exchanged for back-up reinforcers which it would be difficult to deliver at the time the wanted behaviour occurs. Such 'generalizable' reinforcers (like money) are also useful because they help to prevent reinforcement 'saturation' – even one's favourite chocolate may cease to be attractive after a week. Points systems also include a negative punishment system – loss of points for unwanted behaviours. They are most appropriate for child behaviour problems in the age group 7–12, approximately. In order to secure more reasonable behaviour in the home, 14-year-old Bhavna is awarded points for a number of behaviours including coming home on time, doing her homework and getting up when called. At the end of each week, she can exchange her points for money towards something that she wants (this could be a CD or a piece of clothing, a sleepover, or an agreement to stay out later than usual on Friday). If she fails to do those things she's agreed to (contracts are often used with teenagers – see the next section) then points are removed.

Contracts formalize the agreements people make to change their behaviour. They provide reinforcement for clearly specified desired behaviours. Sometimes contracts include a penalty clause, such as fine or a chore, for some undesired behaviour or for failure to comply with the contract.

Contracts are typically the end result of considerable negotiation between the parties, facilitated by the social worker who needs to model key negotiation skills (listening skills, communication skills, turn taking, empathy, etc.). She must make sure that everyone understands the point of view of other parties, why their behaviour is seen as unreasonable (if this is the case), how it is experienced by each person and what each person would like to see change (probably the most important). Clarity and specificity are crucial. 'Being more reasonable' is not good enough. Contracts have to spell out what being reasonable means for a particular person in a particular household. Thus, parents who must say what changes they want and must be prepared to listen to the changes that their teenager might also want. Both parties may have to compromise. Start small if you can (sometimes things are so critical that you have no option but to go for the 'biggies'), encourage people to choose things that are highly likely to be possible (including perhaps things they already do), and make sure that everyone understands what is being asked of them, and how it will be monitored. Contracts don't have to be signed, but this usually helps, as it endows a sense of ownership and commitment. Finally, avoid framing contracts in a contingent manner, i.e. if he does X, she will do Y, because the moment one thing goes wrong the contract collapses.

*Punishment*

Although 'punishment' is a technical term, most consequences designed to suppress behaviour are in fact aversive. Therefore, punishment is not generally recommended for a variety of reasons:

- It may have serious side effects, such as anxiety, depression, aggression, imitation of the behaviour of the person who delivers the punishment, avoidance of the person who delivers the punishment.

- It does not help the person being punished to learn any new, useful behaviour to take the place of the unwanted behaviour.

- People seem to habituate to punishment so that in order to be effective the punishment would have to increase in intensity over time.

- There is more than enough punishment in the lives of most people, without adding to it.

That said, there are times when punishment may have to be considered: when it is necessary to stop some unwanted behaviour rapidly, because it is dangerous, or when other methods (such as replacing the behaviour with an alternative, positive behaviours) would probably take too long. One type of punishment that is unlikely to produce harmful side effects is 'negative' punishments such as fines or loss of points when used within a programme that is mainly one of positive reinforcement. Care needs to be taken with the use of the term punishment, which many people associate with physical punishment, humiliation and other, hurtful exchanges. There is enough unhappiness in people's lives morally to prohibit it being organized by social workers, and in certain circumstances physical punishment, such as slapping, is illegal (e.g. for children in care).

*Operant extinction*

If the worker can identify what is currently reinforcing a particular problem behaviour, and stop the reinforcement immediately and completely, then the behaviour will reduce and eventually cease. But first it may well increase – this is known as the extinction burst (or spurt). The parents who realize that rushing up to Kasha's room whenever she calls out to them in the evenings, taking her milk and biscuits and reading her stories, has been reinforcing her behaviour, will probably find that when they try to ignore her, that her yelling initially gets louder and longer. If they hold out, then will find that it gradually decreases, and eventually ceases. If they give in, they will have reinforced a more substantial problem. Thus, ensuring that people have the support and resources to see cognitive behavioural programmes through is an important consideration.

Differential reinforcement combines the ignoring of inappropriate behaviour, and the reinforcement of alternative, incompatible behaviour, for example, playing nicely with a sibling, instead of arguing.

Hannah's foster carer was at her wit's end. Hannah would never let her talk with anyone else, however firmly she told her to wait until she'd finished talking – Hannah just kept on interrupting, putting her face right in front of her, and talking over either her foster carer or her companion. Hannah's foster carer decided that she would ignore her when she interrupted her conversations with other people (however difficult it proved, and however Hannah responded), but would respond quickly and positively when she waited for an appropriate pause. After one or two extremely persistent episodes, in which Hannah thrust herself in front of her carer's face and talked (louder and louder – the extinction burst), Hannah's foster mother found an opportunity to respond to her when she herself was not talking. Hannah soon learned to turn take. Insofar as her behaviour might have been fuelled by anxiety or insecurity, such an intervention also taught Hannah that her foster carer was none the less attentive just because she was talking to someone else, and it extended the range of activities that she and her foster carer could subsequently enjoy together.

Time out is a variant of extinction which has been shown to be particularly effective in dealing with child behaviour problems (in conjunction with positive reinforcement for desirable behaviours). Time out involves removing the child from all sources of positive reinforcement. The child is asked to do something, say tidy his toys away. If he tidies them then he is reinforced (praised). If he fails to comply, he is asked again with a warning (e.g. if you don't put your toys away then you will go into time out). If the child complies this time then he is reinforced. If not, he is placed in time out (somewhere that holds no distractions or interest, but also no worries, e.g. the bottom step of a stair, a corner) and made to stay there quietly for a brief period of time. Time out does not start until the child is quiet and compliant in time out, and does not usually continue for more than two or three minutes. When released from time out, the process begins again, if appropriate, i.e. if the starting point was an instruction with which the child did not comply. It is tough for parents. Time out needs careful planning and support. The social worker will ensure that the use of time out is explained to the child, including what he or she must do in order to be released from time out, e.g. stay there quietly for two minutes.

### BASED ON RESPONDENT CONDITIONING

Desensitization involves repeatedly pairing a new, unproblematic response with a stimulus that has previously aroused a problematic one (e.g. anxiety, anger), until the problem response has been replaced by the new one. The new response is typically one that is incompatible with the one it is replacing, e.g. feeling relaxed instead of anxious.

Systematic desensitization begins with the construction of a hierarchy of problematic situations ranked in order of difficulty. The person is then taught a response (usually) relaxation. He or she is then helped to imagine each situation in turn, beginning with the least worrying. When the person can manage this he or she is taken on to the next. Eventually the client repeats this 'imaginal exposure' in real life.

Claire was agoraphobic. She could not take her children to school, and was unable to take them to the doctors, do shopping or find work. So, Claire's social worker first got her to list ten scenarios that would make her very anxious. She then helped Claire to rank these in ascending order of concern. Next she taught Claire to relax, and then to imagine each scenario while staying relaxed. If she was unable to do so, they went back to the previous scenario (or slipped another one in to reduce the gap). Eventually, when Claire could manage to imagine each stage in the hierarchy, they arranged for her to practise each one, sequentially, in real life ('in vivo').

*Graded exposure*

This version of desensitization begins with producing a short hierarchy of anxiety-provoking situations, and working through it straight away in real life, starting with the most difficult item that someone can manage, without going through the imaginal stage. It is a faster but equally effective therapy, although some people may be reluctant to take what feels an enormous step so early in therapy.

Humour, being with a person you trust, behaving assertively, are examples of alternatives to relaxation. A central feature is introducing (reintroducing) your client into the anxiety-provoking situation (exposure) so that they experience coping.

## BELL AND PAD (TREATMENT OF BEDWETTING)

The bell or buzzer sounds when the child begins to urinate, simultaneously waking the child and causing his or her muscles to contract. After the repeated association of full bladder, waking up and contracting muscles, the child is able to permanently link these three events and the bell can be phased out. It is appropriate when medical conditions are excluded, and circumstances will support it (see ERIC 2007).

## BASED ON SOCIAL LEARNING THEORY

Modelling simply entails demonstrating how to do something. Modelling is an essential component of much cognitive behavioural work. Showing a mother how to give instructions to her child, or how to play with a small child, or even how to ignore, is often much more effective than simply providing information or advice. The effectiveness of modelling has been shown to be enhanced by a number of factors (Bandura 1977). These are:

1.  A model who, in the eyes of the observer, has some standing (e.g. the status and power that come with popularity) is most likely to attract his or her attention to, and influence his or her behaviour (but see point 3).

2.  A model seen to be reinforced for performing a behaviour is more likely to be imitated.

3.  Some point of comparison or similarity between the model and the observer is essential. If the observer perceives the model as utterly unlike him- or herself he or she may well think that they have no chance of acquiring the behaviour being modelled, or, more importantly, of being reinforced for performing the behaviour.

4.  Giving the observer the opportunity to practise the behaviour soon after seeing it being modelled facilitates its establishment in his or her repertoire.

5.  Reinforcing the observer (arranging reinforcement) for performing the new behaviour also helps to establish it – a strategy not peculiar to modelling.

Attention will now turn to some common approaches which are well-established packages of procedures.

Social skills training is often conducted in groups, the main features being modelling and shaping. For example, a group member who is confident about using the telephone to enquire about a job demonstrates this in a role play. Key features of the skill are identified by the group, and then someone who has difficulty with this takes his or her turn to practise the skill in the role play. He or she receives reinforcement and feedback, and further modelling and practice occur until the skill is mastered. Attention may be paid to cognitive factors – learning the social rules, examining and modifying unhelpful self-talk, and so on. Social skills training is relevant for a single situation that someone finds hard to cope with. A woman whose mother interferes with child management, a teenager who dreads meeting his friends again after discharge from a psychiatric unit, someone with a difficult apology to make or upsetting information to impart: these are further examples of potential users of short episodes of social skills training. The procedures can also be very helpful to social workers themselves, preparing for a confrontation with a client or another professional, indeed for any unaccustomed or worrying interchange.

Social skills training has been used to good effect in many social work circumstances including: work with offenders (teaching them pro-social skills, ways of managing aggression, how to deal confidently with their criminal record and so on); parenting (helping parents learn how to deal confidently with officials, including teachers and health professionals); mental health social work (helping clients develop their interpersonal skills, helping them to secure and retain employment, helping them to behave confidently about their health problems in relation to employers, etc.).

Communication training is a variant of social skills training. As indicated earlier (see the discussion of contracts), communications training, whether undertaken directly or indirectly, is a key component of many social work interventions. It is designed to deal with communication problems between people, including interrupting, failing to acknowledge the other person's feelings or talking too much, expressing positive and negative feelings or making requests. It is therefore useful in group work, work designed to improve relationships, whether between parents and children, between parents, children and teachers, or between couples. In a typical session, a social worker might ask key parties to discuss a topic for five minutes (e.g. what to do on Saturday) and then use that to identify and illustrate key communication problems. The social worker would then re-run the discussion, intervening to point out interruptions, ensure that someone has the opportunity to finish what he or she is saying, checking that what was heard was what was said, and perhaps modelling more effective communication.

*Problem-solving training*
Many of the difficulties that arise for people do so as a result of attempts to solve problems. Problem-solving is central to social work. People are not genetically endowed with problem-solving skills. Most of us acquire them by observing others and practising. There are some circumstances in which it pays formally to teach people a structured approach to solving problems or making decisions. Such an approach involves modelling and practice with specific feedback and reinforcement and a variant of shaping – people learn to perform each stage of the process and then put the stages together in a set order (agree to work on a defined problem, list possible solutions, eliminate obviously bad ones, select one, agree details of implementation). The steps to follow are these:

1.    Agree to work on a problem.

2.    Specify the problem (or part of it).

3.    List all the possible solutions you can think of (brainstorming).

4.   Eliminate all obviously bad solutions.

5.   Examine the remaining solutions one at a time.

   (a)  list all possible negative consequences

   (b)  list all positive consequences

   (c)  eliminate if generally negative

   (d)  take next solution on the list and repeat (a)–(c)

   (e)  compare remaining solutions.

6.   Select solution with the most positive consequences.

7.   Agree on details of implementing the chosen solution, using steps 3–6 as needed.

(Adapted from the flow-chart by Turkat and Calhoun 1980)

### BASED ON COGNITIVE THEORY

*Anxiety management and stress-inoculation (anger control)*

WASP: Wait, Absorb, Slowly Proceed. This mnemonic is an example of the kind of self-talk taught in these forms of training. The methods are used mostly in cases where there is not one, but many different occasions for the client to feel upset or anxious and either act inappropriately or else try to escape or avoid. The key components are teaching about the role of cognitions, self-monitoring of self-talk and problem behaviour, problem-solving, modelling and rehearsing of positive and coping self-talk, plus behavioural procedures such as relaxation, and behavioural homework assignments. In anger control, the person learns to analyse the problem situation into its separate stages, to try to interrupt the sequence of events leading to the angry outburst and to develop alternative responses, paying particular attention to the physiological aspects of anger arousal and to the self-talk that accompanies the run-up to an angry outburst. Self-control training can also play a major part in work with some 'compulsive' or impulsive behaviours such as sexual offending and substance misuse. These procedures are used with people who have developed these problems, and also in preventive programmes.

### ELLIS' RATIONAL-EMOTIVE THERAPY

Ellis (Dryden and Ellis 1986) has produced a list of beliefs or attitudes which, he says, may not be held explicitly but are certainly acted upon. For example, 'Everyone must love me', 'I must always do everything perfectly', 'It will be terrible if I make a mistake'. Ellis' A-B-C method involves teaching the client to analyse situations as follows: A is the Activating event (I don't get the job I apply for) and C is the emotional Consequence (I feel very upset and despairing). But it is incorrect to say that event A causes feeling C. In fact, feeling C is caused by belief B, what I say to myself about event A (I am a total failure and nobody wants to employ me). If you want to change feeling C, then you must dispute belief B. For example, 'I would have liked the job, and I am disappointed' is more rational than 'I am a total failure' because 'I know I can do the work, and I can do lots of other things well'. (A useful account of the mechanics of carrying out rational-emotive therapy is to be found in Dryden and Ellis 1986.)

## BECK'S COGNITIVE THERAPY

Beck's (1976) approach has some similarity with Ellis' but it enjoys a much stronger research base (Blackburn, Eunson and Bishop 1986; Fennell 1989; Scott 1989). One main difference is that the worker gently encourages those with whom he or she works to identify and reconsider their beliefs, rather than confronting and arguing vigorously. Mainly used in the treatment of depression, Beck's approach aims to identify and modify 'negative automatic thoughts' relating to the person's current and future situations and to the person's view of him- or herself (for example, 'I'm stupid'; 'Nobody likes me', 'I'll never make any friends'). Exploration of the client's earlier experiences is often undertaken in an effort to tease out the dysfunctional assumptions underlying the 'negative automatic thoughts'.

With the worker's help, the client begins to learn to recognize such thoughts and to assemble contradictory evidence. For example: 'I am good at my job', 'My workmates invite me to go to the club with them', 'I have made a number of good friends in my life'.

Homework assignments require the person to record negative automatic thoughts as they occur, and rate how strongly each one is believed at the time (usually on a 1–10 scale). Later he or she must not only track and rate the negative automatic thoughts, but also dispute them – writing down the arguments and evidence against – and then re-rate them, noting down a more constructive alternative for each. The rationale is that thoughts are key antecedents to mood and behaviour. However, the homework assignments also include behavioural tasks to test out whether the beliefs are valid: for example, will the person's friends accept an invitation or do they really reject him or her? The person also plans and records activities that give pleasure and experience of 'mastery' or personal achievement. Other behavioural procedures are introduced as required.

## A CASE STUDY

The inter-relatedness of learning theories and the interventions derived from them is probably clear by now. Rarely would one only use one technique. The following case example illustrates the point (the assessment details are omitted here for the sake of brevity). Mr and Mrs J had frequent rows; their teenage daughter was constantly demanding money, often came home late and was abusive. Mr J lost his temper with both wife and daughter and sometimes hit his daughter. This case involved a whole series of interventions, beginning with a couple of difficult family interviews in which the student strove in vain to set up a contract dealing with the parent–daughter problems. These efforts were thwarted by serious communication problems and by Mr. J's outbursts of temper. Therefore, the student took a few steps back and set up:

1.  individual sessions with Mr J in order to help him with anger control

2.  family communication training sessions in which modelling and practice were used in order to teach family members to listen empathically to each other and not interrupt, and to express concerns clearly and calmly

3.  problem-solving training so that the family could learn to achieve consensus or compromise solutions first to simple, comparatively non-controversial questions such as what sort of puppy to buy and later to more challenging issues as pocket money amount and rules about coming home late.

Only then could the family contract be worked out and put into operation. Later still, the problem of the rows between Mr and Mrs J was reassessed with a view to possible intervention. It was decided that the frequency of these rows was now so low that this would not be necessary. Four packages of procedures were used in this case (anger control, problem-solving, communication training and family contracting). In all of these, and throughout, the worker was constantly modelling, offering specific reinforcement for specific behaviours, seeking to remove reinforcement from unwanted behaviours and explaining the procedures to the family.

## THE EVIDENCE BASE

We really have no further need of more controlled studies of cognitive-behavioral therapy for a wide range of problems.

This was the conclusion of an editor of a premier US academic journal in 2003. The reality is that evidence for the effectiveness of cognitive behavioural approaches is abundant and increasing. There is no area where researchers have compared these approaches with others and found the other approaches to be superior, with possibly the exception of anti-social personality disorders (see Lees, Manning and Rawlings 1999) and even there a learning theory account may be most parsimonious. Areas where the evidence is particularly strong include children's behavioural problems at home and at school, substance misuse, offending including sex offending, depression, anxiety, sexual problems, family problems, child abuse and failure to thrive.

Where the required social work contribution is to do with assessment alone, including risk assessment or court reports, making a careful cognitive behavioural analysis of current and recent behaviour, and the discipline of being specific, concrete and non-speculative, will lead to a clear account that will enhance the quality of decision-making.

Like any other psychology-based approach, the behavioural approach is severely limited in the face of major social problems such as unemployment, homelessness or poverty, and in dealing with very severe forms of mental illness such as schizophrenia where medical involvement is essential (though even here the use of cognitive behavioural methods is being explored and evaluated).

## WHERE TO FROM HERE?

This chapter necessarily provides a 'headlines' and 'key features' approach to what is a large and complex body of knowledge. The temptation to treat cognitive behavioural approaches as a tool-box into which one can dip for assistance is to be avoided. Learning how to do a careful assessment takes time, as does goal-setting and evaluation. Supporting people with whom one is working is an essential component, which often means being in the places that behaviour occurs, at the time at which it occurs. It does not fit well with a 9–5 ethos. Ethically, it is difficult to defend not requiring all social workers to have a sound knowledge of learning theory, and of the evidence-based underpinning cognitive behavioural interventions. It is important when providing services, and when commissioning them, and is essential in ensuring that social workers make good quality decisions in relation to those with whom they work, or towards whom they have statutory responsibilities. Social work is much more than the application of learning theory, but learning theory has earned its place as an essential component of effective and accountable practice.

## Note

References have not been given for every statement for which there is research evidence available. Only a few key references to key topics and issues have been cited.

## References

Bandura, A. (1965) 'Influence of a model's reinforcement contingencies on the acquisition of imitative responses.' *Journal of Personality and Social Psychology 1*, 589–95.

Bandura, A. (1977) *Social Learning Theory.* Englewood Cliffs, NJ: Prentice Hall.

Beck, A.T. (1976) *Cognitive Therapy and the Emotional Disorders.* New York: International Universities Press.

Beck, A.T. (1987) 'Cognitive therapy.' In J.K. Zeig (ed.) *The Evolution of Psychotherapy.* New York: Bruner Mazel.

Blackburn, I.M., Eunson, K.M. and Bishop, S. (1986) 'A two year naturalistic follow-up of depressed patients treated with cognitive therapy, pharmacotherapy and a combination of both.' *Journal of Affective Disorders 10*, 67–75.

Bloom, M. and Fischer, J. (1982) *Evaluating Practice: Guidelines for the Accountable Professional.* Upper Saddle River: Prentice-Hall, Inc.

Brewin, C.R. (1996) 'Theoretical foundations of cognitive-behavioural therapy for anxiety and depression.' *Annual Review of Psychology 47*, 33–57.

Dryden, W. and Ellis, A. (1986) 'Rational-emotive therapy (RET).' In W. Dryden and W. Golden (eds) *Cognitive-behavioral Approaches to Psychotherapy.* London: Harper & Row.

Ellis, A. (1979) 'The basic clinical theory of Rational Emotive Therapy.' In R. Greiger and J. Boyd (eds) *Clinical Applications of Rational Emotive Therapy.* New York: Van Nostrand Reinhold.

ERIC (2007) *Education and Resources for Improving Childhood Continence* Bristol: ERIC. Available at http://www.eric.org.uk/

Fennell, M. (1989) 'Depression.' In K. Hawton, P.M. Salkovis, J. Kirk and D.M. Clark (eds) *Cognitive Behaviour Therapy for Psychiatric Problems.* Oxford: Oxford University Press.

Lees, J., Manning, N. and Rawlings, B. (1999) *A Systematic Review of Therapeutic Community Treatment for People with Personality Disorders and Mentally Disordered Offenders.* Report 117. York: Centre for Reviews and Dissemination.

Meichenbaum, D. (1985) *Stress Inoculation Training.* Oxford: Pergamon.

Pavlov, I.P. (1927) *Conditioned Reflexes.* Trans. G.V. Anrep. London: Oxford University Press.

Scott, M. (1989) *A Cognitive Behavioural Approach to Clients' Problems.* London: Tavistock/Routledge.

Skinner, B.F. (1953) *Science and Human Behaviour.* New York: Macmillan.

Skinner, B.F. (1971) *Beyond Freedom and Dignity.* Harmondsworth: Penguin.

Teasdale, J.D. (1993) 'Emotion and two kinds of meaning: Cognitive-therapy and applied cognitive science.' *Behaviour Research and Therapy 31*, 339–54.

Teasdale, J.D. (1997) 'The relationship between cognition and emotion: The mind-in-place in mood disorders.' In D.M. Clark and C.G. Fairburn (eds) *Science and Practice of Cognitive Behaviour Therapy. Oxford: Oxford University Press.*

Turkat, I.D. and Calhoun, J.F. (1980) 'The problem solving flow chart.' *The Behavior Therapist 3*, 1, 21.

Watson, J.B. and Raynor, R. (1920) 'Conditioned emotional reactions.' *Journal of Experimental Psychology 3*, 1–14.

Webster-Stratton, C. (1998) 'Parent-training with low-income families, promoting parental engagement through a collaborative approach.' In S.S. Luthar, J.A. Burack, D. Cicchetti and J.R. Weisz (eds) *Developmental Psychopathology, Perspectives on Adjustment, Risk, and Disorder.* New York, Cambridge University Press.

## Further reading

Carr, J.H. and Collins, S. (1992) *Working towards Independence: A Practical Guide to Teaching People with Learning Disabilities.* London: Jessica Kingsley Publishers.

Hawton, K., Salkovis, P.M., Kirk, J. and Clark, D.M. (eds) (1989) *Cognitive Behaviour Therapy for Psychiatric Problems.* Oxford: Oxford University Press.

Herbert, M. and Wookey, J. (2004) *Managing Children's Disruptive Behaviour: A Guide for Practitioners Working with Parents and Foster Parents.* Chichester: John Wiley.

Sheldon, B. (1995) *Cognitive-behavioural Therapy: Research, Practice and Philosophy.* London: Routledge.

## CHAPTER 13

# TASK-CENTRED PRACTICE

*Peter Marsh*

## Introduction

For over 40 years task-centred social work has made a particular contribution to the development of effective problem-solving and participatory practice. Its history is one of the combination of what we would now term 'evidence-based practice' and 'partnership working'. The development of the model has come from within the discipline of social work itself, unlike many other models of practice, and it has been tested, refined and developed by social workers and social work researchers in many different settings.

The origins can be traced to a number of sources, but one of the earliest demonstrates the origins and development within social work very well. In 1963 Bill Reid submitted his doctoral dissertation – a 'study concerned with the treatment operations of caseworkers: what caseworkers do in their efforts to help clients' (Reid 1963, p.1). This study contains the hallmarks of the 40-year development of the task-centred model of practice: a focus on practice research, based on the actions and needs of social workers and their service users.

The 1963 Reid study used an analogue experiment to examine the influence of training and experience, and to see how responses varied when workers were faced with different degrees of service user problem. What effects do the different elements of the practitioner's work have on the service user's problems? What is it that helps the service user in problem-solving? These questions have been at the core of the many studies that have contributed to the building of the model. The 1963 Reid study, for example, asked 65 experienced workers and 56 students to complete an exercise which acted as an analogue of their real-life response to a service user in an interview. The research examined the ways in which their experience affected their responses. The initial exploratory study was followed by the more famous experiment contrasting short-term and longer-term approaches (Reid and Shyne 1969) and by many more studies after that (some are listed in the further reading section at the end of this chapter). The model has been built up by social workers and social work researchers using exploratory and developmental studies, focusing on the impact of particular practice elements on the service user's problem-solving abilities. Each element of the model that is outlined here has some degree of empirical backing for its effectiveness in problem-solving.

## TWO BUILDING BLOCKS

Helen Harris Perlman, one of the early doyennes of social casework and the author of a classic text (Perlman 1956) wrote the Foreword to the 1969 Reid and Shyne study and succinctly summarized the change in the approach to social work development shown in this study. She highlighted the fact that the research looked at the consequence for the service user of certain actions, and did not focus on the intentions of the caseworker (Reid and Shyne 1969, p.8). There is a Snoopy cartoon of a football game, where Snoopy, in the last frame, wails 'How can we lose when we have such good intentions?' Social workers often feel exactly like that. The confusion of the intentions of the worker with the outcome for the service user has hampered social work throughout its development; social work practice is usually well intentioned, but that does not always mean that the outcome is satisfactory and developmental research, based upon consequence and not upon intention, is one vital ingredient of beneficial social work.

Task-centred work has another equally important basic element, based both on effectiveness research and on a value statement. Underlying the approach is an emphasis on partnership with the service user, which is to be sought as far as possible in all aspects of practice (Marsh 1990a): partnership in the sense of a respect for the service user's view, a great deal of effort being put into good communication, an emphasis on agreed aims, a preference for joint actions on problems and a recognition of the abilities of the service user where appropriate. A commitment to this form of partnership is necessary for all task-centred practitioners, and it underpins many of the developments in 'empowerment' (see, for example, Lupton and Nixon 1999, pp.7–31) and in user involvement and participation (see, for example, Kemshall and Littlechild 2000).

## The model

What does a task-centred practitioner do? In brief summary: he or she proceeds by emphasizing the role of the service user in negotiating appropriate programmes of help, with work based on an agreement between the worker and the service user, covering the problems to be addressed, and outlining the goals to be achieved. When necessary these problems and goals will include those specified by legislative duties or by a court. The work then proceeds in a series of incremental steps towards the goals and is subject to regular review. Service user and worker engage in a number of tasks to reach the agreed goals, and these tasks may themselves involve collaboration with other people. The worker may need to help the service user carry out certain tasks by, for example, giving advice, or encouragement, or skill training procedures. Tasks are therefore effective because they are part of an overall action; any one task is unlikely to lead directly to a goal. Time limits for the duration of the work will be negotiated at the outset: if there is a reason for long-term involvement then work can proceed by a series of shorter-term agreements, or the task-centred programme can be changed to a regular pattern of service and the monitoring of that service. The service user will be centrally involved in all stages and aspects of the work and will be encouraged to be an active and participatory partner in the agreement, in the tasks and in the reviews.

The work therefore moves from problems to goals by the use of tasks carried out in a time-limited period and using participatory methods as far as possible. A simple outline, but a complex practice, as we shall see as we look at some of the main elements.

## PROBLEMS

The work begins with an examination of problems through an initial general scan of all of the areas that may need help. As service users are likely to come to social work and social care via other services, and as a significant number of them will be reluctant to be there, this scan is a particularly useful technique: service users may often limit the problems that they present because of their view of the agency or worker function (see Sainsbury, Nixon and Phillips 1982). Task-centred work begins with an examination of the width of the problems and not the depth.

After this the problems can be explored in more detail, and the prominent problems should be carefully discussed to establish the current patterns and severity. Without this detail the work may be misdirected and it will be harder to see progress (or the lack of it). The priority of different problems is then established, on the basis of two factors. The first consideration is the priority that the service user, after full discussion and advice, wants to give to different problems. The other consideration is when there are problems that statutory processes require the service user to address, such as the level of care given to children. In general, work should only proceed on the basis of the service user wanting it to, or on the basis of a clear requirement in legislation (usually via a court). Establishing the mandate for work is vital: it can be one based on service user wishes, or legal requirement, or contain elements of both. Service user acceptance of the legislative mandate may, of course, be strictly limited and strategies may need to be devised to deal with this (see Rooney 1988a, 1992). If there is a compulsory legal requirement, and despite all efforts this is not accepted by the service user, then task-centred work cannot be done and some form of supervision will need to be put in place in its stead. The two mandates for work, of service user wishes or of statutory process, link the apparently different worlds of voluntarism and compulsion.

## GOALS

Work sometimes will not proceed beyond the stage of problem exploration, but if it does then the goals of the work need to be established. Agreeing problems is a step on the way to agreeing goals. A problem is *what is wrong* and a goal is *what is needed*, and there is not necessarily a simple and direct connection between *what is wrong* and *what is needed*. For some problems, perhaps most problems, the goal will be a reduction rather than a complete removal of a problem (for example, teenagers and parents may recognize that complete family harmony is unlikely, and many elderly people may be consciously using services to stop things getting worse rather than to make things much better). For other problems the service user may suggest a goal which appears to be only indirectly linked to the problem. The service user's view of what is needed, in the light of the informed discussion with the worker, is the paramount consideration (unless statutory reasons mean that some goals must be imposed).

Goals need to be achievable – it is unjust to work on any other basis. Of course some service users may make their goals too modest and full encouragement for more ambitious goals should be given – this is part of the model's emphasis on building on strengths. But equally it is the case that workers have been guilty in the past of over-ambitious claims for social work action, and service users do not benefit from such ambition.

Goals need to be observable – all parties need to know when they reach them. If service users and workers are going to work hard to achieve goals they need to be able to judge progress towards those goals. Equally the sense of accomplishment, which should be present when the work is successful, will be maximized by a clear and unambiguous achievement of a goal; sorting out what will be defined as success needs to be done at the outset and not at a later stage. Perhaps the best way to make sure that the goal is observable is to ask yourself, and the service user, 'Would a third party be able to judge if we had reached this goal?' Defining relevant, clear, agreed goals is central to task-centred work.

## TIME LIMIT

Reid and Shyne's 1969 study indicated that planned short-term work produced results at least as good as open-ended treatment of longer duration, and suggested that the results of this short-term work were reasonably durable. We all know of the remarkable improvement in effort when we are about to reach a deadline, and presumably this effect plays some role in the relative effectiveness of short-term work. Early work may often be better motivated: as the memory of a problem fades, so the motivation to work on it can also fade. Short-term work is not just a smaller amount of longer-term work: it is a different process. The planned date of ending (or of moving to a new agreement, or to a monitoring stage when contact needs to be long term) is agreed at the start. The time limit should be as short as is reasonable for the problem (with around three months as the maximum).

## TASKS

Tasks are carried out after the problems, goals and time limit have been agreed and they are central to the problem-solving efforts in task-centred work. Tasks are not just the *jobs to be done* that usually occur at the end of most interviews between service users and workers. Tasks are discrete parts of the overall action: a series of incremental steps towards goals (Reid 1978). They are effective as part of that overall action; any one task is unlikely to lead directly to a goal. They are a planned sequence; a set of steps on the ladder from *what is wrong* to *what is needed*.

Different task strategies will be needed for different problems and areas; these strategies are the heart of task-centred practice (Reid 1992).

Tasks are carried out by workers and by service users and the process of problem-solving is a joint one between the two partners. They establish the best way to proceed, they divide up the time period into appropriate stages and they divide up the work between them. Another factor which distinguishes tasks from jobs to be done is the active role that service users play in the task work. Tasks are designed in part to provide ways for skills to be learnt, and for dependency to be avoided (see the examples of tasks in Reid 2000). Service users should always be centrally involved in the development of tasks, and there should normally be a number of tasks that they carry out.

RECORDS AS AN AID TO PARTICIPATION

A participative approach is vital in task-centred work and this can be greatly enhanced by the use of written material – to remind, to inform, to clarify and to provide an account. Unfortunately, records have a poor reputation in social work with the two main areas of recording, the agency records (addresses, finance, movement of children in care and so on) and the practice records (notes about sessions, plans of action and so on) being equally ill regarded by most practitioners. Agency records will be needed for the many purposes they serve, but alongside these 'records for others', the practice records are crucial and they need to receive a much better press from task-centred practitioners. Task-centred records (which of course could be tape recorded if major eyesight or literacy problems make writing impossible) are essential in order to keep the service user informed of progress, to clarify the plans, and to act as aide-memoire for service users and workers in carrying out tasks (Doel and Marsh 1992, Chapter 4; Marsh and Doel 2005, p.37). They are an indispensable tool of practice: a view which represents a considerable challenge to the continuing pressure to make 'recording' primarily about managerial control.

## What the model is not

Before considering aspects of task-centred work in greater detail, we should note that task-centred practice is as prone as any other aspect of social work to being simplified and turned into a parody. A sloppy use of the term 'task-centred' is often evident in discussions about methods. It seems to be confused with a simplistic and surface approach to service user problems – 'I'm only doing task-centred work at the moment; my in-depth work is with these other cases'. Nothing could be further from the truth. Task-centred work is beguiling in its clear structure and apparently straight forwardness, but its application is complex and it is designed to tackle the most difficult problems that face social work service users. It is 'in-depth' when that depth is needed; it is not just appropriate for simple problems.

Task-centred work is also confused with a welfare rights approach to problems, and with the provision of services. Practitioners discuss the fact that this or that case is suitable for a task-centred approach because it involves benefit problems and because it involves an application for some form of service. There is no difficulty in incorporating welfare rights work and service provision in the model but to limit it to these processes is quite unnecessary. The task-centred approach integrates these aspects of work into the overall work with the service user; it is not solely a service or welfare rights model.

## The heart of the model

A good analysis of problems, clarity about the basis for work (service user or court mandate) and clarity of goals are vital initial steps in task-centred practice. The heart of the model lies in the task work that follows this. Tasks were described earlier as the steps on the ladder from problems to goals. They are the building blocks of change in the problem-solving process. They are designed to be cumulative, acting in sequence to move the work from the problem, *what is wrong*, to the goal, *what is needed*.

## THE SEQUENCE OF TASKS

The process of problem-solving is therefore seen as:

PROBLEM

*to* tasks

*to* tasks

*to* tasks

*to* tasks

*to* GOAL

The tasks are a series of steps to the goal, each one designed to provide some progress, and with review of that progress, as we shall see, being an important element that underpins the task process (see Marsh and Doel 2005, p.30).

Tasks may be agreed for the worker, for the service user or, with suitable involvement, for others. They may be reciprocal ('If you do this, I'll do that'); they may be repetitive (a number of visits by the home help to carry out the same general tasks to move towards the goal); they may be joint ('We agree to do the following'). Developing them is a challenging process for both worker and service user. The development will involve service users' experience of successful problem-solving, and their caveats about past failures. The model attempts to build on success and to avoid repeating failures.

The first stage in task development is to consider the general pattern of tasks that is likely to lead to the goal; is there an obvious order to tasks – are there simple and more complex ones, is there a suitable balance of worker and service user tasks? These issues will inform the development of the tasks because of the need to see tasks as part of a sequence and not think of them as one activity that leads directly from problem to goal (although simple problems may sometimes lend themselves to very few tasks). Once a general approach is developed, and the focus of relevant tasks for that session agreed, then there needs to be detailed task planning.

## TASK PLANNING AND ACTION

In 1975 Bill Reid published the report of an experimental study designed to show whether or not a particular approach to task planning aided task completion. The success of the Task Implementation Sequence in this study led to its adoption within the model. It consists of five main steps to be carried out after the general focus of a task has been developed. The first stage is 'enhancing commitment', where the practitioner asks the service user to review the potential benefits of carrying out the task and reinforces and encourages realistic assessments of these benefits. The second stage is 'planning task implementation', where the detail of the work to be done is covered. This should be done with great care, making sure that the plans are as clear as possible.

These two stages are followed by 'analysing obstacles', where all reasonable pitfalls are thought of and ways to handle them are explored. Then the practitioner may move on to 'modelling, rehearsal and guided practice' to help prepare for the task work. Actions could be *modelled* by the worker (or by others), they could be *rehearsed* in the session or they could be *guided* in vivo (for example, the service user could make a telephone call with the worker and the service user, having produced a checklist of what needs to be covered and with the worker listening to the call and able to give advice as needed).

Finally the worker needs to 'summarize' the task development by restarting the task (which should be in clear language) and the plan for implementation. The full process of task work is therefore:

1.    Develop an overall task strategy (in outline) that leads from problem to goal – this will be a prominent factor in early sessions and in the back of the mind in later ones.

2.    For each session (including the one that first agrees goals and time limits) decide on tasks for that session.

3.    For each task follow the Task Implementation Sequence of 'enhancing commitment', 'planning task implementation', 'analysing obstacles', 'modelling, rehearsal and guided practice' and ending with 'summary of the task'.

Task development needs to be undertaken for each task. For some tasks it will be brief and straightforward, for others it may be a lengthy part of the session. Writing is again very useful in this work. Writing down the tasks will clarify understanding, and also act as an aide-memoire for worker and service user in the period between sessions when tasks are to be carried out. Leaving a copy of the tasks with the service user is the ideal way of carrying out this task work (a developmental research project, Social Work in Partnership, has developed self-carbonating sheets for 'agreed goals' and 'tasks' – a useful practical aid to the work – see Marsh 1990b).

Task work is designed to achieve change and also to be part of the 'learning by doing' approach of task-centred practice. Service users' and workers' task work can illustrate how obstacles to problem-solving can be overcome and both parties can learn new strategies for overcoming them. Task development, after the initial session, will always begin with a review of the tasks undertaken since the last session. This review is vital to indicate progress, enhance learning and to provide analysis of obstacles to problem-solving. It offers an opportunity to see how things are going in a real and evident way as the work progresses. It also offers the service user a chance to hold the worker to account through the review of worker tasks in each session (for greater details see Marsh and Doel 2005, Chapter 7).

If tasks are not completed, the reasons for this will need to be considered. The task may be the wrong one for the purpose or there may be obstacles that were not foreseen; these two different issues would require different approaches. If the task was wrong then a new task needs to be created; if there were obstacles, then it may be that guided practice or some other form of aid to task work needs to be undertaken rather than the creation of a new task. If tasks are regularly not done despite this analysis and aid, then it may be that the problem, or the goals, is not a priority for the service user. Persistently undone tasks may indicate the need for detailed review of problems and goals; this review will be greatly aided by the evidence of a number of weeks of discussion and support for tasks that are still incomplete.

The tasks outside the sessions should therefore be thought of as an integral part of the approach, and the overall pattern of the model now looks like this (the sessions are in bold):

**PROBLEM** + task development

    *to* tasks

        *to* **task review**

        + **task development**

            *to* tasks

                *to* **task review**

                + **task development**

                    *to* tasks

                        *to* **GOAL**

## REVIEWS AND ENDINGS

Many parts of the model do, in essence, seek to make social work practice more evident, more explicit and more understandable. Tasks are helpful in this process – they allow the worker's intended actions to be seen, they provide a clear picture of the process of problem-solving and they allow progress (or lack of it) to be judged by service user and worker alike. Review of tasks is part of this process and the concept of review is built into the task-centred model in a number of ways.

Apart from the task review a date for a final review of all the work is established at the start by the creation of a time limit for the work. In addition, each of the task sessions should begin with a brief review of problems to see if changes have taken place (for example, relationships breaking up or disabilities getting worse could significantly affect the service user's view of problems stated at the start of the work). Changes in the problem may also have occurred due to the work on the tasks, and even though this work is not sufficient to meet the agreed goal it may have altered perceptions or improved matters sufficiently so that further work on that problem is not needed. These task sessions of the work should therefore always follow the order: problem review, task review, task development.

Work in the task-centred model will be undertaken within a time-limited period, usually not exceeding three months. Clearly there are occasions when the time limit needs to be extended, but this should only happen if there are delays to problem-solving caused by factors outside the worker's and service user's control (such as the policies or timescales of another agency). In general, if work is to continue beyond the time limit then a new set of agreed goals should be negotiated. This means that work will continue in chunks of three months (or to look at it another way, a substantial review of work, its purpose and content, will take place at this interval within a long-term work package).

There may be a number of circumstances where contact has to be maintained over long periods (a frail elderly person with a range of services, a child in the care of social work services, etc.). This does not necessarily mean that a sequence of agreed goals need to be drawn up at regular intervals as it may well be the case that active intervention in the task-centred model is followed by periods of monitoring which do not involve active work from the practitioner. An elderly person, for example, could well engage in a period of active work and then a network of services could be established with an agreed process of review.

## SPECIALIZED WORK AND THE MODEL

The task-centred model is an evolving one, based on practice research and policy development within social work and social care. There are a number of aspects of the current development of the model which cannot be covered in this introductory chapter, for example the detail of its application in specific settings, work on the use of the model in family problem-solving and its links with family therapy, and recent work on the model and partnership approaches to child care and care of elderly people. The further reading section at the end of the chapter provides a starting point for enquiries into some of these developments.

## Critique

The model has probably received the greatest degree of research attention of any model of practice developed within social work and the results of this research are positive, particularly when taken in comparison with other approaches (Reid and Hanrahan 1981). The model is popular with service users (Gibbons *et al.* 1979), and has been used with a wide variety of service user groups and in all of the settings that social workers work in (Epstein 1988a Reid 1985). It is congruent with anti-discriminatory practice and in its respect for the service user's views it sharpens the focus of ethnic-sensitive practice (Devore and Schlesinger 1981). It is proving its worth in the development of community care approaches and in the partnership-based practice that is developing in social work (Marsh 1990a). But there are limits to the model. Some of the limits could almost certainly be overcome; some of them indicate that different approaches are needed.

## IMPLEMENTATION AND TRAINING

The evidence so far is that training workers to use the model is far from straightforward. In the USA (Reid and Beard 1980; Rooney 1988b) and in the UK (Goldberg, Gibbons and Sinclair 1985) there have been major difficulties in training qualified workers in the use of the model. Taking similar cases and problems, some of the trainees appear able to use task-centred work with most of their service users and some appear hardly able to use it at all. Experience indicates similar problems with students on qualifying courses.

There are probably a number of factors to be considered here. First, despite its apparent simplicity, the model is in fact a complex one, demanding notably thoughtful practice and high levels of skill. It may simply be that some workers cannot manage this, and it may also be that some individuals are more prepared than others to invest the required time and effort. Much of the development work in task-centred practice has used volunteer workers with most workers being evidently committed to developmental work (for example, they have been enrolled in continuing education or research programmes), and these attitudes and abilities may need to be present for good development of task-centred practice. Second, the training may be poor, but current evidence on training is too slim to make sound judgements possible. Too many projects fail to give any detail of the training, and there is very little direct research on training. The successful American programmes provide some 40 hours of input, as well as live and indirect supervision of practice (Epstein 1988) and this level of training is probably needed for genuine practice change. Implementation and training issues, and methods to make successful development and maintenance of task-centred work most likely, have been the focus of 20 years of work by the author and his colleague, Doel (see Marsh and Doel 2005). Providing good training, with effective and continuing personal, team and agency support is vital, not least in periods when social work's professional side can be overwhelmed by administrative requirements.

## RANGE OF WORK

Two areas of work are unlikely to respond well to task-centred practice. The first surrounds those families and individuals who appear subject to constant crises and whose problems appear to change with startling rapidity. The second involves cases where there is a statutory reason for involvement but no recognition by the service user of this statutory mandate (and no other area that the service user wants to work on voluntarily).

The *constant crisis* family is a source of great strain for many workers in social care and social work – as fast as the benefits appeal is sorted out there is a teenager on the streets due to family rows, and as fast as this is dealt with there is a housing crisis, etc. These cases can occupy a great deal of time and give rise to a great deal of concern (not least because other agencies are often demanding that 'something should be done'). The task-centred model is not well suited to the extreme version of this sort of case; by the time one set of goals has been agreed there is a completely new set of problems to resolve and a new set of goals to negotiate. A task-centred worker may find that a number of cases that appear to fall in this category at present could be dealt with on a less crisis-orientated basis, but obtaining cooperation and agreement in some crisis-dominated circumstances is always going to be difficult. There do not appear to be any other models, capable of achieving change, that handle this work well. Perhaps a 'holding' model of practice needs to be articulated and developed. The scale of this part of the workload needs some careful analysis and policies need to be developed to handle it – task-centred practice's contribution is to make the practice problem more evident and clear; it will not resolve it.

The case that requires statutory intervention (children in need of protection, etc.) can, as we have seen, be dealt with perfectly well within task-centred practice. But such cases do require at least some agreement (or at least reasonable acquiescence) from the service user to the mandate given by the court. Situations occur where service users refuse to accept this mandate, allowing social workers access but not agreeing that anything needs to be done. Task-centred work cannot proceed in such circumstances (although in the unlikely event of a separate voluntarily agreed problem it could proceed on this). Work in such circumstances will involve some form of supervision, a cross between monitoring and social policing, and this will need to be acknowledged. Continuing attempts to engage such service users will need to be made but it can be extremely difficult work. We do not know how many of these cases exist but they will no doubt continue to form a small group that will fall outside the remit of the model.

OTHER ISSUES

There is no reason why task-centred work should not be the basis for agreed goals which themselves lead to work within other models of practice. For example, task-centred work is not designed to deal with the personal exploration involved in counselling, but a goal, reached in a task-centred manner, of 'feeling better about the death of my wife, and being able to discuss it with my friends' could be met by a number of sessions of counselling. Similar considerations apply to links with behavioural approaches, where programmes could be set up to reach goals agreed during the task-centred beginning of the work.

## Use

Task-centred work has much to commend it and perhaps four main points should be focused on when considering use of the model.

1.    It provides a conceptual clarity for the basis of social work that is sorely needed by practitioners, managers and service users (and probably others, such as the press, the public and politicians). It highlights the fact that social work practice covers *both* help and social control, so long as great care is taken to recognize the elements of each. Working with this model, service users should be able to understand a great deal more about the service they are getting and be in a better position to influence that service and, as appropriate, to call it to account.

2.    It emphasizes the need to develop practice on the basis of sound evidence: to fashion development in an incremental manner which is open to scrutiny by workers, researchers and others. Changes in practice do not seem to occur predominantly on this basis at present and the service is the worse for this.

3.    It is outcome orientated – the good intentions of the worker are not enough. Despite all the laudable efforts of staff in social care and social work, the outcome of a variety of well-intentioned programmes and practices has not been satisfactory on too many occasions. The development of more effective and partnership-based community and child care services is urgently needed. An emphasis on the effect of the work on the service user is an important part of the coming of age of social work practice.

4.    It provides, inherently within its value base, construction and practice, a voice for service users and carers, right at the heart of the services themselves.

These areas are sound reasons for considering the task-centred approach very seriously. Despite the training and implementation caveats, aspects of task-centred work that particularly feature these areas could probably be developed without major investment – for example, making sure that clearly agreed goals are recorded and that a review of these goals is made. Or workers could develop tasks for part of their existing work, using the task development process within their current approach to practice.

The model can be recommended for wide use within social work and social care in most situations where an active professional intervention is required, and where reasonable training and support for task-centred work can be provided. The strengths of the model and its overall status within social work practice will continue to be explored and developed, but we already know that a significantly better service could be given by much greater use of task-centred approaches.

*Editor's note:* The Handbook also refers readers to the models of intervention which can provide alternatives to what Marsh identifies as a hindrance to applying the last centred model universally.

## References

Devore, W. and Schlesinger, E.G. (1981) *Ethnic-Sensitive Social Work Practice.* St Louis, MO: C.V. Mosby.

Doel, M. and Marsh, P. (1992) *Task-Centred Social Work.* Aldershot: Wildwood House.

Epstein, L. (1988) Personal communication to the author.

Gibbons, J.S., Bow, I., Butler, J. and Powell, J. (1979) 'Clients' reactions to task centred casework: A follow-up study.' *British Journal of Social Work 9,* 2, 203–215.

Goldberg, E.M., Gibbons, J. and Sinclair, I. (1985) *Problems, Tasks and Outcomes.* London: George Allen & Unwin.

Kemshall, H. and Littlechild, R. (eds) (2000) *User Involvement and Participation in Social Care.* London: Jessica Kingsley Publishers.

Lupton, C. and Nixon, P. (1999) *Empowering Practice? A Critical Appraisal of the Family Group Conference Approach.* Bristol: Policy Press.

Marsh, P. (1990a) 'Outline of social work in partnership research.' Unpublished research paper, Sheffield, Social Work in Partnership Programme, University of Sheffield.

Marsh, P. (1990b) 'Records in social work in partnership research.' Unpublished research paper, Sheffield, Social Work in Partnership Programme, University of Sheffield.

Marsh, P. and Doel, M. (2005) *The Task-Centred Book.* Abingdon: Routledge.

Perlman, H.H. (1956) *Social Casework: A Problem-Solving Process.* Chicago, IL: Chicago University Press.

Reid, W.J. (1963) 'An experimental study of methods used in casework treatment.' Ph.D. dissertation, Columbia University.

Reid, W.J. (1975) 'A test of a task-centred approach.' *Social Work 20,* January, 3–9.

Reid, W.J. (1978) *The Task-Centred System.* New York: Columbia University Press.

Reid, W.J. (1985) *Family Problem Solving* New York: Columbia University Press.

Reid, W.J. (1992) *Task Strategies.* New York: Columbia University Press.

Reid, W.J. (2000) *The Task Planner.* New York: Columbia University Press.

Reid, W.J. and Beard, C. (1980) 'An evaluation of in-service training in a public welfare setting.' *Administration in Social Work 4,* 1, spring, 71–85.

Reid, W.J. and Hanrahan, P. (1981) 'The effectiveness of social work: Recent evidence.' In E.M. Goldberg and N. Connelly (eds) *Evaluation Research in Social Care.* London: Policy Studies Institute.

Reid, W.J. and Shyne, A.W. (1969) *Brief and Extended Casework.* New York: Columbia University Press.

Rooney, R.H. (1988a) 'Socialization strategies for involuntary clients.' *Social Casework 69,* March, 131–40.

Rooney, R.H. (1988b), 'Measuring task-centred training effects on practice: Results of an audiotape study in a public agency.' *Journal of Continuing Social Work Education 4,* 4, 2–7.

Rooney, R.H. (1992) *Strategies for Work with Involuntary Clients.* New York: Columbia University Press.

Sainsbury, E.E., Nixon, S. and Phillips, D. (1982) *Social Work in Focus.* London: Routledge and Kegan Paul.

## Further reading

The following selected references provide a starting point for further exploration of task-centred practice, including studies which have informed development in specific areas.

### THE DETAILS OF THE MODEL

Marsh, P. and Doel, M. (2005) *The Task-Centred Book*. Abingdon: Routledge.

Reid, W.J. (1992) *Task Strategies*. New York: Columbia University Press.

### FAMILIES/CHILD CARE

Fortune, A.E. (ed.) (1985) *Task-Centred Practice with Families and Groups*. New York: Springer Publishing.

Reid, W.J. (1985) *Family Problem Solving*. New York: Columbia University Press.

Reid, W.J. (1987) 'The family problem-solving sequence.' *Family Therapy 14*, 2, 135–46.

Rooney, R.H. (1988) 'Socialization strategies for involuntary clients.' *Social Casework 69*, March, 131–40.

### OLDER PEOPLE

Cormican, E. (1977) 'Task-centred model for work with the aged.' *Social Casework 58*, October, 490–4.

Dierking, B., Brown, M. and Fortune, A.E. (1980) 'Task-centred treatment in a residential facility for the elderly: A clinical trial.' *Journal of Gerontological Social Work 2*, spring, 225–40.

### CRIMINAL JUSTICE

Goldberg, E.M. and Stanley, S.J (1979) 'A task-centred approach to probation.' From J.F.S. King (ed.) *Pressures and Change in the Probation Service*. Papers presented to the 11th Cropwood Round Table Conference, December 1978. Cropwood Conference Series No. 11. Cambridge: University of Cambridge.

Marshall, P. (1987) 'Task-centred practice in a probation setting.' In R. Harris (ed.) *Practising Social Work*. Leicester: University of Leicester, School of Social Work.

### IMPLEMENTATION

Goldberg, E.M., Gibbons, J. and Sinclair, I. (1984) *Problems, Tasks and Outcomes: The Evaluation of Task-Centred Casework in Three Settings*. National Institute Social Services Library, No. 47. London: Allen and Unwin.

Marsh, P. and Doel, M. (2005) *The Task-Centred Book*. Abingdon: Routledge.

Rooney, R.H. (1988) 'Measuring task-centred training effects on practice: Results of an audiotape study in a public agency.' *Journal of Continuing Social Work Education 4*, 4, 2–7.

## CHAPTER 14

# CRISIS INTERVENTION

*Amy Clark*

## Introduction

There are several types of crisis which people experience over the life course. These are situational crises, a response to a traumatic event such as accidents, natural disasters and corporate failures; developmental crises, the stages of normal development identified by Erikson (1965); and crises relating to social problems, such as individuals or communities caught up in criminal behaviour, illegal drug misuse or terrorism. Coulshed and Orme (2006) and Payne (2005) identify two categories: maturation and situational crisis. A crisis in confidence is a feature and consequence of experiencing such events.

Situational crises are usually unexpected events such as redundancy, financial problems, moving house due to fire or flood, or relationship difficulties. Developmental or maturational crises involve the eight stages of personality development, each maturational stage characterized by psychosocial crisis. This chapter will consider situational and developmental crises and the impact crisis may have on the people involved, the assessment of it and thereafter the intervention required. In order to do this, it is first necessary to have a definition of 'crisis'. This is not straightforward because people use related words such as 'crisis', 'change', 'critical incident' and 'stress', interchangeably, even though they are not equivalent in meaning or in terms of people's experience (Coulshed and Orme 2006). Thompson (2002, p.14) states that crisis 'is based on the idea that crisis is an upset in a steady state, a moment where our usual coping resources are overwhelmed'. Therefore, situations which threaten existing coping mechanisms require new strategies to be evolved to improve or replace existing ones. Thompson (2005, p.69) describes crisis intervention as 'turning points in people's lives [which] generate a lot of energy that can be used positively to tackle problems'. Crisis can be a time for learning and improving situations. Caplan (1964) defines crisis as a threat to homeostasis. People generally seek balance and stability (homeostasis or equilibrium) in their life but when certain experiences overwhelm crisis can ensue. Rapoport (1970, p.276) defines crisis as 'an upset in a steady state'. This definition is simple and not difficult to remember but there are service users who are constantly upset and lurch from one crisis to another (see Chapter 13 in the present volume). Service users frequently experience periods of internal and external upsets throughout their life. Failure to achieve at school can lead to disaffection in adolescents often resulting in delinquent criminal behaviour and the lack of qualification which can affect employment and earning power. People who live in poverty often experience the worst housing, difficult relationships and illness. This cumulative impact of circumstances puts service users in a vulnerable state. Payne (1968, p.102) states that 'people who suffer a life-time of stress will be more quickly incapacitated by problems'.

O'Hagan (1986) suggests that a crisis is a set of circumstances or conditions for one individual which, however, may not be so for another. An individual is in crisis when a particular event such as loss, change, threat or pain causes him or her to become debilitated by the circumstance.

## Situational crises

Situational crisis is experienced by most people: all of us (but perhaps service users more than most) experience periods of upset throughout life; for example, change in living conditions, personal injury or illness, retirement or change in work practice, difficult financial circumstances, a large mortgage or loan, addition to a family, death of a close relative, divorce or partnership separation. In broad terms, change implies transition from one state to another and the individual may experience initial shock, numbness, denial, disbelief and disorganization; these are reactions people experience in response to change and loss (Bowlby 1969; Kubler-Ross 1969). Parkes (1972) in his research studies of grief in adult life identified five phases of the bereavement process: alarm, searching, mitigation, anger and guilt and gaining a new identity. These stages contribute to the individual's ability to cope with change and loss and to achieve a crisis resolution. Some stressors are predictable and occur gradually, and it is possible to prepare for stressful events and prevent a crisis. Preparations for an exam, planning for retirement, and pre-partnership, premarital counselling are examples of anticipatory work (Golan 1978). Anticipatory work helps people to feel more in control and equipped to deal with transitions and problems.

Before we consider helping others through change it is helpful for us as workers to consider an area of personal change and our own reaction. Self-awareness is a fundamental factor in determining reaction to change. Workers have a responsibility to care for themselves as well as for service users and to recognize stressful circumstances and whether the stressful event is temporary or permanent. People manage stress in various ways and to a considerable extent it is a person's perception of the event, rather than the event itself, which determines the stress they experience.

Johnson (1979) reminds us that stress by itself is not necessarily a crisis. Stress can be caused by any change in an individual's life which departs from normal patterns, and it is only when the level of stress becomes too great or distress occurs that problems are presented.

People can, and do, cope with large amounts of change, pressure, complexity and confusion as long as there are some aspects of their life that remain relatively stable. A more helpful approach to the interaction of stress and crisis is that a crisis occurs when a stressful life event overwhelms an individual's ability to cope effectively in the face of a perceived challenge or threat (Auerbach and Kilman 1977; Everly and Mitchell 1999; Flannery and Everly 2000).

Recent developments in resilience theory are relevant to developmental crisis, loss and change and stress. Most people are resilient and thrive on a certain amount of stress. Newman and Blackburn (2002, p.12) for the purposes of their study used the following definition: 'Resilient children are better equipped to resist stress and adversity, cope with change and uncertainty, and recover faster and more completely from traumatic events or episodes.' Unfortunately this is not every child's experience in this nation and countries around the world. Some families are deprived through poor health, poverty, malnutrition, and drug and alcohol misuse. These circumstances can lead children and adults to feel insecure or aggressive, and to experience low self-esteem and mental health problems. Despite these conditions and social divisions, the majority of people are resilient and learn to adapt and survive. The practitioner's task is helping people who have suffered abuse and deprivation to rise above their circumstances. For some this is more easily achieved than for others. A defining variable is that of resilience. Generally the more resilient a person is, the better their capacity to cope with crisis. Gilligan contends that certain positive qualities within the child, and certain favourable conditions within the social context, may help a child to show resilience in the face of adversity. 'Bearing in mind what has happened to them a resilient child does better than he or she ought to' (Gilligan 2000 cited in Maclean 2003, p.1).

Critical incidents are sudden, unexpected, often life-threatening time-limited events that may overwhelm an individual's capacity to respond. I draw on my own personal memory of a critical incident in July 1988 when the oil platform Piper Alpha blew up in the North Sea. There was a massive explosion and huge fire engulfed the platform. Sadly, 167 men died.

Many hours passed that day before families knew whether their relatives were dead, injured or safe. During these hours relatives experienced a range of emotions including shock, fear and denial (Bowlby 1969). Relatives, colleagues and friends tried to cope constructively by fulfilling normal roles but as the hours passed panic and stress was at an intolerable level. Families were anxious, apprehensive and distressed: some suffered somatic distress such as feeling sick, stomach complaints and headaches. Somatic distress was a feature of Lindemann's (1944) study of grief reaction.

Families were overwhelmed by the sudden horrific death of a relative; feelings of loss, frustration and anger were evident. Some people tried to maintain a state of emotional equilibrium while others could not cope and crisis ensued. Support was sought from relatives, friends, social workers, doctors and clinical psychologists. An ability to share the negative emotional impact of a traumatic event is seen as an important step to recovery. Self-help groups also reveal the emotional aid members can give to one another (Lieberman 1993).

Extreme critical incident stresses may result in personal crisis, traumatic stress and even post-traumatic stress disorder or PTSD (American Psychiatric Association 1994); Everly and Lating 1995; Flannery 1994, 1995). Families of men who died, and survivors too, experienced sleep disturbance and withdrawal from full participation in daily activities and intrusive recollections of the disaster. For days and weeks after the event, television and newspaper column coverage was immense. No doubt some individuals were experiencing situational crisis as well as developmental stage crisis, which compounded feelings of anxiety and confusion. Erikson's (1963) developmental theory relates to maturation stages/crises passed through from birth through to old age. Thompson (2005, p.57) states that 'problems may arise where people have difficulty making the adjustment from one life stage to the next'.

Throughout history there have been natural disasters, which because of the magnitude of the event cannot be dealt with by an individual or organization. On 26 December 2004 approximately 100 miles from the western coast of Indonesia's Sumatra islands a 9.0 magnitude earthquake struck causing a tsunami. The tidal wave engulfed countries, towns and villages. It is estimated that more than 200,000 adults and children lost their lives in Indonesia, Thailand, Sri Lanka, India, the Maldives and Malaysia. Thousands of survivors were homeless and had to scavenge for food and water, and injured people inundated hospitals. Worldwide emergency planning was required and basic needs had to be urgently restored to all populations. Plans had to anticipate that people, particularly orphaned or lost children, might fall prey to infectious diseases. It is difficult to visualize such loss of life and destruction over such a wide area. The scale of such a disaster meant that governments and charities around the world gave personnel and financial assistance.

Social workers have considerable knowledge and skills in assisting and sustaining victims overcome by grief and misery following the aftermath of disasters. Counselling and assistance have been provided to victims of train crashes, the Gulf war, Lockerbie, Piper Alpha, Dunblane and other major tragedies. Theories of crisis, humanistic philosophies, Maslow's (1970) hierarchy of need, concepts, models and guidelines all contribute to practitioners' knowledge and practice skills. The American project, National Organization for Victim Assistance (Young 1995), produced guidelines for crisis intervention services in the aftermath of a disaster.

## Developmental crises stages and resilience

Erikson's (1965) eight psychosocial stages build on Freud's legacy of the development of the ego (see Chapter 5 in the present volume), that past conflicts can be pushed out of our conscious awareness but still affect a person's life. Erikson (1965) suggests that ego development is lifelong and his theory of psychosocial development covers a series of distinct stages through which people pass in a certain order. Each stage pulls the person in different direction and if the person is supported and nurtured a favourable healthy balance should be reached between positive and negative traits.

A maturational crisis may occur at any of these developmental stages because each transitional stage depends to a certain extent on the ability of individuals to achieve a resolution of a previous stage. Some people are unable to make the role change required for a new maturational stage to develop because of lack of nurture and support from parents, teachers, partners, peers or significant others to achieve the skills for the next developmental stage. Maturational crises are predictable and occur gradually; therefore, it is possible to prepare for these transitional stages.

People who are supported through these developmental stages are more likely to become resilient human beings. Resilient people are likely to have good relationships and strong attachments to significant others and to manage adverse circumstances and bounce back from threats or traumatic events. Masten and Coatsworth (1998) identify the characteristic of resilient children as: 'good intellectual functioning, appealing, sociable, easygoing disposition, self-efficacy, self-confidence, high self-esteem, talent and faith'; 'Close relationship to a caring parent figure and extended family network support and socioeconomic advantaged'; 'Resilient children formed bonds with prosocial adults outside the family and attended effective schools' (p.212). These findings are all positive child development factors which are referred to in attachment theory and point to potential pathways in reducing the impact of a crisis. Workers therefore can contribute to such protective factors which encourage resilience in people, by adding resources, bolstering and improving relationships and coaching people to develop skills that build self-efficacy.

## Crisis theory and intervention

Crisis theory and concepts have been elaborated and developed over the past 50 years (Caplan 1961, 1964; Coulshed and Orme 2006; Erikson 1965; Golan 1978; Lindemann 1944; Parad 1958; Parkes 1972; Payne 2005; Rapoport 1970; Roberts 1991; Thompson 1991). Caplan's extensive work on crisis theory formulated a method of intervention which was influenced by writings and research carried out by Lindemann (1944), evidencing how people coped with bereavement crises, Parad (1958), on ego psychology and dynamic casework, and Erikson (1965), on stages of development and maturation points in the lifecycle. Caplan (1964) first used 'crises' as a specific psychiatric term in his book *Principles of Preventative Psychiatry*.

It is important that workers use theory and research to enhance their practice. Underpinning theory and concepts contribute to the worker's ability to assess and search out ways to support people in crisis. Howe (1987, p.9) warns us that 'to show no interest in theory is to travel blind'. Knowledge of the following theories and models is essential to understand and assess the following areas:

1. Psychoanalytic theory (Freud 1986) enables the worker to assess the individual's ego strength and the deployment of defence mechanisms.

2. Developmental stages (Erikson 1965) alert the worker to possible maturation crisis.

3. Concurrent stressors (Holmes and Rahe 19679) aid the worker to recognize stressful life experiences and to be alert to environmental factors.

4. Bereavement, change and loss (Marris 1986; Parkes 1972), aid understanding of stages of grief and contributes to the worker's ability to empathize with the individual's situation.

5. Resilience promotion (Masten and Coatworth 1998) facilitates intervention by providing experiences which boosts resilience in the face of adversity.

6. Social network theory (Caplan 1964) of development both formal and informal increases the likelihood of the individual receiving support.

Crisis theory (Caplan 1964) serves as a foundation and framework to help the worker to understand complex situations and behaviour and to predict future events and what supports might be required.

There continues to be a debate regarding empirical testing of theory and evidence based practice. Payne (2002, p.123) believes that 'social work theory from the "evidence-based" position has sought to promote only a limited range of practice that can be empirically tested'. Sheldon (2000, p.123) suggests that 'developing crushes on favourite theories or approaches sometimes induces us to dis-attend to both inconsistencies within them'. Coulshed and Orme (1998, p.7) suggest that theory implies 'rational thinking, distance and objectivity which contrasts with feeling and living reality of social encounters'. Knowledge gained from theory, concepts, values, ethics and practice skills should be subject to scrutiny. Reflective practice (see Chapter 23 in the present volume) alerts a worker to gaps in practice skills and knowledge as well as acknowledging successful outcome.

Theory such as psychoanalytic theory can provide workers with a useful understanding and potential course of action, but be difficult to test according to experiential scientific methods. People in crisis can reveal signs and symptoms of a fragile ego and excessive use of defence mechanisms such as denial, repression or projection. Defence mechanisms through over use by the individual can fail to fulfil emotional support which might lead to mental illness or obsessions. Cohen (1990, p.284) argues that 'Understanding the variations and sequences of emotion, with the accompanying defences, is at the heart of crisis intervention'. Sheldon (2000, p.65) conversely questions 'why should some kinds of trauma be hard to recover from memory, when most people who have suffered bad experiences have great trouble forgetting the fact'. All egos need protecting some time or another, particularly when people are in crisis from external situation or feeling guilty or overwhelmed by intense feelings (Freud 1986).

Developmental crises are associated with ego psychology and the worker needs to be competent to assess Erikson's maturational stages which play a prominent role in understanding human social and emotional development. Even in the face of development difficulty some people seem to do better than others and function well. Newman and Blackburn (2002, p.4) found in their research that resilience is a capacity that develops through 'transitional periods which bring threats and opportunities'.

The worker needs to take into consideration the constructs of social division such as class, gender, disability, and relationship with family and wider community. Lindemann (1944) discovered that people who suffer from mental illness were more likely to remain well if they had a reliable social network, which provided support, companionship, information, and encouragement. In order to promote resilience it is important that workers help service users to maintain or expand a supportive social network. This is particularly important during the transitional period. People need the opportunity to develop relationships and find that one person who can become their confidant, a committed supporter and mentor. This mentor or significant other can be a person from within the service user's family or outside the family. The mentor should have the capacity to help the person to identify benefits in the face of adversities.

## Crisis intervention

Golan (1978) identifies phases experienced by people in crisis. The first and second phase of a person's crisis is marked by an increase in anxiety in response to the traumatic event. The individual tries to use his or her knowledge and skills to combat and resolve the feeling of anxiety. If the person's coping mechanisms are effective there is no crisis; if they are not effective, the person will experience increased anxiety due to failure of usual coping mechanisms.

In the third phase a person often seeks help from outwith the family or social network and is more willing to receive professional help and learn new ways of coping with their circumstances. Relatives and friends may feel rejected by the person reaching out for professional assistance.

The first task for the worker is to identify the characteristics and severity of the client's experience. Aguilera and Messick (1994) devised a means of deciding whether a person will enter a crisis state. The worker needs to decide if the person experiencing the stressful event has i) a realistic perception of the event; ii) an adequate network; iii) an adequate coping mechanism. If the three balancing factors are present this should result in resolution of the problem, equilibrium regained and no crisis. If one or more balancing factors is absent this can result in problems being unresolved; disequilibrium continues and crisis is present.

Individuals can experience multiple changes, situational and developmental stages at the same time and this can increase the risk of the individual becoming dysfunctional. Holmes and Rahe (1967) suggest that the experience and symptoms of crisis vary significantly from individual and that while there may be certain common features, ultimately the experience is unique to the individual. The signs and symptoms are changes in behaviour, eating and sleeping patterns and other signs to which the worker should attend.

People in the fourth phase of a crisis demonstrate poor concentration, ponder, blame others and search for reasons and answers for the situation they find themselves in. During this phase the individual in crisis is prone to use ego defence mechanisms excessively to relieve anxiety. For example, a person may block from his or her memory the feeling or experiences that caused the emotional pain or reinvent an account of the experience. The worker needs to be aware that a person experiencing anxiety may unconsciously distort reality; however, learning to deal with challenges avoids reality distortion and contributes to a more accurate sense of self and events. People in crisis often need to be reassured that this emotional state is normal and they will be able to think clearly again.

Crisis intervention is normally a short-term method of intervention lasting 6–12 weeks. Initially the worker analyses the balance factors (Aguilera and Messick 1994), and explores whether the service user can give a rational explanation of events, whether they can draw on a supportive social network and do they have the ability to manage and improve their circumstances. Absence of any of the three elements determines if the person is entering a crisis state or is in crisis. It is also necessary to establish a working relationship with the service user helping to decrease their anxiety, and, as far as possible, normalize feelings of loss and grief. During the early stages the service user can be overwhelmed by events and the worker will be required to accept the service user's initial dependency and mobilize resources. The service user and worker should as soon as possible work in partnership; establish a rapport, validating how the individual perceives the crisis. It is important to assess the individual's ability to solve or manage their circumstances. The service user is encouraged to explore their situation, identify and prioritize problems and set goals. Giving positive reinforcement helps to restore cognitive functioning. Supporting the individual to understand the process they are experiencing and reinforcing healthy coping mechanisms contributes to future resolution.

The middle stage is a phase where the service user and worker implement action plans, including making referrals and commissioning providers. Workers need to be alert to the individual changing their account of events and the persistent reliance on defence mechanisms such as rationalization, displacement, projection and denial. The worker should try to reduce possible distortion of the service user's perception of events but be aware of the individual's insecurities and level of self-esteem.

The final stages involve the service user and worker identifying goals achieved but there is the possible emergence of secondary crisis. Crisis intervention and task-centred intervention (see Chapter 13 in the present volume) are focused, time-limited methods which encourage the service user to achieve goals. Endings sometimes trigger memories of past crises and a person can regress to earlier difficulties and experience further sense of loss. It is important to handle this stage sensitively by confirming goals achieved and improved personal functioning. The service user should be more self-aware, and one hopes more resilient, demonstrate new skills and therefore be more able to cope with any future crisis.

There is evidence that crisis intervention is an effective method of intervention for people who have experienced various types of crisis, especially where extreme stress may result in psychological trauma. Crisis intervention is a technique used in the aftermath of major critical incident to assist people to return to adequate functioning and stability. Procedures have evolved from studies of grieving conducted by Lindemann (1944) and the three basic principles in crisis work are immediacy of the intervention, proximity to the occurrence of the event, and the expectancy that the person will return to adequate functioning, and these principles have been elaborated by Caplan (1961, 1964) to include immediacy, proximity, expectancy and brevity. Caplan describes three stages of a crisis:

1.   The impact stage (defining the problem and the impact on the client).

2.   The recoil stage (a period of upset and disorganization).

3.   The adjustment and adaptation (resolution and evaluation of crisis and actions).

Roberts (1990) has seven stages of working through a crisis which are identified in the case study discussed later in this chapter. The goal of crisis intervention is to assist the person in distress to resolve the immediate problem as they perceive it and regain emotional equilibrium. The service user initially might be so distressed that the worker would have to temporarily accept their dependency and make decisions on their behalf, but as far as possible the worker should not take over. Crisis intervention initially requires the worker to be more directive than other methods of intervention. Crisis intervention and task-centred intervention (Reid and Shyne 1969; see also Chapter 13 in the present volume) are frequently compared because of the nature of the planned short-term work.

Working in partnership with the service user should be encouraged so that with varying degrees of support they can be actively involved in decisions and resolving problems. The worker should encourage the service user in crisis to talk about the stressful circumstances, and affirm the normality of their emotional state. As Coulshed and

Orme (2006. p.140) suggest: 'The worker and the client together try to make an assessment of the actual event and the causes that seem to have triggered it.' Sometimes the crisis stirs up unresolved problems from the service user's past but these issues should be attended to after the present crisis is managed or resolved. The focus of crisis is on the here and now and it is important to facilitate the service user's understanding of what has occurred and help them be aware of the impact of the situation. This is achieved by gathering and collating facts and actively listening to the client's account of the circumstances. Coulshed and Orme (2006, p.140) recommend the worker should 'gauge what ego strengths someone has so that their normal coping resources can be gleaned'. The service user therefore needs to be in partnerships in terms of ability to cope, social support network, strengths and needs, and ability to problem-solve. Consideration needs to be given to cultural beliefs: Payne (2005, p.279) and Thompson (1991) noted that the response of different ethnic groups to a crisis event will be culturally determined.

There are various responses to illness, death, divorce and pregnancy within cultural groups and the worker has to be culturally competent and not to minimize the effect of crisis on groups which have different lifestyles or value systems. It is also essential that the worker demonstrates empathy and calmness: it is extremely difficult as a worker to listen to people's sadness and anger.

The practitioner should identify specific problems, set tasks and actively assist the service user to use available resources. If the service user is experiencing difficulty in thinking clearly, and is unable to verbalize solutions to the problem, then it may be helpful to encourage the individual to talk about experiences or events immediately before the distressing event (Coulshed and Orme 2006). This practice helps the service user and worker to communicate and engage and establish the beginning of a relationship. After clarifying the service user's account of the event and identifying the individual's need, the worker should as soon as possible arrange 'concrete help'; the service user might have financial difficulties or require assistance with household tasks. It is likely that the individual is not fulfilling his or her role and responsibility within the family or taking part in outside activities. Extended family members might be affected by the crisis and require support as well. People in a crisis need a worker who will make a commitment to work with them until the problem is resolved.

Identifying individuals' spiritual or religious beliefs can provide a source of strength in times of emotional crisis. Spiritual need is often met through cultural practices such as shared values, beliefs, identification with nature and the ability to nurture can reconnect people to a sense of reality and purpose. The services user's family or religious affiliation may be a good source of support.

Assessment of a service user in crisis is not complete without carrying out a risk assessment. The worker has to decide if the service user needs care, protection and/or resources as a result of the loss or damage experienced. It is also important to identify and predict conditions which increase the probability of further damage while weighing up the risk and uncertainty that further damage might occur. The worker has to take decisions which distinguish uncertainty from probability (see Chapter 11 in the present volume). Brearley (1980) devised a matrix which helps the service user and worker make decisions; the matrix includes predictive hazards (the likelihood of an undesirable occurrence), situational hazards (hazards which exist) and danger (likelihood of outcome), and also service user strengths (personal attributes and social networks). Once the worker has carried out a risk analysis decisions are made and an action plan is implemented.

Practitioners constantly work with people in crisis and so it is not surprising that a crisis intervention approach is frequently the initial starting point of the work. Other methods such as task-centred, cognitive behavioural or psychosocial may need to be introduced at a later stage (see Chapters 12 and 13 in the present volume). An eclectic approach is acceptable and useful but can also lead to confusion. Workers should take care to discriminate between theories that are complementary and those that are not: for example, social workers may choose to use short-term methods, e.g. task-centred casework when long-term intervention might be more appropriate and effective (Payne 1998). Reflection and evaluation enables us to structure our work and identify outcomes while research has provided us with knowledge about what works. A number of juvenile offender research studies found that a psychodynamic approach or unstructured counselling was found to be ineffective as a deterrent and did not reduce recidivism in the long term. A psychodynamic approach provided juveniles with insight and an excuse for not changing their behaviour. Cognitive behavioural approaches (thoughts and behaviour are usually closely connected) were found to be effective with youth in the juvenile justice system (Lipsey 1992).

No matter what method is used, it is important to focus on the service user's strengths and aim to empower them by helping them to acquire knowledge and skill and to take greater control of their life. The link between theory and practice will now be examined by the use of a case example. The reader has the opportunity to reflect on the case study and the method of intervention.

## Case example

### BACKGROUND

The following is an example of work with a service user where the worker used crisis intervention. Mrs Butler came to see a social worker six months after her only son had died: she was feeling desolate. Her son had died suddenly leaving a wife and four daughters whose ages ranged from two to eleven years. The daughter-in-law and granddaughters had come to live with Mr and Mrs Butler after leaving Australia one month after their son's death. Mrs Butler said that the first meeting with her grandchildren was a very emotional experience. The family was experiencing serious overcrowding, living in a two-bedroom multistorey flat.

Mrs Butler was very worried about her daughter-in-law Shirley (aged 33) who complained of tiredness and wanted to sleep most of the time. This behaviour resulted in the grandparents taking responsibility for the children. People react to loss in different ways and many widows experience a psychological numbness, their behaviour becomes almost robot-like. The worker could only speculate that Shirley had experienced a warm, intimate relationship with her husband and now because of her grief was withdrawn and isolating herself: Erikson's maturation stage of intimacy versus isolation (see Chapter 5 in the present volume).

Ruth (aged 11) the eldest granddaughter, was truanting from school and Mrs Butler felt she had failed to deal with this situation. Ruth was grieving and found it difficulty to establish friendships with her peer group; she was also struggling with developmental stage Erikson postulates as being industry versus inferiority (see Chapter 5 in the present volume). It may be that her sorrow and loss of industry caused her to avoid her peer group and become isolated.

Initially Mrs Butler had tried to use her knowledge and skills to support her family (i.e. the first stage of crisis) but did not feel she was effective which resulted in her becoming more anxious. This was a complex emotional situation and the worker had to respond calmly and with clarity. Mrs Butler was now seeking professional help, the middle stage experienced by people in crisis.

The social worker drew on Robert's (1990) seven stages of crises intervention: establish rapport, assess safety needs, identify major problems, deal with feelings, explore possible alternatives, formulate an action plan and provide follow-up by making referrals.

## ASSESSMENT AND ESTABLISHING A RAPPORT

Mrs Butler was very distressed throughout the first interview, constantly asking why her son had been 'taken away' when his family needed him so much. The worker drew on knowledge of mourning (Parkes 1976) and reassured Mrs Butler that her feelings of pain, anger and weeping were acceptable and normal. Lishman (1995, p.65) points out that 'listening, and an empathic response are important components in enabling the client to feel that such emotion can be accepted, expressed and lived with and do not have to be hidden or feared... Such acceptance may be the starting point for a client to learn to live with and manage disabling emotions.'

Mrs Butler's ego strength (Freud 1986) and potential to cope and solve problems were also evaluated. The worker's assessment was that she was grieving for her son, overwhelmed with new responsibilities and generally despairing about her life. It was also clear that Mrs Butler was seeking direction on how to function and fulfil her role as wife, mother and grandmother: i.e. she, at 70, was struggling with maturational change – Erikson's stage of ego integrity versus despair – while demands were being made of her from an earlier developmental stage generativity versus stagnation (see Chapter 5). Generativity for many is a time for nurturing the next generation, attention being directed towards children's well-being. Mrs Butler should have been able to view her life with satisfaction and contentment but she was viewing her life with regret, sadness and disappointment. She was trying to maintain a state of emotional equilibrium but could not cope with the events after her son's death.

## DEALING WITH FEELING PAST AND PRESENT

Additionally, Mrs Butler had some unresolved issues from the past. She shared with the worker that she had not wanted her son to emigrate and was distraught at the time; now these thoughts and feelings were haunting her. She also blamed her husband for encouraging their son to emigrate. The worker listened and empathized with her unresolved feelings from the past while still focusing on the present circumstances. There was evidence that Mrs Butler had been blaming her husband and daughter-in-law for problems since her son's death. She was prone to using ego defence mechanisms excessively to protect herself (ego) from the present circumstances. The worker was also aware that she might be unconsciously distorting reality.

The social worker noticed that Mrs Butler talked very fondly of her granddaughters especial the youngest, Kirsty. Mrs Butler smiled as she repeated the things Kirsty said. She mentioned how her husband and she had spent many hours discussing the pleasure their granddaughters gave them. The worker sensitively commented that she had lost a son and gained four granddaughters. Mrs Butler, after a moment's thought, agreed and said that she would have probably missed all their childhood if their son had lived. Even in death there can be gains (Pincus 1976).

It was important to work in partnership with Mrs Butler in solving the current problems so that she felt actively involved in making decisions, and resolving and managing problems. Mrs Butler also sought permission from her daughter-in-law for her to be referred to social services. Her daughter-in-law and children were suffering loss of husband, father, home, friends, country and finance.

It is important to take into consideration family strengths and needs as well as problems when assessing and constructing goals which need to be 'kept to a minimum' (Coulshed and Orme 2006, p.147).

## MAJOR ISSUES IDENTIFIED
*Goals*

1.    The family need to speak about their grief and loss collectively and individually.

2.    Mrs Butler and Shirley need to join a bereavement support group.

3.    The family require help with household tasks.

4.    Shirley Butler needs to lease accommodation for her and the children.

5.    The family needs to increase their social network.

6.    Ruth and her mother will spend time together and become more involved in leisure pursuits as well as discovering new friends.

*Action plan*

A working agreement was made with Mrs Butler and her daughter-in-law. They agreed to meet for weekly sessions over a six-week period and goals, strategies, tasks and action plans were identified. Payne (2005, p.155) emphasized the importance of analysing networks within social support systems. It was crucial to mobilize internal and external resources quickly. Coulshed and Orme (2006) remind us of the need to attend to the emotional as well as practical and rational dimensions (in a sense, the relationship between the two: how service users think and feel about their immediate circumstances). Referrals were made to housing authorities, Citizens Advice Bureau, family centre, and bereavement counselling services. Golan (1978) thought it was important to set tasks and proposed that workers and service user should explore various options, help select a solution, apply for services, and get used to and gain skills in using services.

Mrs Butler faced a myriad of new situations that had been triggered by her loss. She had to orientate to fulfilling new roles, changing routines, coping with young children and solving problems. In many ways these tasks gave her 'time out' from her grief. Parkes (1972), Kubler-Ross (1969) and Lindemann (1944) all make a major contribution to understanding stages of bereavement: alarm, searching, mitigation, anger and guilt. Gradually her grief was replaced by slow resolution and a return to a feeling of well-being and she gained a new identity. Change and loss theory enhances the workers knowledge of the emotional needs of a person in crisis. Worden (1991) cited activities needed to complete grief work: 'to accept the reality of the loss; to experience the pain of grief; to adjust to a changed environment; to emotionally relocate and move on with life'. Worden promotes the idea that grief is a normal reaction to loss. Workers need to assess whither an individual is experiencing normal grief reaction in coping with a crisis.

Counselling techniques (Worden 1991) were used to help Mrs Butler through her acute grief while at the same time reassuring her that her emotional state was normal. The worker at every opportunity praised Mrs Butler's efforts and encouraged her in all aspects of her life and, as a result, her self-esteem and belief in her competence grew. Mrs Butler was able to learn ways of coping with her grief and new family responsibilities. She was able to acknowledge that her efforts were making a difference and she was working in partnership with her daughter-in-law to problem-solve and devise ways to help them all cope with their loss. Rutter (1985) suggests that people with self-esteem and self-efficacy seem to be cushioned from the worst effects of adversities that may befall them. A resilience-led approach to work with adults in a crisis should focus on the service user's strengths as well as needs, which may help clients identify goals, tasks and a favourable outcome.

## EVALUATION

Before termination the worker and Mrs Butler together reflected and evaluated what had been achieved. The family were able to share their grief and develop ways to cope with day-to-day problems. Shirley leased a house and although there were difficulties managed to rebound from her loss and make social adjustments. Both Mrs Butler and Shirley joined a support group which provided a mutually supportive environment that facilitated a healthy grieving process.

Knowledge of crisis theory and concepts contributed to workers' understanding of how to alleviate acute distress and to improve people's coping skills. Practitioners need to reflect and evaluate the quality of resources and accuracy of their work and take account of the service user and their own emotional response to the process and measure the output experienced by the user of services against outcome achieved.

There is a wealth of literature and research that trace the development of crisis intervention which can enhance workers knowledge and skills. Crisis intervention procedures have evolved from studies of grieving conducted by Erich Lindemann (1944).

Professional competence and empirically tested evidence-based practices are increasingly important in social work, as is reflective practice. Payne (2002, p.123) suggests: 'If we are to practise from knowledge and theory, we must have ways of thinking which turn thinking into practice action. Reflection is a way of doing this.' Reflection is a way of working with a range of practice theories. Thompson (2000) echoes this, and draws on Kolb's (1984) model of experiential learning to promote advocacy of the inclusion of personal life experience in the process. Social workers can draw on formal training as well as experiences in their personal and professional life and are well placed to contribute their considerable expertise and skills working with individuals and families in crisis.

# References

Aguilera, D.C. and Messick, J.M. (1994) *Crisis Intervention: Theory and Methodology* 7th edn. St Louis, MO: Mosby-Year Book.

American Psychiatric Association (1994) *The Diagnostic and Statistical Manual of Mental Disorder.* 4th edn, Washington DC: American Psychiatric Press.

Auerbach, S.M. and Kilman, P.R. (1977) 'Crisis intervention: a review of outcome research.' *Psychiatric Bulletin 84,* 6, 1189–1217.

Bowlby, J. (1969) *Attachment and Loss,* Vol. 1. London: Hogarth.

Brearley, P. (1980) *Admission to Residential Care.* London: Tavistock.

Caplan, G. (1961) *An Approach to Community Mental Health.* New York: Grune and Stratton.

Caplan, G. (1964) *Principles of Preventative Psychiatry.* New York: Basic Books.

Cohen, R.E. (1990) 'Post-disaster mobilization and crisis counselling: guidelines and techniques for developing crisis-oriented services for disaster victims.' In A.R. Roberts (ed.) *Crisis Intervention Handbook: Assessment, Treatment and Research.* Belmont CA: Wadsworth.

Coulshed, V. and Orme, J. (1998) *Social Work Practice. An Introduction.* Basingstoke: Macmillan.

Coulshed, V. and Orme, J. (2006) *Social Work Practice.* 4th edn. Basingstoke: Palgrave Macmillan.

Erikson, E. (1963) *Childhood and Society.* 2nd edn. New York: W.W. Norton.

Erikson, E. (1965) *Childhood and Society.* London: Hogarth Press.

Everly, G. and Lating, J. (eds) (1995) *Psychotraumatology: Key Papers and Core Concepts in Post-Traumatic Stress.* New York: Plenum.

Everly, G. and Mitchell, J. (1999) *Critical Incident Stress Management: A New Era and Standard Care in Crisis Intervention.* Ellicott City MD: Chevron Publishing.

Flannery, J. (1994) *Posttraumatic Stress Disorder: The Victim's Guide to Healing and Recovery.* New York: Crossroad Press.

Flannery, J. (1995) *Violence in the Workplace.* New York: Crossroad Press.

Flannery, R. and Everly, G. (2000) 'Crisis intervention: a review.' *International Journal of Emergency Mental Health 2,* 2, 119–25.

Freud, S. (1986) *The Essentials of Psychoanalysis. The Definitive Collection of Sigmund Freud's Writing.* London: Penguin.

Golan, N. (1978) *Treatment in Crisis Situations.* New York: Free Press.

Holmes, T.H. and Rahe, R. (1967) 'The social readjustment rating scale.' *Journal of Psychosomatic Research 11,* 216.

Howe, D. (1987) *An Introduction to Social Work Theory.* Aldershot: Wildwood House.

Johnson, R. (1979) 'Recognising people in crisis.' In J. Robinson (ed.) *Using Crisis Intervention.* Horsham, PA: International Communication.

Kolb, D.A. (1984) *Experimental Learning: Experience as the Source of Learning Development.* Englewood Cliffs NJ: Prentice Hall.

Kubler-Ross, E. (1969) *On Death and Dying.* New York: Macmillan.

Lieberman, M.A. (1993) 'Bereavement self-help groups: A review of conceptual and methodical issues.' In M.S. Stroebe and R.O. Hanson (eds) *Handbook of Bereavement.* New York: Cambridge University Press.

Lindemann, E. (1944) 'Symptomology and management of acute grief.' *American Journal of Psychiatry 101,* September, 141–8.

Lipsey, M. (1992) 'Juvenile delinquency treatment: A meta-analytic inquiry into the variability of effects.' In T. Cook, H. Cooper and D. Cording (eds) *Meta-analysis for Explanation: A Casebook.* New York: Russell Sage Foundation.

Lishman, J. (1995) *Communication in Social Work.* Basingstoke: BASW/Macmillan.

Maclean, K. (2003) 'Resilience: What it is and how children and young people can be helped to develop it.' *International Child and Youth Care Network Journal 55,* 1–10. Available at: *www.cyc-net.org/cyc-online/cycol-0803-resilience.html*

Marris, P. (1986) *Loss and Change.* London, Routledge.

Maslow, A. (1970) *Motivation of the Personality.* 2nd edn. New York: Harper & Row.

Masten, A. S. and Coatworth, J. D. (1998) 'The development of competence in favourable and unfavourable environments: Lessons from research on successful children.' *American Psychologist 53,* 2, 205–20.

Newman, T. and Blackburn, S. (2002) *Transitions in the Lives of Children and Young People: Resilience Factors.* Report for Scottish Executive Education and Young People Research Unit, No.78. Edinburgh: Scottish Executive.

O'Hagan, K. (1986) *Crisis Intervention: Social Service.* London: Macmillan.

Parad, H.J. (1958) *Ego Psychology and Dynamic Casework.* New York: Family Association of America.

Parad, H.J. (ed.) (1965) *Crisis Intervention: Selected Reading.* New York: Family Service Association of America.

Parkes, C.M. (1972) *Bereavement: Studies of Grief in Adult Life.* Harmondsworth: Penguin.

Parkes, C.M. (1986) *Bereavement: Studies of Grief in Adult Life.* London: Tavistock.

Payne, M. (1997) *Modern Social Work Theory: A Critical Introduction.* Basingstoke: Macmillan.

Payne, M. (2002) 'Social work theory and reflective practice.' In R. Adams, L. Dominelli and M. Payne (eds) *Social Work: Themes, Issues and Critical Debates.* 2nd edn. Basingstoke: Palgrave.

Payne, M. (2005) *Modern Social Work Theory.* 3rd edn. Basingstoke: Palgrave Macmillan

Pincus, L. (1976) *Death and the Family.* London: Faber.

Rapoport, L. (1970) 'Crisis intervention as a mode of brief treatment.' In R.W. Roberts and R.H. Nee (eds) *Theories of Social Casework.* Chicago, IL: University of Chicago Press.

Reid, W.J. and Shyne, A.W. (1969) *Brief and Extended Casework.* New York: Columbia University.

Roberts, A.R. (1990) *An Overview of Crisis Theory and Crisis Intervention.* Belmont, CA: Wadsworth.

Roberts, A.R. (ed.) (1991) *Contemporary Perspective on Crisis Intervention and Prevention.* Englewood Cliffs, NJ; Prentice-Hall.

Rutter, M. (1985) 'Resilience in the face of adversity: Protective factors and resistance to psychiatric disorder.' *British Journal Of Psychiatry 147,* 589–611.

Sheldon, B. (2000) 'Cognitive behaviour methods in social care: a look at the evidence.' In P. Stepney and D. Ford (eds) *Social Work Methods and Theories: A Framework for Practice.* Lyme Regis: Russell House.

Thompson, N. (1991) *Crisis Intervention Revisited.* Birmingham: Pepar.

Thompson, N. (2000) *Theory and Practice in Human Services.* 2nd edn. Buckingham: Open University Press.

Thompson, N. (2002) *Loss and Grief: A Guide for Human Services Practitioners.* Basingstoke: Palgrave.

Thompson, N. (2005) *Understanding Social Work: Preparing for Practice.* Basingstoke: Palgrave Macmillan.

Worden, J. W. C. (1991) *Grief Counselling and Grief Therapy.* 2nd edn. New York: Springer.

Young, M.A. (1995) 'Crisis response teams in the aftermath of disasters.' In A.R. Roberts (ed.) *Crisis Intervention and Time-limited Cognitive Treatment.* Thousand Oaks, CA: Sage.

## CHAPTER 15

# FAMILY THERAPY AND SYSTEMIC PRACTICE

*Steven Walker*

## Introduction

Social workers encounter families in almost every aspect of their practice, whatever the context and whatever the service user group. The family is the focus of health and social policy strategy across a range of central and local government and health service provision, including criminal justice, mental health, community care, youth offending, fostering and adoption, education and primary health care. Families are often stated to be at the heart of government policies that aim to support parents and children to participate equally in society as valued citizens. Family therapy and systemic practice as a form of intervention and the systems theory underpinning it offer an attractive, accessible and flexible approach to social work practice in a variety of agency contexts.

Social workers are at the front line between shortcomings in social policy aspirations and the legitimate needs of families. Among a variety of methods and models of approaches and interventions family therapy has established itself as one of the more popular and effective tools available to practitioners. Family therapy and systemic practice provide both an assessment and intervention framework for use with a range of client groups. They also offer a conceptual instrument for use outside direct contact with service users in understanding the way organizational and structural systems affect the ecology of social work practice.

Social workers have traditionally expressed a keen interest in ways of working with whole families or groups in a variety of practice contexts, whether in child care, child protection, mental health, community care, education, health or disability service user settings. It is widely recognized that social workers need to develop the capacity to undertake assessments and interventions in a broad variety of settings with individuals, families, and groups. Such activity needs to be understood in the context of statutory duties, agency requirements, and the needs and wishes of service users, and must be firmly underpinned by anti-racist and anti-discriminatory practice.

Recent SSI inspections and joint reviews have illustrated the need for social workers to rediscover their core skills of assessment so that decision-making, care planning and intervention are based on sound analysis and understanding of the client's unique personality, history and circumstances. A systems perspective offers a holistic tool for undertaking informed assessment work that takes into full account the wider environmental factors combined with the interpersonal relationship patterns influencing family experience. Government guidance is beginning to recognize the importance of a therapeutic dimension to contemporary practice. It is beginning to be acknowledged that social workers' own therapeutic skills need to be seen as a resource to be used and offered in assessment and intervention (DOH 2000; Walker and Beckett 2004).

Community care reforms, child care fiascos and mental health panics have fuelled the drive towards a managerialist culture in social work reducing the professional autonomy of social workers. The evidence from social work practitioners is for a strong demand for the practical and theoretical resources to equip them to deal with modern family life and rediscover the value of interpersonal relationship skills. In 2000 The Department of Health conceded that assessment and intervention processes have become de-skilling for social workers (DOH/SSI 2000).

## Historical context

Modern family therapy as we understand it is generally credited with emerging in the 1950s as a result of a number of developments in the fields of psychology, communication theory and psychiatry. At a broader level it is also important to acknowledge the socio-economic context of post Second World War economic expansion, population growth and the significance of cultural changes affecting people's attitudes to sex, marriage, leisure and intimate relationships. The 1950s in the developed industrialized countries were therefore a time of rapid sociological change and economic growth, when new ideas were more easily articulated and received (Walker and Akister 2004).

One of the important factors that stimulated the embryonic ideas that were to grow into a new form of psychotherapy was a growing dissatisfaction with the traditional psychoanalytic model of individual therapy. This was combined with new research that demonstrated effectiveness when groups of people were brought together to talk about their problems. Two key figures stand out as influential at this time in moving forward the ideas that were to crystallize in the practice of family therapy. Ludwig von Bertalanffy (1968) was a German biologist who devised a general systems theory that could be used to explain how an organism worked by studying the transactional processes happening between different parts. He understood that the whole was greater than the sum of its parts and that we could observe patterns and the way relationships were organized in any living system.

Gregory Bateson (1973) and others in the USA took this concept of a general systems theory, combined it with the new science of cybernetics and applied it to social systems such as the family. Cybernetics had introduced the idea of information processing and the role of feedback mechanisms in regulating mechanical systems. Bateson used this notion to argue that families were systems involving rules of communication and the regulatory function of feedback that influenced patterns of behaviour within them. In the UK, Ronald Laing (1969) challenged the orthodoxy in psychiatric practice by arguing that schizophrenia was a product of family dysfunction, while John Bowlby (1969) moved from treating individuals to treating families where an individual was displaying mental health problems.

The idea began to take root therefore that individual experiences within families were continually being shaped and influenced by the evolving interacting patterns of communication. Individuals were not therefore determined by early traumatic experiences or distorted developmental transitions, as the prevailing therapeutic orthodoxy argued. Family therapy thinking conceptualized that individual personality and identity could change along with changes in family dynamics. From this common root theory – systems theory – a number of models and methods of family therapy practice evolved through to the present day. The term 'family therapy' was broadened in the late twentieth century to incorporate systemic practice as part of the development of this form of intervention whose principles could be applied to individuals, couples and in groupwork contexts.

## What is a family?

The word 'family' can in itself be misleading if there are a number of assumptions about what a family is. Traditional definitions were very narrow and reflected an era when a heterosexual couple married, had children and lived under the same roof. Nowadays this nuclear family stereotype is surprisingly resilient despite evidence of the diversity of different forms of family life. This is a popular conception of how the family is constituted that is more a reflection of how some traditionalists believe sexual, emotional and parental relationships ought to be structured (Muncie and Sapsford 1997).

In contemporary multicultural society, with its rich tapestry of ethnic diversity combined with rapid sociological transformations, there is a wide and complex variety of 'families' such as extended, kin group and lone parent. These can be further distinguished by parental partnerships: same-sex, cohabiting, adoptive, fostering, separated, divorced, remarried and step-parents. Stretching the definition of family further can include the important roles peers, friends and local community figures perform in shaping and influencing family patterns of behaviour. We can therefore see that apparently simple concepts such as family and support/therapy are more complex the closer we examine them. Flexibility and sensitivity in using family therapy and systemic concepts are required in order to avoid pathologizing non-nuclear family forms.

Social workers interested in family therapy need to question their assumptions about families and the needs of the people inside them. Family therapy is not a tool for maintaining what for some will be a crucible of torment and abuse. It ought to be considered among a range of interventions as a viable way of facilitating change and growth. This could mean enabling a bickering couple to part, a woman to clarify her own needs for separation, a man to seek legal advice to gain custody of his children or a woman to gain strength to leave an abusive partner. Family therapy is not a device for coercing families to stay together come what may. Staying together as a family is only one possible outcome of therapeutic intervention.

An uncritical acceptance of the nuclear family as the norm risks reinforcing social workers failure to acknowledge either the multicultural bases of society or the diverse forms of family forms they will encounter. Social workers need to be constantly vigilant to the differential power relations that feature within and determine family relationships – even in the modern myth of the house-husband or child-centred father. Perceiving the family through a gendered lens will enable a more sophisticated practice to develop and one that resists endorsing traditional familialism or patriarchal relations (Dominelli 2002). The following characteristics have been selected to illustrate the range of more common family therapy approaches and their usefulness to social workers.

## Structural family therapy

Structural family therapy is a therapy of action. The tool of this therapy is to modify the present, not to explore and interpret the past. Since the past was instrumental in the creation of the family's present organisation and functioning, it is manifest in the present and will be available to change by interventions that change the present (Minuchin 1974). The structural family therapist engages with the family system and then sets out to transform it. The main focus of this approach is the family structure with the underlying assumption that the problematic behaviour is related to a fault with the functional normative family structure. Structural family therapists believe that by changing the family structure they can change the position of family members and therefore alter their subjective experiences.

The process of the model is that changes to the structure of the family creates the possibility for further change. The notion that the family system is organized around the support, regulation, nurturance and socialization of its members means that the therapist needs to repair or modify the family's functioning so that it can better perform these tasks. Once a change has been introduced the family will therefore preserve that change by the family's own self-regulating mechanisms. Changes in the multiple interactions between family members will lead to the possibility of change in the experience of the individual.

The characteristics of structural family therapy stem from the classic systemic technique of observing the interactive patterns in a family. Once this baseline of behaviour can be understood as contributing to the problem a structural approach would seek to highlight these, interrupt them when they are happening, and then get the family to re-enact them in different ways that lead to different outcomes. The attraction to social workers in this way of practising family therapy techniques is that it aspires to provide families with problem-solving practical solutions. In a family session therefore the task is to enable the family to try out different ways of doing things – for example, by coaching a parent on how to maintain a boundary or limit the behaviour of their child.

Social workers who are attracted to behavioural approaches to their practice will find certain similarities with structural family therapy in that learning is practical enabling family members to observe their own changes. These are some of the key features (Gorell Barnes 1984):

> *Intensity* – creating a very focused experience of emotionally charged interaction rather than skip over uncomfortable feelings.
>
> *Persistence* – concentrating on these long enough to make a difference to the problem patterns brought to your attention.
>
> *Homework* – taking home tasks which transfer what has been learnt to the home context. This assists the momentum of change.

*Confirmation* – seeing the positive connotations of behaviour and emphasizing people's competence is necessary to challenge negative, fixed ideas.

*Enactment* – requesting a family to move from description to actually showing the problem live in the session, and encouraging people to talk directly to each other rather than through the medium of the social worker.

*Changing space* – literally moving people around in the session. It is especially powerful when a child is being caught in the crossfire between fighting parents, or used as a go-between. Asking the parents to sit and face each other can be simple yet incredibly transformational.

*Creating boundaries* – applicable in situations where age appropriateness and enmeshment are issues. For example, where there is poor individuation it helps family members separate themselves. It can be of value where parents experience small children as tyrannical and out of control, or where adolescents are finding independence difficult.

## Strategic family therapy

One of the guiding principles in strategic family therapy is that problems apparently residing in one individual are frequently associated with the difficulties resulting from a family's need to change and reorganize at transitional stages. These can occur at times such as the birth of a baby or when a young person is considering leaving home (Dallos and Draper 2000). This is particularly the case with older adolescents who present with mental health problems or a history of school refusal. This can indicate a family dynamic whereby the young person becomes symptomatic in order to help parents avoid conflict in their relationship. Thus attention is focused on the young person rather than the parents.

One of the central premises of the strategic approach is that people are essentially strategic in the way that we are involved in predicting how others may think, feel and act. Some writers characterize this as indicative of a constant power struggle in which family members are trying to influence each other and define themselves (Haley 1976). Furthermore, this struggle is not contained to the family but also occurs when the family seek help. In social work practice various family members will seek to influence the social worker and try to gain sympathy or agreement with their particular perception of the problem.

The implication for social work practice is that you can use this approach starting from the basis that parents, for example, will seek to enlist you to their side in a struggle with an unruly adolescent. Colluding with this will only distance you from the adolescent and diminish your effectiveness in resolving the problems between parents and child. The strategic approach recognizes explicitly the dilemmas presented by families who seek help but want to remain in control. These beliefs and premises highlight the role played by attempted solutions to problems which either make matters worse or result in denial of the seriousness of the problem.

The strategic approach, in contrast to the structural approach, does not have a normative concept of the family that should exist according to set hierarchies and sub-systems of parents/children, etc. Rather, the focus with strategic family therapists is on the day-to-day interactions which have resulted in problems, and on the cognitive thinking being applied to solve them. The perceptions people have about these problems invariably influences how they try to tackle them. Attempted solutions and behavioural responses that actually maintain the problem require challenging and shifting with alternatives promoted by the therapist. These are some of the key features of strategic family therapy (Dallos and Draper 2000):

*Staged approach* – a detailed exploration of the difficulties to be resolved is translated into an action plan designed to disrupt embedded problematic sequences. Assessment and reappraisal of the outcomes of intervention is used to revise or continue tasks.

*Directive tasks* – these usually consist of homework that family members are asked to carry out between family sessions. They are most effective when every family member is involved in such tasks. The aim is to alter problematic sequences of interactions. The important point is that the task must be reasonable and fit within the family's repertoire of achievable limits.

*Paradoxical tasks* – this is where the family are asked to do the opposite of what the therapist intends to happen. They are employed when families find it impossible to carry out directive tasks. The aim is to encourage symptomatic behaviour, in other words to try to unblock a cycle of failure and poor motivation and hopelessness. An example is where a family report constant bickering and loud arguments, describing family life as conflictual and uncaring. By suggesting that the family have one huge argument at a regular time each evening presents them with a double bind. If they do then they are demonstrating that they can control their behaviour and are therefore not helpless; if they do not because it feels stilted and manufactured – then they are learning not to argue. Either way change has occurred.

## Systemic family therapy

The development of this model began in Italy in the 1970s where a group of psychiatrists were experimenting with treating individuals diagnosed as schizophrenic in a radically different way to the orthodox methods then employed. They reported better outcomes when they worked with the whole family rather than the individual patient. The central theoretical idea informing this approach is that the symptomatic behaviour of a family individual is part of the transactional pattern peculiar to the family system in which it occurs. Therefore the way to change the symptom is to change the rules of the family.

The goal of this therapy is to discover the current systemic rules and traditional myths which sustain the present dysfunctional patterns of relating, and to use the assumed resistance of the family towards outside help as a provocation to change. Change is achieved by clarifying the ambiguity in relationships that occur at a nodal point in the family's evolution. Systemic therapists do not work to a normative blueprint of how an ideal family should function (Burnham 1986). This approach furthermore emphasizes the importance of the underlying beliefs held by family members about the problem which has affected behaviour. It avoids the perception of blaming the non-symptomatic members of the family by working on the basis that the actions of various family members are the best they can do (Dallos and Draper 2000). These are some of the key features:

*Positive connotation* – this technique is used as an extension of the strategic paradoxical task by reflecting back to the family a positive reason for all their actions. This is supported by providing a rationale for why they behave as they do, and maintains the therapist in a non-judgemental stance. It places the family members on an equal footing thus avoiding scapegoating.

*Hypothesizing* – this is a way of bringing together all the available information prior to the family session and collating it into a coherent whole which is fully circular and systemic. In other words it attempts to explain why the family have a problem. This unproved supposition is tentative and is used as the basis for guiding the family session. The task for the therapist is to confirm or disprove the hypothesis and create a new one if necessary.

*Circular questioning* – this unique style of questioning is both elegant and simple. It requires the therapist to ask questions of one member about the relationship between two other family members. The family will not be used to communicating in this way and are placed in a position of having to speak freely about ideas they would normally keep to themselves. Differences in perception and distinctions in behaviour can be explored and discussed according to the interviewers curiosity and hypothesis.

*Neutrality* – again, this is another distinguishing feature of systemic family therapy practice. It involves the therapist siding with everyone and showing no allegiance or favouritism to any individual family member. Although the therapist may feel distinctly biased towards say, a victim of abuse or domestic violence, the neutrality refers to behaviour during the interview. The aim is to maximize the family's engagement and not collude with blaming behaviour which will undermine the desired change.

*The intervention* – at the end of a family session a prescription or intervention is delivered to all those present and can be mailed to any absent members. It can consist of a paradoxical injunction, simple task or complex ritual designed to interrupt dysfunctional behavioural patterns (Campbell and Draper 1985).

*Team working* – this is not exclusive to systemic family therapy but it is a particular characteristic of this method where the concept of live supervision during a family session is considered essential. One-way screens, videos and audiotapes are used to enable several people to bring their collective experience and knowledge to bear on the presented problems. This helps guard against the individual therapist being drawn into subtle alliances or missing important information during lively sessions. You can adapt this in your social work context by having a colleague join you in some work and act as an observer to the process.

## Brief solution-focused therapy

As the title suggests this approach is primarily aimed at a short-term period of work with the emphasis on encouraging families to recognize their own competencies. The mantra of practitioners using this way of working is 'focus on solutions not problems'. For example, a family or parents often discuss a child or a parent in sweeping generalizations when explaining their problems: 'He's always getting into trouble with teachers', or 'She never does as she is told'. These are recognizable complaints and express less the reality than an overemphasis on the negative, as if the parents are trying to convince you of their case for help and their desperation. Solution-focused therapists turn this idea around and carefully enable the complainants to recall an exception to this general rule about the troublesome child.

Once the family has recognized that exceptions do occur and the person can behave/do as he or she is asked, the focus of the approach is to emphasize these exceptions and help the family to make more of them happen. This requires patience and systematic work to excavate every element surrounding these exceptions so that a family can prepare for them, recognize them, sustain them and reproduce them. These are then translated into clear, recognizable goals that can be specifically described so that everyone involved can perceive them. Goal setting can often be difficult, especially with parents/families with poor self-esteem, lacking in confidence and feeling disempowered. To help overcome this difficulty the 'miracle question' is designed to help families identify specific behaviours and actions that indicate change, rather than talk abstractly about wanting to 'be happy again' or 'like a normal family'.

The miracle question entails asking the family to imagine while they were all asleep a miracle happened and the problem was solved. When they awoke they were not aware a miracle had happened. They then have to describe what is different that tells them a miracle has occurred. In describing the difference they are encouraged to make concrete the conditions for change and by doing so are in fact illustrating the goals they desire. The therapist's job is to work collaboratively with the family's own definition of change and help them devise ways of achieving it. Overall the brief solution-focused approach can be summarized in terms of three rules (Dallos and Draper 2000):

*If it ain't broke don't fix it* – even the most chronic of problems show periods where the troublesome patterns or symptoms are absent or reduced. The therapist needs to have a broad and tolerant view of what is not broke – what are competencies. These can be built upon so that therapy does not become bogged down into attempting to build a pursuit of a utopian family.

*Once you know what works do more of it* – once exceptions and competencies have been discovered then families are encouraged to do more of these. This can lead to a self-reinforcing cycle of success which will start to replace that of failure, incompetence and desperation.

*If it doesn't work, don't do it again – do something different* – Families often become involved in cycles where they cannot see any alternative but to continue to act in the ways they always have, or do more of the same. Searching for the exception, they can be helped to notice an alternative pattern happens occasionally with more positive consequences. This is built upon until it replaces the previous more common negative pattern.

## Common characteristics of family therapy

Whatever method or model of family therapy you choose to adopt there are certain cardinal characteristics that distinguish the practice from other interventions. The following have been selected to provide further detail to the above descriptions and illustrate the pragmatic nature of systemic practice.

### GENOGRAMS/FAMILY TREES

Genograms are a neat, cost-effective and engaging way of introducing the family to a different type of social work practice. Used appropriately at the right time and in the right place they can help focus the whole family in a collaborative exercise that reveals a great deal of information in a non-threatening way. It is a way of addressing issues that are difficult to verbalize by physically drawing a picture or diagram of several generations of the family. Older family members as well as quite young children can join in. Deaths, divorces, separations, births and marriages can all be illustrated and committed to a large sheet of paper that can serve as a map of the family process for use in future sessions. Genograms can give families their first understanding of intergenerational family relationship patterns.

Sibling relationships can be described and discussed in a detached way without forcing a confrontation between two rivalrous young people or colluding with an exclusive and problematic closeness. The opportunity for the family themselves to generate hypotheses or narratives to explain the impact of various events can be offered by means of a detailed and carefully constructed genogram. Beware the attraction of predicting pattern repetition though, as this may result in further individual scapegoating. The value in noting pattern is in the meaning this has for the family concerned (for example, are they actively resisting the repetition of early divorce or child care proceedings, or do they feel that their fate has already been sealed?). Genograms are thus a relatively emotion-free way of collecting information that makes sense to the family and connects them to the therapeutic exploratory process (Goldenberg and Goldenberg 2004).

### VIDEOS/ONE-WAY SCREENS

These are associated with the practice of family therapy and probably go some way to inhibit social workers from getting involved. It can feel de-skilling to have your practice scrutinized so openly. The technology appears de-humanizing and deceitful and it raises proper concerns about confidentiality and informed consent. However, in practice most families are not bothered by the use of videos or one-way screens/mirrors and their use is becoming more common in all kinds of non-statutory and family support settings. If these tools are properly explained and introduced to the participants as a means of helping the workers to be more effective, there are rarely objections. In many cases families can be encouraged to take video recordings home with them to review their own behaviour and learn how negative interactions are started and perpetuated. They can therefore be an additional learning resource and can make a point more powerfully than the verbal reasoning of even the most skilled therapist.

### SUPERVISION/JOINT WORKING

Supervision/joint working is another characteristic of family therapy that distinguishes it from conventional managerial supervision that relies upon mainly verbal feedback from the supervisee. This form of supervision has a number of drawbacks that have been identified over the years, including information selectivity, the power differential between manager/worker, forgetfulness, focus on content rather than process, and differences in theoretical stance. Family therapy on the other hand has had a rare openness in relation to exposing practice to wider scrutiny, compared to individual-oriented therapies.

Video recordings, apart from being used as a way of analysing the complex family patterns of interaction that are impossible to track during an interview, can also be used as a training tool. Family therapy sessions are usually supervised live involving at least another person observing the session and offering feedback and suggestions during the work or at a planned mid-point break. The person/s observing are able to gain a different perspective to the worker involved with the family and spot important aspects that may benefit from a supportive suggestion. This notion has been developed to include the use of reflecting teams whereby the people behind the screen/mirror join the family and the worker in front to openly discuss their perceptions.

### CONTEXT OF PROBLEMS

The context of problems is more than anything perhaps the most defining characteristic of family therapy practice. It means that whatever the problem being presented to you as a social worker using systems theory you will automatically begin to ask a series of questions that are linked to the context of the presenting problem. This relates to not just the family context but the wider professional, public, socio-economic and cultural contexts of the problem. In other words, it is an ecological approach in that it posits not just individuals as interlinked within families but also families as interlinked in communities that are in turn interlinked to class, ethnic groups and cultures (McGoldrick, Pearce and Giordano 1982).

It is a way of beginning the reframing process and looking at the problem from a different angle so that the concept of blame begins to be eroded and replaced with the concept of understanding the patterns that create and maintain the current problem. For example, one favourite question asked by many family therapists at some point to each member of a family is: 'If this problem were to disappear, what problem would be left to concern you?' This illustrates the different way of working compared to approaches that can unwittingly reinforce the family's dependence on a particular problem. Understanding the overall context of the problem offers another way of tackling it rather than seeking to change an individual or indeed trying to change a family.

### CIRCULARITY/PATTERNS

Circularity/patterns are again characteristic of whatever model of family therapy appeals to your style of work. It is a foundational assumption of all family therapists that problematic behaviour is conceived as forming part of a reflexive, circular motion of events and behaviours without beginning or end. Being able to spot the circular process and articulate it in a meaningful way with the family offers a positive way forward. This releases the therapist and the family to think beyond linear causality and blaming or scapegoating behaviour. The important distinction when using this conceptual framework is where abusive adults use grooming behaviour and their power to abuse children and young people.

In these child protection cases and in domestic violence situations the motivation and responsibility need to be firmly located with the perpetrator. The circular understanding of problems offers an elegant explanatory tool for the reasons for the symptoms and other dysfunctional behaviour. Within a family any action by one member affects all other members and the family as a whole. Each member's response in turn prompts other responses that affect all other members, whose further reactions provoke still further responses and so on. Such a reverberating effect in turn affects the first person, in a continuous series of chains of influence (Goldenberg and Goldenberg 2004).

## Contemporary developments

### CONVERGENT PRACTICE

This is characterized as the narrowing of the gap with some traditional psychodynamic theories that have informed individual therapeutic work. This is an interesting development in the sense that the development of family therapy has come full circle round to the original theoretical base from which it sprang. Several contributors have discussed the previously unspoken notion of a combined or integrated family therapy practice that reflects and incorporates elements of psychodynamic therapy (Donovan 2003; Larner 2000; Pocock 1997). This development demonstrates that systems theory is still a flexible, evolving paradigm within which approaches and techniques have remained fixed in some ways and changed in many others.

This should suit social workers who, whilst interested in particular approaches to their work, nevertheless are agile enough to incorporate ideas and skills that can best help clients at particular times. Given the psychoanalytic root of modern psychosocial practice there is a valuable opportunity for social workers to build on a solid theoretical foundation with skills and techniques that can feel relevant to many service users. An example is in the use of interpretation. This is one of the most powerful aspects of a psychodynamic approach that can be seen mirrored in the family therapy technique of a reflecting team conversation.

## FEMINIST APPROACHES

Feminist approaches evolved more overtly during the 1980s as female family therapists began to discuss and write about power and gender relations within families (Goldner 1991; Hare-Mustin 1991; Perelberg and Miller 1990). Their feminist analysis of thera-peutic work revealed that couples were strongly influenced by assumptions about gender roles and expectations within relationships and families. After 30 years of feminist theory and practice in other contexts, these writers and many female family therapists began to articulate a challenge to the gender-neutral concepts in orthodox family therapy theory and practice. Instead of assuming a parity between partners or married couples they incorporated an understanding of the inequality conditioned and socialized into heterosexual relationships that explained domestic violence at one extreme or at the other a stereotype of passive/nurturing female and assertive/emotion-ally distant male.

Where problems occur in relationships they can often be better evaluated through a gendered lens that highlights the contradictions and dilemmas between people who are constrained by powerful concepts of maleness and femaleness. When people fail to con-form to the societal norm of working man and child caring female, this is usually expressed as the female failing. Orthodox family therapists, however well intentioned, would try to reverse the stereotype by seeking to engage the male partner in more child care duties but this in many cases simply reinforced the female's sense of failure. This attempted intervention neglected to understand that for many women success in child care was an important defining characteristic of their femininity from which they gained enormous self-esteem and role satisfaction. The intervention also unwittingly reinforced the male as the problem-solver and the more successful partner.

Social workers using an empowering anti-oppressive framework to their practice will find these concepts resonate with their way of working with women who are abused by violent partners or left to cope with children on their own. Combining feminist fam-ily therapy concepts with social work skills they can overtly address the wider social context of the difficulties and dilemmas faced by women by challenging the prevailing patriarchal assumptions that undervalues child care and the relationship/nurturing skills of women. Helping women recover from such traumas and build self-confidence re-quires patience as well as the ability to reframe them away from notions of individual fault/blame/failure towards an understanding of the social constraints affecting rela-tionship patterns. Using a feminist approach means making explicit throughout your work with clients the power differences between genders and enabling them to tackle the consequent dilemmas in their relationships.

## CONSTRUCTIVISM AND SOCIAL CONSTRUCTIONISM

These two related but different concepts are linked to postmodern theories that have recently begun to challenge some of the orthodox thinking and techniques of family therapy practice. The postmodern thesis rejects the notion that there is a fixed truth or single reality about family process. The postmodern view suggests that each individual constructs his or her personalized views and interpretations of what the family might be experiencing together. Family therapists with a constructivist or social constructionist perspective emphasize the importance of cultural diversity, multiple realities and the acceptance of a wide range of belief systems (Goldenberg and Goldenberg 2004; White and Epston 1990).

Constructivism stems from the study of the biology of cognition which argues that individuals have unique nervous systems that permit different assumptions being made about the same situation. Social constructionism is similar in that it argues that there is no such thing as objective reality, but that what we do construct from what we observe arises from the language system, relationships and culture which we share with others. In practice the constructivist and social constructionist family therapist therefore would be recognized by his or her more collaborative style of working. The focus is on helping the family examine and reassess the assumptions individuals make about their lives rather than focusing on family patterns of communication. Using these approaches involves taking a position of uncertainty and not knowing; instead the therapist joins in the search for workable solutions on an equal basis with the family.

### NARRATIVE THERAPY

Narrative therapy recognizes the natural ability people have to possess, to generate and to evolve new narratives and stories to make sense of their experiences (Freeman *et al.* 1997). The focus of interest is the meanings that families generate to explain and shape possible courses of actions. Traditions within families and cultures are used to guide interpretations of events. Making these more explicit in a more conversational style of therapeutic process helps to validate the family experience rather than seeking to impose a solution or follow a therapist-determined path. The nature of the conversation is the key to this approach. Social workers will note similarities with an exchange model of assessment, empowering and service-user focused work. The approach challenges the way clients are labelled because they are usually superficial, negative and one-dimensional descriptions. The client can begin to accept these limiting descriptions and believing they are 'true' start to behave in ways that confirm the label. Narrative therapy aims to help families by collaborating in developing alternative stories about their lives and replacing a single, problem-saturated belief with a number of different, complex beliefs which open up possibilities.

## Family support and family therapy

Family support can be perceived as an overall aspiration within which particular models and techniques of practice are employed. These models and methods can be rooted in behavioural, psychodynamic or task-centred theories and focus on individuals, couples or the whole family. Family therapists using systems theory might also characterize their work in terms of a range of methods, including, for example, structural, psychoanalytic, systemic, cognitive behavioural, solution focused or constructionist. Equally, the focus can be on the individual, couple or whole family.

Within each overall mode of working there are a wide variety of techniques and approaches. So when terms such as 'family support' and 'family therapy' are used in multidisciplinary professional contexts such as inter-agency meetings or case confer-ences it would not be surprising if participants made a number of different assumptions about what was actually being proposed or had already been tried in practice. Without clarification about what these terms mean the potential for confusion as is high and the possibility that families receive mixed messages and conflicting advice.

This is important in the context of finding ways of working that are relevant and acceptable to service users (Walker 2003). Family support has, for example, had to adapt its historical focus on the traditional nuclear family model. Whereas the more recent practice of family therapy has had to consider the effectiveness of culturally competent methods of working with different family forms, rather than trying to defend its focus on systems rather than individuals. Indeed there is a creative body of literature develop-ing that illustrates how family therapy concepts can be adapted for work with individuals or couples.

Some literature identifies the use to which family therapy ideas have been put, but the influences are described in a linear, rather than circular direction (Kelsall and McCullough 1988; Manor 1991; Reamers and Treacher 1995). Family therapists usually eschew the notion of linearity. On the other hand studies of the effectiveness of family support use systemic concepts such as circularity very similar to the most ortho-dox family therapist (Gardner 1998; Hellinckx, Colton and Williams 1997; Pinkerton, Higgins and Devine 2000). Family support therefore may have something to offer family therapy and vice versa.

In a similar way to the silent discourse between feminism and family therapy that was eventually heard, there seems to be a contemporary lack of dialogue between those practising family therapy and those engaged in family support. Family support tends to be marginalized as an activity without a clear definition, whereas family therapy has spawned specialist journals and requiring advanced clinical qualifications for specific occupational roles. Feminist family therapists began to realize that family therapy was failing to engage with feminist ideas of women's unequal position in the family structure. Practice seemed to be based on a denial of the unequal power relationships underpinning family dynamics and was therefore not truly systemic (Goldner 1985; Hare-Mustin 1978).

Any discussion of the family nowadays which does not incorporate the dimension of gender power would be considered inadequate – especially in the context of child and family social work where practitioners need to fully understand how masculine power is used in overt and covert ways to control, dominate and abuse partners and children. As public and professional debate constantly agonizes over the emotional health of families and how to improve it, family therapy and family support are expanding their reach in the arena of family welfare policy and practice (Gorell Barnes 1998; Statham 2000). Both family therapy and family support aspire to improving practice and engaging in evidence-based evaluation. Both are sometimes perceived as descriptions of therapeutic practice and service delivery format.

Yet there is an absence of open discussion between the two interventions and an unspoken assumption that family support is for the working class practised by unquali-fied or low-paid generic staff, while family therapy is for the middle classes and practised by highly paid post-qualified specialists. By opening up the dialogue between them, it may be possible for practitioners to engage in a mutual learning process to benefit one another, as well as individual and family clients or service users.

## Early intervention and prevention

In the government policy consultation paper *Supporting Families* (DOH 1999) the focus of attention was better support and education for current and future parents as a preventive strategy. Key themes included the intention to improve advice and information to parents, and achieving a reduction in child poverty, while offering financial help for working parents. The policy argued that by strengthening adult relationships and targeting serious family problems, an impact could be made on priority areas such as children's learning, youth offending, teenage pregnancy, and domestic violence. These are all areas that could be enhanced by a family therapy approach that can appraise the inter-relationship between and within them.

Various initiatives aimed at children and their families living in disadvantaged areas, such as the Sure Start programme, are evidence of the practical implementation of the implicit preventive aspects of this policy which are based on evidence of success from the USA Head Start scheme. This demonstrated long-term reductions in anti-social activity, marital problems, child abuse, adult mental health difficulties and unemployment in later life, in a group of children who received the intervention and compared with a group of children who did not receive.

Quantifying the impact of preventive family support work is complex and to achieve systematic results is expensive, therefore there is little in the way of evidence of long-term effectiveness in Britain or the rest of Europe. However, there are signs that, while outcome measures from the Department of Health refocusing initiative projects were intangible, small-scale social action projects could evidence changes in relationships between parents and professionals, how to work in partnership and how to engage positively with parents (Robbins 1998). All of which contributed to supporting families better and was more user-focused.

The lessons for social work practice are for emphasizing empowering strategies, searching hard for creative solutions beyond narrow service-led resources, and refining relationship-building skills. This challenges the service management orthodoxy for short-term focused assessments aimed at identifying risk and need according to a limited range of resources provided by other non-statutory agencies. It offers the opportunity to provide professionally qualified social workers with more satisfying work over longer time periods, and service users the chance to feel respected, valued, contained and supported in a consistent and reliable way. The prospect is for combining the best features of social work practice grounded in a solid psychosocial systems theoretical base.

One way that children's services can tilt the balance away from repressive child protection procedures and illustrate the pragmatic use of systems theory is reflected in the example of family group conferences. Introduced some years ago and borrowing from New Zealand Maori traditional practices, they have challenged the orthodoxy in social services planning which places primacy on the professional social workers power, values and perceptions. The key idea in these conferences is that family meetings are convened where there are concerns about the welfare of a child or children. The family in these circumstances is defined widely and extended family members are encouraged to participate. Their task is to create their own plan for the child of concern by assuming responsibility in deciding how to meet the needs of the child.

Thus the social worker's role changes dramatically from an inspectorial/adversarial role largely prescribed by procedures and a restricted definition of their task, to one more consistent with the skills and knowledge of family therapy. In the context of family group conferences social workers can emphasize communication, negotiation, mediation and facilitation skills that are better informed by a family therapy approach seeking to emphasize problem-solving and highlight the strengths within a family system. Clearly a therapeutic stance is required that means social workers having to embrace the concept of partnership practice and resist the seductive simplicity of deciding what is best for children and their families.

At the heart of the family group conference is a redefinition of social work practice with children and families. It puts into sharp focus a tangible example of the elusive and often ill-defined notion of empowering practice. It is a challenge to social work which is driven by a defensive culture and to social workers who are comforted by the ability to retreat into procedural safety when faced with complexity, uncertainty and the normal swings and roundabouts of family life. On the other hand this approach fits with social workers using a family therapy or systemic approach to their work. The family group conference model proposes limits to the intrusion of the professional planning model. It suggests the model should form the frame within which family decision-making should take place, and that decision-making should be carried out in whatever way is appropriate for each particular family (Morris and Tunnard 1996).

## Evaluation and effectiveness

Research into family therapy can be considered compatible with the process and practice of the model itself. As the modern physical scientists have evolved new ways of thinking about facts and objectivity, so, with systems theory in the social sciences, practitioners can embrace the concepts of progressive hypothesizing – formulating ideas about a family, testing them and then reformulating on the basis of feedback (Dallos and Draper 2000). As we noted earlier, the use of supervision, videotape recording and family tasks offers a rich source of evidence with which to measure and analyse the impact of the therapy. Systems theory also sits comfortably within new paradigms in the social sciences which seek to look beyond observed behaviours and recognize the importance of the meanings and beliefs created by families about their problems and attempted solutions.

There have been increasing numbers of studies of family therapy attempting to measure the effectiveness of this particular therapeutic intervention since it began to be more comprehensively established in the 1970s (Campbell and Draper 1985; Dallos and Draper 2000; Lask and Lask 1979; Reimers and Treacher 1995). On the whole the evidence is consistent that family therapy is a valuable and effective approach to use in a variety of contexts. Before examining some of the studies to gain some detail about how family therapy helped it needs to be acknowledged that most of the studies have been undertaken in 'clinical' settings. There have been relatively few studies of family therapy employed in social work agency contexts. Indeed, the valid evidence base for social work interventions is generally speaking rather thin – but improving.

However, even within the confines of clinical practice it is clear that family therapy has established itself alongside some of the older and more orthodox therapeutic methods and models of intervention as a reliable and acceptable approach. A meta-analysis of the findings of 163 published and unpublished outcome studies on the efficacy and effectiveness of marital and family therapy concluded that the clients did significantly better than untreated control group clients (Shadish *et al.* 1995). Based on a substantial literature search of the available research findings recently some clear findings (Friedlander 2001; Goldenberg and Goldenberg 2004) demonstrate the following:

- Compared with no treatment, non-behavioural marital/family therapies are effective in two-thirds of all cases.

- The efficacy of systemic, behavioural, emotionally focused and insight-producing family therapies is established for marital and adolescent delinquent problems.

- Structural family therapy appears to be particularly helpful for certain childhood and adolescent psychosomatic symptoms.

- There is evidence for the efficacy of family therapy in treating childhood conduct disorders, phobias, anxieties and especially autism.

A major review of consumer studies of family therapy and marital counselling analysed a variety of research including large- and small-scale studies, individual case studies, specific therapeutic methodologies and ethnographic studies (Treacher 1995). These are particularly valuable sources of evidence because while they do not have the same methodological rigour as 'clinical' research studies, they nevertheless reflect a more realistic experience of families in front-line working contexts. The review concluded that practitioners who neglected the service user perspective and undervalued the personal relationship aspects of their family support work in favour of concentrating on inducing change, ran the risk of creating considerable dissatisfaction among service users. This reinforced findings from an earlier study into the effectiveness of family therapy that advised that advice and directive work needs to be balanced with reflective and general supportive elements (Howe 1989). In particular the following conclusions are worth highlighting:

- Families needed an explanation of what therapy was about and how it differed from regular social service contact.

- Families felt they were being investigated, judged, manipulated and maligned and were unable to discuss issues they felt were important.

These studies point up the dilemmas faced by social workers trying to employ therapeutic techniques in the context of a statutory remit which often includes a coercive element to family participation and an inspectorial/monitoring element to the work. Assessment in social work is expected to include a therapeutic element but in the context of determining whether a child is in need or there are child protection concerns, it is understandable if both parents and social workers lose track of the purpose of such assessments. These dilemmas probably also reflect the constraints of time that impose artificial time-scales, which are inherently anti-therapeutic. As with similar studies in other health and social care organizations it is difficult to draw substantive extrapolations from the data examining family therapy in social work practice because they rarely meet research validity and reliability criteria. Thus, attempts to compare findings usually run into methodological problems that negate any meaningful meta-analysis.

In a sense these findings confirm the view that attempting to use family therapy or systemic approaches in social work needs to be thought through, planned and introduced in a way that best fits with the context of service users. Families who have had regular contact with social service departments regarding child care issues will have learned a number of responses to their patterns of contact with, and relationships towards, social work staff. Parents could have a perception of social workers as interfering, undermining nosey parkers, which contextualizes their behaviour and communications with them. On the other hand they could perceive social workers as rescuers, troubleshooters or mediators between them and difficult teenagers. Using a family therapy intervention offers a way of engaging creatively with clients to generate a problem-solving approach over a relatively short timescale to what they perceive as their difficulties.

## References

Bateson, G. (1973) *Steps to an Ecology of Mind*. St Albans: Paladin.

Bowlby, J. (1969) *Attachment and Loss Volume 1*. New York: Basic Books.

Burnham, J. (1986) *Family Therapy*. London: Tavistock Publications.

Campbell, D. and Draper, R. (eds) (1985) *Applications of Systemic Family Therapy: The Milan Approach*. London: Academic Press.

Dallos, R. and Draper, R. (2000) *An Introduction to Family Therapy*. Buckingham: OU Press.

DOH (1999) *Supporting Families*. London: HMSO.

DOH (2000) *The Children Act Report 1995–1999*. London: HMSO.

DOH/SSI (2000) *A Quality Strategy for Social Care* London: HMSO.

Dominelli, L. (2002) *Anti-Oppressive Social Work Theory and Practice*. London: Palgrave.

Donovan, M. (2003) 'Mind the gap: The need for a generic bridge between psychoanalytic and systemic approaches.' *Journal of Family Therapy 25*, 115–135.

Freeman, I., Morrison, A., Lockhart, F. and Swanson M. (1997) 'Consulting service users: The views of young people.' In M. Hill and J. Aldgate (eds) *Child Welfare Services: Developments in Law, Policy, Practice and Research*. London: Jessica Kingsley Publishers.

Friedlander, M., Highlen, P. and Lassiter, W. (2001) 'Content analytic comparison of four export counsellors' approaches to family treatment.' *Journal of Counselling Psychology 32*, 171–80.

Gardner, R. (1998) *Family Support: Practitioners Guide*. Birmingham: BASW and Venture Press.

Goldenberg, I. and Goldenberg, H. (2004) *Family Therapy – An Overview*. Pacific Grove, CA: Thomson Learning.

Goldner, V. (1985) 'Feminism and family therapy.' *Family Process 24*, 31–47.

Goldner, V. (1991) 'Sex, power and gender: A feminist analysis of the politics of passion.' *Journal of Feminist Family Therapy 3*, 63–83.

Gorell Barnes, G. (1984) *Working with Families*. London: Macmillan.

Gorell Barnes, G. (1998) *Family Therapy in Changing Times*. Basingstoke: Palgrave.

Haley, J. (1976) *Problem Solving Therapy*. San Francisco, CA: Jossey-Bass.

Hare-Mustin, R. (1978) 'A feminist approach to family therapy.' *Family Process 17*, 181–94.

Hare-Mustin, R. (1991) 'Sex, lies and headaches: The problem is power.' *Journal of Feminist Family Therapy 3*, 39–61.

Hellinckx, W., Colton, M. and Williams, M. (1997) *International Perspectives on Family Support*. Aldershot: Ashgate Publishing.

Howe, D. (1989) *The Consumer's View of Family Therapy*. London: Gower.

Kelsall, J. and McCullough, B. (1988) *Family Work in Residential Child Care*. Manchester: Boys and Girls Welfare Society.

Laing, R. D. (1969) *Interventions in Social Situations*. London: Philadelphia Association.

Larner, G. (2000) 'Towards a common ground in psychoanalysis and family therapy: On knowing not to know.' *Journal of Family Therapy 22*, 61–82.

Lask, J. and Lask, B. (1979) *Child Psychiatry and Social Work*. London: Tavistock.

Manor, O. (1991) 'Assessing the work of a family centre.' *Journal of Family Therapy 13*, 285–94.

McGoldrick, M., Pearce, J. and Giordano, J. (eds) (1982) *Ethnicity and Family Therapy*. New York: Guilford Press.

Minuchin, S. (1974) *Families and Family Therapy*. London: Tavistock Publications.

Morris, K. and Tunnard, J. (1996) *Family Group Conferences: Messages from UK Practice and Research*. London: FRG.

Muncie, J. and Sapsford, R. (1997) 'Issues in the study of the family.' In J. Muncie, M. Wetherell, M. Langan, R. Dallos and A. Cochrane (eds) *Understanding the Family*. London: Sage.

Perelberg, R.J. and Miller, A.C. (eds) (1990) *Gender and Power in Families*. London: Routledge.

Pinkerton, J., Higgins, K., and Devine, P. (2000) *Family Support – Linking Project Evaluation to Policy Analysis*. Aldershot: Ashgate.

Pocock, D. (1997) 'Feeling understood in family therapy.' *Journal of Family Therapy 19*, 283–302.

Reimers, A. and Treacher, A. (1995) *Introducing User-friendly Family Therapy*. London: Routledge.

Robbins, D. (1998) 'The refocusing children's initiative: An overview of practice.' In. R. Bayley (ed) *Transforming Children's Lives: The Importance of Early Intervention*. London: Family Policy Studies Centre.

Shadish, W.R., Ragsdale, K., Glaser, R.R. and Montgomery, L.M. (1995) 'The efficacy and effectiveness of marital and family therapy: A perspective from meta-analysis.' *Journal of Marital and Family Therapy 21*, 345–60.

Statham, J. (2000) *Outcomes and Effectiveness of Family Support Services: A Research Review*. London: Institute of Education.

Treacher, A. (1995) 'Reviewing consumer studies of therapy.' In A. Treacher and S. Reimers (eds) *Introducing User-friendly Family Therapy*. London: Routledge.

Von Bertalanffy, L. (1968) *General Systems Theory: Foundation, Development, Application*. New York: Brazillier.

Walker, S. (2003) *Social Work and Child and Adolescent Mental Health*. Lyme Regis: Russell House Publishers.

Walker, S. and Akister, J. (2004) *Social Work and Family Therapy*. Lyme Regis: Russell House Publishers.

Walker, S. and Beckett, C. (2004) *Social Work Assessment and Intervention*. Lyme Regis: Russell House Publishers.

White, M. and Epston, D. (1990) *Narrative Means to Therapeutic Ends*. New York: Norton.

## CHAPTER 16

# THEORY, CONCEPTS, FEELINGS AND PRACTICE: THE CONTEMPLATION OF BEREAVEMENT WITHIN A SOCIAL WORK COURSE

*Gerard Rochford*

## Editor's note

I have included this original chapter in the new edition, because it still raises relevant questions about current issues in selection and motivation for social work education, although the content and nature of social work and social work education have changed (Cree 2002). The themes of the original chapter, motivation for social work, loss and change (for social workers, service users and social service organizations) and experiential learning (with the implication of reflective learning) continue to be critical for educators in developing the new socials work degrees. Interestingly, in 1991 Rochford drew on a well-referenced knowledge base: i.e. he used an evidence-based approach.

Rochford's introduction to his chapter remains relevant for current social work education:

> Theory and technique which are taught and then applied by solely cognitive processes will always feel somewhat stiff for the practitioner and be perceived as false and manipulative by the client, as having something done to them rather than engaging in a joint task and will thus re-enact and reinforce their already crippling experience of powerlessness, victimization and alienation. (p.239)

In a sense Rochford anticipates the importance of empowerment, advocacy and the inclusion of users and carers in carrying out the social work task (see Chapter 18 in the present volume).

I shall now briefly consider the three themes of the chapter which I believe still to be relevant.

### MOTIVATION FOR SOCIAL WORK

Rochford demonstrates one aspect of motivation for social work, the 'wounded helper' and, in particular, the experience of loss as a factor in motivation for social work. Cree (1996) found, more broadly, that reasons for entering social work training included having a family background with a commitment to public and social service and having life experiences of loss, illness or disability, and also an adult decision which involved various motivations: vocation to care for individuals, to provide social justice and to 'change the system'.

Cree (1996) also highlighted gender differences: men may enter the profession because promotion prospects are high. Women may enter because the qualities and abilities required are stereotypically female rather than male. Cree (2003) further develops her analysis of how people become social workers and their motivation. She recognizes that 'I have been trying to resolve central contradiction in my own background and upbringing' (p.5).

In Cree (2003) an overarching set of reasons was articulately identified by Holman (2003): the threat of death and consequent loss in the Second World War evacuation (again with issues of loss) and being an 'outsider'. Other contributors (Cree 2003) also identify themselves as 'outsiders', discriminated against and therefore challenging discrimination, as a social worker, in relation to the impact of poverty, gender, ethnicity, sexuality and disability on service users.

Rochford's original analysis of motivation for social work in terms of 'wounded healers' and the relevance of the experience of loss for applicants for social work education remains relevant.

However, in selection for social work we need to assess applicants' suitability for social work practice and their ability to meet the professional requirements of the new degrees. In this assessment we need to make judgements about how much applicants have the potential to use personal experience (in terms of loss but also discrimination and structural inequity) to understand and work constructively with service users. We also need to make a judgement about whether applicants will be able to maintain the boundary between their personal experience and their professional role. If issues of loss or discrimination are very recent and remain raw, there is a danger that the student social worker may be influenced by his or her own needs rather than by those of users of services.

## LOSS, CHANGE AND BEREAVEMENT

Sadly loss, bereavement and unwelcome change remain a constant for all of us and therefore a part of the experience that users of services bring to social workers. Rochford's theoretical analysis of bereavement, mourning and the experience of loss again remains relevant as does his conclusion: 'It is clear that an enabling response to bereaved persons requires sensitive and "risky" use of self, particularly the ability to live within ambivalence and not be tempted to "reason" with contradictory feelings.'

The concept of loss as bereavement in Rochford's chapter needs to be extended. Loss can also include:

- loss by family separation or divorce

- loss of health, for example, by accident, disability or illness

- loss of a job by unemployment, redundancy or retirement

- loss of security, for example, by violence or burglary

- loss of home base by moving house, neighbourhood or geographical location, or by moving from a person's own home to residential care

- loss of country, for example, for asylum seekers.

Such losses may be interlinked, e.g. family separation and consequential problems or ill health may lead to entry to residential care. Loss of country for asylum seekers will probably involve loss of family, job, security and home as well as country.

Reactions to such loss are conceived as varying with the strength and quality of the attachment involved and also of previous attachments. Reactions to the losses people experience which, as discussed, are wider than bereavement, do, however, parallel the stages of mourning which Rochford cites from Parkes (1975).

Marris (1974) extended Parkes' analysis of bereavement to a more general analysis of loss including the meaning of loss for the person who has lost and the link between loss and change. Marris argues that change, whether voluntary or imposed, positive or negative, involves loss as well as gain for those involved.

Changes, which initially appear entirely positive, may also include elements of loss, for example:

- becoming a student and leaving home for an unfamiliar university environment

- slum clearance and leaving a familiar neighbourhood and neighbours

- organizational restructuring and thereby leaving familiar organizational roles.

As Marris (1974) argued. 'Transitions like these involve a loss of their previously taken for granted views of the world, their feeling of security and newly established sense of meaning and purpose' (cited in Lishman 2000, p.202) remains a component of change and the losses that might therefore be incurred.

Change and loss, therefore, involve the following conflicts and tensions:

- the need to consolidate what was important and valuable from the past

- the need to preserve oneself in the face of perceived loss

- the need to re-establish a meaningful pattern of relationships in which the loss has been accepted and integrated

- the need to move on and embrace the future and its requirements for change.
                                                            (Lishman 2000, p.202)

Working with people who have experienced loss requires us to understand ambivalence as Rochford argues 'important not only because ambivalence is of the essence of grief but because it introduces the paradox of understanding *cognitively* the powerful processes of *irrationality*' (p.246, my emphasis; a theme explored further in this volume in Chapters 5 and 6).

Such understanding requires social work students and social workers to engage in a process of developing self-awareness and reflection (see Chapter 23 in the present volume, for Fook's analysis of critical reflective practice).

## SELF-AWARENESS AND REFLECTIVE PRACTICE

An essential element of suitability for social work is a capacity to reflect on and be aware of how our own experience, of structural issues such as poverty, ethnicity and disability, of personal and family issues and of loss have influenced us, and therefore make a clear boundary between our own personal experiences, how we experienced them and how this can help us to begin to understand and empathize with service users' experiences. We also need to understand that we cannot assume our experiences mirror those of service users or act *out* on their behalf agendas which are essentially ours.

Fook, in Chapter 23 in the present volume, examines and analyses reflective practice and social work. In the United Kingdom reflective practice has drawn heavily on Schon (1983), with his distinction between *on* and *in* action (Lishman 2002). Reflection *on* action means reflecting afterwards, and could include the following questions:

- What previous experience affected how I responded?

- What specifically did I do and why?

- How much was my response influenced by my own history and experience?

- How might I have responded differently?

Reflection *in* action (Schon 1983) is about engaging in such self-awareness and reflection as we are practising and, therefore, being aware of when a response might be a personal rather than a professional one. For example, if I have had a painful and destructive experience of loss which I have not been able to resolve, I need to be able to reflect carefully *in* action and *on* action about whether my responses to a service user's sharing of loss were about my own experience (for example, in trying to deny its impact) or a professional response of listening actively and empathically to the service user.

Reflection and self-awareness need also, as Rochford argues, to be integrated in practice with knowledge base and cognitive skills. Problem-based learning (Burgess and Taylor 2005) is a potential means to enable students to practise integrating their knowledge, evidence base and critical reflection in using their skills in assessment, intervention and evaluation, and can be used in social work education in both universities and social work agencies to prepare students for being more effective in direct practice with users of services.

Rochford's chapter highlights the experience of bereavement as a contributing factor to the choice of social work as a career. Perhaps more importantly we need to think more broadly about the impact of bereavement, loss and change in the lives of people who use our service and their influence on why people may need services. We also need to reflect on our personal experience of loss and change and how this might affect our professional responses in practice with users of service, but also, potentially, in terms of how we respond to organizational change.

## Introduction

The subject of this paper is how to relate theory to practice by contemplating personal experiences of loss. I am not proposing that the approach I take is appropriate to all teaching. I would say, however, that in some areas of social work education and training theory can only be related to practice by using a model of experiential learning which engages the thinking and the feelings of the students concerning their inner lives and the hypothesized inner lives of those with whom they have shared their intimate personal and professional time. It is my view that teaching students how to relate theory to practice, using an experiential model, not only brings the subject to life in a way that purely didactic and cognitive teaching fails to do, but provides a cognitive framework in such a way as to keep alive the relationship of theory to practice as a continuing and internalized process. Theory and technique which are taught and then applied by solely cognitive processes will always feel somewhat stiff for the practitioner and be perceived as false and manipulative by the client, as having something done to them rather than engaging in a joint task, and will thus re-enact and reinforce their already crippling experiences of powerlessness, victimization and alienation.

## Selection

If you use an experiential model of teaching there are issues around student selection that need to be addressed. The selection process must replicate some features of the course, partly so that students will learn what kind of cognitive but more especially affective work will be demanded of them (them selecting us), but also for us to assess their ability to make their feelings available for cognitive work without undue risk or frustration to themselves. In this sense the work of the course begins in the applicants' personal statement, and is elaborated at interview in a way which makes the acceptance of a place a sufficiently informed consent of a particular kind, namely that a good deal of self-enquiry will be demanded of them.

We are familiar with applicants whose personal statements contain nothing personal and where interviewers are unable to reach the applicants' personal feelings about major life events and their work with clients.

And we know too applicants with a powerful desire to help, but whose life events have swamped them with feelings which are all too readily amplified by the experiences and feelings of clients, raising the issues of anger, guilt, and reparation, the potential problems of counter-transference, its value but also its dangers.

Within the two years of a course the one could not be sufficiently reached nor the other sufficiently healed, nor can it be our task with students to attempt this. Being cut off from feeling or flooded with feeling should lead to an applicant being turned down, though selection errors undoubtedly occur at these boundaries.

Between these extremes there are those with sufficient freedom of feeling around not only normal but in some cases tragic life events to make them available to the cognitive task relating to theory, the practice task relating to work with clients, and the encompassing task of turning self, client, theory and practice into a functioning whole.

The recently wounded would-be healer on the mend may be asked to re-apply. The 'cut-off', whose control and fears of his or her own feelings are likely to lead to a purely intellectual grasp of theory and a controlling and phobic response to clients' feelings, would not be.

We may work readily, therefore, with both the unscarred and the sufficiently healed, though I do feel, to paraphrase Winnicott (1971), that although it can be said that if you have been wounded yourself you have greater sympathy with wounded people (though this is not always the case) somehow it would always have been better if we had not been wounded, (though all of us have).

## The tutor's and the supervisor's task

I am talking here about educating students to work with feelings where the resource is the self and the techniques reside in the responses you make to the person in the room – the therapeutic interview. To develop this resource tutors have a legitimate interest in the students' feelings in so far as these are likely to manifest themselves in professional encounters.

Not only tutors but also supervisors have a legitimate interest in students' feelings. It is possible, however, to identify shifts of focus, although both tutor and supervisor have the same field of vision which encompasses the thoughts and feelings of student and client, flowing within and between them. Both tutor and supervisor seek to promote a helpful response which is based on and leads to further elaboration of cognitive and empathic understanding and subsequent responding. The focus for the tutor may be more towards the student, and for the supervisor more towards the client. From time to time it will become clear that a student is in need of psychotherapy or counselling. This, in my view, should never be offered by the tutor or supervisor.

Somewhere in there lies a boundary, between education and grandiose ambition, between the legitimate need to see the student's feelings, and voyeurism, and between being tutor or supervisor and being a counsellor or therapist. Any strict separation between being a tutor and being a counsellor/therapist would no doubt be unhelpful (Fleming and Benedek 1983) but separation there must be. I would suggest that it is in some ways easier for the supervisor, since the focus and priority is the current work with clients for which the supervisor is often accountable.

## Personal analysis and self-reflection

To focus upon the student's feelings per se is both legitimate and vital. I do hold, with Freud (1957a), that no personal work with clients goes further than my own complexes and internal resistances permit. In psycho-analytic education and training the cognitive, personal, and practice tasks have four clear and separable (though not separate) arenas, namely theoretical seminars, case presentations, the personal analysis and the treatment of cases under supervision.

In social work, to make a contribution to the task of applying theory to practice, from the particular theoretical and clinical tradition of psycho-analysis, obviously requires a considerable modification of such a model, especially in that most crucial aspect, the personal analysis.

The theoretical seminar, the case presentation and the direct work with clients under supervision, all have their counterpart in social work education and training. The personal analysis does not.

Yet some of the process and purposes of the personal analysis have to be present if social workers are to work with distressed feelings and if the contribution of psycho-analytic theory to social work education is to be meaningful and more than an intellectual exercise. To do this we have to provide students with situations and experiences which facilitate some of the process and purposes of a personal analysis so that the students' own experiencing becomes an object of study and so that they are able to anchor the fleeting phenomena of experience in the cognitive framework of concepts and theory, to value self-enquiry, see the need and practical value of it, and to have the confidence to generalize from their own experience (Fleming and Benedek 1983). Part of this process is about converting sympathy to empathy so that a permeable boundary is kept between your feelings and the client's, a boundary none the less for being permeable and a closeness none the less for having a boundary. A client's grief will make you sad. But it is the client's grief and your sadness.

It is, I hope, accepted that empathy, by which the distressed feelings presented by the client and the feelings generated and available to the social worker, can be the medium in which work is done without loss of identity – that empathy is both an essential quality and also an educable resource. This can be achieved by making the student's own experience a primary object of study, in such a way as to make the empathic and the cognitive work together (Fleming and Benedek 1983). This must be done in time to prepare the student for placements and for work. And it must be done in a way which enables the student to internalize a process, a skill and a commitment which they will take further with them (Winnicott 1971). This is most vital because, to paraphrase Fleming and Benedek (1983), the social worker may be confronted by any client in any period of their professional life with one or other vulnerable area in their own personality and will be presented with changes caused by ageing, fatigue, illness or other external events which increase the social worker's vulnerability to the challenge of a client's demands. The achievement of the sort of educative process, I advocate, has been well put by Winnicott (1971) – whereby it becomes possible for a serious person to maintain a professional standard even when undergoing very severe and personal strain in private life. This also concerns avoiding burn-out and underlines the need for supervision throughout one's professional life.

This can only be achieved if students are educated to set up within themselves a free but disciplined communication between thoughts and feelings, the past and the present, the conscious and the unconscious of themselves and of the client in the room.

In which experiences and with which theory can we meet with the students for this task? I would suggest that the experience of loss may be especially relevant to the integration of theory, feelings and practice, where the theory to be understood is psychoanalytic theory.

## The experience of bereavement: theory, concepts, feelings and practice

It appears from applicants' personal statements, and from interview material, that a major feature of motivation to do social work is the working through of the experience of loss, both normal and exceptional.

Looking at two recent intakes, from 38 students, ten had suffered the death of their father during childhood or adolescence and a further four had lost their mother, three had suffered the death of a close friend, one had lost a child, at least one had had an abortion, three had been divorced, one twice, and two had been close to persons committing suicide.

The experience of loss and grief is especially fitted for the teaching of theory and practice and for the educative process of putting a cognitive framework to personal experiences and feelings.

The prevailing theoretical perspective is psycho-analytical, a fact of special aptness. The case which first drew Freud to his life's work was a young woman whose symptoms were shown in response to her father's illness and death. Freud comments: '...her symptoms ... correspond to a display of mourning, and there is certainly nothing pathological in being fixated to the memory of a dead person so short a time after his decease; on the contrary it would be a normal emotional process' (Freud 1910). It was this patient who called analysis 'the talking cure'.

The theme brought forth a stream of classic literature: Freud's *Mourning and Melancholia* (1957b), Klein's *Mourning and its Relationship to Manic-Depressive States* (1940), Bowlby's work on *Attachment and Loss* (1975), Marris' *Loss and Change* (1974). A ground base is the idea that mourning is a necessary process in normal healthy living. Glancing back to what I said about applicants rejected, they are often blocked grievers or those for whom the experience of loss is still too raw.

The classic psycho-analytic account of response to loss is Freud's (1957b) *Mourning and Melancholia*, mourning being a healthy response to loss of a loved one, melancholia or depression being its pathological form.

The features of depression are described by Freud as follows:

> The distinguishing mental features of melancholia are a profoundly painful dejection, cessation of interest in the outside world, loss of the capacity to love, inhibition of all activity, and a lowering of the self-regarding feelings to a degree that find utterance in self-reproaches and self-revilings, and culminates in a delusional expectation of punishment. This picture becomes a little more intelligible when we consider that... the same traits are met with in mourning.

Freud goes on to distinguish two forms of melancholia; one in which the lost object is evident but the response not that of healthy mourning, the other in which we cannot see what is lost and it is reasonable to assume that the sufferer cannot consciously perceive it either. He summarizes the main distinction thus: 'in mourning it is the world which has become poor and empty; in melancholia it is the ego itself'. This may be relevant to post-natal depression in which the experience of birth seems to have been not that of adding another life but of emptying out a part of oneself. This suggests a powerful identification between the woman and infant, a projective identification by which the infantile part of herself is projected into the foetus and there identified with. She is then 'emptied' at birth and transformed into a demanding and helpless infant, a further stage in the projective identification.

## The characteristics of mourning

The characteristics of mourning following Bowlby (1961) are usually organized according to stages developmentally described and consistent with those theories which relate present coping processes to early, particularly infantile, experiences. The concept of stages tends to encourage the view that progress is orderly, the stages discrete and that they must all be entered and passed through 'cleanly'. Perhaps also the concept of stages encourages impatience in the family, friend, neighbour or counsellor who look for progress, and fails to capture the ambivalence of feeling, the to-ing and fro-ing, which seems to pervade the experience of bereavement. Maybe the word 'stance' is closer to the tentativeness of the desire to move on and the fear of betrayal which pulls you back.

The stances of a bereaved person will include many of the following features:

- Shock, numbness, dazed withdrawal; denial, disbelief, a feeling of isolation, of being in a dream, of being childlike, of detachment; over-activity or physical collapse. The funeral often marks a transition: loss of religious faith may be experienced. The funeral also takes on the process of idealization, only the good is remembered (Jaques 1955). It is to be noted that denial is predicated upon some level of acceptance, a later stance. All stances have the others beneath and around them, varyingly accessible to empathic work.

- Yearning and protest, pining, weeping and anger; pangs; illusions, misperceptions, dreams and hallucinations of the lost one; psychosomatic symptoms of anxiety and fear, panic, sleeplessness, palpitations, dryness of the mouth; self-neglect. The bereaved may still disbelieve and deny death, speaking as if the dead person were still alive and imminent, trying to get close, to a chair, a bed, a grave; make nostalgic journeys yet showing fear of other haunts which are now dangerous, places which were previously entered, as it were, on the spouse's arm. The impulse to recover, retain, restore the lost one is also a search for reality and the disappointment of the search, as reality insists upon its truth, can engender in the bereaved person a more relaxed sense of internal presence. Perhaps the most disturbing feeling of all is the feeling of triumph, 'I am alive and he is dead'. There are thus disturbances of thought, feeling and perception, which are attended or followed by feelings of foolishness, shame, frustration and anger.

- Despair, apathy and a feeling of emptiness or meaninglessness signal belief in the death. Bitterness, irritation and hostility to others may emerge with, usually muted, expressions of guilt and anger. The bereaved person senses the world as a dangerous place, withdraws and becomes disorganized, aimless. There is a giving up of associations with the lost one, while retaining one chosen 'version' of him, for example, a photograph.

- Re-organization, acceptance and adaption follow. The bereaved person re-emerges, rebuilds social relationships, restores herself. The sense of mourning as a duty is relinquished, an act that may require the 'permission' of a trusted person. It is now possible to reminisce about happy and unhappy times, with an appropriate sense of the lost and the retained. The reality of reminiscence replaces the unreality of denial. The 'good enough' survivors replace the 'resented, intrusive' substitutes.

There are no feelings unique to the loss through death of a loved one. The processes of denial, search and realization, the ambivalence of feeling, the contradictions of thinking and the errors of perception are the familiar experiences of reflective consciousness as we stand amid what was, what is, what we would like and what ought to be. These processes in particular occur not only within the bereaved but within the dying and within those who, in whatever capacity, share intimately the experience of the dying and the bereaved.

## Theory and practice approaching a bereaved person

The psycho-analytical perspective has at least three implications for those, whether family members, volunteers or professionals, who respond to the bereaved. First, bereaved persons cannot be understood except in the context of two resonating sets of relationship, the primary ones of their infancy and the later adult relationships.

Second, bereavement induces a process which in its manifestation and in its internal feel is in some sense a repetition of the separation anxieties of infancy and the attendant guilt as represented in the statement 'My badness drove her away'. Third, an enabling offer cannot be made to a bereaved person except by reaching into our own losses, both of infancy and of adulthood. Hence the special gifts that may be offered by those who have themselves grown from their own mourning, who can approach the bereaved from their own creative wounds. The proper assumption for practice has been put by Freud with nice severity:

> although grief involves grave departures from the normal attitude to life, it never occurs to us to regard it as a morbid condition and hand the mourner over to medical treatment. We rest assured that after a lapse of time it will be overcome, and we look upon any interference with it as inadvisable or even harmful. (Freud 1957a)

I take interference to mean anything which tends to suppress the expression of grief, including drugs commonly prescribed to bereaved persons.

The appropriate therapeutic stance is indicated both implicitly and explicitly by various writers. Klein (1940) says that the normal working through of mourning relates to the way in which the person first deals with this process in infancy. When the good person (mother) has gone she becomes bad and this gives rise to the ambivalence of love and hate. One way of coping with loss is by internalizing the lost person. The paradoxical effectiveness of this process, stressed by Bowlby (1975), is that the ability to tolerate separation-anxiety is a sign of deep attachment. Similarly, in bereavement, deep attachment leads to a corresponding deep loss, but also to the greater likelihood of restitution, as Pincus so movingly illustrates (1974). Deep attachment leads to healthy mourning as the strength of the remembered good person is retained and drawn upon, and as emotion is withdrawn from the really dead person. This parallel process, of letting go and of harvesting, eventually allows the bereaved person to talk with equanimity about both the good and the bad. The reality of the death and the reality of memory both assert themselves. Just as the anger and hatred against the dead revive and spring from infantile feelings, so also the infantile sense that badness drove the mother away can be seen in the bereaved person's guilt and sense of responsibility for the death: 'If only I'd looked after him better', 'If only I'd made him go to the doctor'. Some share of the ambivalent feelings of the bereaved towards the self and the other, will also be felt by friends, neighbours, relatives, helpers and counsellors, however well intentioned and however actually helpful. The irrationality of this may be a further source of guilt later, as the bereaved person recalls this time with some shame. Substitutes for the lost one may expect both thanks and resentment.

It is Parkes' (1975) view that prolonged or delayed mourning is usually attributable to excessive guilt and/or pronounced ambivalence in the relationship to the deceased. Kübler-Ross (1970) sees the somatic symptoms of the bereaved as a failure to work through guilt, and its attendant unconscious punishment. The starting point for Pincus (1974, p.viii) was to 'explore whether…various responses to bereavement might best be understood or even predicted by focussing on the particular relationships which made for unique family patterns'. The extent to which the relationship had been enhancing or depleting, whether the one was engaged with or lost in the other, interdependent or dependent, will find expression in the extent to which losing the other is being lost oneself. The internal representation of these relationships in the survivor will determine whether or not the taking in and giving out of what was good and bad was achieved without depletion, an experience which can then be drawn upon for the work of the restoration of the self in relationship with survivors.

It is clear that an enabling response to bereaved persons requires sensitive and 'risky' use of self, particularly the ability to live within ambivalence and not be tempted to 'reason' with contradictory feelings.

Just as we may understand the neurotic as someone who, due to constitutional, personal and social-environmental forces got stuck within a developmental process which most people travel through so also with particular responses to bereavement. Theoretical understanding of bereavement draws together the reciprocating knowledge of the normal and the abnormal experience, and of adult and child experience. This perspective requires us to listen not only to carefully designed research investigations but also to the analysis of practice experience and the anecdotes of the wise. For even an anecdote, honestly told, is valid data when theory is concerned with a universal phenomenon.

For both theoretical and practice reasons adult loss by death of a loved one cannot be split off from other losses experienced in the life cycle. The loss of infancy, childhood, adolescence, youth, friends, lovers, hopes and the breast's security, all resonate within us. Whether the later versions of these experiences give rise to some internal restoration or further crippling depletion is heavily dependent on early experience, leading to investment of the self in others (over-involvement), for others, (the helping response), or with others (love).

## Working with the experience of loss

Encouraging a psycho-analytic approach to the students' personal losses introduces them to the way of understanding adult relationships and experiences by reference to early primary relationships, and to their abiding primitive and infantile feelings.

It has the power to arouse in them the recognition that loss in its manifestation and its internal feel is in important ways a repetition of the separation anxiety of infancy. And it does this in a way which values their personal experiences for their own sakes and as professional resources. In terms of practice it hopes to arrive quickly at the realization that an enabling offer to persons with distressed feelings can only be made to the extent that we have reached into our own, holding them as separate from the client's but as a resource none the less.

The potential this theme has for facilitating access to feelings is matched by its suitability for cognitive work.

It introduces students in an experiential way to stage theory both in the general way of examining the evolution of their own dependencies, independencies and interdependencies and for many of them the micro-stages of mourning and grief work.

It introduces them through their feelings to a whole array of key concepts – denial, detachment, projection, identification, guilt, the desire for magical restoration, the flight into health, gain from illness, triumph, regression, despair and perhaps most important of all – ambivalence, important not only because ambivalence is of the essence of grief but because it introduces the paradox of understanding cognitively the powerful processes of irrationality.

It gives some access to the defence mechanisms through self-reflection in a way which also enables students to question but also to value their defences, having been protected by them. This helps them not to be provoked by the defences of clients, not to see them as walls to be attacked but perhaps maintained and even when pathological, only to be eased away painfully, gently and truthfully. It helps them to acknowledge bad feelings in others and not to take flight in unhelpful re-assurance or change of subject. It teaches them the emptiness of euphemizing social work encounters in order to save, that is waste, people's feelings.

In terms of its relevance to client groups the contemplation of loss and grief has considerable power for entering the worlds of others.

For example, though there are many more, (abortion, loss of a limb, divorce) in residential child care the theme of loss is both background and foreground to childrens' experience, where private griefs are compounded by public responses.

A study of List D girls (Petrie 1985) shows from a sample of 80 girls that 50 had lost a parent either from death or desertion, and among the remaining 30, 17 had one parent with serious illness. Similar figures were found among 100 List D boys.

Working with families of disabled children involves the loss of the perfect, unrealized child reverberating down the years, at the anniversaries, and at the many lost rites of passage.

At the other end of life, anyone working with the elderly or in hospitals has to enter the world of grief and must therefore be enabled to do this without being overwhelmed by their own resonating feelings.

## The formal task

By addressing loss in lectures and tutorials I have, I believe, identified a theme which unites teacher and student together in mutual experience. By requiring all students to write about bereavement, relating personal and professional experience to concepts and theory, they can discover that one way of acquiring knowledge is not by taking it in but by unlocking it – so they can say, with Freud's patient, 'I've always known it but never thought it', discerning that some forms of unknowing come not from being empty but from being resistant to, or split off from, yet-to-be released feeling which has a habitation but no name.

The format of an essay also, and importantly, leaves students in control of what material they are willing to expose, while at the same time putting them close to feelings and experiences which they can reflect upon but may not wish to write about or share with tutors, though it is important for them to be able to share with someone.

It is part of the journey towards mature hope so tellingly mapped by Searles (1979) who argues that any realistic hope must be grounded in the ability to experience and survive loss. Furthermore he suggests that hope comes into being when one discovers that despair can be shared with a fellow human being, thus fostering a feeling of relatedness rather than of alienation. 'This experiencing of loss and despair leading to hope is also part of the maturational process traversed by every therapist in the evolution of their own personal feelings in relation to patients with whom they become deeply and sustainedly involved' (Searles 1979, pp.484, 502).

The risks that students take and the hard cognitive work they undertake convinces me it is a journey into darkness well worth the illumination.

## References

Bowlby, J. (1961) 'Process in Mourning.' *International Journal of Psycho-Analysis 42*, 317–40.

Bowlby, J. (1975) *Attachment and Loss.* Harmondsworth: Penguin.

Burgess, H. and Taylor, I. (eds) (2005) *Effective Learning and Teaching in Social Policy and Social Work.* London: Routledge and Falmer.

Cree, V.E. (1996) 'Why do men care?' In K.Cavanagh and V.E. Cree (eds) *Working with Men.* London: Routledge.

Cree, V.E. (2002) 'The changing concept of social work.' In R. Adams, L. Dominelli and M. Payne (eds) *Social Work: Themes, Issues and Critical Debates.* 2nd edn. Basingstoke: Palgrave.

Cree, V.E. (2003) *Becoming a Social Worker.* London and New York: Routledge.

Fleming, J. and Benedek, T. F. (1983) *Psychoanalytic Supervision.* New York: International Universities Press.

Freud, S. (1910) *Five Lectures on Psycho-Analysis, Lecture I.* In J. Strachey (ed.) *The Standard Edition of the Complete Works of Sigmund Freud,* Vol. XI, London: Hogarth.

Freud, S. (1957a) *The Future Prospects of Psychoanalytic Therapy.* In J. Strachey (ed.) *The Standard Edition of the Complete Works of Sigmund Freud,* Vol. XI. London: Hogarth.

Freud, S. (1957b) *Mourning and Melancholia.* In J. Strachey (ed.) *The Standard Edition of the Complete Works of Sigmund Freud,* Vol. XIV. London: Hogarth.

Holman, B. (2003) 'Social work in the neighbourhood.' In V.E. Cree (ed.) *Becoming a Social Worker.* London: Routledge.

Jaques, E. (1955) 'Social systems as a defence against persecutory and depressive anxiety.' In M. Klein, P. Heimann and R.E. Money-Kyrle (eds) *New Directions in Psycho-Analysis.* London: Tavistock.

Klein, M. (1940) 'Mourning and its relation to manic-depressive states.' *Contributions to Psycho-Analysis.* London: Hogarth.

Kübler-Ross, E. (1970) *On Death and Dying.* London: Tavistock.

Lishman, J. (2000) 'Loss.' In M. Davies (2000) *The Blackwell Encyclopaedia of Social Work.* Oxford: Blackwell.

Lishman, J. (2002) 'Personal and professional development.' In R. Adams, L. Dominelli and M. Payne (2002) *Social Work: Themes, Issues and Critical Debates.* 2nd edn. Basingstoke: Palgrave.

Marris, P. (1974) *Loss and Change.* London: Routledge and Kegan Paul.

Molina, R. (2003) 'Social work in the neighbourhood.' In V.E. Cree (2003) *Becoming a Social Worker.* London and New York: Routledge.

Parkes, C.M. (1975) *Bereavement: Studies of Grief in Adult Life.* Harmondsworth: Penguin.

Petrie, C. (1985) 'Girls in a List D School.' Unpublished thesis, University of Aberdeen.

Pincus, L. (1974) *Death and the Family.* London: Faber.

Schon, D.A. (1983) *The Reflective Practitioner: How Officials Think or Act.* New York: Basic Books.

Searles, H.F. (1979) 'The development of mature hope in the patient–therapist relationship.' In *Countertransference and Related Subjects.* Madison, CT: International Universities Press.

Winnicott, D.W. (1971) *Therapeutic Consultations in Child Psychiatry.* London: Hogarth Press and The Institute of Child Psychiatry.

## SOME OF THE MATERIAL APPEARED PREVIOUSLY IN:

Rochford, G. (1985) 'Bereavement.' In *Developing Services for the Elderly.* Research Highlights in Social Work No. 3. London: Kogan Page/Jessica Kingsley Publishers.

## CHAPTER 17

# GROUP CARE

## Colin Keenan

This chapter falls fairly naturally into two sections: one dealing with the historical and contemporary context of group and residential care and the other with issues arising from this context and, consequently, with the methods that may most usefully be used in working in such a setting.

## Introduction

The relationship between residential care and the profession of social work has always been an ambiguous and ambivalent one and to this day the conception of social work conducted in residential settings is frequently characterized as 'social care' rather than social work. This implies a somewhat lower level of professional status for both the discipline itself and its practitioners, which can be seen in salary levels and conditions of service. The basis of that distinction is contentious but relatively easy to understand in a historical context.

The residential care of those who needed it emerged from as early as the fourteenth century and was provided in the public sector within the aegis of a succession of Acts commonly referred to as the Poor Laws. These persisted in one form or another until well into the twentieth century and it may be argued that some of their residue is to be found today within attempts to differentiate between social care (provided predominantly in group care settings) and 'professional' or 'statutory' social work which is generally associated with fieldwork (Frost, Mills and Stein 1999).

Throughout the nineteenth century, these laws served to stigmatize those whom they sought to serve: terms and conditions, the criteria of eligibility, were based on the heavily value-laden categorization of users and residents as 'deserving' or 'undeserving'.

In poor houses or work houses, as such establishments were commonly known, it was the residents (initially termed 'inmates') who provided the staffing to services which provided 'indoor relief'. They maintained the fabric of the building, and did the cooking, cleaning and gardening in return for their keep. Their roles and tasks were relatively menial and could never be described as professional.

Residential practice today, however, is different: it is often highly professional, therapeutic and specialized, but to varying extents carries some of the residues deriving from that bygone age.

The conception of group care does not at first sight sit comfortably alongside the principle of individualization which has for almost 50 years been regarded as one of the cornerstones of professional practice in social work (Biestek 1957). The idea of providing help and intervention on a group basis is incompatible with individualization as a principle and it is easy, therefore, to perceive group care practice as being conducted entirely on a group basis. In reality there are many aspects of care provision where very high levels of individualization are required and practised. The provision of intimate personal care for older people, for those with physical and intellectual disabilities and for children demands a level of sensitive individualization which frequently transcends that required in field or community settings.

On the other hand, ambivalence about the principle of individualization can also be found among workers within the group care setting: the oft repeated mantra of 'do it for one, you must do it for them all' is a case in point. This precept negates individuality by the imposition of a 'one size fits all' approach. It is rationalized, if that is possible, by recourse to ill-founded notions of fairness or standardization when in fact what it does is negate the uniqueness of the individual, in a setting where this is already eroded by the dictates of communal living.

In addition to what we know from history, fairly well-documented evidence of the potentially damaging effects of life in institutions (Goffman 1961) has contributed to ambiguity in fieldworkers (who are generally the referring agents, to group care establishments), about the efficacy or even the safety and desirability of their use, particularly in the case of people considered to be vulnerable. Although Wagner (1988) in her influential report into public residential care of older people found strongly in favour of the use of residential care as a 'positive choice', current practice and attitudes appear rather more guarded. The current government emphasis on social inclusion further militates against the use of resources which appear to place people apart from broader society (Scottish Executive 1999).

> More recently the focus has shifted to ways in which places are integrated with local communities. The former institutions became total living environments in which staff and residents could have all their needs met: the concern in today's language of 'social exclusion' has been that residents in particular and staff to a lesser extent were isolated – set apart from others in the community. Yet changing the buildings essential as it is does not guarantee inclusion. (Clough 2000, p.57)

In essence residential establishments or group care environments do not sit happily alongside the positive ideology of inclusion. That does not, however, gainsay the need for such establishments but may help to explain a degree of ambivalence concerning their use. The central issue may very well be one of ideology as much as utility. The changing ideologies surrounding residential care have been apparent for years but evidence for or against the validity of the ideologies and the nature of the service that such establishments provide is scant. It is not, however totally lacking.

This chapter seeks to explore the areas where evidence does exist, examine how it might be used to inform practice and identify where further enquiry may be indicated.

## The context of a group care setting
### A CHAOTIC ENVIRONMENT
In the first place residential establishments are inherently chaotic and can be seen to operate in ways which are consistent with the mathematical truths contained in what is known as *chaos theory*:

> The flapping of a single butterfly's wings today produces a tiny change in the state of the atmosphere. Over a period of time, what the atmosphere actually does diverges from what it would have done. So, in a month's time a tornado which would have devastated the Indonesian coast doesn't happen. Or, maybe one that wasn't going to happen does. (Stewart 1989, p.141)

This demonstrates the core of chaos theory which has come to be defined as *sensitive dependence on initial conditions*. The tiniest change in initial conditions can alter the long-term behaviour of a system (or set of inter-related systems). Thus, if initial conditions are chaotic a small change may be capable of resulting in order and stability. Conversely, if they were initially ordered and stable, a small change could initiate chaos.

There seems to be a resonance with the butterfly model and the kind of knock-on effects that follow when one incident involving an individual or small group of residents and staff ripples throughout the entire establishment. One unexpected and unplanned admission (a relatively small change in initial conditions) can bring chaos to an otherwise stable regime. That has been clear to unit managers for years, but competing demands between different parts of the wider organization and resource exigency can still produce such situations, particularly in the case of unplanned admissions. While unit managers know this, and chaos theory demonstrates its inevitability, organizational imperatives will produce contingency-based practices which run counter to the available evidence concerning service user experience and unit functioning.

### AN INSTITUTIONAL ENVIRONMENT
The essential characteristics of the residential environment have changed little over the last decade or so and still need to be considered today. All residential establishments are institutions and subject to the processes and dynamics that they produce. Although the word 'institution' carries pejorative connotations for many workers, it is difficult to deny the fact that residential establishments are institutions. Some institutions may correspond more directly than others to Goffman's (1961) conception of a total institution, but the extent to which any given establishment is or is not total, is incidental to the fact that it remains an institution. As with fieldwork practice, tensions between the needs of the organization and those whom it seeks to serve arise on a recurrent basis. Residential establishments operate in a tension between the institution's need to maintain itself (through order, stability and predictability) and the needs, wishes and rights of residents for personal space, choice and expression.

### CULTURES AND SUBCULTURES
Institutions by their nature produce cultures and subcultures and their inter-relationship is a defining characteristic of the setting and its impact on the lives and behaviour of residents and staff alike. My own definition of culture is simply 'that which is learned and

shared': this definition offers useful strands about what evidence can be collected – i.e. what is learned, by whom and how? – how is it shared, and by whom, and what effects it has.

Schein (2004) offers the following definition:

> Culture can now be defined as a pattern of basic assumptions invented, discovered or developed by a given group as it learns to cope with its problems of external adaptation and internal integration that has worked well enough to be considered valid and therefore, is to be taught to new members as the correct way to perceive, think and feel in relation to these problems. (Schein 2004, p.119)

The importance of understanding culture and subculture in the group care context can never be over-emphasized. Staff often have one culture and residents another, although this may not necessarily be true of some therapeutic communities. It is the existence of the disparate cultures which needs close attention as the influence of one can significantly colour the view its members hold of the other. Either or both may or may not be grounded in reality. Each will certainly have its own subjective reality. It is, however, important to understand both and the particular dynamic tension that exists between them.

> Like adolescents the world over, the boys in cottage 6 experiment with the roles and values that are integrated into a youth culture. Delinquent boys want to be free of adult controls as do all adolescents. Because of their histories and staff accommodation, they evolve a social organisation built upon force and manipulation.
>
> A pseudo-environment is thus constructed between two social systems [staff and resident] in a common interactional field…the two systems are extraordinarily independent of each other yet complementar. (Polsky 1962, p.149)

The finding that the social structure of the boys' culture was based on force and manipulation has been contradicted by more recent research by Emond (2003), who found that, rather than force and manipulation, the dominant currency in the resident hierarchy was that of peer support, operating unofficially within the culture of the resident group but not necessarily known or understood by staff.

In another, earlier monograph (Emond 1999), which examined the experiences of young people who had been looked after in local authority residential care, concentrating on what they had been led to believe about life after care compared with what they subsequently experienced, Emond discovered a significant divergence between staff and (former) resident cultures. The children reported life after care in terms of escape, freedom or release and in all cases referred to the experience in terms that suggested that for them the period of life in residential care was akin to some sort of ill-defined sentence from which they were ultimately released. They were in essence 'doing time'. Staff paradoxically believed that the children were there to be helped, supported or managed, defining their roles in more conventionally professional or therapeutic terms. In short, the two groups inhabited parallel universes.

This tends to endorse what Polsky argued over 40 years ago, that the two cultures are simultaneously highly influential and interact with each other whilst remaining fundamentally different in character, operating assumptions and world view. The scale of the establishment, its aims and functions, and clientele will all impact on these cultural essentials but nonetheless different cultures will remain and these will impact on staff and residents alike. Menzies Lyth (1988) points to the inherent danger that staff can become so enmeshed in their own culture that that they are blind to the existence, or despondently accepting, of those operating within the resident group.

## CULTURE SHOCK

Culture shock as a phenomenon of transition was identified as early as 1958 (Guanipa 1998) and seems to provide a remarkable resonance with the situation of someone leaving life in the community to enter the bizarre and chaotic world of residential care, particularly for the first time.

> The term culture shock was introduced…to describe the anxiety produced when a person moves to a completely new environment. This term expresses the lack of direction, the feeling of not knowing what to do or how to do things in a new environment, and not knowing what is appropriate or inappropriate … We can describe culture shock as the physical and emotional discomfort one suffers in another country or a place different from the place of origin. Often, the way that we lived before is not accepted as or considered as normal in the new place. Everything is different…. (Guanipa 1998)

The symptoms include:

- sadness, loneliness and melancholy
- aches, pains and allergies
- insomnia, the desire to sleep too much or too little
- changes in temperament, depression … feeling powerless
- anger, irritability, resentment, unwillingness to interact with others
- loss of identity
- lack of confidence
- feelings of inadequacy
- longing for family
- feelings of being lost, overlooked, exploited or abused.

(adapted from Guanipa 1998)

These symptoms reflect the experiences of many, if not most, new arrivals in residential establishments: they are there for all to see but how staff perceive, understand and respond to them is unlikely to be informed by any evidence of culture shock. Instead more-well intentioned, 'common sense' responses can prevail. A recently admitted resident displaying any or all of those symptoms can justifiably be regarded as showing a normal reaction to an abnormal situation: the danger is that the interpretation can be operated in reverse and that person may be perceived as effecting an abnormal reaction to a normal situation.

There has been considerable evidence available for decades that both the process of caring for residents and the environment within which it is conducted impacts significantly upon staff as well as residents. There are aspects of the caring process and the intimacy that it sometimes entails that can force staff to draw heavily upon their own defence systems. Such defences can and do impact on the nature of the relationships between staff and residents. The socialization of individual staff members prior to embarking upon a group care career and in areas of their lives outwith the domain of their employment can conflict significantly with what they experience in their professional roles. Assisting residents to bathe, feed or go to the toilet can run counter to socialization about the boundaries of privacy (Menzies Lyth 1960, 1988). Before a fully evidenced-based appreciation of the process is achieved, this knowledge must be factored into any appraisal of how effectively the process is managed.

## Entry to the group care process
### THE ADMISSION PROCESS
Most if not all service users who ultimately find themselves as residents of group care establishments have experience of social work services prior to admission and in many cases the initial thrust of such work will have been to avoid or delay the process of admission to residential care. Admission to residential care will in such circumstances be represented or perceived as something to be avoided, and when admission does take place, a surrounding aura of failure is hard if not impossible to avoid. The initial goal has not been achieved and the undesired outcome is a reality. This represents a loss for the service user but often for the workers too. This subtext of failure and consequent loss may be rarely acknowledged, yet there is important and relevant knowledge which shows the impact of loss and change. All change, including that perceived as being for the better, Marris (1974) demonstrates, entails aspects of loss. The process of adaptation to change is therefore inextricably linked to that of loss and requires to be mourned (Parkes 1987).

The admission process, therefore, generally involves issues of loss which impact on workers and service users and family and can profoundly influence the nature of service experienced. For example, an older woman previously living in sheltered housing supported by a range of services and by family members can no longer live safely in such circumstances and decides reluctantly that admission to residential care is inevitable. Her son, daughter and grandchildren are in agreement that, rationally and sensibly, admission is the best option. The care manager agrees and quite quickly after that decision, admission is arranged. A range of losses, for all concerned, therefore ensues. For the woman herself, many of the rocks and anchors in her life will disappear, including the familiarity of her home, many of her possessions (she may be able to take some cherished mementoes with her but it is almost certain that she will be unable to take as many of these with her as she might wish), everyday routines and contact with friends and acquaintances. The change also represents, in a stark way, the decline in her capacity to fulfil a range of roles as well as the imminence of her own death. At a rational level, the change may be perceived as being for the better, but the range of losses has to be acknowledged. Her attachments to familiar people, places, objects, rhythms and continuities in life all contribute to what Marris (1996) and Parkes (1987) have conceptualized as the assumptive world: they are the props that help maintain our sense of self and give personal meaning. So, not only does this older woman have to re-appraise her sense of self, but she has to do so with a reducing number of tools to equip her for the task. The familiarity of those props to the assumptive world reduce to be replaced by new and unfamiliar substitutes.

> Those who are most exposed to loss also tend to have fewer assurances and continuities by which to reconstruct the meaning of their lives… Sometimes all our efforts to sustain a controllable structure of purpose and interpretation break down. Some event or series of events shatters the framework of assumptions and intentions on which our structure of meaning has relied. (Marris 1996, p.118)

That is some of what she faces. To manage this change entails grieving and mourning:

> Grieving is a process of reintegration, impelled by the contradictory desires at once to recover the lost relationship and to escape from painful reminders of loss. It is not a simple reaction to the loss of something valued, which could perhaps be replaced but the expression of healing, if painful impulses, by which vital continuities of meaning are eventually abstracted and reformulated. This task of reconstruction is essentially similar whether the structures of meaning fall apart from the loss of a personal relationship of a predictable social context or of an interpretable social world. (Marris 1996, p.119)

Perhaps her son and daughter can help in the process, but the event is not without its losses for them. They have to contend with their own experiences of loss: the familiarity of their mother at home in the community has been replaced by her being apart, in a 'home'. To manage their experience of change and loss, they too need to grieve and mourn, a process which typically elicits feelings which include both anger and guilt. Their mourning in turn may well impact on their capacity to support their mother at a time when she desperately needs it. Such experiences of anger and guilt, while having to be managed by the woman and her family, can also impact on the workers, field and residential, who are involved in the admission experience. There can be a strong and understandable temptation for workers and others to somehow 'take away' the pain of loss. The most counterproductive position is when workers, confronted with pain and confusion, are unable to tolerate it and actively block an incoming or recent admission's expressions of grief. Such attempts are at best futile and at worst counterproductive. The process of loss is inherently painful but one from which growth can ultimately emerge. Turnbull (2000) writes of experiences encountered in child care:

> They were entering residential care, usually on an emergency basis in the middle of a family crisis. At this most vulnerable time, where skilled and sensitive intervention was vital to gain their confidence, children and young people were frequently confronted despite the best efforts of staff, with an environment of confusion… The initial problems which needed to be addressed with young people and their families were being exacerbated by the turmoil of group living. (cited in Smith 2004, p.19)

In the case of a young man with some intellectual disabilities, leaving the sheltered environment of the family home, as his parents are increasingly less able to provide the support he needs, similar dynamics are likely to arise. This situation may be fraught with ambivalence on his part and his parents' part which is likely to add to difficulties in re-solving the issues of loss for all concerned (Parkes 1987).

Thus, the transition from the world outside is inextricably linked to issues of loss and change. The issues facing service users have, at least in broad terms, been identified, can be foreseen and contribute to an evidence-based for group care, but it is doubtful whether they currently inform admission practice. The centrality of change and loss to the admission process is well known and understood. So too are the nature and effects of culture shock. Such knowledge and understanding constitute the evidence base for practice. The extent to which they influence practice is, however, variable. There is evidence from other aspects of social work that even after a commitment to:

> what works had become well established it was very rare for programmes to be subjected to any kind of evaluation at all – an indication that the virtues of local autonomy has been exaggerated and that practitioners, left to their own devices will not bother with evaluating their work. (Smith 2004, p.19)

## THE ENTRY PROCESS

What new residents leave behind and the circumstances in which the transition is effected can be seen to be riddled with contradiction and paradox, but what they enter may, from their perspective, appear chaotic and bizarre. What may seem perfectly sensible and comprehensible to the professionals involved may not appear that way to the new resident.

Without an appreciation of the fact that, in effecting transition from one known and generally well-understood living situation (in circumstances of crisis, contradiction and paradox), to a new one which may be perceived as chaotic and paradoxical, it is difficult to see how to provide effective support. The difficulties may be known, but if they do not inform action, then the process is managed in an arbitrary and uninformed manner.

The vulnerability of service users for the period before and after admission cannot be stressed highly enough. Anyone entering residential care for the first time, no matter how careful the preparation, is effectively making a transition from the known (including familiar surroundings at home, rhythms of life and relationships) to the unknown (or at best, the partially known) where personnel, practices and routines are new, strange and frequently confusing.

People entering residential care are vulnerable on at least three fronts. They are:

- vulnerable because of whatever circumstances have created the need for admission

- vulnerable to the change process itself

- vulnerable because the admission brings about substantial issues of loss and change for friends or relatives.

Friends and relatives have often been a significant part of the newly admitted person's support system. The impact of major change can therefore leave them with feelings and issues to work through and can impact negatively on their capacity to offer support at this crucial time, leading to tensions and clashes in perspective (Mayer and Timms 1970), as illustrated by the following examples.

Wayne (13) has been admitted to Ugiebank, an eight-bed local authority children's home. Despite the dedicated efforts of his field social worker and the best intentions of the Children's Hearing (the statutory body that in Scotland deals with children at risk or in trouble) and his social worker to avoid admission to residential care, he has not been able to cope with his mother's alcohol and amphetamine problems and in increasingly desperate attempts to gain acceptance and approval somewhere, has gained himself some status within a delinquent/criminal subculture. Not being a particularly accomplished or experienced thief he has been caught more often than the Children's Hearing, as the representative of the wider community, has been able to tolerate and finds himself for the first time at Ugiebank. He has been told that he will remain there for only as long as it takes his mother, an unsupported lone parent, to 'get back on her feet' and that his case will be reviewed in a few months. No more specific timescale than that has been given by anyone and he believes that his stay will be relatively brief. Staff on duty at the time of his admission are keen to offer as much reassurance as they can, and, finding it difficult to impart the fact that his stay might very well turn out to be longer than he may antici-pate, take the easier option of colluding with his belief that it won't be too long before he returns home.

Billy is 15 and has been a resident of the unit for a little over three years. He is a very influential person within the resident subculture (see above). Once Wayne is away from staff, Billy approaches him with the most common of all opening gambits: 'What are you in for?'

'Taking mountain bikes and DVDs,' says Wayne.

'Me too,' adds Billy.

'How long have you been in here?' ventures Wayne.

'Three years,' replies Billy.

'But I'm only here till my ma gets back on her feet.'

'Aye, that's what they told me too.'

An older person can expect to find the transition presented in positive ways: 'It'll be just like a hotel, you'll want for nothing.' The reality is of course far from that presented and the old person is likely to see quite starkly the impending onset of the very last part of their life. Death or its imminence is frequently and obviously a major theme but is diffi-cult, painful and sometimes embarrassing for workers to engage with. They frequently avoid engaging with it at all. In both cases the basis of the stay is misrepresented and from the outset will be in contradiction of what the user can see for him- or herself and experiences at first hand. Thus, if we know about culture shock, can identify some of the paradoxes, are familiar with processes of loss and change and all of these have been well documented (Guanipa 1998; Marris 1974, 1996), such knowledge can inform practice. The fact that it frequently does not, goes to the heart of the professional and social ambivalence surrounding residential care.

## Life in the group care environment
### IMPACT ON SELF
Life in group care impacts profoundly on both workers and residents alike (Menzies Lyth 1988) as they both operate in an environment which is known to make severe

demands on the sense of self of anyone involved. Goffman (1961) refers to mortification of self, a killing off of the uniqueness of the individual in order to conform to institutional demand and requirements. Whatever conception of self may be adopted, the consensus is that admission to and life within any institution makes severe demands of it and complex issues of dependency are enacted at conscious and unconscious levels.

The fact that staff generally have more of a life outwith the unit may mean that they are less prone to the forces of institutional life than are residents, but the fact remains that they are still subject to it. This is evidenced by Menzies Lyth (1988). There are levels of intimacy conducted with relative strangers (for example, toileting, bathing and possibly room sharing) which do not normally accord with experience on the outside and can conflict severely with previous socialization. This process of personal intimacy elicits levels of anxiety which are defended by the staff affected. Such defences (e.g. using pressure of paperwork to avoid personal relationships, putting the administrative before the personal or professional task) are often tolerated and sometimes institutionalized in the form of policy and procedure (for example, 'no touch' policies in children's homes). Research by Daniel, Wassell and Gilligan (1999) suggests that no-touch practices may well be antithetical to promoting the resilience needed to maintain and enhance self. The personal intra-psychic needs of workers can impact upon the worker–resident relationship. Where dependency is a significant dynamic in the relationship between resident and staff, the potential for powerful and primitive defences such as transference, counter-transference, projection, displacement and introjection is strong. The powerful and potentially disabling feelings identified by Menzies Lyth (1960, 1988) have to be managed. The extent to which this can be done successfully is inevitably because of differences in the situation of all involved. As workers, because of their status, can be seen to hold more power than residents, the imposition of workers' needs (conscious and unconscious) upon them is an ever-present potential.

Elsewhere in this volume the importance of understanding the process of splitting is identified (see Chapters 5 and 6). A satisfactory sense of self can help resist the splitting pressures of the institutional environment but, conversely, the institutional environment which is heavily imbued with the potential for splitting, can impact upon the self with dangerous negativity. The idea of complete consistency of response by a staff team to any given resident is no more possible than in any family, and inconsistency and mixed messages will abound. These do need to be identified before they can be managed. If workers ignore previous communication by colleagues with a resident they are likely to respond in an under-evidenced way: checking this out constitutes at some level the gaining of the evidence needed to inform intervention.

Workers can develop strong positive and negative feelings about residents and sometimes the friends and families of residents too. The behaviours and expressed needs of residents can be misinterpreted, dismissed or avoided for reasons which defy simple logic but are clear when evidence about the workers' own agendas are reflected on. The expression 'just attention seeking' is often used in a dismissive way which implies that such behaviour from a resident should best be ignored. The reality is that if someone seeks attention, at some level, they need it. Providing this attention may feel threatening, irritating or even disgusting to the worker, but it does not alter the fact that attention is needed by the resident. Consciously and unconsciously such worker–resident agendas as need for approval, ambivalence in trust, authority and intimacy can be picked up by residents both subliminally and at a more conscious level.

## Learning for, about and from group practice
### QUALITY AND VALUE

Learning about practice can only take place in cultures which accept its importance and, in the case of residential care, the subtexts and undercurrents surrounding the setting itself are likely to impede or deflect its contribution.

Argyris (1993) has identified the processes and consequences of the gap between what people in organizations know (or think they know) and what they actually do: what he conceptualizes as the tension between 'espoused theory' and 'theory- in-use':

> *Espoused theory* is the world view and values on which people believe their behaviour to be based.

> *Theory-in-use* is the world view and values implied by people's behaviour or the maps they use to take action.

Knowledge about how workers think and know about the true nature of residential establishments and how this matches with their practice in the admission process and other aspects of a resident's stay needs some congruence and that congruence has to be founded on fact rather than assumptions deriving from dated historical residues. For residential practice to start moving towards an evidence-based approach the gaps between the theories espoused and those in use need to close. Rhetoric is one thing; reality sometimes something entirely different.

These are necessary pre-conditions whose utility has been demonstrated in a range of other organizational settings but because of the level of ideological ambivalence and confusion surrounding group care, their resonance may be even greater in this aspect of social work than some others. For example, the espoused theory may be that except in very exceptional circumstances, admissions should take placed in a planned way, while the theory in use may result in large numbers of 'emergency' unplanned admissions.

In the market-driven culture which has evolved since the creation of a purchaser/provider split (National Health and Community Care Act 1990), residential care has been increasingly commodified as a service to be purchased rather than directly provided by local authorities. Local authority purchasers must currently account for the value of what they purchase within the terms of Best Value legislation. Best Value, which governs services provided or enabled by local authorities, is based on the following principles:

- challenge (justify the whys and hows of the service)

- compare (performance with similar elsewhere)

- consult (with stakeholder interests)

- compete (to provide the most efficient and effective service).

In the creation of a market culture in social work and driven by the dictates of Best Value, there is a concern in many social work agencies that in-house provision of residential care is unable to deliver best value. If what constitutes good quality is ill-defined and poorly measured then the easy (or only) measure to calculate is that of cost.

> In Social Services Departments, for example Best Value reinforced existing pressures to dispose of residential care to other providers because of assessments of local authority labour costs that were considered too high for such services to function efficiently... It seemed likely that a number of authorities would be outsourcing aspects of residential care. (Harris 2003, p.81)

Many have now done so.

Competition is a totem of what Harris (2003) refers to as 'the quasi business regime' but the cherished assumption that competition will always drive down price is by no means beyond challenge and cost has never been the sole criterion on which quality or value can be judged. The determining variable between cost and value is quality and group care establishments have increasingly to demonstrate the quality of the services they provide. The gap between reality and rhetoric, espoused theory and theory in action, will mean that a reliable conception of what constitutes quality is never easily arrived at.

There are of course many measures in place in most establishments and departments which are geared to collecting or measuring evidence of what is perceived as quality. Systems of quality assurance and quality control are part and parcel of the operation of public and private sector providers of residential care and by their nature are inherently evidence based. They seek empirical evidence in relation to identified standards derived from espoused values or theories and are a central part of management information systems. However, they rely heavily on measurement and whereas some aspects of group care – numbers, turnover rates – are relatively easily to quantify, others – such as resident experience, outcomes etc. – are inherently more difficult or even impossible to measure in any meaningful way.

In such circumstances there is a potential danger that practice priorities may be re-aligned to yield evidence of quality performance in the areas that are most readily quantified at the expense of those where it is most difficult. There is agreement among the gurus of quality (e.g. Deming 1986; Ishikawa 1985) that quality can neither be inspected into a system nor imposed from the top down. Nevertheless, many attempts to determine or develop quality in group care are inherently top down and linked to processes of accountability and transparency.

Residential care in this country (with notable exceptions) may well have become vulnerable to the tides of quasi business rationality (Harris, 2003). It has always had an ambivalent relationship with fieldwork and conflicting ideologies within and outwith the wider profession. These not only define the context in which it is practised, but impact on practitioners and service users and can contribute to conceptions of quality which may derive from agendas tangential to or inconsistent with those of residents and workers. These will be difficult to reconcile with the sheer chaotic complexity of the field.

Learning for practice can only take place in cultures which accept its importance and in the case of residential care, the subtexts and undercurrents surrounding the setting itself are likely to impede or deflect its contribution.

Reflective practice and learning cannot be imposed 'top-down'. Nor can it take place without a concerted understanding of how learning takes place. I felt that, to institute a true culture of learning, fear of risk and failure had to be suspended. In organisations, the top-down, mandated, mechanical, bureaucratic effort to control the direction is all too familiar. (Napier and Fook 2000, p.63)

For an organization to develop a learning culture, and to become a learning organization, it needs to reconcile the gaps between what it knows (whether it likes it or not) and what it does (even if this is at odds with what it wants to do).

## Intervention

### MODELS OF INTERVENTION

Most if not all methods and models of intervention used in other social work settings such as task centred, behavioural, and crisis intervention are capable of successful application in group care settings but there are at least two (opportunity led and life-space interviewing) which have been specifically formulated for practice in group care settings.

### OPPORTUNITY LED

Adrian Ward's formulation of *opportunity-led practice* provides a useful framework for intervention that can in many respects be evidence based. It offers a framework ' for thinking about the everyday opportunities for communication and support which arise in therapeutic community work' (Ward 2002, p.111).

The commitment to 'help them review and learn from' is wholly consistent with an evidence-based approach and indeed it is hard to see this approach succeeding without acquisition of the underpinning evidence to review and be learned from. In this respect, this predominantly systemic approach to practice transcends the more strategically-based life-space interview of Redl and Weinmann (in Whittaker 1979), which does not appear to fit quite so naturally with evidence-based precepts. Nevertheless, it is far from inconsistent with it: an understanding of the central strategies and precepts of the life-space interview provides not only useful contextualizing information to practitioners of the opportunity-led approach (2002) but can offer a measure of historical breadth.

Ward's approach is a four-phase one:

- observation and assessment
- decision-making
- action
- closure.

### OBSERVATION AND ASSESSMENT

*Observation*

In weighing up a situation the worker needs to establish as far as possible what is happening, what is being said/done, who is involved and what their current concerns are, what is likely to happen, why now and what should be done? In so doing cognizance should be taken of proxemics, eye contact, tone of voice, etc., all of which in their various ways impact upon the observation process. Knowledge and understanding of interpersonal process need at some level an evidence base to inform the worker fully and as objectively as possible. An unevidenced, gut-level impression may lead coincidentally to the truth but is more likely to distort perceptions on the basis of the agendas that the worker brings to the situation. For example, determining 'who is involved' may not be as straightforward as first assumed.

Angela's mother was due to visit for the first time in months, yesterday. She failed to show. Angela dumps much of her frustration, by stressing the dangers of trusting any adult, on Alison, who is currently giving serious thought to embarking on life with a new family. This sets Alison back and the way this previously abused 14-year-old copes is by sexually provocative behaviour towards some of the boys in the unit. Some can manage it; others can't. Stan and Ed are two of those who struggle with this and they are relatively low down in their peer-group pecking order. They appear to have started a fire in the bin area and are chasing two rather frightened younger girls with bits of blazing cardboard in some kind of 'kiss or dare' performance.

To address 'the who is involved' question needs the worker to have good current knowledge not only of the kind of chains of events that can run on for days, but of how abused children manage stress and the implications of puberty for Stan and Ed, as well as health and safety obligations. At one level, the behaviour of Stan and Ed is unacceptable – it is clearly dangerous and intimidatory – but managing their immediate behaviour directly (which still has to be done) may do little to address its causes and other equally disruptive consequences to Angela's disappointment may well ensue. The small change in initial conditions may have created the current inflamed situation, the sensitive dependence on initial, conditions shows the chaotic nature of life-space process. Here there is a clear need for all evidence to be reflected on and processed in the knowledge of such concepts and issues as ambivalence, aggression, attachment, sexuality, identity, trust, ego-strength, competing rights, group dynamics and many more. Essentially the question prompts the informed worker to seek and reflect on available evidence, look for more and process such evidence in the light of existing knowledge and theory from studies, etc. elsewhere, for example, on the emotional needs and developmental issues of adolescents living in an institution.

The 'what are the current concerns of those involved?' question is equally complex and requires the worker to at least comprehend the possibility that Angela's mother's inability to fulfil her promise yesterday may be a contributory factor to what Stan and Ed are doing today. It is likely that Stan and Ed's current concerns include sexuality, identity and status; Alison's concerns are dependency, trust and the legacy of abuse; and Angela's, dependency, identity and trust. An advanced knowledge of all of these is amenable to evidence and if thereby informed, will contribute to a better assessment of the current situation and assist significantly in addressing 'what is likely to happen?'

Ward's approach to assessment does allow for such an approach: he argues that the worker needs to consider the current atmosphere – the emotional climate of the unit and micro-climates of sub-groups, how the atmosphere may have changed before or during the incident as well as the key concerns of the day. He thinks about who is not involved (e.g. Alison, Alison's abusers, Angela, Angela's mum and others) and asks workers to consider the network of relationships (cultural and subcultural evidence is useful here, e.g. potential status issues for Stan and Ed) (Emond 2003). This too requires the acquisition and processing of evidence. The evidence yielded may well be 'soft' and even contradictory at times but it is better than prejudice, uninformed ideology and 'seat of the pants stuff' if for no other reason than the whole approach has greater inherent rigour in attempting to identify truth as a basis for action than any which does not attempt to do so. Questions about the power and prejudice (Polsky 1962) which permeate all units break down to seeking evidence about who holds power and why, what prejudices are there and how the actions of staff, parents, friends and outsiders influence the situation. Thus, as far as observation and assessment are concerned, Ward's opportunity-led model not only sits comfortably alongside ideas concerning evidence-based practice, it is actually predicated upon assumptions which point us in an evidenced-based direction.

From assessment Ward moves to decision-making. Good decisions are based on good evidence but they also need to be contextualized. Ward identifies three main considerations:

- urgency
- feasibility
- ethics.

Again they need some evidential base to inform the decision-making about what must or can be done now rather than later and to set priorities for this based on a needs hierarchy starting with safety/survival needs. Feasibility is determined by resources of time, space and personnel; the abilities, confidence and skill level of the worker, as well as the quality of the relationship between the worker and those involved. Additionally the worker needs to consider what he or she seeks to achieve, how it fits in with her or his role and the underpinning philosophy of the unit, as well as a practical timescale in devising tactics for managing the situation. Effective responses require ethical consideration in terms of what can be initiated within the law and in correspondence with the rights of service users, workers and others and the central ethics of the profession such as confidentiality must influence any decision about intervention.

Only then can action be initiated. Ward sees this as being of essentially three broad types:

1. Short-term, behavioural (i.e. emotional first aid on the spot); the emphasis is on managing the immediate situation at an individual or group level, remaining calm and appraising what support is available.

2. Longer-term, therapeutic; this is as much about opening up issues and dynamics as seeking to close them down. What arises on the shop floor may have longer-term implications and impact on people who are not present at the time; or it may present opportunities for problem-solving or addressing longer-term group agendas and dynamics.

3. Sustaining the intervention by keeping communication going, remaining open to re-assessment and seeking supervision.

All incidents need to come to some kind of end and, from a professional point of view, that should wherever possible be the product of the worker's efforts. Some markers of that ending should be laid down (e.g. moving to another activity or venue). Closure should, wherever possible, be apparent and readily understood by those involved. Loose ends need to be tied up (and that requires careful consideration about what ideally should be 'over' and what needs to be kept live for subsequent future discussion or intervention). Reflection on the events may raise implications for policy, practice and procedure and should prompt clear thought about what should be recorded, where and how. The workers needs to reflect on their own performance and consider what if anything it portends for their own needs for support and development.

In particular it is useful for providing or creating the climate wherein the opportunities that Ward writes of may be used to best advantage. Opportunity led is perhaps more reactive than some of the more proactive dimensions of the life-space interview and although there are areas of overlap between the two (identified below), life-space interviewing can provide opportunities to gain information and evidence with which to inform opportunity-led work.

### LIFE-SPACE INTERVIEW

The life-space interview which Redl and Weinmann (cited in Whittaker 1979) have referred to as 'therapy on the hoof' and 'the clinical exploitation of everyday life events' can be regarded as a series of goal-oriented (even if the goal is assessment) interventions conducted over a period of time in a range of sub-settings within the same overall setting. A life-space interview is seldom if ever a one-off, time-limited event but a series of encounters, interactions and observations from which emerge themes which can eventually be directed towards therapeutic ends. Its goal is the assimilation by the worker of evidence to inform both proactive and reactive interventions. Thus, knowledge gleaned from conversations, interactions and observations (casual and more purposeful) with a resident over a period of time can provide extremely useful information to the opportunity-led questions of 'What are the current concerns of those involved?' and 'What is the current atmosphere' or 'emotional climate' (see above) of the group. The group comprises people and the baggage they bring with them enacting both historical as well as existential agendas in a complex, often chaotic, interactional field. An informed understanding of these agendas and their possible antecedents, already gained via a life-space approach can bring an additional evidence-based dimension to opportunity led practice.

The opportunity-led model perhaps also implies (but no more than that) a greater emphasis on direct rather than indirect aspects of intervention than does the life-space interview. The life-space conception of 'manipulation of the boundaries of self' can be a helpful proactive adjunct to the management of emerging situations or crises and sits comfortably with the observation and assessment dimensions as well as with longer-term action of Ward's model.

The central components of the life-space model include:

### Reality rub-in

Residents enter what is a strange and confusing world sometimes in a state of culture shock (Guanipa 1998) and when their assumptive worlds may be in disarray (Marris 1996; Parkes 1987). Their capacity to fully appreciate the reality of their situations is under strain. Some may have been admitted because of pre-existing confusional states (e.g. older people), lacking the ego strength to distinguish adequately between reality and fantasy (e.g. children with emotional problems and/or those who have experienced abuse) or with problems of cognition (e.g. people with special learning needs). It is easy for the abnormal in 'real' terms to appear normal in the residential environment and vice versa.

Reality rub-in can be both short and long term and is directed at primary ego functions such as distinguishing reality from fantasy and appreciating consequences to actions. In the short term it can be as simple as presenting an accurate dose of reality (we want to correct a particular distortion and aid communication – e.g. it is Tuesday today; the chiropodist comes on Wednesday, tomorrow). In that sense reality orientation can be considered to be a form of reality rub-in, but reality rub-in is broader in its conception and is more flexible in that it can be included in other goals and approaches, for example, cognitive behavioural programmes or counselling. When an individual chooses a particular course of action it can have consequences for others: learning to appreciate that, particularly in moral terms is part of ego or super ego 'hygiene' (Redl and Weinmann in Whittaker 1979). In the longer term, the lack of opportunity to take meaningful choices is incompatible with that aspect of reality rub-in. As maintenance of self is essential to prevent its mortification (Goffman 1961), regular opportunities and, if necessary, support for reality rub-in are essential preconditions of any healthy life space.

### Symptom estrangement

Many residents find themselves in group care settings as a consequence of behaviour that wider society finds unacceptable. In some cases they themselves do not see their behaviour as problematic but:

> have invested heavily in secondary gain activities to such an extent that the whole ego seems to be allied with their central pathology rather than any one part of the ego taking a stand against it. While this does not mean that the whole ego is sick with the same disease that we are trying to cure, unless its 'uninfected' part can be 'estranged' from the core pathology and converted into an allegiance to seeing that something is wrong, the battle cannot even get started. (Whittaker 1979, pp.242)

Some can be so stuck in a particular role or behavioural set that this can take over their personalities to the extent that the healthy and potentially coping parts are hard to reach.

The technique consists of patiently finding and then nurturing the healthier parts to work against the maladaptive ones. A residential environment is particularly suited to helping because of the opportunities afforded the worker to access the resident at different times of day, in varying moods and circumstances in a range of settings and sub-settings.

Billy (aged 18) had been a persistent glue sniffer since his early teens and had been using amphetamines and other drugs on an escalating basis. As a result of a string of convictions for thefts and shoplifting, he found himself the resident of a probation hostel. Initially he showed little inclination either to change his lifestyle or to accept personal responsibility for his actions. 'I'm a junkie; what else do you expect?' (This is not dissimilar to Miller and Seligman's (1975) concept of learned helplessness.) Through time it emerged that he bore a lot of anger towards a father he had never known and a mother who he felt had abandoned him to foster carers. The anger, although seldom expressed outwardly, was eating away at his fragile sense of self and severely limited capacity for self-esteem. The anger was (at least to some extent) justified and potentially healthy even if it was misdirected. These feelings about parents were patiently explored and eventually directed through a form of life story work to their proper source. Identity strengthened and his capacity to accept responsibility for his actions increased. The potentially healthy parts of his ego worked against the 'junkie' part and he began to turn his life around.

*Value repair and restoration*

Some service users have become socialized into maladaptive, helpless, disruptive or patently antisocial attitudes and behaviours. The nature of residential life is such that it can (subject to constraints identified above) offer opportunities for modelling, management and education in the area of values. This may be needed in the process of 'normalization', for example. There are obvious dangers of workers imposing their own values on dependent, malleable or approval-needy residents. The values restored therefore need to be consistent with professional ethics rather than the idiosyncratic interpretations of right or wrong held by any particular worker.

*New tool salesmanship*

This simply refers to the social skills learning dimension of life-space work. A large part of the task is to assist residents to abandon old, ineffective or inappropriate behaviours for new constructive and effective ones. This is necessary for two reasons. First because the setting is institutional, and can lead to the loss of, or failure to develop, many everyday social skills, there is a need for a corrective antidote to that aspect of institutionalization.

Second, it is common for people who have found their way into residential establishments to have poor levels of social skills from the outset. Given the discrepancy between the 'official' culture and the resident subculture (see above), it is crucial that care plans provide for the teaching of such skills for life beyond the period in group care.

The acquisition of new skills often requires the renunciation of existing ones and it is essential that workers appreciate the loss aspects that such change may entail (Marris 1974). Given that the process of adaptation to change and thereby loss, is that of mourning (Parkes 1996) and this can include the idealization of what has been lost, there is a danger of the subculture making forbidden fruit taste very sweet indeed and sabotaging skills development. The greater the divergence between staff culture and resident subculture, the more likely this will be. For new skills to be 'sold' in any effective way workers need to understand the power both of the subculture and the homeostatic influences of loss and change.

## Conclusion

The effects of the residential environment on 'the self' have been powerfully documented by Goffman (1961), Miller and Gwynne (1972), Townsend (1962), Berridge (1985) and King, Raynes and Tizard (1971). They fall into two broad camps characterized by Davis (1981) as 'optimists' and 'pessimists'. Both recognize the influence of the life-space environment but the pessimists look more to its corrosive potential on the sense of self of the resident. Anyone with a poor sense of self prior to admission or one damaged in the process of admission is vulnerable to invasion by the effects of the confused and confusing artificiality of life-space existence. The interplay between the pathology of the individual and the nature of life space has been described above. It is crucial that the worker recognizes and understands the dynamic relationship between the sense of self or identity and the environment it inhabits. It follows that as much autonomy and opportunity for making real life choices as is possible, be afforded all residents because it is by these means that self and identity are nurtured, maintained and enhanced. By influencing the environment in this way, the worker is able to influence the sense of self of the resident within it.

## References

Argyris, C. (1993) *Knowledge for Action: A Guide to Overcoming Barriers to Organisational Change.* San Francisco, CA: Jossey Bass.

Berridge, D. (1985) *Childrens Homes.* Oxford: Blackwell.

Biestek, F. (1957) *The Casework Relationship.* London: Allen & Unwin.

Clough, R. (2000) *The Practice of Residential Work.* Basingstoke: Macmillan.

Daniel, B., Wassell, S. and Gilligan, R. (1999) *Child Development for Child Care and Protection Workers.* London: Jessica Kingsley Publishers.

Davis, A. (1981) *The Residential Solution.* London: Tavistock.

Deming, W.E. (1986) *Out of the Crisis.* Cambridge, MA: M.I.T.

Emond, H.R. (1999) *'I thought it would be a bed of roses': The Differences between the Perceptions and the Reality of Learning Care.* Glasgow: Centre for Residential Child Care, University of Strathclyde, and The Scottish Office.

Emond, R. (2003) 'Putting the care into residential care.' *Journal of Social Work 3*, 3, 321–39.

Frost, N., Mills, S. and Stein, M. (1999) *Understanding Residential Child Care.* Aldershot: Aldgate.

Goffman, E. (1961) *Asylums.* Harmondsworth: Penguin.

Guanipa, C. (1998) *Culture Shock.* Retrieved 26 January 2007 from http://edweb.sdsu.edu/people/Cguanipa/cultshok.htm.

Guntrip, H. (1971) *Psychoanalytic Theory, Therapy and the Self.* New York: Basic Books

Harris, J. (2003) *The Social Work Business.* London: Routledge.

Ishikawa, K. (1985) *What is Total Quality Control?* Trans. by D.J. Lu. Englewood Cliffs, NJ: Prentice Hall.

King, R.D., Raynes, N.V. and Tizard, J. (1971) *Patterns of Residential Care.* London: Routledge and Kegan Paul.

Marris, P. (1974) *Loss and Change.* London: Routledge.

Marris, P. (1996) *The Politics of Uncertainty.* London: Routledge.

Mayer, J.E. and Timms, N. (1970) *The Client Speaks.* New York: Atherton.

Menzies Lyth, I. (1960) 'The functioning of social systems as a defence against anxiety.' In *Human Relations 13*, 95–121.

Menzies Lyth, I. (1988) *Containing Anxiety in Institutions.* London: Free Association Books.

Miller, E.J. and Gwynne, G. (1972) *A Life Apart.* London: Tavistock.

Miller, W.R. and Seligman, M.E.P. (1975) 'Depression and learned helplessness in man.' *Journal of Abnormal Psychology 84*, 228–38.

Napier, L. and Fook, J. (2000) *Breakthroughs in Practice.* London: Whiting & Birch.

Parkes, C. M. (1987) *Bereavement: Studies of Grief in Adult Life.* Harmondsworth: Penguin.

Parkes, C.M (1996) *Bereavement: Studies of Grief in Adult Life.* London: Pelican.

Polsky, H. (1962) *Cottage 6.* Huntington, NY: Krieger Publishing.

Schein, E. (2004) *Organisational Culture and Leadership.* 3rd edn. New York: Wiley.

Scottish Executive (1999) *Social Inclusion – Opening the Door for a Better Scotland.* Edinburgh: Scottish Executive.

Smith, D. (2004) *Social Work and Evidence Based Practice.* London: Jessica Kingsley Publishers.

Stewart, I. (1989) *Does God Play Dice? The New Mathematics of Chaos.* London: Penguin.

Townsend, P. (1962) *The Last Refuge.* London: Routledge and Kegan Paul.

Wagner, G. (1988) *Residential Care: A Positive Choice.* London: Stationery Office.

Ward, A. (2002) 'Opportunity led work 2, the framework.' *Social Work Education 15,* 3, 40–59.

Ward, A. (2002) 'Opportunity led work: maximising the possibilities for therapeutic communication everyday interventions.' *Therapeutic Communities 23,* 2, 111–24.

Whittaker, J. (1979) *Caring for Troubled Children.* New York: Jossey-Bass.

## CHAPTER 18

# EMPOWERMENT AND ADVOCACY

*Rob Mackay*

## Introduction

Empowerment has increasingly featured in policy papers, official guidance and social work textbooks, yet there still is an uncertainty and even a vagueness as to what it actually means in practice. It has been suggested that while the treatment paradigm dominated social work practice during the 1960s and 1970s, that empowerment emerged from the 1980s onwards as not simply an evolution of social work practice but rather a revolutionary shift towards a new method of working with people (Adams 1996). It is understood as a paradigm of social work that is located within anti-discriminatory practice and anti-oppressive practice.

This chapter will focus on understanding the concept of empowerment, on how we understand power and powerlessness and on arguing that empowerment is not a single event but a process through which a person or a group can gain a sense of control and influence. The chapter will explore a particular framework (Dalrymple and Burke 1995), in which the power of active and faithful listening is stressed. The characteristics of a social worker committed to supporting empowering processes are identified. Finally the chapter explores advocacy, as one route to empowerment in terms of its various types and also the issues involved for social workers in engaging with service users, carers and independent advocates. The structure of the chapter begins with the concept of empowerment and goes on to address empowerment as a process, advocacy and finally threats to empowerment and advocacy.

## The concept of empowerment

The challenge about getting to grips with empowerment is that it involves complex issues of understanding and actions, which go right to the heart of the interaction between the citizen and the state. Empowerment represents different things to different people and therefore is open to questions, debate and disagreements. In other words, it is a contested topic in which an easy simple definition does not exist. This section explores concepts that communicate ideas of power, powerlessness and empowerment.

### STRANDS OF EMPOWERMENT

There are three main strands of ideas that are relevant to an understanding of the factors which may influence degrees of empowerment, which have been referred to by Hirschmann (1970), Means and Smith (1994) and Ramcharan (1997). These three strands (which are not mutually exclusive) help to explain different perspectives on empowerment and an awareness of these can be very helpful to unpack and analyse a complex situation.

### Exit

'Voting with your feet' – originating from the commercial realities of the USA, the idea that as a consumer my only loyalty is to get the best possible value for the money I am prepared to spend. So, if I don't fancy the clothes in M&S I can go to Next, or vice versa. In the social work context this means that service users can potentially switch services – this notion is of course only possible where there are multiple providers and choice is a realistic option. This idea only seems realistic where service users have control or influence over a budget – a current example of this is direct payments.

### Voice

'Having a say' in what is provided by an existing service and attempting to influence changes and improve services does exist within social work and takes many forms at both the individual and institutional levels. These include meetings with individual service users, case conferences, advisory committees, consultation meetings, customer satisfaction surveys, etc. The structures used are not ones of power sharing in relation to decisions, but rather ensuring that the organization is well informed by a range of stakeholders. This approach depends upon the level of active listening by social workers and agencies, to ensure that the voice of the service user is genuinely incorporated into the decision-making process.

### Rights

'Power to exercise rights which we all have' reflects that there are entitlements to services based on legislation, which as citizens we can invoke. These entitlements are based on both legislation and service standards (Morris 1997).

The use of legislative rights can be a powerful strategy for people to feel empowered, but does depend on their knowledge of their rights, as well as support and resources to ensure these rights are enacted. Dalrymple and Burke (1995) advocate using the law as part of enlightened anti-oppressive practice.

### POWER AND POWERLESSNESS

How we understand power and powerlessness is clearly central to empowerment and in the UK (as compared to the rest of Europe), the structural view has been the dominant paradigm since the mid-1980s. The 'PCS analysis' as expressed by Thompson (2001) provides a theoretical underpinning to an understanding of the processes of discrimination in British society. The central idea being that disempowerment occurs at three interconnected levels – the personal, the cultural and the structural (PCS). This influential model is a useful tool to analyse processes of discrimination and oppression at different levels of practice – individual, institutional and societal.

Others writers, such as Friere (Friere and Macedo 2001), O'Brien (O'Brien and O'Brien 2000) and White (White and Epston 1990), add further dimensions of our understanding as to both the processes of discrimination and oppression and the impact on people's lives and identities. In simple terms, these ideas help to create a conceptual three-dimensional map – of people's social identities being hugely moulded by political, social, cultural and institutional factors but at the same time of people who are constantly adapting to the environment around them in an active and problem-solving manner.

Solomon (1976), in reflecting on her practice with oppressed black communities in the USA, argued that personal and political power are related. She identified both direct power blocks and indirect power blocks for African-American people. By 'direct power blocks' she was referring to processes that 'are applied directly by some agent of society's major social institutions' and by 'indirect power blocks' she was referring to internalized negative self-perceptions that are 'incorporated into the developmental experiences of the individual as mediated by significant others' (Solomon 1976, p.21).

Braye and Preston-Shoot (1995), taking a similar line of thought, make a useful contribution by reminding us that there are barriers and defences operated by social workers and their agencies in terms of day-to-day processes and procedures. 'The more powerlessness is reinforced by services which deny felt experience and choice, and the more practitioners expect partnership without addressing the impact of powerlessness, the less users will be empowered' (Braye and Preston-Shoot 1995, p.110). This is help-ful in terms of freeing us to question powerful professional and agency norms as to what constitutes 'appropriate' behaviour and to reframe our expectations as to the 'role' of the service user. This involves a shift from being a passive and grateful recipient of social services to that of being an active and participating partner.

What we can learn from these two contributions indicates that social workers need to engage in a process of listening to the lived experiences of oppressed individuals and groups. By reflecting on this, the direct and indirect power blocks experienced by people should become apparent and this then provides a basis for planning and taking appropriate action (Solomon 1976).

## PROFESSIONAL AUTHORITY AND POWER
A related component to consider in analysing factors that may induce feelings of pow-erlessness is the impact of professional authority and power on relationships between social workers, their employing agencies and service users and carers. In this context a useful question to ponder is: 'What are the sources of authority and power you have as a social worker?'

Hasenfield (1987) identified four main sources of power among social workers:

1.    Power of expertise – This is sometimes known as 'sapiential authority' and is based on the notion that social workers acquire through professional training and contin-uous development a specialized knowledge base. This enables social workers to 'name' and categorize human phenomena, which in itself is an act of power.

2.    Referent power – This is sometimes known as 'the authority of relevance', as other people may defer to a particular worker because of the strength of their personality or because they have very specialized knowledge, e.g. mental health legislation.

3.    Legitimate power – This is the notion that social workers are mandated through legislation, which is translated into agency duties, responsibilities, polices and pro-cedures. Individual social workers only therefore have power through being an agent of their employing agency.

4.   Power over resources and services – This is the 'gatekeeping role' of social workers and their agencies, in which departmental procedures are set out that guide social workers in making decisions as to who gets a service or a resource and who does not.

This also brings to the fore the inevitable tensions that exist for the individual social worker, who if registered is fully accountable to the national code of conduct (SSSC), and on the other hand is also accountable to his or her employing agency which has a different set of perspectives and issues. The late David Brandon had no doubt that most service professionals face 'a fundamental clash of vested interests' (Brandon, Brandon and Brandon 1995, p.31). Brandon *et al.* identify five different sorts of conflict:

*   organizational needs

*   professional obligations

*   managerial agendas

*   personal needs

*   competition of multiple demands.

The implications of this section is that as social workers we must be aware of the power we carry, and also that conflicts of interest will arise so we need to have the skills to manage these ethical dilemmas.

## Empowerment as a process

In this section I want to describe a number of interlinked approaches that can support a process of empowerment, and the skills and ethical qualities and traits required of a social worker.

### CAN A SOCIAL WORKER EMPOWER ANOTHER?

This question invokes considerable controversy and different viewpoints, which is connected with diverse framing of what empowerment means, and therefore with diverse implications for direct practice. The claim by workers that 'I empower my clients' does seem contradictory as it implies that a worker does something active which is difficult to reconcile with a sense of control and influence by the service user. Service user groups and organizations have their own points of views of what constitutes empowerment and what constitutes effective collaboration (Beresford and Trevillion 1995).

Lee's suggestion that: 'the empowerment process resides in the person, not the helper' (Lee 1994, p.13) is helpful as it indicates there might be a role for the helper, but that fundamentally the service user is the main actor in this situation and has ownership of the process. Lee (1994) acknowledges the work of Barbara Solomon in developing and understanding what empowerment means in practice. Solomon suggests that empowerment is:

> a process whereby the social worker engages in a set of activities with the client…that aim to reduce the powerlessness that has been created by negative valuations based on membership in a stigmatised group. It involves identification of the power blocks that contribute to the problem as well as the development and implementation of specific strategies aimed at either the

reduction of the effects from the indirect power blocks or the reductions of the operations of direct power blocks. (Solomon 1976, p.19)

Lee (1994) identifies three interlocking dimensions of empowerment, namely:

1.   a positive sense of self

2.   a critical awareness of the social and political world

3.   more competence supported by resources and strategies.

How do social workers and the processes in which they are involved initiate such an apparently simple empowerment process in the face of considerable challenges and pressures?

First, the model of anti-oppressive practice by Dalrymple and Burke (1995) draws upon a number of writers including Solomon (1976) and Friere and Macedo (2001). In addition, the contributions of narrative practice and person-centred planning offer complementary thoughts and skills. The facility to combine approaches and perspectives offers practitioners a rich and holistic array of resources from which to choose in order to fashion an unique approach to respond to the needs of unique individuals.

Dalrymple and Burke (1995) rightly point out that empowerment is a process of change and this should remind us what we know about change and how best to support people undergoing change. Dalrymple and Burke (1995) also indicate this change process will go though a number of stages to three different levels – these levels are indicated in Figure 18.1 and are necessary to indicate the connections between personal power and political power. These three levels should not be regarded as a series of steps up which a person ascends – that is far too reductionist – but rather as a dynamic interplay of the three levels that at best will offer a rich and rewarding journey for the individual. Each journey will be different for each person, and so some individuals might initiate the process at the level of feelings through been part of a discussion group, while others might initiate the process at the level of action arising out of a particular event, such as attending for the first time a service user led conference.

However, for clarity, I propose to explain this model in a logical fashion by starting with the first level.

The first level is the level of feelings, which emerge as the person is supported in a safe manner to 'tell their story' and in the process finds a voice to express and recall his or her own biography. At this point, the critical point is not so much what the speaker is saying, but rather how the words are being received by others. If the words (and the meaning attached to them) are not recognized for what they are, then they will fall on stony ground and perish; however, if these words are attended to with genuine care and commitment to this individual, then a seed has been sown and germination may begin. O'Brien and O'Brien (2000), in a superb short article, ask the question: 'What does it mean to listen?' and explore the impact on the person:

> People come to *life* [my emphasis] when they make contact with someone who works actively and faithfully to understand what they want to say... Listening is resonating in body, in imagination and in spirit. Listening to people who live with a lifetime of isolation and discrimination is often painful, frightening and exciting. Listening liberates energy. A person's sense of direction grows stronger. (O'Brien and O'Brien 2000, p.15)

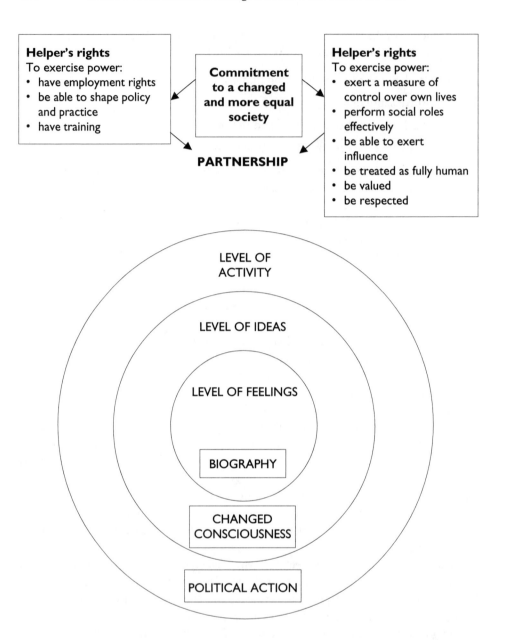

*Figure 18.1 Dalrymple and Burke: a model of anti-oppressive practice*

The authors go on to ask four key questions:

- Where do we listen from?
- What do we listen for?

- How do we listen?

- How can agency managers promote listening?

The compelling point they make is that listening skills should not be attributed to a few gifted individuals, but rather by encouraging a culture of listening within the organization, that this will have a profound effect on the governance of the agency. O'Brien (2005) commented that 'Real change will only come about when those who are unaccustomed to speaking out are heard by those who are unaccustomed to listen.' There is clear and current evidence from social work service users that one of the qualities they value about able social workers is the capacity to listen in an active and faithful manner (Levin 2004).

So, at this first level a positive and life-giving process is initiated within which the person 'telling their story' experiences acceptance and a validation of their feelings, thoughts and perceptions. This does not necessarily trigger a change process, but it does create the potential for an individual to create meaning out of the process of telling his or her own story.

A mental health service user tells of the day 'the penny dropped' when in her mind she began to make the connections between her years of being treated by the psychiatric system for depression and her early years' experience of been adopted. This realization was in part prompted by being encouraged to 'tell her story' by her social worker and being listened to in an attentive and active manner. She was engaging with the level of ideas in which she recognized that within her adoptive family her views were never sought or valued and, similarly, that this was mirrored with the role of a psychiatric patient she was later assigned. She had now begun to make friendships through involvement with a user-led mental health service and so had witnessed other women who had been diagnosed with depression and recognized significant role models in the process of recovery.

This example relates to concepts such as a self-actualization, self-knowledge, self-awareness, self-esteem and self-identity.

Narrative practice perspectives (White and Epston 1990) can also be applied in the same example of the woman with depression by recognizing that a person can have a 'problem-saturated' story of her life that maintain the same identity. However, narrative therapy can support the person to explore other aspects of his or her life and to identify an alternative and more positive story of it. The ability to externalize the problem enables a person to convert personal energy – previously locked into coping with guilt and self-loathing – into that of problem-solving and enhanced capacity. So, a person may unearth capacities that had always been there but had been buried by years of a dominant negative story. For example, somebody who cuts her arms as a way of controlling her voices may have a dominant story based around psychosis, while her alternative story reveals well-worked strategies and methods of survival.

The individual or the group is then in a position to be able to influence a political arena through what Dalrymple and Burke (1995) describe as the 'level of activity'. This often refers to influencing societal and/or institutional policies, processes and procedures, usually done by a group or sometimes as an individual. An example might be a mental health collective advocacy group which is very active in attempting to influence statutory organizations to provide more person-centred services. Dalrymple and Burke

(1995) refer to Solomon (1976) who argues that one of the five skills in empowerment practice is that of facilitating organizational change.

Braye and Preston-Shoot (1995) in their model of empowerment identify a number of key initiatives for change in order to alter the social, cultural and political constituent parts of powerful public organizations and institutions.

> For empowerment in social care to have meaning, the organisational culture must move away from that of power (control of the expert) and role (emphasis on given tasks and procedures) to that of community (learning with users). Such a culture would seek to use and enhance the power and authority held by users, while recognising that professional power and authority remain legally mandated and may have to be exercised. (Braye and Preston-Shoot 1995, p.115)

It is not evident that such a shift in culture has taken place in large public organizations, where the role culture is very much dominant and the pressure of public and political scrutiny is unrelenting.

Equally as valid as the structural perspective is exploring how the level of action can be enacted by the individual person. The Hearing Voices Network, a mutual support system at both local and national level for people who hear voices, has two key principles: self-determination and self-knowledge. The action involved with the Hearing Voices Network is that each individual takes charge of his or her own life and makes choices regarding lifestyle including diet, education, social care and health care. These choices are based on informed decision-making and can involve questioning and challenging opinions and decisions taken by professionals including those in social work. For example, the woman with depression referred to earlier in this discussion might question the anti-depressant prescription and request a social prescription, such as relaxation classes.

The keystone to a social worker's commitment to empowering practice has to be a firm and unflinching grip on social work ethics values and beliefs on an everyday basis. A fair criticism of social workers and agencies and academics is that our espoused values are strong on 'talk the talk', while our values in practice are sometimes more diluted in relation to 'walking the walk'.

Character and virtue ethics suggest that the perceived character of the social worker is crucial to the processes whereby empowerment is supported and encouraged (Ahmad 1990; Banks 2001; Clark 2000; Levin 2004; Singh 1999; Smale, Tuson and Statham 2000). These studies identify the qualities and aspects of the 'character' of the social worker which are valued by service users and carers and contribute in some way to creating an empowerment process.

A social worker for service users and carers needs to be:

- honest

- reliable

- trustworthy

- authentic and genuine.

The social worker needs to:

- accept the person's perceptions as valid

- avoid blaming people for survival strategies

- show genuine interest in the person

- stick with the person

- make time for the person

- recognize his or her own power as a social worker

- be able to recognize his or her own assumptions and question these

- be open to challenge and willing to be wrong

- be prepared to question and challenge others

- be open to change and transformation

- be good at paying attention to the details of processes

- enjoy sharing information

- show warmth and commitment within the relationship

- value networking and mutual support

- be open to learning from mistakes and problems

- be able to engage intensively and at other times 'let' others do the work.

Described and selected in this way this list of qualities may suggest a social worker must have the quality of a saint. It certainly would be unfair to load all the responsibility for empowering practices onto individual social workers. It is pointed out that: 'Lists of virtues can be criticised in the same way as lists of values or ethical principles as being abstract and unhelpful in making everyday ethical decisions' Banks (2001, p.46). The empowerment process, as we have seen, has at its very heart the notion of voice: the idea that a person or a group or a community will develop their own language as a way of expressing their experiences and indicating their choices, preferences, wants and needs. This next section will continue this discussion by looking at the role advocacy can play in helping people to have a voice and to secure rights.

## Advocacy

As Brandon humorously indicates the expectations about advocates and advocacy more generally has never been higher:

> Advocates are becoming the new samurai for reducing social and economic disparities. Health advocates help the socially excluded 'gain access to basic health services, training health professionals to deal more competently with minorities and helping individuals to stand up for themselves' (Coote 2000, p.35). They also leap over tall buildings! (Brandon 2001, p.76–7)

The Advocacy Alliance, which was established in 1981 is a coalition between national charities and the advocacy and the user instrument sector. The Disabled Person (Services,

Consultation and Representation) Act 1986 had provisions for independent representation but these were never implemented by successive governments. So, the idea of advocacy has persisted over 25 years, but its implementation has been constrained due to lack of clear strategies with regard to legal and funding frameworks. However, there are hopeful signs that this is changing and that Advocacy is on the cusp of a major expansion. For example, the Mental Health (Care & Treatment) (Scotland) Act 2003 enshrines a right of access of a patient to advocacy. It places a duty on each local authority and health board to ensure the provision of independent advocacy services. In Scotland there are two agencies funded by the Scottish Executive – Advocacy 2000 and Advocacy Safeguarding Agency – designed to support and to evaluate independent advocacy services.

### WHAT IS ADVOCACY?

'Advocacy' is one of those terms that carries with it different meanings according to the diversity of contexts and roles within which it is being expressed and discussed. It is also confusing because different writers list different types of advocacy and in Scotland the role of an 'advocate' traditionally belongs to a person with a legal training and occupation. It is one of the routes to empowerment by which people may develop a sense of having more influence and control.

At its simplest, advocacy is about making sure that people are encouraged to give voice to their choices and rights through the provision of independent information and support. In other words, that individuals, groups and communities have the capacity – and the opportunity and resources – to be self-advocates.

There are many definitions of advocacy, which probably adds to the confusion, but this one from Brandon *et al.* is useful because it attempts to define both the processes involved and possible outcomes:

> Advocacy involves a person(s), either an individual or groups with disabilities or their representative, pressing the case with influential others, about situations which affect them directly or, and more usually, trying to prevent proposed changes, which will leave them worse off. Both the intent and the outcome of such advocacy should increase the individual's sense of power; help them to feel more confident, to become more assertive and gain increased choices. (Brandon *et al.* 1995, p.1)

### TYPES OF ADVOCACY

1.  *Self-advocacy* – the fundamental and preferred type of advocacy where the person represents their own interests and concerns.

2.  *Group or collective advocacy* – means a self-advocacy group that might be a local group of service users or a group that is linked to a national advocacy organization, such as Who Cares or People First.

3.  *Citizen advocacy* – involves an 'ordinary' citizen, who is trained to be a volunteer advocate and who works alongside a person, usually on a long-term basis. Crisis advocacy works on a very similar basis but the work is limited to a specific problem and so the contact with the citizen advocate is limited in time to that specific issue.

Independent advocacy organizations are responsible for the recruitment, training and support of the citizen advocates. These organizations are usually specific to one area (e.g. mental health, learning disabilities), but can also be generic which makes sense where there is a clear geographical area focus.

4.    *Peer advocacy* – is where an individual is supported by another who has been in a similar position; for example, a psychiatric patient represents another patient.

5.    *Family advocacy* – is where family members speak on behalf of another family member.

6.    *Professional advocacy* – refers to workers whose primary role is that of advocating on behalf of others. Examples include welfare and housing rights workers, as well as those workers who are employed by independent advocacy organizations.

Whatever the type of advocacy, it is useful to recognize there are common processes by which advocacy is enacted.

## THE PROCESS OF ADVOCACY

The notion of the process of advocacy being underpinned by key principles is helpful and influential. This means that how the practice of advocacy is conducted at every stage with service users by advocates is an important consideration, which must be supported by key principles. Therefore, Atkinson (1999) in Brandon and Brandon (2001) refers to principles involving empowerment, autonomy, involvement and citizenship, while Kendrick in Gray and Jackson (2002) identifies what he describes as 'substantive dimensions of integrity' (p.40) that advocates need to employ. He suggests these principles are:

• to be embedded into the way people are responded to

• advocates have a role to 'bear witness' not only to problems experienced by individuals but also to wider community and societal problems

• advocates in speaking on behalf of people have a clear accountability to them

• advocates must be free of conflict of interest in order to influence significant others

• advocates should stick with the process and be reasonably persistent

• advocacy is not about winners and losers

• advocacy is about a respectful process in which different points of view may be heard and expressed in which the interests of the person(s) is pressed and feasible resolutions are sought

• advocates should work for genuine and respectful ways of adding quality to the lives of people

• advocates have a duty to express the voice of those they claim to represent but also to recognize when they may be expressing their own opinions.

The process of advocacy can therefore be informed by reference to these key principles, especially when an advocate is faced with complex and challenging situations. To engage with these issues requires a set of skills, which Bateman (1995) suggests involves interviewing, assertiveness, negotiation, self-management, legal research and litigation.

Sim and Mackay (1997) found there was a very positive response to the use of independent advocates both by service users but also by referring service professionals. For example, 88 per cent of service users considered that because of their contact with an advocate they would be better able to cope with situations that might arise in the future and 84 per cent of professionals felt that advocacy had been helpful to them.

## SOCIAL WORK AND ADVOCACY

Social workers employed in mainstream organizations have traditionally claimed an advocacy role on behalf of their service users. A commitment to social justice is a primary professional value (BASW Code of Ethics) and social workers use advocacy and negotiating skills with regard to powerful local and national welfare and health organizations. However, as employees of organizations social workers have multiple accountabilities, which can produce very real conflicts of interests (Brandon and Brandon 2001). Social workers have an ethical duty to recognize when there is a conflict of interests and to take appropriate measures to deal with this. One point of view is that while social workers can not be independent advocates, they can adopt an advocacy role in certain situations. Brandon and Brandon (2001) in a survey of former social work students makes the distinction between internal and external advocacy work. Examples provided by these students illustrate that conflicts can occur where in terms of professional duties a social worker may attempt to advocate for enhanced service provision within their own agency but this may be resisted by the agency for budgetary reasons. Beresford (1994) is quoted by Brandon and Brandon (2001):

> Can professionals be advocates? Yes but when they have power over individual service users, or responsibilities other than to speak for the person, then there is a conflict of interest, and the person will need an advocate. But, at all times, service workers need to have some awareness of, and try to protect the service user's interests (however imperfectly they do this, given conflicts of interest) and not just leave this to the advocate. (Brandon and Brandon 2001, p.62)

External advocacy includes representing service users directly – writing to a housing agency requesting a housing transfer – and supporting advocacy indirectly by informing service users how to access independent advocacy services or providing accessible information about the complaints procedure.

This brings up the interesting issue as to the relationship between social workers and independent advocates. Do social workers view the advocates as threats or allies? My personal and very local experience suggests this is a very mixed picture, in which there is potential for confusion and conflict between service professionals (not just social workers) and independent advocates. Advocates can experience some service professionals as being hostile, dismissive, patronizing and collusive. Some professionals may regard advocates as encroaching on areas that they traditionally have regarded as their own and may resent this. Some professionals naïvely regard advocacy as simply another service and the advocate as another team member – and therefore react with hurt and anger when the said advocate turns down the offer of a desk in the 'team room' in favour of an independent location that is visible to service users. These tensions may arise because some service professionals may not understand the primary importance of the independence of advocacy and that the essential principle states that the location of control rests with the service user. Basically the advocate is acting as a mouthpiece for the service user to enable his or her opinions, wishes, feelings and choices to be expressed; the role of the advocate does not include making a judgement as to the validity of such opinions.

Social workers therefore need to be knowledgeable about the role of independent advocates. In doing this social workers need to have an authentic commitment to service users who are being supported to find their 'voice' and to express their choices, preferences, feelings and views. This needs to be done with the understanding that critical comments and conflicting perspectives may be a part of this process. It is therefore an area that challenges social workers to have excellent partnership skills with regard to service users and independent advocates.

This chapter has focused in some detail at empowerment and advocacy in practice, so let us now draw back and consider the 'big picture'.

## Threats to empowerment and advocacy

Adams (1996) suggests that there has been a shift away from the treatment paradigm that dominated social work during the 1960s and 1970s towards an empowerment paradigm that has gained ground since the 1980s. It can readily be acknowledged that the language of social work has changed over the past 30 years, but do our espoused values match our actions in practice?

There are suggestions that the social work profession has appropriated the knowledge and experiences of service users without committing itself to authentic partnership working (Wilson and Beresford 2000). So, one threat may come from the uncritical adoption of concepts such as 'empowerment', and the application of these in a bland and general manner. This would be the very antithesis of empowerment.

Another threat is the impact that the use of agency-approved procedures and processes may have in restraining flexible and creative responses to the needs of individuals and groups. The interim report of the 21st Century Social Work Review Group in Scotland identifies a theme from social workers' comments that the development of management systems and controls has had the effect of restricting innovatory and creative responses. From its research the report concludes that: 'It seems that the balance of accountabilities in social work practice has become somewhat skewed, with too much emphasis on accountability to the employer and not enough on individual professional accountability' (21st Century Social Work Review Group 2005, p.30).

In this chapter I have stressed that above all else that empowerment involves a flexible process, in which individuals often gain support and inspirations over a period of time through involvement with self-help group and user-led initiatives. The context of these may be small and informal, although often linked to a wider network, such as the National Hearing Voices Network.

The relationship of social work with issues relating to empowerment and advocacy is complex and ambivalent, given the nature of professional responsibilities and duties at both individual and agency levels. It may be that part of the professional task is having the skills and knowledge to make sense of the tensions that exist between the treatment and empowerment paradigms rather than perceiving these as separate entities.

While recognizing that these professional tensions and dilemmas need to be worked with reflectively, I would like to suggest there are certain core principles, which are non-negotiable for social workers, whatever their job title and official status might be. These include some of the following:

- to commit to building and sustaining a culture of listening

- to safeguard the legal rights of service users and carers

- to acknowledge the power we carry as social workers and to be able to identify the sources of this

- to be authentic and collaborative in our work with service users and carers

- to ensure the professional traits we bring into our work are congruent with that of professional values

- to acknowledge each of us has a responsibility for the culture of our employing team and organization

- to have the requisite skills for working with and resolving complex and challenging ethical dilemmas and value conflicts

- to have the principle of not harming people as a core social work value (Caplan and Caplan 2001)

- to reflect in an enquiring and humble manner that helps to inform and educate future actions.

The practice of referring to core and underpinning principles when confronted with difficult and challenging situations is a sound and well-proven approach in reaching a decision (Reamer 1995).

These principles provide the foundation for ethically-based practice, but we also need excellent reflective and analytical skills to help us exercise sound judgement in situations that are complex and contradictory. The recognition of power and how to use this wisely in the context of partnership working is a central task for contemporary social work practice.


## Conclusion

From this brief overview of empowerment and advocacy, we can recognize that this is a rich and powerful area of activity in which there are many writers, theories and perspectives. I would hope this does not deter the reader, but that such passion and diversity of views is celebrated and valued. The reader is encouraged to avoid the easy surface approach to empowerment and to engage more deeply with the central issues of power and powerlessness in a committed and principled manner. To engage in this we require a level of understanding that is conceptually strong and draws upon an evidence base which is informed by the lived experiences of service users and carers. We need to have the openness and critical ability to reflect on the processes we use and to adapt these in the light of experience. This of course involves acknowledging the power we hold as social workers (individual and institutional) and analysing how this can be used and shared in appropriate and effective ways.

A central point of this chapter is that this work involves a process rather than a single event or a series of neatly planned procedures; it is therefore by definition uncertain and at times quite uncomfortable. This unfortunately goes with the territory and I believe as social workers we need to fully commit ourselves to this process and have the professional characteristics and ethical skills to cope with uncertainty and complexity, as this quotation from Parsloe indicates:

> Flawed as it may be, the thread of power sharing which has run through social work is of fundamental importance if social workers are to put into practice the value they place upon each individual and the accountability they owe to their clients. (Parsloe 1996, p.9)

# References

21st Century Social Work Review Group (2005) *21st Century Social Work Review – Interim Report*. Edinburgh: Scottish Executive. Available at http://csocialworkScotland.org.uk/resources/pub/changing LivesScottishExecutiveResponse.pdf.

Adams, R. (1996) *Social Work and Empowerment*. Birmingham: Macmillan.

Ahmad, B. (1990) *Black Perspectives in Social Work*. Birmingham: Venture Press.

Banks, S. (2001) *Ethics and Values in Social Work*. Basingstoke: Palgrave.

Bateman, N. (1995) *Advocacy Skills*. Aldershot: Arena.

Beresford, P. and Trevillion, S. (1995) *Developing Skills for Community Care: A Collaborative Approach*. Aldershot: Arena.

Brandon, D. and Brandon, T. (2001) *Advocacy in Social Work*. Birmingham: Venture Press.

Brandon, D., Brandon, D. and Brandon, T. (1995) *Advocacy: Power to People with Disabilities*. Birmingham: Venture Press.

Braye, S. and Preston-Shoot, M. (1995) *Empowering Practice in Social Care*. Buckingham: Open University Press.

Caplan, R.D. and Caplan, G. (2001) *Helping the Helpers Not to Harm*. New York: Brunner/Routledge.

Clark, C.L. (2000) *Social Work Ethics*. Basingstoke: Macmillan.

Dalrymple, J. and Burke, B. (1995) *Anti-Oppressive Practice: Social Care and the Law*. Buckingham: Open University Press.

Friere, P. and Macedo, D. (eds) (2001) *The Paolo Friere Reader*. London: Continuum.

Hasenfield, Y. (1987) 'Power in Social Work Practice'. Social Service Review, University of Chicago. In Ahmad, B. (1990) *Black Perspectives in Social Work*. Birmingham: Venture Press.

Hirschmann, A. (1970) *Exit, Voice and Loyalty: Responses to Declines in Firms, Organisations and States*. Harvard: Harvard University Press.

Lee, J.A.B. (1994) *The Empowerment Approach to Social Work Practice*. New York: Columbia University Press.

Levin, E. (2004) *Involving Service Users and Carers in Social Work Education*. Resource Guide No. 2. London: SCIE.

Means, R. and Smith, R. (1994) *Community Care: Policy and Practice*. London: Macmillan.

Morris, J. (1997) *Community Care: Working in Partnership with Service Users*. Birmingham: Venture Press.

O'Brien, J. and O'Brien, C.L. (eds) (2000) *A Little Book about Person Centred Planning*. Ontario: Inclusion Press.

O'Brien, J. (2005) Personal communication.

Parsloe, P. (ed.) (1996) *Pathways to Empowerment*. Birmingham: Venture Press.

Ramcharan, P. (1997) *Empowerment in Everyday Life: Learning Disability.* London: Jessica Kingsley Publishers.

Reamer, F.G. (1995) *Social Work Values and Ethics.* New York: Columbia University Press.

Singh, G. (1999) 'Exploring the theory and practice of anti-racist social work.' Conference speech. Perth, Scotland. (Unpublished)

Sim, A. and Mackay, R. (1997) 'Advocacy – an evaluation.' *Practice 9*, 2, 3–4.

Smale, G., Tuson, G. and Statham, D. (2000) *Social Work and Social Problems.* Basingstoke: Macmillan.

Solomon, B. (1976) *Black Empowerment: Social Work in Oppressed Communities. New York: Columbia University Press.*

Thompson, N. (2001) *Anti-Discriminatory Practice.* 3rd edn. Basingstoke: Palgrave.

White, M. and Epston, D. (1990) *Narrative Means to Therapeutic Ends.* London: Norton.

Wilson, A. and Beresford, P. (2000) '"Anti-oppressive practice": Emancipation or Appropriation?' *British Journal of Social Work 30*, 553–73.

## CHAPTER 19

# SOCIAL WORK AND COMMUNITY DEVELOPMENT

*Alan Barr*

## Introduction

Historically the relationship between social work and community work and development is like an intermittent affair. At times community work and development has been embraced by social work, though perhaps more with warmth than passion, while at others it has been shunned and distanced. But the enthusiasm of community work and development for a close relationship with social work has also blown hot and cold. Community work and development has always had other relationships and suitors. It has been a boundary profession, unclear whether it has an independent identity and professional authority or whether it is a methodology that, like a chameleon, adapts itself to different professional partners. Yet the history of community development and social work are intertwined. Indeed, community work and development is often seen as one of the foundation stones of social work and, in the unitary systems-based practice theories prominent in the 1970s and 1980s (e.g. Goldstein 1973; Pincus and Minahan 1973; Specht and Vickery 1977), as one of three core methods alongside case work and group work.

In this chapter I will review the developing relationship between social work and community work and development in general but give particular attention to recent Scottish experience. This is for two reasons: first because, generally, the level of engagement with community development by social work in Scotland has been much higher than elsewhere. Second, the divergence in policy and practice between Scotland and other parts of the UK in this field has accelerated with devolution.

In the foregoing paragraphs I have used the term 'community work and development'. While this may seem rather clumsy, it is a reflection of the terminological difficulties associated with the field (Popple 1995). I do not wish to divert into a lengthy discussion of definitions of terms but it will be helpful to clarify the conventions which are adopted in this chapter. These follow distinctions identified by Banks *et al.* (2003) who employ the term 'community work' to describe the work done by an occupational group who: 'work with individuals and community groups to identify needs and take action to work towards change in local neighbourhoods and communities of interest' (p.11), and who use the term 'community development' to describe: 'a process of strengthening individuals, groups and organisations to gain the knowledge and power to work towards change in their communities' (p.12). Hence, while community workers promote community development, that process itself involves a wider range of participants and contributors.

In the current period community development is a more prominent aspect of public policy than it has ever been. Yet ironically its influence in social work is at a low ebb. It is as, or more, influential as an aspect of practice in areas such as public health, community safety, social housing, planning, local economic development, environmental improvement and adult learning as it is in social work. Much of this is a reflection of the New Labour commitment to 'modernizing government' through the development of more participatory approaches to both the planning and implementing of public policy. This finds particular expression, in Scotland, in Community Planning and, in England, in Local Strategic Partnerships.

The Local Government Scotland Act (2003) commits Community Planning partnerships (led by local authorities working with health, police, economic development and others) to providing and planning public services not only after consultation between the partners but equally 'with such community bodies or persons as is appropriate' (para 16.1). The Scottish Executive Guidance (2002, para 5) says: 'Community Planning is essentially a process to secure: Greater collective engagement by agencies with communities… Effective joint working between public, private, voluntary and community bodies… Improved connection of national priorities with those at local and neighbourhood level…'

Describing Community Planning as 'a key overarching framework to co-ordinate other partnerships…' the government is placing community participation at the heart of its policies and recognizing a key role for community development in supporting this approach. Hence its Guidance on community learning and development states: 'We have placed our approach to CLD [community learning and development] at the heart of community planning…we want CLD to become a central feature of the way in which planning authorities and service providers engage with communities and citizens' (Scottish Executive 2004a, p.iii).

In England the equivalent policies relate to the development of Local Strategic Partnerships. These are described in the Chapter 5 of Social Exclusion Unit (2001) as single non-statutory, multi-agency bodies that match local authority boundaries and aim to bring together at a local level the different parts of the public, private, community and voluntary sectors. The strategy has released new resources for community development and capacity building. There is a neighbourhood renewal fund including a local small grants scheme for communities that operates across the 88 most deprived neighbourhoods in England.

In Wales there is a parallel Communities First policy in which the same core features are present. The principle of partnership with communities is central and the guidance for this programme (WAG 2001) is more explicit than elsewhere about the balance of community and agency involvement. It states that: 'Partnership membership should be guided by the principle of one third community representatives; one third statutory sector representatives; and the remaining third divided equally between the voluntary and business sectors' (p.14).

These trends are also apparent in Northern Ireland where strong emphasis has been placed on community regeneration in the context of the peace process. In 2003 government in Northern Ireland published its strategy for neighbourhood renewal. The ministerial foreword commits government to a longer-term, sustainable response to the symptoms and causes of deprivation. To do this it argues: 'We must develop a genuine partnership with people in the target neighbourhoods and other key stakeholders in order to empower residents to drive forward renewal in their own areas' (Department of Social Development Northern Ireland 2003, p.3). So, if community development is achieving a greater prominence in public policy than ever before, and if it is seen as a founding influence on the profession, why is its profile in social work currently so low? To understand this it is important to understand the history and tensions of the relationship and to consider how social work and community work themselves are perceived by policy-makers and practitioners.

## Common origins and interests

Though the origins of community development can be traced to several sources, notably the mutual aid and self-help movements associated with urban industrialization through the nineteenth century, the specific link between community development and social work is usually associated with the development from 1883 of the Settlement Movement (Baldock 1974; Hamilton 2001). The significance of this movement was that it was a product of external intervention in disadvantaged communities, that took social welfare beyond simply poor relief or support to individuals and families in difficulty, into providing resources to support the growth of indigenous skills and development of social action. The Settlements later influenced the Community Associations movement of the inter-war period that was promoted by the National Council of Social Service. Community associations were established in the emerging public-sector housing estates with the aim of responding to the dislocating effects on social and recreational life of transition to a new environment.

That both movements have been seen as associated with social work is a reminder that its traditions encompass approaches to social disadvantage which respond to the shared experiences of communities, not just those of individual and families. This history is also an illustration that, in its past, social work has been associated with area-based social regeneration and with informal adult learning and social action as methods of change. It is also a reminder that while social work may justifiably claim this heritage it is not the only profession with legitimate claims to do so.

The identification of social work with these movements is reflected in a continuing theme in social work policy and practice that sees its role as associated with both influencing the community context of practice and drawing on and supporting the capacities of community infrastructure. It was, for example, a major theme of the Seebohm Report on local authority and allied personal services (Seebohm 1968) and of the Scottish Education Department, Scottish Home and Health Department (1966). It emerged again as a major theme in the Barclay Report (Barclay 1982) and, though in a different form, it was evident in the debates and reports preceding the community care legislation of 1990.

## Perspectives on community

Throughout the post-war period then, it is possible to see the fluctuating interest in community development within social work, but it is important also to recognize that this interest does not reflect a consistent perspective on the purpose of a community orientation to social work practice. Interestingly, for example, the Seebohm Report (Seebohm 1968) notes the value of community as a mechanism for establishing and sustaining 'rules which guide social behaviour' and goes on to talk about such rules being 'the basis of strong social control' in relation to delinquency and criminality. Strong communities are therefore seen as a protection against social malaise and the report suggests that this:

> points to the need for social services to engage in the extremely difficult and complex task of encouraging and assisting the development of community identity and mutual aid, particularly in areas characterised by rapid population turnover, high delinquency, child deprivation and mental illness rates and other indices of social pathology. (Seebohm 1968, para. 977)

While this orientation associated social work with intervention in poor communities it can be seen that the underlying explanations of the problems lay in pathological rather than structural theories of poverty. The location of the problem was in community dynamics and characteristics of residents, the objectives of intervention were control and conformity. This perspective which was predominant at the time was shortly to come under heavy challenge from staff of the Home Office Community Development Project or CDP (Loney 1983). That challenge may in part explain some of the ambivalence that has subsequently pervaded the relationship between community development and social work.

The origins of the CDP reflected a very similar theoretical orientation to those of the Seebohm Report. The then Home Secretary launching the programme, talked of 'providing for the care of our citizens who live in the poorest and most overcrowded parts of our cities and towns' and of arresting the 'downward spiral that afflicts so many of these areas' (Hansard 22 July 1968). Yet the evidence of the project itself was to challenge such assumptions. As Hall (1980, p.107) noted, the projects within the CDP programme:

> helped to refute the prevailing notion that deprivation was merely a matter of small pockets in inner urban areas. They helped shift the predominant paradigm from poverty seen in terms of individual misfortune or inadequacy to poverty as a result of powerful structural forces outside the individual's control.

Though such analysis was largely a product of the CDP, its influence in community development was widespread, including in social work.

As Thomas (1984) suggested, the Seebohm Report had ensured the development of community work in the new social services departments in England and Wales while in Scotland the 1968 Social Work Scotland Act, section 12, duty to promote social welfare, had secured a role for it in social work departments. In the latter it was particularly associated with the Social Work Services Group Circular SW11/69, which stated that promoting social welfare involves:

making efforts to encourage the development of conditions whether for individuals, for families or larger groups which will enable them to deal with difficulties as they arise through their own resources or with the help of resources from their own community.

## Theory and practice – a crisis of confidence

The influence of the critique emanating from the CDP was to impact on practitioners in many other settings, including social work. The role and purpose of community development itself was in dispute. While the structural analysis was persuasive the capacity of community development to produce a methodology which could address the structural underpinnings of poverty precipitated a crisis of confidence among many community workers.

Confidence was further challenged by a lively debate about the relationship between the state and community development. The debate revolved around theoretical perspectives on the nature and role of the state itself and the implications of this for locating community development within it. Was it an essentially benign institution or was it a repressive, class-based instrument of the dominant power holders? Was working in state-funded community development, in agencies like social services and social work departments, tacitly accepting that the state was an instrument of social control or was there room for anti-oppressive action that redressed inequality? But if there was room for the latter, coming full circle in the arguments, was there much evidence that the methodology of community development could bring about such change?

On the one hand writers like Cockburn (1977) were arguing from a Marxist perspective that community development was a means by which 'conflict is moderated and converted, wherever possible, into a style of governance'. On the other writers like Henderson, Jones and Thomas (1980) were defending a well-established liberal pluralist perspective defining the role of community workers as 'interjacent' between state bureaucracy and local groups. Henderson and Thomas (1980) were responsible for the most influential practice theory text based on this perspective, the most recent revision having been published as recently as 2002. Others, like Blagg and Derricourt (1982, p.11) were suggesting that community workers needed: 'to see the state as a far more complex and ambiguous formation than hitherto, not reducible to either its purely repressive apparatus or to a simple instrument of the ruling class'. Whatever their position, as Baldock (1982) noted, the 'key boundary in community work...is that between the world of the welfare professions in which they gain the means to live and the movements for change to which they belong' (p.24).

## Scotland and England – divergent trends

The climate of these debates produced ambivalence in social work among community workers and social workers and among employers. By the early 1980s many social services departments in England and Wales were in retreat from community development, though there were significant exceptions, such as Sheffield, where more radical local administrations supported the approach. In Scotland the situation was quite different (Barr

1995); most of the urban-focused regional councils, particularly the largest, Strathclyde, retained more substantial commitment to employment of community workers. Partly this reflected the politics of these councils. Partly it was a reflection of the statutory duties of the 1968 Social Work Scotland Act and associated Guidance on social welfare. But it was also a reflection of a different history of training and professionalization of community work in the context of what, in Scotland, was then known as 'community education'.

Thus a UK-wide survey of community workers in 1984 (Francis, Henderson and Thomas 1984) recorded a ratio of 24.7 community workers per 100,000 population in Scotland compared with 9.7 for the UK as a whole. In Scotland, where qualified, these workers were predominantly trained in community education in whatever sector they were employed. Thus in a social work department like Strathclyde, which at its height employed 400 community workers, the substantial majority of qualified workers were trained in community education. One of the consequences of this was that community workers inside social work had a distinctly different identity from their social work colleagues, lacked identification with the broader tasks of social work and tended to be peripheral to mainstream practice. Not only did this reduce the impact of the approach on mainstream practice but it also reinforced a perception that community work, while it may have been recognized as part of unitary social work theory, was not a method that was part of the practice repertoire of most social workers. Such issues were not peculiar to Scotland. As Baldock (1974, p.110) noted, while social workers may have seen community work as part of their profession 'the majority of community workers appear to reject this assertion'. He went on, 'this rejection is reinforced and rendered emotionally charged by the fact that most social workers are employed by local authorities and by the often misinformed and stereotyped pictures that community workers have of social work'.

## Community social work

By the early 1980s then the picture was a complex one; there was much higher engagement in community work by social work agencies in Scotland than in England but this was not generally conducted by social workers. Hence even where it had a presence it was rarely well integrated into the overall practice of agencies. In this context the emergence of community social work as a practice model was interesting. The model was associated with a neighbourhood or patch-based approach to practice and was given a huge boost by the Barclay Report (Barclay 1982) commissioned from the National Institute for Social Work by the then Secretary of State for Social Services, Patrick Jenkin. The report defined community social work in the following way:

> By this we mean formal social work, which, starting from problems affecting an individual or group and the responsibilities and resources of social services departments and voluntary organisations, seeks to tap into, support, enable and underpin the local networks of formal and informal relationships. (p.xvii)

Though there were prominent dissenters on the committee (Pinker) and some who thought that a more radical model of patch work was required (Brown, Hadley and

White 1982), the approach nonetheless represented a significant challenge to social work and its conception of how social need can be met. It was essentially arguing that the promotion and maintenance of social well-being must ultimately depend on community networks and supports and that the role of social work should be to underpin these rather than take responsibility for trying to meet them all directly. Practice would be focused on prevention rather than reaction to crises, services would be physically located in communities and responsibility for social welfare would be shared with citizens. Hence, the report argued:

> The detailed activities in which community social workers engage may include an increased measure of activities of the kind undertaken by community workers but they will have statutory duties and responsibilities to individuals, families or groups that do not fall within the remit of community workers. (p.xvii)

This was a challenge to both social workers and community workers. It was a change of role for social workers, that would require new skills, and a threat to community workers for two reasons. Some saw it as an encroachment on their specialist territory within social work that would result in further marginalization, others had substantial reservations about the assumptions that lay behind the model. In the context of the economic rationalism of the 1980s, it looked to them to have the potential to be a means of colonizing community effort and organization in the interest of cost reduction to the state (Brenton 1985). Far from being seen as a progressive departure it was treated by many community workers with suspicion. Yet its protagonists promoted it as a radical and empowering form of practice. Cooper (1980), a leading practitioner, describing patch-based community social work in his team, argued:

> experiences showed that there was great potential for community care in a lively partnership of the statutory, voluntary and informal sections of the communities. We developed a theory of community action which incorporated traditional social work values, notions of radical community work and the concept of voluntarism... We wanted to act alongside clients and client groups as members of a community...

To coin a phrase, the response to patch proved patchy. In some areas for a period it came to dominate the organization of social work, in others it had little impact. In Scotland, in authorities like Strathclyde, there was a belief that community social work was already characteristic of practice, but as the earlier evidence indicates the integration of practice methods within the role of a generic social worker was generally absent. Certainly there were patch-based teams, and several purpose-designed area social work offices and 'one-stop shops' were built that would enable local community as well as agency use, but community work remained a distinct and often peripheral aspect of social work practice. For a period in the latter half of the 1980s a range of community social work projects developed and there was a lively dialogue in Scotland (Smale and Bennett 1989) but influence on mainstream practice was not sustained.

As a postscript to this commentary on community social work it is worth reflecting on the criticism made by Hadley and colleagues in their minority contribution to the Barclay Report. They had complained that there had not been 'sufficient acknowledgement of the extent to which community oriented social work represents a significant departure from current practice' and feared that the proposals would not effect 'fundamental changes in attitudes and practices...or fundamental organisational reforms' (Barclay 1982, p.219). In retrospect their comments appear cogently prophetic.

## Community care

Many of the arguments that surrounded community social work were also to emerge as features of the debate at the end of the decade about the development of community care. Indeed the Barclay Report had already argued that: 'it is difficult to over-estimate the importance of the social care that members of communities give to each other' (Barclay 1982, p.200). Community care was to be the next major development in social work that would impact on the debates about community work and social work.

A key driver of the reviews of community care was the so-called 'perverse incentive' in the social security system that made it advantageous to move into residential care rather than stay in your own home (Lewis and Glennester 1996). The terms of reference given to Sir Roy Griffiths in relation to community care were: 'To review the way in which public funds are used to support community care policy and to advise on options which would improve the use of these funds' (Griffiths 1988, p.1). From the start then community workers, among many others, were suspicious about the motivations for the recommendations ultimately presented in the Griffiths Report (Griffiths 1988) and the White Paper, Caring for People (Department for Health 1989).

The reforms ushered in market principles to the provision of care and looked to many to be a reflection of economic rationalism and welfare minimalism, part of a substitution of services by cost-driven alternatives. Yet at the same time the reforms were capturing much more progressive thinking about care provision; they were creating opportunity for service users, frequently removed from society in long-stay residential and health care, to live in and be normal members of communities, and were therefore compatible with demands from the user movement for equality of citizenship (Barnes 1997; Beresford and Croft 1993) and the desire of many practitioners for a user-centred practice. The promise of a statutorily-based care needs assessment and the principle of integrated service development through inter-agency community care planning were attractive to users, carers and professionals. Ironically, despite the economic motivations that lay behind it, the mixed economy of care also held out the possibility of greater diversity and more appropriate forms of care provision.

For community workers within social work the advent of community care was a source of ambivalence. For many it did not appear particularly relevant. Despite their location in social work, the level of attention given by community workers to the disadvantages experienced by care service users was limited. While there was a burgeoning development in the service user movement, particularly in the context of disability, this owed little to the interventions of community workers. The community development and health movement was still in its infancy and tended to focus more on environmental and public health issues than on direct support to community action by service users (Jones 2000). The predominant community work tradition was neighbourhood-based work with a core focus on poverty and the physical environment. It seemed to have largely escaped the attention of most community workers that among the poorest and most systematically disadvantaged groups in society were the very people with whom their social work colleagues in the community care field were engaged. Still further it seemed to have escaped their attention that for such people communities were frequently hostile and unsupportive places (Barnes 1997). Far from embracing care service users and providing the supportive networks envisaged by Barclay, communities commonly marginalize, reject and stigmatize them (Baldwin 1993). If community development has pretensions to addressing exclusion and oppression, these are peculiar omissions.

Frequently, arguments designed to redress the antipathy and/or ignorance towards the potential for community development practice with care users and carers were met with resistance by mainstream community workers (Barr, Drysdale and Henderson 1998; Mayo 1994). Engagement with community care, it was suggested, would be a diversion from the core issues that drove community development. On the other hand, case studies demonstrated that there was much potential for effective community development in the care context in promoting user involvement in service planning and review, and public education, and in applying community economic development skills to community-led care provision. Further this evidence pointed to the importance, from the participant's perspective, of conceptualizing needs in terms of exclusion from full citizenship not merely in terms of consumption of care services (Barr, Drysdale and Henderson 1997; Barr, Henderson and Stenhouse 2001).

Despite the resistance from many community workers, by the mid-1990s the focus of community workers in social work departments had largely transferred to community care issues and groups. However, by this time there had been a huge reduction in the number of such staff. So, whilst there are pockets of good practice, it would be difficult to sustain an argument that community work or social work has embraced the community development opportunities of community care. When social work uses the term 'community care' it is generally not associated with a method of work that seeks to foster collective user responses to their needs, or with establishing networks of support but with the location of service provision. 'Community' is used merely as a counterpoint to 'institutional' care, a context for planning and a setting for assessment and care management of individual users.

The emphasis on care assessment and care management has placed social work in an increasingly bureaucratic, gatekeeping role in terms of access to care services. In such a context the few community workers who are engaged with care users frequently comment that empowering users is a source of potential conflict with their social work colleagues.

## The current picture

The retreat from employment of community workers in social work and social service departments and the association of the residual workforce with carer and user support has been a notable feature of the recent period. A survey of community development workers in the UK (Glen *et al.* 2004) reports: 'We can see that community development workers are responding to the dominant funding and policy issues of social inclusion and regeneration with a shift away from social welfare' (p.7). Thus the retreat from social work has been paralleled by transfer of community work resources into other disciplines, particularly in the context of community regeneration initiatives and in health promotion in the statutory and voluntary sectors. The experience of the Social Inclusion Partnerships (SIPS) in Scotland provides a particularly interesting illustration of the changing perception of the role of community development workers.

Twelve of the 48 SIPs across Scotland have had a thematic focus on specific communities of interest. Several of these have operated directly in social work territory, particularly two which have worked with young people who are, or have been, looked after by local authorities, one that has focused on young carers and another on routes out of prostitution. Other thematic SIPs, focusing on young people, have also had shared interests with social work and many of the area-based projects have supported local community initiatives that serve vulnerable children, young people and adults who are or could be social work service users.

Thus, while social work has become a much less prominent location for community workers, issues of inclusion that are relevant to social work remain a significant aspect of their concerns. Significantly these activities have largely been fostered through inter-agency partnerships working with local communities. Thus, even where the focal client group might have been perceived as the primary concern of social work, as in the case of looked-after children, the partnership response has brought together a wide range of statutory and voluntary agencies including housing, health, education, youth work, employment, psychology, arts and recreation as well as social work. Of course young people's needs have long been recognized as crossing disciplinary boundaries, as is reflected in children's service plans, but a lesson that may need to be learned from the Scottish SIPs is that, if the starting point is the experience of the young person, professional territorialism is challenged. The community development role in such contexts stands outside any one of the service disciplines. Its task is to empower young people effectively to represent themselves in relation to the range of agencies that impact on their lives and to support an integrated agency response.

The idea that community development stands outside specific professions is not new, but a greater appreciation seems to be emerging that it is an approach that can benefit many professions and, more importantly, benefit their collaborative practice. A survey by Glen et al. 2004) vividly illustrated the range of policy areas and types of work with which community workers across the UK are now involved. These include arts, built environment, safety and crime, employment and economic development, environment issues, equalities, health, homelessness and housing, immigration, poverty, play, regeneration, substance misuse and youth work, as well as a continuing but much reduced strand relating to social services and social care.

This broadening focus of development has been reflected in a long-standing debate about whether it is an approach that can be adopted in a range of disciplines or a discipline in its own right. Thomas (1995) has commented on the dilemma that this has created:

> periods since the late 1960's when community development has been successful
> in motivating a large number of occupations that have absorbed and imple-
> mented many of its values and methods...the major objective to influence the

policies and practice of other occupations has been substantially achieved. The cost, however, has been that of marginalising community development as a form of intervention and as a distinctive occupation. (p.33)

The issue of approach or discipline remains a live one. It is well illustrated in the context of community education services, which in Scotland have often been seen as the primary host of community development workers in the field.

In the mid-1990s claims that community education gave substantial attention to community development as against its other elements – youth work and adult learning – were challenged by research commissioned by the Scottish Office (Barr, Purcell and Hamilton 1996). However, the association of community development with regeneration and the emerging Community Planning policies led to new institutional arrangements for it in local government. New departments of neighbourhood or community services increasingly replaced community education departments. They frequently brought together the traditional elements of community education alongside library and information services, and recreation, leisure and arts services, and incorporated community workers who had previously been employed in social work settings. While such departments were generally still concerned with youth work, adult learning and community development the profile of the last has been strengthened. Community education was seen in a ministerial review (Scottish Office 1998a) as an approach rather than a discipline. It was: 'a way of working...its purpose being to promote personal and social development, to build community capacity and invest, and secure investment, in community learning' (p.8).

Five years later when new ministerial (Scottish Executive 2004b) Guidance was published the term 'community education' had been dropped. The field was now described as 'community learning and development' and authority for its development had been transferred from local authorities to community planning partnerships. A primary task was to be the promotion of community engagement in Community Planning across all disciplines. Thus by 2004, not only had community work ceased to be central to social work departments, it had also ceased to be associated particularly with community education services and was rapidly moving into cross-disciplinary departments and partnership structures. Within the wider processes of community planning there would be community learning and development strategies that would be 'a jointly agreed statement to which all Community Planning Partners should contribute and be committed' (p.19).

As the survey data for 2004 (Glen et al.) indicate, similar trends are apparent across the UK. It is interesting for example that when PAULO, the national training organization for the sector, developed occupation standards for community work (PAULO 2003) it described them as identifying 'what is involved in using community development approaches in a variety of contexts' and 'supporting organisations/agencies that promote a CD approach' (p.1).

The adoption of the approach is evident in many fields. The Standing Conference on Community Development, in its strategic framework (2001, p.18) document, notes: 'Many agencies are seeking ways of improving how they relate to, and work with, communities: economic development, planning, housing, leisure services and health are examples.'

Trawling the websites of professional bodies now consistently throws up references to community development. In the context of health, for example, the National Primary and Care Trust Development Programme website provides guidance and illustrations on community engagements; in housing the Chartered Institute for Housing has a range of web-based resources to support community involvement, community cohesion and sustainability; the Arts Council site provides numerous references to arts and community regeneration and inclusion.

## Social work and community work – the future

### WHAT THEN SHOULD THE RELATIONSHIP BE BETWEEN SOCIAL WORK AND COMMUNITY DEVELOPMENT?

As the introduction to this chapter noted the relationship between social work and community development has fluctuated over a long period, but the current climate is not one in which it makes sense to debate the role of community development solely within a specific discipline. We should be considering the relationship between social work and other disciplines in responding effectively, and together, to the experience of citizens. The debate cannot be about social work alone, its clients are also citizens with wider interests whose well-being is promoted by an holistic perspective on their needs and aspirations.

This is the perspective to be found in the partnership-based community regeneration initiatives across the UK highlighted in the introduction to this chapter. These core government policy commitment operate in a model that embraces public participation as a core feature of governance and will therefore require all its partners to develop effective engagement with their users and the wider community. Increasingly characterized by bureaucratic resource management and social control functions, this may be demanding territory for social work despite its historical association with principles of empowerment and social change and its past engagement with community work.

So can social work be let off the community development hook? Can the final divorce decree be issued? The answer has to be no; but social work may have to embrace a polygamous relationship with community work! Community development may no longer be a practice method to which social work can lay any special claim, but the relationship with it as an approach which may increasingly be used to underpin the practice of governance as a whole, needs to be understood. In England the Neighbourhood Renewal Unit makes the case for such joined up working and community involvement in relation to Local Strategic Partnerships when it states:

> Lack of joint working at local level has been one of the key reasons for lack of progress in delivering sustainable economic, social and physical regeneration, or improved public services, that meets the needs of local people. A combination of organisations, and the community, working co-operatively as part of an LSP will have a far greater chance of success. (Neighbourhood Renewal Unit 2007)

The Welsh Communities first programme enunciates similar principles. The Guidance (Welsh Assembly Government) states that the: 'transformation of communities will be driven by local people' and that: 'setting up of partnerships will make sure that those with a stake in improving the lives of people in the most disadvantaged communities work together' (Communities Directorate 2001, p.4).

As noted in the introduction, in Scotland, the Local Government Scotland Act (2003) has made it a legislative requirement that all public services are planned and implemented in consultation not only with partner agencies but equally with bodies representing communities. In the case of social work this means its service users. As the Scottish Executive (2003a) Guidance indicates, a core aim of Community Planning is 'making sure people and communities are genuinely engaged in decisions on public services which affect them' (p.1).

Yet this ought to be well understood by social work in Scotland and evident in its practice, after all, the Scottish Office (1998b) *Modernising Community Care: An Action Plan* said of social work departments: 'Their effectiveness as the lead agency and their ability to work with others, including people who use services, will play a vital role in how well we meet people's needs' (para 1.4). The following year the *White Paper: Aiming for Excellence: Modernising Social Work Services in Scotland* (Scottish Executive 1999) stated as its first objective: 'To involve people who need care, and those who care for them in planning services' (para 1.7), though curiously little was said about how this was to be achieved, perhaps revealing a capacity for good intent that was not supported by strategic planning and resource allocation.

Such an approach is consistent with the professed principles of the social work profession, yet in relation to the application of community development approaches at least, its practice seems to be in retreat from it rhetoric. The British Association of Social Workers states on their website:

> The social work profession promotes social change, problem solving in human relationships and the empowerment and liberation of people to enhance well-being. Utilising theories of human behaviour and social systems, social work intervenes at the points where people interact with their environments. Principles of human rights and social justice are fundamental to social work. (British Association of Social Workers 2007)

In the broader climate of the partnerships-based regeneration and community planning policies across the UK and the specific context of its own objectives, the social work retreat from community development has to be reversed if it is to develop genuinely participatory approaches to its service development. Ironically, despite its history as a host for community development, its mainstream practice may have learned little more about effective participatory practice than most other public service providers. Indeed, in other areas more progress is apparent. In social housing, for example, tenant participation has become a statutory obligation. In the health field across the UK government is giving central attention to public/patient participation. Section 5 of the Scottish national action plan (Scottish Executive 2003) sets out the importance of the participatory approach and states:

> We want to work with the NHS to ensure that a patient focus is embedded in the culture. To make this happen we will ensure that listening, understanding and acting on the views of local communities, patients and carers is given the same priority as clinical standards and financial performance. (p.50)

While social work policy has referred to participatory practice, there appears to be much less commitment to it than is now apparent in other disciplines. This is not to suggest that social work has entirely turned is back on these principles. For example, the Commission for Social Care Inspection states at the start of its vision and values: 'We'll be guided by what they [service users] tell us, and support them to live independent lives with dignity' (Commission for Social Care Inspection 2007). Such a goal is not achievable except with the application of participatory principles. The equivalent Scottish body, the Care Commission, is required by law to consult through a National Advisory Forum at least twice a year, though ironically, given the disadvantages experienced by care users and carers, the Commission is prohibited from making any contribution to the cost of people attending.

But even if there were no such inhibiting factors, such national structures can only be effective if they are underpinned by a participatory culture throughout the care system. There is little evidence of this. In other areas of social work, particularly those involving statutory interventions with children and families or in criminal justice social work, there is even less sign that the implications of participatory governance have been addressed, though examples like the Big Step SIP in Glasgow provide positive illustrations of the potential.

If social work is to recover its interest in community development and public participation, it has to avoid the failures of the past, notably, the marginalization of the approach and its location as the responsibility of a specialist group of staff, ill connected and poorly motivated to engage with the core functions of social work. The task is therefore to challenge social workers themselves to rediscover the third strand of unitary practice and to challenge social work institutions and policy-makers to create the space and allocate the resources to develop this aspect of practice, and to do so in the climate of interdisciplinary collaboration.

In its Guidance (2003a) on its modernizing government initiative in Community Planning the Scottish Executive has said: 'There is still a need for on-going change to working cultures, behaviours, skills and attitudes to achieve effective partnership working and a genuine community focus' (p.1). Similarly the Neighbourhood Renewal Unit (2002) strategy paper on skill development for regeneration: 'The Learning Curve' has stressed the need for people involved in regeneration to 'develop new skills' and 'work on new ways'. Despite its pretensions to have been a custodian of community development and participatory practice, social work is as much in need of giving attention to these changes as any other public service. If it is to be part of the modernized culture, it must take responsibility within its core activities for generating an approach that is committed to participation and empowerment. These words often appear to be part of the mantra of social work, as in the British Association of Social Workers statement of values, yet current practice suggests contradictions that frequently need to be addressed.

To take this approach is not to expect something exceptional from social work but to bring it into line with expectations that policy now places on all public services. Recently the term 'community practice' has been coined to describe this emerging style of public service provision (Banks *et al.* 2003; Butcher *et al.* 1993). This term is used to denote an approach that sees community engagement as part of a wider range of roles, whether in planning, health, housing, social work or many other areas. It has been coined to emphasize the idea that working with communities of place or interest should be an integral part of the practice of many professions. It is this approach that should characterize social work.

## References

Baldock, P. (1974) *Community Work and Social Work* London: Routledge and Kegan Paul.

Baldock, P. (1982) 'Community work and the social service departments.' In G. Craig, N. Derricourt and M. Loney (1982) *Community Work and the State*. London: Routledge and Kegan Paul.

Baldwin, S. (1993) *The Myth of Community Care: An Alternative Neighbourhood Model of Care*. London: Chapman and Hall.

Banks, S., Butcher, H., Henderson, P. and Robertson, J. (eds) (2003) *Managing Community Practice – Principles, Policies and Programmes*. Bristol: Policy Press.

Barclay, P. (1982) *Social Workers their Roles and Tasks*. (The Barclay Report.) London: National Institute for Social Work/Bedford Square Press.

Barnes, M. (1997) *Care, Communities and Citizens*. London: Longman.

Barr, A. (1995) *Practising Community Development*. London: Community Development Foundation.

Barr, A., Drysdale, J. and Henderson, P. (1997) *Towards Caring Communities*. Brighton: Pavilion Press/Joseph Rowntree Foundation.

Barr, A., Drysdale, J. and Henderson, P. (1998) 'Realising the potential of community care – the role of community development.' *Issues in Social Work Education 18*, 1, Spring, 26–46.

Barr, A., Henderson, P. and Stenhouse, C. (2001) *Community Care and Community Development*. York: York Publishing Services/Joseph Rowntree Foundation.

Barr, A., Purcell, R. and Hamilton, R. (1996) *Learning for Change – Community Education and Community Development*. London: Community Development Foundation.

Beresford, P. and Croft, S. (1993) *Citizen Involvement – A Practical Guide for Change*. London: Macmillan.

Blagg, H. and Derricourt, N. (1982) 'Why we need to reconstruct the theory of the state for community work.' In G. Craig, N. Derricourt and M. Loney (eds) *Community Work and the State*. London: Routledge and Kegan Paul.

Brenton, M. (1985) *The Voluntary Sector in British Social Services*. London: Longman.

Butcher, H., Glen, A., Henderson, P. and Smith, J. (1993) *Community and Public Policy*. London: Pluto Press.

Cockburn, C. (1977) *The Local State*. London: Pluto Press.

Commission for Social Care Inspection (2007) *Vision and Values*. CSCI. Available at www.csci.org.uk/about_csci/Who_we_are/vision_and_values.aspx

Communities Directorate (2001) *Communities First Guidance*. Cardiff: National Assembly for Wales.

Cooper, M. 'Interweaving social work and the community.' In R. Hadley and M. McGrath (1980) *Going Local – Neighbourhood Social Services*. London: Bedford Square Press.

Department of Health (1989) *Caring for People: Community Care in the Next Decade and Beyond*. Cmnd. 849. London: HMSO.

Department of Social Development Northern Ireland (2003) *Neighbourhood Renewal – People and Place*. Belfast: Department of Social Development Northern Ireland.

Francis, D., Henderson, P. and Thomas. D. (1984) *A Survey of Community Workers in the United Kingdom*. London: National Institute for Social Work.

Glen, A., Henderson, P., Humm, J., Meszaros, H., Gaffney. M. (2004) *A Survey of Community Workers in the UK*. London: Community Development Foundation.

Goldstein, H. (1973) *Social Work Practice – A Unitary Approach*. Columbia, SC: University of South Carolina Press.

Griffiths, R. (1988) *Community Care – An Agenda for Action*. (The Griffiths Report.) London: HMSO.

Hall, P. (1980) *The Inner City in Context.* London: Heinemann.

Hamilton, R. (2001) 'A hidden heritage – the social settlement house movement 1884–1910.' *The Journal of Community Work and Development 2,* autumn 9–22.

Henderson, P., Jones, D. and Thomas, D.N. (1980) *The Boundaries of Change in Community Work.* London: George Allen & Unwin.

Henderson, P. and Thomas, D.N. (1980) *Skills in Neighbourhood Work.* National Institute Social Service Library 39. London: George Allen & Unwin.

Henderson, P. and Thomas, D.N. (2000) *Skills in Neighbourhood Work.* 3rd edn. London: Routledge.

Jones, J. (2000) *Private Troubles and Public Issues – A Community Development Approach to Health.* Edinburgh, Community Learning Scotland.

Lewis, J. and Glennerster, H. (1996) *Implementing the New Community Care.* Buckingham: Open University Press.

Loney, M. (1983) *Community Against Government.* London: Heinemann.

Mayo, M. (1994) *Communities and Caring – the Mixed Economy of Welfare.* Basingstoke: MacMillan.

Neighbourhood Renewal Unit (2002) *The Learning Curve: Developing Skills and Knowledge for Neighbourhood Renewal.* London: Office of the Deputy Prime Minister.

Neighbourhood Renewal Unit (2007) *Local Strategic Partnerships.* NRU. Available at www.neighbourhood.gov.uk/page.asp?id=531

PAULO (2003) *National Occupational Standards in Community Development Work.* London: Lifelong Learning UK. www.lifelonglearninguk.org/documents/standards/cdw_nos.pdf

Pincus, A. and Minahan, A. (1973) *Social Work Practice: Model and Method.* Itasca, Il: F.E. Peacock Publishers Inc.

Popple, K. (1995) *Analysing Community Work – its Theory and Practice.* Buckingham: Open University Press.

Scottish Education Department, Scottish Home and Health Department (1966) *Social Work and the Community: Proposals for Reorganising Local Authority Services in Scotland.* Cmnd. 3065 London: HMSO.

Scottish Executive (2002) *Policy Memorandum on the Local Government Scotland Bill.* Edinburgh: Scottish Executive.

Scottish Executive (2003a) *Working Draft Guidance on Community Planning.* Edinburgh: Scottish Executive

Scottish Executive (2003b) *Our National Health: A Plan for Action a Plan for Change.* Edinburgh: Scottish Executive

Scottish Executive (2004a) Ministerial foreword. In *Working and Learning Together: Guidance on Community Learning and Development.* Edinburgh: Scottish Executive.

Scottish Executive (2004b) *Working and Learning Together to Build Stronger Communities.* Edinburgh: Scottish Executive

Scottish Office (1998a) *Communities Change through Learning.* (The Ostler report.) Edinburgh: Scottish Office.

Scottish Office (1998b) *Modernising Community Care: An Action Plan.* Edinburgh: Scottish Office.

Seebohm (1968) *Report of the Committee on Local Authority and Allied Personal Social Services.* Cmnd. 3703. (The Seebohm Report) London: HMSO.

Social Exclusion Unit (2001) *A Commitment to Neighbourhood Renewal – National Strategy Action Plan.* London: Cabinet Office.

Smale, G. G. and Bennett, W. *Pictures of Practice Volume 1: Community Social Work in Scotland.* London: National Institute for Social Work.

Specht, H. and Vickery, A. (eds) (1977) *Integrating Social Work Methods.* London: Allen & Unwin.

Standing Conference on Community Development (2001) *Strategic Framework for Community Development.* Sheffield: Standing Conference on Community Development.

Thomas, D.N. (1984) *The Making of Community Work.* London: George Allen & Unwin.

Thomas, D.N. (1995) *Community Development at Work: A Case of Obscurity in Accomplishment.* London: Community Development Foundation.

WAG (2001) *Communities First Guidance.* Cardiff: Welsh Assembly Government.

# Section 4: The Context of Assessment and Intervention

## CHAPTER 20

# SOCIAL WORK WITH CHILDREN AND FAMILIES: A CASE STUDY OF THE INTEGRATION OF LAW, SOCIAL POLICY AND RESEARCH IN THE DEVELOPMENT OF ASSESSMENT AND INTERVENTION WITH CHILDREN AND FAMILIES

*Robert Buckley*

## Introduction

Social work with children and families is arguably one of the most challenging areas of practice in terms of the issues it seeks to address and the demands that are made on staff. It is certainly the most topical and indeed controversial, as a web search through recent social work related news events will evidence.

Adult attitudes towards children and childhood are extremely complex and accommodate a fluid and diverse range of views and perceptions. The shaping of individual attitudes is also a dynamic and multifaceted process that is a combination of experiential, educational, cultural and societal influences. These assorted influences derive from childhood experiences of being parented within our own families, relationships with our extended family and wider experience of childhood in general. In addition family composition is much more complex. Increased divorce rates, second marriages and the growing number of reconstituted families mean that a significant number of children experience family life differently from the stereotypical notion of a family as father, mother and two point four children (Daniel and Ivatts 1998).

Educational influences are acutely important in determining adult attitudes towards children ranging from how we experience socialization with our peers at school to the acquisition of knowledge through studying the plethora of child-related and child-centred subjects available at various academic levels. Adult perspectives on children and associated issues are also determined by major news events concerning children and media presentation and sometimes the misrepresentation of children.

Finally undertaking the role and responsibility of being a parent is important in developing individual attitudes about childhood. Caring for children is a difficult process that occurs on a number of different levels: individual, family and community and societal. Each in turn is linked to custom, practice, culture, policy and legislation. This chapter highlights the developmental context of social work intervention with children and families and provides an overview issues that are central to current legislation, policy and practice.

The chapter aims to provide an understanding of the practice and policy context of social work with children and families by highlighting some of key themes and tensions facing child welfare agencies and practitioners. The chapter will focus on three broad themes: social work and the role of the state, the child protection agenda and developments in child care practice.

## Social work and the role of the state

The role of the state in family life and the role of social work are inextricably linked and have been since the early stages of the Welfare State. The government circular that accompanied the 1948 Children Act described the role of the state very succinctly: 'To keep the family together must be the first aim, and the separation of the child from his parents can only be justified when there is no possibility of securing adequate care for that child in his own home' (quoted in Fisher, Marsh, Phillips *et al.* 1990, p.18).

The emphasis was on the importance of the state in supporting parents to carry out their parental responsibilities. While the range of issues facing the child welfare system may have become increasingly complicated, challenging and controversial the role of the state in supporting and enabling families has arguably remained the same since then.

Fox Harding (1997) provides a comprehensive account of the how different perspectives about the role of the state in family life and the role of social work have shaped policy and practice in child care and child protection over the years. She identifies the following positions:

- *'The laissez faire'* perspective argues the virtue of parental responsibility and that state intervention in family life should be kept to the absolute minimum.

- *'The kinship defender'* perspective argues that state intervention has an important role to play in the upbringing of children but that it must be facilitative and supportive of natural families. Intervention by the state should be directed at helping families overcome deficiencies in child rearing which can be largely but not exclusively linked to social exclusion and structurally oppressive practice.

- *'The society as parent'* perspective holds that society has a moral and legal obligation to protect children. This position also argues that children have a right to grow up in a stable secure environment and if circumstances exist whereby the care offered by natural parents is deficient and harmful the state should provide long-term alternative care, even if this means severing ties with natural parents in some situations.

- *'The children's rights'* perspective argues that historically social work practice has not been truly developed within a child-centred framework. The role of the state and indeed the child welfare system has at best been insufficiently child centred and at worst oppressive towards children. This value position argues that policy, legislation and practice need to respond to the challenge of developing a system that is inclusive.

Colton, Sanders and Williams (2001) provide a very useful four-stage model of how the focus of child care policy and practice has evolved over time. They argue that before 1970 the emphasis was on developing foster care provision and reducing the placement of children in residential care. By the 1970s the focus was on the importance of children being part of a permanent family. The third phase was in the 1980s, with change in policy and practice being aimed towards maintaining children in their biological families. The final stage was that of family continuity where children were viewed as part of a family network and where the extended family is considered as an importance resource in child care provision. Horner (2003) has suggested a fifth stage of 'family stability' with an integrated recognition of contributions that can be made by birth, extended and substitute families.

Following almost two decades when government intervention in family life was deliberately minimalist, the late 1990s saw a rekindling of state intervention in family life through positive and progressive family policies aimed towards addressing issues such as childhood poverty and social exclusion (Fawcett, Featherstone and Goddard 2003). Hill (2004) has noted the gradual shift in attitude towards public policy and the almost widespread acceptance of the role of the state in defining, providing and monitoring an array of welfare services for children and families. Some policy initiatives and services are universal, such as child benefit, while other provision, such as child protection legislation and guidance, is targeted at children considered to be the most vulnerable and at risk of maltreatment. The rights of children have also received greater attention on a global scale culminating with the passing of the UN Convection on the Rights of the Child and the reaching of a degree of 'international consensus' about the objectives and role of state intervention in family life (Pinkerton 2001).

## THE UN CONVENTION ON THE RIGHTS OF THE CHILD

A significant political watershed in the specific recognition of children within a legislative and social policy context was the passing of the United Nations Convention on the Rights of the Child (Ruxton 1996). The UN Convention was ratified by the UK government in December 1991 and has subsequently underpinned major child care legislation such as the Children (Scotland) Act 1995 and the Children Act 2004 (Daniel and Ivatts 1998; Tisdall 1997). Despite this ratification of the Convention it has been suggested that successive UK governments have been slow to wholeheartedly demonstrate commitment and implementation of the convention in full (Fawcett *et al.* 2004).

## CHILDHOOD POVERTY

Since the beginning of the welfare state, successive governments have attempted with varying degrees of success to address a wide range of family related matters via social policy initiatives and new and revised legislation (Fawcett *et al* 2004). Although philosophical and political differences exist about the desirable level of state intervention in family life, there is recognition that social policy plays a strategic role in society in terms of underpinning and achieving social change and social control (Miller 2003; Walker and Walker 1998).

Any discussion of child welfare provision might be considered incomplete without some focus on the issue of childhood poverty. In March 2005 the Department of Work and Pensions' report *Households Below Average Income* announced a drop of half a million children living in poverty between 1997 and 2005 as a result of government policy initiatives to address the issue. According to the Institute for Fiscal Studies' report on child poverty by Brewer *et al.* (2005), although government polices were undoubtedly making an impact, the measures were not fully meeting their own child poverty targets and a significant number of children are still living in poverty. This was further endorsed in March 2005 by a Save the Children Fund report in Wales which argued that on closer scrutiny policies might not be impacting on families as quickly as might be anticipated, given its findings that 25 per cent of children are living in households on or just below the poverty line. Research undertaken by Bradshaw (2003) and Sutherland, Sefton and Piachaud (2005) for the Joseph Rowntree Trust further endorsed the fact that childhood poverty is still a major social problem within the UK and remains relevant to the child welfare system.

## LEGISLATION

For over 15 years the Children Act 1989 had been the principal legislation governing social work with children and families in England and Wales. Over time supplementary and revised measures such as the Leaving Care Act 2000 and the Adoption and Child Act 2002 have come into operation. The most recent overhaul of child care legislation, the Children Act 2004, is currently in the process of being implemented.

The Act contains a range of major reforms such as the introduction of the office of Children's Commissioner for England in keeping with the introduction of similar posts already in operation in Scotland, Wales and Northern Ireland. It also establishes Local Safeguarding Children's Boards to replace Area Child Protection Committees as well as refining legislation on children and young people's service plans and private fostering. The Act also places a duty on local authorities to ascertain the views of children involved with the care system as well as an additional duty to promote the educational achievement of looked after children.

The 2004 Children Act also has provision which attempts to restrict the use of physical chastisement on children by abolishing the parental defence of reasonable chastisement in criminal and civil proceedings. Although the legislation falls short of making physical punishment of children illegal it marks a fundament shift in the balance of rights between children and parents on the issue of punishment. In Scotland the issue was tackled differently when in October 2003 the Scottish Executive outlawed specific forms of physical chastisement such as shaking a child, hitting a child on the head and striking a child with an implement. The very introduction of any restrictive measures on the physical chastisement of children represents a major breakthrough. Government recognition of the link between our culture of child rearing that endorses violence as a legitimate method of controlling children and the physical abuse of children is to be viewed positively. In the UK we have been slow to recognize this connection, in contrast with other countries such as Sweden where it has been unlawful to punish children physically since 1979 (Durrant 1999).

In Scotland the legislative framework underpinning work with children and families is the Children (Scotland) Act 1995, although it also has been augmented by other legislation such as the Protection of Children (Scotland) Act 2002 and the Anti Social Behaviour, etc. (Scotland) Act 2004. Currently the Scottish Executive (2005) is in the process of consultation and review regarding the very essence of social work with children and families and the operation of the Children's Hearing system.

The different legislative frameworks within the UK are an important feature of our historical, cultural and political background and, although there are specific operational differences, the practice and policy issues that child care legislation strives to address are relevant to the whole of the UK. Accordingly legislation has tended to follow the same philosophical policy and practice template. The exception to this is in the field of youth justice where the Scottish Children's Hearing system has traditionally maintained a welfare approach to youth offending, in contrast to the rest of the UK where the welfare of the young offender has been less central in the decision-making process (Goldson 2004).

## The child protection agenda

The protection of children has been pivotal to social work practice with children and families since the 1970s. During this time the focus of the system has widened from the initial concerns about the non-accidental injury of babies and infants to addressing a diverse range of maltreatment issues such as the emotional abuse of children, physical neglect and the array of exploitation that constitutes sexual abuse (Hanks and Stratton 1997; Pritchard 2000).

Physical abuse has been a major concern of child care practice since the report into the death of Maria Colwell (DHSS 1974). Indeed, many of the key elements of the child protection system, such as written inter-agency guidelines, case conferences, the child protection register and the formation of local Area Child Protection Committees, emanated from the reforms generated following the inquiry report (Corby 2002). Since 1974 there have been a number of inquiry reports into the death of individual children. While primarily concerned with the individual case management issues some broader themes have emerged, the most critical being inter-agency and interdisciplinary working and communication (Corby 2002).

The death of Victoria Climbié and the subsequent inquiry report (Laming 2003) demonstrated that despite advances in policy and practice in the 30 years since the death of Maria Colwell in 1973, deficiencies in inter-agency communication are invariably crucial factors in the system's failure to protect any child. The report also illustrated the importance of early recognition and response by all professional staff who encounter potentially suspicious injuries in children. The similarities in the issues raised by the Colwell and Climbié inquiry reports almost 30 years apart is unquestionably a justifiable critical indictment of the child welfare system's ability to protect these individual children.

Working with parents with addiction problems undoubtedly represents one of the major challenges facing practitioners (Kroll and Taylor 2003; Scottish Executive 2003). The inquiry report into the death of Caleb Ness (O'Brien 2003) highlighted the challenge of protecting children of parents where there is a history of one or both having significant addiction problems. This report also illustrated the particular tensions involved in working within a practice framework that attempts to balance the conflicting needs and rights of parents and of children.

We also need to recognize that some child deaths may not be preventable nor will risk indicators be present. The report into the death of Carla Nicole Bone (Black and Burgham 2003) did not highlight any professional issues or inter-agency deficiencies that contributed to that particular child's death, yet the media coverage was still couched in fairly negative and critical terms.

Inquiry reports have served an important role in highlighting policy, procedural and operational deficiencies in practice (Hill 2003; Lawrence 2004). The lessons for staff in different professions concerned with the welfare of children are often salutary. However, without wishing to appear complacent or dismissive of inquiry reports, they have to be read and absorbed within the wider context of the overall system. While there is no counter-argument to the fact that we must closely monitor, review and strive to improve child protection services, we must also avoid being hypercritical in our evaluation of child protection intervention. For example, although critical of a number of aspects of the operation of the child protection system, the Department of Health's *Child Protection: Messages from Research* (1995) did cite low rates of re-abuse for children who came to the attention of the child protection services as a positive indicator of the system's ability to protect children. The findings indicated that although some aspects of the system were flawed it was nonetheless managing to protect the vast majority of children within its jurisdiction, yet the focus of discussion was on the more critical comments about the system. More recently, *Safeguarding Children* (2005), the second Joint Chief Inspectors' Report highlighted that overall the child protection system was responding appropriately to the needs of the children it served.

Physical neglect is another form of child maltreatment that is central to current practice. The number of children placed on the Child Protection Register within this category had increased during the 1990s (Department of Education and Skills 2003b; Department of Health 1998b). One possible explanation for this rise may well be linked to the increased focus and concern about the impact of parental drug usage and addiction on children.

Emotional abuse is notoriously difficult to determine. It is also potentially very long lasting in terms of the possible effects on children (Iwaniec 1996). There is evidence to show that there has been increased use of this category by Child Protection Case Conferences in placing children's names on the Child Protection Register (Department of Education and Skills 2003b; Department of Health 1998b). This may be indicative of greater recognition of emotional abuse and its effects as well as an increased willingness and confidence on the part of child welfare professionals to make use of this category. Alternatively it might illustrate the dominance of a procedurally orientated child protection agenda in practice and a tendency to locate family dysfunction within a child protection framework.

Since the mid-1980s, working with sexual abuse and related issues has proved to be an extremely emotive and controversial aspect of social work. The relatively sudden emergence of sexual abuse as an issue in the 1980s resulted in not only public shock and disbelief but also in the recognition of sexual exploitation as a major danger for children in society. It also led to increased media interest, culminating in 16.5 million viewers watching the BBC's *Childwatch* programme on 30 October 1986 (La Fontaine 1990).

Events in Cleveland in the summer of 1987 and the resultant inquiry report (Butler-Sloss 1988) were highly significant in determining attitudes, policy and legislation in relation to sexual abuse. Criticism was directed at social workers for being authoritarian and acting prematurely without sufficient evidence. This was in contrast to much of the previous criticism levelled at the social work profession for not taking decisive action and allowing children to remain in dangerous situations (Fox Harding 1997). The aftermath of Cleveland led to the realization that a greater political response was required in response to the public concerns about child protection issues (Lawrence 2004). The government response was to commission major research into the operation of the child protection system in England and Wales (Department of Health 1995). In addition the inquiry report findings (Butler-Sloss 1988) also greatly influenced the emergency child protection provisions of the 1989 Children Act.

Within child protection practice there were important developments in terms of understanding and working with the effects and trauma experienced by children who disclosed sexual abuse (Bagley and King 1990; Faller 1989). The therapeutic dimension of practice, however, was overshadowed by the procedural and legalistic framework (Lawrence 2004; Pinkerton 2002). The Department of Health (1995) research demonstrated that the child protection system was 'front loaded' in that a disproportionate amount of time and energy was spent on the investigative and case management side of intervention and too little was spent on supporting children and families. At the same time a major challenge for practitioners was acquiring new knowledge and skills to work with different dimensions of sexual abuse following its rediscovery in the late 1980s.

The child protection agenda has continued to evolve and grow in complexity as new thresholds have been crossed in our understanding of the extent to which adults will exploit and abuse children. An illustration of this that struck at the very heart and soul of the social work profession was the unearthing and subsequent revelations about various forms of abuse in residential child care (Leicestershire County Council 1993; Staffordshire County Council 1991; Waterhouse, Clough and le Fleming 2000). More recently, attention has been drawn to the extent of the use of child pornography and dangers of the internet as resources in the exploitation of children for adult gratification.

## SEX OFFENDERS

The management and treatment of sex offenders is primarily the responsibility of the police, the probation service and the criminal justice social work services. There is a major challenge in balancing the human rights and civil liberties of accused persons and offenders with the wider protection of children (Calder 1999). The passing of the Sex Offenders Act 1997 and the subsequent introduction of the sex offenders' register was arguably the first concerted attempt to respond to the controversial and multifaceted challenge of protecting children and endeavouring to manage sex offenders within the community. In contrast, the Human Rights Act 1998 seeks to protect individuals from actions that are discriminatory and against basic human rights. In applying restrictive measures on offenders, courts, agencies and practitioners have to be mindful of the wider issue of human rights. The UK criteria for registration were further strengthened by the provisions within the Sexual Offences Act 2003 as concern about the supervision and monitoring of sex offenders grew following a number of high-profile sexually motivated attacks on children.

A major issue surrounding the sex offenders register is the question of who should get access to it. There are two schools of thought. One takes the stance that we should deploy or at least develop the idea imported from the US of 'Megan's Law', whereby under the umbrella of freedom of information and the public's right to know, the names of the sex offenders are accessible, so that parents are aware if a known paedophile is living in their area and can take appropriate precautions to protect their own children. The opposite view represents the situation we have adopted currently within the UK: that only designated professionals from key child protection and criminal justice agencies should have access to the register. This is a highly emotive and contentious issue that is likely to remain a central issue and source of debate for the foreseeable future.

The challenge of effectively monitoring people who are considered to pose a risk to children has evolved a further level of complexity in terms of protecting children from abuse within education or care settings. The Protection of Children Act 1999 created a register of people considered unsuitable to work with children. People are placed on this register if they have been convicted or have received a caution for an offence against a child. The management of the registration of people considered to be unsuitable to work with children and placed on List 99 became increasingly complex and controversial. The Soham murders generated widespread media coverage and in turn captured the emotions of the general public, probably helping develop a stronger societal sense of collective responsibility about the need to introduce robust measures to protect our children. The resultant Bichard Inquiry (2003) not only highlighted a number of specific errors in the vetting of the Soham killer to work with children but cast doubts about the wider operational deficiencies with List 99. To date the operation of List 99 remains a highly charged and topical issue.

The failure of the criminal justice system in administering effective justice to children and child witnesses has been identified for some time (Plotnikoff and Woolfson 1995; Utting 1997). Plotnikov and Woolfson cited the considerable time gaps between disclosure of abuse, the case coming to trial and the eventual successful prosecution of the alleged offender. Spencer and Flin (1993) and more recently Stuart and Baines (2004) have highlighted the serious disservice the criminal justice system inflicts on children who are victims of abuse. Stuart and Baines cite Home Office figures which show that convictions for gross indecency towards children fell from 42 per cent in 1985 to 19 per cent in 2001. This was despite the fact the level of recorded offences of gross indecency against children more than doubled in the same period. These figures show no difference to the findings of Utting (1997).

Criminal proceedings are notoriously lengthy and complicated and need to ensure that alleged offenders are processed within a system that is fair and has the confidence of the wider society. Despite an array of procedural changes within the child protection investigation system aimed at easing the plight of child witnesses, such as children giving evidence in chief and the videotaping of interviews, it remains insufficiently child centred (Spencer and Flin 1993; Stuart and Baines 2004). The second Joint Chief Inspectors' Report *Safeguarding Children* (2005) highlighted a number of initiatives aimed at safeguarding children in criminal proceedings but also reported that overall the criminal justice system only offered 'partial' safeguards when dealing with children and that further work was required. Perhaps we have to consider the possibility that the traditional adversarial approach of the criminal justice system is not suited to the needs of children. There may also be a more general children's rights issue about how adults perceive children and how we have traditionally exercised power and control over them. Willow *et al.* (2004) have highlighted the tensions between viewing children as welfare dependants in need of support, care and protection, and viewing them as young citizens with the potential to play actively, participate in society and influence policies which impact on children; they also argue that we are only just beginning to embrace the latter position. A telling illustration of this differential is the contrast between the state's readiness and willingness to introduce fast-track initiatives to deal with children who are deemed to be serial offenders and the failure to introduce a similar fast-track process within the criminal justice system where children are victims of child abuse related crimes.

Advances in technology also pose a considerable challenge in the protection of children from sexual exploitation. The accessing of child pornography via the internet and the use of chat rooms in order to groom potential victims is a major issue. Parents and children have had to be educated in the potential dangers of the internet from a child protection perspective. The proposed creation of the Home Office administered Centre for Child Protection on the internet to replace the National Crime Squad's Hi-technology Crime Unit demonstrates the perceived scale of the problem. There is also a challenge to the criminal justice and legal system in terms of reframing and redefining sex offences against children, as evidenced by the conviction and imprisonment of a paedophile at Alloa Sheriff Court in January 2005 for sexual offences against a child he was in the process of grooming via a chat room but never actually met (Howarth 2005).

## Developments in child care practice

Although the strong focus on the child protection agenda since the late 1980s is entirely justified, some concern has been expressed about the dominance of child protection issues to the exclusion of the wider discussion of the needs of children and social work that is directed at supporting children and families (Department of Health 1995; Parton 1991). The result has been a change of emphasis in terms of trying to locate child protection practice within a more integrated continuum of services that are more holistic and directed at children's needs. This position was reflected in the publication in 2000 of the Department of Health's *Framework for the Assessment of Children in Need* (Colton, Sanders and Williams 2001).

Notwithstanding the child protection agenda, the child welfare system has reflected societal changes and has become increasingly complex. Historically there has been continued evidenced-based concerns about the role and effectiveness of the child care system (Department of Health and Social Security 1985, 1991; Rowe and Lambert 1973).

There have been a number of legislative changes and policy initiatives to try to improve the care experiences of looked-after children. The main thrust in the attempt to improve care planning, recording and decision-making came in the form of the looked-after children materials introduced by the Department of Health in 1995, which are being used by 90 per cent of local authorities in England and the majority of authorities in Wales and Northern Ireland (Colton *et al.* 2001). In Scotland the materials are being used by 85 per cent of local authorities (Scottish Executive/Social Work Services Inspectorate 2004). As the child welfare system has evolved in the complexity of issues it seeks to address there have been major policy and practice implications in key areas of service provision such as foster care, residential child care, adoption and through care provision.

## THE ASSESSMENT FRAMEWORK AND THE ASSESSMENT OF CHILDREN IN NEED

Informed and skilled assessment is central to social work in all areas of practice (see Chapters 7–10 in the present volume). In recognition of this a wide range of procedural guidance has been published in order to standardize and de-mystify what goes on during the assessment process (Department of Health 1988, 1991, 2000). Practitioners, however, need to recognize that these assessment guidelines are only really of value when used in conjunction with a sound theoretical knowledge base and sufficiently developed professional assessment skills.

Howarth (2004) has noted that historically the main focus of social work was directed at children deemed to be at risk of 'significant harm' and that other aspects of child care work were overlooked. As previously discussed it could be argued that professional concerns about child protection, while completely understandable, did, to an extent, hijack social work practice with children and families. The *Framework for the Assessment of Children in Need and their Families* was published by the Department of Health (2000) in an attempt to facilitate a change in practice towards a more holistic assessment of children and need. The framework presents assessment as a three-dimensional interaction between:

- the child's developmental needs

- parenting capacity

- family and environmental factors.

The assessment framework has been operational for five years at the time of writing and forms the basis of assessment work within child care practice. Howarth (2004) provided a comprehensive analysis of how the framework can be best unitised and the degree of professional sophistication required in effectively integrating knowledge and skills.

## LOOKED-AFTER CHILDREN

The national statistics of the Department of Education and Skills (2005) indicate that there were 61,100 children and young people 'looked after' in England with just under 64 per cent (39,400) subject to Care Orders. There was a 19 per cent increase in the number of looked-after children in England between 1994 and 2004. During the same period the number of voluntary placements under section 20 of the Children Act 1989 remained constant. There was also a minor increase in the number of young people subject to detention under youth crime provision. The biggest development, a 30 per cent increase in the use of Care Orders between 1994 and 2004 (Department of Education and Skills 2005), raises some questions and may suggest a shift in the threshold of the application of legislation as a means of social control in family life. The Department of Health (1996) and Harris (1997) noted the tendency towards more procedurally defined and legalistic intervention to the detriment of more supportive and therapeutic work with children and families.

Between 2000 and 2004 the number of children on the Child Protection Register who are also looked after fell from 23 per cent of registration to 13 per cent as at 31 March 2004 (Department of Education and Skills 2005). Creighton (2003), however, highlighted the correlation between 'looked after children' and child protection, citing the fact that 62 per cent of the children and young people 'looked after' at 31 March 2003 were as a result of child protection concerns.

The introduction of the looked-after children materials was in response to research and increasingly concerned views about the inadequacy of social work records for children within the care system. There was also an expectation that the operational use of the materials would facilitate greater partnership between local authorities and parents, carers and children. Research into the effectiveness of the materials has been inconclusive in determining if better records are being maintained or, more importantly, if the materials have facilitated a greater sense of participation and involvement among children and young people (Garret 1999; Jackson 1998; Wheelaghan et al. 1999). Another criticism in practice is the interface and duplication of information collated within the looked-after children materials and the assessment framework (Ward 2001). Thomas (2005) cites the decision to incorporate the tried and tested elements of both assessment systems within the new 'integrated children's systems' as significant in developing comprehensive and meaningful welfare provision to children and families.

## FOSTER CARE

Triseliotis, Shireman and Hundleby (2000) maintain that there is a traditional public perception of fostering and foster carers that is at odds with the demands and reality of the task. Foster care is the cornerstone of resource provision for looked-after children. The type of placements required is diverse, ranging from emergency placements, temporary fostering, respite care, specialist teenage fostering schemes and medium to more permanent provision (Sellick and Howell 2003).

The role of foster carer requires the ability to multi-task in the extreme. The ability to communicate with children, sound observational skills, emotional warmth and resilience and the capacity to work within an inter-professional framework are essential requirements. Working inclusively and in partnership with natural parents is particularly demanding (Triseliotis, Borland and Hill 2000). In addition the stress and demands of providing care to children who have been abused took some time to register with many agencies and practitioners (Macaskill 1989).

In our multiracial society the placement of children from ethnic minority backgrounds is a particularly controversial aspect of practice (Berridge 2001). There are a disproportionate number of children from ethnic minorities living away from home and an acute shortage of carers from different ethnic groups.

The increased demands and nature of fostering has inevitably led to a recruitment and retention crisis with local authority foster carers. The demands on resources often mean that there is restricted movement, with short-term placements invariably ending up longer than intended thus creating a shortage of resources at admission (Sellick and Howell 2003). In response the voluntary sector and not-for-profit organizations such as Barnardo's and Foster Care Associates have developed high-quality specialist family placement projects.

## RESIDENTIAL CARE

The provision of good quality residential care has been a major challenge over the years (see also Chapter 17 in the present volume). Since the 1970s residential care has changed dramatically, with a move from large institutional provision to smaller units. Historically residential care has been devalued and come under attack because of trends in practice, as evidenced by some local authorities who decided to close down all residential child care provision in their area (Kearney 1992; Thomas 2005).

The image of residential care provision has also suffered as a result of the number and nature of high-profile cases of abuse within care settings (Utting 1991, 1997; Waterhouse et al. 2000). Retrospectively the discovery that a significant number of children in residential care had been subjected to maltreatment was perhaps additionally difficult to comprehend. No apology or increased vigour in the selection of staff can be enough for children who were removed from home because of their own vulnerability and subsequently subjected to abuse and exploitation from the very people society had entrusted to provide safe care.

Despite this major indictment residential care has also continued to offer positive realistic needs-led options for many young people (Department of Health 1998; Utting 1991). It is at best naïve and at worst negligent to gear practice resources for children looked-after away from home, exclusively towards family placement. Children's needs are complex and diverse and for some these will be best met via good quality residential care provision (Berridge 2001; Thomas 2005).

## ADOPTION

Legislation, policy and practice have continually evolved to respond to the complex contextual framework of adoption practice. Since the Second World War there has been a decline in the number of babies placed for adoption. There is less stigma in society about illegitimacy/single parenthood and young women, in situations of unplanned pregnancy, exercising choice in deciding to keep their babies. Despite medical advances such as IVF, there were and still are many couples who experience fertility problems and for whom adoption provides the only viable way of having a family (Tirseliotis et al. 1997).

The late 1970s saw adoption and permanency planning become a keystone of practice in many local authorities and in some voluntary child care organizations. Specialist Family Placement Teams or Homefinding Teams were established in many authorities along with Family Placement Projects in the voluntary sector (Parton 1991; Thomas 2005). The slogan 'no child is unadoptable' became the vanguard of adoption practice. Exponents of the approach argued that it was child centred and allowed many children the opportunity of security and stability within a family environment. Opponents argued that the approach was unnecessarily confrontational, against natural justice and shifted the emphasis of practice from the essence of the child welfare system of supporting families in the community (Parton 1991).

The question of mixed-race adoption placements has become increasingly significant. Triseliotis *et al.* (1997) highlight three perspectives on mixed-race placements:

*   *the pragmatist view,* which argues that, given the limited resources, if a placement meets a child's needs, then differences in ethnic background between carers and child should not hold back the placement

*   *the integrationalist view,* which states that children can be placed with parents from a different ethnic origin provided there is clarity about issues of ethnicity and the child's ethnic identity is not compromised

*   *the separatist view,* which argues that placing children in families of different ethnic origins is indicative of structural racism.

There is greater understanding in social work practice of ethnicity and the importance of racial identity in family placement work. Nonetheless the recruitment of adopters from different ethnic groups remains a major deficiency in practice.

For many couples, adopting a child from overseas became an attractive alternative option to the stress of continued medical treatment or engaging in the uncertainty of the assessment process of legally approved adoption agencies. Overseas adoption is a value laden and emotive subject with very polarized perspectives. One view is that by adopting a child from a country in chaos the adoptive parents are rescuing that child from a life of potential strife and trauma as well as meeting their own needs to be parents. The converse view is that rather than removing individual children from their home environment we should be providing aid and assistance to help improve their living conditions and life experience in their own country (Triseliotis *et al.* 1997).

The resurrection and re-branding of permanency planning is a major force in adoption practice. This refocusing on permanency has its roots in government and the Quality Projects initiative. The UK government set a target of achieving a 40 per cent rate of adoption of children from the looked-after population (Rushton 2003) and the introduction and increased use of concurrent planning is also a potentially significant practice development.

## THROUGH-CARE PROVISION

This is a relatively new arena of social work practice. The 1988 Social Security Act removed the provision of automatic Supplementary Benefit payments to young people between 16 and 18 years of age (Thomas 2005). The result was that local authority social service departments were forced to examine the level of financial support they could provide to young people leaving the care system. Although some good practice initiatives existed which tried to ensure that attention was paid by agencies to the development of supportive leaving care packages, the overall level of provision and commitment of resources was piecemeal. This was the background of specific legislative provisions within the Children (Scotland) Act 1995 and the Leaving Care Act 2002.

Despite this positive shift in recognizing the need for comprehensive through-care provision, there are a number of challenges for practitioners (Social Services Inspectorate

1997; Utting 1997). The work of agencies such as the Social Exclusion Unit (1998) has focused attention on the difficulties facing many young people leaving care. Despite the provisions within the Leaving Care Act 2000 there still remains a disconcerting correlation between young homeless people and previous involvement in the care system (Fawcett, Featherstone and Goddard 2004).

## YOUTH JUSTICE

Youth crime is prominent within the wider political agenda and consequently youth justice is a very significant area of current social work practice. Historically there has been a significant difference between Scotland and the rest of the UK in tackling this social problem (Goldson 2004). Since 1971 Scotland has been served by the Children's Hearings system, which is underpinned by a philosophy of a welfare approach and does not seek to differentiate between the needs and deeds of children (Norrie 2002)

Historically the welfare approach to youth justice was not exclusive to Scotland and underpinned the philosophy of the 1969 Children and Young Persons Act. Goldson (2004) argues that the resources were never fully deployed to develop the system and the approach subsequently failed. The result was a complete change of emphasis towards a justice model approach to youth crime

Hill and Tisdall (1997) provide a comprehensive account of different models of approach to youth justice.

1.  *The welfare approach* – views the welfare of the child as the prime consideration and argues that the causes of delinquent behaviour and child abuse and neglect are the same: therefore little distinction should made between children who offend and those in need of care and protection. If the causes of delinquency can be identified, policies can be directed to reducing levels of delinquent behaviour. The approach encourages the use discretionary power by decision-makers and children who commit similar offences may not necessarily be treated the same.

2.  *The justice approach* – considers individuals to be responsible for their own action and delinquent behaviour as a matter of free will and individual choice. The criminal justice system should be concerned primarily with the nature of the offence and distributing proportionate responses to specific offences. Sentencing should be fixed and people convicted of the same offence should be treated equally.

3.  *The restorative approach* – views crime as an act against another person or the community and recognizes that responsibility for crime involves a social and individual dimension. The approach emphasizes restitution of wrongs and losses such as physical harm, property loss and mental trauma to the mutual benefit and interest of the community, the victim and ultimately the offender.

Youth justice is a contentious and controversial issue in society and is likely to command a central location within the political agenda for some years. Between 1998 and 2003 there were four major pieces of legislation passed about youth in England and Wales: the Crime and Disorder Act 1998, the Youth Justice and Criminal Evidence Act 1998, the Criminal Justice Act 2003 and the Anti-social Behaviour Act 2003. In addition to setting up Youth Offending Teams to work with young people who offend and develop preventative strategies, the Crime and Disorder Act 1998 established the Youth Justice Board to oversee the operation of the youth justice system.

Fawcett *et al.* (2004) have suggested that a welfare approach is not automatically compatible with the concept of children's rights: 'at first sight it might seem that a more legalistic, authoritarian approach to youth justice is the most antithetical to children's rights' (p.106). They go on to stress a problematic consequence of welfare approaches: 'By drawing in potential offenders and minor offenders to the child welfare system they often assumed a supervisory function for the state on sometimes dubious grounds. (p.106).

In Scotland there are concerns that the welfare approach to youth offenders of the Children's Hearing system is under threat (NCH Scotland 2004; McGhee, Mellon and Whyte 2004). In an attempt to meet the needs of young offenders a number of projects based on a restorative justice approach were established in the late 1990s (Scottish Executive 2002b). Increasingly the political agenda on youth crime has driven recent policy and practice initiatives (Scottish Executive 2002a) such as fast-track court proceedings for youth crime and the introduction of a range of provisions within the Anti-social Behaviour (Scotland) Act 2004.

## Conclusion

This chapter has endeavoured to highlight the range of activity that constitutes child care social work practice. It has also sought to illustrate the often competing and conflicting demands faced by policy-makers and practitioners given the complexities of family life in the twenty-first century. The account is not exhaustive and could have additionally focused on a range of other child care topics such as:

- children and young people as carers

- education and welfare issues

- children and health care issues

- children with disabilities

- the mental health of children and young people

- issues of race and ethnicity

- the particular challenges for young asylum seekers.

The historical dilemmas in child care work such as care and control, compulsion and collaboration, voluntary support and statutory intervention, and prevention and protection have evolved and remained at the core of social work with children and families. Policy, practice and legislation may have developed in response to societal needs and demands and had been informed by research, but the issues on the agenda of the child welfare system are now increasingly complicated. This is not helped by the perpetual recruitment and retention problems particularly faced by local authorities in this area of practice, nor by the fact that possibly the most challenging, confrontational and emotionally draining area of practice is often carried out by the least experienced and newest recruits to the profession.

While certain sectors within the child care system function under pressure in what can feel a state of perpetual crisis, as we have seen there have been numerous positive and often underplayed developments in policy and practice over the years.

## References

Bagley, C. and King, K. (1990) *Child Sexual Abuse: The Search for Healing.* London: Routledge.

Berridge, D. (2001) 'Foster Families.' In P. Foley, J. Roche J and S Tucker (eds) *Children in Society: Contemporary Theory, Policy and Practice.* Milton Keynes: Palgrave.

Bichard, Sir M. (2003) *The Bichard Inquiry Report.* London: Home Office. Available at www.bichard inquiry.org.uk/report.

Black, N. and Burgham, A. (2003) *Report into the Life and Death of Carla Nicole Bone.* Aberdeen: North East Scotland Area Child Protection Committee.

Bradshaw, J. (2003) 'Poor Children.' *Children and Society Special Issue 17, 3, 173–84.*

Brewer, M., Goodman, A., Shaw, J. and Shepherd, A. (2005) *Poverty and Inequality in Britain: 2005.* London: Institute of Fiscal Studies. Available at www.ifs.org.uk/publications.php?publication_ id=3328.

British Association of Social Workers (2007) *Code of Ethics.* Birmingham: BASW. Available at www.basw.co.uk/Default.aspx?tabid=64

Butler-Sloss, E. (1988) *Report of the Inquiry into Child Abuse in Cleveland 1987.* London: HMSO.

Calder, M.C. (1999) *Assessing Risk in Adult Males who Sexually Abuse Children.* Bath: Russell House Publications.

Colton, M., Sanders, R., and Williams, M. (2001) *An Introduction to Working with Children: A Guide for Social Workers.* London: Palgrave.

Corby, B. (2002) *Child Protection: Towards a Knowledge Base.* Milton Keynes: Open University Press.

Creighton, S. J. (2003) *Child Protection Statistics: Child Protection Outside the Home.* London: NSPCC. http://www.nspcc.org.uk/Inform/Online Resources/Statistics/CPStats/3Outside-pdf-gf25476.pdf

Daniel, P. and Ivatts, J. (1998) *Children and Social Policy.* Basingstoke and London: Macmillan.

Department for Education and Skills (2004) *Annual Statistical Report.* at http://www.dfes.gov.uk/rsgateway/ DB/vol/v000444/index.shtml

Department for Education and Skills (2005) *Children looked after in England (including adoption and care leavers: 2004–2005.* London: HMSO. Available at http://www.dfes.gov.uk/rsgateway/DB/SFR/5000615/index.shtml

Department of Health (1988) *Protecting Children: A Comprehensive Guide for Social Workers Undertaking a Comprehensive Assessment* London: HMSO.

Department of Health (1991) *Placement Outcomes in Child Placement: Messages from Current Research and their Implications.* London: HMSO.

Department of Health (1995) *Child Protection: Messages from Research.* London: HMSO.

Department of Health (1995) *Child Protection: Messages from Research.* London: HMSO.

Department of Health (1998a) *Caring for Children Away from Home – Messages from Research.* London: HMSO.

Department of Health (1998b) *Children on Child Protection Registers as at 31st March 1998.* London: HMSO.

Department of Health (2000) *The Framework for the Assessment of Children in Need and their Families.* London: HMSO.

Department of Health and Social Security (1985) *Social Work Decisions in Child Care: Research Findings and Their Implications.* London: HMSO.

Department of Education and Skills (2003b) *Referrals, Assessment and Children and Young People on the Child Protection Register in the Year ending 31st March 2003.* London: HMSO. Available at www.dfes.gov.uk/rsgateway/DB/VOL/v000444/index.shtml.

Department of Work and Pensions (2005) *Households Below Average Income.* London: HMSO.

DHSS (1974) *Report of the Inquiry into the Death of Maria Colwell.* London: HMSO.

Durrant, J.E. (1999) 'Evaluation of the Swedish corporal punishment ban.' *International Journal of Child Abuse and Neglect 23*, 435–48.

Fawcett, B., Featherstone, B. and Goddard, J. (2004) *Contemporary Child Care Policy and Practice*. London: Palgrave-Macmillan.

Faller, K. (1989) *Child Sexual Abuse: An Interdisciplinary Manual for the Diagnosis, Case Management, and Treatment*. London: Macmillan.

Fisher, M., Marsh, P. and Phillips, D. with Sainsbury, E. 'Rethinking child care policy.' In S. Morgan and P. Righton (eds) *Child Care: Concerns and Conflicts*. London: Hodder & Stoughton.

Fox Harding, L. (1997) *Perspectives in Child Care Policy*. 2nd edn, London and New York: Longman.

Garret, E.M. (1999) 'Mapping child-care social work in the final years of the 20th century: A critical response to the Looked After Children system.' *British Journal of Social Work 29*, 1, 27–47.

Goldson, B. (2004) 'Differential justice? A critical introduction to youth justice policy in UK jurisdiction.' In J. McGhee, M. Mellon and B. Whyte (eds) *Meeting Needs, Addressing Deeds – Working with Young People who Offend*. Glasgow: NCH Scotland.

Hanks, H. and Stratton, P. (1997) 'The effects of child abuse: Signs and symptoms.' In K. Wilson and A. James (eds) *The Child Protection Handbook*. London: Baillière-Tindall.

Harris, R. (1997) 'Child protection, child care and child welfare.' In K. Wilson and A. James (eds) *The Child Protection Handbook*. London: Baillière-Tindall.

Hill, M. (2003) 'Issues in social policy: Children.' In P. Alcock, A. Erskine and M. May (eds) *The Student's Companion to Social Policy*. 7th edn. Oxford: Blackwell.

Hill, M. and Tisdall, K. (1997) *Children and Society*. Harlow: Prentice Hall.

Horner, N. (2003) *What is Social Work: Contexts and Perspectives*. Exeter: Learning Matters.

Horwarth, J. (2004) *The Child's Needs: Assessing Children in Need*. London: Jessica Kingsley Publishers.

Howarth, A. (2005) 'Outrage over two year term for man who had "cybersex" with girl.' *The Scotsman*, 26 January.

Institute for Fiscal Studies (2005) 'Government misses child poverty targets.' Press release 9 March 2005. Available at www.ifs.org.uk

Iwaniec, D. (1996) *The Emotionally Abused and Neglected Child: Identification, Assessment and Intervention*. Chichester: Wiley.

The Joint Chief Inspectors (2005) *Safeguarding Children: The Joint Chief Inspectors' Report on Arrangements to Safeguard Children*. Newcastle: Commission for Social Care Inspection. Available at www.safeguardingchildren.org.uk/docs/safeguards_fullprint.pdf.

Kearney, B. (1992) *The Report of the Inquiry in Child Care Policies in Fife*. London: HMSO.

Kroll, B. and Taylor, A. (2003) *Parental Substance Misuse and Child Welfare*. London: Jessica Kingsley Publishers.

La Fontaine, J. (1990) *Child Sexual Abuse*. Cambridge: Polity Press.

Laming, Lord Justice H. (2003) *The Victoria Climbié Inquiry Report*. Cm5730. London: The Stationery Office.

Lawrence, A. (2004) *Principles of Child Protection: Management and Practice*. Maidenhead: OUP/McGraw-Hill Education.

Leicestershire County Council (1993) *The Leicestershire Inquiry*. Leicester: Leicestershire County Council.

Macaskill, M. (1989) *Fostering the Sexually Abused Child*. London: BAAF.

McGhee, J., Mellon, M. and Whyte, B. (2004) *Meeting Needs Addressing Deeds: Working with Young People Who Offend*. Glasgow: NCH.

Miller, J. (2003) 'Social policy and family policy.' In P. Alcock, A. Erskine and M. May (eds) *The Student's Companion to Social Policy*. 2nd edn. Oxford: Blackwell.

NCH Scotland (2004) *Where's Kilbrandon Now: Report and Recommendations from the Inquiry*. Glasgow: NCH Action for Children.

Norrie K. McK. (2002) *Children's Hearings in Scotland*. 2nd edn. W.Green/Edinburgh: Sweet and Maxwell.

Parton, N. (1991) *Governing the Family: Child Care, Child Protection and the State*. Basingstoke: Macmillan.

Pinkerton, J. (2001) 'Developing partnership practice.' In P. Foley, J. Roche and S. Tucker (eds) *Children in Society: Contemporary Theory, Policy and Practice.* Milton Keynes: OUP/Palgrave.

Pinkerton, J. (2002) 'Child Protection.' In R. Adams, L. Dominelli and M. Payne (eds) *Critical Practice in Social Work* Basingstoke: Palgrave.

Plotnikoff, J. and Woolfson, R. (1995) *Prosecuting Child Abuse: An Evaluation of the Government's Speedy Progress Policy.* London: Blackstone Press Limited.

Pritchard, C. (2000) *The Child Abusers: Research and Controversy.* Milton Keynes: Open University Press.

O'Brien, S. (2003) *Report of the Caleb Ness Enquiry.* Edinburgh: Edinburgh and the Lothians Child Protection Committee.

Rowe, J. and Lambert, L. (1973) *Children who Wait.* London: BAAF.

Rushton, A. (2003) *The Adoption of Looked After Children: A Scoping Review of Research.* London: SCIE. Available at: www.scie.org.uk/publications/knowledgereviews/kr02.pdf

Ruxton, S. (1996) *Children in Europe.* London: NCH Action for Children.

Save the Children Fund (2005) *The Well Being of Children in Wales.* London: Save the Children: Available at: http://www.savethechildren.org.uk/scuk/jsp/resources/details.jsp?id=2662&group= resources&section=publication&subsection=details

Scottish Executive (2002a) *Scotland's Action Programme to Reduce Youth Crime.* Edinburgh: Scottish Executive.

Scottish Executive (2002b) *Youth Justice in Scotland – A Progress Report for all those Working for Young People.* Edinburgh: Scottish Executive.

Scottish Executive (2003) *Getting Our Priorities Right: Good Practice Guidance for Working with Children and Families Affected by Substance Misuse.* Edinburgh: Scottish Executive. Available at: www.scotland.gov.uk/library5/education/gopr-00.asp

Scottish Executive (2003) *Scotland's Action Programme to Reduce Youth Crime.* Edinburgh: Scottish Executive. Available at www.scotland.gov.uk/library3/justice/sapt-00.asp

Scottish Executive (2003) *Children, Physical Punishment and the Law: A Guide for Parents in Scotland.* Edinburgh: Scottish Executive. Available at: www.scotland.gov.uk/library5/justice/cppl-00.asp

Scottish Executive (2003) *Putting Our Communities First.* Edinburgh: Scottish Executive. Available at: www.scotland.gov.uk/consultations/social/pocf-00.asp

Scottish Executive/Social work Services Inspectorate (2004) *Looked After Children in Scotland: Good Parenting – Good Outcomes – Report on the File Audit of Local Authorities' Use of the Looked After Children Materials.* Edinburgh: Scottish Executive.

Scottish Executive (2005) *Getting it Right for Every Child: Proposals For Action.* London: HMSO. Available at: www.scotland.gov.uk/Publications/2005/06/20135608/56098

Sellick, C. and Howell, D. (2003) *Innovative, Tried and Tested: A Scooping Review of Good Practice in Fostering.* London: SCIE. Available at: www.scie.org.uk/publications/knowledgereviews/kr04.pdf

Social Exclusion Unit (1998) *Rough Sleeping.* Cm4008. London: The Stationery Office.

Social Services Inspectorate (1997) *When Leaving Home is also Leaving Care: An Inspection of Services for Young People Leaving Care.* London: The Stationery Office.

Social Services Inspectorate, Commission for Health Improvement, HM Inspectorate of Constabulary, HM Crown Prosecution Inspectorate, HM Magistrates' Courts Inspectorate, Ofsted, HM Inspectorate of Prisons, HM Inspectorate of Probation (2004) *Safeguarding Children: The Second Joint Chief Inspectors' Report on Arrangements to Safeguard Children.* Newcastle: Commission for Social Care Inspection.

Spencer, J. and Flin, R. (1993) *The Evidence of Children.* London: Blackstone Press.

Staffordshire County Council (1991) *The Pindown Experience and the Protection of Children: The Report of Staffordshire Child Inquiry 1990.* Stafford: Staffordshire County Council.

Stuart, M. and Baines, C. (2004) *Progress on Safeguards for Children Living Away From Home: A Review of Action since the People Like Us Report.* York: Joseph Rowntree Foundation. Available at: www.jrf.org.uk/bookshop/eBooks/1859352561.pdf

Sutherland, H., Sefton, T. and Piachaud, D. (2005) *Poverty in Britain: The Impact of Government Policy since 1997.* York: the Joseph Rowntree Foundation. http://www.savethechildren.org.uk/scuk/jsp/resources/details.jsp?id=2697&group=resources&section=news&fromgroup=news&newssection=newslibrary&subsection=details&pagelang

Thomas, N. (2005) *Social Work with Young People in Care.* Basingstoke: Palgrave.

Tisdall, E. K. (1997) *The Children (Scotland) Act 1995: Developing Policy and Law for Scotland's Children.* The Stationery Office – Edinburgh.

Triseliotis, J., Borland, M. and Hill, M. (2000) *Delivering Foster Care.* London: British Association of Fostering and Adoption.

Triseliotis, J., Shireman, J. and Hundleby, M. (1997) *Adoption: Theory, Policy and Practice.* London: Cassell.

Utting, Sir W. (1991) *Children in Public Care.* London: HMSO.

Utting, Sir W. (1997) *People Like Us: The Report of the Review of the Safeguards for Children Living Away from Home.* London: The Stationery Office.

Walker C. and Walker A. (1998) 'Social policy and social work.' In R. Adams, L. Dominelli and M. Payne (eds) *Social Work: Themes, Issues and Critical Debates.* London: Macmillan.

Ward, H. (2001) 'The developmental needs of children: Implications for assessment.' In J. Horwath (ed.) *The Child's World: Assessing Children in Need.* London: Jessica Kingsley Publishers.

Waterhouse, R., Clough, M. and le Fleming M. (2000) *Lost in Care: Report of the Tribunal of Inquiry into the Abuse of Children in Care in Former County Council Areas of Gwynedd and Clwyd since 1974.* London: Department of Health.

Wheelaghan, S., Hill, M., Borland, M., Lambert, L. and Triseliotis, J. (1999) *Looked After Children in Scotland.* Social Work Research Findings No. 30. Edinburgh: Scottish Executive.

Willow, C., Merchant R., Kirby, P. and Neale, B. (2004) *Young Children's Citizenship: Ideas into Practice.* York: Joseph Rowntree Trust. Available at: www.jrf.org.uk/bookshop/eBooks/1859352243.pdf

## CHAPTER 21

# INTERDISCIPLINARY PRACTICE

*Terry McLean*

## Introduction

Increasingly, government expects services to be delivered to the general public in an integrated manner. This chapter will explore the implications of this policy for the various agencies and professions involved. Consideration will be given to the factors which facilitate and hinder interdisciplinary practice. The impact of professionalism on interdisciplinary practice will be evaluated along with an examination of interdisciplinary team process issues. Particular emphasis will be given to consideration of the difficult issues of authority and leadership within interdisciplinary teams.

Although it is not intended to provide a review of published research regarding the effectiveness of interdisciplinary practice, some reference will be made to research findings. Common problems associated with interdisciplinary practice will be identified and possible solutions considered. The later part of the chapter will focus on interprofessional education, which is receiving increased attention within universities, where interdisciplinary practice skills and concepts are being taught to groups of students belonging to a range of professions.

## Why collaborate?

### THE POLITICAL DRIVERS

Within the UK the government has made it abundantly clear that it expects a greater degree of integration of service delivery which will require agencies and disciplines to work much more closely together. There are various reasons for this policy drive. The government believes that public money would be spent more effectively if there was more collaboration and less duplication. It also believes that if agencies and disciplines work more closely together, service users would receive better integrated and holistic care. This belief is reflected in a wide range of government initiatives including *Getting it Right for Every Child* (Scottish Executive 2005).

With regard to child protection, staff working within social work, education and health are under enormous pressure to improve levels of collaboration. In relation to community care this direction is paralleled by the Scottish Executive's (2001) endorsement of the *Joint Future Group Report*, which required the introduction of Single Shared Assessments and the joint resourcing and joint management of services provided to all the community care service user groups. It is possible to argue that the level of integration between health and social work required to achieve joint resourcing and joint management is not a long way off from the creation of a single department.

## BARRIERS

Members of different disciplines are employed by different agencies; therefore, before going on to examine interdisciplinary processes, it is important to give some consideration of inter-agency processes.

If effective inter-agency collaboration was easily achieved, why have successive governments become so frustrated by what they perceive as a lack of progress in this area? The fact is agencies do not naturally collaborate (Hudson 1987). All organizations strive to maximize their level of autonomy. Collaboration involves a loss of autonomy and the investment of scarce resources, particularly in the form of staff time. Hudson identifies a range of factors which predispose agencies to collaborate:

1. *Interorganizational homogeneity* – if agencies have similar structures and values they will find it easier to collaborate.

2. *Domain consensus* – if agencies can agree on what each will do and will not do, effective collaboration is more likely.

3. *Absence of alternative resources* – if the only way an agency can get access to additional resources necessary to fulfil key objectives is by collaborating with another agency, it is more likely to engage in this activity.

4. *Network awareness* – agencies often hold inaccurate views of other agencies, underpinned by negative stereotyping. If, however, an agency can acquire a realistic view of another agency's priorities and strengths, it has a better basis for evaluating how best to collaborate.

5. *Organizational gain* – agencies are unlikely to invest scarce resources in time-consuming collaboration unless they perceive that concrete benefits are likely to accrue.

6. *Trust* – any new collaborative venture is likely to be influenced by earlier experiences of collaboration. Where these earlier experiences have generated a high level of mutual trust, this will positively influence the new venture.

## DEFINITION OF TERMS

Having briefly considered inter-agency processes, the remainder of the chapter will consider the implications of individuals who are drawn from a range of disciplines working and learning together. Various terms are used to describe this activity, the most common of which are 'interdisciplinary' and 'multidisciplinary' practice. These two terms are often used interchangeably but the following definitions perhaps indicate a useful discrimination between them:

• *Multidisciplinary practice* – a team of professionals working together for the benefit of the patient/service user but retaining their professional autonomy.

• *Interdisciplinary practice* – a team of professionals working as a collective for the benefit of the patient/service user.

## Professionalism

### ITS IMPACT ON INTERDISCIPLINARY PRACTICE

It is not possible to understand interdisciplinary practice without first understanding the phenomenon of professionalism. Loxley (1997) acknowledges that a division of labour is a reasonable approach for the management of complexity. However, a particular division of labour, whatever its initial usefulness, can over time become less functional. Inevitably, these divisions or professional specialisms endeavour to acquire a permanent role and control over a particular set of resources. This can lead to a narrow and fragmented view of how to assess and meet need. Integrated care is only possible if the divisions created by professional specialisms are transcended. However, attempts to overcome these professional divisions will often be regarded by the professions involved as threats and therefore resisted.

Loxley (1997) identifies the two key themes of power and culture as central to this process of professional specialisms seeking permanence and autonomy. Professions achieve the power to maintain degrees of autonomy by acquiring social and political influence. Claims of altruism are a method of gaining social approval and a justification for clinical freedom. Political influence is gained by a profession if it succeeds in being perceived by government as central in meeting its welfare agenda. The management of interdisciplinary collaboration needs to incorporate an understanding of the ways in which professions will attempt to exert power so as to maintain autonomy, mark out a particular domain, control resources and claim authority and expertise.

Professions also maintain power by developing and sustaining an occupational culture. This process allows professions to identify themselves as different and distinct from other professional groupings. According to Loxley, an occupational culture will often consist of: 'a collection of shared assumptions, customs and distinct models of reality, which mark out boundaries between those who belong inside and those others who are outside' (p.55).

Another key element in the development of an occupational culture is the establishment of a professional identity which begins during training and is maintained in employment. The establishment of a clear sense of professional identity is vital because it imparts confidence and role clarity, both of which are crucial when working closely with other professions. Paradoxically, it is confidence and clarity about professional identity which are often threatened when practitioners are expected to collaborate closely with other disciplines. Therefore, anxiety regarding a potential erosion of professional identity will often significantly hinder the development of closely integrated interdisciplinary teams. This anxiety can generate conservatism and role rigidity.

### MODELS OF PROFESSIONALISM

Another dimension to the understanding of the impact of professionalism on interdisciplinary practice is consideration of the particular ways a specific profession manifests its professionalism.

Jones and Joss (1995) describe a range of models of professionalism. They argue that these various models can coexist within organizations, but there is often one dominant model. Two models of most interest are the professional as technical expert and the professional as reflective practitioner.

The technical expert has the following characteristics:

1.   Uses theories derived from systematic knowledge. These theories are developed through scientific enquiry.

2.   Esoteric knowledge has been acquired and is only possessed by one profession.

3.   Practice theory is explicit and based upon techniques and expertise applied to problems.

4.   The value base is that of technical rationality. The approach is problem centred rather than service user centred.

5.   An objective approach to relationships with service users is central.

6.   With regard to professional development, knowledge and academic theory are valued, as are rules and guidance.

The reflective practitioner has the following characteristics:

1.   Uses a range of theories but recognizes there is no single right answer to most social problems.

2.   Has a specialist knowledge base. Uses all sources of knowledge available including relevant information from service user.

3.   Practice theory is based on process and interpersonal theories. New roles are created out of practice to make new sense of uncertainty or unique and conflict ridden situations.

4.   The value base is user centred, socially constructed and holistic.

5.   Relationships with service users are collaborative based on ongoing dialogues, sharing meanings and a reflective contract with the service user.

6.   Professional development is a process of experiential learning by doing, observing, reflecting, conceptualizing and experimenting. Abstract conceptualisation leads to new models and principles to be tested and refined.

Both models have their strengths but it is likely that most social workers would be more comfortable adopting a reflective practitioner style. Doctors and other health practitioners, on the other hand, may perceive themselves as technical experts. It will not be uncommon for both approaches to be present within interdisciplinary teams.

If this divergence is acknowledged and valued it has the potential to enhance the creativity of the team. Equally, it has the potential to be a source of frustration and conflict. For example, doctors and physiotherapists may wish to seek specific solutions to specific problems as quickly as possible, whereas social workers, influenced by concepts such as empowerment and choice, may wish to take time to allow the service user to arrive at his or her own solution.

Returning to the theme of professional specific control and autonomy, this process can often be seen most clearly with regard to systems involving referral and assessment. If a profession can control the referral process and the allocation of new work it is able to influence workload volume and prioritization. Equally, if a profession can control its assessment process it can influence how a problem is understood and dealt with.

However, the prevailing political context referred to earlier is making it increasingly difficult for professions to maintain a high level of control over referral and assessment. As already stated, the Scottish Executive (2001) endorsed the recommendations of the Joint Future Group with regard to the introduction of Single Shared Assessment for all the community care service user groups. It was considered that previously, service users/patients were over-assessed by a range of professions, leading to a duplication of effort and fragmented service delivery.

Single Shared Assessments are required to be:

- undertaken by *one member of the multi-agency team* (the most appropriate professional) drawing on contributions from other members of the team as necessary. Contact with the service user for assessment purposes should be through the lead professional. If the assessment points to the need for specialist opinion this should be sought, building on the basic information already collected

- a passport to the *full spectrum of community care services* with no subsequent re-assessment necessary unless needs change.

Loxley (1997) identifies that approaches such as the introduction of single shared assessments require a collaborative approach to referral, assessment and intervention. This is specifically sanctioned and required by government. The Scottish Executive's approach to the introduction of Single Shared Assessments carried out by integrated health and social care teams is replicated in other parts of the UK.

## Teamwork

### DEFINITION

Having examined the nature of professionalism, it is now necessary to consider interdisciplinary teams, which are introduced by a brief consideration of teamwork.

A team is a group of people who share common objectives and who need to work together to achieve them (Woodcock 1989).

Increasingly, interdisciplinary practice takes place within the context of teams. These teams can involve loose arrangements or can be highly structured. All teams are highly complex entities. This complexity is greatly increased if team members belong to a range of professional disciplines. As a means of evaluating a team's effectiveness, Woodcock (1989) outlined stages of team development:

*Stage 1 – undeveloped*

- where feelings are not dealt with
- where there is poor listening
- where weaknesses are covered up
- where there are unclear objectives

- where there is low involvement in planning
- where bureaucracy exists
- where the leader makes most decisions.

*Stage 2*

- where the team discusses risky issues
- where the team considers wider options
- where the team members are able to raise their own personal feelings
- where the team members are able to show concern for others
- where the team members listen to what is being said.

*Stage 3*

- where there is evidence of methodical working
- where there are agreed procedures
- where there are established ground rules.

*Stage 4 – the mature team*

- where there is a high degree of flexibility
- where appropriate leadership exists
- where maximum use is made of individual abilities
- where development is seen as a priority
- where the needs of the individual are met.

## Interdisciplinary teamworking

When interdisciplinary teams are created the hope is that the range of perspectives and skills present within the team will contribute to create an integrated approach to service delivery. For this to happen the interdisciplinary team would need to be operating at the Stage 4 level of maturity. This requires confident and secure group members, as well as skilled leadership.

A common source of confusion, when considering interdisciplinary teamwork, often surrounds the use of the term 'team'. Ovretveit (1993) usefully discriminates between three different types of teams:

1.  *Client teams* – 'A client team is all those serving one client at one time, sometimes co-ordinated by a Care Manager. The client team may change over time however each member contributes to work with the client and will need to relate to colleagues in doing this' (p.58).

2.   *Network association team* – 'A voluntary association of service providers, relating to cross-refer, or to co-ordinate work with clients, or for other purposes. There is no agreed and binding common policy, and usually each network participant is part of another team, placed in a different place and managed by a professional line manager' (p.63).

3.   *Formal multidisciplinary team* – 'A working group with a defined membership of different professions, governed by an agreed and explicit team policy, which is upheld by a team leader' (p.64).

This typology demonstrates that care provision need not be dependant on a permanent team arrangement. However the advantage of a formal team is that they provide a stable basis for the delivery of a comprehensive range of services.

Miller and Freeman (2003) examined the working of six interdisciplinary teams within the following range of settings: neuro-rehabilitation, medicine, child development assessment, diabetics, general practice and community mental health. Their research findings demonstrated that effective collaborative working was only present in one team. In two others, part of the defined team consistently worked collaboratively, whereas other members were observed to be peripheral. The characteristics of effective collaborative working which the researchers observed were the following:

• A highly developed vision of teamworking and a shared philosophy of patient care.

• All relevant team members were expected to contribute to the problem-solving and decision-making processes about their particular patients.

• There was shared responsibility for team actions.

• Communication was multilayered: information and knowledge sharing and the acknowledgement of professional concerns were all recognized as vital for the development of effective teamwork.

• Role understanding was also multilayered: team members felt it was important that they knew what a role comprised, how it was performed and what the underpinning rationales for action were.

• Role boundaries were flexible according to patient requirements, with team members learning skills and knowledge to ensure continuity of care.

• A pool of team skills and knowledge had developed enabled by joint practices such as joint notekeeping, assessment, monitoring, evaluating and therapeutic intervention.

The research team further observed that the greater the level of collaboration across the whole team, the more frequently the following practices were observed:

• continuity and consistency of care from one professional to another

• a reduction of ambiguous messages between team members and between them and their patients/service users and carers

- appropriate referral, both in terms of who was referred to and the timing of that referral

- a wide range of knowledge being used on which to base team decisions

- a problem-solving approach across the team being used to determine care programmes.

Miller and Freeman (2003) concluded that there was a range of reasons as to why the majority of the teams of the research study were unable to achieve effective teamworking. Complex organizational structures were undermined by traditional professional hierarchies. Interpersonal relationships were undermined by power structures and differences in beliefs about teamworking. These interpersonal tensions were heightened by the need for professional roles to be redefined as a result of government policy such as the introduction of the Single Shared Assessments referred to earlier.

Brown, Tucker and Domokos (2003) evaluated the impact of an integrated and co-located health and social care team on older people living in the community. This research found that, compared with traditional arrangements, the assessment process was completed more quickly, but there was no discernable impact on the clinical outcomes for service users/patients. The authors note the dearth of research evidence regarding the effectiveness of joint working, despite this being received wisdom, and speculate that although the team being studied was co-located it was not sufficiently integrated to have an impact on clinical outcome.

If interdisciplinary teams frequently fail to realize their full potential, despite this style of working being a central plank of government policy, it is important to analyse why this should be the case. Ovretveit (1993) generated a list of common problems for interdisciplinary teams, as well as identifying sources of failure.

## Common problems within interdisciplinary teams

- Team meeting problems: poor chairing, frequent absences, avoidance of issues, no agreed decision-making processes.

- 'Emergency work' driving out longer-term more effective work, or too much long-term work.

- Difficulty allocating new cases because members brought their old caseloads to the team.

- No team influence over closure decisions.

- Team members taking referrals or work separately from the team.

- A lack of common awareness of agreed priorities and of ways of implementing priorities.

- No forum for in-depth case discussions of selected cases.

- Separate professional information and records systems, or difficulties getting information from others.

- Insufficient administration support, and inadequate team base.
- Leadership with no authority.

(Ovretveit 1993, p.192)

### HOW TO MAKE A TEAM FAIL

- Practitioners in the same profession continue to meet and work together as a single-profession team.

- Each professional or professional group has its own referral procedures and work priorities.

- Profession specific managers maintain close control over practitioners.

- Many members are only part-time in the team, with the rest of their time allocated to one or more different areas or different services.

- There is no team base – contact and communication points, records and secretarial support are all at different sites.

- There is no team leader position with a responsibility for team operations.

- There are no team objectives or priorities, but only general statements of intent.

- There is no decision-making procedure within the team for treatment decisions, workload management, management issues or developing planning proposals.

- There is no formal annual review by higher management of team operations and achievements.

- No plan exists for the wider service of which the team is a part, and there is no individual or group with the clear responsibility for creating one.

(Ovretveit 1993, p.200)

## Roles within interdisciplinary teams

Formal work–role responsibilities are defined by Ovretveit (1993) as being, 'the work expected of a person by his or her employers; the ongoing duties, and the tasks which are delegated by higher management from time to time' (p.105). Effective interdisciplinary team work is heavily dependent on mutual clarity about team member roles. This is very difficult to achieve. Staff who have worked alongside colleagues from other disciplines often have an incomplete knowledge of the other's role.

The work roles taken on by staff within an interdisciplinary team are influenced by a wide range of issues including, of course, professional training. In addition to professional training what a worker actually does is influenced by what managers, colleagues, referers, and service users and carers want from them. Ovretveit identifies discrete types of roles undertaken within teams as well as a range of common role problems. Profession-specific responsibility is work carried out exclusively by members of one discipline. Sometimes this work is specified by law such as prescribing or the role of the mental health officer. These profession-specific responsibilities are relatively few, but colleagues from other disciplines need to be aware of them.

A wide range of knowledge and skill is frequently spread across professional boundaries within interdisciplinary teams. Therefore often a range of disciplines can carry out what Ovretveit (1993) describes as common responsibilities. Counselling may be an example of such an activity; however, Loxley (1997) warns against assuming that the use of the same term means the same service response. Nevertheless it is clear that many roles can be undertaken by more than one professional discipline. Potentially this fact enables an interdisciplinary team to deliver flexible and integrated care. Unfortunately, however, it can also form the basis for ambiguity and competition between disciplines.

Ovretveit's (1993) third category of role type is care coordination, where one person coordinates the inputs of other colleagues. This role is frequently given to a care manager or, within the care programme approach, a key worker who is a member of a community mental health team.

Ovretveit (1993) identifies a range of common role problems within interdisciplinary teams as follows.

## NO CARE COORDINATION, OR CONFUSED OR DISPUTED COORDINATION

Sometimes members of each discipline can become so preoccupied with their particular input that no one within the team takes responsibility for ensuring the service user/patient is receiving integrated and coordinated care. One member of staff should be given responsibility for coordinating the input of colleagues from both within and outwith the team. Achieving a negotiated clarity about this can be difficult, particularly with regard to the input of colleagues who do not belong to the team.

## SKILLED DILUTION OR DE-SKILLING

Skilled dilution comes from not using skills which one has acquired through training, usually profession-specific skills. For example, a nurse who becomes heavily involved in Single Shared Assessments and care coordination may consider that her/his skills in wound management have become eroded. Skilled dilution is not necessarily a problem if the team member is acquiring other skills that are more valuable to the team.

## CONTESTED ROLE OVERLAP

Role overlap is where two or more members have skills and knowledge in common. As stated earlier this can enhance team flexibility. However, it can become problematic in the following situations:

1.  Two or more team members do the same work and duplicate each other.

2.  No one does the work – each assumes that someone else is doing it.

3.  If a range of disciplines can do the work equally well it can be difficult to decide which is the most appropriate discipline to undertake the work.

4.  One discipline contests as to whether another discipline has necessary competence to undertake the work.

### REDUCED ROLE AUTONOMY

Joining in an interdisciplinary team will inevitably involve some loss of role autonomy for the practitioners involved. If not managed sensitively this can become a major source of resentment and division.

### ROLE OVERLOAD

A common source of stress within interdisciplinary teams is staff feeling that they are required to take on too wide a range of roles.

## Ways forward

### MANAGING DIFFERENCES

A key factor in determining the success or failure of an interdisciplinary team is how effectively differences between team members are managed. When a new interdisciplinary team is formed the staff involved will frequently have different employers, experience, skills, pay, status and power. These differences are potentially a source of creativity and energy. However, for a range of reasons these differences are often minimized or denied. For example, team members may be anxious that an explicit acknowledgement of differences may fragment the team. Denial of differences is also a way of trying to avoid professional competition and jealousy. There may also be an anxiety that if differences in skills, expertise and experience are openly acknowledged within the team this may lead to one or more professions becoming more influential and others losing autonomy.

These attempts to maintain a fragile team cohesiveness can have a high cost in terms of reduced team creativity and productivity. Ovretveit (1993) vividly describes the processes involved within teams who deal with differences in either a positive or negative manner. First, if differences between the range of professions comprising the team can be explicitly recognized, within an atmosphere of mutual respect and trust, this will increase the team's ability to discuss and generate solutions thereby enhancing service delivery.

In contrast, if professional differences are denied or minimized, this may generate mistrust, making it difficult for team members to overtly disagree with one another, thereby reducing the likelihood of creating networks and enhanced service delivery. A fragmented and polarized team is a more likely outcome.

Figure 21.1 demonstrates that the acknowledgement or denial of differences between professions within interdisciplinary teams can generate either creative or destructive circular processes. Effective team building and leadership early in the life of a new interdisciplinary team can help ensure that teams get the full benefit of the presence of a range of disciplines.

### CLARITY REGARDING REQUIRED LEVEL OF INTEGRATION

Another critical factor in determining how successful an interdisciplinary team will be is whether service managers and team members are clear about the level of team integration required in order to achieve anticipated team goals. This level of clarity is not always present.

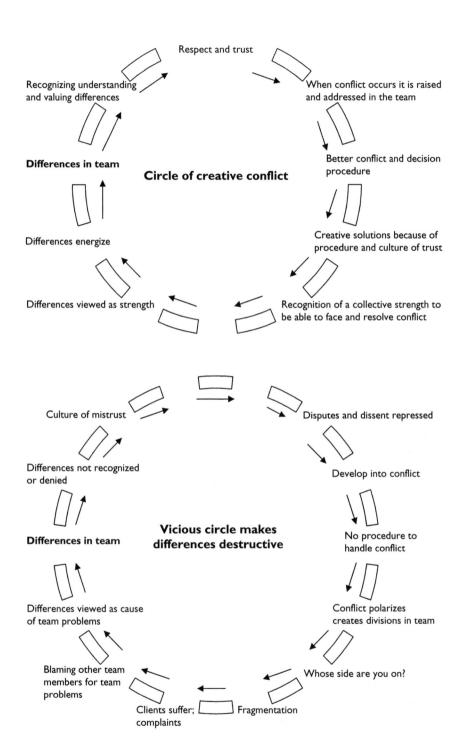

Figure 21.1 Team culture and procedures make differences creative or destructive

Interdisciplinary teams vary enormously with regard to the level of integration which exists between team members. Ovretveit, Mathias and Thompson (1997) described two types of teams which demonstrate this variance of level of integration.

- Collective responsibility teams:

    ○ Team members are accountable as a group for pooling and using collective resources to meet priority needs of a population.

    ○ There is one-door entry for all professional services.

    ○ The allocation for assessment and intervention is determined by team approved priorities.

    ○ All professionals are managed by one team leader.

- Coordinated profession teams:

    ○ A network of separately organized and separately accountable professional services is created to improve coordination and communication.

    ○ Different professions have their own priorities and are separately financed and separately managed to provide specific services.

    ○ Different professions have different referral routes.

    ○ Individual professions maintain a significant degree of autonomy.

Both types of teams have advantages and disadvantages. It is easier for health and social work managers to negotiate the creation of a coordinated profession team because this will involve considerably less disruption to traditional ways of working. The creation of a coordinated profession team is also likely to generate less resistance among the professions involved as it requires fewer changes in working practices and there is less of a threat to their autonomy.

The creation of a collective responsibility team is more ambitious, requiring substantial changes to existing systems and making considerable changes to the working practices of the various disciplines involved. Therefore, negotiating the creation of this type of team is much more difficult. However, it could be argued that the expected benefits of joint working demanded by government in relation to integrated care and effective use of resources, are more likely to be delivered by a collective responsibility team.

### INTERDISCIPLINARY LEADERSHIP

As well as managing interprofessional difficulties and being clear about the required level of team integration, another key factor in achieving effective interdisciplinary teamwork is the presence of effective and appropriate leadership.

Ovretveit (1993) considers that 'one of the biggest mistakes is to believe that interprofessional and interagency conflict, rivalries and protectionism can be avoided by not defining a team leader role' (p.122). Ovretveit et al. (1997) believed that many interdisciplinary teams were poorly managed, with no one given overall responsibility for considering the collective interdisciplinary resources of the team and managing these resources in relation to service user needs. Clearly, in the creation of interdisciplinary teams, senior health and social work managers need to try and agree on how authority is to be allocated within these teams. Ovretveit (1993) describes alternative ways of doing this.

- Team coordinator:
  - Responsible for: chairing team meetings; upholding and reviewing team policy.
  - Accountable to: a manager or group carrying out the above responsibilities.
  - Authorized to: seek information about team member's actions to check if it is in line with agreed team policy; ask for changes in behaviour which are against team policy; report to team managers if changes are not forthcoming.
  - No authority to overrule case decisions of colleagues.
  - Paid to: carry out these responsibilities instead of case work, or in addition to a reduced caseload.

- Team manager:
  - Responsible for: delegating work to and managing team members.
  - Accountable to: a manager or group for their performance and for the performance of the staff team.
  - Authorized to: assign and review work; identify team training needs; initiate disciplinary action.
  - Paid to: carry out these responsibilities instead of casework. May carry a small caseload.
  - Staff may be given access to senior colleagues from the same profession for consultation.

The most common type of leadership role within interdisciplinary teams is that of team coordinator, partly because it is the most easily negotiated by senior health and social work managers and partly because it is often most palatable to the various professions involved. This is because senior managers do not have to hand over explicit line manager control of their employees to someone from another organization and practitioners have more autonomy if they are not being explicitly line managed within the team by someone who may belong to another discipline.

However, just as collective responsibility teams might be more likely to deliver integrated services, the same goal might be better achieved by teams who have managers with explicit authority over all team members. Ultimately the style of leadership should match what is expected of an interdisciplinary team. If the team is expected to be highly integrated this requires the presence of explicit team leadership.

## STAFF SUPERVISION
This is often a highly contentious issue within interdisciplinary teams and is clearly linked to the style of leadership adopted. Terms such as 'supervision', 'accountability' and 'autonomy' can be interpreted in different ways by different professions, which adds

to the difficulty in creating coherent management systems within interdisciplinary teams. Different professions are used to different levels of autonomy and different styles of supervision.

The 21st Century Social Work Review Group (Scottish Executive 2006) discovered that many social workers experienced supervision from social work managers to be primarily focused on workload management. This is less likely to be the case for health care professionals. Within social work the Review argued for the adoption of the term 'consultation incorporating performance management, staff development and staff support' (p.59).

Ovretveit *et al.* (1997) argued that the confusion surrounding supervision within an interdisciplinary context is heightened by professional politics. They defined the phenomenon of 'functional political interpretation' where an ambiguous term such as 'supervision' is interpreted in a particular way by a particular professional grouping so as to further their own interests and maximize autonomy.

Part of the confusion stems from its use within management to describe the monitoring and control of practitioner performance. Within the professions the emphasis on supervision tends to be educational and developmental. This confusion can only be resolved by explicit discussion within interdisciplinary teams of what is understood by the term 'supervision', so that coherent systems of supervision can emerge which meet the needs of everyone. Ovretveit *et al.* (1997) considered that the word supervision can be used to describe the following four tasks:

- *Clinical advice* – 'The practitioner seeks out another, often more experienced practitioner to discuss client's problem, and get their advice. The practitioner remains accountable and responsible for their decisions and the advisor does not assume any responsibility for the case' (p.27).

- *Clinical supervision* – 'In this type of supervision a senior staff member has responsibilities for overseeing a practitioner's clinical decisions about client treatments, and is accountable for the practitioner's clinical work. They have the authority to require regular reports, to direct and overrule the practitioner's clinical actions with the client' (p.27).

- *Management monitoring* – 'Sometimes supervision is used to describe a person in a monitoring role who checks that a practitioner has followed administrative procedures, including those with a bearing on their clinical work, such as performing a care management role in a required way' (p.7).

- *Full management* – 'Some supervisors are full managers, and supervision can mean full management where the manager is accountable for all aspects of the practitioner's work, including clinical decisions. For this they need the authority to appoint the practitioner, assign work, and undertake performance assessments. If they feel they do not have the expertise to judge clinical performance they will delegate this work to someone who has, but they still remain accountable for the practitioner's clinical decisions' (p.28).

Ovretveit *et al.* argue that in principle all the above four tasks can be carried out by someone who does not belong to the same profession as the practitioner. Clearly this is a highly contentious issue. Many practitioners will not accept that someone from a different profession has the expertise to evaluate their practice. If the decision is made to appoint a team leader with line management responsibility for all of the professions represented within the team, each discipline can be allowed access to a senior colleague outwith the team for consultation and staff development, with the team leader retaining ultimate accountability for the practitioner's work.

## PLANNING AND MANAGING INTERDISCIPLINARY TEAMS

In considering how to maximize the benefits of interdisciplinary practice it is insufficient only to consider the nature of professionalism and team functioning. Interdisciplinary teams do not emerge out of thin air. They are the product of a planning and management process engaged in by senior managers within a range of agencies.

Ovretveit *et al.* (1997) are critical of the manner in which some interdisciplinary teams are planned and managed. They describe a familiar sequence in the following manner:

- problems in team work

- attention to team organization

- agreeing team operational policy and procedures

- clarification of services the team should offer

- adjustment of team services in relation to other services provided in the area

- assessment of the needs of the population

- readjustment of team staffing with regard to the mix and amount of various professions.

(Ovretveit *et al.* 1997, p.37)

The above was contrasted with a reverse and preferred sequence with regard to planning and management:

- Assessment of the needs of the population.

- Plan and arrange separate services to meet the most pressing needs.

- Describe the role and purpose of the team as a key part of the range of services, and where the team base will be.

- Describe which professions and skills are required and the amount of each.

- Agree the details of how the team will be organized.

(Ovretveit *et al.* 1997, p.37)

Ovretveit *et al* (1997) argue that new interdisciplinary teams are sometimes expected to operate within a policy vacuum. It is their contention that senior managers should create a policy framework containing the following elements:

- *The needs that are to be served by the team* – This should be more specific than, for example, 'adults with mental health problems'. Guidance should be given as to the categories of need or care programmes and some indication of the proportion of resources to allocate to different types of clients with different problems.

- *Team purpose and work* – It should be made clear whether the team is expected to be a network for coordinating separate professional services or whether the team is a collective responsibility team.

- *Team catchment and boundaries* – This would describe the population the team is expected to serve and give guidance about boundary interface with other services.

- *Base(s)* – The initial policy document should make it clear where team members and their offices and records are to be based.

- *Team membership* – This should specify the number of staff from each profession, their grade and time allocated within the team. The role of each team member should be specified.

- *Referrals to and access to the team* – This should specify the sources from which the team accepts referrals, including whether the team accepts self-referrals. It should also specify whether any team member can accept referrals separately from the team meeting.

- *Team processes and decision-making* – This should specify how decisions are made at each stage of the service user pathway from referral to closure.

- *Care coordination* – This should specify how coordination is to be carried out both between the team and other services. It should also specify whether formal care coordinator roles are to be established within the team.

- *Team leader role* – Of all the policies requiring to be defined, this is considered by Ovretveit *et al.* as the most important. Responsibilities and levels of authority need to be explicitly defined.

- *Supervision, professional advice and quality of professional practice* – This should specify how practitioners get access to advice with complex cases and about how the quality of practitioners' work will be improved.

- *Case records and work recording* – Details of recording expectations should be specified. It is argued that within integrated teams there should be one and only one case file for each client which should be held at the team base.

- *Team management and reviews* – This should specify how and when team performance will be assessed.

- *Team targets and milestones* – Achievement targets to be reached by the team should be set at six-monthly intervals.

## A model for interdisciplinary collaboration

Clearly interdisciplinary practice is a highly complex activity and a range of models have been developed which aim to identify the key elements which contribute to successful interdisciplinary collaboration.

Bronstein (2003) offers, from an American perspective, a model of interdisciplinary collaboration incorporating a range of components. Her preferred definition of interdisciplinary collaboration is 'an effective interpersonal process that facilitates the achievements of goals that cannot be reached when independent professions act on their own' (p.229). The five components of her interdisciplinary collaboration models are as follows:

- *Interdependence* – Refers to the existence and dependence on interactions between different professionals where each is dependent on the other for the successful completion of roles and tasks.

- *Newly created professional tasks* – Refers to new collaborative acts, projects or initiatives that can achieve more than could be achieved by professionals acting independently. Ideally these activities should extend the skills base of each participant.

- *Flexibility* – Goes beyond interdependence and refers to the deliberate occurrence of role blurring. Examples of flexibility would include seeking productive compromises and the modification of roles as professionals, thereby responding creatively to a changing context.

Bronstein (2003) argues that integrative teams require flexibility and role blurring, maintaining that roles taken 'should depend not only on professional's training but also on the needs of the organisation as well as service users and carers' (p.301).

- *Collective ownership of goals* – Refers to the shared responsibility and the whole process of reaching goals, including design, delivery and achievement of goals. Bronstein identifies collective ownership of goals as a key indicator of successful collaboration.

- *Reflection of process* – Refers to practitioners' attention to their process of working together. This includes explicitly discussing working relationships and processes as well as providing productive feedback in order to strengthen collaborative relationships and effectiveness. Bronstein argues that the ability to reflect on process enhances a team's ability to be successfully integrative.

As well as identifying these five key components of effective interdisciplinary collaboration, Bronstein (2005) also defines four major influences on interdisciplinary collaboration:

- *Professional role* – As stated earlier practitioners need a strong sense of their own professional identity in order to successfully collaborate with other professions. However, Bronstein identifies that successful teamwork can be hampered by too strong an allegiance to either one's professional discipline or the interdisciplinary team. Effective collaboration requires a commitment to both.

- *Structural characteristics* – Includes such issues as a manageable caseload, an agency culture that supports interdisciplinary collaboration, administrative support and a reasonable degree of professional autonomy.

- *Personal characteristics* – Those relevant to interdisciplinary collaboration would include trust, respect and understanding and informal communication between collaborators. In particular, trust is seen as critical for successful collaboration.

- *History of collaboration* – If participants have a past positive history of collaboration the ensuing optimism will increase the likelihood of the new collaborative venture being successful.

An overview of Bronstein's model is displayed in Figure 21.2.

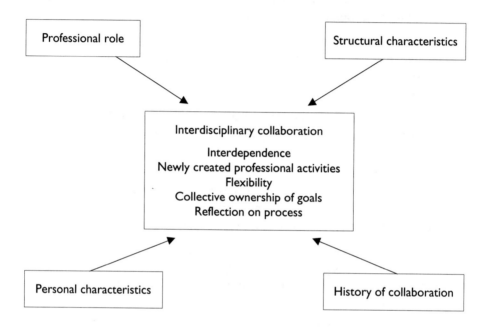

Figure 21.2 Influences on interdisciplinary collaboration

## Interprofessional education

With the widespread move towards integrated services within the UK, clearly many professionals will spend their working lives within interdisciplinary teams. This fact has major implications for universities which provide professional courses and has led to an expansion in the provision of interprofessional education in an attempt to better prepare practitioners for the demands of interdisciplinary working.

Barr (2005), in his review of interprofessional education commissioned by the Learning and Teaching Support Network for Health Sciences and Practice, defined interprofessional education as 'occasions where two or more professions learned from each other to improve collaboration and quality of care' (p.67).

Barr has attempted to develop a competency-based model for interprofessional education. He distinguishes between:

- *Common competencies* – those held in common between all professions.

- *Complementary competencies* – those which distinguish one profession from another.

- *Collaborative competencies* – those necessary to work effectively with others.

Barr provides the following examples of collaborative competences:

- Describe one's roles and responsibilities clearly to other professions and discharge them to the satisfaction of others.

- Recognize and observe the constraints of one's role, responsibilities and competence, yet perceive needs in a wider context.

- Recognize and respect the roles, responsibilities and competence of other professions in relating to one's own, knowing when, where and how to involve those others through agreed channels.

- Work with other professions to review services, effect change, improve standards, solve problems and resolve conflict in the provision of care and treatment.

- Work with other professions to assess, plan, provide and review care for individual patients and support carers.

- Tolerate differences, misunderstandings, ambiguities, shortcomings and unilateral change in another profession.

- Enter into interdependent relationships, teaching and sustaining other professions and learning from and being sustained by those other professions.

- Facilitate interprofessional case conferences, meeting, teamworking and networking.

(Barr 2005, p.16)

Barr was a member of the Cochrane Collaboration, which evaluated the impact of interprofessional education on the organization and delivery of care. Using the Cochrane criteria (Cochrane Collection 2006), only the most rigorous evaluations of interprofessional education were included in the study and none demonstrated a measurable impact on the organization and delivery of care. Barr is also a member of the Interprofessional Education Joint Evaluation Team which used a less rigorous criteria for inclusion in their study (Barr 2004). Although the range of available evidence was limited, this study concluded that 'in favourable circumstances and in different ways interprofessional education can contribute to improving collaboration and practice' (p.30).

In considering interprofessional education at different stages, Barr suggests the following proposition:

The earlier the interprofessional learning in participants' experience, the less they are in a position to share and the more the teacher needs to provide. The later the learning, the more the participants would be able to set their own agenda and call upon their own resources. Objectives for interprofessional education before qualification might be preventative – mitigating the risk of developing prejudices and negative stereotypes, and preparatory, laying foundations for subsequent interprofessional learning and practice. Objectives for interprofessional learning after qualification might be more ambitious – effecting change and improving services. (Barr 2005, p.32)

## Summary and conclusion

Interdisciplinary practice has been considered within a political and interagency context. The nature of professionalism and a range of interdisciplinary team processes have also been examined. The difficulties associated with interdisciplinary practice have been identified but particular attention has been given to explaining how to maximize the likelihood of success in this endeavour.

In conclusion, although governments often have unrealistic expectations of the impact of interdisciplinary practice on service delivery, this approach will clearly remain a key aspect of government policy for the foreseeable future. The hoped-for benefits of joint working are more likely to be realized if:

- Students within all disciplines at undergraduate level are *jointly* taught interdisciplinary practice concepts and skills both within the university and during placements.

- Practitioners within interdisciplinary teams are provided with adequate leadership and training.

## References

Barr, H. (2005) *Interprofessional Education: Today, Yesterday and Tomorrow (Revised edition) – A Review commissioned by the Learning and Teaching Support Network for Health Sciences and Practice.* London: The UK Centre for the Advancement of Interprofessional Education. Retrieved from www.health.heacademy.ac.uk/publications/occasionalpaper/occp1/revised.pdf.

Bronstein, L. (2003) 'A model for interdisciplinary collaboration.' *Social Work Vol 48*, 3, 297–306.

Brown, L., Tucker, C. and Domokos, T. (2003) 'Evaluating the impact of integrated health and social care teams on older people living in the community.' *Health and Social Care in the Community 11*, 2, 85–94.

Cochrane Collection (2006) 'Glossary.' In: *Cochrane Collaboration: The Cochrane Library, Issue 2.* Oxford: Update Software.

Hudson, B. (1987) 'Collaboration in social welfare: A framework for analysis.' *Policy and Politics 15*, 3, 175–82.

Jones, J. and Joss, R. (1995) 'Models of professionalism.' In M. Yelloly and M. Henkel (eds) *Learning and Teaching in Social Work.* London: Jessica Kingsley Publishers.

Loxley, A. (1997) *Collaboration in Health and Welfare: Working with Difference.* London: Jessica Kingsley Publishers.

Miller, C. and Freeman, M. (2003) 'Clinical teamwork: The impact of policy on collaborative practice.' In A. Leathard (ed.) *Interprofessional Collaboration: From Policy to Practice in Health and Social Care.* Hove: Brunner-Routledge.

Ovretveit, J. (1993) *Coordinating Community Care: Multidisciplinary Teams and Care Management.* Buckingham: Open University Press.

Ovretveit, J., Mathias, P. and Thompson, T. (eds) (1997) *Interprofessional Working for Health and Social Care.* Basingstoke: Palgrave.

Scottish Executive (2001) *Scottish Executive's Response to the Report of the Joint Future Group.* Edinburgh: Scottish Executive. Available at: www.scotland.gov.uk/library3/social/fngr-00.asp

Scottish Executive (2005) *Getting it Right for Every Child.* Edinburgh: Scottish Executive.

Scottish Executive (2006) *Changing Lives: Report of the 21st Century Social Work Review.* Edinburgh: Scottish Executive.

Woodcock, M. (1989) *Team Development Manual.* (2nd ed) Aldershot: Gower Publishing.

## CHAPTER 22

# WORKING WITHIN THE ORGANIZATIONAL CONTEXT OF DYNAMIC CHANGE

*Fiona Feilberg*

## Introduction: context of change

The content and form of social work has changed dramatically over the last decade. Changes to the context of social work include organizational expansion and transformation of structures, the increasingly diverse focus of social work, increased regulation along with increasing expectation of responsiveness to users, increased focus on joint working and expectations of evidenced-based practice. There have also been dramatic changes in social work training to match changing realities in the social work field.

In the past periods of profound change were followed by more stable times allowing for consolidation of the change. In today's 'turbulent environment' (Emery and Trist 1965, p.21) the one constant for most organizations is how to cope with change while achieving results and retaining committed and engaged staff. Change is constant and ubiquitous with the only thing that doesn't change being the reality of change itself. This situation may feel new to us and certainly the pace has increased: however, as early as 1973 Schön indicated, 'The loss of the stable state means that our society and all of its institutions are in continuing processes of transformation. We cannot expect new stable states that will endure even for our lifetimes' (Schön 1973, p.28). Organizations face permanent 'white water' (Vaill 1996) where the pace of work is not always smooth but often fast-flowing and tempestuous. Theoretical models of change need to be applicable within that context.

It is important to understand the process of change and its implication for individuals working within organizations and networks in order to develop effective working practices. Martyn (2000) argues that the reflective practitioner needs to focus on developing the skills and knowledge required to manage change rather than waste time and energy on resisting change.

## Models of change

### TRADITIONAL MODELS OF CHANGE

Traditional organizational development theorists such as Lewin (1947) concentrated on understanding and analysing planned change where there was a deliberate decision to change something; a strategic plan was developed and then members of the organization were mobilized to bring about the change. However, it is clear from our own experiences of it that change is not as straightforward as this. Lewin (1945, p.30) recognized there was resistance to change and that 'the conditions of group life and the forces which bring about change or which resist change should be investigated.'

Lewin saw work taking place within a 'system' of roles, attitudes, behaviours, norms, and other factors, any and all of which could cause the system to be in disequilibrium. A system is a set of elements which together form a whole entity, orderly, functional and interrelated. A system is functional as a whole entity with the components and attributes contributing to the working of the whole. In order to understand the system we need to understand not only each component, but also the interactions between them and how they fit together within the whole. For Lewin, resistance to change was a systems phenomenon. Systems maintain an internal balance and attempt to return to that balance if any element changes. Individuals' resistance was seen as only one part of the picture which could be tackled by involving workers in planning for change and sharing power.

Lewin (1947) saw change as a threefold process of *unfreezing, change* and then *refreezing.* Unfreezing required a shaking-up of the system as the stability was based on an equilibrium supported by opposing driving and restraining forces, which Lewin called a 'force-field'. Lewin's notion of force-field analysis encapsulates his systems perspective. For change to occur the overall force-field had to be altered because just adding a driving force towards change would produce an immediate counter-force to maintain the equilibrium. A force-field analysis would identify forces towards the change and those resisting change. Then, by building on the positive forces already within the system and addressing the restraining forces, the climate for change would be developed after which the system could be refrozen in a new equilibrium. (An example of a force-field diagram can be found at http://syqne.com/qualitytools/toolbook/Force/do.htm.)

This can be a useful model for helping staff and students to clarify the context of a change and to plan responses to planned change; however, it is less helpful in working within less planned and controlled changes. Much change now is transformational change where both strategies and the beliefs and values on which they are based change at the same time. It is not simply a case of finding new alternative ways of resolving a short-term operational challenge more effectively but of radically altering the provision of services and sometimes the assumptions on which the provision of services is based. Given the rapidly changing environment, understanding and achieving transformational change is essential for long-term survival (Schön, 1995), and refreezing in the face of continual change is not likely to be an effective strategy. 'Lewin's (1947) idea of what organisational change consists of, freeze, movement, refreeze needs to become freeze, movement, *reframe,* highlighting the need to reformulate the organisation in an open-ended way rather than restore it to some pre-existing state' (Huffington 2004, p.65, original emphasis).

Lewin's model seemed to indicate that there can be a rational process of identifying forces for and against the change and then agreeing a consensus for action. Following Lewin, organizational theorists, such as Peterson (1980) and Kotter (1996), also focused on rational approaches to change, looking at detailed strategic planning with the involvement of staff being focused on the practical aspects of the change. Along with this rational approach there was recognition of the need to involve staff at a deeper level and this concentrated on the need to create a vision to mobilize staff behind planned changes. The creation and communication of a 'vision' may well be helpful in energizing and mobilizing staff, as is detailed strategic planning. However, a focus on detailed plans and a perceived future is not enough in itself. In a context of continual change it becomes less feasible to rely on models which imply that much change is under our control. In the present context, 'the key question is whether change is ever internally driven, or whether it is primarily determined by external events...most change now seems driven by changes in the environment' (Obholzer and Miller 2004, p.36).

For a manager one of the most frustrating aspects of the job can be the resistance to change that emerges within the team. The manager will present what he or she thinks is a well-reasoned and planned-out suggestion for a change in service which would be of benefit to the staff and the clients and is linked to the value base of the organization. Despite the manager's efforts there will generally be a long drawn out process of discussion and disagreements which have to be attended to before the staff can accept the change. It is important to understand why this process is inevitable if changes are not to be imposed on staff. In order to do so other models for understanding organizational change are required.

### STAGE MODELS OF ADJUSTMENT TO CHANGE

In order to understand and assist individuals adjust to change the impact of changes at a psychological level need to be explored. A successful change process will involve rational planning, but also requires time and psychological adjustment. Particularly helpful in understanding this process has been the work of Marris (1974) and Bridges (1991).

Marris (1974) identified the fact that all change, even that which is viewed as positive, involves loss and therefore requires adjustment to that loss. Resistance is a necessary part of the process of change and 'every attempt to pre-empt conflict, argument, protest by rational planning can only be abortive: however reasonable the proposed changes, the process of implementation must still allow the impulse of rejection to play itself out' (p.166).

Most people familiar with Marris (1974) are aware of the key statement that all change involves loss. However, his approach is much more sophisticated than this. Marris also indicated that the same objective change event can be experienced differently by different individuals. Even for individuals who are generally positive about the changes there will be ambivalent feelings around the perceptions of the potential for growth and development and the perception of the impact of the loss of the familiar. However, for those who see the change primarily as a loss there will be the greatest need for adjustment.

There are close links to Bowlby's (1969) three-stage model of responses to loss: the urge to recover the lost object, disorganization and finally reorganization. Change is experienced as loss because of our attachment to the familiar. Not only are we attached to individuals but to the patterns and structures of our lives. For many, the work that they do and the organization for which they work can be closely linked to their identity and changing the patterns within work can be intensely threatening. This identification can vary in strength but 'can result in an organisation becoming a subordinate attachment figure for some people and a principal attachment figure for others' (Stapely 1996, p.52).

Marris (1974) indicates the need to allow time for the process of adjustment. Individuals need to acknowledge and accept the losses involved in the change and reconstruct their perceptions of the world to one in which the change is real. Links between the past and the present take time to process. Imposing the change and providing too little time for exploration can lead to a crystallization of resistance or an unthinking commitment to the new state.

Bridges (1991) developed a similar approach to understanding the management of change within organizations and how change impacts on groups of people. Bridges made a clear distinction between change and transition. The change is an event that can be indicated clearly, described and planned for, whereas transition is the longer process of psychological adjustment to the change:

> It isn't the changes that do you in, it's the transitions. Change is not the same as transition. Change is situational: the new site, the new boss, the new team roles, the new policy. Transition is the psychological process people go through to come to terms with the new situation. Change is external, transition is internal. (Bridges 1991, p.2)

Bridges' aim is to provide a model for understanding the process of transition and to indicate how staff can be managed through this process. He argues that this process occurs in three stages: ending, neutral zone and new beginnings.

The first stage, *ending*, primarily looks at acknowledging and dealing with the reality of loss. There is often a sense of a loss of professional identity and disenchantment with the organization. Staff need time to reaffirm the value of the past and then to begin to let go of the past by expressing feelings, both positive and negative, about the change. Workers can be supported during this stage by clarifying what is over and what is not and by beginning to make links between what has gone before and what is to come.

The second stage *neutral zone*, is characterized by anxiety, confusion and uncertainty. This is the most confusing stage as entering this stage indicates that those involved have let go of the past but have not yet entered the new reality. There can be very strong feelings at this stage and people can become polarized between those who want to rush forward and those who want to move back to the past. Paradoxically this can be the most creative stage as within this chaotic stage innovative ideas can emerge. It can be a difficult stage to manage but recognition of the need for the adjustment and search for new meaning make it easier to help individuals emerge from it.

The final stage, *beginnings* is a time of readjustment to and acceptance of the new state. There is full recognition of losses as having happened but also of their replacement with acceptable alternatives. People make the new beginning only if they have first made an ending and spent some time in the neutral zone, yet many organizations try to start with the beginning rather than finishing with the old first.

Rarely, of course, is it as simple as working through the three stages. Just as Marris (1974) saw the ability to adjust as linked to the individual's perceptions of the change, within an organization different groups may be in different zones of change. Skynner

(1989) saw this as a positive feature of organizational transitions. Those who are surging forward need the stabilizing influence of those who are still at the early stages of adjustment to keep them linked with reality. Skynner likened this to a roped-up climbing team where the leader seeks out the route forward but needs the steadying influence of those behind if they take a wrong route. Within this analogy different individuals can be leading the change at different times with different individuals stabilizing the move forward.

Hoyle (2004) studied organizational change within a number of organizations and looked at the range of reactions encountered and how these were affected by the responses of those leading the change. She identified a spectrum of response types ranging from sycophant to saboteur. The two extremes are exemplified by those who are unable to explore the change. These are defensive responses which defend the individuals from having to experience the psychological process of adjustment to the change. 'Those who cannot engage with the change, believing their personal survival is at stake, either blindly oppose it or blindly embrace it' (Hoyle 2004, p.104).

Hoyle does not go on to look at why some individuals are unable to tolerate change and move from the extreme defensive positions. However, it is likely that the explanation is more rooted in individual than in group and organizational experiences. There are some individuals whose patterns of attachments, object relations experiences and life-cycle development have left them much less able to adjust to change. The chapters in this text which explore individual development can contribute to an understanding of why some individuals remain resistant to change despite being given support and opportunities to express their views. Both the sycophants and the saboteurs maintain their positions because, for them 'reality is too painful or too complex and their desires too precious to forsake' (Gabriel 1999, p.224).

Fortunately, not all individuals cling so desperately to extreme defensive positions. Hoyle (2004) identifies two more productive responses: negative challenging and positive challenging. These are seen in teams and in individuals who are able to think creatively and contribute ideas about how the change could be implemented. However, from the case material Hoyle explores she concludes that if positive or negative criticisms are not taken into account, groups can quickly move to the two defensive stances. Those who had been making criticisms from a positive position of commitment to the change move to a position of sycophancy if any criticism comes to be seen as disloyal and undermining. Similarly, those who are less positive about the change but contributing helpful negative points move to a position where they see any grudging acceptance as commitment to a change they now oppose fully. So, though allowing time to express ideas and explore feelings about the change will not help those who cannot give up their defensive positions, it can prevent others from aligning with them. It can also make clearer to the team the isolated 'unreal' positions that the sycophants and saboteurs actually hold.

Hoyle (2004) also looks at the danger of the change leader becoming a sycophantic advocate of the change. As many changes are now generated externally there is a great deal of pressure put on managers to implement the changes without allowing themselves time to work through the personal and professional implications of the changes. Particularly if the manager is well aware of the need for staff to discuss, process and challenge the change, it may be tempting to attempt to avoid this difficult experience by promoting the change and, consciously or unconsciously, giving the message that any disagreement or criticism is not acceptable. This leads to a staff team unable to deal maturely with the reality of change, unable to process the effects of change and less able to contribute to the development of work within the new context. 'Denying the reality of internal differences affects the capacity to think and reflect' (Mosse and Roberts 1994, p.155). The result is likely to be an unhealthy polarisation of unthinkingly positive advocates and negative rejecters of the change.

Managing change can appear a daunting task for managers particularly as they also need to deal with their own psychosocial adjustment to loss. Hughes and Pengelly (1997) argue that managers need to acknowledge their own mixed feelings about changes and yet also act. They should feel able to share their own feelings but without colluding with team members in resisting change. Good external supervision, or consultancy, can aid managers with this process.

## TRANSITIONAL APPROACHES TO CHANGE
Transitional approaches change to draw together a range of perspectives in order to develop a coherent approach to the management of change. They have developed and drawn on the work of earlier organizational theorists, and have devised their own specific focus on understanding organizations, which has included incorporating elements of psychodynamic theory, systems theory and social construction models.

Transitional approaches challenge the premise of planned change and focus on the complexity, instability and uncertainty of an organizational system and its environment. Planned change models are criticized for primarily focusing on the task and not paying sufficient attention to deeper process issues. The central idea of transitional approaches is that organizational change is essentially a psychosocial process. This implies that any change has to take place at two levels at the same time: the external and internal. The psycho component includes the values, beliefs, hopes, defence mechanisms, ideas and ways of thinking which determine how an individual perceives external reality and shapes their actions towards this perceived reality. The social component includes the services, organizational structure, culture, rules, networks procedures, and the political and financial environment which contribute to the external reality. These two components continually interact, creating the organization within which change occurs.

There is within changing organizations a 'double-task' (Bridger 2001): the need to undertake the practical tasks involved in the change effectively while at the same time providing facilitating conditions to make the adjustment to change a positive developmental process. 'In other words, there is a continual interaction between the external objective features of the situation, and the "internal" subjective experience, and it is precisely this interaction that constitutes the psychological framework of transitional process' (Ambrose 2001, p.6).

Within a transitional model the organization has to focus on both the task to be done and the process of adjusting to the impact of the change if it is to be successful. In the present context management theorists have tended to focus more directly on the task and function of the organization at the expense of the psychodynamic component. Understanding of the subjective experience of change for individuals and groups requires an understanding of the psychodynamic elements of the individual and group experience of being part of the organization.

The development of the psycho-analytic aspects of the transitional approach has been ongoing from the 1950s, drawing on and developing from the seminal works of Jaques (1955), Menzies Lyth (1960), Bion (1961) and Klein (1958). Jaques and Menzies linked the unconscious resistance to change to individuals reliance on the existing structures of the organization as these structures served the psychodynamic purpose of lowering anxieties about the 'suffering and pain' of clients. The systems within an organization provide a means of distancing oneself from the immediacy and difficulties of the 'impossible task' (Roberts 1994). Jaques (1955) and Menzies Lyth (1960) describe how organizations establish social defences, for example, through routinization of procedures, to contain the anxiety generated by the work.

Obholzer (1994, p.87) argues that 'defence mechanisms can be divided into two categories, personal and institutional'. Though an individual's patterns of defences are their own they often chose workplaces which 'fit' with these. In addition, the individual's personal defensive stance will come to represent not just that individual but one group perspective within the organization. Individuals are often drawn to social work because of their own need to make things better – and to feel better themselves, which may only be a partially conscious motivation. At a conscious and unconscious level an individual's identity and the organizational task can become intertwined. These approaches mesh well with Marris' (1974) view that we are all resistant to change because of our attachment to structures of meaning that are familiar to us and part of our 'assumptive world'. He refers to 'boundaried' groups serving as a defence against external dangers and the internal distress of disruption of the familiar.

The contribution of Bion (1961) and Klein (1958) to the transitional approach is to more clearly identify particular defensive positions. Bion argued that understanding group dynamics involves the same knowledge as understanding individuals. Within groups Bion identified three positions, 'basic assumptions' which affect group functioning: *dependency, fight–flight*, and *pairing*. A group using the dependency defence will expect the leader to come up with decisions and will avoid making decisions themselves. Discussion even in the leader's absence is about what the leader would do or should do. A group using the fight or flight defence will assume there is a danger to be attacked or to be avoided but there is still the assumption that the leader should devise the response. The group may protest angrily but without actually planning out any specific action. The final defensive position of pairing is based on the belief that whatever the problems now some event in the future will solve them. The group acts as if a pairing between two members of the group or with the leader and some external person will solve all the problems of the group.

In an organizational culture where dependency assumptions predominate there will be a culture of subordination to the leader; in an organizational culture where flight–fight assumptions predominate there will be a culture of paranoia and aggressive competitiveness; and where pairing assumptions predominate there will be a culture of collusion (Stokes 1994). Bion (1961) suggests that the work group gets caught up in a level of emotionality and unconscious processes which takes it away from the task and reality. As all groups swing from attending to the task to the different assumption positions one of the aims of working with groups is to identify the assumptions and refocus on the task.

Bion (1961) suggests links between the basic assumptions he identifies and Klein's paranoid-schizoid position, which is a defensive position similar to the flight–fight assumption. The responses from this position are called 'projection' and 'splitting'. Splitting and projection create divisions between groups with each group feeling that it is all good and the other group all bad. This is commonly seen between, for example, day centres and hostels, health and social work teams, different work groups within organizations, and between workers and management. There may be some genuine criticisms of the decisions of management or work of the other group which can serve as a justification of the projection and create a 'valency' for the projection. However, the lack of recognition of any positive contributions would indicate that projection is being used. This can allow the projectors to feel valued in the good work they are doing as it is the other professionals who are not doing their job effectively. 'Instead of reflecting on what is most appropriate issues are polarised around right and wrong' (Roberts 1994a, p.58). Often the projection focuses on differing values within each group, with each claiming the moral high ground. This is not to say that there are not genuine differences but they are not looked at, or critically discussed, as the position becomes polarized.

In working within organizations it is important to recognize the use of projection. Sometimes when there are organizational issues that the workers 'cannot' explore there can be another level of splitting. For instance, in residential units it is possible for the young people to become seen as all bad with the staff team seeing themselves as united and skilled and merely thwarted in the face of the worst young people, or worst young person, ever. Again there may be genuine difficulties working with the young people but the polarization of staff versus young people would seem to indicate a use of projection and splitting.

Sometimes, where an individual or a group of workers feels overwhelmed by changes or the enormity of the task they face, they may take on board the projected feelings and become de-skilled and helpless. It may seem surprising but accepting the projected views of the team or service as incompetent can serve to relieve anxieties about the task, because as it is now clear that the team are not able to work effectively, the team no longer have to try.

A further defensive position Klein (1958) identifies is the depressive position. Despite its name this is seen to be a position of mature functioning where an individuals own feelings and reactions are owned by them despite the pain in recognizing elements of good and bad in ourselves, in others and in the world. This mature position is hard to hold on to and whenever self-esteem or identity is threatened the more primitive defences re-emerge. Organizations can become stuck in defensive pathological behaviour which, unless worked through, can be repeated and replayed leaving the organization in an impasse and unable to engage with the work. It is natural for people to want to avoid an anxiety-provoking exploration of issues as the creativity needed to shift the status quo is uncomfortable. Individuals would rather arrive at the end point without the experience of getting there. What is needed is an approach to working through the process of change which takes into account the psychological aspects of change and provides a structure to support individuals in through this adjustment.

## Application of the transitional method

The transitional approach to change looks at what is required to develop a structure within which the interplay between defensive positions and mature positions, and the task can be explored effectively. Bridger (2001) called the process 'double tasking'. He says that an organization is not just 'purpose orientated' but is also a 'learning and self-reviewing' entity. It needs not only to review its aims, take stock in relation to the external environment and the opportunities and constraints therein, but also to pay attention to the psychological responses of the members of the organization. This brings the two elements together – an activity task together with a reflective task – with a need to find a balance between the two. Too much focus on the reflective task leads to a lack of impetus and focus, while too little focus on reflection leads to hostility or dependency. Focus on content and focus on process are interdependent in achieving group objectives.

In order to be able to work productively with both process and content the correct 'environment' in which to take stock and review has to be created. There is a need to provide a safe environment in which to undertake the transitional process. Within this space members can stand back and reflect on their feelings about the situation in ways that reduce stress and conflict and can lead to development and change.

Within this 'holding' (Winnicott 1989) environment another person can act as a 'container' (Bion 1967) for projected feelings. The recipient of the projected feelings has to be able to hold on to the anxieties and then, through facilitating the articulation of thoughts and feelings which have seemed intolerable, develop in the group the capacity to think and hold on to anxiety more effectively in order to address the task. 'Containing' is not about avoiding task but allowing views and feelings to be expressed in order that they do not get in the way of the functions of the organization. In the present task-driven organizational culture, taking time to reflect, review and express feelings is often seen as a luxury. However, this can be an essential part of energizing workers and creatively responding to change. Moylan (1994, p.58) describes a team which tended to blame their difficulties on 'incompetent management on whom they seemed angrily dependent...projecting all their feelings of helplessness and incompetence arising from the work itself into the management group'. Once they were given the space to express these feelings, they began to be more able to address the problems directly and act autonomously.

Time is needed to share with colleagues the impact on us as workers of proposed changes, ongoing issues, and responses to difficult experiences with clients. In many teams the manager is the individual who takes on the containing, holding function and who creates the thinking and feeling space for the team members. Within the training arena the practice teacher will often have that role for the student. It is important that the manager or practice teacher is able to 'hold' anxieties and criticisms and to recognize these as part of a positive process rather than an attack. The manager or practice teacher needs to recognize that the person who seems to be most obstructive or difficult is often serving a function not just for him or herself but for the team he or she is, by expressing ambivalent feelings for all the team; this person needs to be 'heard' and responded to for them all.

This transitional model allows for the fact that in the present context we cannot know clearly what the future will look like, though we know that it will continue to change. Awareness of the transitional process can confirm the need for managers to allow exploration of complexity, avoid suppression of the chaos too soon and provide a space within which to find a balance between action and review. It may sound as though the role of management can be an overwhelming one. There is no doubt it is a challenging role but if a transitional approach is developed over time the creation of a reflective culture will take some of the responsibility from the manager. The culture of reflection and expression of views once established can become the part of the role of the team and require less management attention. 'Sharing and processing experiences, suspending judgements, engaging with conflicts, challenging and exploring differences of perspective both overt and covert' contributes to 'cultivating a culture of corporate reflection at group, team, network and individual level' (Huffington, James and Armstrong 2004, p.77).

In addition, within any organization there are structures and systems, such as team leading, project management and work groups, which encourage the development of 'holding' skills within other individuals and individuals who naturally exhibit skills in helping others through the transitional process. It is important to recognize and value these individuals and build on their skills. Positioning individuals who have good holding and containing skills in key roles can ease the demands on the manager to take total responsibility.

In the present climate increasingly change is imposed or the pace of change leaves little time for discussion. When there has been no space for preparatory review it is important to create time for discussion of the process and task issues that have emerged as a result of the change. The danger of minimizing the impact, or ignoring the need to look at the change because there is nothing that could have been done about it, is that workers will become increasingly distanced from the work of the organization. They may lose commitment to the wider aims of the organization and increasingly do what they have to in a disengaged manner or focus only on what they as individuals want to do.

In looking at the management of change Amado and Amato (2001) identify the key features of transitional change as follows: there is potential for learning and development through the change; unconscious processes within individuals and the organization must be taken into account and worked through; the end point is not determined; the process will make the emerging reality more in touch with the individual participants; and the emergent change will be will be owned and shaped by the knowledge and skills of the workers.

In addition to formal group avenues to explore transitional change, individuals reflective and adaptive skills can be developed within supervision. Rushton and Natton (1996, p.371) call this the 'empathic-containing function of supervision'. Supervision can be a major source of support, learning and development. Within supervision the supervisor/practice teacher can provide a reflective space within which the worker/student can explore the impact of the work on themselves. Negative views and feelings can be expressed with a confidence that they won't be rejected for these views but given space to work them through to resolution and sometimes identifying new solutions to problems. The supervisor can hold on to intolerable feelings for the worker so that the worker can explore them through his interactions with the supervisor. For example:

if a manager is made anxious by a colleague and recognises this has been projected into him, he may hold on to the disturbing feelings while he tries to understand the situation. In a good outcome situation the manager may help the colleague deal with the situation to a point where he can once again function autonomously. (Raffaelli and Harrow 2005, p.263)

Just as important is the quality assurance function of supervision at the tasks and roles of the worker. Supervision mirrors group transition management in involving a 'double tasking' role in looking at both the practical and the emotional components of the work in a balanced way. For students on placement a key role of supervision is to provide an experience of 'double tasking' which can, not only contribute to development on place-ment, but also serve as a model for personal and professional development throughout their career.

## Transitional approaches and complexity
### MANAGING AT THE BOUNDARY
Increasingly social work students move rapidly into team management roles and it is im-portant for them to understand the complexity of management positions and the skills required of them. The practice teacher is in a key position to assist them in developing an understanding of organizations.

Organizations have had to become more open systems in order to be able to respond to the dynamic change environment as information and influences from the external world need to be able to enter the system. For many organizations the management of the flow of influences and information is filtered through the boundary via the manager. Boundary management is a complex role where the manager has to identify sufficiently with the team, with fellow managers, with the wider organizations and with other agencies whose input is important to the work. The manager has to look inwards and outwards simultaneously and avoid being drawn too exclusively into either system. The manager can be the focus of criticism from the team and from the wider environment for neglecting their interests, but however comfortable it might be to commit to one or the other, the role requires a balancing of both.

In working with organizations often workers argue that all would be well if commu-nication was improved and they knew what was going on. Improving channels of communication is clearly necessary for some organizations; however, this is not about being flooded with all information but all relevant information. The manager has a key role in filtering information effectively:

Leadership is about managing a quite sensitive 'titration' process-too much ex-ternal reality overwhelms in-house values and the strengths of the past are lost, too little titration of reality leaves the organisation at the risk of being bogged down, irrelevant and at work conceptually and financially bankrupt. (Obholzer and Miller 2004, p.36).

In the face of the complexity involved in management at the boundary it can be reassuring to remember that 'creativity is inherent to systems operating at the edge of disintegration' (Stacey 1996, p.177) and that anxiety in an organization must not be too contained or there will be no possibility of change or creativity.

## NETWORKING AND LESS TANGIBLE ORGANIZATIONS

Though the manager in many organizations does have a key responsibility for managing the boundary in the more open systems that have developed more recently, this responsibility has become disseminated more widely. With increasing inter-agency working and with the devolving of responsibility for projects and teams working with the inner and the external world is a skill that others need to develop. Like the manager, the worker has to manage the membership of more than one system while not being subsumed fully in either. It can be as difficult to achieve for the workers as for the manager. 'More initiative is now required… more innovative capability, more flexibility and more recognition of the need to co-operate' (Bridger 2001, p.141).

Working effectively within networks, collaborative working, has been a policy requirement for some time. However in reality there is more often a situation where professionals work together while still holding on to traditional divisions of knowledge and authority (multi-professional working) rather than sharing knowledge and ideas more innovatively (interprofessional working). For social work interprofessional work is not a new aspiration as there are social work practitioners within hospital teams, prisons and so on for many years. However this does not mean that collaborative work has necessarily resulted from this close contact. There has been an assumption that allocating workers from different professional backgrounds to the same 'team' would automatically lead to collaborative working. However, though there is often collaboration across administrative boundaries there is less evidence of professionals sharing knowledge and fully integrating procedures. In looking at the present context of social and health care, Owens, Carrier and Horder (1995) conclude that the pattern is still one of multiprofessional rather than interprofessional working.

Despite a recognition that genuine collaborative working is something to aspire to, it carries with if many of the difficulties of managing at the boundary of systems and of the taking-up of the defensive positions to manage anxiety which have already been outlined. Though working in networks may provide workers with more independence and autonomy it can also arouse strong feelings about identity and lack of belonging. Traditionally, individuals' allegiances have been to their own agency or profession, and within a multidisciplinary team there are often difficulties in managing dual membership.

> Each group membership carries a greater or lesser degree of sentience or emotional significance (Miller and Rice 1967). From this stems loyalty and commitment to the group's aims. Inevitably individuals with membership in more than one group will have trouble with conflicting demands from the various groups they belong to, and their dominant sentience may shift over time. (Roberts 1994b, p.191).

Like managers working at the boundaries of organizations, individuals need to hold on to and balance links to their professional identity, to their home agency and to the collaborative group. Too much loyalty to the home agency leads to splitting and projection, competition and fragmentation; while too much loyalty to the collaborative group leads to lack of identity, challenges to the value base and possible merging at a de-skilled level. Within networks, where an individual can feel isolated and less clear about their role, it is more likely that individual defences will come into play. There is a danger that members of different professional groups will see the other as a dangerous threat to their values and professional position. In order to minimize this, it is important that workers have a clear sense of their professional identity.

The potential difficulties in managing dual membership are similar to the difficulties of dual management. It is important to be clear about lines of accountability. If different professionals refer everything back to the home agency and do not accept the appointed leader, they may be effectively unmanaged within the network. Sufficient authority needs to be delegated to the network leader and this needs to be sanctioned both within the group and outside.

Miller, Freeman and Ross (2001) studied a range of interprofessional 'teams'. Most of these they found to be fragmented rather than integrated. Their findings from looking at the more successfully integrated team are helpful in identifying what allowed this team reach a more integrated perspective. Their findings fit well with the model of managing transitional change, as that team was able to create a 'transitional' space within which individuals shared and processed experiences, and explored differences in perspective while also valuing the role of the other professionals. For network teams to work effectively there needs to be clarity about the roles of the different professionals, and a valuing of them based on recognition that each profession has its own specific unique contribution to make. The professional themselves needs to have a clear perception of their own role as their can be some flexibility at the boundary of the role only if the worker is clear about where the boundary is i.e. what is core and what is peripheral. In collaborative work, it is important for each professional to retain certain unique areas of skill and knowledge in order to maintain a clear identity, while sharing the remaining aspects with others.

Within a collaborative team, as within any other group endeavour, anxieties need to be expressed, and issues fully explored, without people either retreating to a fixed professional stance or giving up their professional identity. In trying to develop collaborative work partners can become:

> so preoccupied by the nature and/or requirements of their own work that partnership cannot get off the ground or the energy and commitment released by partnership leads to a watering down or abandonment of real differences related to the nature of the work. (Huffington, James and Armstrong 2004, p.76).

Collaborative working requires

> time and space for…staff not only to talk about and evaluate the work but also to explore personal experiences related to work, to look at the way they work together, at the reciprocal influences and interdependencies of that work, and the suitability of the 'package' offered in view of the objectives. (Vansina-Cobbaert 2005, p.43)

This open reviewing allows individuals to learn about other professionals' ways of thinking and working and also to get feedback on how they are perceived and can contribute to the shared task. The work can then become genuinely collaborative.

Cooper and Dartington (2004) argue that we are living in a world where the traditional organization is vanishing and that individual investment is now in the work itself, with any work setting becoming a temporary location for practising professional competence. Organizations are no longer complete in themselves. 'They provide a structure of a kind, around which networks and alliances of workers can cluster. However they do not have clear boundaries with those at the periphery of one network being at the centre of another' (Cooper and Dartington 2004, p.142). For workers to flourish within this transitional state they need to have a clear sense of their own role and professional identity. The transient networks will only fully support the workers if they can provide transitional space within which the network can not just fulfil the practical aspects of the work but also serve a 'containing' function for workers from different professional backgrounds.

## Conclusion: the role of training for the world of dynamic change

Interprofessional working encourages professionals to share their skills; however, this can only be done when morale is high and when different professions do not feel threatened by others. This threat may be 'real', as workers from different professions may take on what have been seen as traditional social work roles. Similarly the impact of imposed changes on structures and services because of policy initiatives has left some social workers feeling a loss of status, position and familiar role. It is not surprising in this context that there is both psychological and intellectual resistance to change.

However, it is clear that interprofessional methods of working are going to form a significant part of social work and if the opportunities for work are to be utilized most effectively workers need to develop skills in collaborative working. As already indicated, this requires a clear sense of professional identity, equal status with other professional and a willingness to value the contribution of others. The training of present students needs to make them aware of and able to work within networks. The development of network placements may go some way towards meeting this need. 'Network placements offer learning and opportunities that reflect the changing reality of social work and prepares students for the changing world' (Batchelor and Boutland 1996, p.102).

It can be argued that while working within a range of settings it will be difficult for students to develop a defined social work identity. This identity development will require skilled supervision. As in any other management of transitional development supervision will need to provide a boundaried space in which students can make sense of and reflect on their experiences, develop professional identity and clarify their roles.

In a world of change and transitions adaptive organizations will be best placed to meet the contradictory requirements of maintenance and change. The concept of 'transitions' and the requirements for structuring transitional change have application at many levels. It has relevance for individual development, social work training, team development, organizational adjustment and for working within networks. Practice teachers have a key role in orientating students to their position within changing organizations and in developing their understanding of and ability to function productively within the complexity of this change.

The transitional model is a positive approach recognizing the opportunity to engage with and develop through rather than be buffeted by change. It is a model that recognizes change as a constant that we live within and, rather than seeking a steady state, appreciates that 'dynamic stability' (Hughes and Pengelly 1997) is a reality in the ever-changing world.

# References

Amado, G. and Amato, R. (2001) 'Some distinctive features of transitional change.' In G. Amado and A. Ambrose *The Transitional Approach to Change*. London: Karnac.

Ambrose, A, (2001) 'An introduction to transitional thinking.' In G. Amado and L. Vansina (eds) *The Transitional Approach to Change*. London: Karnac.

Batchelor, J. and Boutland, K. (1996) 'Patterns that connect.' In N. Gould and I. Taylor (eds) *Reflective Learning for Social Work*. Aldershot: Arena.

Bion, W.R. (1961) *Experiences in Groups*. London: Tavistock Publications

Bion, W.R. (1967) *Second Thoughts*. London: William Heinemann. Reprinted London: Karnac Books (1984).

Bowlby, J. (1969) *Attachment and Loss, Vol. 1*. New York: Basic Books.

Bridger, H. (2001) 'The working conference design.' In G. Amado and A. (eds) (2001) *The Transitional Approach to Change*. London: Karnac.

Bridges, W. (1991) *Managing Transitions: Making the Most of Changes*. Reading: Addison-Wesley.

Campbell, D. (2000) *The Socially Constructed Organisation*. London: Karnac.

Cooper, A. and Dartington, T. (2004) 'The vanishing organisation: Organisational containment in a networked world.' In C. Huffington, D. Armstrong, W. Halton, L. Hoyle and J. Pooley (eds) *Working Below the Surface: The Emotional Life of Contemporary Organisations*. London: Karnac.

Emery, F.E. and Trist, E.L. (1965) 'The causal texture of organizational environments.' *Human Relations 18*, 21–32.

Gabriel, Y. (1999) *Organizations in Depth*. London: Sage.

Hoyle, L. (2004) 'From sycophant to saboteur-responses to organisational change.' In C. Huffington, D. Armstrong, W. Halton, L. Hoyle and J. Pooley (eds) *Working Below the Surface: The Emotional Life of Contemporary Organisations*. London: Karnac.

Huffington, C. (2004) 'What women leaders can tell us.' In C. Huffington, D. Armstrong, W. Halton, L. Hoyle and J. Pooley (eds) *Working Below the Surface: The Emotional Life of Contemporary Organisations*. London: Karnac.

Huffington, C., James, K. and Armstrong, D. (2004) 'What is the emotional cost of distributed leadership?' In C. Huffington, D. Armstrong, W. Halton, L. Hoyle and J. Pooley (eds) *Working Below the Surface: The Emotional Life of Contemporary Organisations*. London: Karnac.

Hughes, L. and Pengelly P. (1997) *Staff Supervision in a Turbulent Environment: Managing Process and Task in Front-line Supervision*. London: Jessica Kingsley Publishers.

Jaques, E. (1955) 'Social systems as a defense against persecutory and depressive anxiety.' In M. Klein, P. Heimann and R. Money-Kyrel (eds) *New Directions in Psychoanalysis*. London: Tavistock.

Klein, M. (1958) 'On the development of mental functioning.' *International Journal of Psychoanalysis 39*, 84–90.

Kotter, J. (1996) *Leading Change*. Boston, MA: Harvard Business School Press.

Lewin, K. (1945) 'The research center for group dynamics at Massachusetts Institute of Technology.' *Sociometry 8*, 126–36.

Lewin, K. (1947) *Resolving Social Conflicts*. New York: Harper.

Marris, P. (1974) *Loss and Change*. London: Routledge & Kegan Paul.

Martyn, H. (2000) *Developing Reflective Practice: Making Sense of Social Work in a World of Change*. Bristol: Polity.

Menzies Lyth, I. (1960) 'Social systems as a defense against anxiety.' In Menzies Lyth, I. (1988) *Containing Anxiety in Institutions: Selected Essays.* London: Free Association Books.

Miller, E.J. and Rice, A.K. (1967) *Systems of Organization: Task and Sentient Systems and Their Boundary Control.* London: Tavistock Publications.

Miller, C., Freeman, M. and Ross, N. (2001) *Interprofessional Practice in Health and Social Care.* London: Arnold.

Mosse, J. and Roberts, V. Z. (1994) 'Finding a voice: differentiation, representation and empowerment in organisations under threat.' In A. Obholzer and V.Z. Roberts (eds) *The Unconscious at Work: Individual and Organisational Stress in the Human Services.* London: Routledge.

Moylan, D. (1994) 'The dangers of contagion: Projective identification processes in institutions.' In A. Obholzer and V.Z. Roberts (eds) *The Unconscious at Work: Individual and Organisational Stress in the Human Services.* London: Routledge.

Obholzer, A. (1994) 'Fragmentation and integration in a school for physically handicapped children.' In A. Obholzer and V.Z. Roberts (eds) *The Unconscious at Work: Individual and Organisational Stress in the Human Services.* London: Routledge.

Obholzer, A. and Miller, S. (2004) 'Leadership, followership and the creative workplace.' In C. Huffington, D. Armstrong, W. Halton, L. Hoyle and J. Pooley (eds) *Working Below the Surface: The Emotional Life of Contemporary Organisations.* London: Karnac.

Owens, P., Carrier, J and Horder, J. (eds) (1995) *Interprofessional Issues in Community and Primary Health Care.* London: Macmillan.

Peterson, R.A. (1980) 'Entrepreneurship and organization.' In P. Nystrom and W. Starbuck (eds) *Handbook of Organizational Design, Vol. 1.* Oxford: Oxford University Press.

Raffaelli, D. and Harrow, J.A. (2005) 'Self-action research. An institution reviews itself.' In G. Amado and L. Vansina (eds) *The Transitional Approach in Action.* London: Karnac.

Roberts, V.Z. (1994a) 'The self-assigned impossible task.' In A. Obholzer and V.Z. Roberts (eds) *The Unconscious at Work: Individual and Organisational Stress in the Human Services.* London: Routledge.

Roberts, V.Z. (1994b) 'Conflict and collaboration: Managing intergroup relations.' In A. Obholzer and V.Z. Roberts (eds) *The Unconscious at Work: Individual and Organisational Stress in the Human Services.* London: Routledge.

Rushton, A. and Nathan, J. (1996) 'The supervision of child protection work.' *British Journal of Social Work 26,* 357–74.

Schön, D.A. (1975) *Beyond the Stable State. Public and Private Learning in a Changing Society.* Harmondsworth: Penguin.

Schön, D.A. (1995) 'The new scholarship requires a new epistemology.' *Change 27,* 27–34.

Skynner, R. (1989) *Institutes and How to Survive Them.* London: Routledge.

Stacey, R.D. (1996) *Complexity and Creativity in Organizations.* San Francisco, CA: Barrett-Koehler.

Stapely, L.F. (1996) *Personality of the Organisation: A Psycho-Dynamic Explanation of Culture and Change.* London: Free Association Books.

Stokes, J. (1994) 'The unconscious at work in groups and teams.' In A. Obholzer and V.Z. Roberts (eds) *The Unconscious at Work: Individual and Organisational Stress in the Human Services.* London: Routledge.

Vaill, P.B. (1996) *Learning as a Way of Being: Strategies for Survival in a World of Permanent Whitewater.* San Francisco, CA: Jossey-Bass.

Vansina-Cobbaert, M.J. (2005) 'A therapeutic community: A space for multiple transitional change.' In G. Amado and L. Vansina (eds) *The Transitional Approach in Action London:* Karnac.

Winnicott, D.W. (1989) *Psychoanalytic Explorations.* London: Karnac Books.

# Section 5: Reflective And Evidence-Based Practice

## CHAPTER 23

# REFLECTIVE PRACTICE AND CRITICAL REFLECTION

*Jan Fook*

## Introduction

It has been argued that there is an increasing need for reflective practice, given a growing 'crisis' in the professions (Gould 1996; Schon 1983). This crisis revolves around an increased questioning of professional authority and infallibility. Aligned with this there have been moves to manage professional practice through more objective, routinized and measurable systems of accountability (Fook, Ryan and Hawkins 2000, p.242). It might be argued that the essentially subjective processes of critical reflection are antithetical to the more technocratized systems of managerialism. However, I would argue that the move towards reflective practice can be seen as part of the same imperative – to make professional practice more accountable through ongoing scrutiny of the principles upon which it is based.

For this reason, the ability to reflect upon practice in an ongoing and systematic way is now regarded as essential to responsible professional practice. There has been some criticism that 'reflective practice' has simply become a new, and uncritical, orthodoxy (Ixer 1999), possibly because it can be enacted in many and varied ways, and is used so widely, across many different professions and disciplines (Fook, White and Gardner 2006). In this chapter, therefore, I aim to provide enough basic detail about reflective practice and critical reflection for new social work students and practice teachers to begin to use the process in their own practice. I begin by outlining the basic theory and origins of critical reflection, illustrating this with a detailed example of how it can be used in practice learning and teaching, and indeed as an underpinning for ongoing professional practice. I finish by discussing some of the issues for learning which emerge.

## Reflective practice and critical reflection – definitions

The terms 'reflective practice' and 'critical reflection' are often used interchangeably. Both involve an ongoing scrutiny of practice based on identifying the assumptions underlying it. 'Reflective practice' emerges principally from the work of Donald Schon (for example, 1983 and 1987), who was one of the first to alert us to the crisis in the professions often represented by the perceived gap between formal theory and actual practice. In Schon's thinking, reflective practice was a way of reducing the gap, by unearthing the actual theory which is embedded in what professionals do, rather than what they say they do.

Many writers also make a distinction between reflection and *critical* reflection (Fook and Askeland 2006a). The idea of critical reflection seems to be more associated with writers in the education field, in particular adult education (e.g. Brookfield 1995; Mezirow 1991). Part of the difficulty in pinning down exactly what reflective practice and critical reflection mean may be due to the fact that there has been a great deal of development of these concepts in widely varying fields, from the health and welfare professions to law, management, business and education, and from both research and practice traditions.

Critical reflection is defined in various ways. Mezirow (1991), distinguishes critical reflection as unearthing deeper assumptions or 'presuppositions' (p.12). Brookfield (1995, p.8) emphasizes that what makes reflection *critical* is the focus on power. 'Critical', in this sense, is about the ability to be transformative, 'to involve and lead to some fundamental change in perspective' (Cranton 1996, pp.79–80). We can further extend this to encompass an awareness of how assumptions about the connection between oneself and social context/structure can function in powerful ways, so that awareness of these assumptions can provide a platform for transformative action (e.g. Fook 2002; Kondrat 1999). These latter understandings are associated with a critical social theory tradition (Agger 1998). This is the perspective that I adopt in this chapter and in my own work more generally, because I feel it is most compatible with the theoretical traditions of the social work profession, and with the change aspirations of many current practising professionals.

Critical reflection and reflective practice are therefore not mutually exclusive, but are based on similar assumptions and processes of thinking. I like to think of critical reflection as being a subset of reflective practice. Critical reflection is reflective practice which focuses on the power dimensions of assumptive thinking, and therefore on how practice might change in order to bring about change in the social situations in which professionals work. In order to be able to *critically* reflect, obviously one must be able to reflect. However, not all reflective practice will lead to critical reflection – that is, to fundamental changes. While this chapter will outline general reflective processes and thinking, it will also discuss some of the issues involved with critical reflection specifically.

In order to understand the idea of critical reflection and the processes involved, it is helpful to explore the main traditions of thinking from which it arises. I have identified four main ones which are involved: reflective practice, reflexivity, postmodernism and deconstruction, and critical social theory. These traditions are not mutually exclusive, and of course share many commonalities. It is helpful to understand some of the basic tenets of each of these traditions in order to build up a more complex understanding of the theoretical underpinnings of critical reflection. In addition, a better understanding of some of this thinking will enable us as learners to make more substantial connections between our own assumptions and our social and cultural contexts. In the following section I will detail each of these main traditions and their major contributions to the idea of critical reflection.

## The theoretical background of critical reflection

### REFLECTIVE PRACTICE

In the professions, the idea of reflective practice is often credited initially to Argyris and Schon (1976) and later to Donald Schon (1983 and 1987). These works form much of the initial basis for subsequent later writings in the professional learning traditions, such as nursing (e.g. Rolfe 2000; Taylor 2000). In education literature, the work of Dewey (1933) tends to be cited as originating the idea of reflection (Cranston 1996, p.76; Mezirow 1991). Mezirow (1991, p.5) notes that for Dewey 'reflection referred to (Dewey 1933, p.9) "assessing the grounds (justification) of one's beliefs", the process of rationally examining the assumptions by which we have been justifying our convictions'.

Schon (1983, 1987) emphasized the importance of acknowledging that professional knowledge involves both 'technical rationality' (rules) and professional artistry (reflection in action). Part of the 'crisis' for professionals arises from the fact that very often the 'theory' or rules espoused by practitioners, is quite different from the 'theory' or assumptions embedded in the actual practices of professionals. Reflective practice therefore involves the ability to be aware of the 'theory' or assumptions involved in professional practice, with the purpose of closing the gap between what is espoused and what is enacted, in an effort to improve both. A process of reflective practice, in this sense, also serves to help improve practice, by helping to articulate and develop practice theory. In this sense also, reflective practice can be seen as a process of researching practice theory, by developing it directly from concrete practice. From Schon's initial idea of reflective practice, a reflective approach has been developed (e.g. Fook 1996), which encompasses the recognition of the intuitive, the artistic and the creative in professional practice. The role of the emotions is also often emphasized (Fook 1999a).

Put in terms of the reflective practice tradition, *critical* reflection involves a focus on assumptions about power. This includes the many ways power operates, and a person's own power and relationship to it. In addition, focusing on the intuitive and artistic aspects of one's practice also unearths the role of emotions in supporting particular assumptions. A simple reflective approach is useful in helping pinpoint important and indeed formative assumptions. What it can lack, however, is a detailed analysis of how power operates, and in particular the role of personal power in relation to social and structural contexts and constraints. This can be illustrated with a particular example, say the personal experience of loss or grief. Simple reflection might unearth assumptions about the personal meaning of the loss to a person. However, critical reflection, in addition to noting the meaning of the loss might also note how assumptions about social factors might also influence the experience. For instance, the person might feel social expectations to grieve in a certain way, or pressure to relate to other loved ones. The person may feel his or her own lack of power in the face of such pressures. In this example, reflection and critical reflection are complementary. Critical reflection simply *also* notes how a person's assumptions may carry power dimensions.

### REFLEXIVITY

The idea of reflexivity comes from different traditions again, and is often associated with social science research (Marcus 1994) in fields like anthropology (for example, Rosaldo

1993). It has been developed more recently in the health and human service professions (e.g. Taylor and White 2000). Reflexivity, or a 'turning back on itself' (Steier 1991), has been defined in various ways. White's version of reflexivity (2002, p.10) emphasizes the ability to look both inwards and outwards to recognize the connections with social and cultural understandings. This is similar to my own version, which involves the ability to recognize that all aspects of ourselves and our contexts influence the way we research (or create knowledge) (Fook 1999b). I am using the idea of research here to refer to all the different ways in which we create knowledge – some occur on a more formal and systematic basis, yet others are used daily, and often in unarticulated ways to make sense of immediate surroundings. In this sense, research, or knowledge creation, is integral to the daily business of living.

Therefore, in order to be reflexive, we need to be aware of the many and varied ways in which we might create, or at least influence, the type of knowledge we use. There are at least four ways this might happen. First, knowledge is *embodied and social in nature* – it is mediated by our physical and social lenses. So our physical states and our social positions will influence how we interpret and select information, and indeed how we are socially interpreted and interacted with. Similarly, knowledge is also mediated by our own *subjectivity* – our particular being, experience and social position will influence what phenomena we see and how we see them. Third, there is a reactivity element – the knowledge we obtain is at least partly determined by the kinds of tools and process we use to create it. So our own beliefs about what constitutes legitimate knowledge and its legitimate creation, and the types of methods we should and do use, will influence what we find out. For example, information gathered from observation may be quite different from that gained through a conversation. And, last, knowledge is also *interactional* – it is shaped by historical and structural contexts.

Using the idea of reflexivity then, critical reflection is a way of researching personal practice or experience in order to develop our understandings of how ourselves as knowers or makers of knowledge. This in turn helps us make specific connections between ourselves as individuals and our broader social, cultural and structural environment, by understanding how our ideas, beliefs and assumptions might be at least partially determined by our social contexts.

## POSTMODERNISM AND DECONSTRUCTIONISM

The influence of postmodern thinking brings with it particular ways of thinking which to some degree transcend yet complement those associated with reflexivity. For the purposes of this chapter I also include poststructural thinking as well, in that there are common threads which are useful to our understanding of critical reflection (Fook 1999a).

By postmodernism, I am referring simply to the questioning of 'modernist' (or linear and unified) thinking (Parton 1994). It represents a questioning of the idea that knowledge must be arrived at in a progressive way, and that it is non-conflictual. Thus postmodern thinking alerts us to the relationship between knowledge and power (an analysis useful in critical reflection). By pointing up the role of dominant discourses in creating what is perceived as legitimate knowledge (and therefore power) postmodernism sheds light on where power rests and how it is maintained by focusing on how certain thinking, and its association with certain groups, might function to strengthen the position of that group in relation to others. Poststructuralists also alert us in particular to the role of language in forming our knowledge. The way we speak about things, what we choose to label and what is not labelled, and the relationships we imply through the language we use, all have a role in marking what is legitimate and what is thus powerful.

In particular, the tendency to construct binary opposites, that is to create paired categories of phenomena that are total, mutually exclusive and oppositional (e.g. 'male' and female') is an important element in language-making (Berlin 1990). It often underlies how we make difference, and is therefore a crucial part of identity-making, and by implication, inclusion and exclusion. For instance, we often attribute inferiority to the second part of a binary category (e.g. 'female' is inferior to 'male' by definition) and indeed the second part of the binary is often defined in terms of the first (e.g. females are defined as 'not male'). Thereby the first category in the binary opposite retains primacy.

In addition, language (and dominant discourse) also has a role in silencing multiple and marginal perspectives, since it is often only the major (unified) voice which is recognized or recorded historically.

In broad terms then, postmodern and poststructural thinking recognizes that knowledge can be socially constructed. By assuming that particular knowledge is linear and unified, we can unwittingly support a dominant power base, and unwittingly participate in preserving these power relations through the very language which we use to speak about our world. Thus postmodern thinking opens up an awareness of the possibilties for contradiction, change and conflict in thinking, by recognizing that many different experiences can be legitimate, and by providing the basis from which to question accepted dominant ways of thinking.

From a postmodern and poststructural angle then, critical reflection can be aided by deconstructing our thinking in order to expose how we participate in constructing power. This opens the way for us to explore conflicts and contradictions which may have been previously silenced. In particular, it is useful in helping to explore difficulties in practice which are brought about because of perceived (binary) dilemmas or tensions, such as where we have reached an impasse in practice because we believe there is a fundamental dilemma or conflict involved. For example, social workers often conceptualize a basic dilemma in their work as being between 'care' and 'control'; or about 'value-based practice' versus 'outcome-driven practice', as if the two categories are mutually exclusive. Postmodern thinking can lead us to question these divisions, to formulate perhaps more complex ways of working. However, what postmodern and poststructural thinking lacks in its contribution to critical reflection is details about the evaluative aspects – how do we determine which forms of power actually preserve or challenge domination, and how we might change this, need further explication. For this we need to turn to critical social theory.

## CRITICAL SOCIAL THEORY

There are aspects of the work of many different theorists which share some commonalities with this category (e.g. Marx, Marcuse, Habermas (Agger 1998)). For our purposes here, I focus on the common themes of critical social theory. I have paraphrased and summarized these (Fook 2002) from Agger (1998) as follows. Critical social theory recognizes that domination is both personally experienced and structurally created. Therefore, individuals can participate in their own domination, by holding self-defeating beliefs about their place in the social structure, their own power and possibilities for change. Social change must therefore be both personal and collective. This involves a recognition that knowledge often has an empirical reality, but the way that knowledge is used and interpreted may be constructed (socially and personally). Therefore, in bringing about social and personal change, communication and dialogue are important to enable new shared understandings to be created.

Critical social theory provides a broader framework for understanding what critical reflection can and should help achieve. By making connections between the personal and structural, and emphasizing the importance of communication, critical social theory points to how a critical reflection process might help us forge bridges between our own experience and that of others to bring about desired social changes. As Mezirow points out: 'precipitating and fostering critically self-reflective learning means a deliberate effort to foster resistance to…technicist assumptions, to thoughtlessness, to conformity, to impermeable meaning perspectives, to fear of change, to ethnocentric and class bias, and to egocentric values' (1991, p.360).

In practical terms, a critical perspective on critical reflection simply involves the idea that when dominant social understandings or assumptions are exposed (through a reflective process) for the political (or ideological) functions that they perform (i.e. that they exist for political reasons in supporting the status quo, apart from whatever inherent truth they might have), the individual who holds those assumptions is given a choice. Once these hidden ideas are exposed, people who hold them are thus given the power to change them (Fook and Askeland, 2006a).

## An example of the critical reflection process

The theoretical traditions outlined above can be used to devise a process and model of critical reflection. In this section I will describe just such a process, which I have been developing over a period of some years, and which I currently use in the continuing education of practising health and welfare professionals.

### THE AIM OF THE CRITICAL REFLECTION PROCESS

As we said earlier, the aim of critical reflection is to assist the learner to unearth and unsettle assumptions (particularly about power) and thus to help identify a new theoretical basis from which to improve and change a practice situation. In essence, this is the critical reflection process: a reflective analysis, particularly of power relations, which leads to change effected on the basis of new awareness derived from that analysis. It is important to emphasize these *two* aspects of the critical reflection process – *analysis* and *change*. In the process the learner is effectively researching their own practice, and developing their own practice theory directly from their own experience. Not only does this function to evaluate and scrutinize practice, it also teaches the learner the process of learning directly from their own concrete practice. In other words, they are learning to create theory which is applicable to practice.

Elsewhere I have likened the overall critical reflection process to a first stage of deconstruction and a second stage of reconstruction (Fook 2002). It is also similar to a conscientization process (Alfrero 1972), in which a person shifts from a more fatalistic stage in which the 'facts' dominate to a final stage of understanding the causal links between 'facts' and social circumstances. With this model of critical reflection there is a further stage which links this new critical awareness with possibilities for action.

## CRITICAL REFLECTION QUESTIONS

Questions are derived from the above four theoretical traditions (reflective practice, reflexivity, postmodernism and critical social theory) to assist in critically reflecting on a specific piece of practice. Below are some examples. From a reflective practice tradition, questions might include: What was I assuming? What beliefs did I have about power (e.g. mine, other people's)? What are my most important values coming across and how do these relate to power?

From a reflexivity standpoint, we might ask: How did I influence the situation? What preconceptions did I have and how might these have influenced what I did or interpreted? How did my presence make a difference? What sort of power did I think I have, and how did I establish myself in the situation? What were my beliefs about power and how did these affect what I did or chose to see?

Using a postmodern/deconstructive perspective, we might ask: What language/words/patterns have I used? Have I used any binary opposites, and what is the basis for these? What perspectives are missing? What are my constructions of power? What is the relationship between my beliefs about power and the mainstream or dominant view? How have I constructed myself in relation to other people, or power?

A critical stance would place the emphasis on how the critical reflection process can bring about change. We might therefore ask questions like: How has my thinking changed, and what might I do differently now? How do I see my own power? Can I use my power differently? Do I need to change my ideas about myself or the situations in which I work?

Clearly each perspective provides different ways of asking critical reflective questions, but there is also a great deal of commonality. It is not important to differentiate the traditions each type of question is related to, but instead to use these theoretical underpinnings, and the analyses they provide, in an integrated and inclusive way. Using many different ways of questioning will, one hopes, maximize the potential meaningfulness of critical reflection to diverse types of learners. There is in fact no prescribed or formulaic way to undertake critical reflection, and indeed the field is characterized by many different process, techniques and exercises which can be used to further critical reflection. It is as much about the enabling climate which is created, as it is about techniques which are used. The highly diverse nature of critical reflection has been criticised (Ixer 1999) but I would argue that this is in fact one of its primary strengths. Since it is highly adaptable to situation, place, learner and educator, its flexibility potentially allows it maximum effectiveness.

## THE CLIMATE OF THE CRITICAL REFLECTION PROCESS

Given the potentially flexible nature of critical reflection, it is important to structure the process to some degree in order to maximize opportunities to unearth and unsettle assumptions in order to bring about some change. And since there is potentially much personal and professional risk involved in scrutinizing deep-seated assumptions, the climate needs to be enabling and respectful of this.

I therefore think it is important to establish a culture in which it is safe and acceptable to be open and to expose professional vulnerabilities for the sake of learning. Elsewhere this has been termed a climate of 'critical acceptance' (Fook, Ryan and Hawkins 2000, p.230). When I engage in a critical reflection process with colleagues, I am explicit about a set of 'ground rules' to which I establish mutual agreement. There is not room to include the whole list here but some important rules include: confidentiality; respect and acceptance; non-judgementalism (the purpose of critical reflection is to help unearth assumptions, not to make evaluations of actions); focus on 'responsibility' (to influence and respond to the situation) rather than 'blame' (for controlling or causing the situation); openness to other, perhaps contradictory perspectives does not mean having to give up one's own perspective; separating the reflective analysis from the need to make changes or take action.

## THE STRUCTURE OF THE CRITICAL REFLECTION PROCESS

In the model of critical reflection I have developed I ask participants to meet as a small group (usually up to ten people), and I ask each participant to present a piece of practice which was crucial to them in some way. This serves as the 'raw' material for reflection. I then structure the process in two stages. The first focuses on the analytical stage: exposing and examining the hidden assumptions. The second stage focuses on turning an awareness of these hidden assumptions into new ways of understanding practice, our power, and how we might challenge and change our environments accordingly.

The process essentially involves a small group of participants who assist each other to critically reflect on their practice in a confidential setting facilitated by someone versed in the approach. The process normally begins with an introductory session (approximately one and a half hours in length) in which the facilitator lays the groundwork for the programme. This might consist of formal group introductions, some theoretical background and a discussion of ground rules as well as an outline of the process. This is usually presented in an informal and interactive manner. This is followed by a modelling of the first stage of the critical reflection process by the facilitator, in which the facilitator presents her or his own practice material ('critical incident', as discussed below) and asks the group to assist her or him critically reflect upon it, using the questions which have been outlined as a guide. This might last up to one hour. This modelling is vital in establishing a group climate of trust, and ensuring that interaction is egalitarian. The facilitator may then spend a brief time discussing the process and clarifying the participants' understanding of it.

I ask people to present their piece of practice experience in the form of a concrete 'critical incident'. The critical incident technique is widely used, and in varying ways (Brookfield 1995; Davies and Kinloch 2000). In the critical reflection process that I use, I ask that it be kept deliberately concrete, as someone's 'story' or 'narrative' about an event in which they were involved, and which was significant to them in some way. 'Critical' in this sense simply refers to something which was crucial or significant to the person. I ask that they describe, in writing, why it was critical (or their reasons for choosing it), the background or context of the incident and the actual incident. It is vital to use a brief, concrete incident from the person's own practice because it allows them ultimately to keep the focus on further concrete possibilities for their own practice, without being distracted by overly abstracted ways of theorizing practice. Participants bring written versions of the incident for distribution to group members, so that the written version can also be reflected upon, as verbal interaction also takes place.

Participants present their critical incidents in two stages according the process outlined above. They are normally allotted at least half an hour per presentation. Thus, overall the programme takes approximately the equivalent of two and a half days. Normally the first session, which includes the introduction and the facilitator's modelling, takes a half day, then the next two sessions take one day each, usually split by a period of at least a week to allow further intervening reflection.

The first stage focuses on analysing the story of the incident. The whole group asks critical reflective questions based on the four theoretical traditions outlined above. The facilitator tries to ensure that each participant reaches a point where they feel able to articulate some major assumptions which have been unearthed, and can identify some major piece of learning which they wish to take away and reflect further upon. During and at the end of the first session, the facilitator also draws out some of the commonalities of discussion, taking care to make connections between personal and social experiences. At the end of the first stage, the facilitator also ensures that the group as a whole understands their tasks for the second stage. Before the second stage, each participant reflects further on the thinking which has been unearthed in this first stage. In the second stage, they present their revised 'theory of practice' again (allowing approximately at least half an hour each), with a view to devising specific practice strategies from it. The group assists this process by asking a series of questions focused on how practice and thinking may change or be different, compared to their original conception of the incident. Often they may focus on how they would handle it now, given their new set of reflections. The facilitator may encourage them to put a 'label' in this new set of actions and reflections, thus engaging in the process of creating their own personal 'theory of practice'.

## General outcomes and uses

What are some of the claimed benefits of critical reflection? They include an increased capacity for research and knowledge-building (Hess 1995, pp.65, 81), better knowledge application (i.e. the ability to use previous knowledge in new cases) (Hess 1995, p.75), the ability to create contextually appropriate responses (Fook and Napier 2000), improved practice, the creation of new practice possibilities (Hess 1995, p.80) and an increased capacity to practice in change and uncertainty (Fook and Napier 2000).

Analysis of evaluation results from my own critical reflection groups conducted over the last four years indicates the following broad trends:

- Increased collegiality, at a variety of levels including between managers and workers, between workers and supervisors, between colleagues within an organization and between colleagues in differing organizations. This was often brought about by gaining support from colleagues, and therefore a better sense of connectedness with them. An openness to new or other perspectives also encouraged this. Former 'enemies' are more likely to be seen as possible allies, and individuals are more likely to look for cooperative, rather than oppositional, ways of working.

- A motivation and desire to find different ways of working with colleagues, especially where there had been previous conflict.

- A re-energizing of interest in and commitment to the job, through a reawakening of basic values and an ability to prioritize work on this basis. This was often experienced as better morale.

- Finding new strategies and options to deal with long-standing dilemmas.

- Finding the motivation to act on long-standing dilemmas which had previously 'frozen' action.

- many participants speak of being 'liberated', usually from assumptions about what 'professional' practice should be. They often come to realize that they have constructed 'professional' practice in such a way that it limits how they can relate to service users (e.g. Lowth and Bramwell, 2001).

## Applications specific to practice teaching/learning

It is clear that the critical reflection can be adapted in many different ways to suit the particular purposes and contexts of practice teaching and learning. The model I have described in this chapter might be used as a component of a university-based teaching programme, or alternatively as a continuing education or peer supervision programme organized for practitioners. It might be adapted using different tools in place of the critical incident (such as 'stories' or 'narratives' of practice, journal entries, case notes/studies, process recordings, observations or taped recordings of interactions). In short, any type of record of practice might be used as potential raw material for systematic critical reflection. Hypothetical stories might be used (Lehmann 2003) to avoid problems of confidentiality. Critical reflection may be done as 'self-critical reflection' (Mezirov 1998) – a process conducted by oneself on one's own material. It can easily be adapted for use in one-to-one supervision sessions, or as a model for peer supervision or learning groups. Alternatively, individuals might make arrangements with their own 'critical friend' – a friend or colleague whom they trust to assist them in more systematic reflection. Interactions may be face-to-face, but also conducted by phone, written or online.

What is most important to emphasize about the use of critical reflection for teaching and learning purposes however, is not technique or technology, but is rather much more about approach. As an overall approach, *critical reflection emphasizes the idea that we are all both teachers and learners*, even though our formal roles or statuses might be more differentiated. This is an important point – *effective critical reflection can only take place in a climate which is egalitarian and participatory*. Knowledge creation, through ongoing reflection on experience, is something which never stops in a committed practising professional at any level. Furthermore, the critical reflective attitude is about being always prepared to question (and change) deep-seated assumptions and practices.

In terms of practice teaching and learning, this places the onus on all players to be aware of, and take responsibility for, the learning environment which is created. This means we all need to ask ourselves, as students, managers, university academics, supervisors, senior practitioners, colleagues or new workers, how we can best create a climate for critical reflection, in the various settings in which we work. This will of course involve implementing some new technologies and processes for learning, but it may also simply involve being prepared to question and change ourselves in far more fundamental ways.

## Conclusion and issues for learning

In conclusion it is fitting to consider some of the criticisms of, and potential difficulties with, critical reflection as an approach and process.

The threat posed by exposing one's professional practice to detailed scrutiny and questioning holds simultaneous potential for harm and good. Elsewhere (Fook and Askeland, in press b) my colleague, Gurid Aga Askeland, and I argue that because critical reflection is also about unearthing deep-seated assumptions which are culturally held, the capacity for unsettling and threat may be too great, and may work against learning potential. The trick is to get the balance right by minimizing the risk and maximizing the learning. Alternatively it may be the case that many participants may not be 'robust' or resilient enough to expose their vulnerabilities in a public way. It may be that critical reflection is not appropriate for everyone. Its culture and values may not be compatible with some people. For others (both teachers and learners) there may not be enough structure. In addition, some workplace cultures may actively work against a culture of critical reflection by exploiting individual workers' vulnerabiities.

Another perceived difficulty of the critical reflection process is its reliance on many theories. Therefore, in practice it can potentially unearth *any* assumptions about *anything*. And indeed some of these assumptions and related experiences may be outside the mandate of the group to deal with. For example, past painful personal experiences may be unearthed which it would be highly inappropriate for a professional learning group to handle. For this reason, it is important to place boundaries on the group's discussion, and to give participants the right to draw boundaries themselves. At the same time, the ability to be open-ended in what is unearthed can be a potential advantage, in that, without too many preconceptions about what to focus on, some crucial but hitherto deeply hidden assumptions may be uncovered. This is another reason why a critical reflection process can take many different forms, and have many different outcomes, depending on the theoretical perspectives of participants, and their ability to delve deeply for important assumptions.

It has also been argued that reflection is a highly individualized activity, its outcomes difficult to generalize to other people and situations. It is also a highly diversified activity, its processes lacking clarity of detail. It is therefore difficult to measure its outcomes, so therefore it seems impossible to assess its success (Ixer 1999). In addition, the reflective approach and its practice seem to fly in the face of current managerial and cost-cutting trends. Some argue that reflection takes too much time in a climate of maximum efficiency. Its outcomes are often open-ended and unpredictable in regimes which value concrete forward planning and budgeting. Furthermore it encourages self-examination and the disclosure of vulnerablities and limitations (Hess 1995), which can undermine the competitive edge of services. Last, it fosters holistic and contextual ways of knowing in economic contexts requiring scientific proofs of effectiveness and 'evidence'.

My response to these claims is not to disagree, but to point out that they constitute all the more reason to identify the benefits of critical reflection, both in 'hard' and 'soft' terms, and to persevere in developing the ways in which a critical reflective ability can be shown to improve practice responsiveness. Far from being an alternative in opposition to evidence-based practice, critical reflection may in fact be a very accessible process which can contribute to articulating the evidence base of practice.

## Note

Some of the ideas in this chapter have also been developed in Fook, J. (2004) 'Transformative possibilities of critical reflection.' In L. Davies and P. Leonard (eds) *Scepticism/Emancipation: Social Work in a Corporate Era*. Aldershot: Ashgate, pp.16–30.

## References

Agger, B. (1998) *Critical Social Theories*. Boulder, CO: Westview.

Alfrero, L.A. (1972) 'Conscientization.' *New Themes in Social Work Education*. New York: International Association of Schools of Social Work.

Argyris, C. and Schon, D. (1976) *Theory in Practice: Increasing Professional Effectiveness*. San Francisco, CA: Jossey-Bass.

Berlin, S. (1990) 'Dichotomous and complex thinking.' *Social Service Review,* March, 46–59.

Brookfield, S. (1995) *Becoming a Critically Reflective Teacher*. San Francisco, CA: Jossey-Bass.

Cranton, P. (1996) *Professional Development as Transformative Learning*. San Francisco: Jossey-Bass.

Davies, H. and Kinloch, H. (2000), 'Critical incident analysis: Facilitating reflection and transfer of learning.' In V.E. Cree and C. Macauley (eds) *Transfer of Learning in Professional and Vocational Education*. London: Routledge.

Dewey, J. (1933) *How We Think*. Chicago, IL: Regnery.

Fook, J. (ed.) (1996) *The Reflective Researcher: Social Theories of Practice Research*. Sydney: Allen & Unwin.

Fook, J. (1999a) 'Critical reflectivity in education and practice.' In B. Pease and J. Fook (eds) *Transforming Social Work Practice: Postmodern Critical Perspectives*. Sydney: Allen & Unwin, Sydney.

Fook, J. (1999b) 'Reflexivity as method.' In J. Daly, A. Kellehear and E. Willis (eds) *Annual Review of Health Social Science*. Vol. 9 Bundoora: La Trobe University.

Fook, J. (2002) *Social Work: Critical Theory and Practice*. London: Sage.

Fook, J. and Askeland, G. (2006a) 'The "critical" in critical reflection.' In S. White, J. Fook and F. Gardner (eds) *Critical Reflection in Health and Welfare*. Maidenhead: Open University Press.

Fook, J and Askeland, G. Aga (2006b) 'Challenges of critical reflection: Nothing ventured, nothing gained.' *Social Work Education.*

Fook, J. and Napier, L. (2000) 'From dilemma to breakthrough: Retheorising social work practice.' In L. Napier and J. Fook (eds) *Breakthroughs in Practice: Social Workers Theorise Critical Moments in Practice*. London: Whiting & Birch.

Fook, J., Ryan, M. and Hawkins, L. (2000) *Professional Expertise: Practice, Theory and Education for Working in Uncertainty*. London: Whiting & Birch.

Fook, J., White, S. and Gardner, F. (2006) 'Critical reflection: A review of current understandings and litera-ture.' In S. White, J. Fook and F. Gardner (eds) *Critical Reflection in Health and Welfare*. Maidenhead: Open University Press.

Gould, N. (1996) 'Introduction: Social work education and the "crisis" of the professions.' In N. Gould and I. Taylor (eds) *Reflective Learning for Social Work*. Aldershot: Arena.

Hess, P. (1995) 'Reflecting in and on practice.' In P. Hess and E.J. Mullen (eds) *Practitioner-Researcher Partner-ships*. Washington: NASW Press.

Ixer, G. (1999) 'No such thing as reflection.' *British Journal of Social Work 29*, 513–27.

Kondrat, M.E. (1999) 'Who is the 'self' in self-aware? Professional self-awareness from a critical theory per-spective.' In *Social Service Review 34*, 4, 451–77.

Lehmann, J. (2003) *The Harveys and Other Stories*. Bendigo, Australia: St Lukes Innovative Resources.

Lowth, A. and Bramwell, M. (2000) 'Dedicated to the memory of Susan.' In L. Napier and J. Fook (eds) *Breakthroughs in Practice: Social Workers Theorise Critical Moments*. London: Whiting & Birch.

Marcus, G.E. (1994) 'What comes (just) after "post"? The case of ethnography.' In N.K. Denzin and Y.S. Lin-coln (eds) *Handbook of Qualitative Research* London: Sage.

Mezirow, J. (1991) 'How critical reflection triggers learning.' In J. Mezirow (ed) *Fostering Critical Reflection in Adulthood*. San Francisco, CA: Jossey-Bass.

Mezirov, V. (1998) 'On critical reflection.' *Adult Education Quarterly 98*, 3, 185–98.

Parton, N. (1994) 'Problematics of government': (post) modernity and social work.' *British Journal of Social Work 24*, 9–32.

Rolfe, G. (2000) *Research, Truth and Authority*. London: Macmillan.

Rosaldo, R. (1993) *Culture and Truth*. London: Beacon Press.

Schon, D. (1983) *The Reflective Practitioner*. London: Temple Smith.

Schon, D. (1987) *Educating the Reflective Practitioner*. San Francisco, CA: Jossey-Bass.

Steier, F. (ed.) (1991) *Research and Reflexivity*. London: Sage.

Taylor, B. (2000) *Reflective Practice*. Buckingham: Open University Press.

Taylor, C. and White, S. (2000) *Practising Reflexivity in Health and Welfare*. Buckingham: Open University Press.

Taylor, I. (1996) 'Reflective learning, social work education and practice in the 21st century.' In N. Gould and I. Taylor (eds) *Reflective Learning for Social Work*. Aldershot: Arena.

White, S. (2002) 'Auto-ethnography as reflexive inquiry.' In I. Shaw and N. Gould (eds) *Qualitative Research in Social Work*. London: Sage.

## CHAPTER 24

# RESEARCH, EVALUATION AND EVIDENCE-BASED PRACTICE

## Joyce Lishman

This chapter examines the knowledge base of social work including the role of research in underpinning social work practice and policy and the need for social workers to engage in the evaluation of the effectiveness of both their practice and the policy requirements underpinning it. It then explores how research and evaluation contribute to the key policy requirement that in social work, social care and social work education we engage in evidence-based practice (Fisher 2002).

The chapter explores the contribution of both research and evaluation to the knowledge base of social work. It explores what we mean by 'research', its importance in social work practice and some tensions which can arise in its application. It similarly explores what we mean by evaluation and the dilemmas involved in evaluating how effective practice is. It explores how blurred the boundaries are between research and evaluation and why there continues to be a gap between what we know from both research and evaluation and the integration of this knowledge in practice, despite the clear professional requirement that we should be research-minded practitioners and work from an evidence base (Scottish Executive 2006) and a more pragmatic view that, if we had been more willing to engage in ongoing evaluation of the effectiveness of our practice, we would be less vulnerable to what may seem rather crude external monitoring.

In short there is a professional and policy requirement that we need to demonstrate how we account for our practice and how effective we are, i.e. how we examine and account for the outcomes of our practice for service users and clients.

So finally the chapter examines evidence-based practice: how research and evaluation contribute to it, some of the complexities involved in defining evidence in social work, and, therefore, how we can best adopt a research-minded and evidence-based approach.

### The knowledge base of social work

Research and evaluation are an integral component of the development of the knowledge base of a profession. As Sheppard (1998, p.763) argues: 'The pursuit of suitable and firm knowledge foundations has long been a preoccupation of many academics and practitioners in the field of social work. It is not, however, one which has commended a great deal of consensus.' Historically a major perceived weakness of social work as a profession has been its lack of a distinct and specific knowledge base and its reliance on knowledge from other disciplines, e.g. the social sciences. The ESRC-funded (Economic and Social Research Council) seminar series, Theorising Social Work Research (1999–2000), clearly challenged such historical perceived weaknesses and presented a robust argument for a specific knowledge base for social work.

However, understanding of what constitutes the knowledge base of social work is, like the nature of social work, contested.

The *Oxford English Dictionary* (OED) defines 'knowledge' as:

> Intellectual acquaintance with, or perception of, fact or truth: the fact, state or condition of understanding.

> Theoretical or practical understanding of an art, science, language, etc.

> The sum of what is known. (p.1093)

In a sense these definitions highlight some problematic aspects of knowledge in social work. In particular the concept of fact as a universal objective truth, (challenged in the natural sciences; Popper 1969) is problematic in social work where individuals' perceptions, judgements, interpretations and meanings contribute critically to developing understanding and knowledge of the field. In social work therefore, 'scientific knowledge' based on experiment and the positivist paradigm of causality deals not with truth and certainties, but rather with probabilities. For example, *Messages from Research* (Department of Health 1995) provided the practitioner in child protection with a comprehensive empirical knowledge base to underpin practice but did not, and could not, prescribe any certainty in individual interventions. As a Malcolm Sargent Social Worker I had a very sound knowledge base about the impact of bereavement (Parkes 1975) but struggled with applying it to individuals and their families (Lishman 1990).

Helpfully Schon (1987) questions the concept of a knowledge base for professional practice which depends only on positivist experimental research, using techniques which are describable, testable and replicable, and which assures objectivity and neutrality. Rather, Schon emphasizes the uniqueness, uncertainty and potential ethical conflicts of each new practice encounter and argues for the development of practice knowledge based on reflection, on and in action.

For the individual practitioner or user or client there is no set causal link between a problem or situation, a response and an outcome, because individuals, their problems and situations are unique.

The tensions involved in defining the knowledge base of social work also refer to definitions of research and evaluation and their inter-relationship.

## Research in social work

The *Oxford English Dictionary* defines 'research' as: 'An investigation directed to the discovery of some fact by careful study of a subject: A course of critical or scientific enquiry' (p.1712).

What do these definitions imply for social work? An immediate question is: what do we mean by facts? As already highlighted, in examining what knowledge in social work is, individual perceptions, meanings and judgements in social work matter but do not constitute 'facts' as viewed from a scientific, experimental positivist paradigm.

Also, research about users' satisfaction or dissatisfaction and more general views about the services they are offered or would like (research which focuses on perceptions and meanings) may not equate with 'harder' statistical data about outcome measurement, e.g. reduction in offending, child abuse or crimes committed by people with serious mental health problems.

Research relevant to social work often deals with broad questions – e.g. the relationship of life chances, health and education with social class, and with access to health and social service provision. It has also addressed effectiveness in child protection (Department of Health 1995), in criminal justice (Smith 2002a) and in models of community care and care management (Fisher 1997).

It is essential that as professional social workers we familiarize ourselves with such relevant research overviews and draw on them but this kind of research also presents dilemmas for individual practitioners. Research findings usually deal with probabilities but they do not tell me about how I, as an individual worker, should best work with a particular individual or family and research findings may not address resource issues and their implications.

Research which is more immediately accessible to practitioners is that which we can apply to our own practice. It addresses and identifies particular problems in social work service and practice delivery. For example, it examines parental participation and involvement in decision-making processes about child protection (Department of Health, 1995), and the characteristics and experiences of particular user groups (Lindow and Morris 1995) and carers (Stalker 2003).

## Evaluation in social work

In the *Oxford English Dictionary* 'to evaluate' is defined as follows: 'To find out the value of: To find the numerical expression for' (p.640). Evaluation involves similar or equivalent dilemmas and tensions to those involved in the use and application of research findings. Evaluation focuses on effectiveness, at a personal level, as well as a service delivery level. At a personal level it involves individual practitioners accounting for what they do, in terms of the process and outcome of their intervention. It involves questioning values, processes and effectiveness, and reflection *in* and *on* action (Schon 1987; Chapter 23, present volume). It may include research (Shaw and Lishman, 1999) but the key for a practitioner should be:

- *How* am I doing what I am doing?

- *Why* am I doing what I am doing?

- *How* could I be more effective?

- *How* can I ensure my practice is outcome focused while recognizing the complexity of what will contribute to outcomes (successful or not) for users of social services?

Some of the answers to these questions may lie outwith the individual practitioner's control and be subsumed in evaluation of the organization within which they practice. At the organizational or service delivery level evaluation may almost inevitably focus on efficiency and effectiveness, meeting targets, performance indicators and Best Value requirements. It may also draw on the independent evaluation of small-scale specific projects, and practitioner research (Everitt 2002).

This chapter will confine its examination of evaluation to that of practice rather than service delivery because its purpose is to explore why we should incorporate research mindedness and evaluation in our practice and how we can best address the evidence-based practice policy agenda.

Evaluation *in* practice needs to include user feedback, lessons from research and performance indicators, but also a critical recognition of the impact of resource and broader organizational issues on individual or team practice. The questions posed for individual practitioners do need to be applied to service provision and projects where the 'I' becomes a 'we' but the 'how', 'why' and 'how effective' questions remain.

Why should we incorporate evaluation into practice (Shaw and Lishman, 1999)? We need as a profession to demonstrate professional accountability, responsiveness to users and clients, and that we are meeting government imperatives: we need evidence to demonstrate our effectiveness that social workers do make a difference.

## Research and evaluation: the blurring of boundaries

The definitions of 'research' and 'evaluation' from the *Oxford English Dictionary* highlight key shared issues in relation to social work research and evaluation between qualitative and pluralistic 'critical' enquiry and quantitative experimental 'scientific research'.

The distinction between research and evaluation is not clear: this is for good reason. Research relevant to social work frequently asks broad questions, for example, about the effect of structural characteristics, e.g. poverty in the lives of users of social work services/social work. Research has also increasingly explored clients', users' and carers' perceptions of social work practice and service delivery (see, for example, Evans and Fisher 1999; Rees and Wallace 1982; Stalker 2003). Further research has focused on how social work practice may lead to more effective outcomes, e.g. in criminal justice to reduce offending (McGuire 1995) and in child care to inform assessment and good practice with children who are looked after (Scottish Office 1997). Such research is difficult to distinguish from evaluation, which is essentially about examining how effective practice and services are in meeting prescribed goals and contributing to successful outcomes (e.g. reducing re-offending, preventing child abuse).

However, definitions of evaluation in terms of prescribed goals and successful outcomes are problematic. Who defines goals and effectiveness? Are they defined by service users, by carers, by practitioners, by managers, by inspectorates (social services or multiprofessional), by government audit performance indicators, or by Care Commissions? What other factors – e.g. societal, structural or health – may limit how effective a social work intervention may be? Is evaluation only about goals and outcomes or does it also include processes, user and practitioner perspectives and meaning and reflection on and in practice?

The boundaries between research and evaluation are blurred in terms of purpose and of findings or outputs. They are even more blurred in terms of the methodologies they draw on. As Shaw argues in Shaw and Lishman (1999).

> the boundaries are indistinct and the range of methods overlap. There are some methodological activities that are likely to be used mainly in research, some mainly in evaluation, and others in evaluating practice. But some methods are used by practitioners in all three contexts. (p.18)

Research and evaluation in social work represents a continuum. Evaluation tends to be about effectiveness and outcomes including user and practitioner evaluation, not just of outcomes, but also of processes. Research also examines effectiveness and outcomes, but frequently from an external (empirical) perspective. However, user-led research (Evans and Fisher 1999) involves much more of a participatory, inclusive research agenda. In general research is not limited to the effectiveness agenda and examines, for example, wider structural and policy issues which provide the underpinning context within which social work is practised.

Research and evaluation in social work draw on the same methodological repertoire. In terms of exploration of questions and problems relevant to social work practice and service delivery, they share a considerable common ground in the continuum suggested. However, at the extreme, research is more likely to explore structural factors relevant to social work users and carers and empirical studies of 'what works'. At the other extreme evaluation may be very practice focused, individual and qualitative. Both extremes have a part to play in the development of social work practice and service delivery. The common agenda and overlap in the continuum of research and evaluation is the focus for the rest of this chapter.

## Research and evaluation: the methodological repertoire

Inevitably any description and analysis of research and evaluation perspectives in social work does not do full justice to the complexity of the questions to be addressed. This chapter draws on the Shaw and Lishman (1999) paradigms because they are inclusive and recognize the contribution of a range of methodologies to research and evaluation in social work.

Shaw and Lishman (1999) argued that there are three broad paradigms in evaluation: a quantitative approach, a qualitative approach and a participatory empowering approach.

Each approach/paradigm uses particular research methodologies, e.g. quantitative, qualitative, experimental, ethnography, case study, and participatory research. The qualitative paradigm also includes a reflective practice approach.

The quantitative approach to evaluation in social work focuses on empirical practice (Reid 1994), also referred to as research-based or scientific practice. The characteristics of this approach have been case monitoring and evaluation – through single system designs, the application of scientific perspectives and experimental design to methods of practice, and application to practice of knowledge based on interventions whose effectiveness has been demonstrated through the research methods identified (i.e. from a scientific, experimental perspective). The quantitative approach to evaluation is particularly relevant to social work models of intervention with a clear focus on very specific outcomes, e.g. task-centred casework (see Chapter 13 in the present volume) and cognitive behavioural models (see Chapter 12 in the present volume).

The strengths of the approach include both the explicitness of specifying a client's or service user's problem, recording change during intervention and as a result evaluating the success of the intervention, and the more general introduction to social work critical analysis of practice of the importance of specifying aims and goals of intervention, of working with clients and service users within specific and explicit contracts, of the use of time-limited intervention and review, and of the evaluation of intervention in terms of outcomes reviewed against original specified aims.

The weaknesses are that, first, the very specific, clear and measurable outcomes may not reflect the complex and messy problems which social work practice encounters.

Second, the quantitative approach fails to recognize that what social work offers is contingent on the context. Any rigorous analysis of 'what works?' has to question the context of the programme, and what elements of it work for which people in what particular circumstances (Smith 2002a, 2002b).

The characteristics of qualitative research include the utilization of a range of social science methods, including ethnography, discourse analysis, case studies and narrative enquiry, the contribution of practitioners to the construction of social work knowledge and the use of Schon's model of reflective practice (1987).

The strengths of qualitative research in social work include the recognition of the need for research and evaluation in social work to address the role of values and judgements about good practices and processes; the recognition of the importance of meaning and perceived experience in social work encounters, and not solely of prescribed outcomes; the recognition of the importance of the voice of the consumer, user or client in evaluating the experience of receiving a social work service (Beresford and Croft 2001) and the importance of the 'narrative'. *Changing Lives* (Scottish Executive 2006), while emphasizing the critical importance of an outcome focus and an evidence base, also recognizes the importance of relationship-based social work, i.e. process as well as outcome.

A further strength of a qualitative approach in social work to research and evaluation is a recognition of workers' understanding and perception of assessment, process, decision-making and intervention, in the light of their professional, ethical and knowledge base, as well as wider organizational and resource influences and constraints.

The potential weaknesses of this approach include a lack of clarity about specific purposes of intervention and related outcomes, and a focus on individual, specific experience, rather than data which is generalizable. A further potential weakness is that the emphasis is on individual experience and change which may be seen as irrelevant, when in policy terms success may be measured at political and programme level by relatively crude quantitative indicators.

Finally we need to consider the contribution of participatory and empowering research and evaluation (Dullea and Mullender 1999), not yet an established paradigm in social work research and evaluation, but an approach which begins to address the power and authority imbalance between managers, practitioners and users or recipients of services in the evaluation of practice and services (Humphries 2003).

Examination of participatory and empowering evaluation needs to take realistic account of the complexity and diverse purposes of social work practice with its divergent purposes of care, protection, control and empowerment.

Participatory research included the following characteristics:

- People are seen as experts in their own lives.

- The strengths of local people are used to plan action for change based on communally owned values.

- Research is user led (Evans and Fisher 1999).

The participatory research paradigm is grounded in inclusiveness. It draws on a range of theories including feminist theory and methodology, the social model of disability, people first and equal people perspectives in the field of learning disabilities, and the psychiatric survivor movement and the challenge to mental health/psychiatric knowledge as derived from medical research and practice. It also draws on theories derived from children's rights and perspectives; theorizing and knowledge about gay and lesbian choices, lifestyles and behaviours; and theorizing about race and ethnicity.

The strengths of this approach are clear:

- The inclusion in a research/evaluation agenda of the voices of people who may be excluded by race, gender, disability, mental health, age, learning disability or poverty, or a combination of these factors.

- The emphasis and promotion of the user contribution, and potentially control, of the evaluation agenda.

- The social inclusion, in policy and practice development, of previously excluded voices.

- The recognition of the need for accountability of practitioners to service users, not just to employing organizational hierarchies.

It highlights the importance that users of services attribute to processes and relationships as well as outcomes (Scottish Executive 2006).

Potential weaknesses are conflicts between user requirements and needs and resource allocation, conflicts between user perceptions and social work legal requirements in terms of risk assessment and protection (for example, in relation to children), and conflicts between empowerment and the protection and control purposes of some aspects of social work.

Each of these paradigms involves the use of a specific research methodology or of a range of methodologies. Research and evaluation emerge as clearly interlinked. However, considerable areas of research – for example, in social policy, sociology, law and psychology – have not been addressed, not because they are not relevant: they provide contextual knowledge, crucial to understanding the social, legal and political context of social work which impinges the overall effectiveness of social service provision. Instead the emphasis in this chapter is on research or research methodology specifically applied to social work practice and service provision. The need to address effectiveness and attention to outcomes, however, cannot be entirely disentangled from the broader social, legal, political and resource context.

## Research, evaluation and social work practice: the gap

In exploring definitions of research and evaluation the chapter assumes agreement about the necessity of their underpinning practice and its development. However, an examination of the historical context of social work shows that the link is not self-evident. There continues to be a gap between the practice of social work and social work research and evaluation (Everitt 2002; Shaw and Lishman 1999). There are a number of potential reasons for this gap.

First we have to consider the general context of social work and why and how it may contribute to the gap between practice and research and evaluation. Lyons (1999) argues:

> Social work is difficult because the subject matter is problematic and the form and quality of the response is determined not just by the values, knowledge and skills of workers and manager, but also by the demands of government and the perceptions of other professionals, the press and the public.

Social work currently operates in a political context which is critical of post-war welfarism and has embraced market forces, consumerism and managerialism in the public sector; it emphasizes the need for regulation, audit, performance monitoring and inspection. Social work operates in an economic and financial context of concern about containing public sector spending and a consequent emphasis on efficiency savings and ensuring value for money. Social work also operates in a context of rapid and repeated legal and organizational change.

Parton (1999) examines contrasting perspectives in relation to social work practice: social work as a 'rational technical' or social work as a 'practical moral' activity. Were social work simply a 'rational technical' activity, the managerial imperative of regulation, audit, performance, monitoring and inspection would be unproblematic. However, Parton argues the essence of social work is a 'practical moral' activity.

> Social work practice is a complex, uncertain and ambiguous activity which involves an ethical base, legal accountability, responsibility for complex assessment and decision making about relative risks, safety harm and protection and intervention in the lives of people who are in distress, conflict or trouble. (Lishman 2000, p.2)

The tensions between these different purposes and expectations of social work lead to ambiguity and uncertainty in its practice: they render simple definitions of efficient, effective or successful practice problematic and raise issues for how we conceive of an evidence base for practice and how we also manage as practitioners to be outcome focused (how effective are we?).

Questions about the validity and relevance of research and evaluation findings for individual practitioners emerge. First there are questions about potential use of research and evaluation findings. Evaluation may be perceived as a management tool which highlights and punishes poor practice but does not necessarily reward effective practice: unfortunately it may also be perceived as externally driven by efficiency savings for the service or organization. The measurements involved, performance indicators, may not reflect the complexity of the tasks evaluated.

There are questions related to methodology. The criteria for 'success' in social work may be different for users, practitioners, management, researchers and funders. Research knowledge tends to be general and probabilistic: it can therefore be difficult to apply it to an individual case (Fisher 1997). Research, even in randomized control trials, may examine practice in so broad a way that details of difference in methods of practice and intervention, of importance to the individual practitioner, cannot be correlated with effectiveness (Fisher 1997).

For a practitioner there is a real issue about engaging with research and evaluation. It must be relevant to the practitioner's experience of dealing with the details of differences between individual users and clients and their particular situations. Probabilistic indicators of effectiveness have to be reviewed and applied to very different and disparate individual situations. Findings in overview have to be available to practitioners and managers in accessible ways which do not add to information overload.

A key policy requirement in health and social care is that of evidence-based practice (Fisher 2002; Trinder 2000). What constitutes evidence-based practice is closely linked to any discussion of research and evaluation in social work.

## Evidence-based practice: the necessity for research and evaluation in social work

Evidence-based practice was initially conceived in medicine with the following definition:

> the conscientious, explicit and judicious use of current best evidence in making decisions about the care of the individual patients, based on skills which allow the doctor to evaluate both personal experience *and* external evidence in a systematic and objective manner. (Sackett *et al.* 1997, p.71)

MacDonald and Sheldon (1998) draw on Sackett to provide a useful starting point in defining evidence in social work: 'Evidence based social care is the conscientious, explicit and judicious use of current best evidence in making decisions regarding the welfare of individuals'. It is impossible to argue with this definition. As professionals in social work and social care we have a duty to make sure we are using the best possible knowledge and evidence on which to base our assessment and intervention. We should do this with the intention of minimizing adverse consequences to users of our services.

Social work must, as Sackett *et al.* (1997) and Sheldon (1998, 2001) argue, draw on current best evidence, conscientiously (from an ethical base), explicitly (clearly and openly) and judiciously (critically, analytically and carefully balancing and judging the evidence). We must not simply practice on the basis of habit, fad, prejudice or unchecked practice wisdom. However, given the complexity of social work practice, nor should we over-simplify the nature of evidence.

Reasons for using an evidence-based approach, i.e. applying research and evaluation to social work practice, include the need to avoid what have been weaknesses historically. These include:

• Over-reliance on outdated knowledge (including that from qualifying training). This is not confined to social work.

- Over-reliance on practice wisdom which may be selective (what worked in one particular successful case we remember is not necessarily transferable to the rest of our practice).

Further, like other professionals, social workers need to deal with information overload. How to select from the range of 'evidence' available is a real problem. Protocols in medicine attempt to deal with this issue for busy practitioners but have their weaknesses, e.g. they relate to probabilistic effects of a drug on a particular condition and cannot specify its effect on a specific individual or the side effects she or he may experience.

In policy terms reasons, an evidence-based approach (Scottish Executive 2006; Trinder 2002) requires us as practitioners and deliverers of services, in order to meet policy, professional and service user requirements, to address:

- the need to ensure that services and practitioners produce more good than harm

- the need to manage risk and therefore harm (see Chapter 11 in the present volume)

- the need for research-minded practitioners and services to evaluate outcomes, rather than outputs and think carefully, in terms of economy and efficiency, whether the outcomes justify the cost of the inputs and processes.

It appears self-evident that in social work practice and service delivery we should use evidence from research and evaluation, i.e. evidence-based practice, to underpin our practice and enhance its effectiveness. We do need, however, to be cautious in terms of defining evidence-based practice given the complexity identified earlier of research and evaluation in social work: in particular, which research and evaluation methods provide *valid* and reliable evidence.

What are potential reservations from the field about the agenda for evidence-based practice? There are concerns that it may:

- contribute to a managerialist agenda with an emphasis on causal relationships between target setting and outcomes

- fail to address the complex inter-relationships between policy imperatives, resource allocations and practice realities

- involve a lack of attention to the subjective meaning of individuals' experiences, including those of users, carers, and health and social care professionals

- involve a lack of attention to the complexity, messiness and individuality of social work practice.

From a research perspective (Smith 1987, 2002a, 2002b, 2004) there are concerns about the limitations of a positivist, quantitative, experimental approach to evidence-based practice in social work, i.e. the experimental model of natural sciences. In research terms Smith (2004) embraces the need for social work to use evidence as a source of practice but challenges a positivist approach. He argues for a realistic evaluation (e.g. Pawson and Tilley 1997) which stresses that context is crucial in the evaluation of any social programme, not just outcomes. So are the 'mechanisms' which generate change – the choices and capacities which are made available to participants – and their operation is always contingent on context. (Smith 2004, p.30)

More generally, evidence-based practice in social work can lead to a narrow view of evidence, based only on randomized controlled trials which are the 'gold standard' in medicine (Sheldon 2001). Randomized controlled trials do meet the requirements of normal scientific experimental research including random samples, controlled experimental design and therefore moderate confidence in causal relationships. But what are their weaknesses in the social work/social care field? They include the following:

- Randomized controlled trials are probabilistic: they do not tell a practitioner, given the 70 per cent success rate for a group treatment method in criminal justice, who of their individual clients are likely to be one of the 70 per cent of individuals with a successful outcome and who are likely to be in the 30 per cent with an unsuccessful outcome.

- They do not address the need for user/client-led evaluation, which will be based on perceptions of process as well as outcome.

- They do not address the different evaluation agendas of different stakeholders, including users, practitioners, managers, researchers and policy-makers.

- They do not address power differentials in deciding what is to be researched or evaluated and the relative weight attached to the findings.

- They do not address the complexity and uncertainty of social work practice.

- They do not address the context of social work practice (Pawson and Tilley 1997; Smith 2004).

Interestingly this has become a more general issue in health, not just social care, where patient involvement and participation is an important element of policy.

In pharmacy, for example, the concept of evidence-based practice has been extended from an empirical experimental base to include consumer/user evaluation of the treatment of service provided and recognition that partnership with patients is needed to ensure that treatment is effective. For example, if patients fail to complete a prescribed drug regime its experimentally proven clinical effectiveness is of little use.

So what does evidence-based practice mean for social work? How does it connect with practice, research and evaluation? What does constitute evidence-based practice?

First, while it is linked with research and evaluation it needs to embrace a wide range of evidence including theories of meaning (tested in practice), users' and clients' views, and well-established research and evaluation (quantitative and qualitative): these approaches are not disconnected.

We should not abandon hard-won theories of meaning which are not and probably cannot be empirically endorsed, but we should nevertheless use an evidence-based critical approach in relation to them. For example, Erikson (1977) (see Chapter 5 in the present volume) has useful metaphors for life-cycle transitions but they need to be critically reviewed in relation to age, class, gender, ethnicity and culture and the consequent generalizability problems, and the critique must be based on empirical research.

However, Erikson's concepts of transition and life-stage tasks can be useful in terms of understanding our subjective but sometimes common experience.

Second, in relation to empirical evidence, social work has had a historical commitment to attending to the voice of the 'client' (Mayer and Timms 1970), to recognizing the 'meaning' of professional intervention to the recipient (Everitt and Hardiker 1996) and, currently, to engaging in participatory and empowering research (Dullea and Mullender 1999). We should not lose this.

Third, a range of research and evaluation must contribute to the richness of underpinning evidence for social work practice.

We do, in social work, need to examine, as Macdonald and Sheldon (1998) argue, whether outcomes of social work practice are attributable to our interventions or to other factors including time and unrelated change in the lives of service users, which may influence measured outcomes negatively or positively.

Evidence, therefore, should include what methods of assessment and intervention have proved most successful in meeting the specific aims of a particular area of practice or service. Evidence also needs to include how the service user or carer experiences such assessment and intervention, and what other factors have influenced their lives and actions.

Our concept of evidence needs to take account of the range of stakeholders in social work practice and the differential power they can employ. Our concept of evidence also needs to take account of different and conflicting expectations and requirements of social work and social care. For example, it is not possible simultaneously to ensure that no child dies at home through parental violence and neglect and that no child is admitted into care without grounds that meet subsequent legal requirements for proof and evidence. The concept of empowerment for users and carers may not usefully be translated into work with sexual abusers.

Finally, in order to practise in the evidence-based or research-minded way discussed in this chapter, social work practitioners need to become more sophisticated in accessing and critiquing research. Systematic reviews pioneered in medicine and nursing involve reviews of primary research using explicit and systematic criteria to:

*   search, identify, select and evaluate research studies applied to a specific social work focus, e.g. child protection, working with people with learning disabilities

*   draw together and critically analyse the general findings from the review (Cochrane Collaboration 2003).

Systematic reviews may not be currently prevalent in social work but must become an increasing part of the evidence-based practice and research minded practitioners policy agenda (Scottish Executive 2006).

Overall clearly we need to be more outcome focused, while recognizing the complexity of factors contributing to a 'successful' outcome (see Section 2 on assessment and Section 3 on intervention in the present volume). How in integrating a research and evidence-based approach in our everyday practice may the evidence from systematic reviews be usefully incorporated?

What does a systematic review mean and involve? It needs to include attention to ethics and application in a real way to practice: it does not necessarily involve randomized control trials (Morago 2006). It does however mean that as students, practice teachers, practitioners and academics we need to use thorough searches of literature and research to inform our practice.

Because we are all overloaded with too much information, some of it unreliable, we need to make use of pre-appraised research, i.e. existing systematic reviews. The concept of a 'systematic' review (which arose from the 'gold standard' application of randomized control trials to social work) essentially is about how we systematically draw on the best possible evidence available to underpin our work and therefore have clear selection criteria about our evidence base which, for example, distinguish a polemic about 'what I did' from a thoughtful measured piece of qualitative research which fully acknowledges its limitations.

## Conclusions

This chapter has critically examined the tensions for individual practitioners in relation to research, evaluation and evidence-based practice. It explored the blurred distinction between research and evaluation. It suggested that research has a wider focus than evaluation. In particular, research examines the wider social and structural context in which social work is practised and which may limit its effectiveness. The chapter suggests that while evaluation must examine effectiveness and outcomes it needs to include a more reflective and process element, taking account of user, carer, client and practitioner perceptions and theories of meaning. The chapter examines the gap between research and evaluation and practice and suggested reasons for this gap, in particular the complex nature of social work, the individual experience of social work and its effect, and the probabilistic nature of research on effectiveness. Research on effectiveness has also not sufficiently addressed user evaluation of outcomes.

The chapter takes as self-evident the need for research and evaluation to contribute to the evidence base of social work, but argues that the evidence base needs to incorporate more than simply a positivist model. Social workers need to use evidence-based approaches which include evidence from quantitative and qualitative research, but they also need to use theories of meaning (tested with users) and user perceptions. The challenge for researchers and practitioners is how to integrate relatively broad findings from research into individual practice.

The chapter suggested that three broad paradigms, drawn from research methodology, can contribute to the evidence base of our practice. These paradigms are a quantitative approach, a qualitative approach and a participatory empowering approach. Each has strengths and weaknesses but together they all can contribute to the knowledge base of social work, so that evidence of effectiveness can address the complexity of the task, the social and political context, the different perceptions and evaluation of different players and the need to meet criteria of effectiveness. What are the implications for practitioners? These are complicated. Practitioners need appropriate summaries of an overview of research findings provided, for example, by SCIE, Research Highlights in Social Work and the Rowntree Foundation. Practitioners need to work in organizations which promote such research findings as a basis for evidence-based practice but recognize the tensions between research findings based on probabilities and their own decisions about an individual. It still is not entirely clear how many organizations (local authority, voluntary or independent) actively base their policy, service and practice on evidence from research or evaluation.

Finally and briefly, what are the implications for social work students? Qualifying students need to understand the repertoire of research methodology. They need to understand the requirements for evidence-based practice, but also the complexities involved. They need to understand the relevance of the paradigms identified for research and evaluation to underpin their practice. They need to be facilitated to be active participants in the process of seeking out relevant knowledge, research and evidence. They need to understand the concept and process of a systematic review of the literature (Cochrane Collaboration 2003). Post-qualifying education and continuing professional development need further to develop this understanding throughout their professional career.

Research and evaluation in social work are essential, but if they are to be meaningfully integrated into social work, the methodologies and conclusions need to address the complexities of the social work tasks and responsibilities and therefore inform its evidence base.[1]

## Note

1   An excellent start in helping us locate, assess and apply research evidence in child care practice is provided by Barnardos and their *Evidence Guide* – Available at: www.barnardos.org.uk/resources/researchandpublications/theevidenceguide

## References

Beresford, P. and Croft, S. (2001) 'Service users' knowledge and the social construction of social work.' *British Journal of Social Work 1*, 3, 295–316.

Cochrane Collaboration (2003) 'Glossary'. *Cochrane Collaboration, The Cochrane Library, Issue 2*. Oxford: Update Software.

Department of Health (1995) *Messages from Research*. London: Department of Health.

Dullea, K. and Mullender, A. (1999) 'Evaluation and empowerment.' In I. Shaw and J. Lishman (eds) *Evaluation in Social Work Practice*. London: Sage.

Erikson, E. (1977) *Childhood and Society*. London: Fontana.

ESRC (1999-2000) *Theorising Social Work Research*. www.scie.org.uk/publication/misc/tswr/index.asp

Evans, C. and Fisher, M. (1999) 'Collaborative evaluation with service users.' In I. Shaw and J. Lishman (eds) *Evaluation and Social Work Practice*. London: Sage.

Everitt, A. (2002) 'Research and development in social work.' In R. Adams, L. Dominelli and M. Payne (eds) *Social Work: Themes, Issues and Critical Debates*. 2nd ed. Basingstoke: Palgrave.

Everitt, A. and Hardiker, P. (1996) *Evaluating for Good Practice*. Basingstoke: Macmillan.

Fisher, M. (1997) 'Research, knowledge and practice in community care,' *Issues in Social Work Education 17*, 2, 17–30.

Fisher, M. (2002) 'The Social Care Institute for Excellence: The role of a national institute in developing knowledge and practice in social care.' *Social Work and Social Sciences Review 10*, 2, 6–34.

Humphries, B. (2003) 'What else counts as evidence in evidence-based social work?' *Social Work Education, 22*, 1, 81–93.

Lindow, V. and Morris, J. (1995) *Service User Involvement: Synthesis of Findings and Experience in the Field of Community Care*. York: Joseph Rowntree Foundation.

Lishman, J. (1990) 'A child dies.' *Practice 3*, 3 and 4, 271–84.

Lishman, J. (2000) 'What works as evidence for practice? The methodological repertoire of an applied discipline. Cardiff: ESRC Funded Seminar. Available at: www.scie.org.uk/publications

Lishman, J. (2002) 'Personal and professional development.' In R. Adams, L. Dominelli and M. Payne (eds) *Social Work: Themes, Issues and Critical Debates*. 2nd ed. Basingstoke: Palgrave.

Lyons, K. (1999) 'The place of research in social work education.' Paper presented at ESRC-funded Seminar 1, 'Theorising Social Work Research: What Kinds of Knowledge?', on 26 May, Brunel.

MacDonald, G. and Sheldon, B. (1998), 'Changing One's Mind: The Final Frontier? *Issues in Social Work Education 18*, 1, 3–25.

MacDonald, G., Sheldon, B. and Gillespie, J. (1992) 'Contemporary studies of the effectiveness of social work.' *British Journal of Social Work 22*, 6, 615–43.

Mayer, J. E. and Timms, N. (1970) *The Client Speaks*. London: RKP.

McGuire, J. (ed.) (1995) *What Works: Reducing Reoffending: Guidelines from Research and Practice*. Chichester: Wiley.

Morago, P. (2006) 'Evidence based practice: The medicine to social work.' *European Journal of Social Work 9*, 4, 461–77.

Parkes, C. M. (1975) *Loss and Change*. London: RKP.

Parton, N. (1999) 'Some thoughts on the relationship between theory and practice in and for social work.' Paper presented at ESRC-funded Seminar 1, 'Theorising Social Work Research: What Kinds of Knowledge?', on 26 May, Brunel.

Pawson, R. and Tilley, N. (1997) *Realistic Evaluation*. London: Sage.

Popper, K. (1969) *Conjectures and Refutations: The Growth of Scientific Knowledge*. London: RKP.

Rees, S. and Wallace, A. (1982) *Verdicts on Social Work*. London: Edward Arnold.

Reid, W. T. (1994) 'The empirical practice movement.' *Social Service Review 68*, 2, 165–84.

Sackett, D. L., Richardson, S., Rosenberg, W. and Haynes, R. B. (1997) *Evidence Based Medicine: How to Practice and Teach EBM*. Edinburgh: Churchill Livingstone.

Schon, D. (1987) *Educating the Reflective Practitioner*. San Francisco: Jossey-Bass.

Scottish Executive (1997) *Looking After Children: Good Parenting, Good Outcomes*. Edinburgh: Scottish Executive.

Scottish Executive (2006) *Changing Lives: Report of the 21st Century Social Work Review*. Edinburgh: Scottish Executive.

Shaw, I. and Lishman, J. (eds) (1999) *Evaluation and Social Work Practice*. London: Sage.

Sheldon, B. (1998) 'Evidence based social services: Prospects and problems.' *Research Policy and Planning 16*, 2, 16–18.

Sheldon, B. (2001) 'The validity of evidence-based practice: A reply to Stephen Webb.' *British Journal of Social Work 31*, 6, 801–809.

Sheppard, M. (1998) 'Practice validity, reflexivity and knowledge for social work.' *British Journal of Social Work 28*, 763–81.

Smith, D. (2002a) 'The limits of positivism revisited.' *Social Work and Social Sciences Review 10*, 1, 27–37.

Smith, D. (ed) (2002b) *Social work and evidence based practice*. Research highlights 45. London: Jessica Kingsley Publishers.

Smith, D. (ed.) (2004) *Social Work and Evidence-Based Practice*. Research Highlights 45. London: Jessica Kingsley Publishers.

Stalker, K. (2003) *Reconceptualising Work with 'Carers': New Directions for Policy and Practice*. London: Research Highlights 43. London: Jessica Kingsley Publishers.

Trinder, L. with Reynolds, S. (2002) *Evidence Based Practice: A Critical Appraisal*. London: Blackwell.

# THE CONTRIBUTORS

**Jane Aldgate** is Professor of Social Care at the Open University and is Honorary Professor of Social Work at Queen's University Belfast. Jane trained in Scotland as a social worker, and has been in social work education for many years, at the universities of Oxford, Leicester and the Open University. She has researched a wide range of child welfare issues, including family support services, child protection and services for looked-after children. Recent work includes co-editing a new textbook on child development with Wendy Rose, David Jones and Carole Jeffery, *The Developing World of the Child* (published by Jessica Kingsley Publishers in 2006) and studies on kinship care and how children spend their time informing the review of looked-after children in Scotland by the Social Work Inspection Agency, see www.swis.gov.uk.

**Mary Barker** practised as a social worker/manager in Sheffield, Essex and Lancashire. She then taught at the University of Liverpool and the University of Leicester.

**Alan Barr** (OBE) is Co-Director of the Scottish Community Development Centre and Senior Lecturer in the Glasgow School of Social Work. He has 35 years' experience of practice, teaching, research and evaluation in community development. He has worked in the voluntary and statutory sectors. Previous posts include Assistant Director Home Office Community Development Project, Oldham; Principal Officer Community Development for Strathclyde Regional Council Social Work Department. Alan is editor of the *Journal of Community Work and Development* and has published widely in the community development field. He is Vice-Chair of the Community Development Alliance Scotland.

**Judith Brearley** is an organization consultant with the Scottish Institute of Human Relations. Previously she lectured in social work at Edinburgh University.

**Robert Buckley** has been a lecturer in social work at the Robert Gordon University since 1993. Prior to this he had worked as a social worker in Glasgow, Grampian and Northamptonshire. He came to Aberdeen as a senior social worker/team leader in 1987 and spent five years there before joining RGU. He currently retains a practice base as a safeguarder within the Children Hearing System and as a member of the Aberdeen City Council Adoption and Fostering Panel.

**Amy Clark** is a lecturer on the postgraduate Masters course in social work at the Robert Gordon University. She trained as a generic social worker and later as a social gerontologist and has a range of professional experiences in practice, senior social worker training, staff development and management, manager of residential establishments and an inspection officer. Besides being an educator she is currently developing interprofessional work within the Faculty of Health and Social Care.

**Brigid Daniel** is Professor of Child Care and Protection at the University of Dundee. She is the Director of Studies for a large suite of post-qualifying child care and protection training courses. Her research interests and publications are in the field of children's resilience, work with fathers, child development and neglect.

**Ann Davis** works at the University of Birmingham where she is Professor of Social Work and Director of the Centre for Excellence in Interdisciplinary Mental Health. She has researched and published, nationally and internationally, in the fields of service user experiences, social exclusion and mental health. Her most recent publication is a book authored with Viv Cree, *Social Work: Inside Voices*, published by Routledge.

**Fiona Feilberg** has worked in a residential therapeutic community with young people, worked with adults with addictions and managed a day centre for adults with a range of disabilities before moving to the Robert Gordon University in 1997, where she is now involved in course leading, developing and providing short courses for workers in residential childcare and in coordinating and providing consultancy work for individuals, teams and agencies. She has a particular interest in using a psychodynamic approach to understand individuals and to understand and work within organizations. This includes a focus on understanding the impact of change and transitions on individuals within groups and the groups themselves and of the primitive defences that emerge in the context of change and transitions.

**Jan Fook** is Professor in Social Work Studies at the University of Southampton. Until recently she was Professor and Director of the Centre for Professional Development, La Trobe University, where she specialized in conducting short courses in critical reflection.

**Alastair Gibson** is Senior Lecturer in Social Work at the Robert Gordon University and Course Leader of the BA (Hons) in Social Work by Distance Learning. Current teaching interests are human growth and behaviour and interprofessional practice. Social work practice in a variety of hospital and health care settings.

**Pauline Hardiker** was Senior Lecturer in Social Work at Leicester University.

**Patricia Kearney** has worked as a social worker, manager and teacher training; also in the Practice Development Unit of the National Institute of Social Work and then at the Social Care Institute for Excellence.

**Colin Keenan** is Senior Lecturer in Social Work at the Robert Gordon University and Course Leader of the PG Dip/MSc Social Work course. He has been involved in practice, teaching, management and consultancy in the area of group care for over 30 years. His current specific interest is in the application of chaos theory to group care environments and most of his practice experience in the field has been with children and families. His general orientation to practice is evidence-based with psychodynamic leanings.

**Hazel Kemshall** is currently Professor of Community and Criminal Justice at DeMontfort University. She has research interests in risk assessment and management of offenders, effective work in multi-agency public protection, and implementing effective practice with offenders. She has completed research for the Economic and Social Research Council, the Home Office and the Scottish Executive, and both teaches and consultants extensively on public protection and high risk offenders. She has numerous publications on risk, including

*Understanding Risk in Criminal Justice* (2003, Open University Press). She has recently completed an evaluation of multi-agency public protection panels for the Home Office (with Wood, Mackenzie, Bailey and Yates), is currently investigating pathways into and out of crime for young people under an ESRC network (with Boeck and Fleming) and has recently completed work on attrition from accredited programmes for the National Probation Service. She has developed training and guidance materials on high risk offenders for NOMs (with Mackenzie and Wilkinson).

**Joyce Lishman** is Professor and Head of the School of Applied Social Studies at the Robert Gordon University, Aberdeen. She edited the previous edition of the *Handbook of Theory for Practice Teachers in Social Work*. She is the General Editor of the Research Highlights in Social Work series and has a particular interest in evaluation, research and evidence-based practice and how they are utilized in social work practice.

**Geraldine Macdonald** is Professor of Social Work at the Queen's University of Belfast. She was previously Professor of Social Work at Bristol University and Director of Information and Knowledge Management at the Commission for Social Care Inspection.

**Rob Mackay** is Lecturer in Social Work with the Robert Gordon University in Aberdeen. He has a long-standing interest in informal networks, peer support and advocacy activities through involvement with a number of voluntary organizations. His teaching and research interests include disability, mental health, social work values and ethics, empowerment, involvement and participation strategies, narrative practice and the European context of social work. Over the past two years, he has being actively engaged with the RGU project to promote the greater involvement of service users and carers with students and staff of the social work courses.

**Peter Marsh** is Professor and Dean of Social Sciences at the University of Sheffield. He is a social worker, and Professor of Child and Family Welfare at the University of Sheffield. He spent ten years as a lecturer/social worker in a joint post between the university and a community-based team, and is currently working on practice development in participative social work, focusing on family group conferences and on joint working with general practice in primary care. He is professional advisor to the Research in Practice evidence-based services initiative, and heads the resources team for the National Social Work Research Strategy.

**Gill McIvor** is Professor of Criminology at Lancaster University. She was previously Professor of Social Work and Director of the Social Work Research Centre at the University of Stirling. Her research has focused on aspects of social work and criminal justice and her recent books include *Women who Offend, Managing Sex Offender Risk* (with Hazel Kemshall) and *Developments in Social Work with Offenders* (with Peter Raynor).

**Terry McLean** is Associate Head of the School of Applied Social Studies at the Robert Gordon University in Aberdeen. For many years he worked part-time as a social worker at the Department of Child and Family Psychiatry, also in Aberdeen. He teaches interdisciplinary practice to social work and nursing students and is a member of the joint Robert Gordon University/University of Aberdeen Interprofessional Education Group.

**Gerard Rochford** was Professor of Social Work at Aberdeen University and General Editor of the Research Highlights in Social Work series.

**Steven M. Shardlow** is Professor of Social Work at the University of Salford, England, where he is Director of the Institute for Health and Social Care Research. In addition, he is Professor II in Social Work, at Bodø University College, Norway. He is founding Editor-in-Chief of the *Journal of Social Work*. Previously he has worked as a social work practitioner and manager. Current research interests are in the following areas: evidence-based policy and practice; professional ethics; comparative practice in the social professions; professional social work education and practice – especially in respect of practice learning. He has published widely in these fields, including 14 books, and his work has been translated into several languages.

**Michael Sheppard** is Professor of Social Work at the University of Plymouth. Before entering academe he practised as a social worker. His main areas of interest lie in social work theory, child and family care and mental health. Much of this theoretical work has been in the areas of reasoning, knowledge and decision-making in practice. His most recent books are *Prevention and Coping in Child and Family Care* (2004), *Appraising and Using Social Research* (2004) and *Social Work and Social Exclusion: The Idea of Practice* (2006).

**Daphne Statham** was the Director of the National Institute for Social Work and edited *Managing Front Line Practice* in Social Care in the Research Highlights in Social Work series.

**Steven Walker** is currently programme leader in child and adolescent mental health at Anglia Ruskin University. He qualified as a social worker at the London School of Economics and as a family therapist at the Institute of Family Therapy and has practised in London and Essex in child protection and child and adolescent mental health. His recent books include *Social Work and Child and Adolescent Mental Health* (2003, Russell House Publishers) and *Culturally Competent Therapy* (2005, Palgrave).

# SUBJECT INDEX

# AUTHOR INDEX